Mastering Database Programming
with Visual Basic 6

Mastering™ Database Programming with Visual Basic® 6

Evangelos Petroutsos

SYBEX®

San Francisco • Paris • Düsseldorf • Soest • London

Associate Publisher: Richard Mills
Contracts and Licensing Manager: Kristine O'Callaghan
Acquisitions & Developmental Editor: Denise Santoro
Editors: Anamary Ehlen, Pete Gaughan, Linda Good, Nancy Six-smith, and Emily K. Wolman
Project Editors: Pete Gaughan and Emily K. Wolman
Technical Editors: Tony Martin and Dominic Selly
Book Designers: Patrick Dintino and Catalin Dulfu
Graphic Illustrator: Tony Jonick
Electronic Publishing Specialist: Franz Baumhackl
Production Team Leader: Jennifer Durning
Proofreaders: Molly Glover, Nelson Kim, and Patrick J. Peterson
Indexer: Ted Laux
Companion CD: Keith McNeil
Cover Design: Design Site
Cover Illustration: Sergie Loobkoff, Design Site

SYBEX is a registered trademark of SYBEX Inc.

Mastering is a trademark of SYBEX Inc.

Screen reproductions produced with Collage Complete.
Collage Complete is a trademark of Inner Media Inc.

The CD Interface music is from GIRA Sound AURIA Music
Library © GIRA Sound 1996.

TRADEMARKS: SYBEX has attempted throughout this book to
distinguish proprietary trademarks from descriptive terms by following the capitalization style used by the manufacturer.

The author and publisher have made their best efforts to prepare
this book, and the content is based upon final release software
whenever possible. Portions of the manuscript may be based upon
pre-release versions supplied by software manufacturer(s). The
author and the publisher make no representation or warranties of
any kind with regard to the completeness or accuracy of the contents herein and accept no liability of any kind including but not
limited to performance, merchantability, fitness for any particular
purpose, or any losses or damages of any kind caused or alleged
to be caused directly or indirectly from this book.

Library of Congress Card Number: 99-67019
ISBN: 0-7821-2598-0

Manufactured in the United States of America

10 9 8 7 6 5 4

To the loving memory of my father

ACKNOWLEDGMENTS

My gratitude to the talented staff at Sybex, especially developmental editor Denise Santoro for turning a proposal into an actual book; Anamary Ehlen, Linda Good, and Nancy Sixsmith for their keen remarks and constant editing of my revisions; project editors Pete Gaughan and Emily K. Wolman for their graciousness in the final weeks of the project, as the book continued to grow instead of coming to an end; and technical editors Tony Martin and Dominic Selly for seeing that the information provided in this book is correct and accurate—their comments made a big difference.

FOREWORD

Have you ever been so overwhelmed with new technologies that you didn't know how to actually get the job done? If so, you're not alone. Most of us working in the computer world have had the same experience. Personally, I blame it on all the overtime that the developers in Redmond spend thinking of new ways to improve their software. New tools and technologies are useful, but sometimes I just want to shout "Stop!" and get back to work.

Well, you can't stop software companies from releasing products, but in a real-world development situation, you can do the next best thing: pick a set of tools and technologies and stick with it. Most of us are not lucky enough to get paid to just learn new developments in the software universe. Sooner or later, we need to actually use our knowledge to build something. That's where this book can come in handy.

Suppose your boss walks in one morning next week and says, "We want you to head up the project for our new retail sales application. You need to design and implement a user interface so that clerks can enter sales directly into the widget-tracking database. Make sure they can't enter partial orders and that it's multiuser. And oh, yeah, we'd like a Web interface, too." What now?

In a line-of-business application like this one, you'll want to stick to mainstream technologies that are well-understood. In particular, one good way to architect the widget-sales application would be to use Visual Basic for the user interface, ActiveX Data Objects (ADO) for the data-access library, stored procedures to implement business rules, SQL Server for the database, and ASP pages for the Web interface.

Having chosen your toolkit, you could go out and buy a bookshelf full of reference works and set about mastering every detail of ADO and ASP and all the rest. In about six months, your boss would be asking for progress reports, and you might be polishing your resume.

Or you could buy this book.

Evangelos Petroutsos does not attempt in this book to teach you every facet of the technologies that you'll need to use to get a Visual Basic database application up and running. Nor does he insist on always using the most advanced, cutting-edge tools. When he finds no use for something (such as most of the ADO events), he says so and moves on to other topics. On the other hand, he's perfectly willing to do politically-incorrect things like use bound controls if it helps move an application along.

Based on work he's done building actual applications for real customers, Evangelos helps you cut through the mass of information out there to focus on the core concepts you need to learn to make your Visual Basic database applications successful. You'll learn the basics of database design and of the ADO object model. You'll learn the importance of stored procedures and splitting your application into logical tiers. You'll also benefit from much stored-up experience on creating effective user interfaces for straightforward database applications.

By the time you've finished the first part of the book, you should be able to put together working data-entry and data-querying applications. Reading the second part of the book will help you see the direct benefits of otherwise-arcane topics such as data-aware classes and hierarchical Recordsets. You might never have looked at these topics, but you'll see how you can use them to advantage even in simple applications.

Finally, when you're ready to make the leap to the Internet, the third part of the book will help you choose simple, straightforward, cross-browser technologies to do so. When you've finished with this part, you'll be ready to look for more advanced references in the areas that you need to explore further—and you'll be well-prepared to determine what those areas are.

Don't miss the two tutorials on the companion CD-ROM. To me, these are some of the most valuable parts of this book. Often it's useful to watch someone else build a whole application so that you can see the thought process that went into its design. With the tutorials, you can do just that, and you'll end up with code that you can adapt to your own needs.

There's a perfectly good English word that seems to have largely gone out of fashion: practicum. It means "a specialized course that gives you supervised practical experience in a field after you've been exposed to the theory of that field." Consider this book your practicum in building Visual Basic database applications.

Mike Gunderloy

Endicott, Washington

(Author of the *Visual Basic Developer's Guide to ADO, Mastering SQL Server 7.5, SQL Server 7 In Record Time*, and co-author of *Access and SQL Server Developer's Handbook*)

CONTENTS AT A GLANCE

TABLE OF CONTENTS

5   A First Look at ADO

6 Programming with ADO

8   Making the Most of Stored Procedures

PART II   Advanced Data-Access Techniques

10   Shaping Your Data

15 Building IIS Applications

16 Microsoft Transaction Server

INTRODUCTION

A few years ago, when I wrote *Mastering Visual Basic 5*, I included a chapter on the basic concepts of database programming. It was by far the longest chapter in the book. The chapter discussed Data Access Objects (DAO) and addressed the topic of programming Access databases with Visual Basic.

The Visual Basic 6 version of the same book contained two chapters on database programming: one based on DAO and another based on Active Data Objects (ADO). Selecting the topics to include in the discussion of ADO was not simple. VB was being enhanced with new database-related features, but the book could not keep growing; there was simply no room. The need for a book on database programming became obvious—and this is it. *Mastering Database Programming with Visual Basic 6* is the book for VB developers who wish to move into database programming.

Today, Visual Basic is still the most popular programming language, and it's ideal for building database applications. Visual Basic comes with an array of tools for building database applications, the visual database tools, that make it the best environment for developing client/server and multi-tier applications.

Who Should Read This Book

This book is addressed to VB programmers who are interested in developing database applications. It assumes the reader is familiar with Visual Basic but requires no knowledge of databases. Database programming is a very broad topic, so I had to make certain choices as to the topics covered in the book. This book focuses on SQL Server, ADO, and VB code.

SQL Server is well-integrated in Visual Basic's environment, and I expect to see even more SQL Server–specific tools in the next version of Visual Basic. This book doesn't assume knowledge of SQL Server, and it doesn't show you how to get started with SQL Server either. The only SQL Server topic discussed in detail here is Transact-SQL (T-SQL) and stored procedures. T-SQL is SQL Server's built-in programming language. T-SQL complements Visual Basic (or any other language that can access SQL Server databases). Some of the tasks you'd normally implement in VB and execute on the client, can be implemented in T-SQL and executed on the database server. The T-SQL procedures you attach to the database are called stored procedures.

ADO is the latest data-access component and will replace older components such as DAO and RDO. If you haven't developed database applications with VB in the past, there's no reason to waste time with older components that will not even be updated in the future. Even if you're familiar with DAO, you should consider switching to ADO. Other than supporting existing DAO-based applications, your new projects should be based on ADO.

Finally, this book isn't about putting a few controls on the Form, binding them to a database, and thinking you have built a database application. This approach is so deceptively simple that I think the data control shouldn't have a visible interface. You will learn how to use the objects exposed by ADO to actually program the database operations. The no-code approach is a simple method of getting results quickly, but it won't take you far. It's misleadingly simple, and I'm sure none of you believes database applications are built with point-and-click operations.

What's Covered in This Book?

This book is addressed to VB programmers with little or no database experience. It starts with the basics: the principles of database design, VB's visual database tools, and Structured Query Language. As the book progresses, it proceeds to more advanced topics such as Transact-SQL, stored procedures, and hierarchical Recordsets. Toward the end of the book, you will find complex topics such as remote data access and how to use the Microsoft Transaction Server. Finally, the last two chapters of the book detail two examples of complete database applications. These are lengthy examples, which I couldn't fit into any single chapter. Since they combine many of the topics discussed in the book, I've chosen to present them in a separate part of the book.

NOTE   In the course of writing this book, I have used the beta version of ADO 2.5 that came with beta 3 of Windows 2000. Most of the differences between versions 2.1 and 2.5 have nothing to do with databases. ADO 2.5 is the first data-access component that can access semi-structured data like file systems and e-mail systems. These are exciting features, but they're not directly related to database programming. Once you master the basic topics of database programming, especially SQL Server databases, you'll find it easy to understand the new features of ADO 2.5.

Part One: Database Basics

This book is organized in four parts. The first part discusses the basics of databases: how to design them, how to manipulate them with SQL, and how to use Transact-SQL (a programming language built into SQL Server). Then you'll learn how to use the ADO component to write client applications. A client application retrieves a small section of the database, loads it on the client computer, and processes it there. The client application's role is to move as much of the processing away from the server so that the server will have more time to do what it does best: query and update the database.

In the first few chapters of the book, you'll read about the structure of relational databases and how to design them. You'll find detailed discussions of the sample databases you're going to use in later chapters. You'll find a detailed discussion of SQL, and you'll learn about Visual Basic's visual database tools. These tools will help you prepare your application. The more you do with these visual database tools, the less code you'll have to write later.

Stored procedures are discussed in detail in the first part of the book. Many consider this to be an advanced topic, but it isn't. Once you have learned how to implement stored procedures, you'll be able to add custom objects to your database and further simplify the coding of the client applications.

A good deal of the first part of the book is devoted to SQL and T-SQL. As a database programmer, you can't afford to pass these topics. SQL allows you to access any database; T-SQL will help you make the most of SQL Server.

Part Two: Advanced Data-Access Techniques

The second part of the book deals with four fairly advanced topics: hierarchical Recordsets, Remote Data Services (RDS), data-aware Classes, and data-bound controls. The RDS component allows you to build Web pages that contain controls bound to database fields. However, it's limited to Internet Explorer. A data-bound Class is basically a middle-tier component. The Class encapsulates complicated data-access operations, so that your code doesn't have to deal with the complexity of the database. In the last chapter of the second part, you'll learn how to build custom data-bound controls, which will help you standardize the user interface of your client applications. You will also learn how to build custom data controls, with functionality that's unique to your application.

Part Three: Databases on the Web

Each day, more and more companies are making use of the Internet, either building commercial sites or designing Web applications that allow employees to access the corporate database through the Web. In the third part of this book, you'll learn how to use Active Server Pages to build Web applications that access a database on the server through the ADO component. This part provides a quick introduction to VBScript (a subset of Visual Basic) and HTML controls ("light" versions of the basic Windows controls). HTML controls are placed on HTML pages, just as the regular controls are placed on Forms, but you'll learn how Web applications are structured differently than VB applications. I discuss a new type of VB project, an IIS (Internet Information Server). IIS projects allow you to build Web applications right in Visual Basic's IDE. The last chapter in this part is about Microsoft Transaction Server. That material is quite advanced, and you don't really need MTS unless you're developing Web applications, or client applications that will be deployed in very large corporations.

Part Four: Putting Your Knowledge to Work

This part of the book contains two chapters, describing a few sample applications that combine many of the topics discussed in the book. These sample applications are quite lengthy, which is why we placed them in their own chapters.

The DataEntry application demonstrates how to build functional interfaces for browsing and editing multiple tables. The Invoices application demonstrates a simple user interface for placing orders and making transactional updates. You'll see how to implement transactions with ADO as well as with T-SQL stored procedures.

The last application is a Web application that demonstrates all the basic functions of an online bookstore: how to query and update databases from within Web pages, how to implement a shopping basket with cookies, and how to accept orders.

What's on the CD

This book is accompanied by a CD containing:

- The code for all the example projects discussed in the book
- A copy of SQL Server 7 Evaluation Edition
- An appendix with the complete ADO 2.5 object model

You'll find the projects in the CHAPTERCODE folder, and each chapter's projects are in their own folder, named after the project. For example, the Customers project in Chapter 5 is stored in the CHAPTERCODE\CH5\CUSTOMERS folder. All the files needed to open the project and run it in the Visual Basic IDE are stored in this folder.

I suggest that you use the installation software on the CD to copy all projects to your hard disk, duplicating the structure of the CHAPTERCODE folder on your disk. You can run the projects off the CD, but you can't save them on the CD after editing them. To edit a project, you must copy the project's folder to your hard disk and then open the project. Notice that the files copied off the CD have their Read-Only attribute set. To edit any projects you copied manually to your hard disk from the CD, follow these steps:

1. Select all files with the mouse, then right-click your selection.

2. From the shortcut menu, choose Properties to open the Properties dialog box.

3. In the Attributes section, clear the Read-Only box.

Using the Book's Projects

All of the projects in this book use one of the sample databases that come with VB and SQL Server. The information needed to access the database is embedded into the code, usually through the DataEnvironment object (which is discussed in Chapter 4). Other projects set up a connection string with the appropriate information for the connection in the code. The projects that use Jet databases expect to find the sample databases in their default locations. The projects that use SQL Server databases assume that SQL Server is running on the same machine you're using to test them. These projects connect to the database on the local server and use the account *sa* to login (no password). If you have set up your machine differently, or you're using a database server on a LAN, you must change the code (or the properties of the DataEnvironment object) accordingly. All you have to do is change the name of the database server from local to the name of the machine on which SQL Server is running, and set the account name and password. For more information on changing the connection information, see Chapters 3 and 4.

If a project can't connect to a database, it will display an error message. Projects that use the DataEnvironment object to connect to the database will display the error message not only when you attempt to execute them, but also when you attempt to open the DataEnvironment object. To fix them, open the DataEnvironment object, ignore the error message, and then set the name of the database server and the user ID and password. Projects that set up the connection information in their code will display the error message when you attempt to execute them. To fix them, open the project's code window and change the setting of the Connection-String property, as discussed in Chapter 4.

The projects of Chapter 12 and 13 contain custom ActiveX components (data-aware Classes and controls). The first time you open each project, an error message will be displayed indicating that the project's custom component couldn't be located. The component couldn't be found because it's not registered on your system. Ignore the error message and continue loading the project. If the custom component is an ActiveX control, you don't have to take any special action. The component will be registered automatically the first time you execute the project. If the custom component is a Class, you must add a reference to the custom component before you can test it. Open the test Form of the project and add a reference to the custom component through the References dialog box, as explained in Chapter 12.

How to Reach the Author

Despite our best efforts, a book this size is bound to contain errors. If you have any problems with the text or applications in this book, you can contact me directly at 76470.724@compuserve.com.

Although I can't promise a response to every question, I will endeavor to address any problem in the text or examples and will provide updated versions. I would also like to hear any comments you may have about the book regarding topics you liked or disliked, as well as how useful you found the examples. Your comments will help me revise the book in future editions.

Updates

It's quite likely that a Service Pack for Visual Studio will be released after the shipment of Windows 2000. Any changes and/or additions that affect the projects of the book will be posted at the book's section on the Sybex Web site at www.sybex.com. To access this information, simply locate the *Mastering Database Programming with Visual Basic 6* title and follow the link to the Updates section.

PART I

Database Basics

CHAPTER
ONE

1

Database Access: Architectures and Technologies

- Databases and database management systems

- Windows DNA

- Client-server architecture

- Three-tier architecture

- SQL Server

The first chapter in a typical computer book is an introduction to the book's topic. So, this chapter should be an introduction to databases, but it isn't. Databases are the broadest and most diverse area of computer programming. Before I can give you very much detail on what a database is, how to design one, and then how to program it, I must explain some of the key concepts in this field and the numerous acronyms that are used heavily in this book and the online help.

In my attempt to explain all the data access–related technologies at the beginning of the book, I may have oversimplified things. This chapter is for readers who are not comfortable with the various acronyms like OLE DB, ADO, terms like n-tiers, and so on. If you know the difference between OLE DB and ADO, you can skip this chapter and jump to the next chapter, where I discuss the structure of databases.

Databases and Database Management Systems

A *database* is a complex object for storing structured information, which is organized and stored in a way that allows its quick and efficient retrieval. We put a lot of effort into designing a database so that we can retrieve the data easily. The information is broken into *tables*, and each table stores different entities (one table stores customer information, another table stores product information, and so on). We break the information into smaller chunks, so that we can manage it easily (divide and conquer). We can design rules to protect the database against user actions and ask the DBMS to enforce these rules (for example, reject customers without a name). These rules apply to all the items stored in the customers table; the same rules don't apply to the products table and the orders table, of course.

In addition to tables, we define *relationships* between tables. Relationships allow users to combine information from multiple tables. Let's say you store customer information in one table and sales information in another table. By establishing a relationship between the two tables, you can quickly retrieve the invoices issued to a specific customer. Without such a relationship, you would have to scan the entire invoice table to isolate the desired invoices. This view of a database, made up of tables related to one another, is a *conceptual* view of the database. And the database that relies on relationships between tables is called *relational*.

The actual structure of the database on the disk is quite different. In fact, you have no idea how data is stored in the database (and you should be thankful for this). The information is physically stored into and recalled from the database by a special program known as a database management system (DBMS). DBMSs are among the most complicated applications, and a modern DBMS can instantly locate a record in a table with several million records. While the DBMS maintains all the information in the database, applications can access this information through statements made in *Structured Query Language (SQL)*, a language for specifying high-level operations. These operations are called *queries*, and there are two types of queries: selection queries, which extract information form the database, and action queries, which update the database. How the DBMS maintains, updates, and retrieves this information is something the application doesn't have to deal with.

Specifically, a DBMS provides the following functions:

- A DBMS allows applications to define the structure of a database with SQL statements. The subset of SQL statements that define or edit this structure is called Data Definition Language (DDL). All DBMSs use a visual interface to define the structure of a database with simple point-and-click operations, but these tools translate the actions of the user into the appropriate DDL statements. SQL Server, for example, allows you to create databases with a visual tool, the Enterprise Manager, but it also generates the equivalent DDL statements and stores them into a special file, called a *script*.

- A DBMS allows applications to manipulate the information stored in the database with SQL statements. The subset of SQL statements that manipulate this information is called Data Manipulation Language (DML). The basic data-manipulation actions are the insertion of new records, modification and deletion of existing ones, and record retrieval.

- A DBMS protects the integrity of the database by enforcing certain rules, which are incorporated into the design of the database. You can specify default values, prohibit certain fields from being empty, forbid the deletion of records that are linked to other records, and so on. For example, you can tell the DBMS not to remove a customer if the customer is linked to one or more invoices. If you could remove the customer, that customer's invoices would be "orphaned." In addition, the DBMS is responsible for the security of the database (it protects the database from access by unauthorized users).

NOTE   The terms "records" and "fields" are not used in the context of relational databases. We now talk about "rows" and "columns." I'm using the old-fashioned terms because most readers who are new to relational databases are probably more familiar with records and fields. If you have programmed older ISAM databases, or even random-access files, you're probably more familiar with records and fields. I will drop the older terms shortly.

SQL Server is a database management system and not a database. A SQL Server database is a database maintained by SQL Server. SQL is a universal language for manipulating databases and is supported by all DBMSs—we'll examine it in detail in Chapter 4, "Structured Query Language." SQL retrieves selected records from the database and returns them to the client. The set of records returned by an SQL statement is called a *cursor*. If another user changes some records in the database, those changes will not be reflected in the existing cursors. We need a more complicated mechanism that will synchronize the data in the database and the client computer, and this mechanism is *ADO (ActiveX Data Objects)*. We'll get to ADO soon, but first let's discuss Microsoft's view of data access. We'll look at the big picture first, and then at the individual components.

Windows DNA

The one term you'll be hearing and reading about most frequently in the coming months (regarding the release of Windows 2000) is *DNA*. DNA stands for *Distributed interNet Architecture*, and it's a methodology for building distributed applications. A methodology is a set of rules, or suggestions, and not a blueprint for developing applications; it's a recommendation on how to build distributed applications. Since this recommendation comes from Microsoft, you can consider it a very clear hint of the shape of things to come. Follow these recommendations and your applications will not be outdated soon.

A *distributed application* is one made up of multiple components that run on different machines. These machines can be interconnected through a local area network (LAN)—or a few machines on a LAN and a few more machines on the Internet. To make things even more interesting, throw into the mix a second LAN, located a few thousand miles away. So, in effect, DNA is about building applications for the Internet. I'm sure most of you are interested in building database applications that run on a LAN. The Internet? Well, maybe later. Do not panic, because this book is about building database applications for LANs (and a little about the Internet). But if you want to understand how all the pieces fit together, why Microsoft is introducing new access technologies, and why it chooses weird acronyms to describe them, you should start with the big picture.

The big picture starts with the realization that not all information is stored in databases. When most of us are talking about data, we think of databases, rows, and columns—well-structured data that can be easily retrieved. But not all information can be stored in databases. A lot of information is stored in e-mail folders, text documents, spreadsheets, even audio and video files. The ultimate data-access technology is one that can access any information, from anywhere, whether it be a database, an electronic mailbox, a text file, even a handheld device. Ideally, we should be able to access information in a uniform way, no matter where this information resides. And we should also be able to access it from anywhere, meaning the Internet.

Universal Data Access

Microsoft uses the term *Universal Data Access* to describe this idea. The premise of Universal Data Access is to allow applications to efficiently access data where it resides, through a common set of tools. There's nothing new about accessing diverse sources of information today, but how is it done? In most cases, we replicate the information. Quite often, we transform the information as we replicate it. The problem with this approach is that we end up with multiple copies of the same information (a highly expensive and wasteful practice).

At a high level, Universal Data Access can be visualized as shown in Figure 1.1. *Data providers*, or *data stores*, store information, and their job is to expose the data through data services. *Data consumers* receive and process the data. Finally, *business components* provide common services that extend the native functionality of the data providers.

FIGURE 1.1:

Universal Data Access

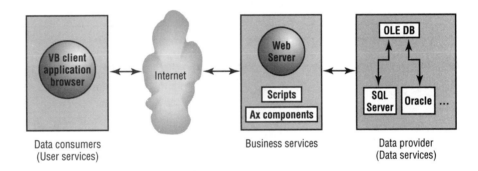

Data consumers
(User services)

Business services

Data provider
(Data services)

A data provider can be a database management system like SQL Server, but it doesn't necessarily need to be. Eventually, every object that stores data will become a data provider.

ADO 2.5, which is currently in beta form and will be distributed with Windows 2000, supports a few special objects for accessing semi-structured data. Semi-structured data are the data you retrieve from sources other than database rows, such as folders and their files, e-mail folders, and so on. These objects are described in the appendix (on the companion CD), but they're not discussed in detail in this book.

For the purposes of this book, data providers are DBMSs. The data consumer is an application that uses the data. This application is usually called a *client* application, because it is being served by the data provider. The client application makes requests to the DBMS, and the DBMS carries out the requests. The data consumer need not be a typical client application with a visible interface. In this book, however, you'll learn how to build client applications that interact with the user. Finally, the service components are programs that read the data from the data source in their native format and transform it into a format that's more suitable for the client application. Universal Data Access requires four basic service components, which are:

Cursor Service The UDA cursor is a structure for storing the information returned by the data source. The cursor is like a table, made up of rows and columns. The cursor service provides an efficient, client-side cache with local scrolling, filtering, and sorting capabilities. The cursor is usually moved to the client (that is, the address space where the client application is running), and the client application should be able to scroll, filter, and sort the rows of the cursor without requesting a new cursor from the DBMS. Figure 1.2 shows a client application for browsing and editing customer data. A cursor with all customers (or selected ones) is maintained on the client. The scrollbar at the bottom of the Form, which is a Visual Basic control, allows the user to move through the rows of the cursor. The fields of the current row in the cursor are displayed on the Form and can be edited.

FIGURE 1.2:

The cursor service is encapsulated into the control at the bottom of the Form.

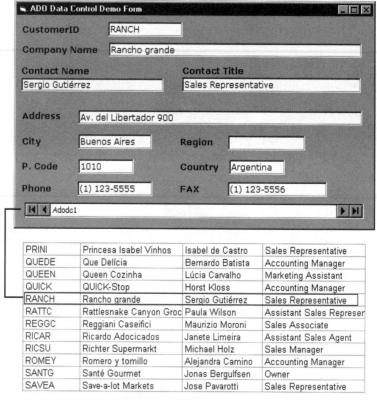

NOTE   For readers who are already familiar with SQL Server, I must point out that the cursors you create with T-SQL statements are different than UDA cursors. The SQL Server cursor contains raw information (the rows extracted from the database with the SQL statement). The UDA cursor contains not only data, but the functionality to manipulate the data. This functionality is implemented mostly with methods for sorting and filtering the rows, navigational methods, and so on.

Synchronization Service   This service updates the database with the data in the local cursor. This service must be able to update the database instantly, as the user edits the data in the cursor, or in batch mode. As you will see later in the book, there are two major types of cursors, those that reside on the server and those that reside on the client. The rows of a client-side cursor are moved to the client and can't be synchronized to the database at all times. It is possible for another user to edit the same rows in the database, while the client application is processing those rows in the client-side cursor.

Shape Service   This service allows the construction of hierarchically organized data. A plain cursor is made up of rows extracted from the database. The data may have come from one or more tables, but it appears as another table to the client; in other words, it has a flat structure. A hierarchical, or shaped, cursor contains information about the structure of the data. A hierarchically organized structure in Access is shown in Figure 1.3. The outer table contains customer information. Each customer has several invoices. Clicking the plus sign in front of the customer's name opens a list of the invoices issued to that customer. Finally, each order has one or more detail lines, viewed by clicking the plus sign in front of an invoice's number.

FIGURE 1.3:

Viewing the records of a hierarchical structure with Access

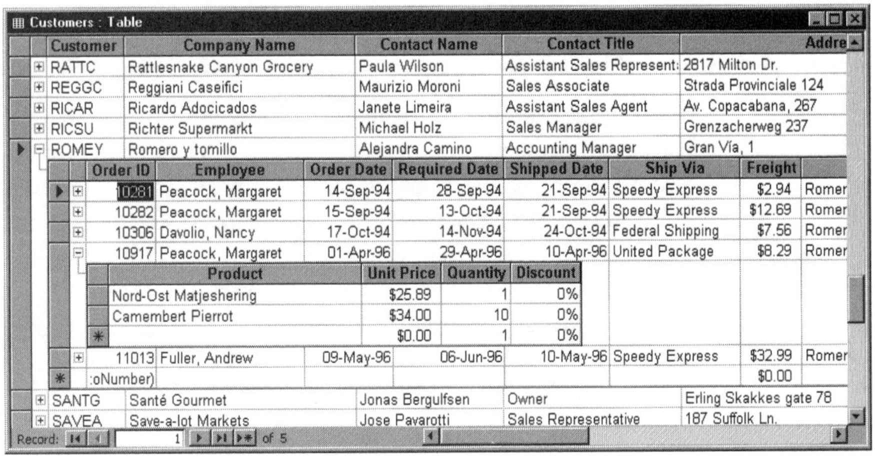

Remote Data Service   This service moves data from one component to another in a multitier environment. You'll understand what this service does when you read about tiers, later in this chapter. For example, in a Web page that queries a database (a page that searches for books with title keywords, author names, and so on), the user enters the search criteria on the page, which is displayed in the browser. This information must be moved to the Web server, then to the database. Obviously, you can't assume that the browser maintains a connection to the database. When it needs to query the database, it must call the appropriate program on the Web server, passing the user-supplied keywords as arguments. A special program on the Web server will intercept the values passed by the Web page, and it will contact the database and extract the desired rows. The result of the query, which is a cursor, must be moved back to the client. Moving information from one process to another is called *marshalling*, and this is where the remote data service comes in, translating the data before passing it to another component. In Part III, you'll see how to use remote data services to write Web pages bound to the fields of a remote database.

More services may be added in the future. Throughout this book, we'll discuss how these services enable you to write client-server applications. The cursor service, for example, is implemented in the Recordset object, which is a structure for storing selected records. You can use the Recordset object's properties and methods to navigate through records and manipulate them. To navigate through the Recordset, for example, you use the MoveNext method:

```
RS.MoveNext
```

RS is a Recordset object variable that represents the cursor on the client.

To change the Address field of the current record in the cursor, you use a statement like the following one:

```
RS.Fields("Address") = "10001 Palm Ave"
```

The cursor service is responsible for scrolling and updating the local cursor (the copy of the data maintained on the client). Depending on how you've set up the Recordset object, the changes can be committed immediately to the database, or you can commit all edited records at a later point. To commit the changes to the database, you can call either the Update method (to commit the current record) or the UpdateBatch method (to commit all the edited records in batch mode). Updating the database takes place through the synchronization server. The component services are totally transparent to you, and you can access them through the ADO objects (the Recordset object being one of them).

To summarize, Universal Data Access is a platform for developing distributed database applications that can access a diverse variety of data sources across an intranet or the Internet. You can think of Universal Data Access as the opposite of a universal database that can hold all types of information and requires that users actually move the information from its original source into the universal database. Let's see how this platform is implemented.

ADO and OLE DB

The two cornerstones of Universal Data Access are ActiveX Data Objects (ADO) and OLE for Databases (OLE DB). OLE DB is a layer that sits on top of the database. ADO sits on top of OLE DB and offers a simplified view of the database. Because each database exposes its functionality with its own set of API (application programming interface) functions, to access each database through its native interface, you'd have to learn the specifics of the database (low-level, technical details). Porting the application to another database would be a major undertaking. To write applications that talk to two different databases at once (SQL Server and Oracle, for instance), you'd have learn two different APIs and discover the peculiarities of each database, unless you use OLE DB and ADO.

OLE DB offers a unified view of different data providers. Each database has its own set of OLE DB service providers, which provide a uniform view of the database. ADO hides the peculiarities of each database and gives developers a simple conceptual view of the underlying database. The difference between ADO and OLE DB is that OLE DB gives you more control over the data-access process, because it's a low-level interface. As far as Visual Basic is concerned, OLE DB uses pointers and other C++ argument-passing mechanisms, so it's substantially more difficult to use than ADO. Actually, most C++ programmers also use ADO to access databases because it offers a simpler, high-level view of the database.

Figure 1.4 shows how your application can access various databases. The most efficient method is to get there directly through OLE DB. This also happens to be the most difficult route, and it's not what VB programmers do. The next most efficient method is to go through ADO, which makes the OLE DB layer transparent to the application. You can also get to the database through ODBC (Open DataBase Connectivity), which is similar to OLE DB, but it's an older technology. If you can program ODBC, then you can program OLE DB, and there's no reason to use ODBC drivers. Many of you are already familiar with DAO (Data Access Objects) and RDO (Remote Data Objects). These are older technologies for accessing databases through ODBC. In a way, they are equivalent to ADO. These components, however, will not be updated in the future, and you should use them only if you're supporting database applications that already use DAO or RDO.

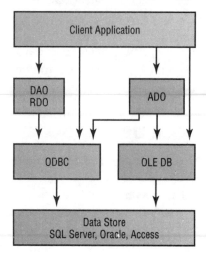

There was a time when DAO was the only way for VB programmers to program databases, and as a result too many DAO-based applications are in use today (and will remain in use for a while). In fact, most VB books in the market still focus on DAO in discussing Visual Basic's data-access capabilities. However, it's an outdated technology, and you should not base any new project on DAO. I wouldn't be surprised if the ADO data control takes the place of the DAO data control in the toolbox of the next version of Visual Basic.

The ADO Objects

Let's switch our attention to the ADO objects. You'll find all the information you need about ADO in the following chapters, so this is a very brief overview to show you how the ADO object model reflects the basic operations we perform on databases. A client application performs the following:

1. Establishes a connection to the database

2. Executes commands against the database

3. Retrieves information from the database

ADO's basic objects correspond to these operations, and they are appropriately named Connection, Command, and Recordset. The Connection object represents a connection to the database. To specify the database you want to connect to, set the Connection object's properties and then call the Open method to actually establish the connection. With the visual database tools, you don't even have to set any properties. You specify the database you want to connect to with point-and-click operations, and VB will prepare the appropriate Connection object for you.

Connection objects are expensive in terms of resources, and establishing a new connection is one of the most resource-intensive operations. It's crucial, therefore, to create a single Connection object in your application and use it for all the operations you want to perform against the database. If you need to connect to multiple databases, however, you must create one Connection object for each database. (This statement isn't universally true. There are situations, as in Web applications, where you can't afford to maintain a Connection object for each viewer. We'll come back to this topic in Part III of the book. As far as client applications are concerned, however, the rule is to establish a connection and maintain it during the course of the application.)

Once you've established a connection to the database, you can execute commands against it. A command can be an SQL statement or the name of a stored procedure. *Stored procedures* are applications written in Transact-SQL (T-SQL, the programming language of SQL Server) and are usually called with arguments. To execute an SQL statement or a stored procedure, you must set up a Command object and then call its Execute method to execute the command. The Command object contains the SQL statement or the name of the stored procedure as well as the required arguments. If the command retrieves information from the database, the results are stored in a Recordset object, and you can access them from within your application through the methods and properties of the Recordset object.

Now that you've seen how an application communicates with the database, we'll turn our attention to the architecture of the database applications that we're going to focus on in this book, the formerly ubiquitous client-server architecture. This architecture is different than DNA, but you need a solid understanding of client-server architecture before you adopt more complicated architectures for your applications. If you're developing database applications to run on a LAN, client-server architecture is adequate.

Client-Server Architecture

Client-server architecture is based on a simple premise: Different computers perform different tasks, and each computer can be optimized for a particular task. It makes sense, therefore, to separate the DBMS from the client application. In a networked environment, the DBMS resides on a single machine. However, many applications access the database, and all clients make requests from the same database. The program that accepts and services these requests is the DBMS, and the machine on which the DBMS is running is the database server. The client applications do not know how the data is stored in the database, nor do they care.

In client-server architecture, the application is broken into two distinct components, which work together for a common goal. These components are called *tiers*, and each tier implements a different functionality. The client-server model involves two tiers. As you will see later in this chapter, you can—and often should—build applications with more than two tiers.

Client-server became very popular because much of the processing is done on the client computer, which can be an inexpensive desktop computer. The more powerful the client is, the more processing it can do. Two clients may receive the same data from the client—sales by territory, for instance. One computer can do simple calculations, such as averages, while another, more powerful, client might combine the data with a mapping application to present complicated charts.

The Two-Tier Model

The first tier of a client-server application is the client tier, or *presentation tier*, which runs on the client. This tier contains code that presents data and interacts with the user, and it is usually a VB application. You can also build client tiers that run in a browser—these are Web pages that contain controls, which are similar to the basic VB controls and allow the user to interact with the database. Figure 1.5 shows a simple client application for browsing and editing customers. This is a VB Form with TextBox controls that display the current customer's fields. Figure 1.6 shows a Web page that does the same. It contains Text controls, which are bound to the customer fields in the database. The VB client application relies on the cursor service, while the Web page relies on the remote data service. These are two of the applications we'll develop in the course of this book.

FIGURE 1.5:

A VB client application for viewing and editing customers

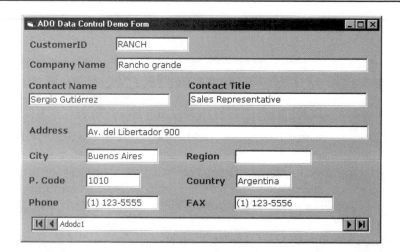

A Web page for viewing and editing customers

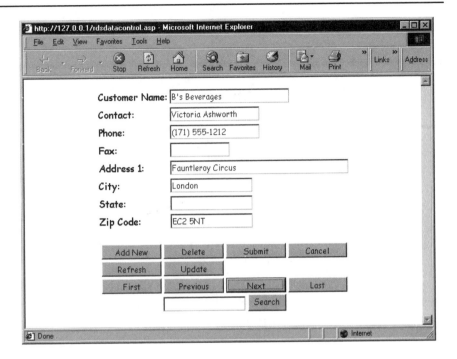

The client application requests data from the database and displays it on one or more VB Forms. Once the data is on the client computer, your application can process it and present it in many different ways. The client computer is quite capable of manipulating the data locally, and the server is not involved in the process. If the user edits the fields, the application can update the database as well. The communication between the client and the server takes place through ADO, which makes it really simple to extract data from and update the database.

The second tier is the *database server*, or DBMS. This tier manipulates a very complex object, the database, and offers a simplified view of the database through OLE DB and ADO. Clients can make complicated requests like "Show me the names of the customers who have placed orders in excess of $100,000 in the last three months," or "Show me the best-selling products in the state of California." The DBMS receives many requests of this type from the clients, and it must service them all. Obviously, the DBMS can't afford to process the data before passing it to the client. One client might map the data on a graph, another client might display the same data on a ListBox control and so on. The server's job is to extract the required data from the tables and furnish them to the client in the form of a cursor. It simply transmits a cursor to the client and lets the client process the information. The more powerful the client, the more it can do with the data. (As you will see later in this chapter, in the discussion of stored procedures, certain operations that are performed frequently, or require the transmission of a very large number of rows to the client, can be carried out by the server.)

By splitting the workload between clients and servers, we allow each application to do what it can do best. The DBMS runs on one of the fastest machines on the network. The clients don't have to be as powerful. In fact, there are two types of clients: *thin* and *fat clients*.

Thin and Fat Clients

Thin clients are less-powerful computers that do very little processing on their own. A browser is a thin client: Its presentation capabilities are determined by the current version of HTML. The benefits of thin clients are their cost (any computer that runs Internet Explorer or Netscape Navigator is good enough) and their connectivity (they can access the database server from anywhere). Another very important—and often overlooked—feature of thin clients is that their presentation capabilities don't vary. A client application that runs within a browser will run on virtually all computers. Thin clients are easy to maintain too, a fact that can lower the cost of deployment of the application.

A *fat client* is a desktop computer with rich presentation features. Because client applications that run on fat clients are far more flexible and powerful, they require more expensive computers to run, and their interfaces can't be standardized. You can make them as elaborate as the available hardware permits.

The Three-Tier Model

The two-tier model is a very efficient architecture for database applications, but not always the best choice. Most programmers develop two-tier applications that run on small local area networks. The most complete form of a database application, however, is one that involves three tiers.

In two-tier or client-server architecture, the client talks directly to the database server. Every application that connects to SQL Server or Oracle, and retrieves some information, like customer names or product prices, is a client-server application. The role of the database server is to access and update the data. Everything else is left to the client. In other words, the client is responsible for presenting the data to the user, parsing user input, preparing the appropriate requests for the database server, and finally implementing the so-called *business rules*. A business rule is a procedure specific to a corporation. Your corporation, for example, may have rules for establishing the credit line of its customers. These rules must be translated into VB code, which will be executed on the client. It is also possible to write procedures that will be executed on the server, but you can't move all the processing back to the server.

Business rules change often, as they reflect business practices. New rules are introduced, existing ones are revised, which means that the code that implements them is subject to frequent changes. If you implement business rules on the client, you must distribute new executables to the workstations and make sure all users on the network are using the latest version of the client software (that is, your applications). If business rules are implemented on the server, you don't have the problem of redistributing the application, but you place an additional burden to the server, tying it up with calculations that it's not optimized for or that could be performed on another machine.

This leads naturally to the introduction of a third tier, the middle tier. The middle tier is an object that sits between the client application and the server. It's a Class (or multiple Classes) that exposes several methods and isolates the client from the server. If many clients need to calculate insurance premiums, you can implement the calculations in the middle tier. Client applications can call the methods of the objects that reside on the middle tier and get the results. The client application need not know how premiums are calculated or whether the calculations involve any database access. All they need to know is the name of one or more methods of the objects that runs on the middle tier.

The main advantage of the middle tier is that it isolates the client from the server. The client no longer accesses the database. Instead, it calls the methods exposed by the objects in the middle tier. A client application will eventually add a new customer to the database. Even this simple operation requires some validation. Is there a customer with the same key already in the database? Did the user fail to supply values for the required fields (we can't add a customer without a name, for example)? Adding orders to a database requires even more complicated validation. Do we have enough items of each product in stock to fill the order? And what do we do if we can only fill part of the order?

A well-structured application implements these operations in the middle tier. The client application doesn't have to know how each customer is stored in the database if it can call the AddCustomer() method passing the values of the fields (customer name, address, phone numbers and so on) as arguments. The middle tier will actually insert the new information to the database and return a True value if all went well, or an error message is an error occurred.

Likewise, the client application can pass all the information of the invoice to the middle-tier component and let it handle the insertion of the new invoice. This action involves many tables. We may have to update the stock, the customer's balance, possibly update a list of best-selling products, and so on. The middle-tier component will take care of these operations for the client. As a result, the development of the client application is greatly simplified. The client will call the NewInvoice member passing the ID of the customer that placed the order, the products and quantities ordered and (optionally) the discount. Or, you may leave it up to the middle tier to calculate the discount based on the total amount, or the items ordered.

The NewInvoice method must update multiple tables in a transaction. In other words, it must make sure that all the tables were updated, or none of them. If the program updates the customer's balance, but fails to update the stock of the items ordered (or it updates the stock of a few items only), then the database will be left in an inconsistent state. The program should make sure that either all actions succeed, or they all fail. You can execute transactions from within your VB code, but it's a good idea to pass the responsibility of the transaction to a middle-tier component.

As a side effect, the middle tier forces you to design your application before you actually start coding. If you choose to implement business rules as a middle tier, you must analyze the requirements of the application, implement and debug the middle-tier components, and then start coding the client application. While this is "extra credit" if you're only learning how to program databases with VB, or you write small applications to be used by a workgroup in your company, it's more of a necessity if you're working as a member of a programming team. By designing and implementing the middle tier, you are in effect designing the client application itself, and the work you do in the middle tier will pay off when you start coding the client application.

The middle tier can also save you a good deal of work when you decide to move the application to the Web. Sooner or later, you'll be asked to develop a site for your company. If the middle tier is already in place, you can use its components with a Web application. Let me describe a component we will develop later in the book. A client application needs a function to retrieve books based on title keywords and/or author name(s). If you specify which of the search arguments are title keywords and which ones are author names, the operation is quite simple. As I'm sure you know, all electronic bookstores on the Web provide a box where you can enter any keyword and then search the database. The database server must use the keywords intelligently to retrieve the titles you're interested in. If you think about this operation, you'll realize that it's not trivial. Building the appropriate SQL statement to retrieve the desired titles is fairly complicated. Moreover, you may have to revise the search algorithm as the database grows.

The same functionality is required from within both a client application that runs on the desktop and a client application that runs on the Internet (a Web page). If you implement a SearchTitles() function for the client application, then you must implement the same function in VBScript and use it with your Web application. If you decide to change implementation of the function, you must recompile the desktop application, redistribute it, and then change the scripts of the Web application accordingly. Sooner or later the same arguments will retrieve different titles on different machines.

If you implement the SearchTitles() function as a middle-tier component, the same functionality will be available to all clients, whether they run on the desktop or the Web. You may wish to extend the search to multiple databases. Even in this extreme case, you will have to revise the code in a single place, the middle tier, and all the clients will be able to search both databases with the existing code. As long as you don't add any new arguments to the SearchTitles() function, the client will keep calling the same old function and be up to date.

It is actually possible to write client applications that never connect to the database and are not even aware that they're clients to a database server. If all the actions against the database take place through the middle tier, then the client's code will be regular VB code and it could not contain any database structures. As you can understand, it's not feasible to expect that you can write a "database application without a database," but the middle tier can handle many of the complicated tasks of accessing the database and greatly simplify the coding of the client application.

The Layers of a Three-Tier Application

The three-tier model breaks the components of the application into three categories, or layers, described below. Figure 1.7 shows a diagram of a three-tier application.

FIGURE 1.7:

A three-tier application

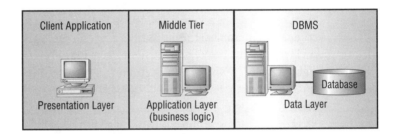

Presentation layer   This program runs on the client and interacts with the user, primarily presenting information to the user. You will usually develop applications for the presentation layer (unless you're on the business services team), and these applications are frequently called *user services*. By the way, user services are not trivial. They can include advanced data-bound controls and, in many cases, custom data-bound controls. Data-bound controls are bound to a field in the database and change value to reflect the field's current value, as the user navigates through the Recordset. When a data-bound control is edited, the new value is committed automatically to the database (unless the control is not editable).

Application layer   Also known as the business layer, this layer contains the logic of the application. It simplifies the client's access to the database by isolating the user services from the database. In addition, you can insert business rules here that have nothing to do with the presentation logic. This layer is designed before you start coding the client application. The components of the application or business layer are frequently called *business services*.

Data layer   This layer is the database server, which services requests made by the clients. The requests are usually queries, like "Return all titles published by Sybex in 1999" or "Show the total of all orders placed in the first quarter of 2000 in California." Other requests may update the database by inserting new customers, orders, and so on. The database server must update the database and at the same time protect its integrity (for example, it will refuse to delete a customer if there are invoices issued to that specific customer).

Three-Tier Applications on the Web

The best example of a three-tier application is a Web application. Web applications are highly scalable, and two tiers of the application may run on the same computer (the client tier runs on a separate machine, obviously). Even though you may never write applications for the Web, you should understand how Web applications interact with viewers.

Figure 1.8 shows a Web application that runs in a browser and contacts a Web server and a database server to interact with the user. The first tier—the presentation layer—is the browser, which interacts with the user through HTML documents (Web pages). A Web page may contain controls where the user can enter information and submit it to the server. The Web page, therefore, is the equivalent of a VB Form. Where your VB application can read the controls' values the moment they're entered, the values of the controls on a Web page must be passed to the server before they can be processed. (It is possible to do some processing on the client, but client-side scripting is beyond the scope of this book).

FIGURE 1.8:

A Web application is a typical example of a three-tier application.

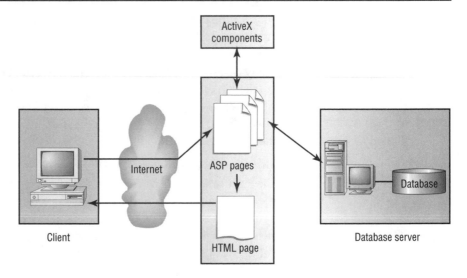

All requests are channeled by the browser to the Web server. Internet Information Server (IIS) is Microsoft's Web server and requires Windows NT or Windows 2000, Server edition. Most of the examples in this book will work with the Personal Web Server, which comes with Windows 98. The material in Chapter 16, "Microsoft Transaction Server," applies only to IIS. IIS is the middle tier (the application layer). The Web server's role is to generate HTML documents and send them to the client. If the Web server needs to access a database, it must contact a DBMS through an ActiveX component. The programs on the Web server are active server pages, written in VBScript.

The DBMS, finally, is the data layer of the application.

Notice that the tiers of a Web application need not reside and execute on different machines. The DBMS may be running on the same machine as the Web server. For testing purposes, you can run all three tiers on the same computer, but when you deploy the application, you will install the client application on multiple workstations. The Web server and the DBMS are frequently installed on the same machine, but they run as two separate processes. Even though they're on the same computer, the DBMS will authenticate the Web server and will not allow it to view information or invoke procedures unless it has the appropriate privileges. As the site grows, you may have to use multiple databases and/or multiple Web servers.

Access and Client-Server Applications

Many readers are probably wondering whether they can develop client-server applications with Access. Access is not a database server. When you contact Access and open a table, the entire table is uploaded to the client computer's memory. (If the table is large, it's uploaded in segments, but the processing takes place on the client.) If five users on the network are all accessing the same information, then five copies of the same table(s) are on the clients, plus the original. To describe Access applications, the term *file-based database* is used, but I prefer the (older) term *desktop database*. To use an Access database, you must have Access or compatible software, such as Excel or a Visual Basic application, installed on the client.

One of the most important differences between Access and SQL Server is how they handle concurrency. SQL Server maintains a single copy of the data. Because all clients must go through the DBMS, SQL Server knows when a record is being edited and prevents other users from deleting it or even reading it. Access must compare the changes made on the client to the original and then decide whether other users can access a row. If a user opens a table and selects a row to edit, no other user can edit the same row. This is a nice feature, unless the user gets an important call or goes out to lunch. Then the row will remain locked indefinitely. As the number of users grows, the overhead is overwhelming, and it's time to upsize the database to SQL Server.

Continued on next page

Access 2000 can be used for developing client-server applications, but this feature of Access relies on SQL Server technology. Microsoft has released the MSDE (Microsoft Data Engine) component, which is client-server data engine. MSDE is fully compatible with SQL Server; it's actually based on the same data engine as SQL Server, but it's designed for small workgroups. You can use MSDE to develop client-server applications with Access 2000 (or VB, for that matter) that can "see" SQL Server databases. These applications are fully compatible with SQL Server and will work with SQL Server if you change the connection information.

SQL Server

Quite a few of you are familiar with Access, and you may have even developed database applications with Access. As I mentioned earlier, however, Access is a desktop database. It can't be scaled up, and it can't accommodate many simultaneous users. To develop real database applications, you should move to SQL Server. SQL Server is Microsoft's DBMS. It's highly scalable and you can use it to develop applications for everything from small networks to thousands of users.

Until recently, Microsoft was pushing Access databases with Visual Basic. Now VB6 comes with all the drivers and tools you need to access SQL Server databases, and the next version of VB will probably rely heavily on SQL Server. So, this is an excellent time to move up to SQL Server. The current version of SQL Server (version 7) runs under Windows 98 and can be easily deployed in a small network. Even if you have no prior experience with SQL Server, I urge you to install the Evaluation Edition of SQL Server on your computer and use the same machine for development and as a database server.

NOTE   Nearly all of this book's examples will work on a standalone computer running Windows 98, but I recommend using Windows NT or Windows 2000.

There are two ways to use SQL Server: as a powerful substitute for Access or as a powerful DBMS (which is what SQL Server is). You can write an application that works with Access, then change its connection to the same database on SQL Server, and the application will work. I know some programmers who upsized their Access database to SQL Server and then changed their DAO-based VB code to work with SQL Server. By the way, converting an application based on DAO to work with ADO is not trivial, but if you write applications based on ADO, you can manipulate Access and SQL Server databases with nearly the same code.

SQL Server has a few unique features that you can't ignore. To begin with, SQL Server has its own programming language, called Transact-SQL (T-SQL). T-SQL is an extension of SQL and it's so powerful that it can do just about everything you can do with VB. T-SQL has no user interface but it supports many data-manipulation functions (similar to the functions of VB) and flow-control statements. It can also access the tables of a database through SQL. In essence, T-SQL combines the power of SQL with the structure of more traditional programming languages. If you don't care about a user interface, you can use T-SQL to implement all of the operations you'd normally code in VB. The advantage of T-SQL is that it's executed on the server and can manipulate tables locally. To do the same with VB, you'd have to move information from the server to the client and process it there. Stored procedures are faster than the equivalent VB code and they standardize client applications, since all clients will call the same procedure to carry out a task.

In effect, it's quite acceptable to implement business rules as stored procedures. Chapters 7, 8, and 9 discuss how to take advantage of stored procedures from within your VB code. Strictly speaking, this information belongs to a book about SQL Server, but I think stored procedures are one of the best reasons to switch from Access databases to SQL Server. A good VB programmer implements the basic operations of the application as functions and calls them from within the application. Practically, you can't implement every data-access operation as a stored procedure, and I urge you to do this. Stored procedures become part of the database and can be used by multiple applications, not just the client application.

Write Better Client Applications with Stored Procedures

If you implement the NewInvoice stored procedure to add new invoices to a database, then you can call this stored procedure from within any VB application that needs to add invoices to the database. If you implement the same operation as a method of a middle-tier component, then you can call this method from within any application—including the Office applications. We will write a stored procedure that adds invoices in a later chapter, and then we'll write a middle-tier component that uses this stored procedure. Because middle-tier components are implemented as Classes, they can be called by any COM-enabled application. In simple terms, this means that every programming language that supports the CreateObject() function can call the methods of the middle-tier component. You will see how to create a script to add orders to the database. If you distribute the application, users don't have to go through the visible interface of the application to add new invoices. They can write a short script to automate the process.

SQL Server also uses triggers. A *trigger* is a special stored procedure that is executed when certain actions takes place. For example, you can write a procedure to keep track of who has deleted a record and when. Triggers are added to individual tables and can be invoked by three different actions: insertions, deletions, and updates. We'll discuss stored procedures and triggers in Chapter 7, and you'll see how you can simplify your VB code by implementing certain operations as stored procedures.

SQL Server Tools

Many of you may not be familiar with SQL Server, so in this section I introduce you to its basic tools. If you don't have access to SQL Server on your company's network, you can install the desktop version on a local machine and use it as a development platform as well. The following section describes how to install SQL Server and related tools on your computer. If you haven't purchased SQL Server yet, you can use the Evaluation Edition on the companion CD, but it will expire three months after installation. For more information on ordering SQL Server 7, visit the Microsoft Web site at `www.microsoft.com/sql`.

Installation

Installing SQL Server is fairly straightforward. Of the available installation options, select the Desktop version. To keep it simple, install SQL Server on the same machine you will use to develop your applications in the course of reading this book. This is a client-server configuration, as SQL Server is a separate program that must be running in order to service client requests. Whether it's running on the same or a different machine, it makes no difference to your application.

If you plan to install and configure SQL Server on a local area network, please consult the product documentation. This is the job of the database's administrator (DBA), who is responsible for maintaining the database as well. SQL Server is nothing like Access, and you really need a DBA to take care of the day-to-day operations.

SQL Server 7 runs under both Windows 95/98 and Windows NT/2000. So, you can really learn how to develop database applications with Visual Basic and SQL Server with a typical desktop system. The Server version of SQL Server that runs under Windows 2000 supports additional features, of course, like full-text search support, replication, and more, but these features are not discussed in this book. You can also install the Microsoft English Query, a component that allows you to query the database with English-language statements like "How many orders were placed in the 1999?" or "Show the titles of all books written by T. S. Eliot." The English Query is not a ready-to-use utility but an environment that must be customized for each database. It's an advanced topic and has very little to do with database programming, so I don't cover it in this book. However, it's a very interesting program, and you should probably take a look at the sample application after you have mastered SQL and database programming.

Once SQL Server has been installed, a new command is added to the Programs menu: SQL Server 7. This command leads to another menu with a few options, including Microsoft SQL Server 7, which leads to a submenu listing SQL Server's tools. The most important tools, which are also relevant to this book's contents, are presented briefly in the following sections.

SQL Server Service Manager

This tool allows you to start and stop SQL Server. To start SQL Server, select Start ➤ Programs ➤ SQL Server 7.0 ➤ Microsoft SQL Server 7.0 ➤ Service Manager, which opens a window where you can start and stop SQL Server. Select the MSSQLServer service in the services box and then click the Start button. If you'd rather have SQL Server autostart every time you turn on your computer, check the option "Auto-start Service when OS starts."

When SQL Server is running, a small icon with a green arrow is added to the system tray. If you attempt to connect to SQL Server from within a client application while SQL Server is not running, you will get an error message to the effect that there's a problem with your network. At this point you must stop the application, start SQL Server through the Service Manager, and then restart the VB application.

Enterprise Manager

The Enterprise Manager, shown in Figure 1.9, is a visual tool that allows you to view and edit all the objects of SQL Server. This is where you create new databases, edit tables, create stored procedures, and so on. You can also open a table and edit it, but the corresponding tools are not nearly as user-friendly as the ones that come with Access. SQL Server databases shouldn't be manipulated directly. Only the DBA should open tables and examine or edit their contents.

Visual Basic includes several visual database tools (discussed in Chapter 3) that allow you to view the structure of your databases, create and edit tables, create and debug stored procedures, and more. Much of what you can do with Enterprise Manager can be done with the visual database tools, except for adding new users, setting user rights, and similar operations. Again, these tasks are the responsibility of the DBA. You will see how to set up a user's profile so that the specific user can execute stored procedures only and other simple tasks in a later chapter. This topic is discussed in Chapter 7, "Transact-SQL."

Expand the folder with the name of the server (TOSHIBA in Figure 1.9) in the left pane, and you will see five folders.

FIGURE 1.9:

The SQL Server Enterprise Manager window

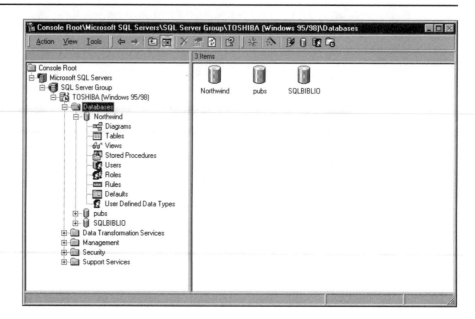

Databases

This folder contains a subfolder for each database. If you select a database here, you will see a list of objects, described below, that are specific to that database.

Diagrams   A diagram is a picture of the database's structure, similar to the one shown in Figure 1.10. You can manipulate the very structure of the database from within this window, which shows how the various tables relate to each other. You can add new relationships, set their properties, add constraints for the various fields (for example, specify that certain fields must be positive), enforce referential integrity, and so on. Don't worry if you are not familiar with these terms; they are discussed in detail in the first few chapters of the book.

To create a new database diagram, right-click on the right window and select New diagram from the shortcut menu. A Wizard will prompt you to select the tables to include in the diagram, and then it will generate the diagram by extracting the information it needs from the database itself. You will find more information on creating tables and diagrams in Chapter 2.

Tables   A table consists of rows and columns where we store information. Databases have many tables and each table has a specific structure. You can edit the columns of each table through the Design window, shown in Figure 1.11. To open the Design window of a table, right-click the table's name and select Design from shortcut menu.

FIGURE 1.10:

A database diagram shows the structure of its tables and the relationships between them.

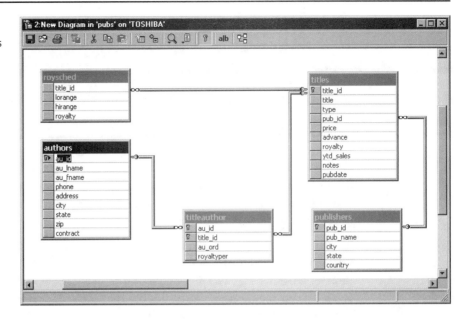

FIGURE 1.11:

The Design window of the titles table

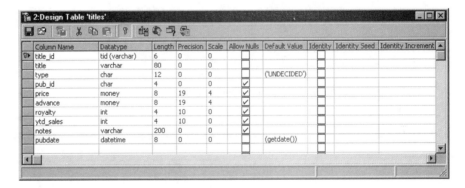

Views   A view is a section of a table, or a combination of multiple tables, and contains specific information needed by a client. If the Customers table contains salary information, you probably don't want every application to retrieve this information. You can define a view on the table that contains all the columns except for the salary-related ones. As far as the client application is concerned, the view is just another table. SQL Server's views are based on SQL statements and they're equivalent to Access queries.

Most views are editable (a view that contains totals, for example, can't be edited). To open a view, select Views in the left pane of the Enterprise Manager, then right-click the desired view's name in the right pane and select Return All Rows from the shortcut menu. The view's rows will appear on a grid, where you can edit their fields (if the view is updateable). To refresh the view, click the button with the exclamation mark in the window's toolbar.

Stored Procedures   A stored procedure is the equivalent of a VB function, only stored procedures are written in T-SQL and they're executed on the server. In this folder, you see the list of stored procedures attached to the database and their definitions. You can create new ones as well, but you can't debug them. To edit and debug your stored procedures, use either the Query Analyzer (discussed in the next section) or the T-SQL Debugger, a tool that comes with VB. Actually, the Stored Procedure Properties window, which will appear if you double-click a procedure's name, contains the definition of the procedure and a button named Check Syntax. If you click this button, the Enterprise Manager will verify the syntax of the stored procedure's definition. It points out the first mistake in the T-SQL code, so it doesn't really qualify as a debugging tool.

Users   In this folder, you can review the users authorized to view and/or edit the selected database and add new users. By default, each database has two users: the owner of the database (user *dbo*) and a user with seriously limited privileges (user *guest*). To view the rights of a user, double-click their name. On that user's Properties dialog box, you can assign one or more *roles* to the selected user (instead of setting properties for individual users, you create roles and then assign these roles to the users). If you click the Permissions button, you will see the user's permissions for every object in the database, as shown in Figure 1.12. It's a good idea to create a user called *application* (or something similar) and use this ID to connect to the database from within your application. This user will impersonate your application, and you can give this user all the rights your application needs.

FIGURE 1.12:

Setting user permissions
for the various objects of a
database

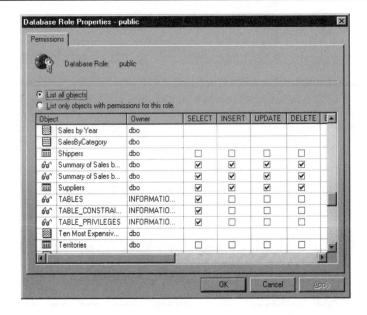

Roles   When you select the Roles item in the right pane, you will see a list with the existing roles. A role is nothing more than a user profile. If multiple users must have common privileges, create a new role, set permissions to this role, and then use it to specify the permissions of individual users.

Rules   SQL Server allows you to specify rules for the values of individual fields of a table. These rules are called CHECK constraints and they are specified from within the Database Diagram window. There's no reason to use this window to specify rules, but it's included for compatibility reasons.

Defaults   Here you can define the default values for any field. The default values are used when no value is supplied by the user, or the application, for the specific field. It is simpler to specify defaults during the design of the table, than to provide the code that checks the user-supplied value and supplies a default value if the user hasn't entered a value for a field.

User-Defined Data Types   This is where the user-defined data types (UDTs) are specified. SQL Server doesn't allow the creation of arbitrary data structures like Visual Basic does. A UDT is based on one of the existing data types, but you can specify a length (for character and binary types) and, optionally, a default value. For example, you can create a UDT, name it ZCODE, and set its type to CHAR and length to five. This is a shorthand notation, rather than a custom data type. UDTs are useful when you allow developers to create their own tables. You can create data types like FNAME, LNAME, and so on, to make sure that all fields that store names, in all tables, have the same length. When you change the definition of a UDT, the table(s) change accordingly without any action on your part.

Data Transformation Services (DTS)

This folder contains the utilities for importing data into SQL Server and exporting data out of SQL Server. The DTS component of SQL Server allows you to import/ export data and at the same time transform it. You will see how to use the DTS component to upsize the Biblio sample database, which comes with both Access and Visual Basic in Chapter 2.

Management

This folder contains the tools for managing databases. The most important tool is the Backup tool, which allows you to back up a database and schedule backup jobs. These tools are also meant for the DBA, and we are not going to use them in this book.

Security

Here's where the DBA creates new logins and assigns roles to users. We are not going to use these tools in this book.

Support Services

This is where you configure two of SQL Server's support services: the Distributed Transaction Coordinator and SQL Server Mail. The Distributed Transaction Coordinator is a tool for managing transactions that span across multiple servers. We will discuss transactions in detail beginning in Chapter 7, but we won't get into transactions across multiple servers.

The SQL Server Mail service allows you to create mail messages from within SQL Server. These messages can be scheduled to be created and transmitted automatically and are used to notify the database administrator about the success or failure of a task. You can attach log files and exception files to the message.

The Query Analyzer

If there's one tool you must learn well, this is it. The Query Analyzer is where you can execute SQL statements, batches, and stored procedures against a database. To start the Query Analyzer, select Start ➢ Programs ➢ SQL Server 7.0 ➢ Microsoft SQL Server 7.0 ➢ Query Analyzer. The Query Analyzer uses an MDI interface, and you can open multiple windows, in which you can execute different SQL statements or stored procedures.

If you enter an SQL statement in the Query Analyzer window and click the Execute button (the button with the green arrow on the toolbar), the window will split into two panes; the result of the query will appear in the lower pane—the Results pane—as shown in Figure 1.13. The statement will be executed against the database selected in the DB box at the top of the window, so make sure you've selected the appropriate database before you execute an SQL statement for the first time. You can save the current statement to a text file with the File ➢ Save As command and open it later with the File ➢ Open command.

In addition to SQL statements, you can execute batches written in T-SQL. A *batch* is a collection of SQL and T-SQL statements. For example, you can enter multiple SQL statements and separate them with a GO statement. Each time a GO statement is reached, the Query Analyzer executes all the statements from the beginning of the file, or the previous GO statement. All the results will appear in the Results pane.

NOTE   SQL statements and batches are stored in text files with the extension .SQL. All of the SQL statements and stored procedures presented in this book can be found in a separate SQL file, each under the corresponding chapter's folder on the companion CD-ROM.

FIGURE 1.13:

Executing SQL statements with the Query Analyzer

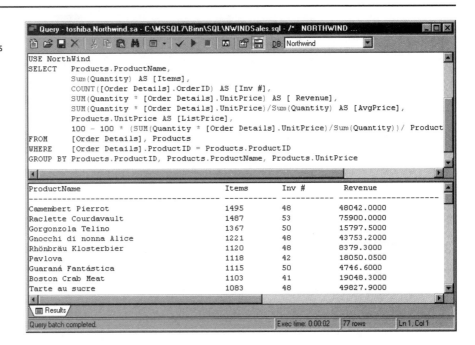

```
USE NorthWind
SELECT    Products.ProductName,
          Sum(Quantity) AS [Items],
          COUNT([Order Details].OrderID) AS [Inv #],
          SUM(Quantity * [Order Details].UnitPrice) AS [ Revenue],
          SUM(Quantity * [Order Details].UnitPrice)/Sum(Quantity) AS [AvgPrice],
          Products.UnitPrice AS [ListPrice],
          100 - 100 * (SUM(Quantity * [Order Details].UnitPrice)/Sum(Quantity))/ Product
FROM      [Order Details], Products
WHERE     [Order Details].ProductID = Products.ProductID
GROUP BY Products.ProductID, Products.ProductName, Products.UnitPrice
```

```
ProductName                      Items       Inv #       Revenue
-------------------------------  ----------  ----------  ----------------------
Camembert Pierrot                1495        48          48042.0000
Raclette Courdavault             1487        53          75900.0000
Gorgonzola Telino                1367        50          15797.5000
Gnocchi di nonna Alice           1221        48          43753.2000
Rhönbräu Klosterbier             1120        48          8379.3000
Pavlova                          1118        42          18050.0500
Guaraná Fantástica               1115        50          4746.6000
Boston Crab Meat                 1103        41          19048.3000
Tarte au sucre                   1083        48          49827.9000
```

Query batch completed.   Exec time: 0:00:02   77 rows   Ln 1, Col 1

By default, the Query Analyzer displays the row output produced by SQL Server: the results and any messages indicating the success or failure of the operation. Most people prefer the Grid view, which is shown in Figure 1.14. To activate this view select Results in Grid from the Query menu. The advantage of this view is that you can change the width of the columns. The grid on the Results Grid tab contains the results of the query, and the messages returned by SQL Server are displayed on the Messages tab.

The Query Analyzer's Grid view

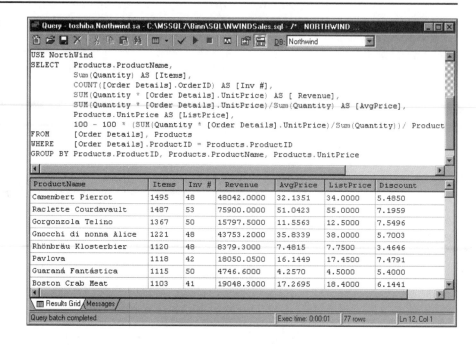

```
USE NorthWind
SELECT    Products.ProductName,
          Sum(Quantity) AS [Items],
          COUNT([Order Details].OrderID) AS [Inv #],
          SUM(Quantity * [Order Details].UnitPrice) AS [ Revenue],
          SUM(Quantity * [Order Details].UnitPrice)/Sum(Quantity) AS [AvgPrice],
          Products.UnitPrice AS [ListPrice],
          100 - 100 * (SUM(Quantity * [Order Details].UnitPrice)/Sum(Quantity))/ Product
FROM      [Order Details], Products
WHERE     [Order Details].ProductID = Products.ProductID
GROUP BY Products.ProductID, Products.ProductName, Products.UnitPrice
```

ProductName	Items	Inv #	Revenue	AvgPrice	ListPrice	Discount
Camembert Pierrot	1495	48	48042.0000	32.1351	34.0000	5.4850
Raclette Courdavault	1487	53	75900.0000	51.0423	55.0000	7.1959
Gorgonzola Telino	1367	50	15797.5000	11.5563	12.5000	7.5496
Gnocchi di nonna Alice	1221	48	43753.2000	35.8339	38.0000	5.7003
Rhönbräu Klosterbier	1120	48	8379.3000	7.4815	7.7500	3.4646
Pavlova	1118	42	18050.0500	16.1449	17.4500	7.4791
Guaraná Fantástica	1115	50	4746.6000	4.2570	4.5000	5.4000
Boston Crab Meat	1103	41	19048.3000	17.2695	18.4000	6.1441

Summary

This chapter was a very broad indeed. It touched a lot of topics, and it probably raised quite a few questions. The following chapters elaborate on all the topics discussed here. Starting with the next chapter, you'll learn how to design databases and how to manipulate them with SQL. Then, you'll see how to use ADO to write database applications that are almost independent of the DBMS you use. Nearly all of this book's application will work equally well with SQL Server and Access databases.

You're probably eager to see some VB code that accesses databases. The next few chapters are not about VB. Before you start writing VB code, you should develop a good understanding of the structure of a database, the role of relationships and how they're used, and SQL. Unless you understand the available tools and what they do, you shouldn't jump into programming. If you decide to skip the second chapter, which discusses the structure of relational databases and how to design relational databases, take a look at the last section of the chapter, which shows how to upsize the Biblio database to SQL Server.

CHAPTER

TWO

2

Basic Concepts of Relational Databases

- Understanding the structure of a database

- Querying relational databases

- Database objects: tables, indexes, views

- Primary and foreign keys

- Relationships

- Database normalization

- Database integrity

If you know what a database is and you have designed simple databases with Access, you can skip this chapter and go on to Chapter 3, "The Visual Database Tools," which covers the tools that come with Visual Basic (and other Visual Studio products). If you haven't done any database programming with Visual Basic, take the time to review this chapter. Before looking at VB's tools, it's important that you learn about the basic principles of database design and familiarize yourself with the basic terms you'll see in the rest of the book: tables and indexes, relationships, primary and foreign keys, referential integrity, and a bunch of other goodies.

This chapter covers the principles of databases and explains the nature of relational databases, why we use a specific methodology to design them, and other related topics, including the normalization of databases. An important part of this chapter is the discussion of the structure of the Northwind and Pubs sample databases, as well as the Biblio database. Northwind comes with both Visual Basic (the Jet version of the database) and SQL Server, while Pubs comes with SQL Server. Biblio is a Jet sample database that comes with Visual Basic, and we'll import it into SQL Server so that we can use it in the examples of upcoming chapters from within both Access and SQL Server.

NOTE To make this chapter easier to read, I will not get into the specifics of the tools that come with SQL Server or Access; there's plenty of information on creating and editing databases with Visual Basic's tools in the following chapter. If you're familiar with either product, however, use the tools you know to examine the sample databases discussed in this chapter.

Why examine the structure of existing databases instead of creating a new one from scratch? Because it's simpler to understand the structure of an existing database, especially a database designed by the people who have designed the data engines themselves. Besides, these databases are used in the examples of the following chapters, so you should make sure you understand their structures.

This chapter introduces the concepts of relational databases. Its purpose is not to teach you how to design corporate databases. The truth is that you needn't even be able to design databases before you start programming them. Quite the contrary: Your experience with database programming will help you develop a solid understanding of databases and their requirements and limitations. Then, you'll find it easier to develop a large database and even become an ER (entity/ relationship) specialist—and make more money, too!

Fundamentals of Database Design

In principle, designing databases is simple. More than anything else, it requires common sense. Databases are meant to solve practical problems faced by corporations on a daily basis: data storage and retrieval. Practical problems call for practical solutions, and databases are not based on mathematics or other abstract concepts.

When designing a database, there are several important points that you should keep in mind. First, any errors in the design of a database will surface later on, when you try to extract data from it. If your data isn't well-organized in the database, you won't be able to extract the desired data (or you'll have to extract a lot of unwanted information along with the useful data).

Another important aspect of databases is integrity. Even the best-designed database can be incapacitated if it's populated with invalid data. If you don't do something to maintain the integrity and consistency of your database, you may never be able to locate data. For instance, if you allow the users of a database to change the name of a company, how will you retrieve the invoices issued to the same company before its name was changed?

Obviously, you can't rely on the users to maintain the integrity of the database. A modern DBMS (database management system) provides built-in mechanisms to help you with this task. Both Access and SQL Server, for example, enforce the integrity of the references between tables. If a customer has placed one or more orders, the DBMS will not allow you to remove the customer from the database. If this customer is removed from the database, the corresponding orders will no longer refer to a valid customer. Later in this chapter, you will see how to incorporate rules for maintaining the integrity of the database right into the database itself.

As you will see as you read on, the design of a database shouldn't be taken lightly. Most problems in database applications can be traced back to the design of the database. Ask any consultant who has stepped into a company to take over someone else's projects and they will tell you how many poorly designed databases are in use out there. Most annoying in these situations is the fact that programmers write questionable code (to put it mildly) to make up for inefficient database design. It goes without saying, of course, that a poorly designed database can't be optimized. The queries will be unnecessarily slow and, in many cases, unnecessarily complicated.

What Is a Database?

A database is one of those objects that is so hard to define, yet everyone knows what it is. Here's a simple definition, which even people with no prior programming experience will understand: A *database* is an object for storing complex, structured information. The same is true for a file, or even for the file system on your hard disk. What makes a database unique is the fact that databases are designed to make data easily retrievable. The purpose of a database is not so much the storage of information as its quick retrieval. In other words, you must structure your database so that it can be queried quickly and efficiently.

Relational Databases

The databases we're interested in are *relational*, because they are based on relationships among the data they contain. The data is stored in tables, and tables contain related data, or *entities,* such as persons, products, orders, and so on. The idea is to keep the tables small and manageable; thus, separate entities are kept in their own tables. If you start mixing customers and invoices, products and their suppliers, or books, publishers, and authors in the same table, you'll end up repeating information—a highly undesirable situation. If there's one rule to live by as a database designer and programmer, this is it: Do not duplicate information.

Of course, entities are not independent of each other. For example, orders are placed by specific customers, so the rows of the Customers table must be linked to the rows of the Orders table that store the orders of the customers. Figure 2.1 shows a segment of a table with customers (top left) and the rows of a table with orders that correspond to one of the customers (bottom right). The lines that connect the rows of the two tables represent *relationships*. The databases we're interested in are called relational, because they're based on relationships. I could discuss other, less efficient database structures, but this isn't a book on the history of databases. All modern databases are relational.

FIGURE 2.1:

Linking customers and orders with relationships

CustomerID	CompanyName	ContactName	ContactTitle
DRACD	Drachenblut Delikatessen	Sven Ottlieb	Order Administrator
DUMON	Du monde entier	Janine Labrune	Owner
EASTC	Eastern Connection	Ann Devon	Sales Agent
ERNSH	Ernst Handel	Roland Mendel	Sales Manager
FAMIA	Familia Arquibaldo	Aria Cruz	Marketing Assistant
FISSA	FISSA Fabrica Inter. Salchichas S.A.	Diego Roel	Accounting Manager
FOLIG	Folies gourmandes	Martine Rancé	Assistant Sales Agent
FOLKO	Folk och fä HB	Maria Larsson	Owner
FRANK	Frankenversand	Peter Franken	Marketing Manager
FRANR	France restauration	Carine Schmitt	Marketing Manager
FRANS	Franchi S.p.A.	Paolo Accorti	Sales Representative
FURIB	Furia Bacalhau e Frutos do Mar	Lino Rodriguez	Sales Manager
GALED	Galería del gastrónomo	Eduardo Saavedra	Marketing Manager

OrderID	CustomerID	EmployeeID	OrderDate	RequiredDate	ShippedDate	ShipVia	Freight
10797	DRACD	7	12/25/97	1/22/98	1/5/98	2	33.35
10825	DRACD	1	1/9/98	2/6/98	1/14/98	1	79.25
11036	DRACD	8	4/20/98	5/18/98	4/22/98	3	149.47
11067	DRACD	1	5/4/98	5/18/98	5/6/98	2	7.98
10311	DUMON	1	9/20/96	10/4/96	9/26/96	3	24.69
10609	DUMON	7	7/24/97	8/21/97	7/30/97	2	1.85
10683	DUMON	2	9/26/97	10/24/97	10/1/97	1	4.4
10890	DUMON	7	2/16/98	3/16/98	2/18/98	1	32.76
10364	EASTC	1	11/26/96	1/7/97	12/4/96	1	71.97
10400	EASTC	1	1/1/97	1/29/97	1/16/97	3	83.93
10532	EASTC	7	5/9/97	6/6/97	5/12/97	3	74.46
10726	EASTC	4	11/3/97	11/17/97	12/5/97	1	16.56

Key Fields and Primary and Foreign Keys

As you can see in Figure 2.1, relationships are implemented by inserting rows with matching values in the two related tables; the CustomerID column is repeated in both tables. The rows with a common value in their CustomerID field are related. In other words, the lines that connect the two tables simply indicate that there are two fields, one on each side of the relationship, with a common value. These two fields are called *key fields*. The CustomerID field of the Customers table is the *primary key*, because it identifies a single customer. The CustomerID field of the Orders table is the *foreign key* of the relationship. A CustomerID value appears in a single row of the Customers table; it's the table's primary key. However, it may appear in multiple rows of the Orders table, because in this table the CustomerID field is the foreign key. In fact, it will appear in as many rows of the Orders table as there are orders for the specific customer. (You'll read more about keys a bit later in this chapter.)

> **NOTE**   This simple idea of linking tables based on the values of two columns that are common to both tables is at the heart of relational databases. It allows us to break our data into smaller units, the tables, yet be able to combine rows in multiple tables to retrieve and present the desired information.

Who Designs Databases?

Since corporations base their day-to-day operations on the quality of their database, when it comes to designing a very large database, most corporations will hire consultants to do the job. Insurance companies, for example, with large computer installations and an army of programmers, database administrators, and all kinds of computer specialists, usually outsource the design of their databases. From time to time, they'll bring in consultants to tune the databases, as well.

There are companies that specialize in database design (though they won't write a single line of code), and they charge a fortune for this service. Professionals who design databases are called ER specialists. ER stands for entity/relationship, a term that emphasizes the importance of organizing data into tables (entities) and establishing relationships between tables.

There's a good chance you may never have to design a corporate database. The database may already be in place, or your company may outsource the design of its main database. Even so, in order to develop applications for an existing database, you should understand its structure and not be intimidated by its size.

In addition to a corporate database, most companies maintain smaller databases with data specific to a department, or even a project. Theory says you must store all your corporate data in the same database, but I have yet to see a corporation that doesn't use multiple databases. Sooner or later you'll be called to develop a small database application, and you should be able to design a simple database.

Exploring the Northwind Database

Before we examine the objects of a database in detail, let's look at the structure of a sample database that comes with Visual Basic, the Northwind database. In the process, you'll develop a good feel for how relational databases are structured, and you'll find the discussion of the objects of a database easier to follow.

The Northwind database that comes with Visual Basic is a Jet database. SQL Server comes with its own, native version of the same database. You can use either Access or SQL Server's Enterprise Manager to examine the structure of this database on your own.

The Northwind database stores sales information: the customers and products of the Northwind Corporation and what products each customer has ordered, along with their prices, discounts, shipping information, and so on. A first attempt to record all of this information might be to enter long lines with every bit of information about each item ordered (and purchased): its price, the quantity ordered, the customer who placed the order, the employee who made the sale, where the item was shipped, and so on. With an exceptionally powerful computer, you'd probably be able to recall all kinds of information from this database. I need not describe why this scheme is inefficient. If a customer's phone number changes, you'll have to scan this long file and replace all instances of the old number with the new one. Clearly, the retrieval of information from this database is anything but efficient; you'd have to write code to scan an enormous table, from start to end, just to locate a few rows. Instead, we'll break the information we want to store in the database into separate tables. Let's start with the tables that make up the Northwind database, and then we'll look at the relationships between the tables.

Northwind Database Tables

The first step in database design is to break the information you want to store into smaller units, the tables, and establish relationships between them. To do so, identify the entities you want to store (products, customers, and so on) and create a table for each entity. A table is a grid: Each row corresponds to a different item, but all items have the same structure. The structure of the table is determined by its columns, and each column represents an attribute of the entity stored in the table. A table that stores products has a column for the product's name, another column for the product's price, and so on. Each product is stored in a different row. As products are added or removed from the table, the number of rows changes, but the number of columns remains the same; they determine the information we store about each product. You can add and remove columns to the table even after you have entered data in them.

The Products Table   The Products table stores information about the products sold by the Northwind Corporation. This information includes the product's name, packaging information, price, and other relevant fields. Additionally, each product in the table is identified by a unique ID number, as shown in Figure 2.2. Product names are easier to remember, but very difficult to enter on a Form. Besides, a product's name can change. Since the rows of the Products table are referenced by invoices (the Order Details table, which is discussed later), each product name change would entail a number of changes in the Order Details table, as well. The product ID that identifies each product need not change; it's a numeric value that carries no meaningful information about the product. Thus by using a unique numeric value to identify each product, you can change the product's name without affecting any other tables.

FIGURE 2.2:

Each line in the Products table holds information about a specific product.

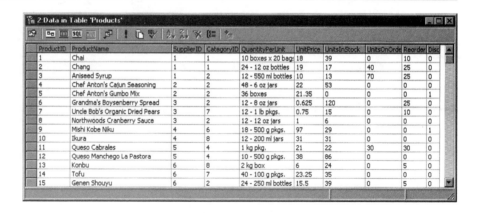

The SupplierID and CategoryID columns contain integer values that point to rows of two other tables, the Suppliers and Categories tables, respectively. These two tables contain information about the Northwind Corporation's suppliers and various product categories.

NOTE   Supplier information can't be stored in the Products table, because the same supplier's name and address would be repeated in multiple products.

Suppliers Table   Each product in the Northwind database has a supplier. Because the same supplier may offer more than one product, the supplier information is stored in a different table, and a common field, the SupplierID field, is used to link each product to its supplier. For example, the products Mishi Kobe Niku and Ikura are purchased from the same supplier, Tokyo Traders. Their SupplierID fields point to the same row in the Suppliers table, as shown in Figure 2.3.

FIGURE 2.3:

Linking products to their suppliers

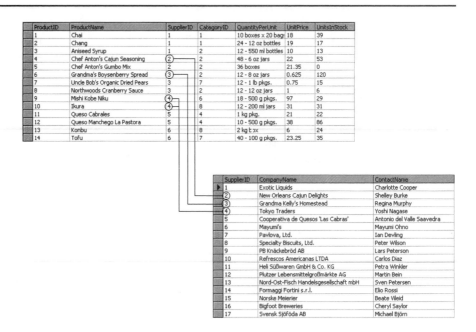

Categories Table   In addition to having a supplier, each product belongs to a category. Categories are not stored along with product names, but in a separate table, the Categories table, whose structure is shown in Figure 2.4. Again, each category is identified by a numeric value and has a name (the CategoryID and CategoryName fields, respectively). In addition, the Categories table has two more columns: Description, which contains text, and Picture, which stores a bitmap.

The Products table (back in Figure 2.2) has a CategoryID column as well, which links each product to its category. By storing the categories in a separate table, you don't have to enter the actual name of the category (or its bitmap) along with each product. The CategoryID field of the Products table points to the product's category, and you can locate each product's category very quickly in the Categories table.

The CategoryID field in the Categories table is the primary key, because it identifies each row in the table. Each category has a unique CategoryID, which may be repeated many times in the Products table. The CategoryID field in the Products table is the foreign key.

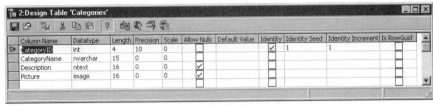

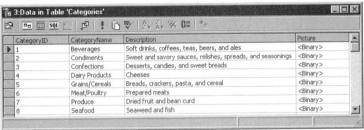

FIGURE 2.4:

The structure of the Categories table (top) and the first few rows of the table (bottom)

Here's what primary and foreign keys do in the Northwind database: When you look up products, you want to be able to locate quickly the category to which they belong. You read the value of the CategoryID field in the Products table, locate the row in the Categories table with the same value in the CategoryID column, and voila!, you have matched the two tables. You can also search the Products table for products that belong to a specific category. You start with the ID of a category and then locate all the rows in the Products table with a CategoryID field that matches the selected ID. The relationship between the two tables links each row of the first table to one or more rows of the second table, and you will see shortly how relationships are defined.

NOTE   The operation of matching rows in two (or more) tables based on their primary and foreign keys is called a *join*. Joins are very basic operations in manipulating tables, and they are discussed in detail in Chapter 4, "Structured Query Language."

Customers Table   The Customers table, shown in Figure 2.5, stores information about the company's customers. Before we can accept an order, we must create a new row in the Customers table with the customer's data (name, phone number, address, and so on), if one doesn't exist already. Each row in the Customers table represents a different customer and is identified by the CustomerID field. This field has a unique value for each row, similar to the ProductID field of the Products table. However, the CustomerID field is a five-character-long string, and not an integer.

CustomerID	CompanyName	ContactName	ContactTitle
DRACD	Drachenblut Delikatessen	Sven Ottlieb	Order Administrator
DUMON	Du monde entier	Janine Labrune	Owner
EASTC	Eastern Connection	Ann Devon	Sales Agent
ERNSH	Ernst Handel	Roland Mendel	Sales Manager
FAMIA	Familia Arquibaldo	Aria Cruz	Marketing Assistant
FISSA	FISSA Fabrica Inter. Salchichas S.A.	Diego Roel	Accounting Manager
FOLIG	Folies gourmandes	Martine Rancé	Assistant Sales Agent
FOLKO	Folk och fä HB	Maria Larsson	Owner
FRANK	Frankenversand	Peter Franken	Marketing Manager
FRANR	France restauration	Carine Schmitt	Marketing Manager
FRANS	Franchi S.p.A.	Paolo Accorti	Sales Representative
FURIB	Furia Bacalhau e Frutos do Mar	Lino Rodriguez	Sales Manager
GALED	Galería del gastrónomo	Eduardo Saavedra	Marketing Manager
GODOS	Godos Cocina Típica	José Pedro Freyre	Sales Manager
GOURL	Gourmet Lanchonetes	André Fonseca	Sales Associate
GREAL	Great Lakes Food Market	Howard Snyder	Marketing Manager
GROSR	GROSELLA-Restaurante	Manuel Pereira	Owner
HILAA	HILARION-Abastos	Carlos Hernández	Sales Representative

Orders Table   The Orders table, shown in Figure 2.6, stores information (customer, shipping address, date of order, and so on) about the orders placed by Northwind's customers. The OrderID field, which is an integer value, identifies each order. Orders are numbered sequentially, so this field is also the order's number. As you will see in the "AutoNumber and Identity Fields" section later in this chapter, each time you append a new row to the Orders table, the value of the new OrderID field is generated automatically by the database. Moreover, this value can't be edited (this is a built-in mechanism for protecting the integrity of the database).

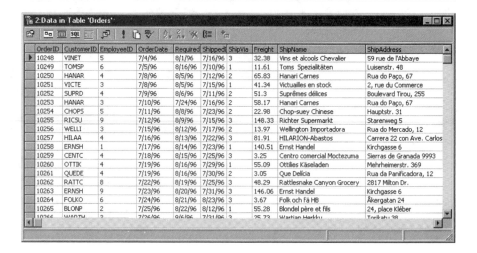

The Orders table is linked to the Customers table through the CustomerID field. By matching rows with identical values in their CustomerID fields in the two tables, we can recombine a customer with his orders.

Order Details Table   You probably have noticed that the Northwind database's Orders table doesn't store any details about the items ordered. This information is stored in the Order Details table (see Figure 2.7). Each order is made up of one or more items, and each item has a price, a quantity, and a discount. In addition to these fields, the Order Details table contains an OrderID column, which holds the order number to which the detail line belongs. In other words, the details of all invoices are thrown into this table and are organized according to the order to which they belong.

FIGURE 2.7:

The Order Details table

2:Data in Table 'Order Details'

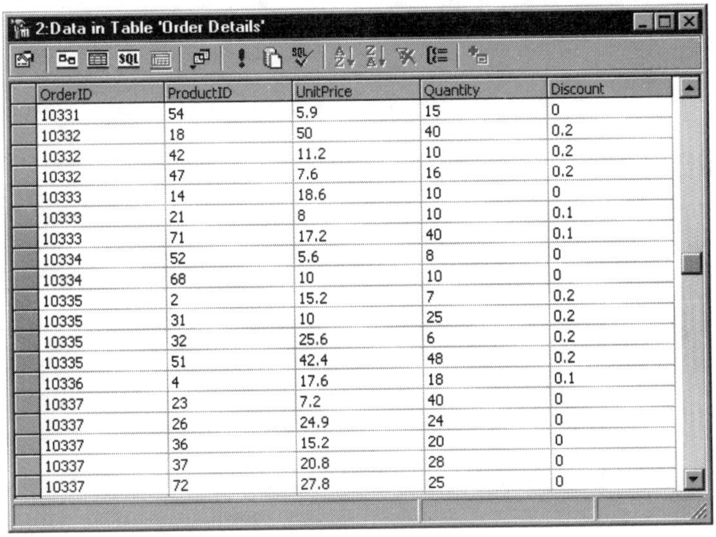

OrderID	ProductID	UnitPrice	Quantity	Discount
10331	54	5.9	15	0
10332	18	50	40	0.2
10332	42	11.2	10	0.2
10332	47	7.6	16	0.2
10333	14	18.6	10	0
10333	21	8	10	0.1
10333	71	17.2	40	0.1
10334	52	5.6	8	0
10334	68	10	10	0
10335	2	15.2	7	0.2
10335	31	10	25	0.2
10335	32	25.6	6	0.2
10335	51	42.4	48	0.2
10336	4	17.6	18	0.1
10337	23	7.2	40	0
10337	26	24.9	24	0
10337	36	15.2	20	0
10337	37	20.8	28	0
10337	72	27.8	25	0

The reason details aren't stored along with the order's header is that the Order and Order Details tables store different entities. The order's header, which contains information about the customer who placed the order, the date of the order, and so on, is quite different from the information you must store for each item ordered. Try to come up with a different design that stores all order-related information in a single table, and you'll soon realize that you end up duplicating information. Figure 2.8 shows how three of the tables in the Northwind database, Customers, Orders and Order Details, are linked to one another.

I should probably explain why the order's total doesn't appear in any table. To calculate an order's total, you must multiply the quantity by the price, taking into consideration the discount. If the order's total were stored in the Orders table, you'd be duplicating information. In other words, you'd be able to retrieve the same information from two different tables, and there's no guarantee that the values will always be the same.

FIGURE 2.8:

Linking customers to orders
and orders to their details

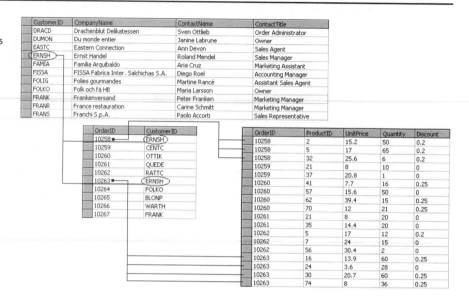

Employees Table   This table holds employee information. Apparently, the employees of the Northwind Corporation work on commission, and we need to know what sales they have made. When a sale is made, the ID of the employee who made the sale is recorded in the Orders table.

Shippers Table   Finally, Northwind Corporation uses three different shippers. The Shippers table holds information about the shippers, and each shipper's ID appears in the Orders table, along with the order date, shipment date, address, and so on.

Understanding Relations

In a database, each table has a field with a unique value for every row. This field is marked with the icon of a key in front of its name, as you can see back in Figure 2.4, and it's the table's primary key.

The primary key does not have to be a meaningful entity, because in most cases there's no single field that's unique for each row. The primary key need not resemble the entity it identifies. The only requirement is that primary keys are unique in the entire table. The IRS probably uses social security numbers to uniquely identify us all, but your corporation can't get this information for all of its customers. Some products may have unique IDs, which can be used as primary keys. Books have ISBN numbers, but not all of them. A thesis cataloged in a library does not have an ISBN, and neither do many useful manuals. Usually, we make up product IDs, which may or may not resemble the actual product's name. Thus the same product may be cataloged with two completely different codes by two different companies. Conversely, the same code may be used for two totally different products by two different companies. However, both codes (IDs) are unique within the framework of each company.

In most designs, we use an integer as the primary key. To make sure they're unique, we even let the DBMS generate a new integer for each row added to the table. Each table can have one primary key only, and this field can't be Null.

NOTE   Most primary keys are made up (either by the user, or by the DBMS itself). Some people make up semi-real keys. For example, I've seen databases that uses ISBN values to uniquely identify most of the books, and fake ISBNs (they start with the digits 000, or 999) to represent the few books that have no ISBNs. This approach will work for a while, especially if you know how to make up ISBNs, but you never know when it will fail. What if another bookseller had the same idea and eventually you have to do business with this bookseller? There's a chance that the two "unique" identification systems will collide with each other. If you can't use a real entity as the primary key, leave it to the system to make unique keys for you. (You'll see how this is done in the upcoming "AutoNumber and Identity Fields" section.) The numeric keys will not help the problem of conflicting IDs, but they do not pretend to be globally unique, like ISBNs.

The related rows in a table repeat the primary key of the row they are related to, in another table. The copies of the primary keys in all other tables are called *foreign keys*. Foreign keys need not be unique (in fact, they aren't) and any field can serve as a foreign key. What makes a field a foreign key is that is matches the primary key of another table. The CategoryID field is the primary key of the Categories table, because it identifies each category. The CategoryID field in the Products table is the foreign key, because the same value may appear in many rows (many products may belong to the same category). When you relate the Products and Categories tables, for example, you must also make sure that:

- Every product added to the foreign table points to a valid entry in the primary table. If you are not sure about to which category the product belongs, you can leave the CategoryID field of the Products table empty. The primary keys, however, can't be Null.

- No rows in the Categories table are removed if there are rows in the Products table pointing to the specific category. This will make the corresponding rows of the Products table point to an invalid category.

These two restrictions would be quite a burden on the programmer if the DBMS didn't protect the database against actions that could impair its integrity. The integrity of your database depends on the validity of the relations. Fortunately, all

DBMSs can enforce rules to maintain their integrity. You'll learn how to enforce rules that guarantee the integrity of your database in the "Database Integrity" section later in this chapter.

Viewing Related Rows in Access 2000

One of the major improvements in Access 2000 is the grid that displays tables. If the table's rows are linked to another table's rows, then a plus sign appears in the first column of the table. In most designs, the primary key is the first column (that's how most people design their tables), so the plus sign appears in front of the primary key. Clicking the plus sign opens a smaller grid containing the rows of the related table.

Figure 2.9 shows the Northwind Customers table (to open this table on your computer, launch Access 2000, open the Northwind database, and, in the Tables view, double-click the name of the Customers table). As you can see, clicking the plus icon in front of a customer's name displays the related rows in the Orders table. These are the orders placed by the selected customer. Access has located all the rows of the Orders table whose CustomerID field matches the value of the CustomerID field of the selected customer in the Customers table. These rows are then displayed in a smaller grid within the original grid.

FIGURE 2.9:

Viewing the orders of a customer

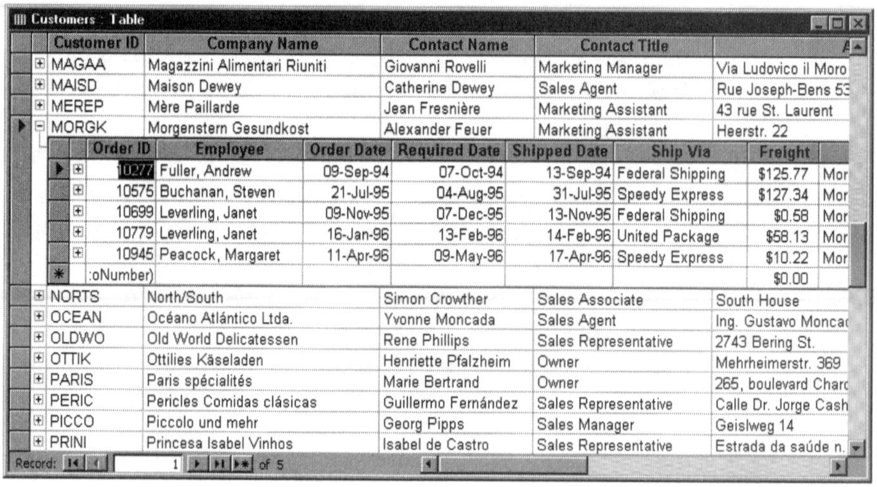

The rows in the small grid are primary keys in another relationship, namely the relationship between the Orders and Order Details tables. To view the related rows of the Order Details table, click the plus icon in front of an order. The rows that correspond to the selected order will appear in yet another grid, as shown in Figure 2.10. Access 2000 allows you to visualize relationships not only in the structure of the database, but in the actual data stored in the tables.

FIGURE 2.10:

Visualizing relationships with Access 2000

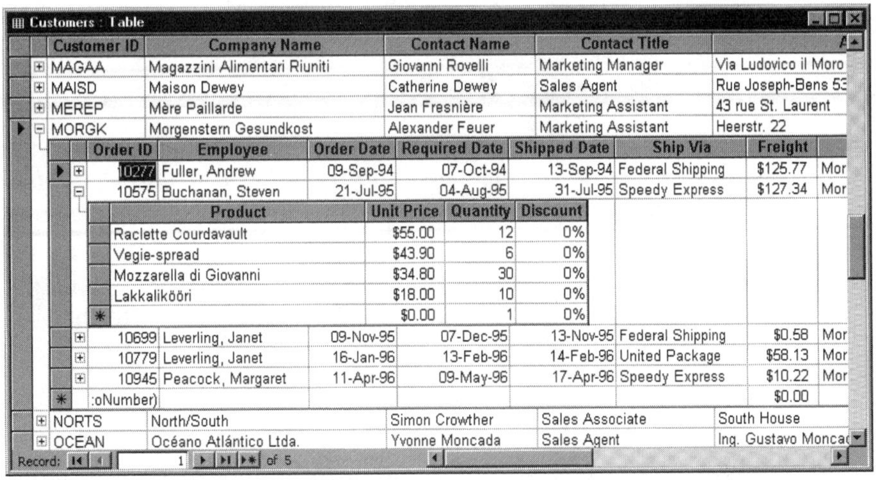

Customers : Table				
Customer ID	**Company Name**	**Contact Name**	**Contact Title**	
⊞ MAGAA	Magazzini Alimentari Riuniti	Giovanni Rovelli	Marketing Manager	Via Ludovico il Moro
⊞ MAISD	Maison Dewey	Catherine Dewey	Sales Agent	Rue Joseph-Bens 53
⊞ MEREP	Mère Paillarde	Jean Fresnière	Marketing Assistant	43 rue St. Laurent
⊟ MORGK	Morgenstern Gesundkost	Alexander Feuer	Marketing Assistant	Heerstr. 22

	Order ID	**Employee**	**Order Date**	**Required Date**	**Shipped Date**	**Ship Via**	**Freight**	
⊞	10277	Fuller, Andrew	09-Sep-94	07-Oct-94	13-Sep-94	Federal Shipping	$125.77	Mor
⊟	10575	Buchanan, Steven	21-Jul-95	04-Aug-95	31-Jul-95	Speedy Express	$127.34	Mor

Product	**Unit Price**	**Quantity**	**Discount**
Raclette Courdavault	$55.00	12	0%
Vegie-spread	$43.90	6	0%
Mozzarella di Giovanni	$34.80	30	0%
Lakkalikööri	$18.00	10	0%
*	$0.00	1	0%

	Order ID	**Employee**	**Order Date**	**Required Date**	**Shipped Date**	**Ship Via**	**Freight**	
⊞	10699	Leverling, Janet	09-Nov-95	07-Dec-95	13-Nov-95	Federal Shipping	$0.58	Mor
⊞	10779	Leverling, Janet	16-Jan-96	13-Feb-96	14-Feb-96	United Package	$58.13	Mor
⊞	10945	Peacock, Margaret	11-Apr-96	09-May-96	17-Apr-96	Speedy Express	$10.22	Mor
*	:oNumber)						$0.00	

⊞ NORTS	North/South	Simon Crowther	Sales Associate	South House
⊞ OCEAN	Océano Atlántico Ltda.	Yvonne Moncada	Sales Agent	Ing. Gustavo Moncad

Record: 1 of 5

NOTE

A note to VB programmers: The control that displays the rows of multiple related tables in Access is not available in the Visual Basic environment. It will probably be included as an ActiveX control with the next release of the language. In Chapter 10, "Shaping Your Data," you'll learn about the MSFlexGrid control, which is similar to the Access control shown in Figure 2.10, and is used to display hierarchical cursors.

Querying Relational Databases

Now let's consider the most common operations you'd like to be able to perform on the Northwind database's tables. The process of retrieving data from the tables is known as *querying*, and the statements you execute against a database to retrieve selected rows are called *queries*. These statements are written in SQL (Structured Query Language), which is discussed in detail in Chapter 4. In this section, we'll look at a few simple queries and how the DBMS combines rows from multiple tables to return the data we're interested in.

Retrieving a Customer's Orders

This is probably the most common operation one would perform on a database like Northwind. To retrieve a customer's orders, start with the customer's ID and locate all the lines in the Orders table whose CustomerID field matches the CustomerID field of the selected row in the Customers table. To retrieve the customer's orders, the DBMS must search the Orders table with its foreign key. To help the DMBS with this operation, you should index the Orders table on its CustomerID field. Both versions of the Northwind database define an index on this field.

Calculating the Total for Each Order

The Orders table doesn't contain the total for each order—and it shouldn't. The totals must be calculated directly from the details. As mentioned earlier, databases shouldn't duplicate information, and storing the totals in the Orders table would be a form of duplication; you'd duplicate the information that's already present in another table. Had you stored the totals along with each order, then every time you changed a detail line, you'd have to change a row in the Orders table, as well.

To calculate an order's total, the DBMS must search the Order Details table with its foreign key (OrderID) and sum the products of quantities times prices for all rows that belong to the specific order (it must also take into consideration the discount). To help the DBMS with this operation, you should index the Order Details table on its OrderID field. Both versions of the Northwind database define an index on the OrderID field.

Calculating the Total for Each Customer

This operation is similar to totaling an order, but it involves three tables. Start with the customer's ID and select all the rows in the Orders table whose CustomerID field matches the ID of the specific customer. This is a list with the IDs of the orders placed by the selected customer. Then scan all the rows of the Order Details table whose OrderID field is in this list and sum the products of quantities times prices.

Performing More Complicated Queries

The kind of information a manager may require from a database can't be classified or enumerated. You can perform complicated queries, such as locating the state in which a specific product is very popular, the best-selling product for each month or quarter, and so on. All the information is in the database, and it's a question of combining the proper fields of the various tables to extract the information you need in order to make better decisions.

Most practical queries involve multiple tables and their relationships. Primary and foreign keys are central concepts in querying databases and, as such, are one of the most important aspects of the design process. As you will see in Chapter 4, the most difficult aspect of SQL is joining multiple tables based on their relationships.

Database Objects

Now that you've been introduced to the basic concepts (and objects) of a relational database by means of examples, you should have a good idea of what a relational database is. You understand how data is stored in separate tables in the database and how the tables are linked to one another through relationships. You also know how relationships are used to execute complicated queries that retrieve data from multiple tables. I'm sure you have questions about specific attributes and techniques, which are addressed in the following sections of this chapter. Let's begin our detailed discussion of the objects of a relational database with the most basic objects, tables.

Tables

A *table* is a collection of rows with the same structure that stores information about an entity such as a person, an invoice, a product, and so on. Each row contains the same number of columns, and each column can store data of the same data type. You can think of a table as a grid or a random access file that stores records. As you know, each record in a random-access file has the same structure, and you can't read or write data to the file unless you know the structure of the records it holds. I probably need not mention this, but any resemblance between tables and random access files ends here.

A DBMS like SQL Server or Access doesn't store tables in separate files. All of the data reside in a single file, along with auxiliary information required by the DBMS to access them quickly. In reality, the DBMS uses more space to store the auxiliary information than for the data itself. The tables in a database are an abstraction; they form a conceptual model of the data. This is how we, humans, view the database. Tables don't reflect the actual structure of the data in the database. Instead, they reflect the entities in our database, and the relations between tables reflect actions (products are *purchased*, customers *place* orders, and so on).

Internally, every DBMS stores information in a proprietary format, and we need not know anything about this format. In effect, this is one of the requirements of the relational database model: *The physical structure may change, but these changes shouldn't affect how we see the database.* Microsoft may change the physical structure of the data in an MDB file, but Access will still see tables and indexes, it will still be able to relate tables to each other using common field values (the primary and foreign keys), and your applications will keep working. You will see the same tables, the same SQL statements will retrieve the same data, and you won't even notice the difference (there will be new features, of course, but existing applications will continue to work without any modifications).

Customers and Suppliers: Same Entities, Different Function

You will notice that the Northwind database's Customers and Suppliers tables have the exact same structure. As far as the operations of an application are concerned, customers and suppliers are two separate entities, and there's no overlap between the two. This is a rather unusual situation, where two different entities have the same (or nearly the same) structure.

Keep in mind that Northwind is a sample database. In a real-world situation, the two tables may not be totally isolated, as the same company may act both as a supplier and as a customer. In other words, it may not only sell to your company, but buy from it as well. In my applications, I use a single table for customers and suppliers. This approach may complicate the programming a little, but it simplifies operations from a user's point of view. If you don't know that a supplier is also a customer, you may end up paying for the items you purchase regularly and never know that the other party is not keeping up with their obligations. There are other practical reasons for treating both customers and suppliers as a single entity, such as preferring a supplier who is also a good customer of yours.

Creating Tables

To create a table, you must specify its structure by declaring its columns: specify how many columns the table has, their names, and their types. No matter what DBMS you're using, here's how tables are created:

1. Make up a name for the table. Table names can be quite long, so you should name them after the entity they represent. Table names, as well as field names, can include spaces as long as you remember to enclose them in a pair of square brackets ([Order Details], [Sales in Europe], and so on) in your code.

2. Make up a name for each column (or field) of the table. Columns are the attributes of the entity represented by the table. The columns of a table that stores customers should probably contain a customer's name, address, phone numbers, electronic address, and so on. The columns of a table that stores invoices should contain an invoice's number, the date of the invoice, shipping address, and so on.

3. Decide the data type for each column. Since different columns store different items of information, their types should match. A column that stores quantities should be defined as integer, while a column that stores prices should be defined as currency. Likewise, a column that stores dates should be defined accordingly.

NOTE   Different DBMSs use different names for the data types they support, yet they support all the basic data types. You'll learn about the data types supported by Access and SQL Server in Chapter 3. When you program databases through the ADO component, however, you can use ADO constants for each type, regardless of the name used by the DBMS to describe each type. Table 2.1, later in this chapter, shows the data types supported by Access and SQL Server and the ADO constant for each data type.

That's all it takes to design a table. If later you decide that you need an additional column, you can always add one without affecting the structure, or the content, of the existing ones. You will see the tools for creating new database from scratch, or edit existing databases, in the following chapter.

When you create a new table, a grid with the names and the attributes of the fields is displayed. Figures 2.11 and 2.12 show the table design grid for both Access and SQL Server. Each row in the grids corresponds to a table column.

FIGURE 2.11:

Designing a table with Access in Design view

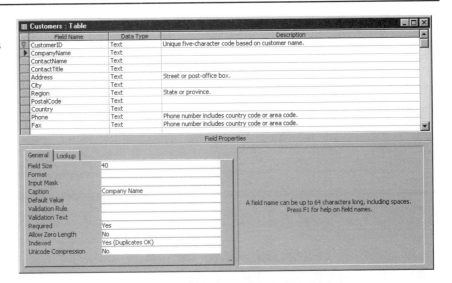

FIGURE 2.12:

Designing a table in SQL Server's Enterprise Manager

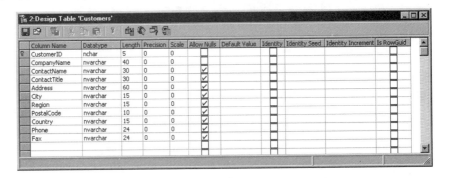

Each column must have a name with a maximum length of 64 characters (for Access and SQL Server databases). The column's data type can be selected from a drop-down list and can have one of the values shown in Table 2.1. Notice that Access and SQL Server don't recognize the same data types (the most common data types, however, are common to both). You won't see the constants listed in Table 2.1 when you design tables with Access or SQL Server, but this is the value you must specify when you program databases with ADO.

TABLE 2.1:   Access and SQL Server Data Types

Constant	Access	SQL Server
adBinary		binary
adBoolean	Yes/No	bit
adChar		char
adCurrency	Currency	money, smallmoney
adDate	Date/Time	Datetime, smalldatetime
adDBTimeStamp	Date/Time	timestamp
adDecimal		Decimal, numeric
adDouble	Double	float
adGUID	ReplicationID	uniqueidentifier
adInteger	Long Integer, AutoNumber	int, Identity
adLongVarBinary	OLE Object	image
adLongVarChar	Memo	text
adNumeric		decimal, numeric
adSingle	Single	real
adSmallInt	Integer	smallint
adTinyInt		tinyint
adVarBinary		varbinary
adVarChar		varchar

Entering Data into Tables

There are many ways to enter data into a database's tables. You can use SQL statements: The INSERT statement appends a new row to a table and sets its fields to the value specified with the command. You can also open the actual table and edit it. Both Access and SQL Server support this type of direct editing. Just double-click the name of an Access table, or right-click the name of a SQL Server and select Open Table ➤ Return All Rows from the shortcut menu. By the way, SQL Server is a DBMS and not a visual environment for accessing and manipulating data. Access is primarily a front-end application, so it's easier to edit Access tables than SQL Server tables. Finally, you can write VB applications that allow users to edit tables through the proper interface. Obviously, this is the recommended method, since it allows you to validate the data and protect the database against user mistakes. You'll find a lot of information in this book on building practical, functional user interfaces with Visual Basic.

Null Values

If you're not familiar with database programming, you probably haven't used Null values yet, and you'll be surprised how important Null values are to databases. A *Null value* means that the actual field value is unknown. A numeric field with a zero value is not Null. Likewise, a blank string is not a Null value either. Nulls were introduced to handle incomplete or exceptional data, and they should be handled in a special manner. A field that has not been assigned a value is considered incomplete. If this field is involved in an operation, the result of the operation is considered exceptional, since it's neither zero nor a blank string. When a new row is created, all of its columns are set to Null, and unless you specify a value, they remain Null. You can modify this default behavior by requesting that certain columns can't be Null. If you attempt to add a new row with a Null value in a column that's not allowed to accept Nulls, the database will reject the insertion. The same will happen if you edit a row and set to Null the value of a column that's not allowed to accept Nulls.

Primary key fields (the fields that link tables to one another), for example, can never be Null. To specify that any other field may not accept the Null value, you must set the Required property in Access to True, or the Allow Nulls property in SQL Server to False. Figure 2.14 shows how to prevent a field (the CompanyName field) from ever being Null in an Access table.

If your tables contain Null values, you should be aware of how the DBMS handles them. When you sum the values of a column with the SUM() function, Null values are ignored. If you count the rows with the COUNT() function, the Null fields are also ignored. The same is true for the AVG() function, which calculates the average value. If it treated the Null values as zeros, then the average would be wrong. The AVG() function returns the average of the fields that are not Null. If you want to include the Null values in the average, you must first replace them with the zero numeric value. These rules apply to both Access and SQL Server.

Null values are so important in working with databases that SQL recognizes the keywords IS NULL and IS NOT NULL (SQL statements are not case-sensitive, but this book uses uppercase so that you can quickly spot the SQL keywords in the examples). To exclude the Null values in an SQL statement, use the clause:

```
WHERE column_name IS NOT NULL
```

You'll learn just about everything you need to know about SQL statements in Chapter 4, but here's a simple example of an SQL statement that retrieves the titles that have a price and ignores the rest of them:

```
SELECT Title, Price
```

```
FROM Books
WHERE Price IS NOT NULL
```

To retrieve the titles without a price, use a statement similar to this:

```
SELECT Title
FROM Books
WHERE Price IS NULL
```

Indexes

OK, so you've created a few tables and have actually entered some data into them. Now the most important thing you can do with a database is extract data from it (or else, why store the information in the first place?). And I don't mean view all the customers or all the products. We rarely browse the rows of a single table. Instead, we're interested in summary information that will help us make business decisions. We need answers to questions like "What's the most popular product in California?" or "What's the month with the largest sales for a specific product?" and so on. To retrieve this type of information, you must combine multiple tables. To answer the first question, you must locate all the customers in California, retrieve their orders, sum the quantities of the items they have purchased, and then select the product with the largest sum of quantities. As you can guess, a DBMS must be able to scan the tables and locate the desired rows quickly. An index is nothing more than a mechanism for speeding up lookup operations.

Computers use a special technique, called *indexing*, to locate information very quickly. This technique requires that the data be maintained in some order. As you will see, the indexed rows need not be in a specific physical order, as long as we can retrieve them in a specific order. If you want to retrieve the name of the category of a specific product, the rows of the Categories table must be ordered according to the CategoryID field. This is the value that links each row in the Products table to the corresponding row in the Categories table.

To search for a value in an ordered list, compare the middle element of the list with the value you're looking for. If the value is larger than the middle element, you know that you need not search in the first (upper) half of the list. The same process is repeated with the bottom half of the list. Again, compare the value with the middle element in the remaining list, and reject one half of the list again. This process repeats until you're left with a single element. This element must be the one you're looking for. If it isn't, then the element you're searching for does not belong to the list.

This searching scheme is called *binary search* and it's the basic idea behind indexing. To get an idea of the efficiency of this method, consider a list with 1024 elements. After the first comparison, the list is reduced to 512 elements. After the second search, the list is reduced to 256 elements. After the tenth comparison, the list is reduced to a single element. It takes only 10 comparisons to locate an element in a list with 1024 elements. If the list had a million elements, it would take just 20 comparisons.

Fortunately, you don't have to maintain the rows of the tables in any order yourself. The DBMS does it for you. You simply specify that a table be maintained in a specific order according to a column's value, and the DBMS will take over. The DBMS can maintain multiple indexes for the same table. You may wish to search the products by name and supplier. It's customary to search for a customer by name, city, ZIP code, country, and so on. To speed up the searches, you can maintain an index for each field you want to search on.

The binary search algorithm described above is a simplified description of how a DBMS locates items in an ordered list. As you have probably guessed, searching an ordered list is the easy part. The difficult part is to make sure that, each time a new row is added (or edited), it's inserted in the proper place, so that the table's rows are always ordered. The details of maintaining ordered lists are far more complicated. SQL Server uses a data structure known as Balanced Trees (B-Trees) to maintain the rows of a table in order at all times and search them. You need not understand what B-Trees are, because this is exactly what a DBMS does for you: it frees you from low-level details and allows you to focus on data, rather than the actual organization of the data on the disk.

The DBMS doesn't actually sort the rows of a table. It keeps a list of numbers, which reflects the order of the elements sorted according to a field. This list is the *index*. Once a table has been indexed, every time you add a new row to the table, the table's indexes are updated accordingly. If you need to search a table in many ways, you can maintain multiple indexes on the same table.

Indexes are manipulated by the DBMS, and all you have to do is define them. Every time a new row is added, or an existing row is deleted or edited, the table's indexes are automatically updated. You can use the index at any time to locate rows very quickly. Practically, indexes allow you to select a row based on an indexed field instantly. When searching for specific rows, the DBMS will take into consideration automatically any index that can speed the search.

Efficiency Issues

Tables are not static objects. Most tables in a database change constantly: new rows are added and existing rows are deleted or edited. This also means that the DBMS must constantly update the table indexes. This process can become quite a burden, so you shouldn't create too many indexes. On the other hand, indexes speed up lookup operations enormously. So, where do you draw the line?

Continued on next page

If you're using Access, you must tune the performance of the database manually. If a table is updated heavily on a daily basis, try to minimize the number of indexes on that table. If a table isn't updated as frequently, but it's used by many queries, you can add many indexes to speed up the queries. Unfortunately, the tables that are used most often in queries are also updated heavily. At any rate, if you're putting too much effort into squeezing every drop of performance out of your Access database, it's probably time to move up to SQL Server.

One of the many tools that come with SQL Server 7 is the Index Tuning Wizard, which helps you decide which indexes to keep and which ones to drop. The Index Tuning Wizard monitors the performance of the database, logs the necessary statistics, and tells you which indexes are responsible for most of the performance. These are the indexes you need in your database; the rest can be dropped at the price of slowing down some queries that are not used as frequently. The Wizard can also create a script with the changes it suggests and implement them immediately. For more information on the Index Tuning Wizard, see SQL Server's online books on the SQL Server CD.

Views

In addition to tables, most databases support views. A *view* is a virtual table: It looks and behaves just like a table, it can be updated too, but it's not an object that exists in the database. It's based on query. Views come to life when they're requested, and they're released when they're no longer needed. Any operations you perform on a view are automatically translated into operations on the table(s) from which the view is derived.

Views enhance the security of the database. Consider a personnel table, which stores information about employees, including their salaries and other sensitive information. While most of the information is public (names, telephone extensions, departments, the projects each employee is involved with, and so on), some fields should be restricted to authorized users only. While you could split the table into smaller ones, SQL Server allows you to create unique views and assign access rights to those views to selected user groups.

You can also use views to hide the complexity introduced by the normalization process and the relations between tables. Users don't really care about normalization rules or relationships. They would rather see a list of customer names, their orders, and the actual product names. This information exists in the database, but it's scattered in four different tables: Customers, Orders, Order Details, and Products. By defining a view on the database, you can maintain a structure that eases your development, yet gives the users the "table" they would rather see.

Updating Tables and Views

Changes in the view are reflected immediately to the underlying table(s). When the underlying tables change, however, these changes are not reflected immediately to the views based on them. Views are based on the data in the tables the moment the query was executed. A view that's based on a table and hides a few of its rows (or columns) is always updateable, as long as it contains the primary key of the table. (As mentioned already, the primary key uniquely identifies a table's row. Without this piece of information, SQL Server wouldn't know which row to update.)

Some views cannot be updated. Views based on SQL statements that combine multiple tables may not be, and views that contain totals can't be updated. Totals are based on many rows and SQL Server doesn't know which order or detail line it must change to affect the total.

Figure 2.13 shows a section of the Invoices view (I have hidden many of the columns by setting their width to zero). Start SQL Server's Enterprise Manager, open the Northwind database folder in the left pane, and click Views under the Northwind database name. The names of all the views defined for the database will be displayed in the right pane. To open a view, right-click on its name and select Open ➤ Return All Rows from the shortcut menu.

FIGURE 2.13:

The Invoices view displays the order details along with customer names and product names.

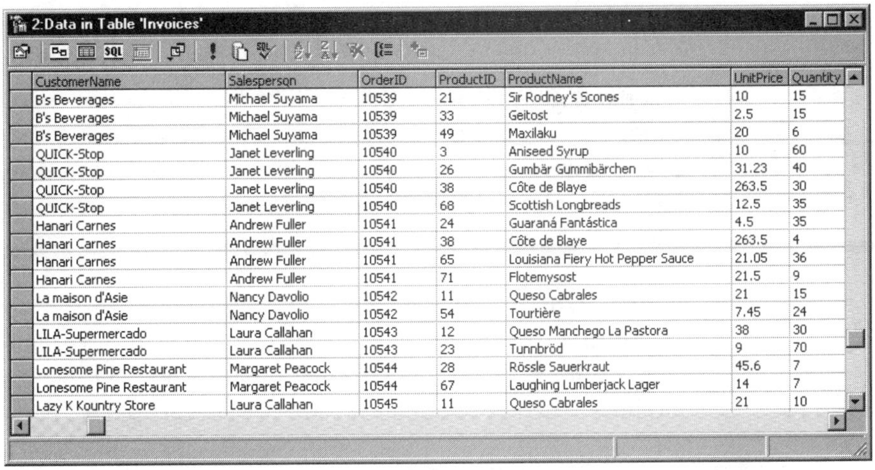

CustomerName	Salesperson	OrderID	ProductID	ProductName	UnitPrice	Quantity
B's Beverages	Michael Suyama	10539	21	Sir Rodney's Scones	10	15
B's Beverages	Michael Suyama	10539	33	Geitost	2.5	15
B's Beverages	Michael Suyama	10539	49	Maxilaku	20	6
QUICK-Stop	Janet Leverling	10540	3	Aniseed Syrup	10	60
QUICK-Stop	Janet Leverling	10540	26	Gumbär Gummibärchen	31.23	40
QUICK-Stop	Janet Leverling	10540	38	Côte de Blaye	263.5	30
QUICK-Stop	Janet Leverling	10540	68	Scottish Longbreads	12.5	35
Hanari Carnes	Andrew Fuller	10541	24	Guaraná Fantástica	4.5	35
Hanari Carnes	Andrew Fuller	10541	38	Côte de Blaye	263.5	4
Hanari Carnes	Andrew Fuller	10541	65	Louisiana Fiery Hot Pepper Sauce	21.05	36
Hanari Carnes	Andrew Fuller	10541	71	Flotemysost	21.5	9
La maison d'Asie	Nancy Davolio	10542	11	Queso Cabrales	21	15
La maison d'Asie	Nancy Davolio	10542	54	Tourtière	7.45	24
LILA-Supermercado	Laura Callahan	10543	12	Queso Manchego La Pastora	38	30
LILA-Supermercado	Laura Callahan	10543	23	Tunnbröd	9	70
Lonesome Pine Restaurant	Margaret Peacock	10544	28	Rössle Sauerkraut	45.6	7
Lonesome Pine Restaurant	Margaret Peacock	10544	67	Laughing Lumberjack Lager	14	7
Lazy K Kountry Store	Laura Callahan	10545	11	Queso Cabrales	21	10

Try editing the Invoices view to see how it behaves. Bring the CustomerName column into view, change the name *Hanari Carnes* into uppercase, and then move to another cell. The customer's name has been changed already, not only in the open view, but in the database as well. If you opened the Customers table, you would see that the changes have already been committed to the database. Yet, the remaining instances of the same name on the view didn't change. That's because the view isn't updated constantly. SQL Server doesn't maintain a "live" link to the database, and it can't update the view every time.

Things can get even worse. Locate another instance of the same customer in the view and change the name to *HANARI CARNES1*. As soon as you move to another cell, the following message will pop up:

```
Data has changed since the Results pane was last updated. Do you
want to save your changes now?
Click Yes to save your changes and update the database
Click No to discard your changes and refresh the Results pane
Click Cancel to continue editing
```

What's happened here? The name of the customer you read from the database was Hanari Carnes, and you changed it to uppercase. This change was committed to the Customers table. Then you attempted to change the name Hanari Carnes into something else again, and SQL Server attempted to update the Customers table for a second time. This time, SQL Server didn't find the name Hanari Carnes there; it had already been changed (to HANARI CARNES). And that's exactly what the message tells you. You have attempted to change a field, but its original value is no longer the same as when it was read.

Of course it isn't. You just changed it, right? But SQL Server doesn't keep track of who's changing what in the database. For all it knows, the changes could have been made by another user, so it simply tells you that the record you're about to change is no longer the same. Imagine if this was a seat reservation application. You'd assign the same seat to two different customers. When you change a row in a table, you must be sure that the row hasn't changed since you last read it.

Confusing? Welcome to the world of database programming! As you can understand, this behavior is not unique to views. It's a major issue in database programming known as *concurrency control*. In a multiuser environment, there's always a risk of two or more people attempting to update the same information at once. The behavior you just witnessed is actually a feature of the database: It lets you know that someone else has already changed the row you read. Otherwise, you'd have to implement the same logic from within your application. I didn't mean to scare you; I just wanted to introduce you to one of the most troublesome aspects of database programming. You'll find more information on the topic of concurrency control and how to handle simultaneous updates in Chapter 9, "Advanced ADO Topics."

NOTE   You can't repeat this experiment with Access. Access may not be as powerful a DBMS as SQL Server, but it has a very flexible user interface, meant to be used by people with little database experience. The CompanyName field is displayed as an element of a ComboBox control. You're forced to select another valid company name from a list with all customer names, but you can't edit the company name directly—unless you're editing the Customers table.

Access Views

Access's views are called queries, and they are basically the same thing. You write a query (an SQL statement) that retrieves selected rows from one or more tables and attach its definition to the database. To work with a query, double-click its name in the Queries window to view a grid with the qualifying rows. There's one major difference between SQL Server views and Access queries. If the query is updateable, the changes you make are committed immediately to the database, and they also update the query's grid. This instant feedback is a nice feature that makes working with Access queries very convenient. Even if another uses changes one of the rows you're viewing, your grid will be updated immediately.

NOTE   If you're wondering why the two products behave so differently, the answer is that Access is a not-so-powerful DBMS, with a user-friendly interface. SQL Server, on the other hand, is a very powerful DBMS, but not a front-end application. You must write applications to access SQL Server's tables and views and not edit them directly. As you will see in Chapter 4, when you fetch a row with your application, SQL Server provides the most recent version of the row. If another user changes the row after you have read it, an error will be generated, and you can handle the conflict from within your code.

Establishing Relationships

Once the information has been broken up logically into separate tables, you must establish relationships between the tables, which is the essence of the relational database model. To relate tables to each other, you use fields with common values. In this section, you'll see how primary and foreign keys are used to establish relationships between tables.

Primary and Foreign Keys

The Categories table has a CategoryID field, which holds a value that identifies each category. This value must be unique for each row of the Categories table, and it's the table's primary key. The Products table also has a CategoryID field, which is set to the ID of the product's category. The two fields have the same name, but this is not a requirement. It's just a convenience for us. The mere existence of the two fields doesn't mean that the two tables are related to each other. You must specify how the tables will be related, as well as which field is the primary key and which field is the foreign key. The primary key is unique to each row, while the foreign key may appear in more than one row. This relationship is called one-to-many, because a single row of the Categories table is usually pointed to by multiple rows of the Products table.

Figure 2.14 shows how SQL Server depicts relationships between tables. To view the relationships between the tables of a database, start the Enterprise Manager and open the desired database in the left pane. Click the Diagrams icon under the database's name and when the Relationships icon appears in the right pane, double-click it. The Relationships diagram will appear in a new window. Each table is represented by a ListBox with the table's field names, and the relationships between tables are represented with arrows. On one end of the arrow is the icon of a key, which indicates the primary key. On the other end of the arrow is the infinity symbol, which indicates the table with the foreign key. The infinity symbol means that there may be many rows pointing to the row with the primary key.

FIGURE 2.14:

The CategoryID field in the Products table is the foreign key, which points to the primary key in the Categories table.

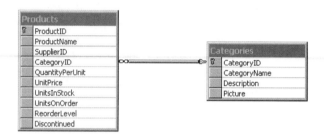

A last note on keys: primary key fields are not used for custom searches. It doesn't make sense to retrieve all customers with an ID of 1000 or less, or the products with an ID between 50 and 75. Primary key fields are used to connect two tables, so we are never interested in their actual value. Here's a simple SQL statement that retrieves the orders placed by the customer Alfreds Futterkiste:

```
SELECT * FROM Orders
WHERE Customers.CompanyName = 'Alfreds Futterkiste' AND
    Orders.CustomerID = Customers.CustomerID
```

This statement tells the DBMS to retrieve the rows of the Orders table that match the following criteria:

- The customer's CompanyName field is the customer's name, *and*

- The foreign key in the Orders table matches the primary key in the Customers table.

This query will return all the rows of the Orders table whose CustomerID field is the same as the CustomerID field of the specified customer's row. Primary and foreign keys are used to match rows in two tables, and their actual values are of no interest to us. (The asterisk is a special character that means "all the fields." You could have specified a comma-separated list of the desired fields in the place of the asterisk).

Viewing and Editing Relationships

To view the relationships of an Access database, switch to the Tables view and select Relationships from the Tools menu. The window shown in Figure 2.15 will appear on your screen, which is quite similar to the Relationships diagram of SQL Server. The relationships between tables are represented with lines, which have the digit 1 on the primary key's side and the infinity symbol on the foreign key's side. In addition, the primary key in each table is printed in bold to stand out.

FIGURE 2.15:

Viewing the relationships in an Access database

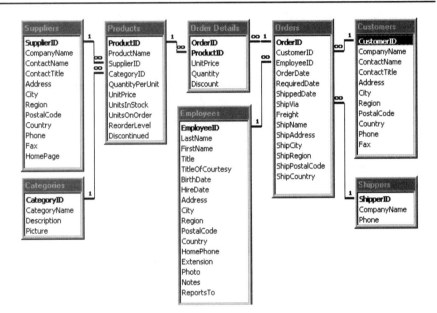

To delete a relationship, right-click its name and select Delete from the shortcut menu (in SQL Server, select Delete Relationship from Database). To view or edit the properties of the relationship, select Edit (or Properties in SQL Server) from the same shortcut menu. The Properties window should specify the primary and foreign keys, and in SQL Server each relationship has a name. Notice that Access relationships are not named.

AutoNumber and Identity Fields

The actual values of the primary key fields are so irrelevant that in most cases we let the DBMS generate their values for us. The DBMS can automatically generate an integer value for a primary key field every time a new row is added. SQL Server uses the term *Identity* for this data type, while Access uses the term *AutoNumber*. If you specify an AutoNumber field in Access, you can specify whether it will be increased by one or by a random value. In SQL Server, you can specify the initial value of an Identity field and its increment.

To create the new value for an AutoNumber or Identity field, the DBMS adds a value (usually one) to the last value of this field in the same table. This operation is simple in principle, but it would be quite a task if you had to implement it on your own. With many users adding rows to the same table, you'd have to lock the table, read the last row's Identity value, add the proper increment, and then commit the newly added row.

More Complicated Relations

Not all relations can be resolved with a pair of primary and foreign keys. Let's say you're designing a database for storing book titles. The structure of the table with the titles is rather obvious. The relationship between titles and publishers is also obvious: Each title has a single publisher and the same publisher may appear in multiple titles. The relationship between publishers and titles is called one-to-many. Conversely, the relationship between titles and publishers is called many-to-one, because multiple titles may point to the same publisher. One-to-many and many-to-one relationships are the same—they follow the order of the related tables.

But how about the relationship between titles and authors? Each book has a varying number of authors; some books have no author, some others may have six authors. Likewise, the same author may have written more than one title. The relationship between titles and authors is called many-to-many. To establish a direct relationship between the Titles and Authors tables, some rows in the Titles table should point to many rows in the Authors table. Likewise, some rows in the Authors table should point to many rows in the Titles tables. To avoid this type of relationship in your design, introduce a new table, which is linked with a one-to-many relationship to the Titles table and a many-to-one relationship to the Authors table.

In our example, we introduced an intermediate table between the Titles and Authors tables: the Title Author table, which contains one row per title-author pair, as shown in Figure 2.16. This table has a very simple structure (you could say that it doesn't even contain any original information). It simply maps books to authors. If a book has three authors, we add three rows to the Title Author table. All rows have the same ISBN (the title's key) and the authors' ID keys.

Intermediate tables like the Title Author table are very common in database design. Practically, there's no other method of implementing many-to-many relations between tables.

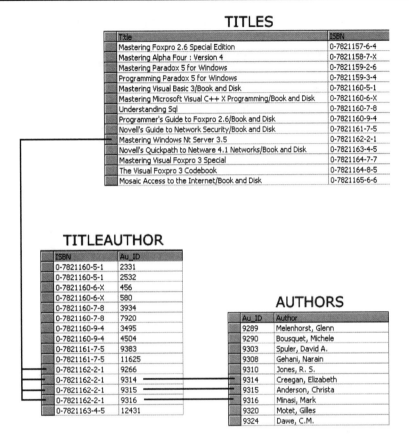

FIGURE 2.16:

Connecting the Titles table to
the Authors table with an
intermediate table, the Title
Author table.

Normalization Rules

By now you have good idea as to how relational databases are designed, and
you could easily design a simple relational database yourself, using the information discussed earlier and your common sense. Most important, you should be
able to understand how information is stored in a database by looking at its relational diagram.

However, there are a few rules in relational database design, known as the *normalization rules*. These rules will help you design a *normalized* database, or at least verify
your design. A database is normalized if it doesn't repeat information and doesn't
exhibit update and delete anomalies. While the number of these rules varies, the
basic normalization rules are just three: the first, second, and third normalization
rules. Don't be surprised, however, if you find as many as half a dozen normalization rules.

A table normalized according to the first rule is said to be in first normal form (1NF). A table normalized according to the second rule is said to be in second normal form (2NF). Notice that a table must be 1NF before you can apply the second normalization rule. Finally, a table that's in 2NF can be normalized according to the third rule, in which case it's said to be in third normal form (3NF). Higher normal forms deal with very specific and rare situations, which most programmers handle on an individual basis.

Database Design Errors

To understand the need for database normalization, I will start with a few common mistakes in database design. These mistakes are so obvious that it doesn't take a degree in computer science to understand why and how to avoid them. Yet, the same mistakes are repeated over and over. You'll find it easy to spot the mistakes in the example designs, which are small in size. In larger databases, even ones with a few dozen tables, it's not as simple to spot the same mistakes.

Let's start with the following simple table for storing information about books:

```
Table TITLES
ISBN    Title    Pages    Topic
```

This table seems perfectly good, until you decide to add a second topic to a title. A book about HTML could be classified under the category "programming," but also under the category "Internet." To add multiple topics, you'd have to repeat each title's data for each category:

```
0144489890    Total HTML    850    programming
0144489890    Total HTML    850    Internet
```

The problem with this table is that certain information is repeated (actually, most of the information is repeated). The primary objective in designing databases is to avoid duplication of information. To avoid this unnecessary duplication, you must move the topics to another table. Some of you may consider adding columns for multiple topics, but then you must make an (arbitrary) assumption as to the maximum number of topics per title and come up with a table like the following one:

```
Table TITLES
ISBN    Title    Pages    Topic1    Topic2    Topic3
```

This table is even worse. In trying to avoid duplicating the table's data, you've introduced duplication of information in the structure of the table itself. As you will see, the first rule in database design is to avoid groups of columns with information of the same type. If you decide to change the name of the "programming" category to something else, like "computer languages," you'd have to change too many rows, in too many places. Some titles may have "programming" under Topic1, others under Topic2, and so on.

To solve the problem of multiple columns of the same type, you introduce two new tables, as shown here:

```
Table TITLES
ISBN   Title   Pages
```

```
Table TITLETOPIC
ISBN   TopicID
```

```
Table TOPICS
TopicID   TopicName
```

This design uses a table that stores topics only. To change the description of a topic, you must change a single row in the TOPICS table. Topics are related to titles through the TITLETOPIC table. If a title must be classified under multiple topics, you will insert multiple lines in the TITLETOPICS table. To find out the topics of a specific title, use its ISBN to search the TITLETOPIC table and extract the rows whose ISBN matches the ISBN of the book. You'll end up with none, one, or a few rows of the TITLETOPIC table. Use the TopicID of these lines to locate the topic(s) of the title. Sounds complicated? It's simpler than it sounds, because all tables are appropriately indexed, and the DBMS will perform the necessary searches for you.

Update and Delete Anomalies

Let's drop the Topic column from our original table design and add some publication information. Here's the structure of another table that holds information about books:

```
Table TITLES
ISBN   Title   Pages   PubYear   Publisher   PubAddress
```

Notice that the publisher's address doesn't belong to the TITLES table. This structure can lead to two highly undesirable situations:

- If a publisher relocates, then you must change the address in not one, but hundreds, perhaps thousands, of records. This is known as *update anomaly*. If you forget to change the publisher's address in a few records, the database will contain bad information. This situation can be avoided by moving the publishers to a different table.

- Even worse, if you delete the last book of a publisher, you will lose all the information about the specific publisher. This situation is known as *delete anomaly*, and it can also be avoided by moving the publishers to a different table.

Here's a better structure for storing the same information:

```
Table TITLES
ISBN   Title   Pages   PubYear   PublisherID
```

```
Table PUBLISHERS
PublisherID    Publisher    PubAddress
```

The PublisherID field is a unique number that identifies a publisher, and it must have the same value in both tables. To find out a title's publisher, you retrieve the PublisherID field from the TITLES table and then locate the row in the PUBLISHERS table that has the same value in its PublisherID field. In effect, the PublisherID field in the PUBLISHERS table is the primary key (it cannot appear in more than one row), and the PublisherID fields in the TITLES table are the foreign keys (they can appear in many rows).

Okay, this is pretty obvious, but why did you have to introduce a new field? Couldn't you use the publisher's name to relate the two tables? Had you used the publisher's name as a key, then you wouldn't be able to change the publisher's name in a single place. If Ventura Press is incorporated and changes its name to Ventura Press Inc., you should be able to change the publisher's name in a single place to avoid update anomalies.

Using a number to identify each row in a table is a very common practice. Numeric IDs need not be changed, so they will not cause any update anomalies. Some readers may think that publishers don't change names, but this type of assumption is too dangerous in database design. Companies merge, they incorporate, and you can't assume their names won't change. Even when such an assumption may appear reasonable, you shouldn't base the design of a database on an assumption.

First Normal Form

This one is very simple. It says that a table shouldn't contain repeating groups. Here's a table that contains all the mistakes of the previous (unacceptable) designs. Let's start with the repeating groups (the book's topics):

```
ISBN  Title  Pages  Publisher  PubAddress  Topic1  Topic2
```

To remove a group from a table, keep the first column of the group and repeat the additional topics in multiple rows of the table. A title with two topics will be stored in this table as follows:

```
ISBN          Title        Pages  Publisher  Topic
01254889391   SQL Server   850    Sybex      Programming
01254889391   SQL Server   850    Sybex      Databases
```

NOTE   The first row contains field names, and the following rows are data. I have omitted the PubAddress column to shorten the lines.

The first normal form doesn't require that a table be broken into multiple tables. It turns some of the table's columns into additional rows. This structure has the following advantages:

No empty fields   If a title belongs to a single topic, then the fields Topic2 and Topic3 in the example would be empty.

No artificial limitations   If a specific title should be located under half a dozen categories, you can add as many lines as necessary to the table.

I've discussed the shortcomings of this design already. The table design is in first normalized form, and you must now apply the second normalization rule.

Second Normal Form

The second normalization rule says that any fields that do not depend fully on the primary key should be moved to another table. The Topic field in the last table structure is not functionally dependent on the ISBN (the primary key). *Functionally dependent* is a math term, meaning that a field is fully determined by the key. A book's page count is functionally dependent on the book's ISBN. If you know the book's ISBN, you can determine the book's page count uniquely. The same is true for the book's publication year. But the topic is not dependent on the ISBN, because the same ISBN can lead to multiple topics.

The second normalization rule requires that the topics be moved to a different table:

Table TITLES
```
ISBN    Title    Pages    Publisher    PubAddress
```

Table TITLETOPIC
```
ISBN    Topic
```

Now, why is this better than the previous table structure? The same ISBN can lead to multiple topics. The TITLETOPIC table doesn't repeat information. Only the primary key is repeated and you can't avoid it. A single title may have multiple topics. This is a one-to-many relationship, and you can't avoid the duplication of the primary key.

However, there's a problem with this table too. Since a book's topic is described with a string, you haven't avoided the update anomaly. If you change the description of a category, you'd have to change many rows in the TITLETOPIC table. To avoid the update anomaly, you must create a separate table with the topics and assign a unique ID to each topic:

Table TOPICS
```
TopicID    Topic
```

To connect each title to one or more topics, you must change the TITLETOPIC table that connects the TITLES and TOPICS tables. The TITLETOPIC table must contain pairs of ISBNs and Topic IDs:

```
Table TITLETOPIC
ISBN   TopicID
```

Third Normal Form

The third normalization rule says that there should be no dependency between non-key fields. In the last table design, you have such a dependency. The publisher's address depends on the publisher, not the book's ISBN. To remove this type of dependency, you must move the publisher information to another table. Since each book must have a publisher, you add the PubID field to the TITLES table and to the new table with the publishers. The PubID field of the TITLES table must have the same value as the PubID field in the PUBLISHERS table. Here's the original table in the third normal form:

```
Table TITLES
ISBN   Title   Pages   PubID


Table PUBLISHERS
PubID   PubAddress


Table TOPICS
TopicID   Topic


Table TITLETOPIC
ISBN   TopicID
```

Figure 2.17 shows the final tables and the relationships between them. As you can see, the normalization rules are simple and resemble the practical rules we derived earlier based on our intuition and common sense. The second and third rules are almost identical—some authors combine them into a single rule. The difference is that the second rule removes the dependencies between the fields and the primary key: you test the dependency of each field against the key field. The third rule removes the dependencies between fields other than the key field.

To summarize, you must use your common sense to split your data into separate tables. Use a separate table for each entity. Then establish relationships between tables (if they can be related, of course). In the process, you may need to introduce additional tables to connect the basic tables of your design. Some tables can't be linked directly. At each stage apply the three normalization rules to your tables to make sure your database is normalized.

FIGURE 2.17:

A normalized database's relational diagram

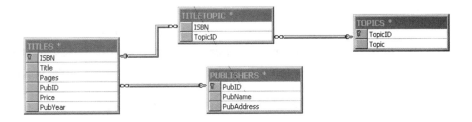

Normalization and Joins

Let's return to the Northwind database for a moment and see how the DBMS uses relations. Each time you connect two tables with a common key, the DBMS must perform an operation known as *join*. It must join the two tables using the primary and foreign keys. Joins are quite expensive operations, and you should try to minimize them. You must also see that the foreign keys used in the join operations are indexed, to help the DBMS with the lookup operations. Some databases may use as many as a few dozen joins to get the desired results out of the database—very slow operations.

As you may notice, there's a conflict between normalization and joins. In a very large database, you may end up with too many related tables, which also means a large number of joins. Many database administrators and programmers will de-normalize their databases a little to reduce the number of joins in the queries. While this is a rather common practice, don't base the design of your databases on this premise. If you ever design a database with many tables, you may have to trade off some normalization for fewer joins. No hard rules here, just use common sense.

Previous versions of SQL Server had a limit of 16 joins in a single SQL statement. SQL Server 7 supports a very large number of joins, but I think even 16 joins are too many. If an operation requires too many joins, you can create an intermediate table or two with fewer joins and then join these tables. Obviously, these operations shouldn't be performed frequently. If some of your queries require many joins, you should probably revise the design of the database. For more information on joins, see "Joining Tables" in Chapter 4. At any rate, this type of problem arises with corporate databases, which are designed by teams of ER specialists.

Database Integrity

The major challenge in database design is maintaining the integrity of the database. Designing a database is only the beginning; you must also make sure that the database is kept in good shape at all times. The burden of keeping a database in good shape is shared by the database administrator (DBA) and the programmers.

As a programmer, you must make sure that all the data your code places into the database are valid. This is quite a task and would require an enormous amount of validation, but, as you'll learn in this section, the database itself can help.

Modern databases include tools that allow you to protect the integrity of the database from within. Access and SQL Server, for example, let you incorporate rules that enforce database integrity. By specifying each column's type, you're actually telling the database not to accept any data that don't conform. If a user or an application attempts to assign a numeric value to a field that stores dates, the database will reject the value to protect data integrity.

The rules for enforcing the integrity of a database can be classified into three categories, which are described next.

Domain Integrity

The first, and simplest, type of integrity is *domain entity*, a fancy term that means each column must have a unique type. If a column holds dates, then users shouldn't be allowed to store integers or Boolean values in this column. As you already know, when you create a table you must declare the data type for each column. If you attempt to assign a value of the wrong type to a column, the database will reject the operation and raise a trappable runtime error. As far as your application is concerned, you can either test the data type of a user-supplied value against the column's data type, or intercept the runtime error that will be raised and act accordingly.

Entity Integrity

The second type of integrity is *entity integrity*, which means that an entity (a customer, product, invoice, and so on) must have a valid primary key. If a table's primary key is Null, then no rows in other tables can be connected to this row. All DBMSs can enforce this type of integrity by not allowing the insertion of rows with Null keys, or by preventing changes that would result in a Null value for a primary key. All you have to do to enforce this type of integrity is set the Nullable property of the column that's used as primary key to False. Actually, you don't even have to set the Nullable property, because neither Access nor SQL Server will accept Null values for primary key fields.

Referential Integrity

This is one of the most important topics in database design. Designing the database is a rather straightforward process, once you have understood the requirements of the corporation (the information that will be stored in the database, how it will be recalled, and the relations among the various tables). Just as important, if not more important, is ensuring that the various relationships remain valid at all times.

Relationships are based on primary and foreign keys. What will happen if the primary key in a relationship is deleted? If you delete a row in the Customers table, for instance, then some orders will become orphaned; they will refer to a customer who doesn't exist. Your applications will keep working, but every now and then you'll get incorrect results. Nothing will go wrong in calculating the total for an existing customer, for example.

If you calculate the grand total for all customers, you'll get one value. If you calculate the grand total for all the detail lines, you'll get a different value. This inconsistency shouldn't exist in a database. Once you realize that your database is in an inconsistent state, you must start examining every table to find out why and when it happened and what other reports are unusable. This is a major headache that you want to avoid. And it's simple to avoid such problems by enforcing the database's referential integrity.

Problems related to the referential integrity of the database can be intermittent, too. If the deleted customer hasn't placed an order in the last 12 months, all the totals you calculate for the last 12 months will be correct. If you receive a (very) late payment from this customer, however, you won't be able to enter it into the database. There's no customer to link the payment to!

Enforcing Referential Integrity

Both Access and SQL Server can be programmed to enforce referential integrity. If you enforce the integrity of the relationship between Customers and Orders, for example, when an application attempts to delete a customer, the database will raise a runtime error and not allow the deletion of the record. If the customer has no orders in the Orders table, then the application will be allowed to delete the customer. This action will not impair the integrity of the database, because there are no related rows.

The good news is that you don't need to write any code to enforce referential integrity. When you specify a relationship, you can also specify that the integrity of the relationship be enforced. In Access, select a relationship in the relational diagram, right-click it, and select Edit from the shortcut menu to open the Edit Relationships window shown in Figure 2.18. Select the primary and foreign keys in the two related tables, then check the Enforce Referential Integrity option, which tells the Jet engine that it shouldn't change (or delete) the primary key if there are foreign keys referencing it.

Access can enforce referential integrity as well as cascade updates and deletes.

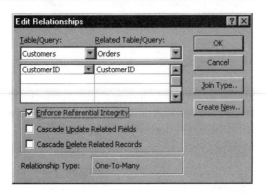

SQL Server can also enforce referential integrity, rejecting any changes in the primary key if this key is referenced by another table. Open the Properties window of a relationship by right-clicking the arrow that represents the relationship between two tables in the Relationships diagram, then selecting Properties from the shortcut menu. Click the Relationships tab, which is shown in Figure 2.19, and check Enable Relationship For INSERT And UPDATE. The Check Existing Data On Creation option is valid when you create a new relationship between two tables that contain data already. It tells SQL Server to make sure that existing data does not violate the new relationship.

FIGURE 2.19:

Specifying the properties of a relationship in a SQL Server database

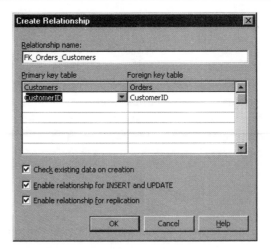

Cascade Updates and Deletes

In Access, you can also use *cascade updates* and *cascade deletes*. These options are not available in SQL Server. When the Cascade Delete option is in effect, you can delete a customer, but all related rows in every table in the database will also be deleted. If you use cascade deletes to enforce referential integrity, then all the orders placed by the specific customer in the Orders table must also be deleted. As each row in the Orders table is deleted, it must take with it all the related rows in the Order Details table as well.

Cascading updates are a less drastic method of enforcing referential integrity. When you change the value of a primary key, Access changes the foreign keys in all tables related to the updated table. If you change a customer's ID, for example, Access will change the OrderID field in the Orders table for all orders placed by that customer.

NOTE   If the primary key is an AutoNumber field, you need not turn on cascading updates, since AutoNumber fields can't change. Cascading deletes are valid, because Auto-Number fields can be deleted.

Triggers

SQL Server does not support cascaded updates because it uses a better mechanism: triggers. A *trigger* is a procedure that's invoked automatically, like an event. For example, you can write a trigger that runs every time a row is updated and takes the appropriate action. If a user changes the primary key, the trigger could reject the changes, cascade deletes and updates (by deleting or updating the related records), or take any other action you deem appropriate. Triggers are commonly used to store information about the changes made to a table's rows, such as the name of the user and the time of the action. In the case of deletions, the trigger could save the original row into an auxiliary table.

Triggers are implemented in T-SQL, which is an extension of SQL and covered in detail in Chapter 7, "Transact-SQL." T-SQL is a mix of SQL statements and more traditional programming statements such as control flow statements, loop structures, and so on. In Chapter 7, I discuss the CascadeCustomerDelete trigger, which is invoked automatically every time a row is deleted in the Customers table. This trigger deletes all the rows in the Order Details table that correspond to customer orders being deleted. After the detail lines have been deleted, the trigger deletes the rows of the Orders table that correspond to orders placed by the same customer. Since the details of these orders no longer exist, you can delete the order without violating the integrity of the database. Finally, the trigger deletes a row from the Customers table.

In the description of the Northwind database, earlier in this chapter, I mentioned that the order totals are not stored in the Orders table, because this design would duplicate information. If your applications spend a lot of time calculating order totals, you may consider saving each order's total in a field of the Orders table. If you do so, you must write a trigger that's invoked every time a row in the Order Details table is added or edited. This trigger must calculate the total of the order and update the corresponding field in the Orders table. The trigger will be fired no matter how the row is added or edited, and it ensures that the Orders table reflects the changes in the Order Details table at all times.

The Pubs Database

The Pubs database is a sample database that comes with SQL Server, and it is used almost exclusively in the examples of SQL Server's online help. The tables of the Pubs database contain very few rows, but they were designed to demonstrate many of the operations we perform on databases. I use this database in a lot of the examples in this book. Following are descriptions of the tables of the Pubs database:

titles This table holds book information. Each book is identified by the title_id field, which is neither its ISBN nor an Identity field but a made-up key. This table also contains a column named ytd_sales (year-to-date sales), which is the number of copies sold in the current year. Since there's no information about the total sales, we'll assume that this column contains the total sales for each title.

authors This table contains author information. Each author is identified by the au_id field (which is the author's social security number), as well as contact information (phone number, address). The last column in the authors table is the contract column, which indicates whether the author has a contract or not.

titleauthor This table connects titles to authors. Its rows contain pairs of title IDs and author IDs. In addition, it contains each author's order in a title, along with the author's royalty split per title. The title ID BU1032 appears twice in this table, which means that this title has two authors. The first one is the author with ID 409-56-7008, and his share of the royalties is 60 percent. The second author has the ID 213-46-8915, and his share of the royalties is 40 percent. The same person is the single author of another title (ID BU2075) and gets 100 percent of the royalties generated by this title.

roysched This table stores the information needed to calculate the royalties generated by each title. Books earn royalties according to a royalty schedule; the royalty escalates as sales increase. The title with ID BU1032 has a breakpoint at 5,000 copies. For the first 5,000 copies, it will make a royalty of 10 percent. After that, this percentage increases to 12 percent. The title with ID BU2075 has many breakpoints (10 percent for the first 1,000 copies, 12 percent for the next 2,000 copies, 14 percent for the next 2,000 copies, 16 percent for the next 3,000 copies, and so on). Figure 2.20 shows the relationships between the tables of the Pubs database involved in calculating royalties. The royalty breakpoints are shown in Figure 2.21.

FIGURE 2.20:

Linking titles, authors, and royalties in the Pubs database

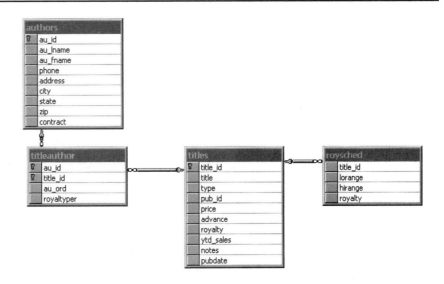

FIGURE 2.21:

Applying the relationships of Figure 2.20 to some actual data

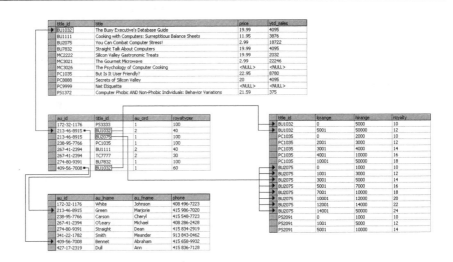

pub_info   This table holds information about the publishers. Each publisher is identified in the pub_id field, and the same value is repeated in the titles table.

stores   This table stores the names and addresses of a number of book-stores to which sales are made. Each store is identified by a store ID (stor_id field). This table is linked to the sales table.

sales   The sales table contains sales information. The stor_id field holds information about the store to which the sale was made, the ord_num field is the order's number, and title_id and qty are the title and quantity sold. Unfortunately, this table doesn't contain all the sales, and you can't find out how many copies of each title were sold by adding quantities in this table.

discounts   This table holds the initial, usual, and volume discounts for each store. Each discount range is determined by a low and high quantity. The initial discount is 10.5 percent. For a volume discount, a store must order 100 or more copies. In addition, you can store specific discounts for each store in this table.

The remaining tables of the Pubs database have to do with employees and jobs and are not used in this book's examples. The employees table holds personnel information and the jobs table holds job descriptions.

The Biblio Database

This sample database comes with Access and Visual Basic, but not SQL Server. The Biblio database is quite large in number of records (it contains more than 8,000 titles), and it's a good database for testing your applications and SQL statements. The structure of this database is quite simple, and we'll go briefly through its tables and relationships. Then we'll import the Biblio database into SQL Server.

The Biblio database is a typical bookstore database, without sales information. We'll use this database later in the book to build an online bookstore. Take a look at the relational diagram of the database (see Figure 2.22) and explore it on your own. We have discussed the basic structure of this database in previous sections.

FIGURE 2.22:

The relational diagram of the Biblio database

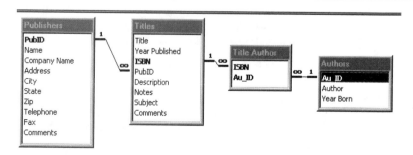

The Titles table stores book titles, using the book's ISBN as the primary key. Publishers are stored in the Publishers table, and they are related to the Titles table through the book's ISBN. Authors are also stored in a separate table, the Authors table, but this table can't be directly linked to the Titles table. Each book may have any number of authors, so there's a table between Titles and Authors, the Title Author table. To add a new author to a book, you add a new line to the Title Author table, with the ISBN of the book and the ID of the author.

Should Primary Keys Be Integers?

This database uses the book's ISBN as the primary key. You'll probably read that primary keys should be integers, because the DBMS can handle them faster than strings. This is true, but SQL Server is extremely efficient when it comes to indexing. If it makes sense to use a meaningful field in the table as the primary key, do it. As long as the field's length doesn't exceed 50 characters, you will not notice any delay. I'm not sure this is the case for a table with a billion rows, but for a moderately sized database, it's okay to use noninteger primary keys. You may not have noticed it, but all of the sample databases that come with either VB or SQL Server include tables that use noninteger primary keys. I can't see why the folks at Redmond would have gone to the trouble of making up keys, if an AutoNumber or Identity field makes a more efficient primary key.

Importing the Biblio Database into SQL Server

In the following chapter, I will use the Biblio database in SQL Server, as well as the other sample databases that come with VB and SQL Server, so it would be a good idea to port the database from Access into SQL Server (or *upsize* it, to use a trendy expression). If you have used Access in the past and plan to switch to SQL Server, you may wish to upsize some of your own databases too.

This last section takes you through the steps of importing an Access database into SQL Server. While you'd usually leave this type of operation to the database administrator, it's fairly simple and you should be able to perform it on your own. Besides, importing the database into SQL Server can be scripted in VBScript, and you may wish to learn a little more about the process.

NOTE   VBScript is Microsoft's scripting language and is incorporated into many of its products. As a VB programmer, you can add scripting capabilities to your own applications with the help of the Scripting control. VBScript is identical to Visual Basic, but it lacks a visual user interface.

To import data from another database into SQL Server, use the Data Transformation Services (DTS). DTS is a component of SQL Server that allows you to import data from different databases and text files, as well as export data to other databases. To import the Biblio database from Access, follow these steps:

1. To start the DTS Import Wizard, right-click the Databases folder and select All Tasks ➤ Import Data from the shortcut menu. Click Next to skip the welcome screen.

2. In the Choose a Data Source screen, specify the source of the data (the Biblio Access database). In the Source box, select Microsoft Access, and in the File Name box enter the path to the `Biblio.mdb` file. Or click the button next to the File Name box and locate the database file through the File Open dialog box. Click Next.

3. In the Choose a Destination screen, choose the database that will accept the data. The destination must be the Microsoft OLE DB Provider for SQL Server. Specify the name of the server on your network—or (`local`), if you're running SQL Server on the same machine—as well as the authentication type. In the Database box, select New to create a new database that will accept the Biblio database. As soon as you select the New entry in the Database drop-down list, the Create Database dialog box will appear (see Figure 2.23). The same dialog box appears when you create a new SQL Server database.

FIGURE 2.23:

The Create Database
dialog box

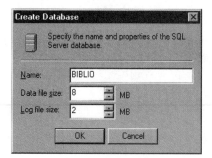

4. In the Create Database dialog box, specify the name of the new database and its initial size. Eight megabytes are more than enough for the Biblio database, and a log file size of 2MB is also plenty. Click OK, and SQL Server will create the new database and return to the Choose A Destination screen. Click Next to move on.

5. In the Specify Table Copy or Query screen (see Figure 2.24), specify whether to copy the Access database's tables into the new database, or to select specific rows from the database's tables with one or more queries. You want to

copy all the rows of the Biblio tables in the new database, so check the first option and click Next.

FIGURE 2.24:

On this screen of the Wizard, you must specify whether SQL Server will copy all rows or selected ones.

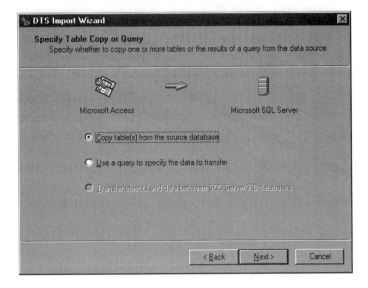

6. In the Select Source Tables screen (see Figure 2.25), specify which tables will be transferred. Each time you select a table by clicking in front of its name, a similarly named table is added to the Destination Table column. Check all source tables in the first column. You can also change the name of the destination table, but there's no need to change the names of the Biblio database.

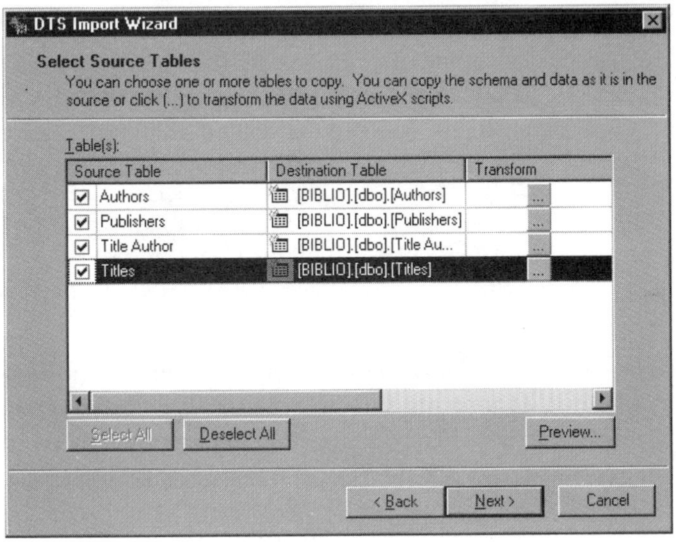

FIGURE 2.25:

The Select Source Tables screen of the Wizard

7. The buttons in the Transform column of the Select Source Tables screen let you specify transformations on the data as it is imported into SQL Server. Click the button of the column you want to transform, and you'll be prompted to specify the transformation (in most cases, a simple data type change). The Column Mappings and Transformations window contains two tabs. The Column Mappings tab (see Figure 2.26) shows the definitions of the rows of the selected table. You can change some of the definitions, or even exclude some of the columns. If you want to omit a column, click the table's name in the Destination column and select "ignore."

FIGURE 2.26:

The Column Mappings and Transformations window

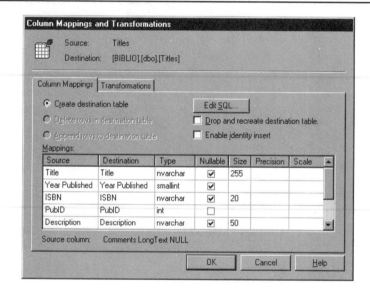

8. On the Transformations tab, you can specify whether the source columns will be copied directly or transformed as they are copied into the destination columns. If you check the second option, the text box on the window will be enabled. Here you can enter a script to transform the data as it's transferred. The script is a short program written in VBScript that manipulates the fields of the source and destination fields.

9. Click OK to return to the Column Mappings and Transformation Wizard. There's no need to specify any transformations, so let the Wizard translate the table definitions and transfer all rows for you.

10. Click OK to return to the DTS Wizard and click Next to specify when the data import will take place. Select Run Immediately to import the database immediately. If you plan to import the same data in the future, check Save DTS Package. SQL Server will create a script automatically so that you

won't have to go through all the screens of the Import Wizard again. If you choose to save the DTS package, you'll be prompted to enter a name for the package.

11. Click Next again to see the last screen. Confirm your intention to import the database and click Finish. SQL Server will start transferring data asynchronously, and it will display the progress of the operation on the Data Transferring screen.

After the transfer has completed, you will see the number of rows of each table transferred into the new database. If any errors occur during the transfer, the process of importing the corresponding table will be aborted. The Wizard will tell you how many rows it transferred successfully, and you can open the original table to find out what's wrong with the specific row.

Summary

This concludes the introduction to databases. In the following chapter, you will learn to use the visual database tools. Using these tools, you can design databases right in Visual Basic's IDE. The visual database tools allow you to manipulate SQL Server and Oracle databases (edit tables, establish relationships, and create queries) as if you were working with Access databases. I know you're eager to write some VB code, but these tools will make things a whole lot simpler.

CHAPTER

THREE

3

The Visual Database Tools

- The visual database tools

- Connecting to a database

- The Data View window

- The Database Designer

- The Database Diagram

- The Query Designer

- The Source Code Editor

So far you've learned about database drivers, basic database access components, and the principles of relational databases. Before we start building database applications that use the data-bound controls to access a database, we should look at the visual database tools. These tools come with Visual Basic 6 and Visual Studio 6, and some of them (like the Query Designer and the Database Diagram) are included in SQL Server. They are very important tools that simplify many phases of application development, and I discuss them now so that we can use them in the following chapters.

Think of this chapter as reference material. Read it to understand what each tool does, follow the examples, and don't worry if it raises a few questions. The tools discussed here will help you follow the examples of the following chapters and they will ease your way into developing database applications. The Query Designer, for example, is a tool that lets you generate SQL statements with point-and-click operations. If you're not familiar with SQL statements, the Query Designer is an excellent starting point. Use it to ease your way into more complicated SQL statements and stop using it after you have mastered SQL, if you find it easier to just type your SQL statements.

> **NOTE**
>
> To make this chapter more useful to the majority of the book's readers, I introduce many topics that are discussed in detail in following chapters. For those of you already familiar with topics like SQL statements, stored procedures, and so on, this chapter is both a review and a summary. If you haven't designed a database in the past, or if you don't know SQL, then follow along. You'll learn how to design with visual tools, and in the following chapters, we'll get into real programming.

Some topics discussed here may be advanced, but they are central in programming the SQL Server. To build efficient, scalable applications with SQL Server, you must master these topics. SQL Server will be a major aspect of the new version of Visual Studio, and MSDE is already available for those of you who want to build highly scalable applications. None of these topics are difficult or out of the ordinary. Once you've learned SQL, you'll be ready to write your own stored procedures and triggers. In the meantime, you'll be able to do just about everything with the visual database tools.

A First Look at the Visual Database Tools

The *visual database tools* of Visual Basic simplify operations like database design and the extraction of data from a database. They are not programming tools. They're tools to help you prepare the application for coding. The more you do with these tools, the less VB code you'll have to write later on. It's not unlike building regular applications with Visual Basic, if you think about it. Have you ever considered how much functionality you bring into your applications when you drop a control from the toolbox on a Form and then set the properties of the control in the Properties window? We'll start with a quick review of the visual database tools and then we'll explore each tool separately.

The Data View Window   The Data View window lets you specify connections to one or more databases and visualize the structure of the database(s). Figure 3.1 shows a typical Data View window with a single Connection object to the Northwind database. Once you've established a connection to the database, you can view its objects and create new ones. The Data View window is nothing more than a switching point you use to select the objects you want to work with. These objects are the tables, views, stored procedures, and so on. The Data View window is a container for database connections and database objects.

FIGURE 3.1:

A typical Data View window

The Database Designer   The Database Designer is the tool for designing databases. If every DBMS comes with its own set of tools for designing databases, who needs another one? Every VB programmer, that's who. This tool allows you to access SQL Server and Oracle databases alike, and perhaps more databases in the future. The interface is the same and you don't have to learn another database design environment. If you have designed Access databases in the past, you're ready to design SQL Server databases with the Database Designer. It's that simple.

The Database Designer consists of the Table Designer, a tool for creating tables, and the Relational Diagram window (shown in Figure 3.2), which is a tool for establishing relationships between tables. As I mentioned earlier, the Database Designer is a tool for designing databases, not creating new ones. To create a new database, you must still use the DBMS, SQL Server, or Oracle. After the database has been created, you can use the Database Designer to build the database (define its tables, relationships, and so on).

FIGURE 3.2:

Use the Database Designer to view the structure of the tables and to establish relationships between them.

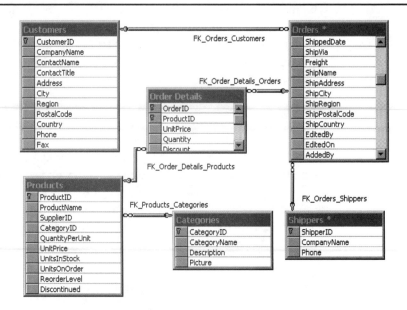

The Query Designer   This is a great visual tool, especially for people who are not familiar with SQL. The Query Designer, shown in Figure 3.3, allows you to build SQL statements with point-and-click operations. You just drop the tables you want to include in the query on a pane of the Query Designer, select the fields you want to use in the query, and finally specify the constraints. The Query Designer is an intelligent and very flexible tool, and you'll probably use it more than any other visual database tool. Even programmers familiar with SQL statements use the Query Designer to design queries, especially if they involve many field names from multiple tables, to minimize typing mistakes.

The Query Designer is based on a fairly old technology, known as Query by Example (QBE), and it's not a new tool either. It was included in Office 95, and many of you may have used it already.

The Source Code Editor and T-SQL Debugger   The Source Code Editor allows you to create new stored procedures and triggers, or edit existing ones. You can also execute and debug stored procedures from within the Visual Basic environment. The Source Code Editor doesn't really qualify as a visual tool, but stored procedures and triggers are subroutines, like VB routines, which you must write on your own. Both stored procedures and triggers are written in T-SQL, and the Source Code Editor is a simple editor for T-SQL.

You can test your procedure by clicking the Execute button on the Source Code Editor. When you do so, the T-SQL Debugger window will appear (see Figure 3.4). The T-SQL Debugger is an interactive environment for debugging T-SQL procedures, and its tools are very similar to Visual Basic's debugging tools.

FIGURE 3.3:

A typical Query Designer window

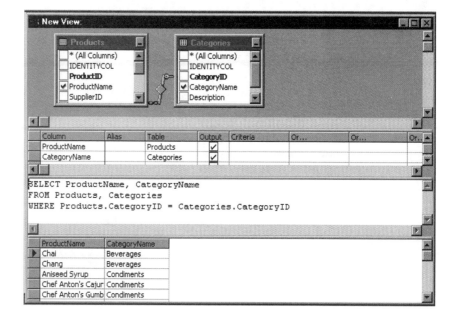

FIGURE 3.4:

The T-SQL Debugger lets you debug your stored procedures interactively.

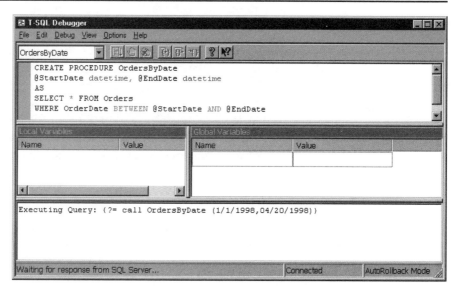

In the following sections, we will explore each one of these tools. But first we'll review the methods for establishing connections to databases. No matter what you're going to do with a database, you must connect to it first.

Connecting to Databases

There are many ways to connect to a database, but for the most common databases you have two options: either through the ODBC driver, or through the OLE DB driver. If you want to access SQL Server or Oracle databases, use the OLE DB driver, which is faster. Other database manufacturers will develop OLE DB drivers for their products, which will be installed automatically during the program's setup.

ODBC is the older driver, and there are many applications that use it today. It's a well-established driver and there are ODBC drivers for most databases. The DAO (Data Access Objects) component, for example, uses the ODBC driver to connect to databases. For your new applications, you should switch to OLE DB, because this is the new data access mechanism and Windows DNA is based on OLE DB. ODBC will not be enhanced in the future, while OLE DB is being improved constantly. Incidentally, the DAO component is not discussed in this book. Microsoft supports it, but there are no plans to enhance the DAO component or existing ODBC drivers.

You have two ways to connect through the OLE DB driver:

- Specify the name of an external file that stores information about the connection. This file is known as a *data link file* and has an extension .udl. The problem with this approach is that you must prepare a different link file for each user on the network.

- Specify a *connection string*, which passes all the information needed by the driver to establish a connection to a database. This information includes the name of the machine on which SQL Server is running, authentication information, and the name of the database. The problem with this approach is that you must hardcode all the information needed to connect to the database. Of course, you can prompt the user for his ID and password. Most developers use the connection String method and prompt users for their ID and password.

Using Data Link Files

To create a data link file, open the folder where you want to create the file and right-click on an empty area. In the shortcut menu, select New, then Microsoft Data Link. A new file's icon will appear in the folder with the name `New Microsoft Data Link.udl`. Rename this file accordingly, but don't change its extension. Then right-click the data link file and from the shortcut menu select Properties (or just double-click the file's icon).

The Data Link Properties window contains four tabs:

Provider   This is where you specify the provider that will be used to connect to the database.

Connection   This is where you specify the data source of the connection (the database to which you want to connect).

Advanced   Use this tab to specify some advanced connection options.

All   This tab contains all the attributes of the connection (most of them have been specified on the other three tabs), and you can edit their values.

These tabs are discussed in detail in the following section, where we'll discuss the connection string method. The two methods use the same Properties pages, because, no matter which method you choose, the information required to connect to the database is the same. The contents of the tabs change depending upon the provider selected on the first tab.

Using Connection Strings

The connection string is a long string that contains all the attributes of the connection. To create a connection string, you must open the Data View window, right-click the Data Link icon, and from the shortcut menu select Add Data Link. You will see the Data Link Properties window, which has the same four tabs discussed earlier.

The Provider Tab   The Provider tab contains all the database drivers installed on your system. The Microsoft Jet 3.51 (4.0) OLE DB Provider is used with Access databases. ADO installs two OLE DB drivers, one for SQL Server and another one for Oracle databases. The OLE DB Provider for ODBC Drivers is used with databases that have an ODBC driver only.

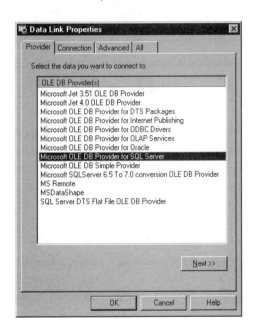

Select the OLE DB provider for your database and switch to the Connection tab.

The Connection Tab   On the Connection tab, you must provide the information needed to contact the database. To establish a connection to an Access database, you simply specify the name of the MDB file with the database and, optionally, the user ID and password for the database. You must specify the name of the server on which the DBMS is running. The drop-down list should display the names of the database servers on the network, but it doesn't always work. If you don't see any server names in this list, you must enter it yourself. If you're using the same machine to run SQL Server and develop your applications, you can supply the string "(local)".

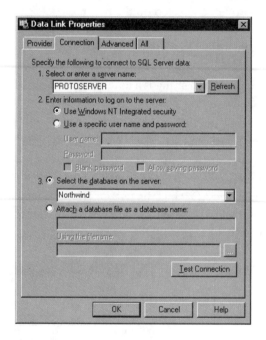

Then specify the authentication information. On Windows 98 machines, you must supply a user ID and a password. On Windows NT machines, you can let the operating system authenticate the user. The Allow Saving Password option stores the password into the connection string. The password is not encrypted, so it's not a good idea to store passwords in the connection string. By the way, data link files are not encrypted, either.

Next, provide the name of the database you want to use. Assuming you have entered the name of the server, the user ID, and the password, you can select the name of the database from the drop-down list. Alternatively, you can specify the name of the MDF file that stores the database. If you want to specify the path name of the MDF file of a database, you must also specify a descriptive name for the database.

The Advanced Tab   On the Advanced tab, you can set the network settings for the Impersonation and Protection levels (these settings are used with Remote Procedure Calls), the connection timeout (the number of seconds before a connection attempt times out), and the access permissions.

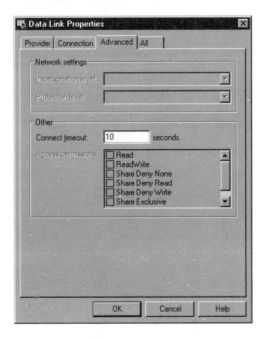

These permissions, shown in Table 3.1, apply to Access databases, but not SQL Server databases. You can check none, one, or more options:

TABLE 3.1: Access Permission Settings (Jet Databases Only)

Setting	Description
Read	The database is opened for reading only.
ReadWrite	The database is opened with read and write permissions.
Share Deny None	The application that opens the database can't deny access to other applications.
Share Deny Read	The application that opens the database can prevent other applications from opening the database in read-only mode.
Share Deny Write	The application that opens the database can prevent other applications from opening the database in write-only mode.
Share Exclusive	The application that opens the database can prevent other applications from opening the database at all.
Write	The database is opened for writing only.

The All Tab   This tab displays all of the initialization parameters of the selected OLE DB provider. To edit a value, select it with the mouse and click the Edit button.

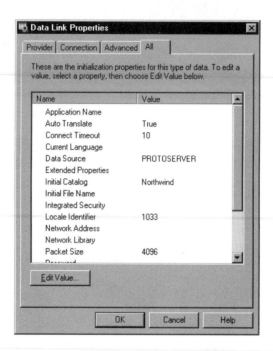

Connecting to the Northwind Database

To connect to the Northwind database, start a new VB project, and in the New Project window select Data Project. The new project has a Form, as usual, and a new folder called Designers (see the Project window in Figure 3.5). Under the Designers folder are two objects, DataEnvironment and DataReport. The DataEnvironment object lets you connect to a database and specify the commands that you will execute against the database. Presumably, some of these commands will select rows from one or more tables, which you can display on your application's user interface or edit. The DataReport object lets you design custom reports based on the commands of the DataEnvironment object. The DataEnvironment object is described in detail in Chapter 6, "Programming with ADO." The DataReport Designer is an ActiveX Designer for putting together reports with point-and-click operations, which is not discussed in this book.

The DataEnvironment object contains the various objects you need to connect to a database and program it from within your VB code. These objects are similar to the ones of the Data View window. Unlike the objects of the Data View window, however, they can be accessed from within your VB code. As you will see in the last section of this chapter, you can drag the objects you have created in the Data View window and drop them on the DataEnvironment window.

FIGURE 3.5:

The components of a new Data Project

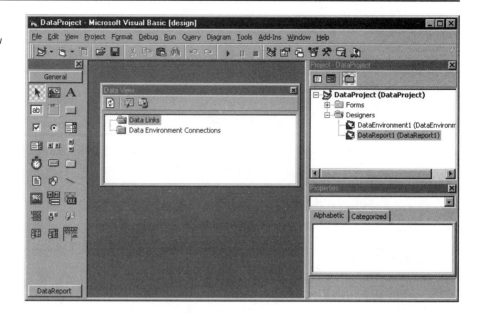

Before you can see the visual database tools in action, you must connect to a database and create a few commands that retrieve information from the database. Open the Data View window by clicking its button on the toolbar (it's the icon of a database with a magnifying glass). By default, the Data View window contains two folders, which are initially empty and which both store connections to databases. The Data Links folder contains connections you establish through the Data View window. The Data Environment Connections folder stores connections you have specified through the DataEnvironment Designer.

You can establish a connection to any database on your system, following the steps outlined in the section "Connecting to Databases," earlier in this chapter. Follow the steps below to establish a connection to the SQL Server Northwind database, to make sure you can follow the examples of this chapter. Following similar steps, you can connect to an Oracle or Access database.

> **NOTE**   If you choose to use an Access database, keep in mind that Access databases do not support stored procedures and triggers.

1. Right-click the Data Link icon and select Add a Data Link from the shortcut menu.

2. On the Provider tab of the Properties dialog box, select the provider Microsoft OLE DB Provider for SQL Server.

3. Switch to the Connection tab and specify the name of the server on which the SQL Server is running, the authentication parameters, and then the name of the database (Northwind). Notice that no database names will appear in the Initial Catalog drop-down list before you specify a user ID and a password. Unless, of course, you choose the Windows NT integrated security option.

4. Click the Test Connection button at the bottom of the window to make sure everything works, and then click OK to close the Properties dialog box.

You've established a connection to the Northwind database through the Data-Link1 Data Link object. Right-click the connection's icon on the Data View window, select rename, and set the connection's name to something more meaningful, like NWConnection. The Data View window's Data Link is not a synonym for a data link file and Data View will not create a new ULD file.

If you don't have SQL Server installed on your system, or you want to test drive the visual database tools with an Access database, you must select the Microsoft Jet 4.0 OLE DB Provider in the Provider tab and specify the path to the NWind.mdb file in the Connection tab. This version of the OLE DB provider is installed with the Service Pack 3 of Visual Studio. If you don't have version 4.0 installed on your system, you can still use version 3.51, which comes with VB6.

Using the Data View Window

Once you have established a connection to a database, the objects of the specified database will appear in the Data View window automatically. The database objects are stored in folders, according to their type. For SQL Server and Oracle databases, you will see the following folders:

Database Diagrams   This folder holds the relational diagrams of the database. Each database must have at least one relational diagram, where you must specify how the various tables are related to each other. To specify new relationships, right-click the Relationships icon and select New Diagram. To edit an existing one, right-click it and select Open.

The reason you can have multiple database diagrams is to group tables and their relationships. If the database contains many tables, you can create a different diagram for each group of interconnected tables. Individual tables may belong to multiple diagrams, as long as the relationships in all diagrams are consistent.

Tables   This folder contains all the tables of the database. You will see in the next section how you can add new tables to the database, or edit existing ones. If you have connected to a database that has just been created but not yet designed, you can add all the tables and their relationships from within the Database Designer. To design a new table, right-click the Tables icon and select New Table. To edit an existing one, right-click its name and select Design. You can also open a table and see its rows on a grid. You can even edit the rows of the table on this grid, right from within Visual Basic's environment.

You use the Tables folder to access the triggers of the database. Triggers are specific to tables, and they are listed under the table they belong to. If you expand a table in the Data View window, you will see its fields. If the table contains triggers, their names will also appear after the list of the table's fields. To design a new trigger, right-click the Tables icon and select New Trigger.

Views   This folder contains the views already attached to the database. If you expand a view, you will see its columns. To design a new view, right-click the Views icon and select New View. To edit an existing one, right-click its name and select Design. You can also open a view by double-clicking its name; you will see its rows on a grid. If the view is updateable, you can edit its rows (or the ones you're allowed to edit) right from within Visual Basic's environment.

Stored Procedures   This folder contains the stored procedures already attached to the database. To view the definition of a stored procedure, double-click its icon to open the Stored Procedure Design window. If you click the plus sign in front of a stored procedure's name, the item will expand to show the input and output parameters of the stored procedure.

NOTE   All the objects under a Data Link in the Data View window are stored in the database and are not specific to the project. Even if you remove a Data Link from this window, all the changes you made to the database through that link will not be lost. This is a difference between the visual database tools and the DataEnvironment object. The objects you attach to the DataEnvironment's window are specific to the project, not the database.

If you have established a connection to an Access database through the Microsoft Jet 3.51 OLE DB Provider, you will see the Tables and View folders only (the Views folder contains all the queries in the database). Access databases have no triggers. If you have used version 4.0 of the provider, then you will see a Stored Procedures folder with the parameterized queries. They are as close to stored procedures as an Access object can get.

Using the Database Designer

This section discusses the Database Designer and uses the Northwind database for the examples. Instead of designing new tables, we'll edit the tables of the North-wind database, examine the existing constraints and relationships, and add new ones. I will assume you have established a connection to the SQL Server North-wind database and that its name is NWConnection.

There is no Database Designer window per se among the visual database tools. There are three tools for designing database objects:

- The Database Diagram window, where you can view and edit the relation-ships between the tables of the database

- The Design Table window, where you can edit the tables of the database

- The Table Property Pages, where you can view and edit table properties like indexes, constraints, and so on

Through the windows of the Database Designer, you can design SQL Server and Oracle databases, but you can't edit the tables of an Access database.

Open the Data View window, create the NWConnection Data Link (if you haven't done so already), and then expand the Data Link and the folders under it. To open a table in design mode locate it in the Tables folder, right-click its icon and select Design. Figure 3.6 shows the Products table in design mode. If you haven't noticed yet, working with the visual database tools means many windows are open at the same time. A resolution of 1024×768 is really necessary.

FIGURE 3.6:

The Products table in design mode

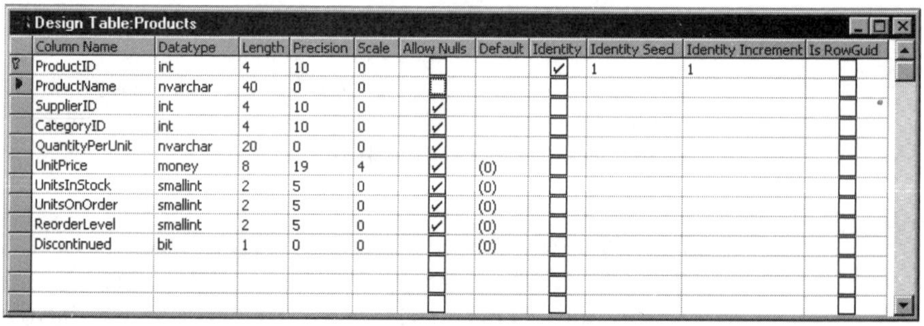

Column Name	Datatype	Length	Precision	Scale	Allow Nulls	Default	Identity	Identity Seed	Identity Increment	Is RowGuid
ProductID	int	4	10	0			✓	1	1	
ProductName	nvarchar	40	0	0						
SupplierID	int	4	10	0	✓					
CategoryID	int	4	10	0	✓					
QuantityPerUnit	nvarchar	20	0	0	✓					
UnitPrice	money	8	19	4	✓	(0)				
UnitsInStock	smallint	2	5	0	✓	(0)				
UnitsOnOrder	smallint	2	5	0	✓	(0)				
ReorderLevel	smallint	2	5	0	✓	(0)				
Discontinued	bit	1	0	0		(0)				

Each table column has a name and a data type, and every data type has a length. The length of most data types is fixed and you can't change it. Integers are stored in four bytes, datetime columns are stored in eight bytes, and so on. The varchar and nvarchar data types are variable length strings, and you specify their maximum length in the Length column. The same is true for binary columns. Some numeric types have Precision and Scale attributes. The Precision attribute is the number of digits used to represent a numeric data type—the total number of digits in the number. The Scale attribute is the number of fractional digits of a numeric data type (the number of digits to the right of the decimal point).

The Allow Nulls column must be cleared for fields that can't be Null. Primary key fields, for example, can't be Null. Before you specify the table's primary key, you must clear its Allow Nulls attribute. Depending on the data you intend to store in the table, other non-key fields may not be allowed to accept Null values. An order's date, for example, is usually not allowed to be Null.

To set the table's primary key field (if any), right-click the gray box in front of the column name and select Set Primary Key from the shortcut menu. The table's primary key field is identified by a key icon.

In the Default Value column you can specify a default value for the field, which is assigned automatically to each new row, if no other value is specified. The default value could be a value of the same type as the column, or a function returning the same data type. The default value for the OrderDate field in the Order table could be the following expression, which returns the current date and time:

```
GetDate()
```

The last few columns in the design grid are called Identity, Identity Seed, Identity Increment, and Is RowGUID. Primary key fields are usually set to integer values, and we let the database assign a unique integer value to the key field of each row added to the table. To specify that SQL Server should automatically assign values to a field, check the box in the Identity column. If this box is checked for a column, you can specify the initial value (Identity Seed) as well as the increment (Identity Increment). The last box, Is RowGUID, should be checked if the corresponding column is global identifier: a value that's unique not only in the context of the table, but in the entire database.

This is how you design tables. So far, it's quite simple, almost intuitive. Tables, however, are more than collections of columns. To ensure the integrity of the database, you should be able to impose restrictions on the values of the various columns, specify indexes and key fields, and finally create relationships between primary and foreign key fields. To view the properties of a table, right-click somewhere on the table's design window and select Properties from the shortcut menu. The Properties dialog box has three tabs, which are explained next.

TIP
To view the Properties pages of a table, you must first open the table in design mode and then right-click the table's design window. If you right-click the table's name in the Data View window and select Properties, you will see a dialog box with the table's name and its owner name, not the Table Properties window.

The Tables Tab

The Tables tab, shown in Figure 3.7, enables you to select any table from the drop-down list and change its name by entering the name in the Table Name box. The next two boxes will display the value PRIMARY, unless the Database Administrator has split the database into multiple files. Leave these boxes to the DBA. (In short, a SQL Server database can be stored in multiple files, but this will not affect your code. The conceptual view of the database remains the same, whether its tables are stored in one or more tables).

FIGURE 3.7:

Use the Tables tab of a table's Properties dialog box to specify constraints.

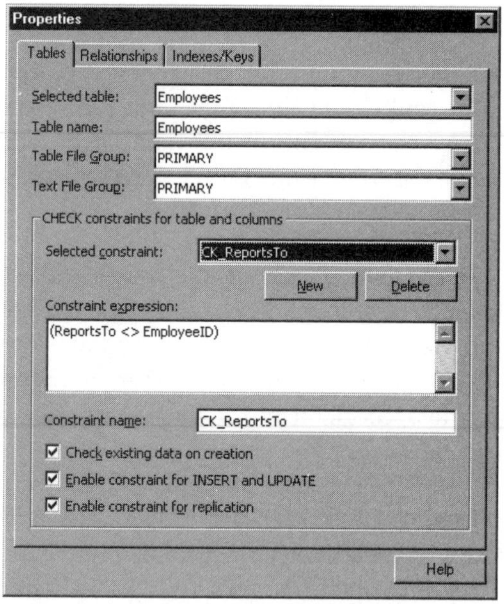

In the lower half of this tab, you can specify any number of constraints for the selected table. Each constraint is identified by a name (so that you can lift the constraint and re-impose it later) and a definition. To add a new constraint, click the New button, enter a name for the constraint, and type its definition in the appropriate text boxes. The definition of the constraint is an expression, similar to how you would express the same constraint in VB. Most constraints are of the following form:

```
Discount > 0 And Discount < 1
```

This expression, which involves relational and logical operators, tells SQL Server that the discount should have a value between 0 and 1. To specify that the Unit Price field should be positive, use the following constraint:

```
[Unit Price] >= 0
```

The Employees table contains a slightly more complex constraint, which requests that the employee's birth date is less than the current date:

```
([BirthDate] < getdate())
```

NOTE   This is a textbook example. A constraint like this one doesn't really protect your data at all.

You may not have noticed it, but the Employees table is a bit unusual: it references itself. It contains a field named ReportsTo, which is the ID of another employee. In most corporations, employees do not report to themselves, so a more meaningful constraint for the Employees table would be one that prevents the ReportsTo field from being the same as the EmployeeID field. Can you imagine what would happen if you created a hierarchy of employees based on who reports to whom and one of the employees referred to himself? To remedy this unlikely situation, you can add a new constraint with the following definition, as shown in Figure 3.8:

```
(ReportsTo <> EmployeeID)
```

Name this constraint CK_ReportsTo and check it out. First, you must close the Employee design grid and then open the same table for editing by double-clicking its name. If you attempt to make the ReportsTo field equal to the EmployeeID of the same row, the update will be rejected.

FIGURE 3.8:

This error message will appear if you enter a value that violates the CK_Reports-To constraint.

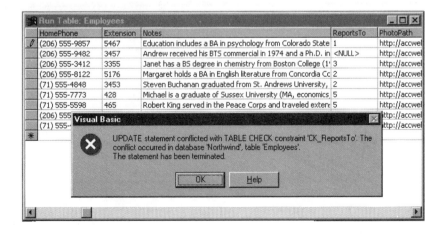

The Relationships Tab

Relationships are the most important aspect in the design of a relational database. Not only must you specify the correct relationships for the joins you'll execute later in your queries, you must also establish rules for the integrity of the references between tables. This tab is discussed in the section "Using the Database Diagram," later in this chapter.

The Indexes/Keys Tab

Use the Indexes/Keys tab, shown in Figure 3.9, to manipulate the indexes and keys of your tables. Each table is indexed on one or more columns and usually has one primary key. From the Selected Index box, you can select one of the selected table's indexes. To create a new index, click the New button. Each index has a name, a definition, and a few attributes, which are specified in the lower section of the tab. The definition of the table is the name of one or more columns. If you anticipate that your applications will be searching for customers by name, index the Customers table on the LastName field. When you index a table on a field, you are practically ordering the table according to the field(s) involved in the index. The rows of the table are not rearranged, but they are retrieved in the order specified by the index. You can also index a table on two or more fields. If the field you're indexing on isn't unique, like the last name, you can specify additional keys. It is possible to index a table on the last name and first name fields, so that rows with the same last name are clustered together and ordered according to first name.

FIGURE 3.9:

Use the Indexes/Keys tab of a table's Properties dialog box to specify new indexes and key fields.

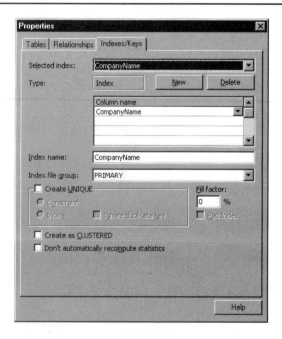

The Create UNIQUE check box lets you specify that an index is unique. The index on the LastName field, for example, can't be unique. It's quite possible for two or more contacts in the Customers table to have the same last name. An index based on a field like a product's ID or a book's ISBN is unique. This field is used as a primary key, and primary keys are by definition unique. There are situations, however, where a field can't be used as a primary key, yet it must be unique. Let's say you're maintaining a table with teacher IDs and room numbers. Since a teacher can't be in two different rooms at the same time, you can specify that the combination TeacherID + RoomNumber is unique. If you don't want to create an index on these two columns, check the Constraint option. If you want to be able to search the table with the field combination TeacherID + RoomNumber (or with the field TeacherID only), then create a new index by checking the Index option.

The Create As CLUSTERED check box lets you specify that an index will be created as clustered. Each table can have only one clustered index, and this index must be based on the field that's used most often for searching. Clustered indexes are very efficient, because SQL Server stores rows in the same order as dictated by the clustered index. In other words, the physical order of the rows is the same as the logical order of the key values. As a result, when SQL Server searches the B-tree structure of the index, it locates the actual data, not a pointer to the data. To maintain a clustered index, SQL Server works a little harder every time a new row is added, but operations that involve the clustered index are performed very efficiently.

Using the Database Diagram

To view and edit the relationships in a database, switch to the Data View window and expand the Database Diagram folder. The first item is called Relationships. To view the relationships in a database, double-click the Relationships icon. If there's no relational diagram for the database, right-click the Database Diagrams icon and select New Diagram.

The Database Diagram window will appear on the screen. Now drop the tables you want to include in the diagram from the Data View window on the Database Diagram window. Tables are represented by boxes, which contain each table's field names. Primary key fields are marked with the icon of a key in front of their name, as shown in Figure 3.10.

Each relationship is represented by an arrow connecting the two linked tables. In a normalized database, we have two types of relationships:

- One-to-many (or many-to-one)
- One-to-one

FIGURE 3.10:

The Relational Database
diagram of the Northwind
database

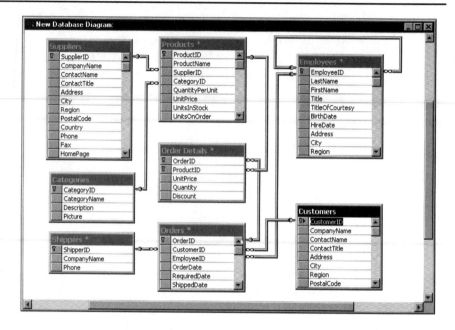

On the unique side of the relationship, there's an icon of a key, because we have a key field. On the other side we have, usually, the symbol of infinity. The "many" side of a relationship is a foreign key. The relationship between Publishers and Titles is a typical one-to-many relationship: each publisher may appear in multiple titles. Each title, however, has a single publisher. One-to-one relationships are not as common. When there's a unique mapping between the rows of two tables, these tables can be combined into a single table. The resulting table has the same number of rows as the larger of the two and more columns than either of the original tables. If you rest the pointer on a relationship, you'll see its name and the names of the two tables it links. To view the labels of the relationships, right-click somewhere on the pane and select the Show Relationship Labels command from the shortcut menu.

NOTE   Conceptually, you could have many-to-many relationships. The relationship between books and authors is a many-to-many one. Some titles have multiple authors, while the same author may appear in multiple titles. Many-to-many relationships can't be implemented with primary and foreign keys, and they are broken into two one-to-many relationships with the introduction of another table. As you recall from our discussion of the Biblio database, the Titles and Authors tables are linked with the [Title Author] table. The Titles and Authors tables are not related directly. Titles are linked to authors through the [Title Author] table, which holds pairs of ISBN and author IDs. The relationship between Titles and [Title Author] table is one-to-many (the same ISBN may appear in multiple rows of the Authors table). The relationship between the [Title Author] and Authors tables is also one-to-many (the same author may appear with multiple ISBNs).

To view more information about a relationship, right-click its line and select Properties. You will see the Table Properties window with the Tables, Relationships, and Indexes/Keys tabs, which we discussed already. The Relationships tab is shown in Figure 3.11 (it depicts the relationship between the tables Orders and Order Details).

FIGURE 3.11:

The Relationships tab of the Properties dialog box

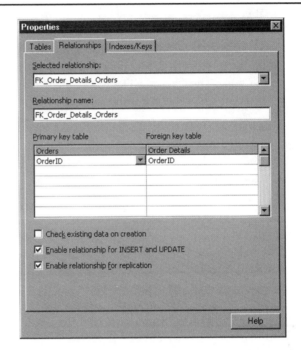

On the Relationships tab you'll see the name of the selected relationship, the two fields involved in the relationship (the primary and foreign key), and three options for enforcing the integrity of the relationship at the bottom.

- The Check Existing Data On Creation check box tells SQL Server to make sure that the existing rows don't violate the relationship. If a pair of primary/ foreign keys violates the relationship (the foreign key in a row points to non-existing primary key), a warning will be displayed and the relationship will not be added to the database. You must manually correct the offending row(s) and then attempt to establish the relationship again.

- The Enable Relationship For INSERT And UPDATE check box tells SQL Server to abort any insert or update operation that violates the integrity of the relationship.

- The last check box, Enable Relationship For Replication, tells SQL Server to apply the constraint when the foreign table is replicated to a different database.

To establish a new relationship between two tables, drag one of the two fields involved in the relationship and drop it on the other field. If you open the Relationships window of the Northwind database, you will notice that there's no relationship between the tables Orders and Customers. In its current form, the Northwind database will not prevent you from entering a new order without customer information (or an invalid customer ID). You can edit the Orders table right now and see that you can change the CustomerID field of any row without consequences. (The real consequences will become quite obvious in the future, when you'll attempt to match customers to their orders). To add a relationship between the two tables, drag the CustomerID field of one table and drop it on the CustomerID field of the other table. The Database Designer is intelligent enough to figure out which is the primary field and which is the foreign one.

As soon as you drop the field, the Create Relationship window will appear. The default name of the relationship is FK_Customers_Orders and all three options at the bottom of the window are checked by default. In most cases, all you need to change is the name of the relationship.

Scripting Your Changes

There is a very useful bit of information hidden in SQL Server's documentation on scripting your changes. As a programmer, you should never work with the production version of a database (all of us have made a few quick and trivial changes, but you should never work with the actual database). The DBA will see that you work on a copy of the production database. The DBA will also have to approve any changes to the database. When you change the design of the database by editing its tables or the relationships between tables, the Save Change Script command in Visual Basic's File menu will be enabled. Use this command to save a script with your changes. The DBA can examine the script and then execute it against the production database to implement the changes. Actually, the DBA will wait to make sure both the new and existing applications work, then implement the changes to the "real" database.

Add a new relationship to the Northwind database, or edit a table slightly. Then open the File menu and select the Save Change Script command. The dialog box shown in Figure 3.12 will appear with the script of the changes. You can't change the script, but you can save it to a disk file. Click the Yes button to save the script, so that the same changes can be implemented on the production version of the database.

FIGURE 3.12:

Saving a script file with the
changes you made to the
database

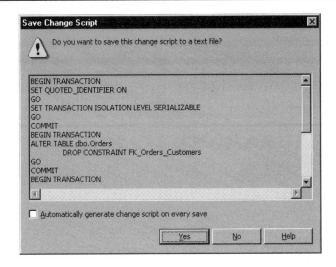

The core of the script that adds a new relationship is shown here:

```
ALTER TABLE dbo.Orders ADD CONSTRAINT
        FK_Orders_Customers FOREIGN KEY
        (
        CustomerID
        ) REFERENCES dbo.Customers
        (
         CustomerID
        )
```

This script tells SQL Server to add a new constraint to the database. The constraint
is named FK_Orders_Customers, and it says that the CustomerID field of the Orders
table is a foreign key referencing the CustomerID field of the Customers table. This
is SQL code you could have written yourself, but you'd rarely get it right the first
time. So, keep working with the visual tools and let VB script your changes.

To summarize, the Database Designer is a collection of tools that allows you to:

- Create new tables and edit existing ones

- View and edit the rows of an existing table

- Establish constraints for the individual columns

- Create new indexes and edit existing ones

- Establish new relationships between tables and edit existing relationships

These are all the operations you need to design a new database or refine the design of an existing one. Even the simplest DBMS provides these capabilities, and you can design databases for various DBMSs from within Visual Basic's environment. The Database Designer can handle Access, SQL, and Oracle databases—you have a common tool for all these different types of databases.

Using the Query Designer

The most important, and most common, operation you'll be performing on a database is querying it. To query a database, you must write commands in a special language, the Structured Query Language (SQL), and execute them against the database. In this section, we will build SQL statements using another visual tool, the Query Designer. Using the Query Designer, you build SQL with point-and-click operations, while it creates the equivalent SQL statement, which you can copy and use in your VB code. The Query Designer is an excellent tool for what it does, but as a programmer you probably will not want to rely on visual tools only; eventually, you will master SQL so that you can just type in your queries.

With the Query Designer you can use a visual query diagram to drag tables into the query and specify which fields will appear in the query's output with point-and-click operations. In addition, you can limit the number of rows returned by the query by specifying search criteria on a grid. The Query Designer will generate the SQL statement that implements your query and display it in a separate pane. Finally, you can execute the query to find out whether it works as intended. The query will be executed against the database, so be sure you don't execute *action queries* (queries that modify the database) against a production database. Keep in mind that, if you change any of the sample databases by executing action queries against them, you may not get the same results as in the examples in the following chapters. It's quite safe, however, to execute *selection queries*, which retrieve rows and display them in the lower pane of the Query Designer's window. Many programmers simply enter the SQL statements in the Query Designer's middle pane and execute it; you don't have to specify the statements visually. An interesting feature of the Query Designer is that it can build the visual representation of an SQL statement, and you can tweak the query with the visual tools.

The Query Designer's Window

To start the Query Designer, right-click the View icon in the Data View window and select New View from the shortcut menu. The Query Designer window that opens has four panes, shown in Figure 3.13.

The panes of the Query Designer's window

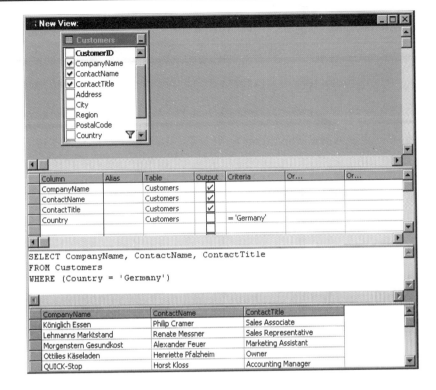

The Diagram Pane

This is where you display the tables involved in the query. Tables are represented by boxes, which list the table's columns. To add tables to a query, simply drag them from the Data View window and drop them on the Diagram pane. As soon as you add a new table, it is linked automatically to the existing ones, if a relationship exists between the new table and any of the existing ones. By default, the Query Designer creates inner joins. (The types of joins are explained in Chapter 4, "Structured Query Language," but this is an important detail.) You will see the various types of joins and how to change the default join type shortly.

The Grid Pane

The Grid pane contains a spreadsheet-like grid in which you specify criteria for limiting the number of rows and the columns to be included in the query (like orders placed in a specified interval, books published by a specific publisher, and so on). If you want to calculate totals (sums, counts, averages), you specify them on the Grid pane.

The SQL Pane

The SQL pane displays the SQL statement for the current query. The SQL statement implements the query you've specified visually on the Diagram pane. You can edit the SQL statement, or you can enter your own SQL statement from scratch. When you do so, Query Designer places the tables involved in the query on the Diagram pane and fills the selection criteria.

If you're new to SQL, you'll probably use the Diagram pane to create queries visually and then see the SQL statements generated automatically by the Query Designer. If you're familiar with SQL, you'll probably enter the SQL statements manually (or you may use the Diagram pane to avoid entering long lists of field names and then edit the initial statement).

The Results Grid

Once the SQL statement has been specified, either in the Diagram pane or in the SQL pane, you can execute the query and view the rows it returns. To execute a query, use the Run command from the Query menu. You can also right-click the SQL or Diagram pane and select Run from the shortcut menu. Or, you can right-click the SQL pane and select Verify SQL Syntax from the shortcut menu to make sure your SQL statement is correct. This doesn't mean you'll get the results you want, but you can verify your SQL statements, especially the action queries.

At this point, the Query Designer will generate the appropriate SQL statement and display it on the SQL pane. If you have entered the SQL statement, the Query Designer will update the Diagram pane accordingly. Then, it will proceed to execute the query and display the qualifying rows in the Results grid at the bottom of the window.

WARNING If the query changes one or more rows of a table (an action query), it will not return any rows, and nothing will be displayed on the Results grid. The database, however, will be updated. If needed, test your action queries with temporary tables, or even a copy of the database. Most queries are selection queries, and they can be safely tested. But many of us are so used to testing selection queries in the Query Designer that we may invoke the Run command without realizing we're running an action query.

Building Simple Queries

If you're not familiar with SQL, you must build a few queries with the Query Designer to see what it can do for you. This will help you get started, and you may choose to use this tool on a regular basis.

The simplest type of a query is one that retrieves a number of fields from selected rows in a single table. To retrieve the names of the companies in Germany and their contacts from the Northwind database, follow these steps:

1. Arrange the Data View and Query Designer windows on your screen so that they're both visible. Then drag the table(s) you need in your query from the Data View window and drop them on the Query Designer's Diagram pane. For this example, you'll need the Customers table only.

2. Check the names of the fields you want to appear in the query's output. Check the fields CustomerID, CompanyName, ContactName, and ContactTitle. The names of the fields will appear in the Grid pane, where you must specify the restrictions of the query—namely, that you want to select only the rows in which the Country field is "Germany."

3. Click the first blank line in the Grid pane and select the Country field in the drop-down list of all fields that will appear. Then move to the Criteria column and enter this expression:

   ```
   = 'Germany'
   ```

   This is the only criterion we will apply to the query. Since all customers will be from Germany, we don't want to include the Country field in the output. To exclude a field from the query's output, clear the corresponding box in the Output column.

   As soon as you move the cursor to another cell, the SQL pane will be updated. The SQL statement that implements the query you specified with the visual tools is:

   ```
   SELECT CompanyName, ContactName, ContactTitle
   FROM Customers
   WHERE (Country = 'Germany')
   ```

4. Open the Query menu and select Run to execute the query. The qualifying rows of the Customers table will appear on the Results pane, as shown in Figure 3.13.

If you want to specify multiple criteria for the same field, enter them in the columns with the Or . . . heading. All the criteria will be combined with the OR operator. To select all customers from Germany and Italy, for example, enter the following expression in the column to the right of the Criteria column:

```
= 'Italy'
```

If you want to specify criteria with different columns, repeat step 3 with a different field name. To select customers from Germany and Berlin, you can select the City field in the next available row of the Grid pane, and enter the following expression in the Criteria column:

```
= 'Berlin'
```

Don't forget to clear the Output box for the City field, because we don't want to include the city name in the output.

To retrieve all customers from Berlin, you need not specify the country restriction. In general, city names are not unique, so you should specify the country as well.

Building Queries with Aggregate Functions

In this section, we'll include aggregate functions in SQL statements using the visual tools of the Query Designer. Before we do this, however, let's quickly review aggregate functions.

SQL can calculate aggregates on selected fields. An *aggregate* is a function that counts rows, calculates sums and averages, and performs a few more common math operations used to summarize data. SQL supports the following aggregate functions:

AVG()	Returns the average of the values in a column
COUNT()	Returns the count of the values in a column
MAX()	Returns the highest value in a column
MIN()	Returns the lowest value in a column
SUM()	Returns the sum of all values in a column

NOTE   Chapter 4 shows how these functions are used in SQL statements.

Now, let's revise our first query, so that instead of all customers in a specific country, it will return the number of customers in each country. Start a new View, drop the Customers table on the Diagram pane, and check the CompanyName and Country fields. This query will return all the customers along with their country.

Simple Aggregates

To replace the CompanyName field with the count of customers in each country, open the Query menu and check the Group By option. A new column with the heading Group By will be inserted between the Output and Criteria columns in the Grid pane. All cells in this column will be assigned the value Group By. We want to group all customers by country, so we need not change the Group By specification in the Country row. In the CompanyName row, and under the Group By column, select the Count option (click this cell with the mouse and select Count from the drop-down list). Notice that the summation symbol will appear next to the Company-Name field and the grouping symbol will appear next to the Country field. The corresponding SQL statement is:

```
SELECT COUNT(CompanyName) AS Expr1, Country
FROM Customers
GROUP BY Country
```

This statement tells SQL Server to group all rows of the Customers table according to the Country field, so that customers from the same country are grouped together. Then, it must count the rows in each group. The result of the query is a list of country names and customer counts, as shown here (only the first few countries are included in the list):

```
3       Argentina
2       Austria
2       Belgium
8       Brazil
3       Canada
```

The clause AS Expr1 is an alias for the first column of the result. To display a more meaningful column name, use an alias like "Customers" or "Number of Customers."

Other aggregate functions are just as easy to use. If the CompanyName field was a numeric one, you could calculate the average with the AVG() function, or the total for all rows in the group with the SUM() function.

Aggregates on Multiple Tables

Let's build one more query with an aggregate, this time a query involving two tables. This query will retrieve the category names and the count of products in each category. Right-click the Views folder and select New View; the Query Designer will appear on the screen. To build this statement, you need the Categories and Products tables. Drop these two tables from the Data View window onto the Tables pane of the Query Designer. You want a list of category names and the number of products in each category, so check the field CategoryName in the Categories table. You don't want to include the ID of the categories in the output list, and you aren't going to include any fields of the second table—you'll only count the products.

Open the Query menu in the Visual Basic IDE and check the Group By option. This command will group the results according to the selected field in the Categories table. As soon as you check the Group By option, the grouping symbol will appear next to the name of the CategoryName field in the Categories table. If you expand the first cell in the second row of the grid pane, you will see the item COUNT(*), in addition to the field names. The COUNT() function returns the number of items in the current group. Whether you count a single field or all the fields doesn't make any difference. Open the Query menu again, select Run, and observe the results of the query in the lower pane of the Query Designer. The corresponding SQL statement will appear in the SQL pane of the window, as shown here:

```
SELECT Categories.CategoryName AS Expr1, COUNT(*)
    AS Expr2
FROM Categories INNER JOIN Products ON
    Categories.CategoryID = Products.CategoryID
GROUP BY Categories.CategoryName
```

The INNER JOIN statement combines rows from two tables based on a common field value (the CategoryID field in this example) and it's discussed in the next section. Here are a few lines of the output produced by this statement:

```
Beverages       11
Condiments      11
Confections     13
```

Building Multi-Table Queries

Queries are rarely that simple. Most queries involve multiple tables linked to one another and restrictions that apply to fields or more than one table. Let's build a query that retrieves all the customers, along with their orders and the products they have purchased. This query involves four tables: Customers, Orders, Order Details, and Products, because the Order Details table contains product IDs, not their actual names. The specification of this query sounds complicated, but building the query is not difficult using the visual database tools.

Right-click the Views folder and select New View from the shortcut menu. Then switch to the Data View window. While both tools (the Query Designer and the Data View) are visible on the screen, drop the tables on the Diagram pane. The Query Designer will automatically link them together based on the existing relationships, as shown in Figure 3.14. It will also prepare the core of the SQL statement and display it on the SQL pane. Notice that the selection list is empty. Start checking the names of the fields you want to include in the output and watch the selection list of the SQL statement grow. Check the following field names in the corresponding tables:

Table	Selected Fields
Customers	CompanyName
Orders	OrderID, OrderDate
OrderDetails	UnitPrice, Quantity, Discount
Products	ProductName

FIGURE 3.14:

The Query Designer can link tables to each other based on the primary/foreign key definitions in the database.

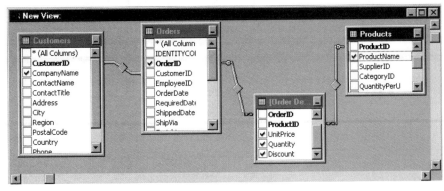

The Query Designer will generate a long selection list:

```
SELECT Customers.CompanyName, Orders.OrderID,
       Orders.OrderDate, [Order Details].UnitPrice,
       [Order Details].Quantity, [Order Details].Discount
```

All field names are prefixed by the name of the table they belong to, with a period between the table and field name. The FROM clause of the SQL statement is a long list of inner joins. Joins are discussed in detail in Chapter 4, but here's a brief explanation of the join operation. A join combines rows from two tables based on the values of a field that's common to both tables (usually, a primary and foreign key combination). The rows of the Customers and Orders tables are joined as follows: SQL Server will scan all the rows of the Customers table. Each row of the Customers table will be linked to one or more rows of the Orders table, whose CustomerID field has the same value as the CustomerID field of the current row in the Customers table. If the customer with ID of "BLAUS" has five matching rows in the Orders table, five new rows will be appended to the output. These five rows will have the same CustomerID, but a different OrderID. Tables are linked automatically to each other in the Diagram pane based on the relationships between the tables.

The Query Designer will also populate the Selection Grid with the fields you have checked, as shown in Figure 3.15. Now right-click somewhere on the Diagram pane and select Run from the shortcut menu to see the output of the query.

FIGURE 3.15:

The result of a query we specified with the Query Designer's visual tools

CompanyName	OrderID	ProductName	UnitPrice	Quantity	Discount
Furia Bacalhau e Frutos do Mar	10551	Pavlova	17.45	40	0.15
Furia Bacalhau e Frutos do Mar	10551	Steeleye Stout	18	20	0.15
Furia Bacalhau e Frutos do Mar	10551	Gula Malacca	19.45	40	0
Furia Bacalhau e Frutos do Mar	10604	Chocolade	12.75	6	0.1
Furia Bacalhau e Frutos do Mar	10604	Lakkalikööri	18	10	0.1
Furia Bacalhau e Frutos do Mar	10664	Ikura	31	24	0.15
Furia Bacalhau e Frutos do Mar	10664	Gnocchi di nonna Alice	38	12	0.15
Furia Bacalhau e Frutos do Mar	10664	Louisiana Fiery Hot Pepper Sauce	21.05	15	0.15
Furia Bacalhau e Frutos do Mar	10963	Camembert Pierrot	34	2	0.15
Galería del gastrónomo	10366	Louisiana Fiery Hot Pepper Sauce	16.8	5	0
Galería del gastrónomo	10366	Original Frankfurter grüne Soße	10.4	5	0
Galería del gastrónomo	10426	Gnocchi di nonna Alice	30.4	5	0

The query's specification may sound complicated, and the SQL statement that implements it is quite lengthy, but we were able to build it by simply dropping four tables on the Diagram pane and selecting the names of the fields to be included in the output.

Entering SQL Statements

Let's exercise the Query Designer's SQL pane. The following SQL statement retrieves all the product names and their categories from the Customers table. Clear your SQL pane and enter this statement:

```
SELECT ProductName, CategoryName
FROM Products, Categories
WHERE Products.CategoryID = Categories.CategoryID
```

The WHERE clause tells SQL Server to link the two tables with their ProductID field. In effect, it retrieves all the product names from the Products table, along with the name of the category they belong to from the Categories table. You could read this statement as, "Show pairs of product names and categories by matching the CategoryID field in the Products and Categories tables."

Let's verify the syntax of the statement. Right-click the SQL pane and select Verify SQL Syntax. The Query Designer will confirm the correctness of the statement. In verifying the syntax of the statement, the Query Designer will populate the Diagram pane with the tables and the selected fields, as well as the Selection grid, as shown in Figure 3.16.

FIGURE 3.16:

The Query Designer can populate the Diagram pane and Selection grid based on the contents of the SQL pane.

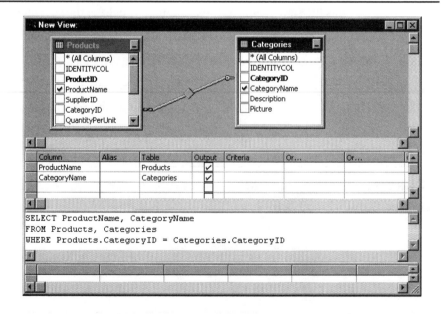

To see the results of the query, right-click the Diagram pane and select Run from the shortcut menu (or open the Query menu and select the Run command). The Result pane will be populated with the names of the products and their categories.

As you have certainly noticed, the Query Designer uses the JOIN keyword to implement all the queries that combine multiple tables. The WHERE clause limits the selected rows (like products with a price of $10 or less, customers from a specific country, and so on). The proper clause to link two tables is the INNER JOIN, but many people use the WHERE clause because it's simpler. As you will see in Chapter 4, this is a dangerous practice, which you should avoid. Or, at least be sure when you can use the WHERE clause in the place of a JOIN. Using the WHERE clause in the place of the JOIN operator is a widely (ab)used technique.

The Query Designer will replace the WHERE clause with an INNER JOIN operation. The two are equivalent, but the JOIN keyword has several variations. The INNER JOIN links the rows that match in both tables. A product, however, may not have a matching category. The INNER JOIN will ignore this product. To include this product in the query, even without a category, you must use the LEFT JOIN keyword. This keyword will return all the rows of the left table (the Products table), even if they have no matching rows in the right table (the Categories table). If you want to retrieve all the product names and all the category names, use the FULL OUTER JOIN keyword. This operation will return all the products with matching categories, the products without a category, and the categories that are not referenced by any product.

To change the type of a join, right-click the symbol in the middle of the line that connects the two tables in the Diagram pane. The shortcut menu, shown in Figure 3.17, contains the options Select All Rows from Products and Select All Rows from Categories. If you check the first option, the Query Designer will generate a LEFT OUTER JOIN (it will include all products and the matching rows from the Categories table). If some products don't have a category, they will still appear in the result. If you check the second option only, then a RIGHT OUTER JOIN will be created. This join will include the products that have a category only, as well as all categories, regardless of whether they have matching products. If you check both options, then a FULL OUTER JOIN will be created. This join returns all rows from both tables, regardless of whether there's a matching row in the other table.

FIGURE 3.17:

Specifying the type of a join in the Diagram pane of the Query Designer

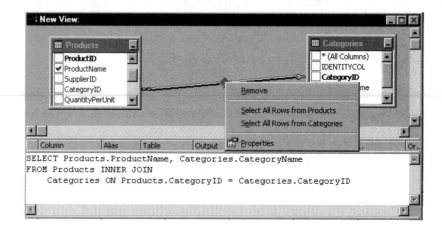

The Source Code Editor

The last of the visual database tools isn't really visual. The Source Code Editor is a text editor customized for entering Transact-SQL statements, and it's the tool you'll be using to write your own stored procedures and triggers. The following two sections introduce stored procedures and triggers. You'll also learn how to debug your stored procedures with the T-SQL Debugger. Stored procedures and triggers are not trivial topics, and they're discussed in detail in Chapter 7, "Transact-SQL." In this section, I will use simple examples to show you what T-SQL can do for your application. These examples will conclude our overview of the database objects and the tools to manipulate them.

Working with Stored Procedures

A *stored procedure* is a program in T-SQL that queries or updates the database. In its simplest form, a stored procedure is a query, which is stored in the database itself. A simple query that retrieves the names of the customers need not be implemented as a stored procedure. Some queries can get quite complicated, however, and it pays to implement those as stored procedures and save them to the database. After a stored procedure has been designed and tested, it becomes an object of the database. In addition, SQL Server compiles the stored procedure and executes is faster than the equivalent SQL statement.

To demonstrate how to use the T-SQL Debugger to debug your custom stored procedures, we'll use a sample stored procedure that comes with the Northwind database. Open the Stored Procedures folder on the Data View window and double-click the icon of the SalesByCategory stored procedure. You will see a Design window for stored procedures, as shown in Figure 3.18.

FIGURE 3.18:

Editing stored procedures in
Visual Basic's development
environment

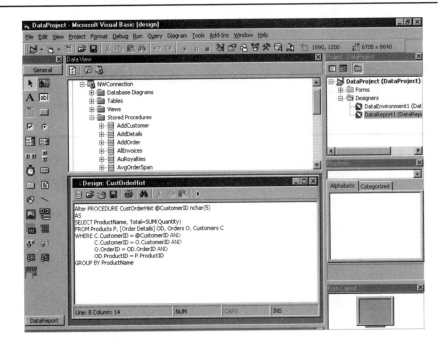

Stored procedures are written in T-SQL, which is a mix of SQL and more traditional programming structures, like IF statements, loops, and so on. As a VB programmer, you'll have no problem learning and using T-SQL.

The SalesByCategory stored procedure accepts two input parameters, the *@CategoryName* and the *@OrdYear* parameters. They are the names of a category and the year, in which the total is calculated. The two variables are declared right after the declaration of the procedure. Notice that the *@OrdYear* parameter has a default value of 1998, should you call the stored procedure without supplying a value for this argument.

The first three lines examine the value of the *@OrdYear* parameter. If it's not in the range 1996 through 1998, the procedure ignores the original value (which is in error) and calculates the total of the specified category for 1998:

```
IF @OrdYear != '1996' AND @OrdYear != '1997' AND @OrdYear != '1998'
BEGIN
    SELECT @OrdYear = '1998'
END
```

This code looks more like Pascal, rather than Visual Basic, but you can easily understand what it does. All you need to know to understand this procedure is that all T-SQL variable names begin with the @ sign.

The rest of the code is an SQL statement that combines the Products, Categories, Orders, and Order Details tables to calculate the total sales for a specific category in a year's period. I'll interrupt the discussion of stored procedures momentarily to show you how to test the SQL statement with the Query Designer.

Testing SQL Statements with the Query Designer

To start the Query Designer, switch to the Data View window, right-click the Views icon, and select New View. If the Query Designer window completely over-laps the stored procedure Designer window, click Ctrl+Tab to switch to the stored procedure's window. Select the SQL statement and then switch back to the Query Designer and paste the text into the SQL pane.

The statement can't be executed as is. The two variable names are not recognized by SQL. Only T-SQL can handle variables. To test the statement, you must replace the variable names with actual values. Replace the variable *@CategoryName* with the string *Beverages* and the variable *@OrdYear* with the value *1998*. Then execute the query by selecting the Run command from the Query menu. You'll see a message to the effect that the ORDER BY clause can't be used with this type of query (you can't use the ORDER BY keyword with a view). The View will be generated as expected, but the ORDER BY keyword will be ignored (even though it will remain in the definition of the view). The statement will be processed and you'll see the total sales for each product in the specified category in the Results pane.

Executing and Debugging a Stored Procedure

We'll now return to the stored procedure Designer window and execute the Sales-ByCategory stored procedure. If you edit the stored procedure, you must save it to the database before you execute it. To save the stored procedure, click the Save to Database button on the window's toolbar (it's the third button from the left). Once the procedure as been stored into the database, you can execute by clicking the Execute button (the last button on the window's toolbar).

Before the stored procedure is executed, you'll be prompted to enter the values of the expected parameters with the window shown in Figure 3.19. Enter the desired values in the last column and click OK to continue.

FIGURE 3.19:

Supply the parameters of a stored procedure in the Para-meters window.

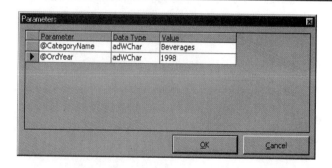

After clicking the OK button on the Parameters window, you will see the T-SQL Debugger window, shown in Figure 3.20. The T-SQL Debugger is a tool for debugging stored procedures (or T-SQL code in general). It allows you to define breakpoints, single-step through a procedure, and monitor the values of the variables in the code. As I've mentioned earlier, T-SQL is a mix of SQL statements and traditional programming statements. The T-SQL Debugger isn't much help with SQL statements. A SQL statement is passed to the SQL Server for execution, and you can't execute it in segments. Every SQL statement is a single statement, although it's usually entered in many lines of text. The other statements of T-SQL are similar to the control-flow statements of VB, and you can execute them one at a time.

FIGURE 3.20:

Use the T-SQL Debugger to debug complicated stored procedures.

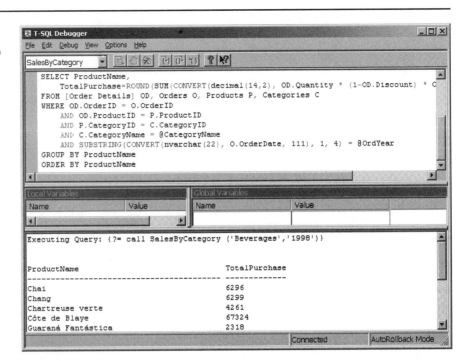

T-SQL Debugger: Special Requirements

If you haven't used the T-SQL Debugger yet, there's a good chance it will not work the first time you use it. This tool has a special requirement: it will work only if you connect to the database through Windows NT authentication.

Continued on next page

This is not always enough either. On many systems, you'll get a generic error message and the T-SQL Debugger will crash. To find out more information on the problem, open the Event logger and locate a fatal error issued by SQL Server. This error is logged by Windows NT (or Windows 2000 Server) if the file `MSSDI98.DLL` is not in the `BINN` folder under SQL Server's folder (usually `C:\MSSQL7`).

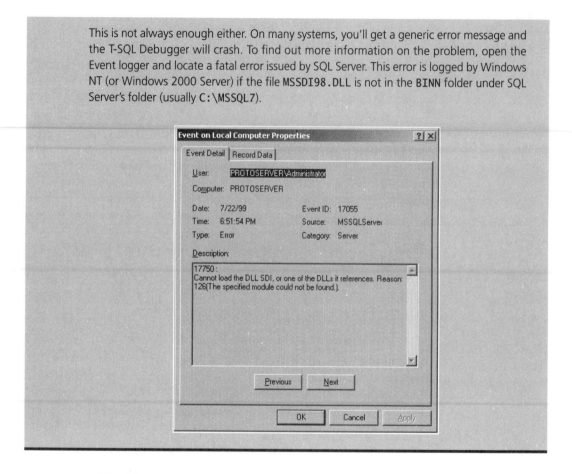

The debugging commands are similar to the ones of Visual Basic. You can single-step through the statements of a stored procedure, set breakpoints, and examine the values of the local variables during execution.

Working with Triggers

Triggers are very similar to stored procedures, but they are invoked automatically. Triggers are invoked by the following actions: the insertion of a new row in a table, the deletion of an existing row, and the update of an existing row. You cannot specify any other actions to invoke a trigger. Moreover, triggers are attached to tables. Only an action on a specific table can invoke a trigger, and you can't execute a trigger from within another trigger or stored procedure (unless the procedure or trigger performs an action that fires a trigger automatically).

To see a table's triggers, expand the Tables folder and then expand a table by clicking the plus sign in front of its name. Triggers are marked with a special icon (a box with a wave-like pattern), as shown in Figure 3.21. Double-click the trigger's name to see its definition. The triggers shown in Figure 3.21 will not appear in your system, but you'll see how to build them in this section, as well as in Chapter 7.

FIGURE 3.21:

Viewing the Orders table's triggers

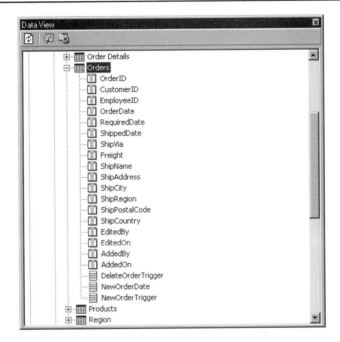

The Northwind database doesn't include any triggers. To create a new one, right-click the table and select New Trigger from the shortcut menu. In the Edit window, you will see the following text:

```
Create Trigger Orders_Trigger1
On dbo.Orders
For /* Insert, Update, Delete */
As
     /* If Update (column_name) ...*/
```

This is the skeleton of a trigger's code; you must insert your code. As I mentioned already, the Source Code Editor is not a visual tool; you must enter your code and test the trigger manually.

Let's implement a trigger to cascade updates and deletes. As you recall from Chapter 2, Access supports cascade updates and deletes, but SQL Server 7.0 doesn't. To cascade the deletion of a customer, you must locate all the orders of the specific customer and delete them. Because orders are referenced by their detail lines, you must first delete the detail lines of these orders. Here's the SQL statement that deletes the details, then the orders, and finally the customer:

```
DELETE FROM [Order Details]
WHERE [Order Details].OrderID = Orders.OrderID AND
      Orders.CustomerID = @thisCustomer
```

The *@thisCustomer* variable holds the ID of the customer who's about to be deleted. You'll see shortly how it's assigned the proper value. After the deletion of the order details, you must delete the orders of the same customer with the following statement:

```
DELETE FROM Orders
WHERE Orders.CustomerID = @thisCustomer
```

Finally, delete the customer with this statement:

```
DELETE FROM Customers
WHERE Customers.CustomerID = @thisCustomer
```

The value of the *@thisCustomer* variable must be set to the ID of the customer who's about to be deleted. T-SQL variables must be declared before they are used:

```
DECLARE @thisCustomer char(5)
SELECT @thisCustomer = CustomerID FROM deleted
```

The second line retrieves the value of the CustomerID column from the deleted row. The trigger is invoked before SQL Server attempts to delete the row, but the deleted collection contains the line that's about to be deleted.

You have constructed the core of the trigger; now insert this code in the Trigger's Design window:

1. Change the name Orders_Trigger1 to a more meaningful name. Since your trigger will be invoked when a customer is deleted, name it CascadeCustomerDelete.

2. Set the action that will invoke the trigger. This action is the Delete action, and the third line must become:

   ```
   FOR DELETE
   ```

3. Insert the T-SQL code that will implement the trigger after the AS keyword. Here's the trigger that will cascade deletions of customers:

   ```
   CREATE TRIGGER CascadeCustomerDelete
   ON Customers
   FOR DELETE
   AS
       DECLARE @thisCustomer char(5)
       SELECT @thisCustomer = CustomerID FROM deleted
   ```

```
DELETE FROM [Order Details]
        WHERE [Order Details].OrderID = Orders.OrderID AND
        Orders.CustomerID = @thisCustomer
DELETE FROM Orders
        WHERE Orders.CustomerID = @thisCustomer
DELETE FROM Customers
        WHERE Customers.CustomerID = @thisCustomer
```

The Editor window doesn't change SQL keywords into uppercase, but I have edited the code to follow the same notation as in the rest of the book.

Using the Data View Window with Visual Basic

We've covered a lot of ground in this chapter, but not a single line of VB code. The visual database tools are integrated into Visual Basic's environment, but how do they help the VB developer? As I mentioned earlier, the more you do with the database tools, the less code you'll have to write later. Set up your constraints and relationships properly now, and you won't have to worry about maintaining referential integrity from within your code. Write stored procedures for the most common tasks, like adding customers, products, invoices, and so on, and you can call these procedures like methods of the database. Finally, by testing and debugging your queries ahead of time, you can simply copy the SQL statements from the Query Designer and paste them into your code.

To get an idea of how the visual database tools can help you develop database applications, I will go through some examples. These are topics we'll explore in depth in the following chapters, but I'd like to end this chapter with some tangible proof of the usefulness of the tools we've discussed. We won't write any code. We'll continue with the visual approach to database programming.

Creating Command Objects

As you recall, a Data Project contains a Form, as usual, and two Designer objects: the DataEnvironment and the DataReport Designers. The DataReport Designer is a straightforward tool that streamlines the generation of reports. The DataEnvironment object is Visual Basic's gateway to visual database programming. Let's review how you can set up a DataEnvironment object and use it from within your code.

The DataEnvironment object is a container for two types of objects: Connection objects and Command objects. Connection objects are no different than the Data

Link objects of the Data View window. The process of establishing a connection to a database with a Connection object in the DataEnvironment object is the same as the one outlined in the section "Connecting to Databases," earlier in this chapter. A Command object is any database object that returns one or more rows from the database. It can be a stored procedure, a table, or an SQL statement. You can create these objects with the visual database tools and drop them on the DataEnvironment's window. Let's do it.

If you don't have a project with a Data Link to the Northwind database, create one now:

1. Start a new Data Project, open its Data View window, and add a Data Link to the Northwind database. Then double-click the DataEnvironment icon in the Project window to open it in design mode. If you want to access the Customers table from within your VB code, you can do so by creating a Command object that "sees" the Customers table.

2. Delete the Connection1 object in the DataEnvironment window. Right-click its icon and select the Delete command form the shortcut menu.

3. Switch to the Data View window, while making sure that both the Data View and DataEnvironment windows are open. Drag the Customers table's icon under the Tables folder and drop it on the DataEnvironment's window. Figures 3.22 and 3.23 show the two windows before and after the addition of the Customers table to the DataEnvironment object.

FIGURE 3.22:

Open the DataEnvironment object and delete the default Connection object.

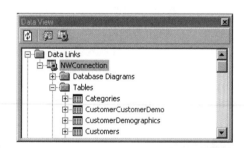

FIGURE 3.23:

When you drop a table on the DataEnvironment object, it brings along its connection to the database.

Because there's no Connection for the Customers table, a new Connection is added to the DataEnvironment object. It is the original connection of the Customers table in the Data View window (only there, it's called Data Link). If you right-click the Connection1 object and select Properties, you'll see the same Data Link dialog box as with the NWConnection object.

The Customers table was appended to the DataEnvironment object. The DataEnvironment is a programmable object that allows you to access the database from within your VB application. However, you can't use the DataEnvironment object to design new database objects, or edit existing ones, just as you can't access the Data View window's objects from within your VB code.

Displaying Rows on a DataGrid Control

Let's use the objects in the DataEnvironment window in a VB application. Close all open windows and open the project's Form in Design mode. Enlarge the Form and place an instance of the DataGrid control on it. Make the control slightly smaller than the Form, as shown in Figure 3.24. We will display the rows of the Customers table on the DataGrid control, and we'll do so by setting a few properties of the control, as explained next.

NOTE

The DataGrid control is added automatically to a new Data Project's toolbox. If you don't see its icon in the toolbox, open the Components dialog box and add the Microsoft DataGrid Control 6.0 (OLE DB) component to your project.

FIGURE 3.24:

Accessing the rows of the Customers table through a DataGrid control

1. Select the control on the Form and switch to the Properties window. Locate the property DataSource and set it to DataEnvironment1. Just expand the list of options next to the name of the property and select the name of the DataEnvironment object in the project.

2. Locate the DataMember property and set it to Customers. The DataSource and DataMember properties specify where the DataGrid control will pump its data from. It will contact the DataEnvironment object and it will request the rows returned by the Customers command. As you will see in the following chapters, all data-bound controls expose these two properties, which allow you to specify the source of their data.

3. To actually display the rows of the Customers table on the control, right-click the control and select Retrieve Fields. This command contacts the database you specified with the DataSource property and reads the structure of the cursor you specified with the DataMember property. It doesn't read any values; just the column specifications. The names of the fields will appear as titles on the fixed row of the DataGrid control. The control will be populated as soon as you run the project.

Press F5 and you will see the rows of the Customers table displayed on the DataGrid control, as shown in Figure 3.24. If you attempt to edit a cell, you'll realize that the fields are locked. To unlock them, stop the project and set a few properties.

Switch to the DataEnvironment window, right-click the Connection object, and select Properties from the shortcut menu. On the Customers Properties dialog box that appears, switch to the Advanced tab, shown in Figure 3.25. As you can see, the Customers table was opened for reading only. Set the Lock property to 3 (Optimistic). Then click OK to close the dialog box.

FIGURE 3.25:

The Customers Properties dialog box (Advanced tab)

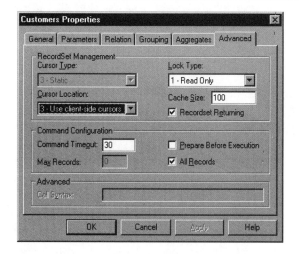

While you're at it, change a few properties of the DataGrid control as well. Switch to the application's Form, select the DataGrid control, and locate the properties with the Allow prefix. The AllowAddNew and AllowDelete properties are False by default. Set them to True, so that you can delete rows and add new ones at run time. The AllowUpdate property is True by default, so you can edit the rows displayed on the control.

Run the project again and this time attempt to edit the fields on the DataGrid control. It works very well, and it's quite useful, too. This simple Form allows you to edit a table with the simplest VB application you can think of. All you had to do was create the Command object in the DataEnvironment object and set a few properties for the DataGrid control.

Viewing Query Results

The DataGrid control isn't limited to tables. You can set it to display the result of any query, similar to the Results pane of the Query Designer. Bring the DataEnvironment and Data View windows into view, open the Views folder in the Data

View window, and drop the Product Sales for 1997 view on the DataEnvironment object. The view object of the Data View window will become a Command object in the DataEnvironment window. Because object names can't have embedded spaces, the spaces are replaced by underscore characters. Switch the Form again, and change the DataGrid control's DataMember property from Customers to Product_Sales_for_1997. Then map the new Command object's fields on the DataGrid control (right-click, then select Retrieve Structure) and run the project.

To edit the fields on the DataGrid control, you must set its Lock property to 3 (Optimistic). Even so, you won't be able to edit this particular view, because it contains aggregates. This is an example of a nonupdateable query, as you recall from our discussion of views in the previous chapter. If it were an updateable query, you'd be able to edit its rows.

Summary

The DataEnvironment can handle stored procedures, too, but I will not show any examples yet. Usually, stored procedures accept arguments and they return results, and this calls for some VB code. This ends our discussion of the visual database tools, which you can use in the following chapters. Whether you want to design a new database, tune an existing database, or create queries or stored procedures, you'll find these tools indispensable.

In the next chapter, we'll switch gears and explore the language for manipulating databases, the Structured Query Language (SQL). SQL is a universal language for manipulating databases (both their contents and their structure) and it's a "must" for a database developer. The Query Designer is a great tool, but it can't substitute a thorough understanding of SQL statements and their syntax.

Structured Query Language

- Selection and action queries

- Executing SQL statements

- Data Manipulation Language

- Joining tables

- Action queries

We have used quite a few SQL statements in the previous chapters, without a formal discussion of the statements and keywords of SQL. It's about time to look at this peculiar language and see what it can do for your application. Even though this chapter doesn't deal directly with VB statements, it covers the language behind every database management system (DBMS), and you should spare the time and effort to learn it. You can generate SQL statements with point-and-click operations (such as Query by Example, which comes with both Access and SQL Server), but they are no substitute for writing your own SQL statements.

Before we proceed, a few words on how SQL is used. Every database comes with a tool for executing SQL statements and displaying the results. When the boss wants some information that can't be retrieved by your company's database application, you can write an SQL statement to retrieve the information. In addition, you can execute SQL statements against a database from within your VB applications. The rows returned by the statement are intercepted by VB, and you can write the code to display them graphically, process them, or place them on an HTML page and send them to a browser.

Structured Query Language (SQL) is a nonprocedural language. SQL doesn't provide traditional programming structures. Instead, it's a language for specifying the operation you want to perform at an unusually high level. The details of the implementation are left to the DBMS. This is good news for nonprogrammers, but many programmers new to SQL wish it had the structure of a more traditional language. You will get used to SQL and soon be able to combine the best of both worlds: the programming model of VB and the simplicity of SQL.

To retrieve all the company names from the Customers table of the Northwind database, you issue a statement like this one:

```
SELECT CompanyName
FROM Customers
```

To select customers from a specific country, you issue the following statement:

```
SELECT CompanyName
FROM Customers
WHERE Country = 'Germany'
```

The DBMS will retrieve and return the rows you requested. As you can see, this is not how you'd retrieve rows with Visual Basic. In that language, you would have to specify the statements to scan the entire table, examine the value of the Country column, and either select or reject the row. Then you would display the selected rows. With SQL you don't have to specify how the selection operation will take place. You simply specify *what* you want the database to do for you—not *how* to do it.

SQL statements are categorized into two major categories, which are actually considered separate languages: the statements for manipulating the data, which form the Data Manipulation Language (DML), and the statements for defining database objects, such as tables or their indexes, which form the Data Definition Language (DDL). The Data Definition Language is not of interest to every database developer, and we will not discuss it in this book. The Data Manipulation Language is covered in depth, because you'll use these statements to retrieve data, insert new data to the database, and edit or delete existing data. Toward the end of this chapter, we'll discuss how SQL Server automatically generates the statements that reproduce the structure of an existing database so that you can create a fresh database during installation.

Selection and Action Queries

The statements of the DML part of the SQL language are also known as *queries*. There are two types of queries: selection queries and action queries. *Selection queries* retrieve information from the database and don't modify the database in any way. All selection queries start with the SELECT statement. *Action queries* modify the data in the database's tables and start with one of three keywords: INSERT, DELETE, or UPDATE.

The majority of this chapter covers selection queries. Action queries are simpler, but the principles of selection queries apply to action queries as well. After all, you rarely modify an entire table unconditionally. You first specify the rows to be modified, and then act on them. As you see, you won't go far without mastering selection queries.

Executing SQL Statements

If you are not familiar with SQL, I suggest that you follow the examples in this chapter and modify them to perform similar operations. To follow these examples, you have three options—SQLEXEC, the Query Analyzer, and Access queries—which are described here.

The SQLEXEC Application

SQLEXEC is a simple VB application that lets you execute SQL statements against a SQL server or Access database, as shown in Figure 4.1. We'll look at the code behind this application later in this book. To open a database, click the Open Database button. The program will ask you which type of database you want to open and the actual database name.

After you open a database, you can enter any SQL statement in the upper box and click the Execute button to execute it against the open database. If the SQL statement is a selection query (a query that retrieves rows from the database), the qualifying rows will appear in the lower grid. If the SQL statement is an action query (a query that updates selected rows in the database), the number of affected rows will appear on the window's title bar, and the grid will be cleared. If the DBMS can't execute the query for any reason, it will return an error code displayed in a message box.

FIGURE 4.1:

The SQLEXEC application enables you to execute any SQL statement against any SQL Server or Access database.

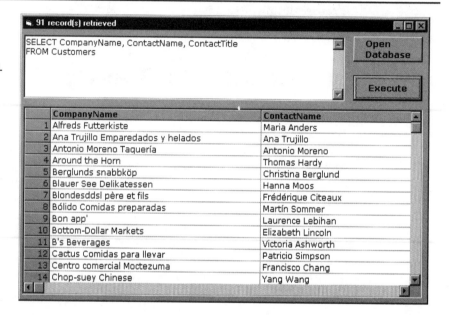

You can review the structure of the open database by clicking the Map Database button. You will see the Database Map window, shown in Figure 4.2, which displays the database's tables. Each time you select a table name with the mouse, its fields are displayed in the right pane. Use this window to quickly look up the field names you need in your query.

You can save SQL statements into files, so that you won't have to type them again. To do so, open the File menu, select Save, and enter the name of a file where the contents of the Query pane will be stored. The statement will be stored in a text file with the extension .sql. The lengthier examples of this chapter can be found in SQL files on the companion CD. Instead of entering the statements yourself, you can load the corresponding SQL file from the CD and execute it. Notice that the SQLEXEC application will not prompt you to save a statement that hasn't been saved yet.

FIGURE 4.2:

The Database Map window of the SQLEXEC application

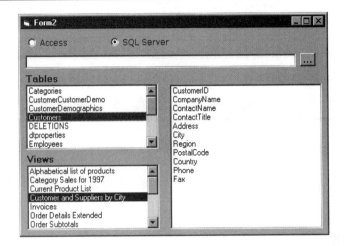

The Query Analyzer

Besides SQLEXEC, you can also use SQL Server's Query Analyzer to follow the examples. Start the Query Analyzer (select Start ➤ SQL Server 7.0 ➤ Query Analyzer), and you will see a Query window. Initially, this window will be empty. Enter the SQL statement you want to execute and then select the desired database's name in the DB drop-down list. The SQL statement will be executed against the selected database. Alternatively, you can prefix the SQL statement with the USE statement, which specifies the database against which the statement will be executed. To retrieve all the Northwind customers located in Germany, enter this statement:

```
USE Northwind
SELECT CompanyName FROM Customers
WHERE Country = 'Germany'
```

Then select the Execute command from the Query menu, or press Ctrl+E to execute the statement. The results will appear in the lower pane, as shown in Figure 4.3. For a selection query, like the previous one, you will see the rows selected and their count at the bottom of the Result pane. If the query updates the database, you will see only the number of rows affected.

To execute another query, enter another statement in the upper pane, or edit the previous statement, and press Ctrl+E again. You can also save SQL statements into files, so that you won't have to type them again. To do so, open the File menu, select Save As or Save, and enter the name of the file where the contents of the Query pane will be stored. The statement will be stored in a text file with the extension .sql. The lengthier examples of this chapter can be found in SQL files on the companion CD. Instead of entering the statements yourself, you can load the corresponding SQL file from the CD and execute it.

FIGURE 4.3:

Executing queries with the Query Analyzer

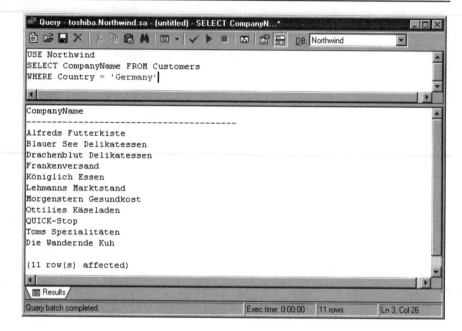

Access Queries

If you don't have SQL Server installed, or you feel more comfortable with Access, you can follow the examples of this chapter using Access. To execute an SQL statement against an Access database, you must first open the database and then create a query to execute. To create a new query, select the Queries tab of the database and press the New button. To edit an existing query, press the Design button.

When you create a new query, Access will display the Query by Example window. This tool allows you to create queries with point-and-click operations. To actually write SQL statements, you must close the Query by Example window and switch to a small text editor where you can enter the statements. In the New Query window that will appear, click OK, and you'll see the first window of the Wizard that takes you through the steps of designing a new query. Click the Close button and then select SQL View from the View window. Enter the SQL statement, as shown in Figure 4.4(a), and then close the window. You'll be prompted to enter a name for the new query. After that, every time you edit a query, you'll be asked to save the changes.

To execute an Access query, select its name in the Queries tab and click the Open button—or double-click the query's name. You will see a new window, like the one shown in Figure 4.4(b), with a spreadsheet view of the results. You can resize columns, hide certain columns, and sort rows according to a selected column's values (to do so, right-click the header of the desired column and select Sort Ascending or Sort Descending from the shortcut menu). Unlike SQL Server, Access allows you to edit the results of a query—as long as the changes you make are feasible and don't violate the integrity of the database. If you display selected customers from the Northwind database, you can change a customer's name. If you display sales totals, you can't change the total for a customer. Access wouldn't know which field(s) to modify.

FIGURE 4.4:

Designing (a) and executing (b) a query in Access

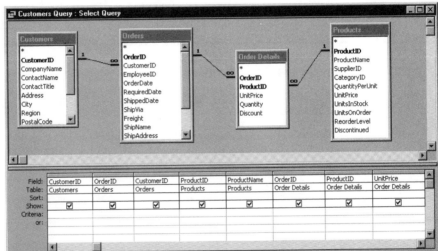

a

b

Data Manipulation Language

The Data Manipulation Language consists of four statements, described in Table 4.1.

TABLE 4.1:   The Data Manipulation Statements

Statement	Action
SELECT	Retrieves records from the database
UPDATE	Updates records in the database
DELETE	Deletes records in the database
INSERT	Inserts records in the database

These statements can get quite complex, because you must also define which records will be selected and acted upon. The selection criteria you specify can apply to multiple tables, and SQL provides many operators and functions that let you specify the desired records. The mechanisms for specifying the desired rows are the same, regardless of whether you simply retrieve them from the database, update, or delete them. The INSERT statement is the simplest one, because it appends rows to a table in the database.

We'll start our discussion of SQL with the SELECT statement. Once you learn how to express the criteria for selecting the desired rows with the SELECT statement, you'll be able to apply this information to other Data Manipulation statements.

The simplest form of the SELECT statement is

```
SELECT fields
FROM tables
```

where *fields* and *tables* are comma-separated lists of the fields you want to retrieve from the database and the tables they belong to. To select the contact information from all the companies in the Customers table, use this statement:

```
SELECT CompanyName, ContactName, ContactTitle
FROM Customers
```

To retrieve all the fields, use the asterisk (*) or the ALL keyword. The statement

```
SELECT * FROM Customers
```

will select all the fields from the Titles table. Figure 4.5 shows the output of a query generated by the Query Analyzer.

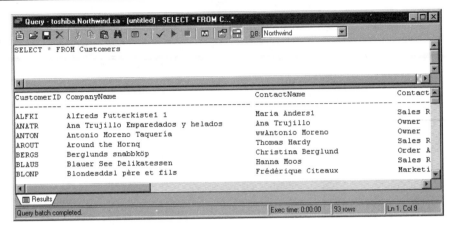

The WHERE Clause

The unconditional form of the SELECT statement we used in last few examples is quite trivial. You rarely retrieve selected columns of all rows in a table. Usually you specify criteria, such as "All companies in Germany," "All customers who have placed three or more orders in the last six months," or even more complicated expressions. To restrict the rows returned by the query, use the WHERE clause of the SELECT statement. The most common form of the SELECT statement is the following:

```
SELECT fields
FROM tables
WHERE condition
```

The *fields* and *tables* arguments are the same as before. The syntax of the WHERE clause can get quite complicated, so we'll start with the simpler forms of the selection criteria.

The *condition* argument can be a relational expression, like the ones you use in VB. To select all the customers from Germany, use the following condition:

```
WHERE Country = 'Germany'
```

To select customers from German-speaking countries, use a condition like the following one:

```
WHERE Country = 'Germany' OR
      Country = 'Austria' OR
      Country = 'Switzerland'
```

Long lines can break anywhere—you can't break words, of course.

Using Multiple Tables

When you combine multiple tables in a query, you should always include the WHERE clause to specify some criteria. Let's say you want a list of all product names, along with their categories. The information you need is not contained in a single table. You must extract the product name from the Products table and the Category name from the Categories table and specify that the ProductID field in two tables must match. The statement

```
USE NORTHWIND
SELECT ProductName, CategoryName
FROM Products, Categories
WHERE Products.CategoryID = Categories.CategoryID
```

will retrieve the names of all products, along with their category names. Here's how this statement is executed. For each row in the Products table, the SQL engine locates the matching row in the Categories table and then appends the Product-Name and CategoryName fields to the result. The rows are matched with the CategoryID field (both rows must have the same CategoryID value). If a product has no category, then it will not be included in the result.

NOTE

Note that when fields in two different tables have the same names, you must prefix them with the table's name to remove the ambiguity. In this book, I have tried to prefix all field names with their table names. This makes the statements lengthier, but they are easier to read, especially if the user is not familiar with the database. Also note that some field names may contain spaces. These field names must appear in square brackets. The Publishers table of the Pubs sample database contains a field named *Publisher Name*. To use this field in a query, enclose it in brackets: `Publishers.[Publisher Name]`. The table prefix is optional (no other table contains a column by that name), but the brackets are mandatory.

This type of restriction is used in nearly every SELECT statement that combines two or more tables. Here's another statement that uses a similar restriction to retrieve data from the Pubs database. It retrieves all the titles from the Titles table, along with the matching publisher:

```
USE Pubs
   SELECT Title, Pub_name
   FROM Titles, Publishers
   WHERE Titles.Pub_ID = Publishers.Pub_ID
```

(Actually, this statement doesn't retrieve all the titles, because some titles may not have a publisher. This topic is discussed in detail in "Joining Tables," later in this chapter).

You can also combine multiple restrictions with logical operators. To retrieve all the titles published by a specific publisher, use the publisher's ID in the WHERE clause, as in the following statement. This time I'm using Access's Biblio database, because it has more data than the Pubs database:

```
USE Biblio
SELECT Titles.Title
FROM Titles
WHERE Titles.PubID=722
```

This statement assumes that you know the publisher's ID—or you look it up in the Publishers table first and then plug it into the statement. A more elegant coding of the same statement would be the following:

```
SELECT Titles.Title
FROM Titles, Publishers
WHERE Titles.PubID=Publishers.PubID AND
      Publishers.Name="SYBEX"
```

This statement combines two tables and selects the titles of a publisher specified by name. To match titles and publisher, it requests that

1. The publisher's name in the Publishers table is *SYBEX*, and

2. The PubID field in the Titles table matches the PubID field in the Publishers table.

Notice that we did not specify the publisher's name (field [Company Name]) in the SELECT list; all the desired books have the same publisher, so we used the PubID field in the WHERE clause, but did not include any information about the publisher in the result.

If you specify multiple tables without the WHERE clause, the SQL statement, will return an enormous cursor. If you issue the following statement,

```
SELECT ProductName, CategoryName FROM Categories, Products
```

you will not get a line for each product name followed by its category. You will get a cursor with 616 rows, which are all possible combinations of product names and category names. This is known as a *Cartesian product* (or *cross-product*) of the two tables and contains all possible combinations of the rows of the two tables. In this example, the Categories table has eight rows and the Products table has 77 rows, so their cross-product contains 616 rows. If you create the cross-product of two tables with a few thousand records, you will retrieve a cursor so large that it's practically useless.

The AS keyword

By default, each column of a query is labeled after the actual field name in the output. If a table contains two fields named CustLName and CustFName, you can display them with different labels using the AS keyword. The SELECT statement

```
SELECT CustLName, CustFName
```

will produce two columns labeled CustLName and CustFName. The query's output will look much better if you change the labels of these two columns with a statement like the following one:

```
SELECT CustLName AS [Last Name], CustFName AS [First Name]
```

It is also possible to concatenate two fields in the SELECT list with the concatenation operator. Concatenated fields are not labeled automatically, so you must supply your own header for the combined field. The following statement creates a single column for the customer's name and labels it *Customer Name*:

```
SELECT CustFname + ", " + CustLName AS [Customer Name]
```

SQL Server doesn't automatically label the combined columns. Access names them Expr1000, Expr1001, and so on. Notice also that Access recognizes two operators for concatenation: & and +. The & operator concatenates the two values, even if one of them (or both) are numeric. The + operator concatenates two arguments if they are strings, but adds them if they are numeric values. SQL Server recognizes a single concatenation operator (the + symbol). If the two values are numeric, they will be added. If they are both text, they will be concatenated. If one of them is numeric, SQL Server will not perform any conversion automatically. You must convert the numeric value to text with the CONVERT() function before you can concatenate the two with the + operator. The CONVERT() function is covered in Chapter 7, "Transact-SQL."

The TOP Keyword

Some queries may retrieve a large number of rows, while you're interested in the top few rows only. The TOP N keyword allows you to select the first *N* rows and ignore the remaining ones. Let's say you want to see the list of the 10 most wanted products. Without the TOP keyword, you'd have to calculate how many items from each product have been sold, sort them according to items sold, and examine the first 10 rows returned by the query.

The TOP keyword is used only when the rows are ordered according to some meaningful criteria. Limiting a query's output to the alphabetically top *N* rows isn't very practical. When the rows are sorted according to items sold, revenue generated, and so on, it makes sense to limit the query's output to *N* rows. You'll see many examples of the TOP keyword later in this chapter, after you learn how to order a query's rows.

The LIKE Operator

Quite often you won't be interested in an exact match. A publisher's name may be followed by several initials, like Inc., SA, and so on. Or you may be interested in retrieving books with specific words in their titles. To handle similar searches, which involve patterns rather than exact matches, SQL provides the LIKE operator, which is a very general pattern-matching operator.

The LIKE operator uses pattern-matching characters, like the ones you use to select multiple files in DOS. The expression "`Sales*`" stands for "All files that begin with the string Sales," while "`*.xls`" stands for "All files with extension .xls." The LIKE operator recognizes a number of pattern-matching characters (or wildcard characters) to match one or more characters, numeric digits, ranges of letters, and so on. The problem is that the wildcard characters are not identical across all DBMSs—but more on this later.

If you are not sure about the publisher's last name, use an expression like the following one:

```
WHERE Publishers.Name LIKE "JOHN WILEY*"
```

This expression will locate all rows in the Publishers table beginning with the string "JOHN WILEY" and followed by any other character(s) (or no characters at all). The search is not case-sensitive, so you need not capitalize the arguments. If you attempt to display all books published by John Wiley in the Biblio database using the equals operator (`Publishers.Name = "JOHN WILEY"`), you'll retrieve only two records. If you use the LIKE operator, as shown in the following SQL statement, you will retrieve 394 titles:

```
SELECT Titles.Title
FROM Titles, Publishers
WHERE Titles.PubID=Publishers.PubID AND
      Publishers.Name LIKE "JOHN WILEY*"
```

The additional records were published by John Wiley & Sons.

You can use the LIKE operator to retrieve all titles about Windows, with a statement like the following one:

```
SELECT Titles.Title
FROM Titles
WHERE Titles.Title LIKE "*WINDOWS*"
```

The two asterisks mean that any characters may appear in front or after the word *Windows* in the title. This is how you code the expression: "The title should contain the word WINDOWS."

This statement will retrieve 884 titles, including titles ranging from "Using dBASE IV for Windows" to "Wicked Windows Comes Alive." To limit the selection to books about Windows programming, use this statement:

```
SELECT Titles.Title
FROM Titles
WHERE Titles.Title LIKE "*WINDOWS*" AND
        Titles.Title LIKE "*PROGRAM*"
```

The rows retrieved by this query are shown in Figure 4.6. By using the string "*PROGRAM*" you can locate titles with the words *Program*, *Programming*, *Programmer*, and so on. This set of titles is more likely to contain all the titles about Windows programming than if you had used the string "PROGRAMMING" in the statement's WHERE clause.

FIGURE 4.6:

Locating titles that contain selected keywords

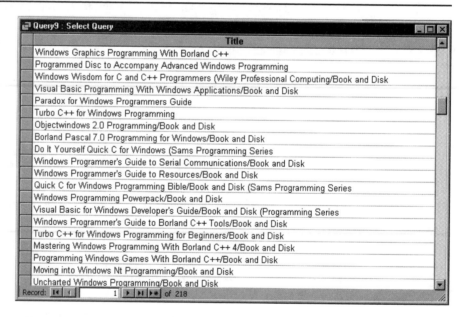

The LIKE operator recognizes many wildcard characters, but the syntax is not uniform across all databases. Even Microsoft's Access and SQL Server use different wildcard characters. If you're using a single product, you'll get used to the notation quickly. If you're consulting for various companies, the syntax of the LIKE operator can be a real problem. The wildcard characters for Access and SQL Server are listed in Tables 4.2 and 4.3.

TABLE 4.2:   Access Wildcard Characters

Wildcard Character	Function
*	Matches any number of characters. The pattern **program*** will find *program*, *programming*, *programmer*, and so on. Notice that the asterisk can be used as the first or last character in the character string, or as both the first and last character. The pattern ***program*** will locate strings that contain the words *program*, *programming*, *nonprogrammer*, and so on.
?	Matches any single alphabetic character. The pattern **b?y** will find *boy* and *bay*, but not *boysenberry*.
[ ]	Matches any single character within the brackets. The pattern **Santa [YI]nez** will find both *Santa Ynez* and *Santa Inez*. This pattern is quite useful in locating possibly misspelled words in a single pass.
[!]	Matches any character not in the brackets. The pattern ***q[!u]*** will find words that contain the character *q* not followed by *u* (they are misspelled words).
[-]	Matches any one of a range of characters. The characters must be consecutive in the alphabet and specified in ascending order (A to Z). The pattern **[a-c]*** will find all words that begin with *a*, *b*, or *c* (in lowercase or uppercase).
#	Matches any single numeric character. The pattern **D1##** will find *D100* and *D139*, but not *D1000* or *D10*.

The Access wildcard characters are the same as the ones used by DOS and Windows for partial file and directory matching (like *.exe, or Sales??.xls). To use the special symbols of Table 4.2 as literal, you must enclose them in a pair of square brackets. You can search for the opening bracket, question mark, number sign, and asterisk as literal in your search argument by enclosing them in square brackets. The closing bracket can't appear inside a pair of brackets (it will close the opening bracket prematurely), but you can use it as a literal on its own. The closing bracket in the argument "abc]" has no special meaning, because there's no opening bracket.

TABLE 4.3:   T-SQL Wildcard Characters

Wildcard Character	Function
%	Matches any number of characters. The pattern **program%** will find *program*, *programming*, *programmer*, and so on. Notice that the asterisk can be used as the first or last character in the character string, or as both the first and last character. The pattern **%program%** will locate strings that contain the words *program*, *programming*, *nonprogrammer*, and so on.

Continued on next page

TABLE 4.3 CONTINUED: T-SQL Wildcard Characters

Wildcard Character	Function
_	(Underscore character) Matches any single alphabetic character. The pattern **b_y** will find *boy* and *bay*, but not *boysenberry*.
[ ]	Matches any single character within the brackets. The pattern **Santa [YI]nez** will find both *Santa Ynez* and *Santa Inez*. This pattern is quite useful in locating possibly misspelled words in a single pass.
[^]	Matches any character not in the brackets. The pattern **%q[^u]%** will find words that contain the character *q* not followed by *u* (they are misspelled words).
[-]	Matches any one of a range of characters. The characters must be consecutive in the alphabet and specified in ascending order (A to Z, not Z to A). The pattern **[a-c]%** will find all words that begin with *a*, *b*, or *c* (in lowercase or uppercase).
#	Matches any single numeric character. The pattern **D1##** will find *D100* and *D139*, but not *D1000* or *D10*.

When performing string comparisons with LIKE, all characters in the pattern string are significant, including leading and/or trailing spaces. To ignore the spaces in the search arguments, use the TRIM() function with Access, and the LTRIM() and RTRIM() functions with SQL Server. LTRIM() and RTRIM() remove leading and trailing spaces, respectively. None of these functions are part of SQL, but both SQL Server and Access recognize functions that remove spaces around a string. Another tricky situation may arise because trailing spaces may exist in a field value. Fields declared as char(20) will contain trailing spaces if the value stored is less than 20 characters long. All fields that store variable-length strings must be declared as varchar.

Some search arguments may include one or more of the special wildcard characters themselves. A column that stores discounts may contain numeric values followed by the percent sign (%), and the underscore character is not uncommon in product codes. To include a wildcard character in the search argument as a regular character, you must repeat the special character. To search for the string, "Up to 50% off the list price," use the following WHERE clause:

```
WHERE Comments LIKE "%up to 50%% off the list price%"
```

What if you want to search for the string "50%"? You want to locate a string that ends with the percent sign, followed by any character. This time you must use the ESCAPE clause. This clause specifies an escape character, which cancels the effect of a special character when placed in front of it. To locate strings that contain the string '50' you use a WHERE clause like the following:

```
WHERE Comments LIKE '%50%'
```

If you want to locate the string "50%", however, you must first select an escape character, which doesn't appear in the search argument (the exclamation mark is used commonly as an escape character). The condition must change to '%50!%%' and followed by the ESCAPE clause:

```
WHERE Comments LIKE '%50!%%' ESCAPE '!'
```

The first and last percent signs in the search argument have the usual meaning (any characters in front or after the string). The exclamation mark tells SQL Server to treat the following percent sign as part of the string and not as a special string. The last SQL statement will retrieve all rows with the string "50%" in their Comments column.

Using the LIKE Operator with ADO

When you execute SQL statements against a database through the Active Data Objects, you must use SQL Server syntax. ADO will handle the special symbols for you when it contacts an Access database. The following statement will not return any rows if you execute it as an Access query:

```
SELECT CompanyName, ContactName, Country
FROM Customers
WHERE Country LIKE '_ermany'
```

The correct statement for Access would be:

```
SELECT CompanyName, ContactName, Country
FROM Customers
WHERE Country LIKE '?ermany'
```

This statement, however, will not work with SQL Server.

The statement that works with SQL Server will also work with Access, if you execute it through ADO. The following VB statements will return the 11 customers from Germany, whether they're executed against SQL Server or Access:

```
cmd = "SELECT CompanyName, ContactName, Country "
cmd = cmd & "FROM Customers "
cmd = cmd & "WHERE Country LIKE '_ermany'"
RS.Open Text1.Text, objConnection
```

The *objConnection* variable represents a Connection object to the Northwind database.

NOTE   For more information on executing SQL statements against a database from within your VB application, see Chapter 5, "A First Look at ADO."

Locating NULL Values

A very common operation in manipulating and maintaining databases is to locate Null values in fields. The expressions IS NULL and IS NOT NULL find field values that are (or are not) Null. A string comparison like the following one will not return Null values:

```
WHERE CompanyName = ""
```

Actually, this statement will return rows in which the CompanyName column was set to an empty string, but not the rows in which it was never assigned a value. They could be rows that were assigned values in the CompanyName field, but these values were deleted later. Perhaps there's a reason to set certain fields to an empty string. To locate the rows which have a Null value in their CompanyName column, use the following WHERE clause:

```
WHERE CompanyName IS NULL
```

A Null price in the Products table means that the product's price was not available at the time of the data entry. You can easily locate the products without prices and edit them. The following statement will locate products without prices:

```
WHERE Price IS NULL
```

If you compare the Price field to the numeric value zero, you'll retrieve the products with zero price (they could be discontinued products, freebies, but certainly not the products that have never had a price).

Here's a more practical example. While you're entering titles in the Biblio database, you may not know a book's publisher and leave this field blank. At a later stage, you can locate all the titles without a publisher and edit them. The following statement will retrieve all the rows without a publisher:

```
SELECT Titles.Title
FROM Titles
WHERE Titles.PubID IS NULL
```

A more useful SQL statement would locate not only titles without publishers, but also titles that point to nonexisting publishers. For example, you may have deleted rows in the Publishers table without removing the corresponding references in the Titles table. This situation should never arise in a well-designed database, but most databases in use today are far from perfect, and freelance consultants face similar problems when they take over someone else's projects. Once you develop a basic understanding of the database, you should examine the rules for establishing referential integrity. The Biblio database, for example, doesn't enforce referential integrity between the Titles and Publishers tables. In other words, it is possible to remove a publisher even though it's referenced by one or more titles.

NOTE   For a detailed discussion of referential integrity and the rules for enforcing referential integrity among the tables of the database, see the "Referential Integrity" section in Chapter 2, "Basic Concepts of Relational Databases."

If you suspect that some titles refer to invalid publishers, use the following statements to retrieve all the titles that have no publisher or refer to nonexisting publishers. This statement retrieves titles without a publisher:

```
SELECT Titles.Title
FROM Titles
WHERE (Titles.PubID IS NULL);
```

The following statement retrieves titles with an invalid publisher:

```
SELECT Titles.Title
FROM Titles, Publishers
WHERE Titles.PubID=[Publishers].[PubID] AND
      Publishers.Name IS NULL;
```

How about combining the two WHERE clauses with the OR operator, so that you can retrieve all the titles with a single statement? The following statement seems valid, but it's not:

```
SELECT Titles.Title
FROM Titles, Publishers
WHERE ((Titles.PubID IS NULL) OR
       (Titles.PubID=[Publishers].[PubID] AND
        Publishers.Name IS NULL));
```

This statement will return an enormous recordset that contains all combinations of titles and publishers. We'll come back to queries that generate large recordsets later in this chapter and discuss them in detail. There's a simple method to combine the results of two or more queries with the UNION operator that combines the unique rows from two recordsets. The UNION operator is discussed in the following section.

Notice that you can't edit the Titles table to create a few titles without a publisher, because the PubID field in the Titles table can't be Null. You must lift the constraint first, then edit the table. After you're done, don't forget to add the constraint back to the database.

The UNION Operator

The UNION operator allows you to combine the results of two separate queries into a single cursor. The final cursor is the union of the cursors returned by the individual queries, and it doesn't contain duplicate rows. Here's how you can combine the rows retrieved by the two previous examples with the UNION operator:

```
(SELECT Titles.Title
    FROM Titles, Publishers
    WHERE Titles.PubID IS NULL)
UNION
    (SELECT Titles.Title
        FROM Titles, Publishers
        WHERE Titles.PubID=Publishers.PubID AND
        Publishers.Name IS NULL)
```

In short, this statement will find all titles with a problem in their publisher entry. The IS NULL and IS NOT NULL expressions are used quite frequently in establishing the integrity of a database; a simple SQL statement can locate the Null values in a table. Later in this chapter, in "The UPDATE Statement," you will learn how to edit these fields in a table with SQL statements.

How about the records that have an invalid publisher ID (a publisher ID that points to a nonexisting record in the Publishers table)? To find the rows of the Title table that point to nonexisting publishers, you must use the IN (and NOT IN) keyword, which is described later in this chapter.

The DISTINCT Keyword

The DISTINCT keyword eliminates any duplicates from the cursor retrieved by the SELECT statement. Let's say you want to find out which countries have Northwind customers. If you retrieve all country names from the Customers table, you'll end up with many duplicates. To eliminate them, use the DISTINCT keyword, as shown in the following statement:

```
SELECT DISTINCT Country
FROM Customers
```

The cursor returned by this statement is shown in Figure 4.7. The NULL entry means that one or more rows in the Customers table have no value in the Country column.

According to our discussion of database normalization, you should have created a separate table for storing country names and forced each row in the Customers table to point to a country name in this new table. You could have done so, but the designers of the Biblio database decided not to go too far with the normalization. I don't store country names in separate tables, because they are not easily misspelled and they usually never change. (With so many new countries popping up on the map, however, I may have to reconsider).

FIGURE 4.7:

Selecting unique country
names from the Northwind
Customers table

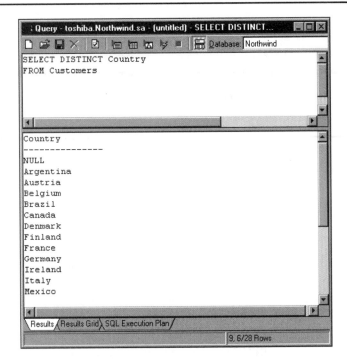

The DISTINCT keyword applies to the list of fields that follow. The statement

```
SELECT DISTINCT Country, City
FROM Customers
```

will retrieve unique country and city names. The above statement retrieves 70 rows.
If you omit the DISTINCT keyword, you'll get 92 rows. There are three customers in
Buenos Aires, Argentina, but this country-city combination appears only once if the
DISTINCT statement is used.

Sorting Rows with the ORDER Keyword

The rows of a query are rarely returned in the order you want them. They are
ordered according to the order in which the column names were specified in the
SELECT statement and the order in which the rows were entered in each table. To
request that the rows be returned in a specific order, use the ORDER BY clause.
The syntax of ORDER BY is

```
ORDER BY col1, col2, . . .
```

You can specify any number of columns in the Order list. The output of the query
is ordered according to the values of the first column (col1). If two rows have identical values in this column, then they are sorted according to the second column

and so on. Let's say you want a list of all customers in the Customers table ordered by country. Since you have multiple customers in each country, you must also define how each group of customers from the same country will be ordered. The statement

```
SELECT CompanyName, ContactName
FROM Customers
ORDER BY Country, City
```

will display the customers ordered by country and by city within each country's section. If you want to order the rows by company name within each country group, use the following statement:

```
SELECT CompanyName, ContactName
FROM Customers
ORDER BY Country, CompanyName
```

Or, you can order them by country, by city within each country, and by company name within each city with the following statement:

```
SELECT CompanyName, ContactName
FROM Customers
ORDER BY Country, City, CompanyName
```

Figure 4.8 shows the output produced by the two SELECT statements.

FIGURE 4.8:

The Northwind companies as retrieved from the Customers table (a) and the same companies ordered by country and city within each country (b)

```
91 record(s) retrieved

SELECT CompanyName, Country, City
FROM Customers
```

	CompanyName	Country	City
1	Alfreds Futterkiste	Germany	Berlin
2	Ana Trujillo Emparedados y helados	Mexico	México D.F.
3	Antonio Moreno Taquería	Mexico	México D.F.
4	Around the Horn	UK	London
5	Berglunds snabbköp	Sweden	Luleå
6	Blauer See Delikatessen	Germany	Mannheim
7	Blondesddsl père et fils	France	Strasbourg
8	Bólido Comidas preparadas	Spain	Madrid
9	Bon app'	France	Marseille
10	Bottom-Dollar Markets	Canada	Tsawassen
11	B's Beverages	UK	London
12	Cactus Comidas para llevar	Argentina	Buenos Aires
13	Centro comercial Moctezuma	Mexico	México D.F.
14	Chop-suey Chinese	Switzerland	Bern
15	Comércio Mineiro	Brazil	Sao Paulo

a

FIGURE 4.8:

(Continued)

The Northwind companies as retrieved from the Customers table (a) and the same companies ordered by country and city within each country (b)

b

Calculated Fields

In addition to column names, you can specify calculated fields in the SELECT statement. The Order Details table contains a row for each invoice line. The invoice #10248, for instance, contains four lines (four items sold), and each detail line appears in a separate row in the Order Details table. Each row holds the number of items sold, the item's price, and the corresponding discount. To display the line's subtotal, you must multiply the quantity by the price minus the discount, as shown in the following statement:

```
SELECT Orders.OrderID, ProductID,
    [Order Details].UnitPrice *
    [Order Details].Quantity * (1 - [Order Details].Discount)
FROM Orders, [Order Details]
WHERE Orders.OrderID = [Order Details].OrderID
```

This statement will calculate the subtotal for each line in the invoices issued to all Northwind customers and display them along with the order number, as shown in Figure 4.9. The order numbers are repeated as many times as there are products in the order (or lines in the invoice). In the following section, "Totaling and Counting," you will find out how to calculate totals, too.

FIGURE 4.9:

Calculating the subtotals for each item sold

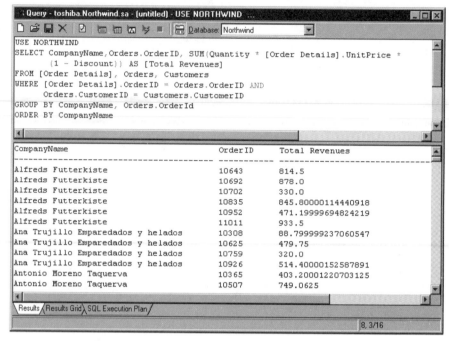

```
Query - toshiba.Northwind.sa - [untitled] - USE NORTHWIND ...
Database: Northwind
USE NORTHWIND
SELECT CompanyName, Orders.OrderID, SUM(Quantity * [Order Details].UnitPrice *
       (1 - Discount)) AS [Total Revenues]
FROM [Order Details], Orders, Customers
WHERE [Order Details].OrderID = Orders.OrderID AND
       Orders.CustomerID = Customers.CustomerID
GROUP BY CompanyName, Orders.OrderId
ORDER BY CompanyName
```

```
CompanyName                           OrderID      Total Revenues
-----------------------------------   ----------   --------------------
Alfreds Futterkiste                   10643        814.5
Alfreds Futterkiste                   10692        878.0
Alfreds Futterkiste                   10702        330.0
Alfreds Futterkiste                   10835        845.80000114440918
Alfreds Futterkiste                   10952        471.19999694824219
Alfreds Futterkiste                   11011        933.5
Ana Trujillo Emparedados y helados    10308        88.799999237060547
Ana Trujillo Emparedados y helados    10625        479.75
Ana Trujillo Emparedados y helados    10759        320.0
Ana Trujillo Emparedados y helados    10926        514.40000152587891
Antonio Moreno Taquerva               10365        403.20001220703125
Antonio Moreno Taquerva               10507        749.0625
```

Results / Results Grid \ SQL Execution Plan /

8, 3/16

TIP

The last SQL statement is too lengthy. You can shorten it by omitting the table name qualifier for the Quantity and UnitPrice fields, since their names do not appear in any other table. You can't omit the table qualifier from the OrderID field's name, because it appears in both tables involved in the query. You can also specify a short alias for the Order Details table name with the AS keyword and then use the alias in the place of the actual table name:

```
SELECT Orders.OrderID, UnitPrice * Quantity * (1 - Discount)
FROM Orders, [Order Details] AS Details
WHERE Orders.OrderID = Details.OrderID
```

Totaling and Counting

SQL supports a number of aggregate functions, which act on selected fields of all the rows returned by the query. The aggregate functions, listed in Table 4.4, perform basic calculations like summing, counting, and averaging numeric values. Aggregate functions accept field names (or calculated fields) as arguments, and they return a single value, which is the sum (or average) of all values.

TABLE 4.4: SQL's Aggregate Functions

Function	Action
COUNT()	Returns the number (count) of values in a specified column
SUM()	Returns the sum of values in a specified column
AVG()	Returns the average of the values in a specified column
MIN()	Returns the smallest value in a specified column
MAX()	Returns the largest value in a specified column

These functions operate on a single column (which could be a calculated column) and they return a single value. The rows involved in the calculations are specified with the proper WHERE clause. The SUM() and AVG() functions can process only numeric values. The other three functions can process both numeric and text values.

These functions are used to summarize data from one or more tables. Let's say we want to know how many of the Northwind database customers are located in Germany. The following SQL statement will return the desired value:

```
USE NORTHWIND
SELECT COUNT(CustomerID)
FROM Customers
WHERE Country = 'Germany'
```

This is a simple demonstration of the COUNT() function. If you want to count unique values, you must use the DISTINCT keyword along with the name of the field to count. If you want to find out in how many countries there are Northwind customers, use the following SQL statement:

```
SELECT COUNT(DISTINCT Country)
FROM Customers
```

If you omit the DISTINCT keyword, the statement will return the number of rows that have a Country field. The COUNT() statement ignores the Null values, unless you specify the * argument. The following statement will return the count of all rows in the Customers table, even if some of them have a Null in the Country column:

```
SELECT COUNT(*)
FROM Customers
```

The SUM() function is used to total the values of a specific field in the specified rows. To find out how many units of the product with ID = 11 (Queso Cabrales) have been sold, use the following statement:

```
USE NORTHWIND
SELECT SUM(Quantity)
FROM [Order Details]
WHERE ProductID=11
```

The SQL statement that returns the total revenue generated by a single product is a bit more complicated. This time we must add the products of quantities times prices, taking into consideration each invoice's discount:

```
USE NORTHWIND
SELECT SUM(Quantity * UnitPrice *(1 - Discount))
FROM [Order Details]
WHERE ProductID=11
```

You will find out that Queso Cabrales sold 706 units, which generated a total revenue of $12,901.77, as shown in Figure 4.10.

FIGURE 4.10:

Using the COUNT() function to calculate sums on numeric fields

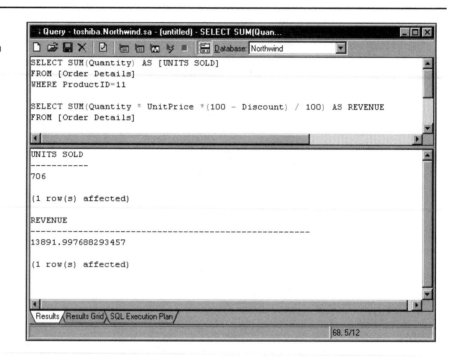

```
SELECT SUM(Quantity) AS [UNITS SOLD]
FROM [Order Details]
WHERE ProductID=11

SELECT SUM(Quantity * UnitPrice *(100 - Discount) / 100) AS REVENUE
FROM [Order Details]
```

```
UNITS SOLD
-----------
706

(1 row(s) affected)

REVENUE
-----------------------------------------------------
13891.997688293457

(1 row(s) affected)
```

Here's a SELECT statement that returns all product IDs along with the number of invoices that contain them, and the minimum, maximum, and average quantity ordered:

```
SELECT ProductID AS PRODUCT,
    COUNT(ProductID) AS [INVOICES],
    MIN(Quantity) AS [MIN],
    MAX(Quantity) AS [MAX],
    AVG(Quantity) AS [AVERAGE]
FROM [Order Details]
GROUP BY ProductID
ORDER BY ProductID
```

Grouping Rows

The aggregate functions operate on all the rows selected by the query. Sometimes you need to group the results of a query, so that you can calculate subtotals. Let's say you need not only the total revenues generated by a single product, but a list of all products and the revenues they generated. The last example in the previous section calculates the total revenue generated by a single product. If you omit the WHERE clause, it will calculate the total revenue generated by all products. It is possible to use the SUM() function to break the calculations at each new product ID as demonstrated in Lising 4.1. To do so, you must group the product IDs together with the GROUP BY clause.

LISTING 4.1   **The ProductRevenues Query**

```
USE NORTHWIND
SELECT ProductID, SUM(Quantity * UnitPrice *(1 - Discount))
      AS [Total Revenues]
FROM [Order Details]
GROUP BY ProductID
ORDER BY ProductID
```

The above statement will produce an output like this one:

ProductID	Total Revenues
1	12788.10
2	16355.96
3	3044.0
4	8567.89
5	5347.20
6	7137.0
7	22044.29
8	12772.0
9	7226.5
10	20867.34
11	12901.77
12	12257.66

NOTE   You will see all 77 product IDs, but I have omitted most of them from the listing.

As you can see, the SUM() function works in tandem with the GROUP BY clause (when there is one) to produce subtotals. The GROUP BY clause is not another ordering mechanism, like the ORDER BY clause. It groups all the rows with the same values in the specified column and forces the aggregate functions to act on each group separately. SQL Server will sort the rows according to the column specified in the GROUP BY clause and start calculating the aggregate functions. Every time it runs into a new group, it prints the result and resets the aggregate function(s).

If you use the GROUP BY clause in an SQL statement, you must be aware of the following rule: *All the fields included in the SELECT list must be either part of an aggregate function or part of the GROUP BY clause.* Let's say you want to change the previous statement to display the names of the products, rather than their IDs. The following statement will display product names, instead of product IDs. Notice that the ProductName field doesn't appear as an argument to an aggregate function, so it must be part of the GROUP BY clause.

LISTING 4.2	The ProductRevenues1 Query

```
USE NORTHWIND
SELECT ProductName,
       SUM(Quantity * [Order Details].UnitPrice *
       (1 - Discount)) AS [Total Revenues]
FROM [Order Details], Products
WHERE Products.ProductID = [Order Details].ProductID
GROUP BY ProductName
ORDER BY ProductName
```

These are the first few lines of the output produced by this statement:

ProductName	Total Revenues
Alice Mutton	32698.38
Aniseed Syrup	3044.0
Boston Crab Meat	17910.63
Camembert Pierrot	46927.48
Carnarvon Tigers	29171.87
Chai	12788.10
Chan	16355.96
Chartreuse verte	12294.54
Chef Anton's Cajun Seasoning	8567.89
Chef Anton's Gumbo Mix	5347.20
Chocolade	1368.71
Côte de Blaye	141396.74

If you omit the GROUP BY clause, the query will return the total revenue generated by all the products in the database. If you remove the GROUP BY clause, you must also remove the ProductName field from the SELECT list, as well as the

ORDER BY clause. For more information on using aggregate functions, see the following sidebar, "How to Use Aggregate Functions."

You can also combine multiple aggregate functions in the SELECT field. The following statement will calculate the units of products sold, along with the revenue they generated and the number of invoices that contain the specific product:

```
SELECT ProductID AS PRODUCT,
    COUNT(ProductID) AS [INVOICES],
    SUM(Quantity) AS [UNITS SOLD],
    SUM(Quantity * UnitPrice *(1 - Discount)) AS REVENUE
FROM [Order Details]
GROUP BY ProductID
ORDER BY ProductID
```

The COUNT() function counts how many times each product ID appears in the Order Details table. This value is the number of invoices that contain a line with the specific product. The following SUM() functions calculate the total number of items sold and the total revenue they generated. The SQL statement and the output it generated in the Query Analyzer are shown in Figure 4.11.

FIGURE 4.11:

Combining multiple aggregate functions in the same SELECT list

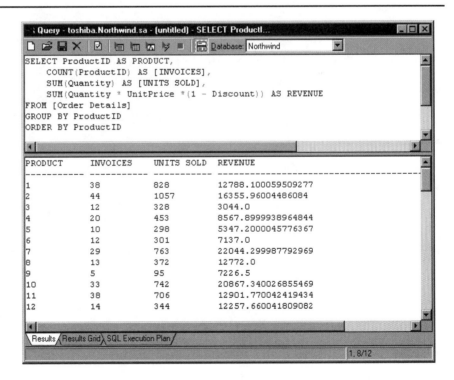

How to Use Aggregate Functions

Aggregate functions can be used only in the list of fields following a SELECT statement, or in a HAVING clause (this clause is discussed later in this chapter). They can't be used in a FROM or a WHERE clause. Moreover, if a SELECT list includes an aggregate function, then you can't include other fields in the same list, unless they are part of an aggregate function, or they are part of a GROUP BY clause. The statement:

```
SELECT ProductID,
    SUM(Quantity * UnitPrice *(1-Discount)
    AS REVENUE
FROM [Order Details]
WHERE ProductID=11
```

will not display the product ID along with the revenues generated by the specified product. Instead, it will generate the following error message:

```
Column 'Order Details.ProductID' is invalid in the select list
because it is not contained in an aggregate function and there is
no GROUP BY clause.
```

If you attempt to execute the same statement as an Access query, the error message will be:

```
You tried to execute a query that doesn't include the specified
expression 'ProductID' as part of an aggregate function.
```

To avoid this error message and display both the product ID and the revenues it generated, use the GROUP BY clause, as in the following statement. It doesn't make much sense to group a single product, but it will do the trick and you'll get the desired output.

```
SELECT ProductID,
    SUM(Quantity * UnitPrice *(1 - Discount)
    AS REVENUE
FROM [Order Details]
WHERE ProductID=11
GROUP BY ProductID
```

The following SELECT statement returns all product IDs along with the number of invoices that contain them, and the minimum, maximum, and average quantity ordered:

```
SELECT ProductID AS PRODUCT,
    COUNT(ProductID) AS [INVOICES],
    MIN(Quantity) AS [MIN],
```

```
      MAX(Quantity) AS [MAX],
      AVG(Quantity) AS [AVERAGE]
  FROM [Order Details]
  GROUP BY ProductID
  ORDER BY ProductID
```

Limiting Groups with HAVING

The HAVING clause limits the groups that will appear in the cursor. In a way, it is similar to the WHERE clause, which limits the number of rows that will appear in the result cursor. However, the HAVING clause can only be used in a GROUP BY clause, and any fields used in the HAVING clause must also appear in the GROUP BY list, or as arguments in an aggregate function.

The following statement will return the IDs of the products whose sales exceed 1,000 units:

```
USE NORTHWIND
SELECT ProductID, SUM(Quantity)
FROM [Order Details]
GROUP BY ProductID
HAVING SUM(Quantity)>1000
```

If you want to see product names instead of IDs, you must add a slightly longer statement that includes the Products table and maps them to the ProductIDs in the Order Details table with a WHERE clause:

```
USE NORTHWIND
SELECT Products.ProductName, [Order Details].ProductID,
       SUM(Quantity) AS [Items Sold]
FROM Products, [Order Details]
WHERE [Order Details].ProductID = Products.ProductID
GROUP BY [Order Details].ProductID, Products.ProductName
HAVING SUM(Quantity)>1000
ORDER BY Products.ProductName
```

Use the WHERE clause to include additional restrictions. To retrieve all the "expensive" products with large sales volume, replace the WHERE clause in the last example with the following one:

```
WHERE [Order Details].ProductID = Products.ProductID AND
      Products.UnitPrice >= 50
```

(We consider products that cost $50 or more to be expensive.) A more reasonable method to isolate the expensive products would be to calculate the average price and then use it to select products whose regular price exceeds the average product price. We'll come back to this example in the next section of the chapter.

IN and NOT IN Keywords

The IN and NOT IN keywords are used in a WHERE clause to specify a list of values that a column must match (or not match). They are more of a shorthand notation for multiple OR operators. The following is a simple statement that retrieves the names of the customers in Germany, Austria, and Italy (16 rows in all):

```
USE NORTHWIND
SELECT CompanyName
FROM Customers
WHERE Country='Germany' OR
      Country='Austria' OR
      Country='Italy'
```

This statement is verbose as is. Imagine if we wanted to select orders that contained one of many products, or customers from all European countries. The same statement could be rewritten with the help of the IN keyword as follows:

```
USE NORTHWIND
SELECT CompanyName
FROM Customers
WHERE Country IN ('Germany', 'Austria', 'Italy')
```

The second statement is shorter, and therefore easier to read and edit.

Subqueries

The IN and NOT IN keywords can also be used with subqueries. A subquery is a regular query whose result cursor is used as part of another query. Let's say you want to find the products that have never been ordered by Austrians. The first step is to create a list of products that have been ordered by companies in Austria. Here's the statement that returns the IDs of these products:

```
USE NORTHWIND
SELECT DISTINCT ProductID
FROM [Order Details], Customers, Orders
WHERE [Order Details].OrderID = Orders.OrderID AND
      Orders.CustomerID = Customers.CustomerID AND
      Customers.Country = "Austria"
```

This statement returns a list of product IDs that have been sold to companies in Austria. We want the product IDs that do not appear in this list, and we can get these rows with another statement that uses the NOT IN operator to locate IDs that do not belong to the list returned by the above query. This query will become a subquery for the following statement:

LISTING 4.3   **The SalesOutsideAustria query**

```
USE NORTHWIND
SELECT ProductID, ProductName
FROM Products
WHERE ProductID NOT IN
    (SELECT DISTINCT ProductID
     FROM [Order Details], Customers, Orders
     WHERE [Order Details].OrderID = Orders.OrderID AND
           Orders.CustomerID = Customers.CustomerID AND
           Customers.Country = "Austria")
```

The entire SQL statement that retrieves the products sold in Austria was enclosed into a pair of parentheses and became the list for the NOT IN operator.

You may think there's a simpler method. If you change the equals sign in the subquery to not equals, you will get the products that have never been sold to Austria. If you change

```
Customers.Country = "Austria"
```

to

```
Customers.Country <> "Austria"
```

you will get the products that have been sold everywhere but Austria. This is a different set than the set of products not sold in Austria. Chances are that every single product in the database has been sold to at least another country, regardless of whether it's been sold to an Austrian customer or not.

Here's another example that uses subqueries. This time we'll construct three lists. One with countries that are unique to customers (countries we sell to, but never buy from), another one with countries that are unique to suppliers (customers that we buy from but never sell to), and a third list with countries that are common to both customers and suppliers (countries we buy from and sell to). The results of the three queries are shown in Table 4.5. The blank cells are not part of the cursor; I left them blank to simplify comparisons between rows.

TABLE 4.5: Countries Unique to the Customers and Suppliers Tables

Unique Customer Countries	Unique Supplier Countries	Common Customer/ Supplier Countries
Argentina		
	Australia	
Austria		
Belgium		
		Brazil
		Canada
		Denmark
		Finland
		France
		Germany
Ireland		
		Italy
	Japan	
Mexico		
	Netherlands	
		Norway
Poland		
Portugal		
	Singapore	
		Spain
		Sweden
Switzerland		
		UK
		USA
Venezuela		

The columns of Table 4.5 were filled with three separate SQL statements, which are quite similar. The first two queries that display unique countries use a subquery to locate the countries that appear in the other table and then exclude them from the final cursor. The third query, which generates the list of common countries, uses a subquery to locate customers in the Suppliers table and then uses them to select the same countries in the Customers table. Here are the three SQL statements:

Unique Customer Countries:

```
SELECT DISTINCT Country FROM Customers
WHERE Country NOT IN (SELECT Country FROM Suppliers)
```

Unique Supplier Countries:

```
SELECT DISTINCT Country FROM Suppliers
WHERE Country NOT IN (SELECT Country FROM Customers)
```

Common Customer/Supplier Countries:

```
SELECT DISTINCT Country FROM Customers
WHERE Country IN (SELECT Country FROM Suppliers)
```

The following statement is another example of the HAVING clause. This statement retrieves the total items sold of the products that are more expensive than the average price. This statement uses a subquery in the HAVING clause to calculate the average price and limit the qualifying groups to those that contain expensive products:

LISTING 4.4   **The ProductsAboveAverage query**

```
USE NORTHWIND
SELECT Products.ProductName, Products.UnitPrice,
       SUM(Quantity) AS [Items Sold]
FROM Products, [Order Details]
WHERE [Order Details].ProductID = Products.ProductID
GROUP BY [Order Details].ProductID, Products.UnitPrice, Products.Pro-
ductName
HAVING Products.UnitPrice >
            (SELECT AVG(Products.UnitPrice) FROM Products)
ORDER BY Products.ProductName
```

The output of the ProductsAboveAverage query is shown in Figure 4.12.

FIGURE 4.12:

Sales for products with prices above average

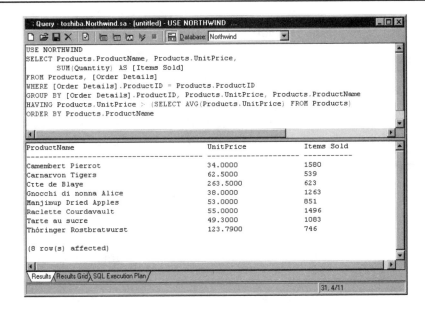

The BETWEEN Keyword

The BETWEEN keyword lets you specify a range of values and limit the selection to the rows that have a specific column in this range. The BETWEEN keyword is a shorthand notation for an expression like

```
column >= minValue AND column <= maValue
```

To retrieve the orders placed in the first quarter of 1997, use the following statement:

```
USE Northwind
SELECT OrderID, OrderDate, CompanyName
FROM Orders, Customers
WHERE Orders.CustomerID = Customers.CustomerID AND
      (OrderDate BETWEEN '1/1/1997' AND '3/31/1997')
```

The list of orders includes the ones placed on the first and last date of the specified interval.

Access queries that involve dates expect that date values are delimited by with the # sign. The equivalent Access query should be written as

```
USE Northwind
SELECT OrderID, OrderDate, CompanyName
FROM Orders, Customers
WHERE Orders.CustomerID = Customers.CustomerID AND
      (OrderDate BETWEEN #1/1/1997# AND #3/31/1997#)
```

You can use the BETWEEN operator to specify a range of numeric values (like prices) and string (from A through E, for example). The statement

```
USE Northwind
SELECT CompanyName
FROM Customers
WHERE CompanyName BETWEEN 'A' AND 'E'
```

will retrieve all customers with a company name that begins with A, B, C, or D and a company named E (if such a company exists). A company name like Eastern Connection is alphabetically larger than E and it will not be included in the cursor. To include companies whose name starts with E use a statement like

```
USE Northwind
SELECT CompanyName
FROM Customers
WHERE CompanyName BETWEEN 'A' AND 'EZZZ'
```

The last statement can be rewritten with the LIKE operator:

```
SELECT CompanyName
FROM Customers
WHERE CompanyName LIKE '[A-E]%'
```

Examples

This is a good point to present a few practical SQL statements that combine several of the keywords discussed so far. The following examples are useful to people who maintain databases and are responsible for the integrity of their data.

Specifying constraints during the design of the database is never adequate. Bad data will inevitably creep into the database. If you're in charge of the database, you must search for bad data from time to time to catch mistakes early enough so that you can fix them. For example, a program that imports titles from text files into the Biblio database might assign a few hundred authors to a given title, or assign the same author to every book that doesn't have an author. You can retrieve the titles with more than three authors, or the titles of the most productive authors. If you are familiar with the information stored in the database, you will be able to spot many common mistakes. An author with two dozen or more titles isn't just another name to a bookseller. Likewise, a large number of titles with more than half a dozen authors is a good indication that the data-entry mechanism may not be working perfectly.

Books with Multiple Authors

This example uses the Biblio database, and it's an Access query. The exact same SQL statement will work with the Biblio database on the SQL server, provided you have ported the database, as discussed in Chapter 2, "Basic Concepts of Relational Databases." We are going to locate books with multiple authors using the COUNT() function to count the number of authors for each book. How do you convert the English statement "for each book" into an SQL statement? Simply, by grouping the results according to ISBNs (you can't use titles, because there could be multiple books with the same title). Since you don't care about the author names, just their count, you are not going to use the Authors table. The author count can be extracted from the Title Author table.

Let's start with the SELECT statement:

```
SELECT Titles.Title, COUNT([Title Author].Au_ID
FROM [Title Author], Titles
WHERE Titles.ISBN = [Title Author].ISBN
```

This statement can't be executed, as the first two fields in the SELECT list do not appear in an aggregate function or a GROUP clause. To make a valid SQL statement, we must add a GROUP BY clause, as shown here:

LISTING 4.5   The MultipleAuthors Query

```
SELECT Titles.Title, Count([Title Author].Au_ID)
FROM [Title Author], Titles
WHERE Titles.ISBN=[Title Author].[ISBN]
GROUP BY Titles.Title, [Title Author].ISBN
```

If you execute this query against the Biblio database, you'll get the list of titles in the Titles table along with the number of authors per book, as shown in Figure 4.13.

To display the titles with multiple authors, append the following HAVING clause to the previous statement:

```
HAVING COUNT([Title Author].ISBN) > 1
```

FIGURE 4.13:

The output of the MultipleAuthors query

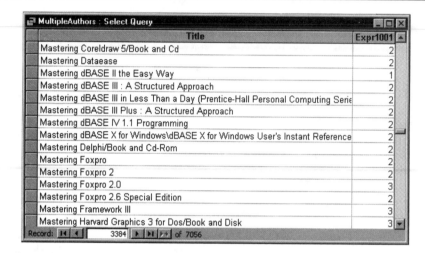

Authors with Multiple Books

The next example is not too different from the previous one. This time we'll locate the authors who have written more than one book. We want to display author names and the number of books they have authored (or co-authored). We are not interested in the actual titles they have written, so we are not going to use the Titles table in our query. The SELECT statement includes a field name and a count:

```
SELECT Authors.Author, Count([Title Author].ISBN) AS Books
FROM [Title Author], Authors
```

The rows of the two tables must have a matching field, which is the book's ISBN. In addition, the Authors.Author field must appear in a GROUP BY clause. Here's the complete SQL statement:

LISTING 4.6   **The BooksByAuthor Query**

```
SELECT Authors.Author, Count([Title Author].ISBN) AS Books
FROM [Title Author], Authors
WHERE Authors.Au_ID=[Title Author].[Au_ID]
GROUP BY Authors.Author
```

Again, if you want to limit the authors displayed to those who have authored more than a single book, use a HAVING clause:

```
HAVING COUNT([Title Author].ISBN) > 1
```

Customers, Orders, Details

The last example of this section involves four of the tables in the Northwind database. We are going to write a statement that retrieves all customers, their orders, and each order's details in a single report. The desired output is shown next. Notice that I have abbreviated customer and product names, so that all the information fits on a single line on the page. The actual cursor contains many more lines than the ones shown here:

Company	OrderID	Product	Price	Qty	Disc	ExtPrice
Alfreds	10643	Rössle	45.60	15	25	513.00
Alfreds	10643	Chartreuse	18.00	21	25	283.50
Alfreds	10643	Spegesild	12.00	2	25	18.00
Alfreds	10692	Vegie	43.90	20	0	878.00
Alfreds	10702	Aniseed	10.00	6	0	60.00
Alfreds	10702	Lakkalikööri	18.00	15	0	270.00
Alfreds	10835	Raclette	55.00	15	0	825.00
Alfreds	10835	Original	13.00	2	20	20.80
Alfreds	10952	Grandma's	25.00	16	5	380.00
Alfreds	10952	Rössle	45.60	2	0	91.20
Alfreds	11011	Escargots	13.25	40	5	503.50
Alfreds	11011	Flotemysost	21.50	20	0	430.00
Ana	10308	Gudbrandsdal	28.80	1	0	28.80
Ana	10308	Outback Lager	12.00	5	0	60.00
Ana	10625	Tofu	23.25	3	0	69.75
Ana	10625	Singaporean	14.00	5	0	70.00
Ana	10625	Camembert	34.00	10	0	340.00
Ana	10759	Mascarpone	32.00	10	0	320.00
Ana	10926	Queso	21.00	2	0	42.00
Ana	10926	Konbu	6.00	10	0	60.00
Ana	10926	Teatime	9.20	7	0	64.40
Ana	10926	Mozzarella	34.80	10	0	348.00

As usual, we'll start with the list of the desired columns:

```
SELECT CompanyName, Orders.OrderID, ProductName,
    [Order Details].UnitPrice AS Price,
    Quantity, Discount * 100 AS Discount,
    Quantity * (1 - Discount) *
    [Order Details].UnitPrice AS SubTotal
FROM Products, [Order Details], Customers, Orders
```

The desired fields are the company name (CompanyName), the invoice's ID (OrderID), and each invoice's details: product name, price, quantity, discount, and extended price. The extended price is a calculated field, which is computed as follows:

```
Quantity * Price * (1 - Discount)
```

Next, we must provide the restrictions to match selected fields in all four tables. If not, the Cartesian product generated by this query will be enormous. The restrictions are as follows:

- Each product ID in the Order Details table must match with a row in the Products table:

  ```
  [Order Details].ProductID = Products.ProductID
  ```

- Each order ID in the Order Details table must match with a row in the Orders table:

  ```
  [Order Details].OrderID = Orders.OrderID
  ```

- Each customer ID in the Orders table must match with a row in the Customers table:

  ```
  Orders.CustomerID = Customers.CustomerID
  ```

Finally, we must sort the rows of the cursor by CompanyName and OrderID, so that each customer's invoices appear together within the customer's section. Here's the complete SQL statement that retrieves customer, order, and detail information from the Northwind database:

LISTING 4.7   **The AllOrders query**

```
USE NORTHWIND
SELECT CompanyName, Orders.OrderID, ProductName,
    [Order Details].UnitPrice AS Price,
    Quantity, Discount * 100 AS Discount,
    Quantity * (1 - Discount) *
    [Order Details].UnitPrice AS [Ext. Price]
FROM Products, [Order Details], Customers, Orders
WHERE [Order Details].ProductID = Products.ProductID AND
    [Order Details].OrderID = Orders.OrderID AND
    Orders.CustomerID=Customers.CustomerID
ORDER BY Customers.CompanyName, Orders.OrderID
```

NOTE   You have seen SQL statements that calculate all kinds of subtotals, but how about totals? You would probably want to see the total for each invoice, customer totals, and the grand total in the report of this example. It is possible to build subtotals and grand totals, and you'll see how this is done in the section "The COMPUTE BY Statement" in Chapter 7."

Publishers, Books, Authors

Let's end this section with a similar SQL statement that retrieves all the titles in the Biblio database and orders them by publisher. Within each publisher, the books will be sorted by title and author. The desired format of the statement's output is shown next:

Company Name	Title	ISBN	Author
AK PETERS LTD	A Physical Approach. . .	1-5688101-3-X	Levitus
AK PETERS LTD	Colour Principles . . .	1-5688100-9-1	Cowan
AK PETERS LTD	Colour Principles . . .	1-5688100-9-1	Shumaker
AK PETERS LTD	Computer Facial Anim. . .	1-5688101-4-8	Parke
AK PETERS LTD	Computer Facial Anim. . .	1-5688101-4-8	Werner
AK PETERS LTD	Computer Graphics . . .	1-5688100-8-3	Brown
AK PETERS LTD	Computer Graphics . . .	1-5688100-8-3	Pressman
AK PETERS LTD	Fundamentals of . . .	1-5688100-7-5	Hampe
AK PETERS LTD	Fundamentals of . . .	1-5688100-7-5	Hoschek
AK PETERS LTD	Fundamentals of . . .	1-5688100-7-5	Lasser
AK PETERS LTD	Fundamentals of . . .	1-5688100-7-5	Schumak
AK PETERS LTD	Languages for . . .	0-8672045-0-8	Ayer
AK PETERS LTD	Languages for . . .	0-8672045-0-8	Myers
. . .			
SYBEX Inc	Microsoft Access . .	0-7821176-5-1	Getz
SYBEX Inc	Microsoft Access . .	0-7821176-5-1	Gilbert
SYBEX Inc	Microsoft Access . .	0-7821176-5-1	Litwin
SYBEX Inc	Microsoft Access . .	0-7821176-5-1	Reddick
SYBEX Inc	Microsoft Access . .	0-7821176-2-7	Getz
SYBEX Inc	Microsoft Access . .	0-7821176-2-7	Powell
SYBEX Inc	Microsoft Access . .	0-7821121-3-7	Briggs
SYBEX Inc	Microsoft Access . .	0-7821121-3-7	Powell

It would be nice to display all the authors of any given book under its title, without repeating the book's title, ISBN, and publisher. This is not possible with straight SQL, but you will find out how to format a cursor in Chapter 7, "Transact-SQL." In Chapter 10, "Shaping Your Data," you will learn how to create hierarchical recordsets, which have a tree structure.

Let's return to our example and generate the list shown above, with the statements and keywords you have learned so far. The statement should select the following fields:

```
SELECT Titles.Title, Publishers.Name, Authors.Author
FROM Titles, [Title Author], Authors, Publishers
```

This is the simpler part of the desired statement. Now you must construct the WHERE clause to relate the titles with their publishers and authors. The clause for combining titles and publishers is quite simple:

```
WHERE Titles.PubID = Publishers.PubID
```

To connect titles and authors, you must take into consideration the Title Author table, which sits between the Titles and Authors tables:

```
WHERE Titles.ISBN = [Title Author].ISBN AND
      [Title Author].Au_ID = Authors.Au_ID
```

The complete statement that combines the three restrictions is shown next. I have added an ORDER BY clause to order the titles alphabetically. The output of the AllBooks query is shown in Figure 4.14.

LISTING 4.8   The AllBooks query

```
SELECT Titles.Title, Publishers.Name, Authors.Author
FROM Titles, [Title Author], Authors, Publishers
WHERE Titles.PubID = Publishers.PubID AND
      Titles.ISBN = [Title Author].ISBN AND
      [Title Author].Au_ID = Authors.Au_ID
ORDER BY Titles.Title
```

FIGURE 4.14:

Executing the AllBooks query with SQLEXEC

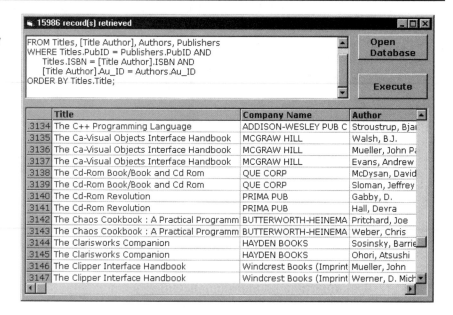

Joining Tables

The WHERE clause allows you to connect two or more tables, based on the values of two columns in the two tables. The WHERE clause, however, should be used to express constraints involving one or more tables, and not for connecting tables—although many programmers use the WHERE clause almost exclusively. The proper method of linking tables is the JOIN operation. Before we look at the JOIN operation, let's discuss the shortcomings of the WHERE clause that lead to the need for a more elaborate mechanism for connecting multiple tables.

The two columns involved in the WHERE clause are usually the primary key in one table and a foreign key in the other table. When you connect the Titles to the Publishers table, for example, you request that the Publisher table's primary key (Publishers.PubID) is equal to a foreign key in the Titles table (the Titles .PubID field):

```
WHERE Titles.PubID = Publishers.PubID
```

The columns you use to combine the two tables need not be indexed, but it helps if they are. If you omit the WHERE clause, the query will return the cross product of the rows in the two tables (that is, all possible combinations of the rows in the two tables).

Combining multiple tables with the WHERE clause, though, will not work if one the two columns contains Null values. In this example, the Publishers.PubID column can't have a Null value, but the Titles.PubID can. The titles with a Null value in the PubID column won't match with any row in the Publishers table, and they will be left out. You may not need these rows, but in most cases we want all the titles, regardless of whether they have a publisher or not. The same is true for authors. The AllBooks query retrieves all the titles with author(s) from the Biblio database. However, it will reject all the titles without author. You can verify this by looking up the title "Database Processing," which has no author. This title will not be included in the query.

Let's exercise the AllBooks query, repeated here:

```
SELECT Titles.Title, Publishers.Name, Authors.Author
FROM Titles, [Title Author], Authors, Publishers
WHERE Titles.PubID = Publishers.PubID AND
      Titles.ISBN = [Title Author].ISBN AND
      [Title Author].Au_ID = Authors.Au_ID
ORDER BY Titles.Title
```

This query returned 15,959 rows when I executed it on my system. Since there are 8,531 titles in the Biblio database, most of these titles have two or three authors. This result, however, doesn't include titles without authors. When I retrieved the titles and their authors using joins, the query returned 17,449 rows. This difference of 17,449 − 15,959 = 1,490 rows must be the number of books without author. (If you have edited the Biblio database, you will get different numbers, but you will be able to verify the difference). To verify this conclusion, we must count the number of titles without author directly from the database. To do so, we'll count the titles whose ISBN doesn't appear in the Title Author table. First, we must retrieve all the ISBN values from the Title Author table. This query is quite simple:

```
SELECT DISTINCT ISBN FROM [Title Author]
```

Then, you must retrieve all the titles whose ISBN doesn't appear in the result of the above query. Even better, you'll simply count the rows of the Titles table, whose ISBN does not belong to the first query's result:

```
SELECT COUNT(Title)
FROM Titles
WHERE Titles.ISBN NOT IN
      (SELECT DISTINCT ISBN FROM [Title Author])
```

If you execute this statement against the Biblio database (use the Access database if you haven't ported it to SQL Server), it will confirm our calculations (it will report 1,490 titles).

The question now is how we can retrieve all the titles, regardless of whether they have an author or not. The operation of combining multiple tables is known as *join*, and it can be coded with the JOIN operation. The JOIN operation was designed specifically to combine multiple tables. The WHERE clause does the trick in simple situations, but it doesn't always work, as the previous example demonstrates.

> **NOTE**   Many tables can be joined with the WHERE clause because of their nature. The Orders and Order Details tables can be joined with the WHERE clause, because we can't have an order without details (an order without details would indicate a serious flaw in the design of the database). Sometimes, programmers take this convenient circumstance for granted and abuse the WHERE clause. You should try to implement all your joins with the JOIN operation and use the WHERE clause to limit the number of qualifying rows. It's not coincidental that JOIN is an operation, while WHERE is a simple keyword.

The JOIN operation combines columns of two tables where the rows have a matching field. Its syntax is

```
FROM Table1 INNER JOIN Table2 ON Table1.col = Table2.col
```

> **NOTE**   You can ignore the INNER keyword for now; you will see shortly that there are various types of joins, and you must specify the type of join you want to perform with another keyword.

The two columns need not be matched with the equals operator, although this is the most common method of matching multiple tables. You can use any of the relational operators (>, >=, <, <=, and <>). The JOIN operator may appear only in a

SELECT statement's FROM clause, which is why I've included the FROM keyword in the statement's syntax. In addition, you can combine multiple restrictions with the logical operators. For example, you may require that a pair of columns match exactly and another pair are different:

```
FROM Table1 INNER JOIN Table2 ON Table1.col1 = Table2.col1 AND
     Table1.col2 <> Table2.col2
```

This statement retrieves all the rows whose col1 column in Table1 matches *col2* in Table2 and excludes from this set the rows whose col2 values are different.

Types of Joins

SQL supports two types of joins:

> **Inner Join**   This join returns all matching pairs of rows in the two tables and discards unmatched rows from both tables. This is the default if no join type is specified.

> **Full (or Outer) Join**   This join returns all rows normally returned by the INNER JOIN operation plus rows from either the left or right table that do not meet the join condition. A full join would return all titles with their publishers, as well as the titles without a publisher. Rows with unmatched columns in either table are set to NULL. In the titles/publishers example, titles without a publisher would appear with a Null value in the publisher's column.

Both inner and full (or outer) joins can be modified by specifying which table to be used as the basis for the join. For example, we may want to retrieve all rows of one table and the matching rows of the other table. Therefore, joins can be further classified according to the order in which they look up the tables involved in the operation:

> **Left Join**   This inner join returns all of the records from the first (left) of two tables, even if there are no matching values for records in the second (right) table.

> **Right Join**   This inner join returns all of the records from the second (right) of two tables, even if there are no matching values for records in the first (left) table.

To demonstrate the different types of joins, I have constructed a trivial database with two tables: a table with city names (Cities) and a table with country names (Countries). Each country has a unique ID, which is used by the Cities table to indicate the country to which a city belongs to. The CountryID field is a primary key in the Countries table and foreign key in the Cities table. Here's the structure of the two tables and their contents:

Cities Table

CityName	`varchar(50)`
CountryID	`int`

Countries Table

CountryName	`varchar(50)`
CountryID	`int`

Table 4.6 shows all the entries in the two tables of the database and their mapping. If a city isn't mapped to a country, then the second column has a Null value in this city's row. If a country isn't mapped to a city, then the first column has a Null value in this country's row.

TABLE 4.6: Cities and Countries in the CITIESDB Database

CityName	CountryName
NULL	Argentina
NULL	China
NULL	France
NULL	Japan
Alexandria	Egypt
Barcelona	NULL
Berlin	Germany
Cairo	Egypt
Chicago	USA
Frankfurt	Germany
Hamburg	Germany
London	UK
Madrid	NULL
Manchester	UK
New York	USA
Rome	Italy
San Francisco	USA
Venice	Italy
Zurich	NULL

As you can see, the Cities table contains cities that don't belong to any country (Barcelona, Madrid, and Zurich), and the Countries table contains countries that are not referenced by any row in the Cities table (Japan, France, Argentina, and China). Let's join the two tables using all the variations of the JOIN keyword.

INNER JOIN

This first query uses an INNER JOIN keyword, which retrieves matching rows only:

```
USE CitiesDB
SELECT Cities.CityName, Countries.CountryName
FROM Cities INNER JOIN Countries
        ON Cities.CountryID = Countries.CountryID
ORDER BY Countries.CountryName, Cities.CityName;
```

The result of the query is shown here—12 rows of cities that are mapped to a country. Cities that don't belong to any country are not included in the result.

CityName	CountryName
Alexandria	Egypt
Cairo	Egypt
Berlin	Germany
Frankfurt	Germany
Hamburg	Germany
Rome	Italy
Venice	Italy
London	UK
Manchester	UK
Chicago	USA
New York	USA
San Francisco	USA

LEFT JOIN

If you replace INNER JOIN with LEFT JOIN in the previous statement, the query will retrieve all the cities, regardless of whether they map to a country or not. If a city isn't mapped to a country, then the corresponding row in the second column will contain a Null value. This query will return 15 rows in all (the number of rows in the left table). The statement that retrieves all cities is

```
USE CitiesDB
SELECT Cities.CityName, Countries.CountryName
FROM Cities LEFT JOIN Countries
     ON Cities.CountryID = Countries.CountryID
ORDER BY Countries.CountryName, Cities.CityName
```

Here's the result of the query:

```
CityName              CountryName
----------------
Barcelona             NULL
Madrid                NULL
Zurich                NULL
Alexandria            Egypt
Cairo                 Egypt
Berlin                Germany
Frankfurt             Germany
Hamburg               Germany
Rome                  Italy
Venice                Italy
London                UK
Manchester            UK
Chicago               USA
New York              USA
San Francisco         USA
```

RIGHT JOIN

If you use RIGHT JOIN, the query will retrieve all the countries, regardless of whether they map to a city or not. If a country isn't mapped to a city, then the corresponding row in the second column will contain a Null value. This query will return 16 rows in all (the number of rows in the right table). The statement that retrieves all countries is

```
USE CitiesDB
SELECT Cities.CityName, Countries.CountryName
FROM Cities RIGHT JOIN Countries
     ON Cities.CountryID = Countries.CountryID
ORDER BY Countries.CountryName, Cities.CityName
```

Here's the result of the query:

```
CityName              CountryName
----------------
NULL                  Argentina
NULL                  China
Alexandria            Egypt
Cairo                 Egypt
NULL                  France
Berlin                Germany
Frankfurt             Germany
Hamburg               Germany
```

```
Rome                Italy
Venice              Italy
NULL                Japan
London              UK
Manchester          UK
Chicago             USA
New York            USA
San Francisco       USA
```

FULL JOIN

The FULL JOIN keyword returns all the rows of both tables. All cities have a country value (even if it's a Null value), and every country has a city value (even if it's a Null value). Country names are repeated as needed. The result doesn't contain duplicate city names, because a city can't belong to more than one country.

```
USE CitiesDB
SELECT Cities.CityName, Countries.CountryName
FROM Cities FULL JOIN Countries
    ON Cities.CountryID = Countries.CountryID
ORDER BY Cities.CityName, Countries.CountryName
```

The result of this query contains 19 rows, shown here:

```
CityName            CountryName
------------------
NULL                Argentina
NULL                China
NULL                France
NULL                Japan
Alexandria          Egypt
Barcelona           NULL
Berlin              Germany
Cairo               Egypt
Chicago             USA
Frankfurt           Germany
Hamburg             Germany
London              UK
Madrid              NULL
Manchester          UK
New York            USA
Rome                Italy
San Francisco       USA
Venice              Italy
Zurich              NULL
```

The FULL JOIN keyword is not supported by Access, and you can't test the last SQL statement without SQL Server (or any other DBMS that supports full joins). Indeed, full joins are not used frequently, and they may generate quite large cursors.

I hope this simple database has helped you clarify the concept of inner and outer joins. Now we can use these keywords to write a few advanced queries that combine multiple tables with the JOIN operator.

Joining Titles and Authors

Let's return to the AllBooks example (Listing 4.8) and implement it with a JOIN. Since you want all the titles along with their authors, you must use two left joins, one after the other. First, you must join the Title Author and Authors tables with a LEFT JOIN operation. The result will be a virtual table with all the ISBNs on the left and the corresponding author names on the right. Even ISBNs that appear in the Title Author table but have no matching authors in the Authors table will appear in the result. This virtual table must then be joined with the Titles table, with another LEFT JOIN operation. The Titles table will be on the left side of the first join, so that the titles with no entry in the Title Author table will be included in the result. Listing 4.9 shows the query that retrieves all titles and their authors with the JOIN operation:

LISTING 4:9: The TitlesAuthors query

```
SELECT Titles.Title, Authors.Author
FROM Titles
    LEFT JOIN ([Title Author]
        LEFT JOIN Authors
        ON [Title Author].Au_ID = Authors.Au_ID)
            ON Titles.ISBN = [Title Author].ISBN
ORDER BY Titles.Title;
```

This statement is processed as follows: The SQL Server starts by evaluating the innermost join, which combines the rows of the Title Author and Authors tables. This join selects all the rows of the Title Author table and the columns of the Authors table that have the same Au_ID value. If a row in the left table has no matching row in the right table, it is included in the query's result anyway. If a row in the right table has no matching row in the left table, then it is ignored. (This would be an author name that refers to a title that was removed from the Titles table, but the corresponding entries in the Title Author and Authors tables were not removed.) Here's the first join that will be executed by the DBMS:

```
([Title Author] LEFT JOIN Authors
ON [Title Author].Au_ID = Authors.Au_ID)
```

The result of this join is another table—it exists only during the execution of the query. Let's call this table ISBNAuthors. If you replace the expression of the inner-most join with ISBNAuthors, the original query becomes

```
SELECT Titles.Title, Authors.Author
FROM Titles
    LEFT JOIN ISBNAuthors
            ON Titles.ISBN = [Title Author].ISBN
ORDER BY Titles.Title;
```

After the creation of the innermost join, the DBMS will execute another join. This time it will join the Titles table with the result of the previous join, and it will combine the rows of the Titles table with the rows returned by the join already executed by matching their ISBNs. The rows retrieved by the TitlesAuthors query are shown in Figure 4.15.

FIGURE 4.15:

Displaying all titles in the Biblio database and their authors

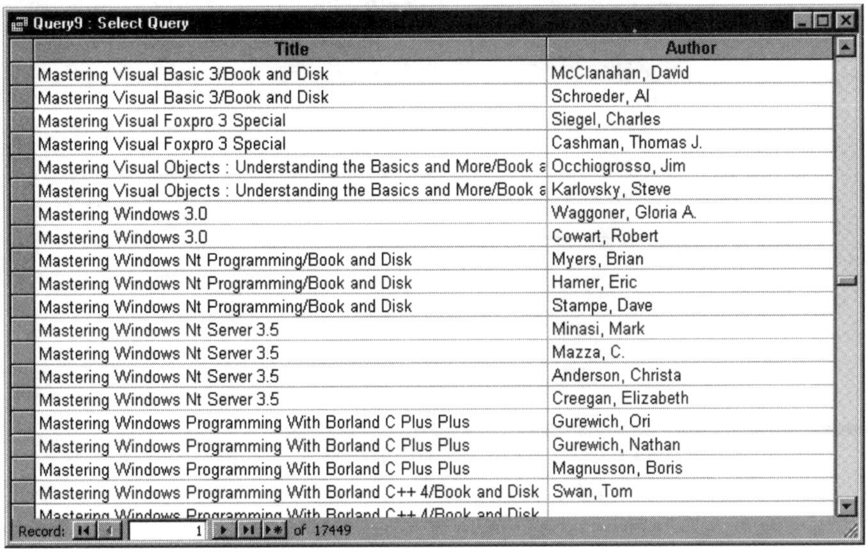

Title	Author
Mastering Visual Basic 3/Book and Disk	McClanahan, David
Mastering Visual Basic 3/Book and Disk	Schroeder, Al
Mastering Visual Foxpro 3 Special	Siegel, Charles
Mastering Visual Foxpro 3 Special	Cashman, Thomas J.
Mastering Visual Objects : Understanding the Basics and More/Book a	Occhiogrosso, Jim
Mastering Visual Objects : Understanding the Basics and More/Book a	Karlovsky, Steve
Mastering Windows 3.0	Waggoner, Gloria A.
Mastering Windows 3.0	Cowart, Robert
Mastering Windows Nt Programming/Book and Disk	Myers, Brian
Mastering Windows Nt Programming/Book and Disk	Hamer, Eric
Mastering Windows Nt Programming/Book and Disk	Stampe, Dave
Mastering Windows Nt Server 3.5	Minasi, Mark
Mastering Windows Nt Server 3.5	Mazza, C.
Mastering Windows Nt Server 3.5	Anderson, Christa
Mastering Windows Nt Server 3.5	Creegan, Elizabeth
Mastering Windows Programming With Borland C Plus Plus	Gurewich, Ori
Mastering Windows Programming With Borland C Plus Plus	Gurewich, Nathan
Mastering Windows Programming With Borland C Plus Plus	Magnusson, Boris
Mastering Windows Programming With Borland C++ 4/Book and Disk	Swan, Tom
Mastering Windows Programming With Borland C++ 4/Book and Disk	

Record: 1 of 17449

Publishers, Books, Authors

The next example (Listing 4.10) extends the previous one by including the Publishers table. This time we'll add a third join to connect titles and publishers. This intermediate table will then become the first (left) table of another join that returns titles, publishers, and authors.

LISTING 4.10   The AllTitlesJOIN query

```
SELECT Publishers.[Company Name], Titles.Title, Authors.Author
FROM (Titles LEFT JOIN Publishers
      ON Titles.PubID = Publishers.PubID)
      LEFT JOIN ([Title Author] LEFT JOIN Authors
          ON [Title Author].Au_ID = Authors.Au_ID) ON
      Titles.ISBN = [Title Author].ISBN
ORDER BY Publishers.[Company Name], Titles.Title
```

Customers, Orders, Details

This example will retrieve sales-related information from the Northwind database. We want to retrieve all customers, invoices, and invoice details in a query with the following structure:

CustomerName	OrderID	ProdName	QTY	Price	Disc	SubTot
Alfreds Futt.	10643	Rössle	15	45.60	0.25	513.0
Alfreds Futt.	10643	Chartreuse	21	18.00	0.25	283.5
Alfreds Futt.	10643	Spegesild	2	12.00	0.25	18.0
Alfreds Futt.	10692	Vegie	20	43.90	0.0	878.0
Alfreds Futt.	10702	Aniseed	6	10.00	0.0	60.0
Alfreds Futt.	10702	Lakkalik	15	18.00	0.0	270.0

NOTE   I have shortened the names of the customers and products so that I could fit the report on the printed page. You can execute the query in the Query Analyzer to see the actual rows returned.

Let's build the SELECT statement that retrieves this information. First, we must select all customers. Within each customer's section, we must list all the orders (their ID and the date they were placed). Finally, within each order's section, we want to list all the details of the specific order. The fields will come from the Customers, Orders, and Order Details tables. Notice that the Order Details table contains product IDs and not actual product names, so we must include the Products table. For each product ID in the Order Details table, we must retrieve the product name from the matching row in the Products table.

Let's start with the Customers table and specify the CompanyName as the first field in the SELECT list. The Customers table must be joined with the Orders table on the CustomerID field. This join will repeat each customer name as many times as there are orders for that customer. The output of the first join will begin something like:

```
Alfreds Futterkiste                    10643
Alfreds Futterkiste                    10692
```

```
Alfreds Futterkiste                        10702
Alfreds Futterkiste                        10835
Alfreds Futterkiste                        10952
Alfreds Futterkiste                        11011
Ana Trujillo Emparedados y helados         10308
Ana Trujillo Emparedados y helados         10625
Ana Trujillo Emparedados y helados         10759
Ana Trujillo Emparedados y helados         10926
```

(The first customer has six orders, the second customer has three orders and so on.) Here's the join that produced the above list:

```
SELECT Customers.CompanyName, Orders.OrderID
FROM    Customers INNER JOIN Orders
        ON Customers.CustomerID = Orders.CustomerID
ORDER BY Customers.CompanyName
```

Now we must bring in the Order Details table and join it with the Orders table on the OrderID field. If the first order has three items, the line

```
Alfreds Futterkiste 10643
```

must be repeated three times. Let's expand the last statement to include the Order Details table. For the purposes of this example, we'll use the UnitPrice, Quantity, and Discount columns of the Order Details table:

```
SELECT Customers.CompanyName, Orders.OrderID,
       [Order Details].ProductID, [Order Details].Quantity,
       [Order Details].UnitPrice
FROM    (Customers INNER JOIN Orders
       ON Customers.CustomerID = Orders.CustomerID)
          INNER JOIN [Order Details]
          ON [Order Details].OrderID=Orders.OrderID
ORDER BY Customers.CompanyName
```

Notice the placement of the parentheses in the FROM clause of the statement. They are not required, but I wanted to emphasize the fact that the first join (the one we designed in the first step) is, in effect, another table. It's called a *virtual table*, because it may not exist in the database, but SQL server must create it in order to join its rows with the Order Details table.

We're almost there. We must now match the Order Details.ProductID field to the ProductID field of the Products table, so that instead of a Product ID, we'll display the actual product name. Here's the final SQL statement:

```
SELECT Customers.CompanyName, Orders.OrderID,
       Products.ProductName, [Order Details].Quantity,
       [Order Details].UnitPrice, [Order Details].Discount,
```

```
            [Order Details].Quantity * [Order Details].UnitPrice *
                (1 - [Order Details].Discount) AS SubTotal
FROM    Customers INNER JOIN Orders
        ON Customers.CustomerID = Orders.CustomerID
        INNER JOIN [Order Details] ON
            [Order Details].OrderID = Orders.OrderID
        INNER JOIN Products ON
            [Order Details].ProductID = Products.ProductID
ORDER BY Customers.CompanyName
```

I have dropped the ProductID field from the SELECT list and replaced it with
the Products.ProductName field. In addition, I have added a calculated field,
which is the line's subtotal (quantity * (price - discount)).

Here's an SQL statement that retrieves the same information, but it calculates
running totals as well.

```
SELECT Customers.CompanyName, Orders.OrderID,
        Products.ProductName,
        [Order Details].Quantity, [Order Details].UnitPrice,
        [Order Details].Quantity * (1 - Discount) *
            [Order Details].UnitPrice AS SubTotal
FROM Customers, Orders, [Order Details], Products
WHERE Orders.CustomerID = Customers.CustomerID AND
        [Order Details].OrderID = Orders.OrderID AND
        [Order Details].ProductID = Products.ProductID
ORDER BY Customers.CompanyName, Orders.OrderID
COMPUTE SUM(Quantity * (1 - Discount) * [Order Details].UnitPrice)
            BY Customers.CompanyName, Orders.OrderID
COMPUTE SUM(Quantity * (1 - Discount) * [Order Details].UnitPrice)
            BY Customers.CompanyName
```

NOTE   The COMPUTE statement is recognized by SQL Server only and is discussed in the
section "The COMPUTE BY Clause" in Chapter 7. You can't execute this statement against the Access Northwind database.

The Query Engine of SQL Server (or Access) is optimized for joins, which are
the most common operation you will be performing against your databases. To
help the Query Engine, you should consider indexing the columns involved in
the most common queries.

Action Queries

In addition to selection queries, SQL supports a few statements for action queries. We use action queries to manipulate the contents of the database. You can perform three types of actions: insertions, updates, and deletions. SQL provides three action statements, one for each action: the INSERT, UPDATE, and DELETE statements. Their syntax is simple, so you don't have to learn any additional keywords. As you can guess, actions are not performed unconditionally on all rows of a table. The rows that will be affected by an action query are specified with the appropriate WHERE clause. Most of the information covered in the previous sections applies to action queries as well.

A substantial difference between selection and action queries is that action queries do not return any rows. When you execute an action query with the Query Analyzer, you will see the number of rows affected in the Results pane. Access takes a different approach. It executes the action query, but doesn't immediately update the table. A message box first informs the user how many rows will be changed by the query. At this point you can commit the changes or cancel the action query.

The SQLEXEC application doesn't report the number of rows that will be changed, but it displays the number of rows that were affected by the action query on its title bar.

The DELETE Statement

Let's start with the simplest action query, which is the deletion of one or more rows of a table. The DELETE statement deletes entire rows, and you need not specify a field list. However, you must specify the rows to be deleted. The syntax of the DELETE statement is

```
DELETE FROM table_name
WHERE condition
```

where *table_name* is the name of the table from which the qualifying rows will be removed. Only the rows that meet the *condition* specified by the WHERE clause will be deleted. The statement

```
DELETE FROM Customers
WHERE Country = 'Germany'
```

will remove all German customers from the Northwind database. The WHERE clause of the DELETE statement (as well as of the other action statements) can get as complicated as you can make it. You can also omit it entirely, in which case all the rows will be removed from the table. In this case, you don't even have to use the FROM keyword. Just specify the table's name with a statement like the following one:

```
DELETE Categories
```

This statement should delete all the rows of the Categories table. However, the DELETE statement is subject to the referential integrity rules incorporated into the database. The rows of the Categories table are referenced by the rows of the Products table, and the DBMS (Access or SQL Server) will refuse to delete them. If a category is not referenced by any product, then it will be deleted.

An unconditional statement will delete all rows of a table that are not referenced as foreign keys in another table. If you're using SQL Server, there's a more elegant alternative, namely the TRUNCATE TABLE statement, which removes the same rows, only faster. To remove all categories that are not used as foreign keys in the Products table, use this statement:

```
TRUNCATE TABLE Categories
```

The INSERT Statement

The INSERT statement inserts a new row into a table. The complete syntax of the INSERT statement is

```
INSERT table_name (column list) VALUES (value list)
```

This statement will add a row to the table *table name* and assign the specified values to the row's fields. The two lists must be enclosed in parentheses, as shown above. The first value in the *value list* is assigned to the first column in the *column list*, the second value in the *value list* is assigned to the second column in the *column list* and so on. Obviously, the two lists must match each other: They must have the same number of items, and the values' types must match the types of the columns. Identity fields cannot be specified in the *column list*. The DBMS will assign values to these fields automatically.

To insert a new customer in the Customers table, use the following statement:

```
INSERT (CustomerID, CompanyName, ContactName)
    VALUES ("SYBEX", "Sybex, Inc.", "Tobias Smythe")
```

This statement doesn't assign values to all the columns of the new row. Only three of them will have a value. You can always update a table row with the UPDATE statement, which is discussed next. The columns that are not listed in the *column list* will take their default value (if they have one) or the Null value. If a column does not have a default value and it's not nullable, then you must explicitly assign a value to it.

If you are going to supply a value for each field in the new row, then you can omit the *column list*, as long as you supply them in the proper order.

Another mechanism for passing column values to the INSERT statement is to SELECT them from another table. Let's say you want to insert the contacts from the Customers table into the PhoneBook table. The first step is to retrieve the required information from the Customers table:

```
SELECT ContactName, Phone, Fax
FROM Customers
```

This list can then become the *value list* of an INSERT statement:

```
INSERT PhoneBook
SELECT ContactName, Phone, Fax
FROM Customers
```

This form of the INSERT statement allows you to insert multiple rows at once.

The UPDATE Statement

The last action statement is the UPDATE statement, which can update columns in selected rows. The UPDATE statement can affect multiple rows, but it still acts on a single table, and its syntax is:

```
UPDATE table_name
    SET column1 = value1, column2 = value2, . . .
WHERE condition
```

The following statement will change the Country column of the rows in the Customers table that correspond to German customers:

```
UPDATE Customers
    SET Country = 'Germany'
WHERE Country = 'W. Germany' OR Country = 'E. Germany'
```

Here's a more complicated statement that updates the price of specific products. Let's say a supplier has increased the discount by 5% and you want to pass half of the savings to your customers. The following statement will adjust the prices of the products you buy from the supplier with ID=4 by 2.5%. Here's the UPDATE statement (the result of the execution of the statement is shown in Figure 4.16):

```
UPDATE Products
SET UnitPrice = UnitPrice * 0.025
WHERE SupplierID = 3
```

FIGURE 4.16:

When updating rows through the Query Analyzer, the number of updated rows is displayed in the Results pane.

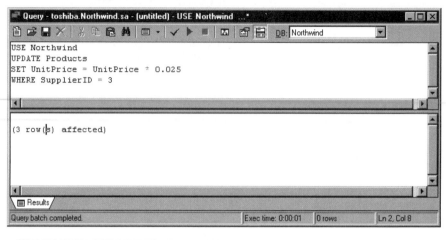

Summary

The SQL statements we have explored so far are not specific to SQL Server or Access. They are supported by both DBMSs, and all of the examples in this chapter will work with both SQL Server 7.0 and Access 97/2000. We'll come back to SQL in Chapter 7, where we'll explore SQL Server's extensions to standard SQL. In that chapter, you'll learn SQL Server's built-in programming language, Transact-SQL (T-SQL), which combines the power of a nonprocedural language, SQL, with the flexibility of traditional programming languages.

In the next two chapters, however, we'll switch to VB. It's time to put together all the information presented so far to build some database applications. Chapter 5, "A First Look at ADO," and Chapter 6, "Programming with ADO," discuss the basics of data access with the ADO component, and you'll build your first database applications.

CHAPTER
FIVE

5

A First Look at ADO

- How ADO works

- ADO's main objects

- The Connection object

- The Recordset object

- The Command object

- Basic Recordset operations

- Updating databases

It's time now to get into some real database programming. In this chapter, we'll explore the ADO component (Active Data Objects), which is Microsoft's standard for data access. As you recall from Chapter 1, the ADO component can access a variety of data sources, including Access and SQL Server databases, as well non-Microsoft databases such as Oracle and Sybase. Most important, the ADO component will eventually replace DAO (Data Access Objects) and RDO (Remote Data Objects), which are older data access technologies. If you start developing new database applications today, use the ADO component to be sure it will work with tomorrow's operating systems and databases.

NOTE   ADO belongs to the core services of Windows 2000, and you need not redistribute it with your applications. This means that ADO is here to stay, and it will be substantially enhanced in the future.

While most VB programmers use the DAO component, and there's an enormous base of applications that work with this component, this book isn't about DAO. DAO is an older technology, designed and optimized for Jet Engine (Access) databases and, as such, it's not the most efficient tool for programming SQL Server. I will stress the differences between DAO and ADO whenever I think this will help programmers experienced with DAO, but I will not show how to program with DAO. If you're already familiar with DAO, learning ADO will be a breeze. If you're new to database programming, there's no reason to learn an old data access technology. ADO is more elegant, can access more databases, and it's the tool Microsoft suggests for data access today.

Another reason for focusing on ADO is that this component is an ideal companion for both SQL Server and Access databases. In later chapters, you will learn how to make the best of SQL Server's features, like writing and calling T-SQL stored procedures, triggers, and other advanced features. Although nothing has been officially announced about the next version of Visual Studio, SQL Server is expected to be a major part of it.

NOTE   I don't start this chapter with a discussion of the data-bound controls. These controls will come in handy later, but they are deceivingly simple. Learning how to write simple applications with data-bound controls isn't going to help you develop a solid understanding of the principles of database programming. If you familiarize yourself with the ADO objects early enough, you will understand how the data-bound controls work and when to use them.

How Does ADO Work?

ADO is a component for accessing databases. It exposes a few very flexible objects, which expose their own properties, methods, and recognize events. The structure of the ADO object model reflects the operations you perform on a database, and you can even guess these objects and their names once you understand what it takes to access and update a database. In this chapter we'll explore the objects of the ADO object model and the role of each object in establishing a connection to a database and manipulating its tables.

To use the ADO objects in an application, you must first add a reference to the ADO component to your application. Start a Standard EXE project and then select Project ➤ References. In the References window, locate Microsoft ActiveX Data Objects 2.*x* Library and check the box in front of it. The ADODB component will be added to your project, and you can now declare variables to represent its components.

NOTE 2.*x* is the version of ADO installed on your system (2.0, 2.1, or 2.5). If you have version 2.0, you must update to version 2.1. Visual Basic 6 came with ADO 2.0, but Service Pack 3 includes ADO 2.1; this version is also installed automatically with Internet Explorer 5.0. At the time of this writing, the current version of ADO is 2.1, and ADO 2.5 is in beta. This version will be installed with Windows 2000, but Microsoft should distribute a version for Windows 98/NT, probably immediately after the release of Windows 2000. Visit the site **www.microsoft.com/data** for the latest information and download ADO 2.5 when it becomes available. The projects in this book will work with ADO 2.1/2.5, and only a few projects include features not supported by ADO 2.0.

Alternatively, you can create a Data Project that automatically includes a reference to the ActiveX Data Objects. The Data Project contains two ActiveX Designers as well—the DataEnvironment and DataReport Designers. The DataEnvironment Designer was discussed briefly in Chapter 3, "The Visual Database Tools," and you'll find more information on this object and how to use it in your application in Chapter 6, "Programming with ADO."

Connecting to a Database

The first step to using ADO is to connect to a database. Using the Connection object, you tell ADO which database you want to contact, supply your username and password (so that the DBMS can grant you access to the database and set the appropriate privileges), and, possibly, set more options. The Connection object is your gateway to the database, and all the operations you perform against the database must go through this gateway. The Connection object encapsulates all the functionality of a Data Link and has the same properties. As discussed in Chapter 3, when you drop an object, like a table or a stored procedure, from the Data View window onto the DataEnvironment window, it takes with it its link to the database. The Data Link object of the Data View window automatically becomes a Connection object in the DataEnvironment window. Unlike Data Links, however, Connection objects can be accessed from within your VB code. They expose a number of properties and methods that allow you to manipulate your connection from within your code.

If you open the Code window of a new Data Project (or a standard EXE project to which you have added a reference to the ADODB library), you can declare a Connection object with the following statement:

```
Dim Conn AS New ADODB.Connection
```

As soon as you enter the period after ADODB, you will see a list with all the objects exposed by the ADO component, and you can select the one you want with the arrow keys. Declare the *Conn* object in the Code module's Declarations section. Then place a command button on the Form, name it Connect to Access, and in its Click event enter the following:

```
Sub Command1_Click()
    Conn.ConnectionString =
        "Provider=Microsoft.Jet.OLEDB.4.0;" & _
        "Persist Security Info=False;" & _
        "Data Source = C:\Program Files\VB98\Nwind.mdb"
    Conn.Open
End Sub
```

NOTE   You can enter the value of the ConnectionString property in a single, long line, if you wish.

You have just established a connection to the Access NWind database. The ConnectionString property of the Connection object contains all the information required by the provider to establish a connection to the database. (I will explain the parameters of the ConnectionString property shortly. I will also show how to use the DataEnvironment Designer to build this string in Chapter 6.) As you can see, it contains all the information you specify on the Connection Properties tabs with point-and-click operations in text format. Just remember that the Connection-String property tells the Connection object where it should connect. Don't forget to set the value of the Data Source parameter to the path of the NWind database on your system.

If you want to connect to the SQL Server version of the same database, change the value of the ConnectionString property to the following:

```
Conn.ConnectionString =
    "Provider=SQLOLEDB.1;Persist Security Info=False;" & _
    "User ID=sa;Password=xxx;Initial Catalog = Northwind"
```

Don't forget to set your User ID and Password in this string. If SQL Server is running on a different computer, you must specify the computer's name on the network with the Data Source attribute as follows (EXPERTNEW is the name of the SQL Server workstation on my LAN and you should replace it accordingly):

```
Conn.ConnectionString =
    "Provider=SQLOLEDB.1;Persist Security Info=False;" & _
    "User ID=sa;Password=xxx;Initial Catalog = Northwind;" & _
    "Data Source=EXPERTNEW"
```

To establish the connection, call the Connection object Open method.

NOTE All projects on the companion CD use the setting "(local)" for the Data Source. In other words, I'm assuming you have SQL Server installed on the local machine. I expect most readers will not use the corporate server for training purposes. For your convenience, a time-limited version of SQL Server 7 is included on this book's companion CD.

WARNING If you plan to distribute your applications, you must prompt the user for the name of the server machine on which SQL Server runs. Database applications are not usually distributed massively. Most developers install the applications on the client's network themselves and customize the database as well. If an application attempts to connect to a server that's not present on the network, the connection will time out and an error message will be displayed. You must change the ConnectionString property and try again.

Executing a Command

After you have connected to the database, you must specify one or more commands to be executed against the database. A command could be as simple as a table's name, an SQL statement, or the name of a stored procedure. If you specify the name of a table, the DBMS will return all the rows of the table. If you specify an SQL statement, the DBMS will execute the statement and probably return a set of rows from one or more tables. If the SQL statement is an action query, some rows will be updated, and the DBMS will report the number of rows that were updated, but it will not return any rows. The same is true for stored procedures. If they select rows, these rows will be returned to the application. If they update the database, they may return one or more values.

TIP

As I have mentioned, you should prepare the commands you want to execute against the database ahead of time and, if possible, in the form of stored procedures. With all the commands in place, you can focus on your VB code.

You specify the command to be executed against the database with the Command object. You can also use the Command object to specify any parameter values that must be passed to DBMS in the case of a stored procedure, whether the command will be executed synchronously or asynchronously, and a host of other options. One of the basic properties of the Command object is the ActiveConnection property, which specifies the Connection object through which the command will be submitted to the DBMS for execution. It is possible to have multiple connections to different databases and issue different commands to each one. Depending on the database to which you want to submit a command, you must use the appropriate Connection object. Connection objects are a significant load on the server, so don't use multiple connections to the same database in your code.

Selection queries return a set of rows from the database. The following SQL statement will return the company names of all customers in the Northwind database:

```
SELECT CompanyName FROM Customers
```

As you recall from Chapter 4, SQL is a universal language for manipulating databases. The same statement will work on any database (as long as the database contains a table called Customers and this table has a CompanyName column). Therefore, it is possible to execute this command against the SQL Server Northwind database and the Access NWind database to retrieve the company names. If you have edited one of the two databases, then the same command may return a different set of rows.

NOTE

For more information on the various versions of the sample databases used throughout this book, see the sections "Exploring the Northwind Database," "The Pubs.Database," and The Biblio Database" in Chapter 2.

Let's execute a command against the database using the *Conn* object you've just created to retrieve all rows of the Customers table. The first step is to declare a Command object variable and set its properties accordingly. Use the following statement to declare the variable:

```
Dim Cmd As New ADODB.Command
```

Then set its CommandText property to the name of the Customers table:

```
Cmd.CommandText = "Customers"
Cmd.CommandType = adCmdTable
```

The second statement tells ADO how to interpret the command. In this example, the command is the name of a table. You could have used an SQL statement to retrieve selected rows from the Customers table, such as the customers from Germany:

```
CMDText = "SELECT ALL FROM Customers"
CMDText = CMDText & "WHERE Country = 'Germany'"
Cmd.CommandText = CMDText
Cmd.CommandType = adCmdText
```

By setting the CommandType property to a different value, you can execute different types of commands against the database.

Retrieving and Manipulating Data

The set of rows retrieved by an SQL statement are represented by an object that's known as a *cursor* (in SQL Server), or a *Recordset* (in ADO). There's a fine distinction between the two objects, which will become clear after you see a few examples (especially the stored procedures in Chapter 7, "Transact-SQL").

Here are some quick definitions:

- A *cursor* is a set of rows retrieved from one or more tables; it's the raw information supplied by the DBMS, and it lives on the server.

- A *Recordset* is an ADO object that stores these rows. The Recordset object may reside either on the server or on the client. In addition to the selected rows, the Recordset object provides the functionality (properties and methods) to access these rows.

The Recordset object hosts the rows returned by the DBMS in response to the execution of a command, and it has the structure of a table, with rows and columns. You use the properties and methods of the Recordset object to access the records of a table. A fundamental concept in programming Recordsets is that of the *current row*: In order to read the fields of a row, you must first move to the desired row. The Recordset object supports a number of navigational methods, which allow you to locate the desired row, and the Fields property, which allows you to access (read or modify) the current row's fields.

The Recordset object is at the heart of database programming, since most of the operations you perform on a database take place through this object. A typical application sets up a connection to a database and executes commands through this connection, but it spends most of its time processing the rows returned by the DBMS.

After establishing a connection to the database and preparing the Command object, you can execute the command and retrieve the cursor. Before you do so, however, you must prepare an object where the cursor will be stored. This object is a Recordset variable, which must be declared with the following statement:

```
Dim RS As ADODB.Recordset
```

Then execute the command with the Execute method and assign the cursor returned to the RS variable:

```
Set RS = Cmd.Execute
```

The Execute method of the Command object accepts a number of optional arguments, which are discussed in "The Command Object," later in this chapter. This simple form of the method is all you need to execute an existing Command object.

At this point, the rows of the Customers table can be retrieved through the *RS* object variable. The Recordset object exposes a number of properties and methods for manipulating the rows of the cursor. The RecordCount property, for example, returns the number of rows in the cursor (provided the cursor resides on the client). When the Recordset variable is first created, it's positioned at the first row of the cursor. To move to another row, use one of the Move methods (MoveNext, MovePrevious, and so on). Once you're on the desired row, you can access its fields through the Recordset object's Fields collection. The number of fields in the cursor is RS.Fields.Count. To access the first field in the current row, use the expression RS.Fields(0).Value. The name of this field is RS.Fields(0).Name and its data type is RS.Fields(0).Type. The Recordset object is substantially more complicated than the other ADO objects, so I'll discuss its basic members before I present any meaningful examples.

How "Fresh" Is My Cursor?

If you're not familiar with database programming at all, you may think that the Recordset object is a special type of Grid control and that you can access any row and any field as you would access the cells of a Grid control. That's not true. Cursors are complex objects, and you can't map them to a static structure. One of the most difficult concepts in database programming is the "freshness" of a cursor—unfortunately, it's one of the first concepts you must master.

The rows of a cursor are not static. While one user is viewing customer information on his workstation, another user may be inserting or deleting rows. It is even possible for a user to edit the very row another user is viewing. Theoretically, you could map the rows of a cursor to a grid-like control, but it would have to be a terribly smart and efficient control to reflect the changes in the database in real time. You'd also need a powerful server to keep track of who's viewing what, so that it could update each user's window. Besides, we don't have the bandwidth required to keep so many cursors alive.

Continued on next page

The short of the story is that cursors are subject to a number of limitations, and you must choose the right type of cursor for your application. Some cursors reflect the contents of the database the moment they were created, and other cursors remain constantly up to date by "seeing" the deletions and insertions made by other users. As you can guess, the more flexible cursors are the most expensive ones as well (an "expensive" cursor is one that requires many resources on the server).

As you will see, you can execute a command directly through the Connection object, or specify the command to select some rows with the Recordset object itself. You will learn about these shortcuts and when to use them in Chapter 8. In the meantime, I suggest that you:

- Use the Connection object to establish a connection.

- Use the Command object to execute a command.

- Use the Recordset object to access and process the rows retrieved by the command.

ADO's Main Objects

In the following sections, we'll look at the three major objects of ADO in detail. We'll examine the basic properties and methods you'll need to manipulate databases, and you'll find examples of how to use each object. ADO objects also recognize events, which are discussed in Chapter 9, "Advanced ADO Topics," along with other advanced ADO topics, like Recordset persistence, batch updates, and transactions.

Figure 5.1 summarizes the Active Data Objects model. If you're familiar with DAO, you'll agree that ADO is simpler, consisting of three main objects. Each object, however, exposes a large number of properties and methods, which are discussed in this and following chapters. The Connection object is the simplest one, because its role is to establish a connection to the database. The Command object exposes a Parameters collection, which contains information about the parameters of the command to be executed. The Recordset object exposes the Fields collection, through which you can access the fields of the rows it contains. The Errors collection is a property of the Connection object, and it contains the information about the most recent error (the Error object is discussed in Chapter 9).

FIGURE 5.1:

The ADO object model

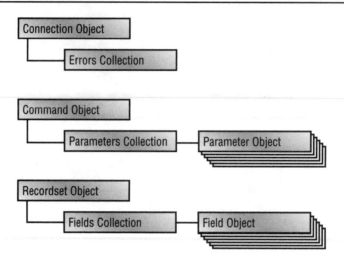

The Connection Object

The Connection object establishes a connection to a database, which is then used to execute commands against the database or retrieve a Recordset. Its most important property is the ConnectionString property, which specifies the database you want to connect to. To establish a connection through a Connection object, call its Open method. When you no longer need the connection, call the Close method to close it. To find out whether a Connection object is open, use its State property.

The ConnectionString Property

The ConnectionString property is a long string with several attributes separated by semicolons. A typical connection string for connecting to the Access NWind database is:

```
Provider=Microsoft.Jet.OLEDB.4.0;
Data Source=C:\Program Files\VB98\Nwind.mdb
```

NOTE   The connection string shown here is entered as a single line, but it had to be broken to fit on the page.

To connect to the SQL Server Northwind database, use the following connection string:

```
Provider=SQLOLEDB.1;User ID=sa;password=;
Initial Catalog=Northwind;
Data Source=EXPERTNEW
```

Here are the attributes you must define in a connection string:

Provider   The name of the provider is the OLE DB driver that ADO will use to access the database. For Access databases it's Microsoft.Jet.OLEDB.4.0, and for SQL Server databases it's SQLOLEDB.1. For Oracle databases, use the MSDORA provider. To access databases that have no native OLE DB provider, use the ODBC interface. ODBC was Microsoft's original provider for many databases. The MSDASQL is an OLE DB provider for ODBC data sources. This provider's name is MSDASQL.1. In Chapter 10, "Shaping Your Data," you'll learn about the MSDataShape provider, which you must use to build hierarchical Recordsets.

User ID   The user's ID is needed by the provider to establish the proper rights for accessing the database.

Password   The user's password is needed by the provider to validate the user.

Integrated Security   If you plan to use the Windows NT Integrated Security, omit the User ID and Password attributes and set the Integrated Security attribute to `Integrated Security=SSPI`.

Data Source   The name of an Access database—the full path to the MDB file where the database is stored. If you are using SQL Server, this is the name of the machine on which SQL Server is running.

Initial Catalog   SQL Server databases are not stored in separate files like Access databases. Use the Initial Catalog attribute to specify the name of a SQL Server database.

In practice, you'll never have to build connection strings from scratch. You can use the ADO Data Control Property Pages or the DataEnvironment Designer to build this string for you. Both objects will guide you through the steps of building the connection string with point-and-click operations, and they are discussed later in this chapter. Establishing a connection to a database through the ADO object is similar to creating a data link with the visual database tools, which are discussed in Chapter 3.

DSN-Based Connections

When you set the connection string manually, you are building a so-called DSN-less connection. DSN is the data source name by which a data source is known to your computer. Windows allows you to create a DSN for a database and then use the DSN name to connect to the database. Let's say you've created a DSN with the name NWINDDB, which represents the Northwind database on SQL Server. To connect to this database, use the following simple connection string:

```
DSN=NWINDDB
```

This is much simpler than specifying the attributes of the DSN explicitly, but it's not as convenient when you develop applications that will be deployed on many workstations. The DSN must be specified on each workstation. If your corporation uses a single database, you can request that all workstations are set up with the appropriate DSN. Moreover, DSN-based connections use the ODBC drivers, and they are slower than OLE DB. If your database supports OLE DB, then you shouldn't use this method. DSNs are used when applications are attempting to contact a remote server, because we don't want to include login information in the client application. Web applications, for instance, use this technique to contact a database on the Web server.

Setting Up a Data Source for SQL Server

To set up a data source for SQL server, follow these steps:

1. Open the Control Panel (select Start ➤ Settings ➤ Control Panel) and double-click the ODBC Data Source (32-bit) icon. In the ODBC Data Source Administrator window, select the System DSN tab (see Figure 5.2). The Data Source you set up on this tab will be visible to all users who connect to the current machine.

FIGURE 5.2:

The System DSN tab

Note that the System Data Sources list in this ODBC Data Source Administrator window will be different (and probably shorter) on your machine.

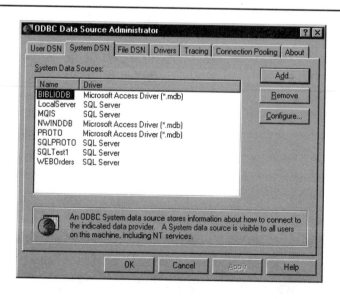

2. To create a new data source, click the Add button. In the Create A New Data Source window, you must select the provider for the new data source. Select SQL Server and click Finish.

3. In the next window, specify a name for the data source. This name will appear in the ODBC Data Source Administrator window, which is a description of the data source and the name of the machine where SQL Server is running. You can also select the "local" option if you have SQL Server installed on your workstation. Click Next.

4. In the window shown in Figure 5.3, specify whether SQL Server will use Windows NT or SQL Server's authentication to verify users attempting to connect to the data source. If using SQL Server, you must specify a Login ID (username) and a password, and then click Next.

FIGURE 5.3:

The Create A New Data Source authentication window

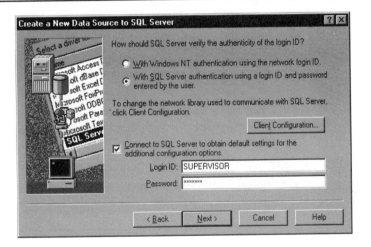

5. In the next window, you must specify the database for the new data source. Check the Change The Default Database To check box and select Northwind from the drop-down list. Click Next.

6. In the last window of the Wizard, you can specify various properties. Do not change any of the options on this window. Just click Finish, and the initial window will appear again, this time with the new data source's name.

Setting Up a Data Source for an Access Database

Setting up a data source for an Access database is simpler. Start as before, click the Add button on the ODBC Data Source Administrator window, and this time select Microsoft Access Driver. In the ODBC Microsoft Access Setup window, specify a data source name and a description. Click Select and you will be prompted to select an MDB file through a File Open dialog box. Locate the NWIND.MDB file on your disk and click OK. When you return to the ODBC Microsoft Access Setup window, click OK, and you're done.

Let's return to the methods of the Connection object.

The Open Method

After you have specified the ConnectionString property of the Connection object (or a DSN), you must call the Open method to establish a connection to the database. If you have already specified the ConnectionString property, call the Open method without any arguments, as shown here (*CN* is the name of a Connection object):

```
CN.Open
```

The Open method accepts a number of optional arguments. The complete syntax of the Open method is

```
CN.Open ConnString, UserID, password, options
```

The *ConnString* argument is identical to the ConnectionString property. In other words, you can pass the connection string as an argument directly to the Open method. The *UserID* and *password* arguments, if specified, override the values of the equivalent attributes of the connection string. The *options* argument lets you specify that a connection should be established asynchronously. The topic of asynchronous connections is discussed in Chapter 8, "Making the Most of Stored Procedures."

To open a connection to the NWINDDB Data Source with the Open method, use the following statement:

```
CN.Open "DSN=NWINDDB"
```

The Close Method

Use the Connection object's Close method to close an open connection. The Connection is not actually released, but remains alive in memory and can be used again later. To remove the Connection object from memory, set it to Nothing:

```
Set CN = Nothing
```

The Close method applies to all ADO objects. You can close them and reopen them later with the same or different settings. For example, you can close a Recordset object and reopen it later with a different data source. As with all VB objects, it's a good practice to release them from memory by setting them to Nothing when they're no longer needed.

The Recordset Object

The Recordset object is at the heart of every VB application that manipulates databases. In short, the Recordset is a programmable object where cursors are stored. Through the Recordset object, you can manipulate the rows of a cursor, view their fields, and update the underlying tables. An important aspect of Recordsets is that you can choose their location—whether they will reside on the server, or whether they'll be downloaded to the client.

Another important property of Recordsets is that they can be disconnected from their source. You can create a Recordset and then break the connection to the server. You can still process the Recordset on the client, and when you are done (or when you can connect to the server again) you can update the underlying tables. The topic of disconnected Recordsets is discussed in Chapter 9.

We'll start our discussion of the Recordset object by looking at the various types of cursors. There are several types of cursors, and each type has its advantages (and disadvantages). In addition, cursors can live on either the client or the server. Choosing the proper cursor type and location is an important part of application design.

Cursor Properties

To understand the role of the CursorType and CursorLocation properties, consider for a moment the nature of a database. A database is a dynamic object that changes constantly. While you're viewing a table's records, other users add new records and edit or delete existing ones. How can you be sure you're viewing the latest information? In fact, you can't. For some applications, you don't need up-to-the-second information. An application that analyzes last quarter's sales to help a manager revise sales plans doesn't have to be notified about the deletion of a record because a customer returned a few items. These actions don't change the big picture. On the other hand, an application that makes hotel or flight reservations must be able to see what goes on in the database. If not, the same seat may be assigned to two different passengers.

The sales application that doesn't have to constantly monitor the database is not very difficult to implement. The second application is more demanding. It must monitor the database for changes and make sure that no other application can update the record(s) it's changing. Different applications have different requirements, and these requirements are reflected by the cursor-related properties as well as by the LockType property. The LockType property is discussed in the section "Concurrency Control," later in this chapter. First, we'll explore the cursor properties because of the effect they have on the performance of the application.

Cursors are categorized according to their type (the CursorType property) and where they reside (CursorLocation property). The type of the cursor determines how "fresh" the cursor is—that is, whether the application can see changes made to the cursor by other users or not. If the cursor resides on the client, then its type is static. All other types apply to cursors that reside on the server.

The CursorType Property

ADO supports four types of cursors, and you can specify the desired cursor type by setting the value of the CursorType property to one of the constants shown here:

Constant	Description
adOpenForwardOnly	Creates a forward-only cursor
adOpenKeyset	Creates a keyset-driven cursor
adOpenDynamic	Creates a dynamic cursor
adOpenStatic	Opens a static cursor

Forward-Only Cursors (*adOpenForwardOnly*)   When you create a Recordset object by calling the Command object's Execute method or the Recordset object's Open method, ADO creates this default cursor. This cursor can be scanned forward only, and it's suitable for one-pass operations (such as displaying the rows on a control, performing calculations that involve consecutive rows, and so on). Forward-only cursors are quite limited, but they are less expensive than other types of cursors because the provider doesn't need to store information about the location of the rows already "seen" by the Recordset. If you don't need to move back and forth in the cursor, use a forward-only cursor. It's the least demanding type of cursor for the server and much faster than any other cursor type (see the RecordsetScan project, described later in the chapter).

Static Cursors (*adOpenStatic*)   This cursor type is a little more flexible and expensive than the forward-only cursor. The static cursor is a snapshot of the database the moment the cursor was created, and, unlike the forward-only cursor, it can be scanned in both directions. However, you can't see modifications made to the rows by other users after the creation of the cursor, nor will you see any new rows added since you've opened the static cursor. Moreover, if a row is deleted since you've opened the cursor, your application will keep thinking that the row is still part of the cursor. To refresh a static Recordset, use the Resync or Requery method (discussed later in this chapter).

WARNING   When you open a cursor on the client, the qualifying rows are moved from the server to the client. This cursor is static. Other applications may change one or more of the qualifying rows in the database, but the corresponding rows in your cursor will not be updated. ADO will not generate an error message if you attempt to open another type of cursor on the client; it will simply ignore the setting and open a static cursor.

Keyset Cursors (*adOpenKeyset*)   When a keyset cursor is created, the server doesn't extract the actual rows (field values) from the database. Instead, it creates a list of keys to the rows that belong to the cursor and uses these keys to access the fields of the current row as needed.

The number of keys (which is the same as the number of rows in the cursor) doesn't change while the cursor is open. This means that a keyset cursor can't see additions made by other users. If another user adds a new row to a table and this row happens to qualify as a member of the cursor (a row that would have been selected by the command, if it were available at that time), you will not see this row through a keyset cursor. We say that the *membership* of the cursor is *fixed*. This means that the number of rows cannot change once the cursor has been created.

The advantage of keyset cursors over static cursors is that they can see changes and deletions made by other users. Each time the user moves to another row of the cursor, ADO must fetch the row from the database. If the row has been changed, then the latest version of the row will be fetched. If the row was deleted in the meantime, ADO will skip this row.

Keyset cursors can be scanned in either direction, because the list of keys is maintained by the server while the cursor is open.

Dynamic Cursors (*adOpenDynamic*)   This is the most flexible, and most expensive, type of cursor. It's similar to the keyset cursor, in the sense that its rows are not read from the database when the cursor is created; they are accessed as needed with the help of pointers to the actual rows.

The membership of a dynamic cursor is not fixed. If another user adds a new row after the creation of the cursor, a key for the new row is inserted into the cursor, into its proper position (the same position this row would have been inserted if it were available at the time of the cursor's creation). If the new row belongs to the segment of the cursor that has been scanned already, your application will not see it unless it moves back through the rows, or scans them from the beginning again. If the new row is inserted ahead of the current row, your application will see it as it scans the rows of the cursor, even though it wasn't there when the cursor was created.

Notice that keyset and static cursors have fixed memberships and they can report the number of rows. Dynamic cursors do not the report the number of rows, because their membership is not fixed. The number of rows may change at any time. For more information on retrieving the number of rows in a Recordset, see "The RecordCount Property" later in this chapter.

The Cursor's Location

Another aspect that affects performance and efficient resource usage is the cursor's location. A cursor can be located either on the server or on the client, depending on the value of the CursorLocation property:

Constant	Description
adUseClient	Opens a client-side cursor
adUseServer	Opens a server-side cursor

Server-side cursors provide better concurrency control. Use client-side cursors when the application must move back and forth in the cursor. If you must implement a lookup table in your application, you should also use a client-side cursor. (A lookup table is a cursor with publisher IDs and names, which is used to look up publisher IDs and retrieve publisher names to display on a Form). The rows will be downloaded once, and the application can use them all the time. If the Recordset contains too many rows, you should leave it on the server and read rows as needed.

TIP

I'll get back to the issue of choosing the right type of cursor and using cursors efficiently later in the book, but here's the most important tip: Don't use large cursors. Try to download only the rows that will be used by the client application. Users can't work with thousands of rows at once, so you must provide the appropriate interface, where users can specify the information they really need (like the products of a category, the books of a publisher, and so on). If an application needs to modify a large number of rows, then try to implement the changes on the server with an SQL statement or a stored procedure.

Concurrency Control

The last factor to consider in setting up a cursor is the type of *locking*, or *concurrency control*. Concurrency control determines what will happen when two users attempt to update the same row. An application reads a row and displays its fields on a Form. Another application (which could be a copy of the same application running on a different workstation) reads the same row as well. Both users edit some fields and they are ready to commit the changes to the database. Which application will update the database and what will the other application do? (The easy answer is that the last user wins, but it's not always that simple. Users may wish to know that a row has been changed since they last read it; they may even want to see the edited row.)

To specify how ADO should handle concurrency, use the Recordset object's Lock-Type property. This property can have one of the values described in Table 5.1.

T A B L E 5 . 1 : LockType Property Settings of the Recordset Object

Constant	Description
adLockReadOnly	Use this type of locking to open the cursor for reading-only, if the application need not update its rows. The user, or application, does not update the rows and many users can view the same rows at the same time. In effect, this type of locking avoids the concurrency problem altogether.
adLockPessimistic	This is the strictest form of concurrency control. The row is locked when an application starts editing the row. Other users can read the row, but can't edit it. The lock is released after the row is updated by the application that placed the lock on it.
	This type of locking should be used in special cases only. Use it to change an order's details or other infrequent and very sensitive operations. Moreover, applications that use this type of locking shouldn't keep the lock in effect for a long time. You must make sure that the lock is released as soon as possible, so that other users can access the locked row.
adLockOptimistic	This is the most common locking technique. The database places a lock on the row(s) while it's updating them. This lock lasts for an instant only. This type of locking is based on the assumption that the chances of two users editing the same row are very small. Indeed, this is the most common situation, but your code must be able to handle situations where two users attempt to update the same row at once.
adLockBatchOptimistic	Some applications can download a Recordset to the client, break the connection to the server, update multiple rows, and then attempt to commit all the changes to the database by establishing a new connection. This method is used with disconnected Recordsets.

In the next few sections we'll go through all the basic properties and methods of the ADO objects. The information in this chapter will enable you to write basic applications using the ADO objects, as well as the data-bound controls of Visual Basic.

Basic Recordset Properties

In the following few sections you'll learn about the basic properties of the Recordset object. Unlike the properties we discussed already, these following properties are available at run time only, and you'll use them to access the underlying tables.

The RecordCount Property

The RecordCount property returns the number of records in the Recordset. Do not count on this property to return the exact number of records. Some providers do not report the number of records read. Moreover, records are not downloaded immediately to the client. The server sends the first few records, so that the application can start processing them, and it continues downloading records. In this case, the number of records reported by the RecordCount property will not be final. If you need to know the exact number of records in a Recordset object, issue the MoveLast method to make sure the Recordset has been fully populated and then read the RecordCount property.

You should also keep in mind that databases are not static. As soon as you read the RecordCount property, another user may add or delete records, which might affect your Recordset. A dynamic cursor's RecordCount property is –1. This is ADO's way of telling you that it doesn't make any sense to request the number of rows of a dynamic cursor, because new rows may be added even as the DBMS is counting the qualifying rows. If the cursor resides on the client—in which case it's a static cursor—we know that the number of rows isn't going to change, even if new rows are added to the underlying table(s). If the cursor resides in the server, and its membership is not fixed, then ADO reports the value –1.

Many programmers tend to use this property a lot, but it's not necessary. To iterate through the rows of a Recordset, use a While ... Wend loop, never a For ... Next loop. If you want to find out how many records have a specific property, use the appropriate SQL statement; don't create a Recordset with the qualifying rows. To find out the number of orders placed in the first quarter of 1997, for example, use an SQL statement with the COUNT() function, instead of iterating through the rows of the Orders table.

The RecordCount Project   To experiment with the RecordCount property returned by the various types of Recordsets and providers, use the RecordCount project, which is shown in Figure 5.4. This project allows you to specify the type of cursor, then create an actual Recordset object and examine its RecordCount property. Each time you change one of the cursor properties, the Show Count button is disabled. In addition, the Recordset's properties will appear on the Form's title bar. These settings are retrieved from the Recordset object, and they may not match the settings you've specified. If you specify a client-side cursor that's not static, ADO will automatically change its type. You must click the Fetch Records button to create a Recordset with the new settings. This action will enable the Show Count button, which you can click to see the value of its RecordCount property.

Client-side cursors report the number of rows they contain, because all the rows have been moved to the client. Even if new qualifying rows have been added to the database, these rows will not become part of the client-side cursor unless you refresh it, of course. The RecordCount property of client-side static cursor, in effect, returns the number of rows moved to the client.

FIGURE 5.4:

The RecordCount project lets you experiment with the RecordCount property of the various Recordset types.

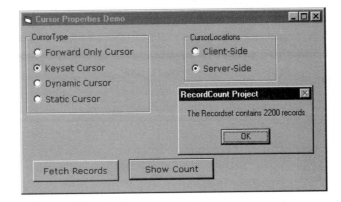

A forward-only cursor does not report the number of rows, because it doesn't know how many rows qualify. This cursor fetches the next row as needed, and it doesn't know how many rows qualify until it has visited the last qualifying row. At this point, some of the rows already fetched may not qualify (they may have been edited, or deleted by another user).

A dynamic Recordset does not report its number, because its membership is not fixed. Even if you scan the entire cursor to find out the number of rows, new ones may be added, or existing ones deleted, as you work with it. The value –1 means that you shouldn't attempt to count the cursor's rows.

Keyset cursors have fixed membership, so they report the correct number of rows. This value of the RecordCount property is the number of rows that qualified when the cursor was created. Even if new rows were added after the creation of the cursor, you won't be able to see them through the keyset cursor. However, you will see the changes made by other users to the qualifying rows. The RecordCount property of a keyset cursor doesn't change, even if one or more rows are deleted.

You can open the RecordCount project to see how it sets up the cursor properties of the Recordset and then opens it. It uses the *CN* Connection variable to establish a connection to the Northwind database from within the Form's Load event, which is shown in Listing 5.1.

LISTING 5.1   The Form's Load Event

```
Private Sub Form_Load()
    'CN.ConnectionString = _
            "Provider=Microsoft.Jet.OLEDB.4.0;" & _
            "Data Source=C:\VB98\Nwind.mdb"
    CN.ConnectionString = "Provider=SQLOLEDB.1;" & _
            "ID=sa;password=;Initial Catalog=Northwind"
    CN.Open
```

```
        CType = adOpenStatic
        CLocation = adUseServer
    End Sub
```

To connect to the Access NWind database, uncomment the first line and comment out the second one. The *CType* and *CLocation* variables (they map the Recordset's CursorType and CursorLocation properties) are declared in the Declarations section of the Form, and they're set each time you check another option button on the Form.

The code behind the Fetch Records and Show Count buttons is shown next. Notice that the program uses the CursorLocation and CursorType properties of the *RS* object to find out the actual properties of the cursor. As you will notice, the properties reported by the Recordset object may not match the ones you've specified. If you test this project with different providers, you will discover that not all providers support all cursor types. If you attempt to open a dynamic cursor with the Jet provider, ADO will automatically change the Recordset's type to static. The CLocationName() and CLocationType() functions convert the constants that identify the cursor's location and type from integer values to strings.

LISTING 5.2   **Fetching Records**

```
Private Sub Command2_Click()
    If RS.State = adStateOpen Then
        RS.Close
    End If
    RS.CursorLocation = CLocation
    RS.CursorType = CType
    RS.Open _
        "SELECT * FROM Customers WHERE Country='Germany'",_
        CN, CType
    bttnCount.Enabled = True
    Me.Caption = "CursorDemo (" & _
            CLocationName(RS.CursorLocation) & ", " & _
            CTypeName(RS.CursorType) & ")"
End Sub
```

LISTING 5.3   **The Show Count Button**

```
Private Sub bttnCount_Click()
    MsgBox "The Recordset contains " & _
            RS.RecordCount & " records", _
            vbOKOnly, "RecordCount Project"
End Sub
```

The RecordsetScan Project   The RecordsetScan project demonstrates the differences between the various types of Recordsets by timing how long it takes to scan the rows of the Order Details table of the Northwind database. The Form of the application, shown in Figure 5.5, lets you specify the type and location of the Recordset. The program sets up the proper Recordset object to retrieve the rows of the Order Details table of the Northwind database. Then, it iterates through the rows of the cursor with the MoveNext method and times the operation. Run the application and check out how long it takes to scan the various types of Recordsets. The forward-only cursor is clearly the fastest one.

FIGURE 5.5:

The RecordsetScan project

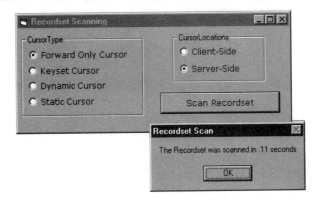

Most of this project's code is similar to the code of the RecordCount project. Instead of requesting the value of the RecordCount property, it scans the cursor's rows with the MoveNext method. (The MoveNext method advances to the next row of the Recordset and is discussed in "Navigating through Recordsets," later in this chapter). Here's the code behind the Scan Recordset button:

LISTING 5.4   **Scanning the Recordset**

```
Private Sub Command2_Click()
    If RS.State = adStateOpen Then
        RS.Close
    End If
    RS.CursorLocation = CLocation
    RS.Open "[Order Details]", CN, CType
    Me.Caption = "CursorDemo (" & _
                CLocationName(RS.CursorLocation) & ", " & _
                CTypeName(RS.CursorType) & ")"
    T1 = Timer
    While Not RS.EOF
        RS.MoveNext
```

```
        Wend
        MsgBox "The Recordset was scanned in " & _
                Format(Timer - T1, "###.00") & _
                " seconds", , "Recordset Scan"
    End Sub
```

The forward-only cursor was scanned in well under a second on my system, but it took several seconds for all other types of cursors. Despite its limitations, the forward-only cursor is extremely efficient. A client-side cursor is scanned even faster, because the rows have been moved to the client and they're processed there.

The While .... Wend loop iterates through the rows of the *RS* Recordset. The MoveNext method takes you to the next row in the Recordset, and it's the only navigational method supported by forward-only Recordsets. The navigational methods of the Recordset object are discussed in "Navigating through Recordsets."

The Supports Method

ADO is a universal data access mechanism. Using the same objects, you can view and manipulate many different databases. As neat as this may sound, it poses a few special problems. Because not all DBMSs support the same functionality, some programs that work with SQL Server may not work with Access, Oracle, or other databases. Or, the same applications may behave differently when they access different databases. You can find out from within your VB code whether a Recordset is capable of a certain operation with the Supports method. The syntax of the Support method is

```
    RS.Supports(option)
```

This expression returns a True/False value that indicates whether the Recordset object supports the specified option. The *option* argument can have one of the values shown in Table 5.2.

TABLE 5.2:   The Support Method's Argument Values

Constant	Description
adAddNew	Indicates whether the Recordset supports the addition of new records with the AddNew method
adApproxPosition	Indicates whether the Recordset supports absolute positioning with the AbsolutePosition and AbsolutePage properties
adBookmark	Indicates whether the Recordset supports bookmarks
adDelete	Indicates whether the Recordset supports record deletion with the Delete method
adFind	Indicates whether the Recordset supports the Find method
adIndex	Indicates whether the Recordset supports the Index property

Continued on next page

TABLE 5.2 CONTINUED: The Support Method's Argument Values

Constant	Description
adHoldRecords	Indicates whether changes you have made will remain in effect when you fetch more rows
adMovePrevious	Indicates whether the Recordset supports backward navigation. If this property returns False, you can't call the methods MoveFirst, MovePrevious, Move, and GetRows
adNotify	Indicates whether the Recordset can raise events (provided it has been declared with the WithEvents keyword)
adResync	Indicates whether the Recordset can be refreshed with the Resync method
adUpdate	Indicates whether the Recordset can be updated with the Update method
adUpdateBatch	Indicates whether the Recordset can be disconnected

The ADOCursors Project   The ADOCursors project, shown in Figure 5.6, demonstrates the operations you can perform with the various cursor types. In the CURSOR TYPE section you can select the type of the cursor, and in the CURSOR LOCATION section you can select the location of the cursor. After setting the cursor's properties, you can click one of the buttons on the Form.

FIGURE 5.6:

The ADOCursors project demonstrates the capabilities of the various types of Recordsets.

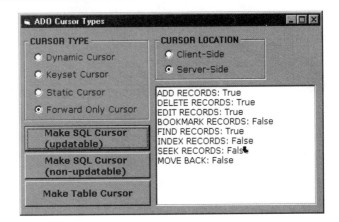

The top two buttons create a SQL Server cursor—an updateable and non-updateable one. The updateable cursor is created with the following SQL statement:

```
SELECT CompanyName, ContactName, ContactTitle, OrderID
FROM Customers, Orders
WHERE Orders.CustomerID=Customers.CustomerID
```

This statement selects all the customers in the Northwind database and the IDs of their orders.

The SQL statement that generates a non-updateable Recordset is a bit more complicated. This statement selects the total items purchased by each company. It may not be the most useful information you can extract from the Northwind database, but it's a valid SQL statement nevertheless.

```
SELECT CompanyName, Sum(Quantity)
FROM Customers, Orders, [Order Details]
WHERE Orders.CustomerID=Customers.CustomerID AND
      [Order Details].OrderID=Orders.OrderID
      GROUP BY CompanyName
```

This Recordset can't be updated. The number of items sold is calculated by adding all the quantities from the Order Details table. It doesn't make sense to increase the total number of units. ADO doesn't know whether you want to add more items to a specific order, or whatever you may have in mind. This Recordset can't be updated, not because of its properties, but due to its nature. If the command is such that it excludes the update of the Recordset, then the Supports(adUpdate), Supports(adAddNew), and Supports(adDelete) methods return False.

The last button opens the Customers table. This Recordset is always updateable, because it represents a table's rows. Don't forget to set the LockType property of the Recordset to a value other than adLockReadOnly.

The program sets up the appropriate Recordset object taking into consideration the properties specified on the Form by the user. The actual code that creates a non-updateable cursor is shown next.

LISTING 5.5   **Making a Non-updateable Recordset**

```
Private Sub Command1_Click()
    Set RS = New ADODB.Recordset
    Set CN = New ADODB.Connection
    CString = "Provider=SQLOLEDB.1;" & _
              "User ID=sa;password=;" & _
              "Initial Catalog=Northwind;Data Source=(local)"
    CN.ConnectionString = CString
    CN.Open
    RS.CursorType = CType
    RS.CursorLocation = CLocation
    RS.ActiveConnection = CN
    RS.LockType = adLockOptimistic
    RS.Open "SELECT CompanyName, Sum(Quantity) " & _
        "FROM Customers, Orders, [Order Details] " & _
        "WHERE Orders.CustomerID=Customers.CustomerID " & _
        "AND [Order Details].OrderID=Orders.OrderID " & _
        "GROUP BY CompanyName"
```

```
        ShowRSProperties
        Set CN = Nothing
        Set RS = Nothing
End Sub
```

The ShowRSProperties subroutine displays the current Recordset's features on a TextBox control, with the following statements:

LISTING 5.6   **Querying a Recordset's Capabilities**

```
Sub ShowRSProperties()
    Text1.Text = _
            "ADD RECORDS: " & RS.Supports(adAddNew) & vbCrLf
    Text1.Text = Text1.Text & "DELETE RECORDS: " & _
            RS.Supports(adDelete) & vbCrLf
    Text1.Text = Text1.Text & "EDIT RECORDS: " & _
            RS.Supports(adUpdate) & vbCrLf
    Text1.Text = Text1.Text & "BOOKMARK RECORDS: " & _
            RS.Supports(adBookmark) & vbCrLf
    Text1.Text = Text1.Text & "FIND RECORDS: " & _
            RS.Supports(adFind) & vbCrLf
    Text1.Text = Text1.Text & "INDEX RECORDS: " & _
            RS.Supports(adIndex) & vbCrLf
    Text1.Text = Text1.Text & "SEEK RECORDS: " & _
            RS.Supports(adSeek) & vbCrLf
    Text1.Text = Text1.Text & "MOVE BACK: " & _
            RS.Supports(adMovePrevious)
End Sub
```

The Bookmark Property and CompareBookmarks Method

The Bookmark property is among the most commonly used properties of the Recordset object. A *bookmark* is a value that uniquely identifies the current row in a Recordset object. You can store the Bookmark property into a variant variable, so that you can return to the specific record. The following code segment bookmarks the current record before adding a new one. If the user decides to cancel the addition of the new record, the application will return to the last valid record:

```
currentRecord = RS.Bookmark
{code to add new record}
RS.CancelUpdate
RS.Bookmark = currentRecord
```

The Bookmark property is not the record's position in the Recordset. It will not change value even if records are deleted or inserted. However, it reflects the relative order of records in the Recordset. To find out whether a record is ahead of another in the Recordset, use the CompareBookmarks method, whose syntax is:

```
RelOrder = RS.CompareBookmarks (bookmark1, bookmark2)
```

The value returned by the CompareBookmarks method can have one of the values shown in Table 5.3.

TABLE 5.3: Values Returned by the CompareBookmarks Method

Constant	Description
adCompareLessThan	The first bookmark is before the second one.
adCompareEqual	The two bookmarks are equal (they represent the same record).
adCompareGreaterThan	The first bookmark is after the second one.
adCompareNotEqual	The order of the bookmarks is unknown.
adCompareNotComparable	The two bookmarks can't be compared.

The Bookmark property is not supported by forward-only Recordsets, because this type of Recordset can only be scanned forward (even if you could bookmark records, you wouldn't be able to return to them).

The Fields Collection

This is probably the most important property of the Recordset object, and it represents the fields (columns) of the Recordset. The Fields collection is made up of Field objects, each representing a separate field (column). This property is a collection, and it exposes the standard properties of a collection, shown in Table 5.4.

TABLE 5.4: Members of the Fields Collection

Member	Description
Count property	Counts the number of fields in the Recordset
Item property	Selects a specific field by an ordinal number (`RS.Fields.Item(0)`) or by the field name (`RS.Fields.Item("ContactName")`)
Append method	Appends a new Field object to a Fields collection. Use this property to construct Recordsets from within your code.
Delete method	Removes a Field object from a Fields collection. This method can be used only with Recordsets you create from within your code and not with Recordsets based on actual tables.
Refresh method	Reads the definitions of the Field objects in a Fields collection directly from the database

You can access and manipulate the attributes of a field with the following properties of the Field object.

ActualSize

This property returns the actual size of a field's value. It is used with character and binary fields and returns the actual length of the data, rather than the maximum size of the field. To find out the maximum length of a field, use the DefinedSize property. If a field's definition is char(100) and it holds the value "Visual Basic Programming", the ActualSize property will return 24. The DefinedSize is 100, regardless of the value stored in the field.

Attributes

This property indicates some special characteristics of a Field object. The special characteristics are listed in Table 5.5.

TABLE 5.5: The Attributes Property Values of the Field Object

Constant	Description
adFldMayDefer	Indicates that the field value is not read from the database when you land on a new row. Instead, the actual value is read when the specific field is referenced.
adFldUpdatable	Indicates that the field can be updated
adFldUnknownUpdatable	Indicates that the provider doesn't know whether the field can be updated or not
adFldFixed	Indicates whether the field contains data of fixed length
adFldIsNullable	Returns True if the field can accept Null values
adFldMayBeNull	Returns True if the field can return Null values
adFldLong	Returns True if it's a long binary field. Use the AppendChunk and GetChunk methods to write to or read from this field.
adFldRowID	Indicates that the field is a record ID
adFldRowVersion	Returns true if the field uses timestamps to track updates
adFldCacheDeferred	Returns true if the provider caches the values of the fields and subsequent reads are done from the cache

The Attributes property is a combination of one or more of the constants listed in the Table 5.7. To find out a specific property, use a statement like the following one:

```
If (RS.Fields(3).Attributes And adFldRowsID) = adFldRowID Then
    {the field is a row ID, process it accordingly}
End If
```

DataFormat

This property is an object that specifies how the field will be formatted when displayed on a data-bound control. VB6 supports the DataFormat object, which allows you to control the formatting of the fields when they're displayed on a control (such as a TextBox control) on the Form.

DefinedSize

This is the size (in bytes) of the column. The size of numeric fields is fixed and you need not change it. See "ActualSize" earlier in this section for more information.

Name

This is the field's name. When you want to display all the fields on a control that's not data bound, you can use the Name property to display the field names as headers, with a loop like the following one:

```
For Each fld In RS.Fields
    Print fld.Name
Next
```

NumericScale, Precision

These two properties apply to numeric fields only. The NumericScale property specifies the number of decimal places (number of digits to the right of the decimal point). The Precision property specifies the total number of digits. The Numeric-Scale and Precision properties are read-only for Recordsets based on existing tables and read-write for Recordsets you create from within your code.

OriginalValue

This property returns the value of a field before it was changed. You can use this property to restore a single field's value (normally, you should never have to restore changes to individual fields). Use the CancelUpdate method to undo the changes made to the current record.

Type

Returns a constant that represents the field's data type. The types recognized by ADO are listed in Table 5.6. Notice that no single provider supports all data types, but ADO should be able to handle any data type it may run into.

TABLE 5.6: ADO Data Types

Constant	Access	SQL Server	Visual Basic
adBigInt			
adBinary		binary	Variant
adBoolean	Yes/No	bit	Boolean
adBSTR			
adChapter		Field is a Recordset	
adChar		Char	String
adCurrency	Currency	money, smallmoney	Currency
adDate	Date/Time	Datetime, smalldatetime	Date
adDBDate			
adDBFileTime			
adDBTime			
adDBTimeStamp	Date/Time	timestamp	Variant
adDecimal		decimal, numeric	
adDouble	Double	float	Double
adEmpty			
adError			
adFileTime			
adGUID	ReplicationID	uniqueidentifier	
adIDispatch			
adInteger	Long Integer, AutoNumber	int, Identity	Long
adIUnknown			
adLongVarBinary	OLE Object	image	Variant
adLongVarChar	Memo	text	String
adLongVarWChar			
adNumeric		decimal, numeric	
adPropVariant			
adSingle	Single	real	Single
adSmallInt	Integer	smallint	Integer
adTinyInt	Byte	tinyint	Byte
adUnsignedBigInt			
adUnsignedInt			
adUnsignedSmallInt			
adUnsignedTinyInt			
adUserDefined			
adVarBinary		varbinary	
adVarChar		varchar	
adVariant			
adVarNumeric			
adVarWChar			
adWChar			

The adChapter constant is not a data type per se; it signifies that the field is a Recordset. In Chapter 10, "Shaping Your Data," we'll discuss hierarchical Recordsets, and as you will see, it is possible to create Recordsets that contain smaller Recordsets. For example, you can create a Recordset with customer information and specify that a specific column holds the orders of the each customer. Obviously, this column can't be a simple field. It's an entire Recordset. This field's type is adChapter, and you must handle it as a Recordset, rather than as a regular field.

UnderlyingValue

This is the field's current value in the database. This property does not always return the same as the OriginalValue property. If another user has changed the field value since you read it, the UnderlyingValue will return the value written to the database by the other user. The OriginalValue will return the value your application read from the database when the Recordset was created. These two properties are identical after the execution of the Resync method.

Value

This property reads, or sets, the value of a specific column. To change the value of the third field in the current row of the RS Recordset, use this statement:

```
RS.Fields(2).Value = new_value
```

The value you supply must be compatible with the field's type. To read the value of the same field and store it into a variable, use this statement:

```
var_name = RS.Fields(2).Value
```

Handling Null Values

In most cases, you want to know if a field's value is Null before you use it in your code. If you attempt to assign a field's value to the Text property of a TextBox control, or the Caption property of a Label control, a runtime error will occur if the field happens to be Null. Use an If statement like the following one to avoid the runtime error:

```
Text1.Text = ""
If Not IsNull(RS.Fields(2)) Then
    Text1.Text = RS.Fields(2)
End If
```

If you want to display the <NULL> value in the TextBox instead of a blank string, replace the first line with the following one:

```
Text1.Text = "<NULL>"
```

You will frequently use the following lines, which print the field names of a cursor and the field values under them. You will see the same code many times in this book, in most cases displaying this information on a FlexGrid control:

```
For iCol = 0 To RS.Fields.Count - 1
    MSFlexGrid1.TextMatrix(0, iCol) = RS.Fields(iCol).Name
Next
While Not RS.EOF
    For iCol = 0 To RS.Fields.Count - 1
        If Not IsNull(RS.Fields(icol)) Then
            GridLine = GridLine & _
                RS.Fields(iCol).Value & vbTab
        Else
            GridLine = GridLine & vbTab
        End If
    Next
    MSFlexGrid1.AddItem GridLine
    RS.MoveNext
Wend
```

The first loop prints the headers (field names) and the second loop goes through the rows of the cursor and displays their values in columns, under the corresponding headers. The code shown here doesn't attempt to print Null values, but not all fields can be displayed. Binary fields (like images) should be handled differently, and you must insert the appropriate code to handle them.

Creating Custom Recordsets

The properties of the Recordset object are not read-only. It is possible to create Recordset objects from within your code by attaching Field objects to the Fields collection and setting their properties accordingly. The following statements create a few Field objects, set their properties, and append them to the Fields collection of the *RS* Recordset variable. After the *RS* Recordset has been set up, you can insert new records and manipulate your data with the Recordset's objects. In "Saving Recordsets," later in this chapter, you'll learn how to save this Recordset on a disk file and open it later.

```
RS.Fields.Append "StateName", adChar, 2
RS.Fields.Append "StateAbbr", adChar, 20
RS.Open
RS.AddNew Array("StateName", "StateAbbr"), Array("AL", "Alaska")
RS.Update
RS.AddNew Array("StateName", "StateAbbr"), Array("AZ", "Arizona")
RS.Update
. . . {add more rows}
```

```
RS.MoveFirst
While Not RS.EOF
    Debug.Print RS.Fields(0) & "    " & RS.Fields(1)
    RS.MoveNext
Wend
```

Being able to create your own Recordsets from within your code allows you to apply many of the techniques discussed in this book in applications that don't justify the cost of the database, yet they can benefit from data-bound controls. Practically, you can replace random access files with custom Recordsets and use the methods and properties of the Recordset object to manipulate their records.

The Command Object

The Command object carries information about the command to be executed. This command is specified with the control's CommandText property, and it can be a table name, an SQL statement, or the name of a SQL Server stored procedure or Access query (stored procedures and Access queries are discussed in Chapter 7). To specify how ADO will interpret the command specified with the CommandText property, you must assign the proper constant to the Command-Type property. The CommandType property recognizes the constants shown in Table 5.7.

TABLE 5.7: Settings of the CommandType Property

Constant	Description
adCmdText	The command is an SQL statement.
adCmdStroredProc	The command is the name of a stored procedure
adCmdTable	The command is a table's name. The Command object passes the following string to the server:
	SELECT * FROM table_name
adCmdTableDirect	The command is a table's name. The Command object passes the name of the table to the server. This option is more efficient than the adCmdTable option.
adCmdUnknown	The command type is unknown (the DBMS will try to figure it out and execute it).

You must also use the Command object to specify parameter values, if the stored procedure requires one or more input parameters, or it returns one or more output parameters. For more information on specifying parameters with the Command object, see Chapter 8, "Making the Most of Stored Procedures."

The Command object exposes very few properties. In addition to the Command-Text and CommandType, it exposes the State property, which indicates the current state of a command, and it can return one of the constants shown in Table 5.8.

TABLE 5.8: Values Returned by the State Property of the Command Object

Constant	Description
adStateClosed	The Command object is closed.
adStateOpen	The Command object is open.
adStateExecuting	The Command object is executing.
adStateFetching	The Command object is fetching rows.

Use this property when you execute commands asynchronously to find out the command's progress.

NOTE   The topic of asynchronous execution of commands is covered in Chapter 8.

The examples of this chapter use the Command object to access tables. The two statements that specify the table to be opened are:

```
CMD.CommandText = "Customers"
CMD.CommandType = adCmdTable
```

To execute an SQL statement against a database use the following statements:

```
CMD.CommandText = "SELECT ContactName, ContactTitle " & _
    "FROM Customers " & _
    "WHERE Country = 'Italy'"
CMD.CommandType = adText
```

Basic Recordset Operations

To access the fields of a specific row in a Recordset, you must first locate the desired row, and then access the Fields through the Fields collection. To locate a row, the Recordset object exposes a number of navigational methods (the Move methods), as well as a Find and a Seek method, which can locate one or more rows based on any criteria you specify. These two methods apply to the current Recordset only. You can't retrieve more rows from the underlying tables, even if they match your criteria.

Navigating through Recordsets

To navigate through the rows of a Recordset, use the Move method and its variations. The MoveFirst, MovePrevious, MoveLast, and MoveNext methods take you to the first, previous, last, and next rows in the cursor respectively. These methods do not accept any arguments, but using them is not quite trivial. All four methods ignore deleted rows. The MoveFirst method, for example, takes you to the first nondeleted row in the cursor. If all rows have been deleted, then the MoveFirst or MovePrevious method will also set the BOF property to True. Likewise, the MoveLast and MoveNext methods will also set the EOF property to True, when you go past the last row in the Recordset. The EOF (End of File) and BOF (Beginning of File) properties indicate that you have reached the end or the beginning of the file, respectively. These two properties are discussed in the following section.

The Move method allows you to specify the row you want to move to. The syntax of this method is:

```
RS.MoveNext NRecords [, Start]
```

The first argument, *NRecords,* is the number of rows you want to advance in the cursor. To move two rows ahead of the current one, call the Move method as follows:

```
RS.Move 2
```

This statement is equivalent to calling the MoveNext method twice. To move two rows behind the current one (toward the beginning of the cursor), use the statement:

```
RS.Move -2
```

This statement is equivalent to calling the MovePrevious method twice.

The second argument of the Move method is optional, and it can be a valid bookmark or one of the constants shown in Table 5.9. A bookmark is a special value that uniquely identifies a row in a cursor (see the discussion of the Bookmark property earlier in the chapter). This argument specifies the row relative to which the Move method will advance.

TABLE 5.9:   Values of the Move Method's *Start* Argument

Constant	Description
adBookmarkCurrent	Moves with respect to the current row
adBookmarkFirst	Moves with respect to the first row
adBookmarkLast	Moves with respect to the last row

Forward-only cursors do not allow moving backward or moving by more than one row at a time. The MoveFirst, MovePrevious, and MoveLast methods can't be used with a forward-only Recordset.

EOF and BOF Properties

While scanning a Recordset, you must monitor these two properties, which let you know whether you've reached the beginning (BOF) or the end (EOF) of a Recordset. The two properties return False, unless you've moved ahead of the first record or beyond the last record. These two properties allow you to scan a Recordset and know when to stop. The following loops scan a Recordset in both directions and stop when the end has been reached:

```
' Scan from beginning to end
RS.MoveFirst
While Not RS.EOF
    {process current row}
    RS.MoveNext
Wend

' Scan from end to beginning
RS.MoveLast
While Not RS.BOF
    {process current row}
    RS.MovePrevious
Wend
```

TIP

Use these properties to find out whether a Recordset contains any records or not. If a Recordset is empty, then both EOF and BOF properties return True.

The EOF property is used by other operations as well. In the next section you will read about the Find method, which can locate records based on some criteria you supply. If the Find method can't locate any records that match your criteria, it will set the EOF property to True to indicate that it completed unsuccessfully.

Absolute Positioning in a Recordset

When you work with ADO Recordsets, you can query the position of the current row in the Recordset, or even move to a specific row, which will become the Recordset's current row. Not all types of Recordsets support absolute positioning, and it shouldn't matter to your application either. As a matter of principle, you shouldn't write applications that rely on the absolute positions of the records. However, when you work with client-side cursors that can report the number of rows they contain (the RecordCount property), you can use the AbsolutePosition property to let users know approximately where they are in the Recordset, or allow them to move quickly near the location of the desired row (provided that rows are ordered somehow).

In addition to absolute positioning in a Recordset, ADO supports *paged Recordsets*—the type of Recordsets displayed on Web pages when the results of a query are too many to be displayed on a single page. The Web server displays 20 or so records and a number of buttons at the bottom of the page that allow you to move quickly to another group of 20 records. This technique is very common in Web applications, and ADO supports a few properties that simplify the creation of paged Recordsets. They are the AbsolutePage, PageSize, and PageCount properties, which are described in this section. After the descriptions of the properties, you'll find an example that demonstrates all the absolute positioning properties.

The AbsolutePosition Property

Use this property to find out the absolute location of a row in a Recordset or to move to this row quickly. The relative position of the current row in the Recordset is given by the property `RS.AbsolutePosition / RS.RecordCount`. As you can guess, the AbsolutePosition property can be used only with cursors that also support the RecordCount property.

The PageSize Property

The PageSize property returns or sets the number of records in a page and is used to create paged Recordsets. The PageSize property doesn't break a Recordset into smaller sets; it simply divides the Recordset into logical sections. Every time you set the AbsolutePosition property, the corresponding page of PageSize rows is fetched.

The PageCount Property

This property returns the number of pages in a Recordset and is equivalent to the expression `RS.RecordCount / RS.PageSize`. If the Recordset doesn't support the page-related properties, then the PageCount property returns the value –1.

The AbsolutePage Property

This property returns or sets the absolute page in the Recordset. When this property is set, ADO moves automatically to the first row in the page. To move to another row in the same page, use the Move methods as usual. Notice that the partitioning of the Recordset in pages is artificial. If you call the MoveFirst method, you'll be taken to the first row in the Recordset (even if it doesn't belong to the current page), and the MoveLast method will take you to the last row in the Recordset. To scan the PageSize rows in a page, you must call the MoveNext method as many times as there are rows in the page (PageSize). If you keep calling this method, you'll land on rows outside the current page without any warnings.

The CacheSize Property

When you work with paged Recordsets, you should consider setting the CacheSize property, which is the number of records read into the client computer's memory at once. The default value of this property is 1.

When you build paged Recordsets from within your VB code, you should set the CacheSize property equal to the PageSize property, so that the entire page is read into the cache and you can manipulate its rows on the client without delays.

The CacheSize property has some annoying side effects you should be aware of. As you know, keyset cursors can see changes made by other users to the underlying tables. When you move to another row in the Recordset, ADO fetches the row from the database into the Recordset. If the Recordset's CacheSize property is 100, ADO will fetch rows in groups of 100. This means that another user may change the ninetieth row of the Recordset after it has been read, and before you land on this row. You will not see the current version of the row, but rather the version that was read into the cache. You will find more information on setting the CacheSize and when this action is necessary in the following chapter.

The PagedOutput Project   The PagedOutput project demonstrates the use of the ADO Recordset properties for absolute positioning. The ListBox on the Form of Figure 5.7 displays 20 rows of the Orders table at once. The user can request the previous and next pages using the two buttons at the bottom of the Form. The Scrollbar control above the buttons reflects the position of the current page in the Recordset. To move quickly to another page, the user can slide the scrollbar to the desired location (say, three-quarters down the Recordset).

FIGURE 5.7:

The PagedOutputDemo project demonstrates the properties for absolute positioning in a Recordset object.

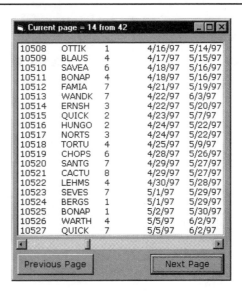

The Recordset object contains the rows of the Orders table, but it doesn't retrieve all of them at once. I defined a page size of 20 records and set the CacheSize property to 20 as well, so that all the rows of the current page are read into the local cache at once. The current page's number is displayed on the Form's title bar, along with the total number of pages in the Recordset.

When the Form is loaded, the code sets the parameters of the Recordset object and displays the first page's rows:

LISTING 5.7   **Setting Up a Paged Recordset**

```
Private Sub Form_Load()
    ADOCN.ConnectionString = "Provider=SQLOLEDB.1; " & _
            "User ID=sa;password=;Initial Catalog=Northwind"
    ADOCN.Open
    ADORS.CursorLocation = adUseClient
    ADORS.CursorType = adOpenStatic
    ADORS.ActiveConnection = ADOCN
    ADORS.CacheSize = 20
    ADORS.Open "Orders"
    ADORS.AbsolutePage = 1
    currentPage = 1
    ADORS.PageSize = 20
    HScroll1.Min = 1
    HScroll1.Max = ADORS.PageCount - 1
    HScroll1.Value = currentPage
    ShowRecords
End Sub
```

The code behind the two navigational buttons is shown next.

LISTING 5.8   **Navigating through the Recordset's Pages**

```
Private Sub Command1_Click()
    If currentPage > 1 Then currentPage = currentPage - 1
    ADORS.AbsolutePage = currentPage
    HScroll1.Value = currentPage
    ShowRecords
End Sub

Private Sub Command2_Click()
    currentPage = currentPage + 1
    If currentPage = ADORS.PageCount Then currentPage = ADORS.PageCount - 1
    ADORS.AbsolutePage = currentPage
    HScroll1.Value = currentPage
    ShowRecords
End Sub
```

The *currentPage* variable is declared in the Declarations section of the Form, so that it can be manipulated by any routine in the project. The two navigational buttons adjust the current value of the Scrollbar control as well. Finally, when the user changes the Scrollbar control, the following lines are executed:

LISTING 5.9   Moving to a Page with the Scrollbar Control

```
Private Sub HScroll1_Change()
   If HScroll1.Value = currentPage Then Exit Sub
   ADORS.AbsolutePage = HScroll1.Value
   currentPage = HScroll1.Value
   ShowRecords
End Sub

Private Sub HScroll1_Scroll()
   ADORS.AbsolutePage = HScroll1.Value
   currentPage = HScroll1.Value
   ShowRecords
End Sub
```

It's good practice to program the Scroll event along with the Change event, so that the user can get some feedback while scrolling the control's button.

This technique is used with Web applications that retrieve rows from a database and display them on multiple pages. Its implementation is a little more involved, because you can't have global variables in a Web application. You will see how to create paged output for Web applications in the online bookstore application, which is described in Chapter 18.

Searching and Filtering Rows

The navigational methods of the Recordset object are pretty limited. Being able to move to the next and previous records isn't going to be much help when you're working with a cursor that contains hundreds (and possibly thousands) of records. To locate the desired record quickly, you can use the Find method, or apply a filter to the cursor to further limit the rows.

The Find Method

The Find method searches the Recordset to locate a record that matches some user-supplied criteria. The syntax of the Find method is:

```
RS.Find criteria, [skipRecords], [searchDirection], [start]
```

The first argument, *criteria*, is an expression that specifies a field name and its desired value. The field name must be related to the value with a comparison operator, such as

```
Country='Germany'
```

or

```
UnitPrice > 100
```

The Find method does not allow the use of logical operators. In other words, you can't combine multiple criteria with the operators AND and OR. Use the Filter method to perform more complicated searches.

DAO provided the FindFirst and FindNext methods to locate the first and the following records meeting certain criteria. This type of functionality is now supported by the Filter method. Use the Find method to locate a record or two, but if many records match your search criteria and you want to iterate through them, apply a filter as described in the following section.

After locating the first record, chances are that you want to view other records that match the same search criteria. If you sort the records according to the search field, you can use a While … Wend loop to iterate through the records that match the same search criteria. Let's say you want to locate customers by country. Instead of opening the Customers table, use an SQL statement to retrieve the rows of the table sorted by country:

```
SELECT DISTINCT Country FROM Customers ORDER BY Country
```

If you call the Recordset's MoveNext method after a successful search, you'll be taken to the next record that matches your criteria, similar to the DAO's FindNext method. To scan and display all the customers from Germany, for example, you can use the following statements:

```
RS.MoveFirst
RS.Find "Country='Germany'"
If RS.EOF Then
    MsgBox "No record found"
Else
    While RS.Fields("Country") = 'Germany'
        List1.AddItem RS.Fields("CompanyName")
        RS.MoveNext
        If RS.EOF Then Exit Sub
    Wend
End If
```

Notice that the Find method is issued once, but the following records match the search criteria of the Find method, because all customers from Germany are located in consecutive rows (that's how we extracted them from the table). When the

Country field is no longer 'Germany' then we know we are done with all the customers from this country.

The FindDemo project, shown in Figure 5.8, demonstrates this technique. When the Form is loaded, the names of all countries are loaded on a ComboBox control. The user can select a country with the mouse and then click the Locate Customers In button to display all the customers whose Country field is the same as the selected country.

FIGURE 5.8:

Use the FindDemo project to experiment with the Recordset object's Find method.

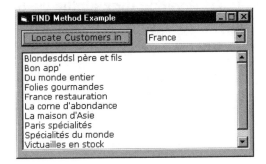

Here's the code that's executed when the Form is initially loaded:

LISTING 5.10   The FindDemo Project's Form_Load Event Handler

```
Private Sub Form_Load()
    ConnString = "Provider=SQLOLEDB;Password=;" & _
                 "User ID=sa;Initial Catalog=Northwind;" & _
                 "Data Source=(local)"
    CN.ConnectionString = ConnString
    CN.Open
    cmdString = "SELECT DISTINCT Country " & _
                "FROM Customers ORDER BY Country"
    RS.CursorType = adOpenDynamic
    RS.CursorLocation = adUseServer
    RS.Open cmdString, CN
    While Not RS.EOF
        If Not IsNull(RS.Fields("Country")) Then _
                Combo1.AddItem RS.Fields("Country")
        RS.MoveNext
    Wend
    Combo1.ListIndex = 0
    If RS.State = adStateOpen Then
        RS.Close
    End If
    cmdString = "SELECT * FROM Customers ORDER BY Country"
    RS.CursorType = adOpenDynamic
```

```
        RS.CursorLocation = adUseServer
        RS.Open cmdString, CN
    End Sub
```

When the button is clicked, the program reads the selected country from the ComboBox control and finds the first record from this country. Then it scans the following records with the While … Wend loop for as long as the Country field remains the same:

LISTING 5.11   **Iterating through the Customers of the Same Country**

```
Private Sub Command1_Click()
    country = Combo1.Text
    List1.Clear
    If Combo1.Text = "" Then Exit Sub
    RS.MoveFirst
    RS.Find "Country='" & country & "'"
    If RS.EOF Then
        MsgBox "No record found"
    Else
        While RS.Fields("Country") = country
            List1.AddItem RS.Fields("CompanyName")
            RS.MoveNext
            If RS.EOF Then Exit Sub
        Wend
    End If
End Sub
```

The ComboBox control used in this example is not data-bound. It was populated with the appropriate code from within the Form's Load event. Notice that the ComboBox control's Style property was set to DropDown List, so that users can't enter country names that don't exist in the database.

The Index Property and the Seek Method

The Seek method is similar to the Find method: It locates a row in the Recordset based on a field value. However, the Seek method uses an index to locate the desired row much faster. Before you can use the Seek method, you must specify the name of the index that should be used. To specify an index, use the Index property, as follows:

```
RS.Index = "ByCountry"
```

where *ByCountry* is the name of an index that has already been defined. The index must exist already—you can't create an index by specifying one or more column names. Not all providers support the Index property, so make sure the

Index property (as well as the Seek method) is supported before you call it, using the Supports property.

The syntax of the Seek method is:

```
RS.Seek KeyValues, SeekOption
```

The *KeyValues* argument is an array of variants, and it should contain one value for each column in the index. The Seek method will locate the row in which all fields that are part of the index match the specified values. The *SeekOption* argument can have one of the values shown in Table 5.10, which determine how the field values will be compared to the key values.

TABLE 5.10: Values of the Seek Method's SeekOption Argument

Constant	Description
adSeekAfterEQ	Locates the first key that is equal to or larger than the specified value(s)
adSeekAfter	Locates the first key that is larger than the specified value(s)
adSeekBeforeEQ	Locates the first key that is equal to or smaller than the specified value(s)
adSeekBefore	Locates the first key that is smaller than the specified value(s)
adSeekFirstEQ	Locates the first key that is equal to the specified value(s)
adSeekLastEQ	Locates the last key that is equal to the specified value(s)

If the Seek method does not find the desired row, the EOF property is set, but no runtime error is generated. The Seek method can only be used with server-side cursors.

The Filter Property

The Filter property allows you to select certain records in the current Recordset, either for viewing purposes, or to operate on them as a group (to delete or update them as a group, for example). The Filter property recognizes more complicated criteria than the Find method, as you can combine multiple comparisons with logical operators. The syntax of the Filter property is:

```
RS.Filter = filter
```

The expression *filter* involves one or more field names and/or constants combined with relational operators. In simpler terms, it's an expression like the ones you would use with an If statement. The following filter expression will isolate the rows whose OrderDate field's value falls in the first quarter of 1997:

```
RS.Filter = "OrderDate >= '1/1/1997' And OrderDate <= '3/31/1997'"
```

You can also combine Visual Basic variables to build the filter expression, because it's parsed at runtime and then passed to ADO. The following statement will select the orders placed in a user-supplied interval:

```
RS.Filter = "OrderDate >= '" & startDate & _
             "' And OrderDate <= '" & endDate & "'"
```

If the variables *startDate* and *endDate* are assigned the values 1/1/1997 and 3/31/1997 respectively, the last two examples are identical.

This property acts like a method too, because the Recordset is filtered as soon as you apply the filter. If the filtered version of the Recordset contains one or more records, then you'll be placed on the first filtered record. To remove a filter, you can either supply an empty string to the Filter property, or the constant adFilterNone.

If the original Recordset is very large, ADO will take some time to filter out the unwanted rows, especially if the expression is complicated and involves many columns. You should avoid downloading large Recordsets to the client and filtering them there; build the corresponding SQL statement and retrieve the rows you want from the database. If an application applied many different filters to the same Recordset (for example, an application that builds different graphs based on subsets of the same Recordsets, like sales per year, per country, and so on), it's probably more efficient to download the Recordset and then filter it repeatedly on the client.

Once a filter has been applied to a Recordset, the usual navigational methods apply to the filtered records. Likewise, the Find method will not find any matching records outside the filtered ones. To return to the original Recordset and apply a new filter, you must first remove the filter by setting the Filter property to adFilterNone.

The Sort Property

This is another property that works like a method. As soon as you supply a value to this property, the records of the current Recordset will be sorted according to the field(s) you have specified. The syntax of the Sort method is

```
RS.Sort = field_list
```

where *field_list* is a comma-separated list of field names. To sort the rows of the Customers table according to the contact name, use the following statement

```
RS.Sort = "ContactName"
```

To contact the rows by country and then by name within each country, use the statement

```
RS.Sort = "Country, ContactName"
```

By default, rows are sorted in ascending order. To change the order of the sort, use the DESC keyword:

```
RS.Sort = "ContactName DESC"
```

You can also combine the DESC and ASC keywords in the same statement:

```
RS.Sort = "Country ASC, ContactName DESC"
```

> **NOTE**   This property can be used with client cursors only. When you sort the rows of a client cursor, a temporary index will be created for the fields specified in the Sort property. This will speed up not only sorting, but searching operations as well.

Sorting a large Recordset will take some time, so you must avoid sorting rows on the client. You should try to download the desired rows in the desired order (use the ORDER BY clause in your SQL statements). If the rows must be sorted differently once on the client, use the Sort method.

Saving Recordsets

In this section, we'll look at a group of related properties that allow you to "persist" Recordsets (store their rows locally on the client and retrieve them even after the connection to the server has been terminated). The methods discussed in this section allow you to read the rows of a Recordset in an array or a long string, even save them to a disk file. You can do the same using the Fields collection, but you have to take into consideration each field's type, and this complicates the code. The following methods extract the rows of a Recordset and store them in an array, a long string (which you can save to a local file), or a disk file.

The GetRows Method

The GetRows method retrieves the rows of a Recordset (or a subset of it) and stores their fields into an array. The array returned by the GetString method has as many columns as the Recordset has fields and as many rows as the Recordset. You can access this array from within your code and generate complicated reports, but any changes you make to the array will not be written back to the database (or even the Recordset object). The syntax of the GetRows method is:

```
array = RS.GetRows rows, start, fields
```

All arguments are optional. The *rows* argument determines how many rows you want to retrieve. To retrieve all values, use the value –1 (or the constant adGetRowset), which is the default value of this argument. The *start* argument determines the bookmark of the row from which the GetRows method should start, and it can have one of the values shown in Table 5.11. The rows before *start* will be ignored. This argument can be set to one of the following constants. Use the constant adBookmarkLast to retrieve the last row only.

TABLE 5.11: Values of the GetRows Method's *start* Argument

Constant	Description
adBookmarkCurrent	Starts at the current record
adBookmarkFirst	Starts at the first record
adBookmarkLast	Starts at the last record

The last argument, *fields*, is an array of field names (or ordinal position numbers), which will be included in the result. Use this argument to select a subset of the Recordset's rows.

To retrieve an entire Recordset and store it in the Records() array, you must begin by declaring the array as follows:

```
Dim Records()
```

You should not specify any dimensions. The GetRows method will dimension the array appropriately. The array's elements are variants, even if all the selected fields are of the same type. To move the rows of the Recordset to the Records array, use the statement:

```
Records() = RS.GetRows
```

You can request the number of columns and rows of the Records array with the following statements:

```
Cols = UBound(Records, 1)
Rows = UBound(Records, 2)
```

For an example of the GetRows methods, see the SaveRecordset project at the end of this section.

GetString Method

The GetString method retrieves a number of rows from a Recordset and stores them into a string variable. You can specify the column and row delimiters, so that the string can be later parsed with VB code. This method can also be used to create an HTML table with a Recordset's rows. The syntax of the GetString method is

```
RS.GetString stringFormat, rows,_
        colDelimiter, rowDelimiter, NullExpression
```

The arguments *colDelimiter* and *rowDelimiter* are strings that will be inserted at the end of each column and each row respectively. To create an HTML table with the Recordset's rows, use the delimiters "<TD>" for columns and "<TR>" for rows (see "The GetStringDemo Project").

The last argument, *NullExpression*, lets you specify the value that will replace the Null field values.

The following lines read an entire Recordset and store it into a string variable as an HTML table:

```
HTMLText = "<HTML><TABLE BORDER=1>" & vbCrLf & "<TR><TD>"
HTMLText = HTMLText & RS.GetString(, , "<TD>", vbCrLf & _
            "<TR><TD>", "N/A")
HTMLText = HTMLText & vbCrLf & "</TABLE></HTML>"
```

The HTML variable can be used as is to display the table on a browser.

Save Method

The Save method saves the rows of the current Recordset to a disk file. You can save the rows on your local computer, disconnect from the database, and work with them while disconnected. I'll have a lot to say about working with disconnected Recordsets in Chapter 11. The syntax of the Save method is

```
RS.Save filename, persistFormat
```

The argument *filename* represents a disk file, and the *persistFormat* argument can have one of the values listed here:

Constant	Description
adPersistADTG	The Recordset is saved in a proprietary format.
adPersistXML	The Recordset is saved in XML format.

NOTE   If a filter is in effect, then only the rows selected by the current filter will be saved. To save all the rows, make sure you have removed any filter from the Recordset by setting the Filter property to adFilterNone. If the Recordset is hierarchical, then only the child Recordset (and its child Recordsets) will be saved. Hierarchical Recordsets are discussed in Chapter 10.

NOTE   The Save method does not close the file, so that any changes you make to the Recordset after the call to the Save method will also be saved to the file. The file remains open for as long as the Recordset is opened, thus no other applications can access this file. Usually, we close the Recordset immediately after saving it to a disk file.

The *adPersistADTG* option stores the data using a proprietary format. To read the Recordset, you must use the Open method of the Recordset object and specify the name of the file instead of a table name of an SQL statement. The *adPersistXML* option saves the rows in XML format, and it's supported by ADO 2.1 and 2.5. Notice also that only ADO 2.5 can save hierarchical Recordsets. The XML format is a specification for global exchange of structured data. XML will be a major aspect of the next release of Visual Studio, but at this point you need a good understanding of XML to use the XML files produced by ADO to build Web pages. You can open the XML file created by the Save method with Internet Explorer to see what they look like.

The GetStringDemo Project

The GetStringDemo project demonstrates the three methods discussed in this section: GetString, GetRows, and Save. The Form of the project, shown in Figure 5.9, has three buttons. Each one exercises a different method. When the Form is loaded, it retrieves selected columns of the Customers table into the *RS* Recordset variable with the following SQL statement:

```
SELECT CompanyName, ContactName, City, _
       Country FROM Customers ORDER BY CompanyName
```

FIGURE 5.9:

The GetStringDemo project demonstrates the GetString, GetRows, and Save methods of the Recordset object.

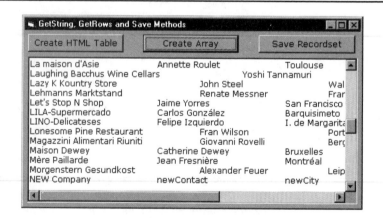

The Create HTML Table button calls the GetString method and uses the HTML table tags to create an HTML table. The HTML code is displayed in the Form's TextBox control. Here's the code that builds the HTML table:

```
Private Sub Command1_Click()
    HTMLText = "<HTML><TABLE BORDER=1>" & vbCrLf & "<TR><TD>"
    HTMLText = HTMLText & RS.GetString(, , "<TD>", _
               vbCrLf & "<TR><TD>", "N/A")
    HTMLText = HTMLText & vbCrLf & "</TABLE></HTML>"
    Text1.Text = HTMLText
End Sub
```

The Create Array button stores the Recordset into the Records() array. Then the Records() array is scanned and its elements are displayed in the TextBox control. Each row is displayed on a new line, and consecutive columns in the same row are separated by a Tab character. The code of the Create Array button is shown here:

```
Private Sub Command2_Click()
Dim Records()
    RS.MoveFirst
    Records() = RS.GetRows
    Cols = UBound(Records, 1)
    Rows = UBound(Records, 2)
    MsgBox "The array contains " & Rows & _
           " rows of " & Cols & " columns each"
    Text1.Text = ""
    TRow = ""
    For iRow = 0 To Rows - 1
        For iCol = 0 To Cols - 1
            TRow = TRow & Records(iCol, iRow) & vbTab & vbTab
        Next
        Text1.Text = Text1.Text & TRow & vbCrLf
        TRow = ""
    Next
End Sub
```

The last button, Save Recordset, saves the Recordset in two different files, using the ADTG and XML format. First, it deletes the existing files and then calls the Save method twice, the first time with the adPersistADTG option and the second time with the adPersistXML option. Here is the code behind this button:

```
Private Sub Command3_Click()
On Error Resume Next
    Kill "c:\records.ADTG"
    Kill "c:\records.XML"
On Error GoTo 0
    RS.Save "c:\records.ADTG", adPersistADTG
    RS.Save "c:\records.XML", adPersistXML
End Sub
```

Updating Databases

Let's see how you can edit the database using the Recordset object. Obviously, a Recordset that was opened as read-only can't be updated. All other types of Recordsets are updateable. Recordsets based on SQL statements that involve aggregates can't be updated either, but I'm assuming you won't attempt to update a Recordset that's not updateable by its nature.

Updating a record is not always a straightforward process. What happens if a user changes the record after you have read it? And what will happen if the record you're about to update has already been deleted by another user? This is a difficult topic and will be discussed in detail in Chapter 9, "Advanced ADO Topics." In the current chapter, you will learn the basics of updating databases through the ADO objects. In the following chapter you'll learn how to use the methods discussed here along with the data-bound controls to build functional user interfaces.

For the remainder of this chapter, all Recordsets are opened with the adLock-Optimistic option. This locking mechanism is based on the assumption that the chances of two users updating the same record at the same time is very small—it's a very realistic assumption for most practical situations. While you're changing a record, other users can access it, too. The record is locked while it's being updated, which is a very short time indeed.

Inserting New Rows

To insert a new record to an open, updateable Recordset, you must call the AddNew method. This method can be called without any arguments, in which case it appends a new row to the Recordset and makes it the current row. You can assign values to the new row's fields through the Fields property. Or, you can call the AddNew method with the following syntax:

```
Recordset.AddNew field_list, value_list
```

where *field_list* is a comma-separated list of fields and *value_list* is a comma-separated list of values. Each value is assigned to a field based on the order in which fields and values appear in the two lists. The first value is assigned to the first field, the second value to the second field, and so on.

The *field_list* need not contain all the fields in the cursor—and it usually doesn't. However, you must specify all the fields that can't accept Null values. If you don't, the DBMS will reject the operation with a trappable runtime error. To add a new customer to the Customers table of the Northwind database, use a statement like the following one:

```
RS.AddNew ("CustomerID", "CompanyName"), _
          ("SYBEX", "Sybex, Inc.")
```

This statement will append a new row to the *RS* Recordset, which presumably contains the rows of the Customers table. Only two of the new row's fields are set: the CustomerID (which can't be Null) and the CompanyName fields.

The Update Method

The new row isn't updated immediately. To commit the changes, you must call the Recordset object's Update method, or move to another row. The Update method doesn't require any arguments. It simply commits a new row, or the changes you made to an existing row (see the Edit method, described in the following section) to the database. Moving to another row has the same effect: it commits a new row to the table, or the changes you made to an existing row. It's a good idea to disable the navigational methods while users are editing a row, or adding a new one, and then commit the changes by calling the Update method explicitly when the OK button is clicked. I'll have a lot to say about building user interfaces in the following chapters.

The CancelUpdate Method

If you decide not to commit the new row to the database, call the CancelUpdate method. This method doesn't require any arguments. It simply deletes the newly added row, or reverses the changes you made to an existing row.

After calling the Update method, the newly added row becomes the current row in the cursor. After calling the CancelUpdate method, the last valid row you visited becomes the current record.

Editing Rows

To edit the fields of the current row, use the Fields property. Just assign values to the fields you want to change and then call the Update method to commit the changes to the database. If you move to another row without calling the Update method, then the changes will be committed as well. To reset the fields to their original values, call the CancelUpdate method.

NOTE   If you have programmed with DAO in the past, keep in mind that ADO doesn't support an Edit, or equivalent, method. You don't have to tell ADO that you're about to edit a row. As soon as you change a field's value, ADO places the row in edit mode and saves its current status, so that you can undo any changes with the CancelUpdate method later.

The EditMode Property

When an edit or an addition operation is underway, the EditMode property is set accordingly. This property can have one of the values listed in Table 5.13 and is read-only.

TABLE 5.13: Values of the EditMode Property

Constant	Description
adEditNone	Indicates that no editing operation is in progress
adEditInProgress	Indicates that data in the current record has been modified but not yet saved
adEditAdd	Indicates that the AddNew method has been invoked, but the new record is in a buffer and no new record has been saved in the database

Since the ADO Recordset property doesn't support a method to prepare the current row for editing, you must examine the EditMode property from within your code to find out whether an edit operation is underway. The EditMode property is set to adEditInProgress as soon as you change a field value in the current record. This setting remains in effect until either the changes are committed to the database, or canceled with the CancelUpdate method.

The following statement reads the value of the CompanyName field of the current row in the RS Recordset:

```
Debug.Print RS.Fields("CompanyName")
```

To change the value of the same field, simply assign a new value to the same expression:

```
RS.Fields("CompanyName") = "Sybex, Inc."
```

Deleting Rows

To delete one or more rows from a Recordset, call the Delete method. The Delete method can remove either the current record or a group of records. To delete the current record, just call the Delete method without any arguments. To delete multiple records, use the following syntax of the Delete method:

```
RS.Delete [recordsAffected]
```

The *recordsAffected* optional argument can have one of the values shown here:

Constant	Description
adAffectCurrent	(default) Deletes the current record only
adAffectGroup	Deletes all the records selected by the current Filter (see "The Filter Property" earlier in this chapter)
adAffectAllChapter	Deletes all the child Recordsets of the current Recordset (for more information on hierarchical Recordsets, see Chapter 10)

If you want to delete multiple records, you can select them with the Filter property and then delete them en masse by calling the Delete method with the *adAffect-Group* argument. This technique will work only if the records you want to delete have a common characteristic, so that they can be selected with the Filter property.

You can also update a database with the UPDATE, INSERT, and DELETE SQL statements as well. Just build the appropriate SQL statement in your application and then execute it against the database through the Command object. You can even write stored procedures that accept the necessary information as arguments and update the database by executing the appropriate SQL statements. A stored procedure isolates the client application from the database, so that the client application doesn't manipulate the database directly. It calls stored procedures to add/edit/delete rows, and the stored procedure performs all the validation and updates the database. The same stored procedure can be called from many places in your code too. These topics are discussed in detail in later chapters. Actually, a major aspect of this book is to show you all the options and help you choose the approach that will work best for each application.

Summary

This concludes our discussion of the basic properties of the ADO objects. The more difficult topics will be postponed until Chapter 9. In the next chapter, you'll find examples of using the ADO objects from within your VB applications. You'll learn about the data bound objects and the ADO Data control, and you'll see how you can put together all the information presented so far to build data entry and browsing applications. In later chapters you will find information on more advanced ADO topics, as well as examples of functional user interfaces.

Programming with ADO

- The DataEnvironment Designer

- The ADO Data Control

- The Data Form Wizard

- Creating simple and functional data-entry Forms

- Examples

In this chapter, you'll learn how to program the ADO object model, but we won't start from scratch. You'll use the DataEnvironment Designer to establish a connection to the database and prepare the commands you'll execute against the database. You'll also learn how to use Visual Basic's ADO Data Control and the data-bound controls to build user interfaces with drag-and-drop operations.

As you know, Visual Basic provides several tools for preparing the various objects you need in your database applications. The visual database tools, for example, let you refine the design of the database, build your SQL statements with point-and-click operations, and debug your stored procedures. The DataEnvironment Designer lets you design the Connection and Command objects you need to access your data. The ADO Connection object is identical to the Connection object in the DataEnvironment window, which in turn is equivalent to a Data Link in the Data View window. The ADO Command object is the same as the DataEnvironment's Command object. The ADO Recordset object, finally, can't be mapped to an object in the DataEnvironment window. Every time you call the Command object's Execute method, however, the DataEnvironment object creates a Recordset object, which you use in your code to manipulate the rows of the underlying table(s). The difference between the DataEnvironment objects and the visual database tools is that DataEnvironment objects can be accessed from within your VB code, where the visual database tools are used to prepare the database for coding. As you may recall from Chapter 3, these tools can exchange information, and you can drop objects from the Data View window onto the DataEnvironment window.

At the beginning of this chapter, we will explore the DataEnvironment object in depth. Then, we'll look at the ADO Data Control and the data-bound and data-aware controls and how you can use them to build your user interface. In the last section of this chapter, we'll build applications using the ADO objects only. More advanced examples will appear in following chapters.

The DataEnvironment Designer

We first discussed the DataEnvironment Designer in Chapter 3, along with the visual database tools. In this section you'll see how to create Connection and Command objects with the DataEnvironment Designer, and then how to use these objects in a VB application.

Start a new Data Project, open the Project menu, and select DataEnvironment Designer. You can also add a DataEnvironment Designer to a Standard EXE project by selecting Project ➤ More ActiveX Designers ➤ DataEnvironment. The Data-Environment Designer (I'll call it DE Designer from now on) will be placed in the Designers folder in the Project window. To activate the DE Designer, double-click its icon. The DataEnvironment1 window, as shown in Figure 6.1, appears on your screen.

The top icon in the window (DataEnvironment1) represents all three ADO objects: Connection, Command, and Recordset. Think of it as your gateway to a database. To access any of these objects from within your code, you must use the DataEnvironment1 object.

Creating Connection Objects

The first subordinate object is a Connection object (Connection1), which must be set to point to the desired database. Let's make it point to the Northwind database.

1. Right-click the Connection1 icon and select Rename from the shortcut menu. Rename this object to *Northwind*.

2. Right-click the same object and select Properties from the shortcut menu. The Data Link Properties pages will appear, similar to Figures 6.2 and 6.3, but initially empty.

3. In the Provider tab, select the desired data provider (the DBMS that will provide the data). For a SQL Server database, select Microsoft OLE DB Provider for SQL Server. For an Access database, select Microsoft Jet 4.0 OLE DB Provider. If there's no OLE DB provider for your database, you can still access it through the OLE DB Provider for ODBC Drivers.

4. Switch to the Connection tab and enter the name of the server on your LAN (the name of the machine on which SQL server is installed). The Refresh button will not work; you must type the name of the server. If SQL Server is running on the same machine as you're using to develop applications, you can leave this box blank. Supply your username and password (or check the button Use Windows NT Integrated Security). This information will enable the DE Designer to connect and query the database.

FIGURE 6.2:

The Data Link Properties pages (Provider tab) after the Connection object is set to point to the Northwind database

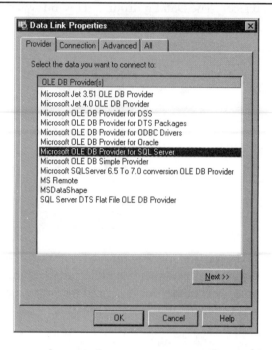

FIGURE 6.3:

The Data Link Properties pages (Connection tab)

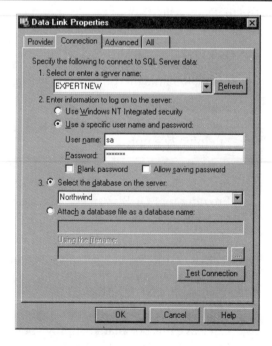

5. Select a database on the server, or attach an SQL Database file as a database. Don't worry about the last option (your DB Administrator will let you know whether and when you'll have to use this option). In the drop-down list under Select the Database on the Server, select the name of the Northwind database.

6. Click the Test Connection button to make sure the connection is working. You should see a message box informing you that the test was successful. If not, verify the information that you have entered.

NOTE   If you want to connect to an Access database, the Connection tab will be different. Simply locate the `NWIND.MDB` file on your hard disk through a File Open dialog box and select it.

---

7. In the Advanced tab, set the Connect Timeout property. If the connection can't be established in the specified time interval, the Connection object will time out. Don't change the value of this property (the default value is an empty string) unless you're working over a slow connection.

8. When done, click OK.

You have just established a connection to the Northwind database through the DE Designer. Select the Northwind connection object in the DataEnvironment window. Then open the Properties window and observe that the DE Designer has set the ConnectionSource property to the same value you set the ConnectionString property to, manually, in the section "The Connection Object," in the previous chapter.

From now on, you can add the DE Designer to your projects and use it to establish a connection to the Northwind database. If you want, copy the connection string property built by the Designer and use it in your code. To view the connection string built by the DE Designer, select the Connection object in the DE Designer's window and then select the ConnectionSource property in the Properties window. The Northwind Connection object's ConnectionSource property is:

```
Provider=SQLOLEDB.1;Persist Security Info=False;User ID=sa;
Initial Catalog=Northwind
```

The Data Source item is missing from the ConnectionSource property, because the database is running on the local machine.

Creating Command Objects

In addition to using the DE Designer to create Connection objects, you can also use it to access tables, execute queries and stored procedures against a database, and more. To execute a command against the database, you must create the appropriate Command object. Let's create a Command object to open a table.

1. Right-click the Northwind object and select Add Command from the shortcut menu. The Command1 object will be appended to the Northwind Connection. Rename the Command1 object to AllCustomers by selecting Rename from the object's shortcut menu.

2. Right-click the AllCustomers icon and select Properties from the shortcut menu. The Properties pages will appear, as shown in Figure 6.4. This window contains six tabs, but we are not going to examine all of them in this chapter. Some of them are required for advanced operations and are discussed later in the book.

FIGURE 6.4:

The General tab of the Command object's Properties pages

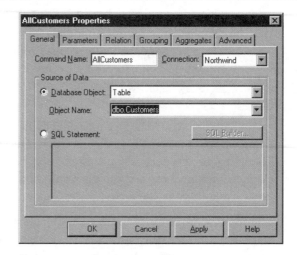

3. On the General tab, you will see the names of the Connection and the Command. The DE Designer can establish multiple connections to databases and execute different commands against each one. In the Source of Data section, specify the command, which can be a table's name, stored procedure, or SQL statement. Select Table from the Database Object drop-down list and then select the Customers table from the Object Name drop-down list. Click OK to close the Command Properties window.

The remaining tabs are used to create hierarchical Recordsets and are discussed in Chapter 10, "Shaping Your Data." On the last tab of the Command object's Properties pages, you can set the type and location of the cursor, as well as the locking mechanism. It is also possible to set these properties in the Properties window of the Command object (in the lower right corner of the IDE, not shown here).

Specifying a Recordset with an SQL Statement

If you choose to specify the desired Recordset with an SQL statement, you can check the SQL Statement option on the General tab and then click the SQL Builder button. This will open a new window, which is very similar to the Query Designer of the visual database tools. However, you can't drop tables from the Data View window on the SQL Builder. You must specify the select statement yourself, then right-click somewhere on the SQL pane and select Verify SQL Syntax. The SQL Builder will verify the syntax of the statement and will also populate the Tables pane. If you don't know how to write your own SQL statements, or you would rather use a visual tool, you can still use the Query Designer (you can access it any time from the Data View window), design your query with point-and-click operations, and then copy the SQL statement and paste it on the Query Builder's window.

If you switch to the Advanced tab, shown in Figure 6.5, you will see that the default Recordset created by the DE Designer is read-only and resides on the client. The Cursor Type option is disabled, because all client-side cursors are static by definition. The Read-Only option is a very good choice, although we are going to change it. You must set the Lock Type to Optimistic, so that you can edit the Customers table.

FIGURE 6.5:

The Advanced tab of the Command Object's Properties pages

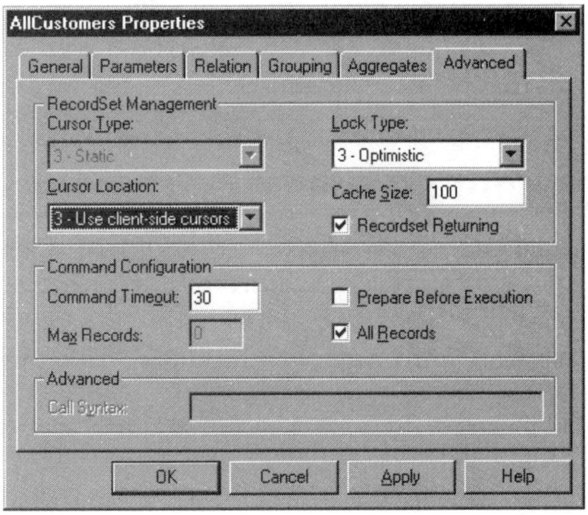

The read-only cursor is your best choice as far as locking goes, because it avoids concurrency problems. To edit the underlying table(s), you should prepare the appropriate stored procedures, as discussed in Chapter 7, "Transact-SQL," and let SQL Server handle the updates. You will see examples of updating tables with stored procedures in Chapter 7, and there will be more elaborate examples in Chapter 17, "Building an Invoicing Application."

WARNING   If you're using Access and the OLE DB Provider for the Jet Engine, you should be aware of the following: the Command objects inherit the CursorLocation property of the Connection object. The CursorLocation property of the Connection object is by default client-side. If you change the CursorLocation property of the Recordset object, you will get a runtime error to the effect that the application uses arguments of the wrong type, or arguments that are in conflict with one another. This means that the Connection and Command objects have different settings for their CursorLocation property. You must set the CursorLocation property of the Connection object before you add any Commands to it. To change an existing Recordset's cursor location, you must first change its Connection object's CursorLocation property. If you're using the OLE DB driver with SQL Server, the CursorLocation property of the Recordset object overwrites the setting of the same property of the Connection object. To change the CursorLocation (and CursorType) of a Connection or a Command object, select the corresponding object in the DataEnvironment window and locate the property name in the Properties window. If you ever have to change the cursor's Properties, delete the existing Command object and create a new one.

The Advanced tab also has a check box named Recordset Returning. Check this box if the command returns a Recordset (which is what most commands do, anyway). If the command updates a table or doesn't return a Recordset, you should clear this box. Not that ADO will return a Recordset when it shouldn't, but it will have to figure out the type of the command and decide whether it should return a Recordset or not. This involves some overhead, which you can avoid by setting the Recordset Returning option on the Advanced tab.

Programming the DataEnvironment Objects

So, you have created a connection to a database, and you can view its tables through the appropriate Command objects. But what good are these objects for your application? In this section you'll learn how to access the objects of the database through the objects of the DataEnvironment window from within your VB code.

Switch to the project's Form and open it in design mode. Place a Command button on the Form and then double-click it to open the Code window. In the Command1_Click() event handler, enter the name of the Designer object followed by a period:

```
DataEnvironment1.
```

Visual Basic will display a list with the members of the DataEnvironment object; select the one you need with the arrow keys. The DataEnvironment1 object exposes the members shown in Table 6.1.

TABLE 6.1: Members of the DataEnvironment Object

Object Name	Description
AllCustomers	A method you must call to open the AllCustomers Recordset. The AllCustomers method is equivalent to the Execute method of an ADO Command object.
Commands	A collection with all the Command objects of the DataEnvironment1 object. The first item in the Commands collection has an index value of 1, not 0.
Connections	A collection with all the Connection objects of the DataEnvironment1 object. The first item in the Connections collection has an index value of 1, not 0.
Name	The DataEnvironment object's name
Northwind	The Northwind Connection object. The DE Designer creates a separate object for each connection and names it after the Connection object.
Recordsets	A collection with all the Recordset objects of the DataEnvironment object. The first item in the Recordsets collection has an index value of 1, not 0.
rsAllCstomers	The AllCustomers Recordset object, which is an ADO Recordset object. The DE Designer creates a separate object for each Recordset and names it after the Recordset object. This Recordset object is initially empty, and you must call the AllCustomers method to populate it.

The DE Designer creates all the ADO objects required to access the specified table. All you have to do is call the AllCustomers method to populate the rsAll-Customers Recordset and then work with it. Let's write a few lines of code to print the basic properties of each object. In the command button's Click event handler, enter the lines shown in Listing 6.1.

> **NOTE**
>
> The following listing is also available on the companion CD in the DEDemo project file in Chapter 6 folder. Please be sure to edit the Connection object so that it points to the Northwind database on your computer.

LISTING 6.1   Exercising the Basic DE Members

```
Private Sub Command1_Click()
Debug.Print "DataEnvironment Object Name:   " & _
            DataEnvironment1.Name
Debug.Print "Number of Commands in the DE object: " & _
            DataEnvironment1.Commands.Count
For i = 1 To DataEnvironment1.Commands.Count
    Debug.Print "    Command #" & i & ":   " & _
            DataEnvironment1.Commands(i).Name
    Debug.Print "                    " & _
            DataEnvironment1.Commands(i).CommandText
Next i
Debug.Print "Number of Connections in the DE object:   " & _
            DataEnvironment1.Connections.Count
```

```
For i = 1 To DataEnvironment1.Connections.Count
    Debug.Print "                    " & _
            DataEnvironment1.Connections(i).ConnectionString
Next i
Debug.Print "DataEnvironment Object Name:    " & _
            DataEnvironment1.Name
Debug.Print "            Connection String:    " & _
            DataEnvironment1.Northwind.ConnectionString
Debug.Print "Number of Recordsets in the DE object:    " & _
            DataEnvironment1.Recordsets.Count
For i = 1 To DataEnvironment1.Recordsets.Count
    Debug.Print "  Connection #" & i & ":  " & _
                DataEnvironment1.Recordsets(i).DataMember
    Debug.Print "                    " & _
                DataEnvironment1.Recordsets(i).Source
Next i
' DISPLAY COLUMN NAMES
Debug.Print "rsCustomers Recordset Columns"
For i = 0 To DataEnvironment1.rsAllCustomers.Fields.Count - 1
    Debug.Print DataEnvironment1.rsAllCustomers.Fields(i).Name;
Next i
Debug.Print
' DISPLAY COLUMN VALUES
DataEnvironment1.AllCustomers
DataEnvironment1.rsAllCustomers.MoveNext
While Not DataEnvironment1.rsAllCustomers.EOF
    For i = 0 To DataEnvironment1.rsAllCustomers.Fields.Count - 1
        Debug.Print _
            DataEnvironment1.rsAllCustomers.Fields(i).Value & _
            vbTab;
    Next i
    DataEnvironment1.rsAllCustomers.MoveNext
    Debug.Print
Wend
End Sub
```

This listing contains very long expressions, but you should be accustomed to Visual Basic's object hierarchies by now. You can shorten these long expressions by using intermediate variables. For example, you can assign the `DataEnvironment1` `.rsAllCustomers` object to a Recordset object variable, *RS*, and replace all instances of the lengthier Recordset expression with the variable name RS. First, declare an ADO Recordset variable and set it to the Recordset object of the DE Designer:

```
Dim RS As ADODB.Recordset
Set RS = DataEnvironment1.rsAllCustomers
```

After this declaration, you can rewrite long lines like the following one:

```
DataEnvironment1.rsAllCustomers.MoveNext
```

as:

```
RS.MoveNext
```

Alternatively, you can use the With structure:

```
With DataEnvironment1.rsAllCustomers
    While Not .EOF
        For i = 0 To .Fields.Count - 1
            Debug.Print .Fields(i).Value & vbTab;
        Next
        .MoveNext
        Debug.Print
    Wend
End With
```

Here's the output produced by the listing shown earlier. The headings will not be highlighted in the Immediate window; I've placed them in bold so they stand out in the text:

```
DataEnvironment Object Name:   DataEnvironment1
Number of Commands in the DE object:    1
    Command #1:    AllCustomers
                   select * from "dbo"."Customers"
Number of Connections in the DE object:    1
Provider=SQLOLEDB.1;Persist Security Info=False;User ID=sa;Initial Cat-
alog=Northwind;Locale Identifier=1033;Connect Timeout=15;Use Procedure
for Prepare=1;Auto Translate=True;Packet Size=4096;Workstation
ID=EXPERTNEW
DataEnvironment Object Name:   DataEnvironment1
        Connection String:      Provider=SQLOLEDB.1;Persist Security
Info=False;User ID=sa;Initial Catalog=Northwind;Locale Identi-
fier=1033;Connect Timeout=15;Use Procedure for Prepare=1;Auto Trans-
late=True;Packet Size=4096;Workstation ID=EXPERTNEW
Number of Recordsets in the DE object:    1
    Connection #1:
                   select * from "dbo"."Customers"
rsCustomers Recordset Columns
CustomerID
CompanyName
ContactName
ContactTitle
Address
City
Region
PostalCode
```

```
Country
Phone
Fax
ALFKI    Alfreds Futterkiste Maria Anders
         Sales Representative
         Obere Str. 57   Berlin        12209
         Germany
         030-0074321 030-0076545
ANATR    Ana Trujillo Emparedados y helados
         Ana Trujillo
         Owner    Avda. de la Constitución 2222
         México D.F.      05021    Mexico
         (5) 555-4729     (5) 555-3745
```

As you can see, the DataEnvironment Designer is a visual tool that allows you to prepare the objects you need to access the desired data in the database with point-and-click operations. Once the appropriate objects have been set up, you can use them from within your code to access the actual data. The DataEnvironment's objects correspond to ADO objects, and you can now use them in your VB code. In this section's example, you saw how to read the fields of the cursor. Had you specified an SQL statement instead of a table name, you'd be able to retrieve not just a table's rows, but combine rows from multiple tables based on any criteria you wish. You can also set up commands to modify a table's rows (a non-Recordset-returning command), a topic discussed in the following section.

Updating Tables through the DataEnvironment Objects

You can experiment with data modification operations on your own, using the objects exposed by the DE Designer. For example, you can use a loop like the one in Listing 6.2 to iterate through the rows of the Customers table and replace the country names with proper case strings (use uppercase for the first character and convert the following to lowercase). To update the Country fields, place another command button on the Form and enter the following code in its Click event handler:

LISTING 6.2   **Updating Fields through the rsAllCustomers Object**

```
Private Sub Command2_Click()
DataEnvironment1.AllCustomers
While Not DataEnvironment1.rsAllCustomers.EOF
    DataEnvironment1.rsAllCustomers.Fields("Country") = _
    UCase(Left(DataEnvironment1.rsAllCustomers.Fields _
            ("Country"), 1)) & _
            Mid(DataEnvironment1.rsAllCustomers.
                    Fields("Country"), 2)
```

```
                    DataEnvironment1.rsAllCustomers.MoveNext
        Wend
        End Sub
```

The code doesn't take into consideration abbreviations like U.K. or country names with multiple words like United States; you can write a more elaborate VB routine to change the strings.

If you attempt to execute these lines, you may get an error message indicating that the provider does not support the requested operation. The problem is with the default Recordset generated by the DE Designer. Switch to the Advanced tab of the AllCustomers object's Properties pages and change the locking type from Read-Only to Optimistic.

Let's build another Command object that updates selected rows in the Products table. We'll add a simple command that increases the price of all products in the Condiments category by 10 percent (the ID of the Condiments category is 2). Create a new Command object under the Northwind Connection object and name it ChangePrices. Open the new object's Properties pages and, in the General tab, check the SQL Statement button and enter the following SQL statement:

```
UPDATE Products
SET UnitPrice = UnitPrice * 1.1
WHERE CategoryID=2
```

If you switch to the Advanced tab, you'll see that the Recordset Returning option button is cleared. The DE Designer figured out that the Command doesn't return a Recordset and cleared the option button. To execute this command, place a Command button on the Form and insert the following line in its Click event handler:

```
Sub Command3_Click()
    DataEnvironment1.ChangePrices
End Sub
```

Run the application again, and click the newly added button; the prices of the selected products will be updated instantly. This time, the work will be carried out by Access. ADO will simply pass the command to Access, and Access will execute it. The advantage of using SQL statements to update the tables is that you don't have to move each row to the client, edit it, and then send it back to the server. The operation is faster and doesn't burden the network with unnecessary traffic.

NOTE To summarize, the DataEnvironment Designer exposes a method for each Command object, which has the same name as the Command object, and a Recordset property, which has the same name as the Command object with the "rs" prefix. If you have created an object named *AllCustomers*, the DataEnvironment will create an *AllCustomers* method and an *rsAllCustomers* Recordset. Call the AllCustomers method to populate the rsAllCustomers Recordset. The rsAllCustomers object is an ADO Recordset, and you can manipulate it through the properties and methods discussed in the previous chapter. To access the Recordset object with the customers, use the expression `DataEnvironment1.rsAllCustomers`. Just append a period to the previous expression followed by the name of the property or method you want to call. `DataEnvironment1.rsAllCustomers.Recordcount` is the number of rows in the cursor, and `DataEnvironment1.rsAllCustomers.Fields` is a collection object with the current row's fields.

Building Forms with Data-Bound Controls

Now that you've learned how to create ADO objects in code, or with the help of the DataEnvironment object, you're ready to build Forms to display the data and allow the user to interact with the application and edit the data. You can write code that maps a field to a TextBox control and use the control's value to update the corresponding table in the database, but this is not necessary. For instance, you can simply tell Visual Basic that a specific TextBox must be bound to the CompanyName field of the Customers table and Visual Basic will do the rest. Namely, it will update the control every time you move to another row. If you edit the control's contents, the new value will overwrite the existing one in the database.

As you probably know, many of the standard controls of Visual Basic can be bound to a data source. A TextBox control, for example, can be bound to a specific field in the data source, and every time you move to another row, the control's contents change to reflect the field's value. If the cursor is updateable, you can edit the control and update the value of the underlying field in the database. These controls are called *data-bound*. To bind a control on your Form to a specific field in a database, you must set their DataSource, DataMember, and DataField properties. These properties are referred to as *data-binding* properties and are explained in the following section.

One of the functions of the DataEnvironment object is to populate a Form with data-bound controls that display the fields of a Command object. All you have to do is drop a Command object on the Form, and it will automatically create all the required data-bound controls. It sounds too simple to be true, doesn't it? You'll see the limitations of this simple approach to database programming, and then we'll move on to some "real" database programming. I'm not suggesting you ignore the data-bound controls, but you shouldn't expect to build real applications with point-and-click operations. Let's see how the DE Designer can simplify the most tedious step in database application design and then look at some examples.

Binding Controls to Database Fields

In this section we'll discuss the properties that allow you to bind a control to a field in the database (the data-binding properties) and how the data-bound control behaves as you navigate through the Recordset. Switch to the project discussed in "Programming the DataEnvironment Objects," earlier in this chapter. (If you haven't created it yet, open the CustomersDE project on the companion CD.) The DataEnvironment window contains the Northwind Connection object and the All-Customers Command object. You're all set to display the customer data on a Form. Switch to the project's Form and, while both the DataEnvironment window and the Form are visible on your screen, drop the AllCustomers object on the Form. The DataEnvironment Designer will create a data-bound control for each field. Figure 6.6 shows what your screen should look like.

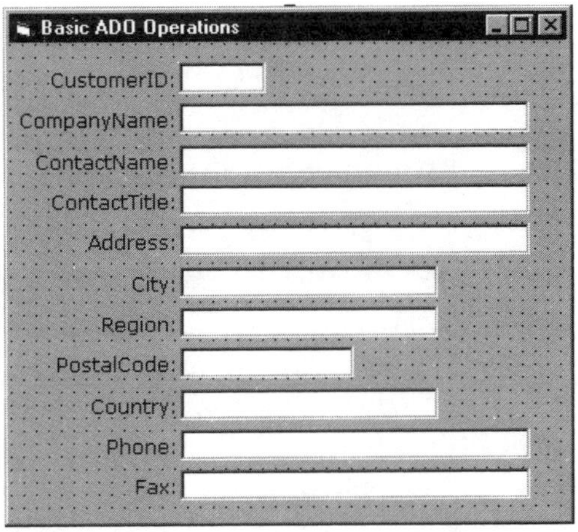

FIGURE 6.6:

The DE Designer can create a Form with the data-bound controls to display the fields of a Recordset.

As you can see, the DE Designer has created the outline of a data-entry Form. Each field in the Recordset is mapped to a TextBox control on the Form, through its data-binding properties, which are explained next:

> **DataSource** This property specifies the name of the Command object through which the control binds to the database. Its value is usually the name of a DataEnvironment object, but it can also be the name of an ADO Data Control (this control is discussed in "Using the ADO Data Control" later in the chapter). All the TextBox controls on the Form are bound

through the DataEnvironment object and their DataSource property is set to "DataEnvironment1."

DataMember If the control is bound to a database field through a Data-Environment object, this property is set to the appropriate Command object. In our example, the DataMember property for all TextBox controls on the Form is the name of the AllCustomers Command object. If the DataSource property were the name of an ADO Data Control, you wouldn't have to set this property.

DataField Use this property to specify which field will be bound to the data-bound control. The Recordset specified by the DataSource and the DataMember properties contains many columns, but each data-bound control can be bound to a single column only. Each TextBox control on the Form is bound to a different column. Notice also that the size of each TextBox control is set to the size of the column it maps.

If you press F5 to run the application, you will see the fields of the first row in the Recordset. There are no navigational tools on the Form, and you can't do much with it. However, it's quite easy to add a few navigational buttons. Place four Command buttons on the Form and set their captions as shown in Figure 6.7. Then insert the code in Listing 6.3 in their Click event handlers.

LISTING 6.3   **The Navigational Buttons**

```
Private Sub bttnFirst_Click()
    DataEnvironment1.rsAllCustomers.MoveFirst
End Sub

Private Sub bttnLast_Click()
    DataEnvironment1.rsAllCustomers.MoveLast
End Sub

Private Sub bttnNext_Click()
    DataEnvironment1.rsAllCustomers.MoveNext
    If DataEnvironment1.rsAllCustomers.EOF Then
        DataEnvironment1.rsAllCustomers.MoveLast
    End If
End Sub

Private Sub bttnPrevious_Click()
    DataEnvironment1.rsAllCustomers.MovePrevious
    If DataEnvironment1.rsAllCustomers.BOF Then
        DataEnvironment1.rsAllCustomers.MoveFirst
    End If
End Sub
```

The four Command buttons are the simplest navigational capabilities you can add to your application.

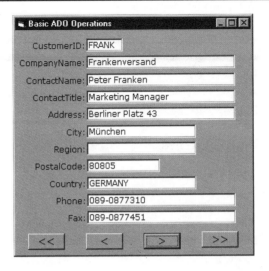

To move to the first, previous, next, and last row, you must call the Recordset object's MoveFirst, MovePrevious, MoveNext, and MoveLast methods respectively. There's a small complication, however. You must prevent the user from moving past the end of the Recordset. The last row in the Recordset is a valid row, and the EOF property isn't set to True when we land on this row. The same is true for the first row in the Recordset—landing on the first row won't set the BOF property of the Recordset object to True. The EOF and BOF properties are set to True only when we attempt to move past the last and first rows in the Recordset.

The row after the last one in the Recordset is not invalid. If you move to this row, the Recordset object automatically appends a new row. The new row's fields will be initially empty, and you can assign values to the fields by entering these values into the appropriate TextBox controls. As far as data-entry applications go, however, this is an unusual behavior. Data-entry operators expect to see an Add or New button on the Form, which they must click to add a new row. Also missing are Edit, Cancel, and OK buttons. To commit changes made to fields in the current row, you must move to another row. Change a few fields and move to the next or previous row. Then return to the row you edited and you will see that the changes have taken effect.

The navigational methods of the Recordset object are quite limited too. Who needs to move to the next and previous row? Users should be able to retrieve rows in many different ways (by entering the first few words in a book's title, a company name, and so on). A product's code or a book's ISBN is a far better choice, provided this information is readily available. When you move to the cash register in a bookstore, the cashier will either scan the book's bar code or type the book's ISBN, which is printed on the book. In other words, you shouldn't try hard to make elaborate user interfaces that allow users to locate items in many different ways, unless you're building an online store. The most practical data-entry Forms are usually the simpler ones. We'll have more to say about building user interfaces later in this chapter, as well as in Chapter 8, "Making the Most of Stored Procedures." In Chapter 17 you'll find a feature-rich application for browsing and editing the books of the Biblio database.

The Customers Project

The built-in functionality of the Recordset object's navigational methods is not always adequate, so let's build a proper application for browsing and editing the rows of the Customers table. The DE Designer has placed the data-bound controls on the Form rather awkwardly. You should move and resize them accordingly to create a more functional, and aesthetically pleasing, Form and set their tab order accordingly (this is a very important aspect of data-entry Forms, as most users prefer the keyboard to the mouse). The Form shown in Figure 6.8 looks much more like a data-entry Form than the Form generated by the DE Designer.

Designing the Form   You already have a DataEnvironment object with a connection to the Northwind database and a command that retrieves the rows of the Customers table. Place a few TextBox controls on the Form, one for each field, and arrange them as you would like them to appear. Place a label with the corresponding field's name in front of each TextBox. Figure 6.8 shows the Form of the Customers project you'll find in this chapter's folder on the companion CD.

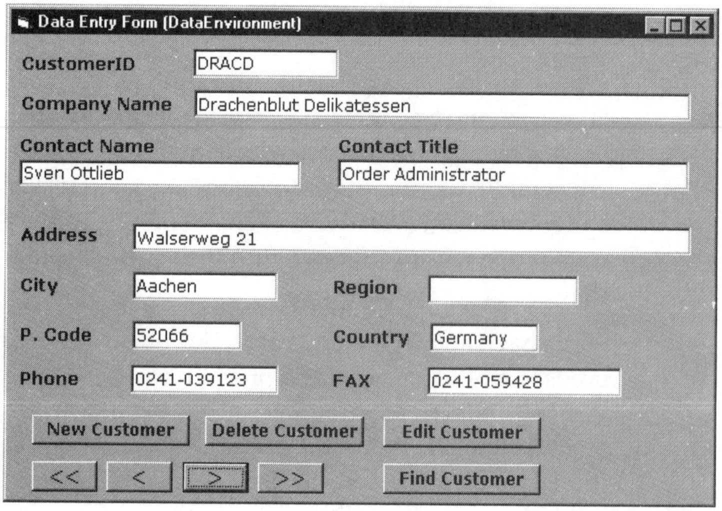

FIGURE 6.8:

The Customers project uses ADO objects to access the Customers table.

Select all the TextBox controls on the Form and set their DataSource property to DataEnvironment1 and their DataMember property to AllCustomers. Then select each TextBox individually and set its DataField to the name of field in its data source. This will bind the TextBox controls to their fields.

Then place the four navigational Command buttons at the bottom of the Form. Insert the code of Listing 6.3 in their Click event handlers. You can already run the project and browse the customers. You can also edit them, but don't do it yet. We'll build a more functional interface for editing the fields.

Now place the editing buttons—New Customer, Edit Customer, and Delete Customer—at the bottom of the Form. The names of these buttons are bttnAdd, bttnEdit, and bttnDelete. Place OK and Cancel buttons as well and name them bttnOK and bttnCancel.

The Form should work in two distinct modes: browsing and editing. In browsing mode, users can navigate through the Recordset and shouldn't be allowed to edit the fields. To prevent the editing of the controls on the Form, you can simply set their Locked property to True. Select all the TextBox controls on the Form again and lock them.

To enter edit mode, the user must click the Add Customer or Edit Customer button. The Edit button signals the user's intention to edit the current row. The application must unlock the controls and hide the navigational buttons, to restrict the user to the current row, and display the OK and Cancel buttons. When done editing, the user must click the OK button to commit the changes to the database or the Cancel button to undo the changes. When either button is clicked, the application must hide the OK and Cancel buttons and restore the navigational buttons again. The Add button works in a similar way: It adds a new row and the user can edit it as before. The operation is completed or terminated with the click of the OK or Cancel button.

Finally, the Delete button should remove the current row and move to the row visited last. This isn't always feasible, because the user may delete many rows, one after the other. We will move to the first valid row in the Recordset and leave it up to the user to locate a row with the Find button or the navigational buttons.

The first three buttons should be initially visible and the OK and Cancel buttons invisible. You also need two routines to show and hide the buttons when the user switches between browse and edit modes—the ShowButtons() and HideButtons() subroutines (which I won't list here). Likewise, you need two more subroutines—LockFields() and UnlockFields()—which turn on and off the Locked property of the data-bound controls. You should protect the user from changing field values accidentally by locking the controls on the Form. The controls will be unlocked only when a row is being edited or a new row is added.

Programming the Buttons   When the New Customer button is clicked, the program must add a new row to the Recordset, unlock the data-bound controls, hide the editing buttons, and display the OK and Cancel buttons. Because the user may change his mind and cancel the addition of the new row, the code must mark the current row, so that it can return to it. Do this by saving its Bookmark property into a Form variable, the *lastRow* variable. Listing 6.4 shows the Add Customer button's Click event handler.

LISTING 6.4   **Adding a New Customer**

```
Private Sub bttnAdd_Click()
    HideButtons
    Unlockfields
    If DataEnvironment1.rsAllCustomers.Supports(adBookmark) Then
        lastRow = DataEnvironment1.rsAllCustomers.Bookmark
    End If
    DataEnvironment1.rsAllCustomers.AddNew
End Sub
```

I used the Supports property to make sure the Recordset supports bookmarks. This isn't really necessary, because we know that a client-side static cursor supports bookmarks. Other Recordset types do not support bookmarks. If the application can change the Recordset type from within its own code, you must make sure it doesn't attempt to call nonsupported properties and methods.

When the Edit Customer button is clicked, you must unlock the data-bound controls and hide the buttons on the Form with the code in Listing 6.5.

LISTING 6.5   **Editing the Current Row**

```
Private Sub bttnEdit_Click()
    HideButtons
    Unlockfields
End Sub
```

Now, let's see what happens when the user ends an operation with the OK button. To save the changes to the database, you must call the Recordset's Update method. If the method can save the changes to the database, you exit. If the Update method can't commit the changes to the database (most likely because a field has the wrong data type), you must display a message. First, distinguish whether the user ends an add or edit operation. This information is returned by the value of the Recordset's EditMode property, which returns one of the values: adEditAdd, adEditDelete, adEditInProgress, and adEditNone. Use this information to display the appropriate error message, should the operation fail. The code for this is shown in Listing 6.6.

LISTING 6.6	**Ending an Edit Operation**

```
Private Sub bttnOK_Click()
On Error Resume Next
DataEnvironment1.rsAllCustomers.Update
If Err.Number <> 0 Then
    If DataEnvironment1.rsAllCustomers.EditMode = adEditAdd Then
        MsgBox "Could not add record." & vbCrLf & Err.Description
    Else
        MsgBox "Could not save changes." & vbCrLf & _
                Err.Description
    End If
    DataEnvironment1.rsAllCustomers.CancelUpdate
    DataEnvironment1.rsAllCustomers.Move 0
End If
ShowButtons
LockFields

End Sub
```

If the user cancels the operation, we simply call the Recordset object's CancelUpdate method, which cancels both the addition of a new row and the editing of the current row and restores the buttons at the bottom of the Form. If the operation that was canceled was an add operation, we return to the last visited row by setting the Bookmark property of the Recordset.

> **NOTE**
>
> Notice the line that calls the Move method, after an edit operation has been canceled. This method forces the Recordset to restore the data-bound controls to the original field values, before they were edited by the user. If you omit this line, then your edits will remain on the screen, and the information on the Form will not match the actual information in the database.

If the Cancel button is clicked, the code must restore an existing row to its original state, or reject the addition of a new row. Listing 6.7 shows the code of the Cancel button's Click event handler.

LISTING 6.7	**Canceling an Edit Operation**

```
Private Sub bttnCancel_Click()
    If DataEnvironment1.rsAllCustomers.EditMode = adEditAdd Then
        DataEnvironment1.rsAllCustomers.CancelUpdate
    Else
        DataEnvironment1.rsAllCustomers.CancelUpdate
        DataEnvironment1.rsAllCustomers.Move 0
```

```
        End If
        ShowButtons
        LockFields
    End Sub
```

To delete the current row, you must call the Recordset object's Delete method, as shown in Listing 6.8. After deleting a row, don't move to the next or previous row. Keep the deleted row on the Form until the user navigates to another row. You can modify the code so that it moves to the next row or to the last valid row already visited.

LISTING 6.8   Deleting the Current Row

```
Private Sub bttnDelete_Click()
    reply = _
        MsgBox("Record will be deleted permanently. Proceed?", _
        vbYesNo)
    If reply = vbYes Then
        On Error Resume Next
        DataEnvironment1.rsAllCustomers.Delete
        If Err.Number <> 0 Then
            MsgBox "Could not delete record." & vbCrLf & _
                    Err.Description
            DataEnvironment1.rsAllCustomers.CancelUpdate
        End If
        On Error Goto 0
    End If
End Sub
```

This is a simple data-entry Form, but it outlines the basic operations. It may not be impressive, but it won't confuse the users. If you want, you can open the project in the Visual Basic IDE and fix the tab order, assign shortcut keys to certain fields, or experiment with any of the features described at the beginning of this section.

You have certainly noticed all the error-trapping code. Any application that accesses databases must be able to cope with all types of errors. Rows may be locked, another user may delete a row before you get a chance to save your edits, and so on. This project will work as long as all the users in your corporation don't edit rows at will, all at the same time. Optimistic locking works best when the Recordset isn't being updated heavily and by many users. This is a very reasonable assumption for most practical situations. Why would two users edit the same invoice, or why would one user edit the row another user is about to delete? However, you should be able to handle all types of unexpected situations, and this complicates your code considerably. We'll return to the topic of handling ADO errors in Chapter 9, "Advanced ADO Topics."

Using the ADO Data Control

The DE Designer is a visual tool that helps you prepare the ADO objects you need to connect to a database. It can also place the appropriate controls on a Form and bind them to a table's columns by setting their data binding properties. However, it won't insert any code for you. You can access the ADO objects it creates as members of the DataEnvironment1 object and manipulate your connection to the database as well as the Recordset retrieved by the various Command objects. The data-bound controls are linked directly to fields in the database and your changes are committed to the database automatically. We are going to build a better data-entry Form, but first let's look at the ADO Data Control and how it's used with the same data-bound controls.

Visual Basic 6 ships with the ADO Data Control, which accesses databases through the ADO objects. The ADO Data Control is your application's visual gateway to a database. You can set it up to "see" any table or query in a database with point-and-click operations, similar to setting up a Data Link in the Data View window. Each ADO Data Control sees a single table in the database (or an SQL statement), and it represents the corresponding Recordset to your application. To view or manipulate multiple Recordsets, you must use one ADO Data Control for each Recordset. Alternatively, you can change the control's RecordSource property to view different Recordsets at different times, but this will complicate your code.

You may be wondering why I haven't discussed the ADO Data Control and the data-bound controls of Visual Basic earlier. Indeed, Visual Basic provides some really cool tools for developing database applications, but this is not how real database applications are built. These tools are great for beginners, but after you use them for a while you'll realize that they are nothing more than wrappers around the ADO objects. Now that you have developed a good understanding of the ADO object model, you'll be able to understand how the ADO Data Control works, when to use it, and how to program it.

To simplify database development, Visual Basic provides two Data Controls that can be used to connect the data-bound controls to a database. These controls are the equivalent of the DataEnvironment object, only they expose some additional functionality. The intrinsic Data Control works with the Data Access Objects (the DAO component), which is practically outdated. The DAO component will not be enhanced in the future (it hasn't been enhanced since version 5 of the language) and it's not discussed in this book. The other control, which we'll discuss in detail, is the ADO Data Control, which is based on the ActiveX Data Objects.

Setting up an ADO Data Control

To add an ADO Data Control to your project, right-click the Toolbox and select ADO Data Control 6.0 (OLEDB) from the Components dialog box. The ADO Data

Control's icon will appear in the Toolbox, and you can place one or more instances of the control on the Form. Once the ADO Data Control has been placed on the Form, you can use it to bind other controls to selected columns in the database.

The ADO Data Control resembles a Scrollbar control. The four buttons correspond to the four navigational methods of the Recordset object (MoveFirst, MovePrevious, MoveNext, and MoveLast). So, the ADO Data Control is visible at run time and allows the user to navigate through the Recordset. Try using this control to navigate through the rows of a Recordset with just a few dozen rows, and you'll see that it's quite inadequate as a navigational tool. However, many programmers use the ADO Data Control to access their databases, but keep it invisible at run time.

To access a database through the ADO Data Control, you must set the following properties of the Data control:

ConnectionString   This string contains all the information required to connect to your database. We have discussed the attributes of the connection string, and I will not repeat them here.

RecordSource   This is a database object, such as a table, query, or stored procedure, that specifies the rows that make up the control's Recordset.

Place an ADO Data Control on a Form and then switch to its Properties window. If you select the ConnectionString property, you will see a button with an ellipsis. Click this button to open the General tab of the control's Property pages. Likewise, if you select the control's RecordSource property and click the button with the ellipsis, the RecordSource tab of the control's Property pages will open. You can also right-click the control on the Form and select ADODC Properties from the shortcut menu to see the control's Property pages.

The General Tab

The General tab, shown in Figure 6.9, lets you specify the database you want to connect to (the control's data source). You can specify a data source with three different methods.

Use Data Link File   Click the Browse button and select the data link file on your hard disk. The process of creating data link files was explained in the section "Connecting to Databases" of Chapter 3.

Use ODBC Data Source Name   With this option you can specify the name of an ODBC Data Source Name (DSN). See the section "DSN-Based Connections" of Chapter 5 for a description of how to set up data sources. You can select an existing DSN from the list, or create a new one by clicking the New button.

Use Connection String   Use this option if you want to supply your own connection string. You can click the Build button to specify the connection string with point-and-click operations. If you click the Build button, you will see the Data Link Properties window, which was also described in the section "Connecting to Databases" of Chapter 3.

FIGURE 6.9:

The ADO Data Control's Property pages (the General tab)

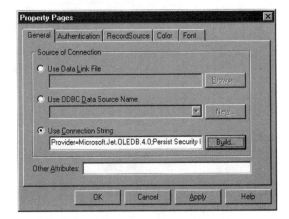

You can use any of the three methods to specify your connection to the database. Just remember that the second method will use the ODBC driver, and you should use it with databases that don't have native OLE DB drivers

The RecordSource Tab

Shown in Figure 6.10, the RecordSource tab lets you specify the control's RecordSource (the rows you want to access through the control). The RecordSource can be the name of a table, the result of an SQL statement, or the name of a stored procedure that returns the desired rows. In the Command Type box, select the type of RecordSource (adCmdText for an SQL statement, adCmdTable for a table's name, and adCmdStoredProcedure for a stored procedure's name). After you have specified the type of command that will return the desired rows, the objects of the specified type will appear in the second ComboBox control, where you can select one with the mouse. If the RecordSource is an SQL statement, you must enter the statement in the Command Text box.

The simplest thing you can do with the ADO Data Control is use it to bind a few controls to the Recordset's fields. As far as data-bound controls are concerned, the ADO Data Control is equivalent to the Command object of the DataEnvironment object. The data-bound controls will use the ADO Data Control to view (and update) a specific field in the database. Unlike the DataEnvironment object, however, the ADO Data Control has a user interface that exposes the navigational methods as buttons. Figure 6.11 shows the relationship between data-bound controls, the ADO Data Control, and the database.

FIGURE 6.10:

The ADO Data Control's
Property pages (the Record-
Source tab)

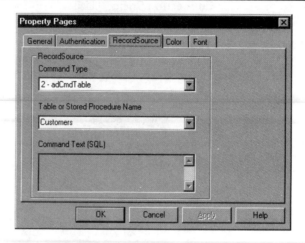

FIGURE 6.11:

Binding controls to database
fields through the Data Control

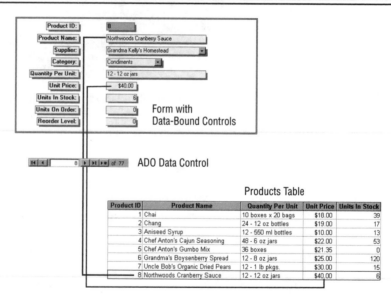

To bind a control to a field, just set the control's DataSource property to the name
of the ADO Data Control and assign the field's name to the DataField property of
the control. If you could execute the following statement every time the ADODC1
Data Control moves to another row of its Recordset, then the Text1 control would
display constantly the current value of the field CompanyName:

```
Text1.Text = Data1.Fields("CompanyName")
```

Likewise, if you could write the Text property of the TextBox control to the database before the control is moved to another row, then you could edit the cursor
through the TextBox control:

```
Data1.Fields("CompanyName") = Text1.Text
```

(By the way, you should also validate the new value before attempting to commit it to the database). These statements are quite valid, but they must be issued from within the proper events. Instead of having to monitor the Data Control's events, Visual Basic does this for you if you bind the intrinsic control to the Data Control.

ADO Data Control Properties

Select the ADO Data Control on the Form, switch to its Properties window, and take a look at its properties. This control combines the basic properties of all basic ADO objects. The ConnectionString and ConnectionTimeout properties are the same as with the Connection object. Set these properties accordingly to connect to the desired data source (or right-click the ADO Data Control to specify its data source with point-and-click operations). The CommandType property is the same as the Command object's property by that name. There's no CommandText property, but only because it has a different name. The source of the cursor underlying the ADO Data Control is specified with the RecordSource property.

As far as similarities to the Recordset object go, notice the CursorLocation and CursorType properties that specify the properties of the cursor, the LockType property that determines how the cursor's rows will be locked, and so on. There's nothing really new about the ADO Data Control. Everything you have learned about the ADO objects applies to the ADO Data Control as well, and you will find it very easy to understand what the ADO Data Control does and how you can manipulate it.

The ADO Data Control and ADO Members

The ADO Data Control is nothing but a wrapper for the ADO Recordset object. Unlike the ADO Recordset object, the ADO Data Control is visible at run time. It exposes its navigational methods with the help of four buttons at the two ends of the scrollbar (as if this is how users navigate through a Recordset). In addition, most properties can be set at design time through the Properties window. Instead of entering the statement:

```
RS.CursorLocation = adUseClient
```

you select the ADO Data Control on the Form and set its CursorLocation property in the Properties window to adUseClient. Sure, it's simpler to set properties with the mouse than writing code, but you should understand that the differences between the ADO Data Control and the ADO Recordset object are superficial. Many programmers don't like the visible interface of the ADO Data Control anyway, and they ignore it altogether. If you'd rather set property values in the Properties window instead of writing code, you can still use the control to simplify the design of the interface and keep the control invisible at run time.

The ADODataControl Project

In this section we'll build a project that uses an ADO Data Control and a few data-bound controls to create a user interface. It's not the most elaborate user interface you can build, but it doesn't require a single line of code. We'll build a project with a single Form for browsing (and editing) the customers of the NWIND database.

1. Start a new Standard EXE project, and rename its Form from Form1 to ADO-DataControlForm and the project from Project1 to ADODataControl.

2. The ADO Data Control is not loaded by default to the Toolbox (unless you create a Data Project). Right-click somewhere on the Toolbox and select Components from the shortcut menu. When the Components dialog box appears, check the box in front of Microsoft ADO Data Control 6.0 (OLE DB). Then click OK.

3. In your project, place an instance of the ADO Data Control on your Form.

4. Right-click the control and select Properties from the shortcut menu. In the General tab of the control's Properties pages, click the Build button to build the appropriate connection string.

5. You will see the Data Link Properties pages, where you can select the OLE DB Provider for SQL Server. Switch to the Connection tab and select the name of the Northwind database. If you don't have SQL Server installed, use the OLEDB provider for Microsoft Jet Engine and select the NWIND.MDB database. The project will work with either data source. Notice that you will not see any database names in the last drop-down list on the Connection tab, unless you have specified your user name and password for the SQL Server. If you select to log in using the Windows NT integrated security option, you don't have to specify user name and ID. Click OK to return to the ADO Data Control's Properties pages.

So far you have specified the properties of the connection. As I mentioned earlier, the ADO Data Control is a Recordset object in disguise, so we must specify the actual data we want to access (the cursor).

6. Switch to the RecordSource tab of the ADO Data Control's Properties pages to specify a table name or SQL query. To specify the type of the command, expand the Command Type drop-down list, and you will see the following options: adCmdUnknown, adCmdText, adCmdTable, adCmdStoredProcedure. Select adCmdTable.

7. Expand the second drop-down list on the RecordSource tab and select the name of the Customers table. Click OK to return to your Form.

You have specified the cursor of a Recordset and you're ready now to bind a few controls to the cursor's fields. Let's design the Form for viewing and editing the fields of the Customers table. The final Form is shown in Figure 6.12.

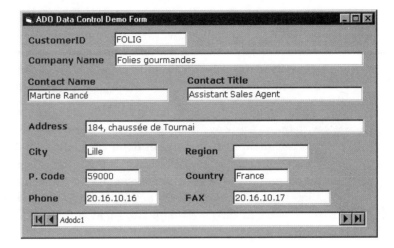

8. Place the Label and TextBox controls on the Form as shown in Figure 6.12. The Label controls will be used to display field names (or other, more descriptive field titles) and the TextBox controls to display the actual field values.

9. Select each TextBox control and set its data binding properties as follows:

    • Set the DataSource of all controls to ADODC1 (the name of the ADO Data Control on the Form).

    • Set the DataField property of each control to the appropriate field name. If you expand the DataField property's drop-down list, you will see the names of the fields in the Customers table, and you can select the desired one with the mouse.

Now run the project and use the ADO Data Control's buttons to navigate through the Recordset. The data-bound controls on the Form not only display the fields on the current row, they also allow you to edit these fields. If you change a few fields on the Form and then move to another record, the changes will be committed to the database. To locate a specific customer, you must keep clicking the Next button of the ADO Data Control until you land on the desired row. Not the best interface for a data-entry application, but we'll return to this topic shortly.

In short, the ADO Data Control exposes the navigational tools we had to code ourselves in the Customers project. Other than that, the two applications are identical. In the next section we'll take a look at the basic properties of the ADO

Data Control's properties, and then we'll explore a few more advanced data-bound controls.

The ADO Data Control's Recordset Property

The ADO Data Control is your gateway to a database. It exposes the basic properties of the Connection object, which allow you to connect to a database, and the basic properties of the Command object, which allow you to retrieve the desired rows. To access these rows, use the Recordset object. This is a property of the ADO Data Control, which in turn exposes the same properties as the ADO Recordset object.

As mentioned earlier, to access the data you must first land on the desired row with one of the Move methods or the Find method. After you set the current row, you can manipulate its fields through the methods of the Recordset object, which are all supported by the ADO Data Control's Recordset property. To iterate through the rows of the Data Control's cursor, use the Move methods. The Fields property allows you to access the fields of the current row. The following expression returns the value of the first field in the current row:

```
ADODC1.Recordset.Fields(0)
```

Likewise, you can assign a new value to this property to update the database:

```
ADODC1Recordset.Fields(0) = new_value
```

To delete a record use the expression:

```
ADODC1Recordset.Delete
```

This method accepts the same arguments as the Delete method of the Recordset object. To commit the changes to the database or cancel the edits, call one of these methods:

```
ADODC1Recordset.Update
```

or

```
ADODC1Recordset.CancelUpdate
```

The ADO Data Control supports two more very important properties, which don't have counterparts in the Recordset object: the EOFAction and BOFAction properties.

The EOFAction Property

Use this property to tell the control how to handle the EOF condition (what to do when the user is already on the last record and clicks the MoveNext button). By default, the ADO Data Control will move to the last record. You can change this default behavior by assigning one of the constants in Table 6.2 to the EOFAction property.

TABLE 6.2:   Settings of the EOFAction Property

Constant	Description
adDoMoveLast	Control moves automatically to the last record.
adStayEOF	Control stays at EOF. The data-bound controls are blank (there are no fields to display), and the EOF property returns True. Use this value when you want to handle the EOF condition from within your code (perhaps jump to the first record in the Recordset).
adDoAddNew	This setting automatically creates a new record and waits for the user to supply values to the fields of the newly added record.

If you set the EOFAction to adDoAddNew to add records to a Recordset, beware of the following:

- The operation can't be canceled without any code. Every time users land on a new record, this record will be committed to the database, so users must provide values for all fields that don't accept Null values.

- Auto-increment fields are not displayed. Although a new value is supplied automatically to every auto-increment field, these values are not displayed (and in most cases, the actual value doesn't make any difference, so avoid displaying auto-increment fields if you can).

The BOFAction Property

Use this property to tell the control how to handle the BOF condition (what to do when the user is already on the first record and clicks the MovePrevious button). By default, the ADO Data Control will move to the first record. You can change this default behavior by assigning one of the constants in Table 6.3 to the BOFAction property:

TABLE 6.3:   Settings of the BOFAction Property

Constant	Description
adDoMoveFirst	Control moves automatically to the first record.
adStayFirst	Control stays at BOF. The data-bound controls are blank (there are no fields to display) and the BOF property returns True. Use this value when you want to handle the BOF condition from within your code (perhaps to jump to the last record in the Recordset).

Notice that there is no option for adding a new row to the Recordset when the beginning of the Recordset is reached, equivalent to the adDoAddNew option of the EOFAction property.

The Data Form Wizard

One of the many Wizards that come with VB is the Data Form Wizard, which builds simple data-entry Forms for individual tables and generates some of the necessary code for you. As you'll see, I'm not too fond of this Wizard. It uses the ADO Data Control's navigational methods (which I think are primitive), it can't handle lookup fields, and it sometimes produces code that doesn't work. Yet, it's not a waste of time to look briefly at the code it generates. I have included this section to show you what can go wrong with this Wizard and warn you before it drives you nuts.

In addition to simple data-entry Forms, the Wizard can produce more complicated Forms with the DataGrid control and Master/Detail Forms. You have already seen how simple it is to use the DataGrid control with your Forms, and you can build Master/Detail Forms using the DataList control and a few lines of code. In Chapter 10, "Shaping Your Data," you'll learn how to build elaborate Master/Detail Forms. Actually, the Data Form Wizard uses the techniques described in Chapter 10 behind the scenes.

Building a Data-Entry Form with the Wizard

Let's build a simple data-entry Form with the Data Form Wizard to see how it does it and what could go wrong. The Data Form Wizard is an add-in, which you must explicitly load. Open the Add-Ins menu, select Add-In Manager, and double-click VB6 Data Form Wizard in the dialog box that appears. Then click OK to return to the Visual Basic IDE. Follow these steps to create a data-entry Form:

1. To start the Wizard, open the Add-Ins menu and select Data Form.

2. In the first window, you can select a profile with your personal settings. For this example, skip this screen.

3. In the next window, select the driver to be used. Select Access and click OK.

4. Select the name of the Access database. Locate the NWIND.MDB file on your hard disk and click OK. The Wizard will set up a connection to the NWIND database, but you can change the ConnectionString property and connect to a SQL Server database.

5. Now select the type of Form you want to create. Select Single Record and check the ADO Code button in the Binding Type section. (If you select the ADO Data Control option, the Wizard will generate an application that's based on the ADO Data Control).

The Wizard will create a Recordset object in code to store the rows of the table you will select. In addition, it will actually create something that looks like an ADO Data Control as the only navigational tool on the Form. I suggest you provide buttons to locate a row (using the Find method), or select the desired row in a Data-Combo or DataList control. (If the Wizard is so partial to the ADO Data Control interface, then why don't we check the ADO Data Control option? You can experiment with the other options on your own, but right now you'll benefit by examining the code that manipulates the ADO objects).

6. In the next screen, select the name of the table (you can't specify a query) and the columns you want on the Form. Select the Customers table and all its columns. Click Next.

7. Specify which buttons you want on the Form:

   Add button Adds a new row to the Recordset (in effect, it saves the users from having to go to the blank row after the last row in the table).

   Update button Commits the changes to the database. If you move to another row, the changes will be committed anyway. If you don't like this behavior, disable the navigational buttons while a new record is being edited and display them again when the user clicks the Update button.

   Delete button Removes the current row from the table. This is a useful button, as the ADO Data Control doesn't allow deletions.

   Refresh button Re-reads the Recordset's rows from the database, so that users can view changes made by other users. If you examine the code, you'll see that the Wizard generates a client-side cursor, which is by definition static. The only way to see changes made by other users is to refresh the Recordset. (Remember, every time a static cursor is refreshed, all rows are moved from the server to the client.)

8. The last screen prompts you to save the settings, but you can safely skip it (unless you plan to use the Wizard to build many Forms). The output of the Wizard is the Form shown in Figure 6.13.

As you can see in Figure 6.13, the Wizard places the fields on the Form in alphabetical order and doesn't size the data-bound controls according to the defined size of the corresponding fields. You can fix the placement of the controls on the Form with the mouse, but this is not all. You must edit the code generated by the Wizard as well.

FIGURE 6.13:

This Form was generated by the Data Form Wizard and is based on the ADO objects.

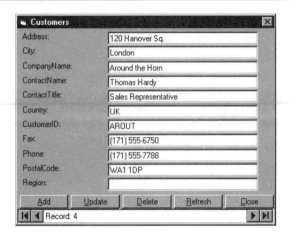

The Code behind the Wizard

The Wizard will create a client-side static Recordset and use optimistic locking. The Recordset is defined in the Form's Load event handler with the statements in Listing 6.9.

LISTING 6.9	Creating an ADO Recordset

```
Dim db As Connection
Set db = New Connection
db.CursorLocation = adUseClient
db.Open "PROVIDER=Microsoft.Jet.OLEDB.3.51;" & _
        "Data Source=C:\Program Files\VB98\Nwind.mdb;"
db.CursorLocation = adUseServer
Set adoPrimaryRS = New Recordset
adoPrimaryRS.Open "select " & _
        "Address, City, CompanyName, ContactName, " &_
        "ContactTitle, Country, CustomerID, Fax, " & _
        "Phone, PostalCode, Region from Customers", _
        db, adOpenStatic, adLockOptimistic
```

When the Add button is clicked, the code hides the other buttons and displays the Update and Cancel buttons only.

An interesting piece of code is the Recordset's WillChangeRecordset event handler, shown in Listing 6.10. This subroutine is invoked every time the underlying table is about to be updated. The WillChangeRecord event can be caused by many different actions, and you must handle each case differently. The Wizard generates generic code, which is shown next. Basically, you have to provide the code for each of the Case statements you want to handle from within your code.

LISTING 6.10   The WillChangeRecord Event Handler

```
Private Sub adoPrimaryRS_WillChangeRecord(ByVal adReason As _
      ADODB.EventReasonEnum, ByVal cRecords As Long, _
      adStatus As ADODB.EventStatusEnum, _
      ByVal pRecordset As ADODB.Recordset)
      'This is where you put validation code
      'This event gets called when the following actions occur
   Dim bCancel As Boolean

   Select Case adReason
   Case adRsnAddNew
   Case adRsnClose
   Case adRsnDelete
   Case adRsnFirstChange
   Case adRsnMove
   Case adRsnRequery
   Case adRsnResynch
   Case adRsnUndoAddNew
   Case adRsnUndoDelete
   Case adRsnUndoUpdate
   Case adRsnUpdate
   End Select

   If bCancel Then adStatus = adStatusCancel
End Sub
```

I suggest you avoid programming this event, if possible. If you write your own data-entry Forms, you can show and hide buttons so that the user can only perform certain actions at any time. For example, you can provide an Add button, which will signal the addition of a new row. At this point you must hide all buttons and display the Save and Cancel buttons only. The user has two choices: commit the changes or cancel the addition of the new row.

To program the WillChangeRecord event, you must provide the code for each action that fired this event. In the case of adRsnMove, insert the code you want to execute if the record is about to be changed because the user has edited the fields and then attempted to move to another row. If you decide not to change the current row, you must set the *bCancel* property to True. At the end of the code, the value of the *bCancel* variable is assigned to the adStatus argument. This action cancels the update of the current row.

The code generated by the Wizard is not bug-free. If you attempt to delete a row of the Customers table, SQL Server will not allow it, because all customers have orders attached to them and the database enforces the relationship between the Customers and Orders tables. The error-trapping routine will catch the error and display the appropriate message. However, when you attempt to move to the next or previous row, a runtime error will pop up, in the subroutine shown in Listing 6.11:

LISTING 6.11   The MoveComplete Event Handler's Code

```
Private Sub adoPrimaryRS_MoveComplete( _
            ByVal adReason As ADODB.EventReasonEnum, _
            ByVal pError As ADODB.Error, _
            adStatus As ADODB.EventStatusEnum, _
            ByVal pRecordset As ADODB.Recordset)
  'This will display the current record position for this
  'recordset
  lblStatus.Caption = "Record: " & _
            CStr(adoPrimaryRS.AbsolutePosition)
End Sub
```

The code attempts to read the absolute position of a row we've attempted to delete. Obviously, the row wasn't removed from the table, but it was removed from the cursor that lives on the client! To fix this behavior, you must call the CancelUpdate method from within the DeleteErr error handler:

```
DeleteErr:
  adoPrimaryRS.CancelUpdate
  MsgBox Err.Description
```

TIP   Although it's not mentioned anywhere in the documentation that the CancelUpdate method works with the Delete method, it does so when the row hasn't been actually removed from the table. The CancelUpdate method cancels the deletion of a row in the Recordset that resides on the client. You'd expect that ADO wouldn't remove the row from the Recordset if it couldn't successfully remove it from the table, but it does. Be aware of this "issue" and call the CancelUpdate method after an unsuccessful deletion. Even if this behavior is fixed in the future, an unnecessary call of the CancelUpdate method shouldn't have any side effects.

WARNING   I mentioned earlier that SQL Server won't let you remove rows from the Customers table, because they are linked to orders. The same is true for the Access version of the same database, unless you've turned on the Cascade Deletes option. In this case, Access will delete all dependent rows in other tables and then the current row in the Customers table.

One last remark about the Form Wizard: It uses client-side cursors by default. If you change the cursor's location, you'll probably have to make more changes in the code. We'll return to the topic of the differences in programming the various types of cursors in Chapter 9, "Advanced ADO Topics."

Creating Simple and Functional Data-Entry Forms

As you may have noticed by now, the ADO Data Control is not the ideal tool for designing data-entry applications. For one thing, you can't delete a record automatically. You must place the appropriate button on the Form and call the Recordset's Delete method from within your code. The method for adding a new record is also awkward. You must move to the last record and then click the Next button again to add a new record. Even worse, after you've decided to add a record, you can't change your mind! There's no way to get out of the new record without actually supplying values to all its fields. The navigational methods of the ADO Data Control are also pretty limited. Being able to move from one record to the next or previous one is not the ultimate navigational tool. Also, fields can be changed at any time. A user may press the spacebar by mistake and edit a field. When the control is repositioned to another record, the changes will be committed to the database. (In fact, there are events that let your application know when the Data Control is about to write to the database, but then you'd have to constantly pester the user with unwanted messages boxes).

So, the no-code approach of the ADO Data Control is inadequate for practical, real-world applications. You can take advantage of the simplicity of this control and the related data-bound controls for data browsing and other simple applications (what many people call textbook applications), but if you want to write "real" data-entry applications, you must supply your own code. Besides, most data-entry applications involve more than one table: titles have publishers and authors, invoices are issued to specific customers and can have any number of detail lines, and so on.

Unfortunately, one of the most tedious, yet crucial, tasks in database programming is designing data-entry applications. Each data-entry application has its own requirements, and you can't design an application that will work with different types of data. Let's consider the Biblio application. Each title has a unique ISBN, which we use as the primary key for the Titles table. It wouldn't be very difficult to design an application that reads an ISBN value and then attempts to locate it in the Titles table. If it's found, the title's fields are displayed, and the user can edit them. If not, a new record is appended and the user must enter the appropriate values.

This approach is too simple. For one thing, users may not always have the ISBN at hand. The application should be able to locate records by title, and perhaps by other fields. The same is true for customers. Again, you may wish to change a customer's phone number, because you found a note on your desk. Searching for a customer with a key, even if this key contains a few characters, is the last thing you want to do. What you need is a mechanism that will look up the table with customer names. A common requirement for every data-entry application is that records can be located in several ways. When you recall records with any field other than a unique key field, it's likely that more than one record will surface. In this case, you should be able to present all the records that match some criteria, along with additional information, and let the user select the desired record.

Many of you are probably thinking that the most complicated tasks in database programming are queries that combine or update multiple tables. As you will see in later chapters, it is possible to create elaborate Forms that allow you to drill down into the orders of a specific customer and then into the details of a specific order without a single line of code. It's really crucial to design robust and functional data-entry Forms. Once the data gets into the database, it's relatively easy to retrieve it. Your data-entry applications, however, must make sure that the data gets to the right place, on time, and in its entirety. Keep in mind the following issues when designing your data-entry Forms.

Speaking from Experience: Advice on Designing Data-Entry Forms

I have been designing data-entry Forms since long before visual tools came along, and I've learned a thing or two about the design of a data-entry application. First, it has to be simple. I've written applications that could look up records based on all kinds of field combinations, only to find that operators were using just a couple of methods to locate the desired records. I've seen too many applications that allow users to select products by name, books by title and so on. The fact is that data-entry operators work with catalogs and they prefer to work with product codes and ISBNs. Data-entry operators are not customers and they don't browse the database; they maintain it.

Also, visual tools don't change the average data-entry operator's routine. Users still prefer the keyboard to the mouse because their fingers are much faster. I've put together a Form in less than an hour and then spent the rest of the day making sure the tab order was correct, enabling the Enter key in specific fields, assigning shortcut keys to various fields, and so on. In short, try to get the mouse out of the picture. There's nothing more annoying to a data-entry operator than having to reach for the mouse. Of course, the various shortcut keys should be consistent across the Forms of an application.

Isolated Operations   When you design data-entry Forms, isolate every operation and use clearly marked buttons to initiate and terminate each operation. To add a new row, the user should have to click the Add button. Likewise, to edit the current row, the user should have to click the Edit button. While the current row is being edited, you should disable the navigational keys. The only options for the user should be the OK and Cancel buttons.

Navigation   Never count on the ADO Data Control as a navigational tool. The Next and Previous buttons we have used in several of this book's examples are totally inadequate. You must provide more direct mechanisms for locating rows. When the user presses the Enter key in a field that's unique, you should use the Seek (or Find) method to retrieve the desired record. Sometimes, users want to go through a series of rows, like the titles of a publisher, customers with a common characteristic (like a purchase in the last quarter), and so on. If you identify such a requirement, you should provide a Form where users can supply their criteria, retrieve the qualifying rows, and only then expose the Next and Previous buttons.

Visual Feedback   Provide some visual feedback, like changing the Form's title bar to indicate the current operation. You can even change the Form's background color to indicate an edit operation—especially if the operation is going to affect multiple rows. It's also important to specify the proper tab order for all controls on the Form and make the OK and Cancel buttons react to the Enter and Escape keystrokes. If the Form contains fields that are not used with the majority of the rows (like a translator field or an optional second topic), remove these fields from the tab order, but assign a hotkey combination to move to them when needed. Also consider changing the color of the TextBox control that has the focus. Make it a light yellow or cyan color—nothing really drastic, but easy to spot on the Form.

Validation   As far as your code goes, make sure you validate all the fields and the user knows that an operation has failed, when it happens. Don't use Visual Basic's error messages; make up your own descriptive error messages instead. End users don't really care whether ADO wasn't able to convert one data type to another, or SQL Server timed out. A message telling them that the current operation failed and giving them the option to retry is adequate. If you get a time-out error, it makes sense to repeat the operation. If you get a more serious error, just pop up a message box telling the user that the program couldn't save the changes to the database and return to the last visited valid row.

As you already know, you can validate the field values the hard way (by implementing all the validation logic in your VB code) and the easy way (by incorporating as many validation rules as you can in the design of the database itself). If you choose the second method, you must include an error-trapping routine to intercept and handle the errors returned by SQL Server. If an application requires too many validations, consider writing stored procedures to update the database.

Data-Aware Controls

Visual Basic comes with a few data-bound controls that can bind to multiple rows. These controls are called *data-aware* and they can't be used without a data source. The TextBox control, for example, may be bound to a field, but it can function on its own outside the context of a database. The data-aware controls, described below, can only be used in conjunction with a database:

> **The DataList control**   This is similar to the ListBox control, but its items are the values of a column in the database (or a query).
>
> **The DataCombo control**   This is similar to the ComboBox control, but its items are the values of a column in the database (or a query).
>
> **The DataGrid control**   This is similar to the MSFlexGrid control and it maps an entire table (or query) on a grid. Unlike the MSFlexGrid control, however, the DataGrid control allows direct editing of its cells, as well as the addition of new rows and the deletion of existing ones. The DataGrid control is similar to the editing grid of Access 95/97, but not as elaborate as the equivalent tool that comes with Access 2000.

The DataList and DataCombo controls are frequently used as lookup mechanisms. They display the values of a specific column, yet they can be bound to another Recordset and synchronize their data with the second Recordset. That's hard to grasp without an example, so I'll provide one.

Let's say you're displaying the titles of the Biblio database using simple databound controls. Most fields can be displayed in TextBox controls, but the Titles table doesn't contain the publisher's name. Instead, it contains the PubID field, which points to the proper row in the Publishers table. You must use the current title's PubID field to look up the publisher's name in the Publishers table and display it on the Form. This isn't a very complicated operation, and you already know how to build an SQL statement that combines titles and their publishers.

But what if you want to be able to edit each title? How would you change the publisher of an existing title, or assign a publisher to a new title? You shouldn't force the users of your application to enter IDs, nor should you force them to enter the exact publisher's name. The solution is to use a ComboBox or a ListBox control, where the user can select the publisher's name. When the Form is loaded, the data-aware control is populated with the values of the Name column of the Publishers table. At run time, the current title's publisher is automatically displayed as you navigate through the titles. The user can change the current title's publisher by selecting another name from the list. Because the data-aware control is bound to the Recordset with the titles, it knows that it must insert the proper publisher ID in the Titles table. The users work with publisher names and don't even know they're viewing information from two separate tables—and why should they? As far as code goes, you don't have to write a single line to implement this operation. However, you must set several properties at design time (you can also manipulate the data-aware controls from within your code, and you'll see how this is done shortly).

There are two steps in using a data-aware control on your Form: first, you must populate it; second, you must specify the field that will be looked up (the publisher's name, in our example) and how this field is mapped to the lookup field (the publisher's ID).

Populating a Data-Aware Control

The data-aware controls that can display more than a single row support the following properties:

RowSource   This property is the name of a data source with the values that will populate the control. It's either the name of a DataEnvironment object or the name of an ADO Data Control.

RowMember   This is the name of a Command object in the DataEnvironment object you specified in the RowSource property. If the RowSource property is the name of an ADO Data Control, you need not set this property.

ListField   This is the name of the column whose values will be used to populate the control.

To experiment with these properties, create a DataEnvironment object to connect to the Biblio database. Then add a Command object to retrieve the rows of the Publishers table (add a new Command object under the Connection object and set its data source to the Publishers table). Place a DataCombo control on the Form, name it Publishers, and set its RowSource to DataEnvironment1, its RowMember property to Publishers, and its ListField property to Name.

If you run the project, the DataCombo control will be populated with the names of all publishers in the Publishers table. The control uses the values of the RowSource and RowMember properties to open a table in the database and retrieves the values of the field specified by the ListField property to populate itself.

Looking Up Fields with a Data-Aware Control

By setting the RowSource (RowMember, if needed) and ListField properties, you can populate the DataCombo or DataList control with the values of a specific column. In the case of the titles example, you can populate a ComboBox control with the names of the publishers. Yet you should be able to bind the publisher names in the Publishers table to the PubID field in the Titles tables, so that each time the user moves to another title, the selected publisher in the DataCombo control will be updated accordingly.

To bind the data-aware control to a specific row of a Recordset, you need to set the DataSource (and DataMember, if needed) and BoundField properties:

> **DataSource** This is the data source of a Recordset that contains the field that will be looked up through the DataCombo control. It's either the name of a DataEnvironment object or the name of an ADO Data Control.
>
> **DataMember** If the DataSource is a DataEnvironment object, set this property to name of the Command object that retrieves the rows from the database. If DataSource is the name of an ADO Data Control, ignore this property.
>
> **DataField** This is the name of a column in the DataSource Recordset that will act as a lookup value.
>
> **BoundColumn** This is the name of the column in the DataCombo control's Recordset that be looked up.

Let's say you've created a DataEnvironment object with two Command objects: one for the titles (the AllTitles command) and another for the publishers (the AllPublishers command). The AllTitles command is used as a data source for a bunch of data-bound controls on the Form. These controls display the fields of the current title. The AllPublishers command is used as a row source for a Data-Combo control. To bind the DataCombo control to the current row of the AllTitles Recordset, you must set the DataSource property of the DataCombo control to the Titles table and the DataField and BoundField properties to the field that's common in both tables (the PubID field). The BoundField property is set to one of the fields of the Recordset specified by the RowSource property, and the DataField is set to one of the fields of the Recordset specified by the DataSource property. The control detects changes in the DataField and sets the BoundField accordingly. In other words, as the user navigates through the rows of the AllTitles table, the AllTitles.PubID field changes value. The DataCombo control monitors this field and when it changes value, the control is automatically repositioned to the row of the AllPublishers Recordset with a matching AllPublishers.PubID field. Figure 6.14 shows how a data-aware control acts as a lookup table between two Recordsets.

Using the DataCombo control to look up publisher names with their ID

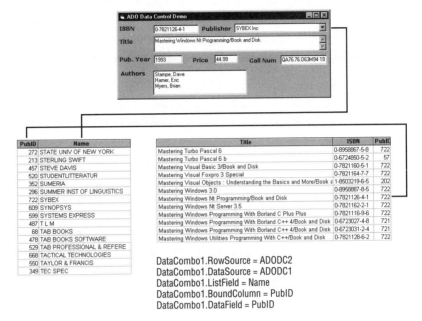

```
DataCombo1.RowSource = ADODC2
DataCombo1.DataSource = ADODC1
DataCombo1.ListField = Name
DataCombo1.BoundColumn = PubID
DataCombo1.DataField = PubID
```

The Titles Project

Let's put all this information together to build a flexible Form for displaying and editing the rows of the Titles table. Figure 6.15 shows a Form with all the fields of the Titles table and an ADO Data Control that binds them to the database. All fields are mapped on TextBox controls, with the exception of the PubID field, which is mapped on a DataCombo control that displays publisher names (instead of IDs), and the title's authors, which are mapped on a DataList control. This project uses the Access Biblio database.

The Titles project allows users to view and edit the titles of the Biblio database.

To design this Form, start a new Data Project, open the DataEnvironment Designer, and set its connection to the Biblio database. You can use the version that comes with VB6, or the SQL Server version (if you have ported the Biblio database into SQL Server, as discussed in the section "Importing the Biblio Database into SQL Server" of Chapter 2). Name the Connection object *BiblioConn*. Then add two commands to the Connection object: one of them to hold the Recordset of the titles and another to hold the Recordset of the Publishers. Name the two Command objects *Titles* and *Pubs* and set their RecordSources to the Titles and Publishers tables, respectively.

Normally, you'd have to place a bunch of Label and TextBox controls on the Form and set their DataSource and DataField properties accordingly. To avoid this repetitive and error-prone task, open the project's Form and then drop on it the Titles Command object from the DataEnvironment window. For each field in the Titles table, a Label and TextBox control will be placed on the Form. The Label control displays the field's name and the TextBox control is bound to the corresponding field. The DataSource, DataMember, and DataField properties will be set automatically to the proper values, which are:

Property	Setting
DataSource	DataEnvironment1
DataMember	Titles
DataField	Each TextBox control's DataField property is set to a different field in the Titles table.

The DataEnvironment Designer has placed the PubID field on the Form—it didn't take into consideration the fact that the Titles.PubID field is a foreign key to the Publishers table. You must remove the PublisherID TextBox and place an instance of the DataCombo control in its place. Don't forget to change the name of the Label control from "PublisherID" to "Publisher."

While you're rearranging the controls on the Form, make the first TextBox control on the Form large enough to hold three or four lines of text and set its MultiLine property to True, because most titles are too long to be displayed on a single line.

To use the DataCombo control as a lookup tool, set its properties as follows:

Property	Setting
RowSource	DataEnvironment1
RowMember	Pubs
ListField	Name
DataSource	DataEnvironment1

DataMember	Titles
DataField	PubID
BoundColumn	PubID

Don't run the application yet—there are no navigational tools on the Form. Place four Command buttons on the Form as shown in Figure 6.15 and insert the navigational code, as shown in Listing 6.3, earlier in the chapter.

Now you can run the application and see how the DataCombo control implements the relationship between the Titles and Publishers tables. As you scroll through the titles, the current title's publisher is selected on the control. You can also change a title's publisher by expanding the DataCombo control and selecting a different publisher name. Although you can select a publisher's name on the DataCombo control, the publisher's ID will be saved in the PubID field of the Titles table.

NOTE   You can't change the publishers yet. The default Recordset of a Command object is read-only. If you want to edit the titles from within this Form, you must change the LockType property of the Titles Recordset. Stop the application, open the Properties pages of the Titles Command object, and in the Advanced tab set its Lock-Type property to 3 – Optimistic.

The Titles project works as advertised, but it can stand some improvement. For one thing, the Pubs Recordset need not be a table. We're only using two fields, the publisher's ID and name (fields PubID and Name), so there's no reason to move any additional information to the client. Edit the Pubs object's properties and set its data source to the following SQL statement:

```
SELECT PubID, Name
FROM Publishers
```

This change isn't going to affect any of the existing controls. The project will work without any additional changes.

The DataCombo control's Style is dbDropDownCombo by default. This means that users can enter information in the control's edit box. However, the control doesn't know how to use this information. In other words, it doesn't know how to append a new row to the Publishers table. If you want users to be able to enter new publisher names, you should place a New Publisher button on the Form. This button must invoke another Form, where users can enter new publishers (not just a name) and then return to the Titles Form and use the new publisher. For the purposes of this demo, set the Style property of the DataCombo control to DropDown List, so that users can select a different publisher but will not be able to enter a new value.

The Lookup Project

The Lookup project, shown in Figure 6.16, uses two DataCombo controls, which display (and allow you to change) the product's category and its supplier. As expected, this operation doesn't require any code; just set the properties of the two DataCombo controls as described later in this section.

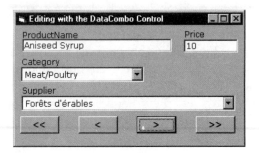

The project uses three ADO Data Controls, which store the three Recordsets: the products, their categories, and their suppliers. All three data controls have the same RecordSource property, which is:

```
Provider=Microsoft.Jet.OLEDB.4.0; _
Data Source=C:\Program Files\Microsoft Visual _
Studio\VB98\Nwind.mdb;_
```

The AllProducts data control's RecordSource property is the name of the Products table. The program uses two fields only (the product's name and price), so you could use a shorter Recordset by specifying an SQL statement.

The AllCategories data control's RecordSource property is the following SQL statement, which retrieves the category IDs and category names from the Categories table:

```
SELECT CategoryID, CategoryName
FROM Categories
ORDER BY CategoryName
```

Finally, the AllSuppliers data control's RecordSource property is another SQL statement that retrieves the supplier IDs and the names of the companies from the Suppliers table:

```
SELECT SupplierID, CompanyName
FROM Suppliers
ORDER BY CompanyName
```

The two DataCombo controls on the Form are used to look up supplier and category names. The properties of the two DataCombo controls are shown here:

Property Name	Setting
DataCombo1.RowSource	AllCategories
DataCombo1.ListField	CategoryName
DataCombo1.DataSource	AllProducts
DataCombo1.DataField	CategoryID
DataCombo1.BoundColumn	CategoryID
DataCombo2.RowSource	AllSuppliers
DataCombo1.ListField	CompanyName
DataCombo1.DataSource	AllProducts
DataCombo1.DataField	SupplierID
DataCombo1.BoundColumn	SupplierID

The three ADO Data Controls are invisible at run time, so you must supply the usual navigational buttons, as shown in Figure 6.16.

Using the DataList Control

The DataList control is similar to the DataCombo control. It displays a number of values from a given table column, and it can be bound to another Recordset. For example, you can create a Form that displays products and use a DataList control to display the names of the categories. As you move through the rows of the Products table, the current product's category is highlighted in the DataList control. This is a very dangerous practice, because it's too easy for the user to select another row in the DataList control and change the current products category. Some users may not even understand what they are doing. They may use the arrow keys to scroll the DataList control and, inadvertently, change the products category.

The DataList control is used frequently as a navigational tool in a Recordset. The ADO Data Control is seriously limited when it comes to navigational capabilities, and so are the methods of the ADO Recordset. If a table doesn't contain thousands of rows, you can display a meaningful field (like a customer's name, product's name, and so on) on a DataList control, which will act as a navigational tool. Figure 6.17 shows the Form of the DataList project, which allows you to select a customer by clicking the company name in the DataList control at the bottom of the Form.

The user interface is quite simple. You can actually edit the fields of the current row (the ones on the Form, at least). The changes will be committed to the database when you select another customer. You can add the usual Add, Edit, and Delete buttons on the Form to prevent the users from updating the tables by mistake.

FIGURE 6.17:

Selecting customers by name from a DataList control

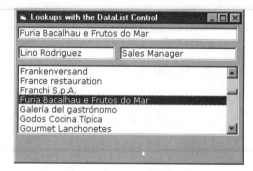

The DataList project's code is quite trivial. It contains a single line of code in the DataList control's Click event handler. Every time the user selects another customer, it sets the Recordset's Bookmark property to the selected item. By setting the Bookmark property of a Recordset, you're actually moving to the specified row. In other words, the selected row becomes the current row. The other controls on the Form are updated automatically, because they are bound to the Customers table through the Adodc1.Recordset object.

```
Private Sub DataList1_Click()
    Adodc1.Recordset.Bookmark = DataList1.SelectedItem
End Sub
```

The Form of the DataList project has a hidden ADO Data Control, which is set up as follows:

Property Name	Setting
ConnectionString	Provider=Microsoft.Jet.OLEDB.4.0; Data Source=C:\Program Files\VB98\Nwind.mdb
RecordSource	Customers
CursorType	AdOpenStatic
CursorLocation	AdUseClient
LockType	AdLockOptimistic

As far as the DataList control goes, all you have to do is set its RowSource and ListField properties, so that it's populated with the CompanyName column of the Customers table:

RowSource	Adodc1
ListField	CompanyName

Examples

In the last section, we'll look at a few examples that combine many of the topics discussed so far. Some of the examples will prepare you for more complicated applications you'll build in later chapters.

The AllTitles Project

This project demonstrates how to use multiple ADO Data Controls on the same Form and how to connect them to each other. On the Form of the ADODCDemo2 project, shown in Figure 6.18, you can display titles along with their authors and publishers. Okay, the Titles table of the Biblio database has close to 8,000 titles, so what good is the ADO Data Control as a navigational tool? This application is meant only to demonstrate the use of the data-aware controls, not how to build a user interface. In Chapter 17 you will see how to build an elaborate user interface for locating books by their title, or ISBN. In the meantime, we'll add Find and Filter buttons to the Form to help users locate the desired titles.

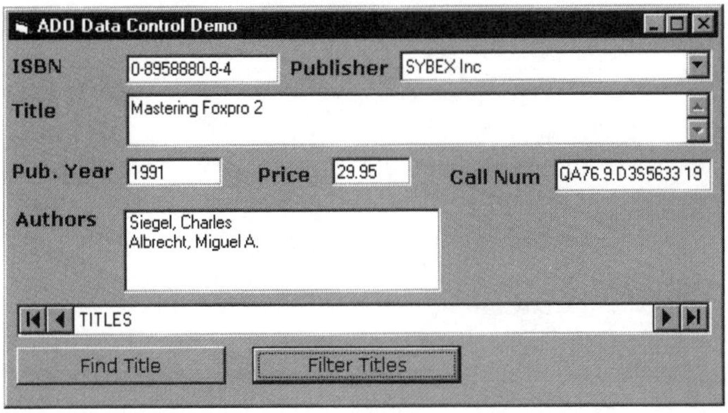

FIGURE 6.18:

The AllTitles project demonstrates how to select a title with the help of a DataList control.

The publishers are displayed on a DataCombo control, and the user can change the current title's publisher by selecting one from this list. The DataCombo control is populated when the Form is loaded and resides on the client. The authors of each title are displayed on a DataList control, whose DataSource property changes every time the user moves to another title.

To retrieve the required information, there are three ADO Data Controls on the Form: one for the Titles table, another for the Publishers table, and a third for the Authors table. Of the three controls, only the Titles ADO Data Control is visible at run time. The RecordSource property of the three Recordsets are shown here:

Name	RecordSource
Titles	Titles table
Publishers	SELECT [Company Name], Name, PubID FROM Publishers ORDER BY [Company Name]
Authors	SELECT Author FROM Authors, [Title Author] WHERE Authors.Au_ID=[Title Author].Au_ID AND [Title Author].ISBN='" & TITLES.Recordset.Fields("ISBN") & "'"

As you can guess, the RecordSource property of the Authors ADO Data Control can't be set at design time. This property is set by the project's code every time a new title is selected with the Titles control (an event signaled by the ADO Data Control's MoveComplete event). To build this statement, you extract the ISBN field's value and use it to locate the appropriate author.

The Titles control is the application's gateway to the Titles table; it "sees" all the rows of the Titles table. Therefore, all the simple data-bound controls should be bound to a single field of this control. Set the data binding properties of the TextBox controls on the Form as follows:

Control Name	DataSource	DataField
txtISBN	Titles	ISBN
txtTitle	Titles	Title
txtPubYear	Titles	PubYear
txtPrice	Titles	Description
txtCallNum	Titles	Comments

NOTE   I've used the names txtPrice and txtCallNum for the last two fields, because it seems that this is the information stored in these two fields. A book's call number is the number used to identify the location of each title in a library.

The other two data-bound controls are not simple. They hold multiple items, and they operate differently. The publishers are displayed on a DataCombo control, so that the user can change a book's publisher by selecting another name form the list. Each time the ADO Data Control is repositioned to another title, the current book's publisher should be selected in the ComboBox control.

The DataCombo control's RowSource property is set to the Data Control that "sees" the Publishers table. To populate the Publishers DataCombo control with the names of the publishers, set its ListField property to the name of the Company Name field in the Publishers table. If you run the application now, you will see that the DataCombo1 control is populated with the names of the publishers, but the selected publisher's name doesn't change to reflect the current book's publisher.

You must now connect the DataCombo1 control to the Titles control, so that every time the control moves to a new row, the corresponding publisher's name is selected automatically. Select the control's DataSource property and set it to Titles (the name of the Data Control with the titles). To synchronize the DataCombo control with the Titles ADO Data Control, you must set the properties DataField and BoundColumn. If you examine the values listed under these two properties in the Properties window, you'll see that the DataField property can be set to any of the fields of the Titles Data Control and the BoundColumn property can be set to any of the fields of the Publishers Data Control. To synchronize the two controls means that every time the Titles control moves to another title, the current book's publisher must appear in the DataCombo control. Synchronize the two controls by selecting the PubID field for both properties. Here's how the DataCombo control works:

- Initially, it's populated with the values of the field specified with the ListField property.

- Then, its DataField property is connected to BoundColumn property. When the field specified with the DataField property changes, the DataCombo control selects the row that matches the field specified with the DataBound property.

- As a result, when the user selects another title, the selected title's publisher appears in the DataCombo control. Likewise, if the user selects another publisher from this list, the new publisher is assigned to the currently selected title.

Now we must do something similar with the authors. We can't use a DataCombo control because a title may have multiple authors. Even if all titles had a single author, we still wouldn't be able to display all author names in a list—this list would be too long and practically useless. The author(s) will be displayed on a DataList control. As discussed already, the Authors Recordset must be updated every time a new title is selected, so that it contains the current title's authors only. This action must take place from within the Titles data control's MoveComplete event. This event is fired by the ADO Data Control every time it's repositioned to another row in the Recordset. Here's the code that updates the Authors data control:

```
Private Sub TITLES_MoveComplete(ByVal adReason As _
            ADODB.EventReasonEnum, _
            ByVal pError As ADODB.Error, _
            adStatus As ADODB.EventStatusEnum, _
            ByVal pRecordset As ADODB.Recordset20)
    Authors.RecordSource = _
            "SELECT Author FROM Authors, " & _
            "[Title Author] WHERE Authors.Au_ID=" & _
            "[Title Author].Au_ID AND " & _
            "[Title Author].ISBN='" & _
            "TITLES.Recordset.Fields("ISBN") & "'"
    Authors.Refresh
End Sub
```

The event recognizes a number of arguments, which we'll cover in Chapter 9. The AllTitles application was implemented with a single line of code. All its functionality is built into the ADO Data Control and the data-bound objects. However, it's pretty limited when it comes to locating a specific title. The Data Control allows you to move to the two ends of the Recordset, or one record at a time. Let's add a few buttons to enhance the application's navigational capabilities. Notice that you can edit most of the fields, but there's no simple method to add to or remove authors from a specific title. We'll come back to this project in Chapter 17, where we'll build a more functional application to manipulate the titles of the Biblio database.

Finding and Filtering Records

Let's make the AllTitles project a little more versatile by adding find and filter operations. Add two buttons on the Form, name them Find Title and Filter Titles, and enter the code in Listing 6.11 in their Click event handlers.

LISTING 6.11   **Finding and Filtering Titles**

```
Private Sub bttnFind_Click()
    prevBookmark = TITLES.Recordset.Bookmark
    FindTitle = InputBox("Enter the desired book's title")
    If FindTitle = "" Then Exit Sub
    TITLES.Recordset.Find "Title LIKE '" & FindTitle & "%'"
    If TITLES.Recordset.EOF Then
        MsgBox "No titles in the database match your criteria"
        TITLES.Recordset.Bookmark = prevBookmark
    End If
End Sub
```

```
Private Sub bttnFilter_Click()
    prevBookmark = TITLES.Recordset.Bookmark
    FilterTitles = InputBox("Enter the first few words" & _
                    " of the titles")
    If FilterTitles = "" Then
        TITLES.Recordset.Filter = adFilterNone
    Else
        TITLES.Recordset.Filter = _
                "Title LIKE '" & FilterTitles & "%'"
        If TITLES.Recordset.EOF Then
            MsgBox "No titles in the database match your criteria"
            TITLES.Recordset.Bookmark = prevBookmark
        End If
    End If
End Sub
```

When clicked, both buttons prompt the user to enter the beginning of the title. When finding titles, you should try to identify the title as best as you can, by entering the entire title, if possible. The Filter operation will locate titles beginning with the keywords you specify, so may enter a single word like *Database* or *Autocad* to locate books based on the first word(s) of their title.

Then the code builds the following expression:

```
"Title LIKE '" & FindTitle & "%'"
```

This will locate records whose titles begin with the user-supplied word(s). The percent symbol at the end of the string denotes that any character(s) may follow. If you specify "Autocad" as the search argument, the above expression will locate titles like *Autocad Power Toolkit* and *Autocad Tutor*, but not *Mastering Autocad*. You can edit the application's source and implement more complicated searches. In Chapter 12 "Data-Aware Classes," we'll build a component for searching the Biblio database. This component will locate books based on title words and/or author names.

The Find method either locates the record (and displays it) or moves to the end of the Recordset. If the property Titles.Recordset.EOF is True after the Find method is called, then the title was not found and the data control is repositioned to the record it was at before the Find method was called. This action isn't initiated by the control. The code stores the Bookmark of the last record it displayed in the *prevBookmark* variable and then sets the Recordset's Bookmark property to this value, to return to the bookmarked record.

The Filter method will ignore records that do not match the filter specification. After the Filter method is called, the data control is repositioned to the first record that matches the filter. If the Filter operation wasn't able to locate any records, the data control will jump to the end of the Recordset and set the EOF property to True. In this case the code returns to last valid record it displayed.

Notice that I've added an extra line in the Titles Control's MoveComplete event handler. This extra line is necessary because an unsuccessful Find or Filter operation will reposition the data control to the end of the Recordset. As a result, a runtime error will be raised when the code attempts to read the current title's ISBN field. To avoid the runtime error, I've inserted the following line:

```
If TITLES.Recordset.EOF Then Exit Sub
```

The ADODCDemo Project

This project demonstrates how to use both the DataCombo and DataList controls to build a functional user interface with rich navigational capabilities. The Form shown in Figure 6.19 displays the most important pieces of information in the Northwind database. The controls on the Form allow you to select a company either by name or with the name of the company's contact. In either case, you must expand the corresponding ComboBox control to select the desired entry. No matter how you select a company, the boxes at the top of the Form will be filled with the proper values. The Orders DataList control will be populated with the numbers of the orders placed by the selected customer. Then, you can select an order by clicking its number to view the order's details.

FIGURE 6.19:

The ADODCDemo project

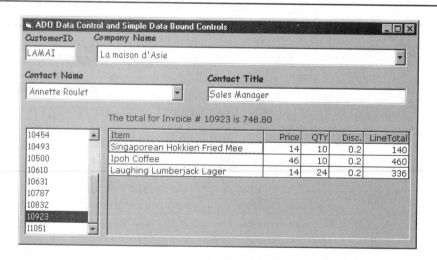

Notice that the contact names are not sorted. To locate a contact, you must enter the first few characters of the contact's name. Since both DataCombo controls are populated with the same Recordset, the order can't change. The order in which the items will appear is determined by the SQL statement that retrieves them from the database.

The ADODCDemo Form uses three ADO Data Controls to "see" the three Recordsets it uses: the customers, the selected customer's orders, and the selected order's details. All three controls, which are invisible at run time, have the same ConnectionString property, which is:

```
Provider=SQLOLEDB.1;User ID=sa; _
Initial Catalog=Northwind;Data Source=(local)
```

The ADODC1 control that sees the Customers table has its RecordSource property set to Customers. The RecordSource property of the other two ADO Data Controls is set from within the code.

The DataCombo control that displays the company names is called CompanyNames, and you can populate it by setting the following properties:

Property	Setting
RowSource	ADODC1
ListField	CompanyName

Likewise, the second DataCombo control that displays contact names on the Form is called ContactNames and its data-binding properties are:

Property	Setting
RowSource	ADODC1
ListField	ContactName

To reposition the ADODC1 control in its Recordset, we must set the corresponding ADO Data Control's Bookmark property, as we did in the examples earlier in this chapter. Every time the user selects another company name in the CompanyNames DataCombo control, the Change event is fired and Listing 6.12 is executed from within this event.

LISTING 6.12   Selecting a Customer with the CompanyName

```
Private Sub CompanyNames_Change()
    On Error Resume Next
    Adodc1.Recordset.Bookmark = CompanyNames.SelectedItem
    On Error Goto 0
End Sub
```

The same statements are executed when a new item is selected in the ContactNames list, as shown in Listing 6.13.

LISTING 6.13   **Selecting a Customer with the ContactName**

```
Private Sub ContactName_Change()
    On Error Resume Next
    Adodc1.Recordset.Bookmark = CustomerNames.SelectedItem
    On Error Goto 0
End Sub
```

The DataList control is called OrderNumbers and is populated with the numbers of the orders placed by the selected customer. This action must take place when a new company is selected. Because a new company can be selected in two ways (either through the CompanyNames or the ContactNames control), we must program the ADODC1 control's MoveComplete event. This event is fired every time a new customer is selected, regardless of how the new customer was selected. In the MoveComplete event of the ADODC1 control, you must execute the following lines:

```
Private Sub Adodc1_MoveComplete(ByVal adReason As _
            ADODB.EventReasonEnum, _
            ByVal pError As ADODB.Error, _
            adStatus As ADODB.EventStatusEnum, _
            ByVal pRecordset As ADODB.Recordset)
    Adodc2.RecordSource = "SELECT OrderID FROM Orders " & _
            "WHERE Orders.CustomerID='" & _
            Adodc1.Recordset.Fields("CustomerID") & "'"
    Adodc2.Refresh
End Sub
```

In this event, you select the rows from the Orders table that correspond to the selected customer's ID with an SQL statement. The SELECT statement is straightforward, except for the fact that you must embed the ID of the selected customer in it.

The ADODC2 control loads the qualifying rows, which are automatically displayed on the DataList control, because this control's RowSource property is set to ADODC2 and its ListField property is set to the name of the OrderID field. Notice that these two properties can be set at design time. Each time the ADODC2 control's RowSource property changes at run time, the DataList control's contents are updated automatically.

The last interesting procedure in this application is the code that populates the MSFlexGrid control with the details of the selected invoice. Each time a new order number is selected, the Click event of the DataList control is fired and Listing 6.14 is executed.

LISTING 6.14   Retrieving an Order's Details

```
Private Sub DataList1_Click()
    Adodc3.RecordSource = "SELECT ProductName AS Item, " & _
            " [Order Details].UnitPrice AS Price, " & _
            "Quantity AS QTY, Discount AS [Disc.], " & _
            "[Order Details].UnitPrice*Quantity AS LineTotal " & _
            "FROM [Order Details], Products " & _
            "WHERE [Order Details].ProductID= " & _
            "Products.ProductID AND " & _
            "OrderID='" & DataList1.Text & "'"
    Adodc3.Refresh
    While Not Adodc3.Recordset.EOF
    Sum = Sum + Adodc3.Recordset.Fields("Price") * _
                Adodc3.Recordset.Fields("QTY") * _
                (1 - Adodc3.Recordset.Fields("Disc."))
        Adodc3.Recordset.MoveNext
    Wend
    InvoiceTotal.Caption = "The total for Invoice # " & _
                        DataList1.Text & " is " & _
                        Format(Sum, "#,###.00")
End Sub
```

The code is quite straightforward; the artificial line breaks we had to insert in the listing make it look long. It retrieves the rows with the selected order's details and displays them on an MSFlexGrid control. After the details have been placed on the MSFlexGrid control, it scans the Recordset with the details (a very short Recordset), calculates the total, and displays it above the grid with the details.

The ADOCodeDemo Project

The ADOCodeDemo project is similar to the ADODCDemo project, but it uses the ADO objects only. While you'll have to write more code, I've included this project as another example of programming with the ADO objects—a simpler method of implementing the same functionality.

To simplify the code of the project, I've prepared a DataEnvironment object with the following objects:

NWConnection   A Connection object that establishes the connection to the Northwind database (the SQL Server database)

AllCustomers   A Command object that retrieves information from the Customers table with the following SQL statement:

```
SELECT CustomerID, CompanyName, ContactName, ContactTitle
FROM Customers
ORDER BY CompanyName
```

The AllCustomers Command, as well as the other Command object in the DataEnvironment1 window, returns a client-side, read-only cursor.

AllOrders   A Command object that retrieves the numbers of the selected customer's orders from the Orders table with the following SQL statement:

```
SELECT OrderID FROM Orders WHERE CustomerID=?
```

AllDetails   A Command object that retrieves the details of the selected order from the Order Details table with the following SQL statement:

```
SELECT ProductName, [Order Details].UnitPrice,
Quantity, Discount
FROM [Order Details], Products
WHERE [Order details].ProductID=Products.ProductID
AND OrderID=?
```

As you can see, the SQL statements used in two of the Command objects expect a parameter value. This means that when you call the AllOrders method to populate the rsAllOrders Recordset, you must pass the value of the parameter. The following statement will retrieve the orders of the selected customer:

```
DataEnvironment1.AllOrders CustID
```

where *CustID* is a variable with the ID of the selected customer.

Although you can access the three Recordsets with expressions like the following one, I've set up two variables to store the Recordsets with the Customers and Orders:

```
DataEnvironment1.rsAllCustomers.Fields(…)
```

The declarations of the variables are shown next:

```
Dim RSCustomers As New ADODB.Recordset
Dim RSOrders As New ADODB.Recordset
```

Let's start by looking at the code in Listings 6.15 and 6.16, which select a customer every time the user clicks an item in the CompanyName or ContactName DataCombo control.

LISTING 6.15   **Selecting a Customer with the CompanyName**

```
Private Sub CompanyNames_Change()
    RSCustomers.Bookmark = CompanyNames.SelectedItem
    txtContactTitle.Text = RSCustomers.Fields("ContactTitle")
    If DataEnvironment1.rsAllOrders.State = adStateOpen _
            Then DataEnvironment1.rsAllOrders.Close
    DataEnvironment1.AllOrders RSCustomers.Fields("CustomerID")
    Set RSOrders = DataEnvironment1.rsAllOrders
    Set DataList1.RowSource = DataEnvironment1.rsAllOrders
    DataList1.ListField = "OrderID"
    ContactNames.Text = _
            DataEnvironment1.rsAllCustomers.Fields("ContactName")
    DataList1.SetFocus
    DataList1.Text = RSOrders.Fields("OrderID")
End Sub
```

LISTING 6.16   **Selecting a Customer with the ContactName**

```
Private Sub ContactNames_Change()
    RSCustomers.Bookmark = ContactNames.SelectedItem
    txtCustomerID.Text = RSCustomers.Fields("CustomerID")
    txtContactTitle.Text = RSCustomers.Fields("ContactTitle")
    CompanyNames.BoundText = RSCustomers.Fields("CompanyName")
End Sub
```

The code isn't complicated, but it's quite lengthy if you compare it to the code of the same application that uses the ADO Data Control.

Finally, when the user selects an order in the DataList control, Listing 6.17 retrieves the selected order's details from the Order Details table and displays them on a MSFlexGrid control.

LISTING 6.17   **Displaying an Order's Details**

```
Private Sub DataList1_Click()
    If DataEnvironment1.rsAllDetails.State = adStateOpen _
            Then DataEnvironment1.rsAllDetails.Close
    DataEnvironment1.AllDetails DataList1.Text
    Set RSDetails = DataEnvironment1.rsAllDetails
    Set DataGrid1.DataSource = DataEnvironment1.rsAllDetails
    While Not RSDetails.EOF
        Sum = Sum + RSDetails.Fields("UnitPrice") * _
                    RSDetails.Fields("Quantity") * _
                    (1 - RSDetails.Fields("Discount"))
```

```
        RSDetails.MoveNext
    Wend
    InvoiceTotal.Caption = "The total for Invoice # " & _
                            DataList1.Text & " is " & _
                            Format(Sum, "#,###.00")
End Sub
```

NOTE   Notice how *rsAllOrders* and *rsAllDetails* Recordsets are populated. The code examines the State property of the corresponding Recordset. If the Recordset is open (that is, if it has been populated already), it closes it first and then re-populates it with a different Recordset by calling the AllOrders and AllDetails methods and passing to it the appropriate argument.

Summary

This example concludes the first chapter that discusses database access with VB and the ADO objects. In the next chapter you'll learn about SQL Server's built-in language, Transact-SQL (T-SQL). T-SQL combines SQL with more traditional programming statements, and it allows you to build procedures that access and process the rows of a database. The advantage of stored procedures is that they are executed by the SQL Server. This means you don't have to move data from the server to client and process them there. As you will see, you can use T-SQL to carry out many of the tasks you'd normally perform with Visual Basic.

CHAPTER
SEVEN

7

Transact-SQL

- The COMPUTE BY clause

- Stored procedures and Access queries

- Writing T-SQL stored procedures

- T-SQL local and global variables, statements, and functions

- Using arguments

- Building SQL statements on the fly

- Implementing business rules with stored procedures

In Chapter 4, you built SQL statements to retrieve and update rows in a database. You also learned all the variations of the SELECT statement. Some restrictions, however, can't be expressed with a WHERE clause, no matter how complicated. To perform complicated searches, many programmers would rather write an application to retrieve the desired rows, process them, and then display some results. The processing could include running totals, formatting of the query's output, calculations involving multiple rows of the same table, and so on.

Most database management systems include extensions, which enhance SQL and make it behave more like a programming language. SQL Server provides a set of statements known as Transact-SQL (T-SQL). T-SQL recognizes statements that fetch rows from one or more tables, flow-control statements like IF … ELSE and WHILE, and numerous functions to manipulate strings, numeric values, and dates, similar to Visual Basic's functions. With T-SQL you can do everything that can be done with SQL, as well as program these operations. At the very least, you can attach lengthy SQL statements to a database as stored procedures, so that you can call them by name. In addition, you can use parameters, so that the same procedure can act on different data. Access supports queries, a similar feature—which combines SQL statements with VBA functions and can accept arguments. Access queries, however, don't recognize flow-control statements and are not nearly as flexible as SQL Server's stored procedures.

In this chapter, we'll explore T-SQL and build stored procedures to perform complicated tasks on the server, simply by calling the stored procedure by name. We'll start with the COMPUTE BY statement, which allows you to calculate totals on groups of the rows retrieved from the database. This statement looks and feels very much like the straight SQL statements discussed in Chapter 4, "Structured Query Language." Yet it's not part of standard SQL—and as such it can't be used with Access queries. It's one of the most important extensions to SQL and you will use it, even if you do not plan to write stored procedures with T-SQL.

Then we'll look at T-SQL in depth. If you're familiar with T-SQL you can skip this chapter and dive to the examples of Chapter 8, "Making the Most of Stored Procedures." If you need to look up a function or how to declare a stored procedure's arguments, you can use this chapter as reference material. If you're new to T-SQL, you should read this material, because T-SQL is a powerful language and, if you're working with or you plan to switch to SQL Server, you'll need it sooner or later. In addition, you'll develop a deeper understanding of database programming with Visual Basic. T-SQL is the native language of SQL Server, and it basically does the same things as the ActiveX Data Objects. By seeing how the basic operations can be implemented in T-SQL and VB, you'll gain a deeper understanding of database programming.

The COMPUTE BY Clause

As discussed in Chapter 4, an SQL statement can return either details or totals, but not both. For example, you can calculate the order totals for all customers with a GROUP BY clause, but this clause displays totals only. Let's say you want a list of all customers in the Northwind database, their orders, and the total for each customer. Listing 7.1 provides an SQL SELECT statement that retrieves the desired information from the database.

LISTING 7.1   **The OrderTotals.sql Query**

```
USE NORTHWIND
SELECT CompanyName, Orders.OrderID,
    SUM([Order Details].UnitPrice *
        Quantity * (1 - Discount))
FROM Products, [Order Details], Customers, Orders
WHERE [Order Details].ProductID = Products.ProductID AND
      [Order Details].OrderID = Orders.OrderID AND
      Orders.CustomerID=Customers.CustomerID
GROUP BY CompanyName, Orders.OrderID
ORDER BY CompanyName, Orders.OrderID
```

This statement calculates the totals for each order. (The Orders.OrderID field is included in the GROUP BY clause because it's part of the SELECT list, but doesn't appear in an aggregate function's arguments. See the sidebar "How to Use Aggregate Functions" in Chapter 4). This statement will display groups of customers and the totals for all orders placed by each customer:

```
Alfreds Futterkiste                  10643    814.5
Alfreds Futterkiste                  10692    878.0
Alfreds Futterkiste                  10702    330.0
Alfreds Futterkiste                  10835    845.80
Alfreds Futterkiste                  10952    471.20
Alfreds Futterkiste                  11011    933.5
Ana Trujillo Emparedados y helados   10308     88.80
Ana Trujillo Emparedados y helados   10625    479.75
 . . .
```

If you want to see the totals per customer, you must modify Listing 7.1 as follows:

```
USE NORTHWIND
SELECT CompanyName,
    SUM([Order Details].UnitPrice *
        Quantity * (1 - Discount))
```

```
FROM Products, [Order Details], Customers, Orders
WHERE [Order Details].ProductID = Products.ProductID AND
      [Order Details].OrderID = Orders.OrderID AND
      Orders.CustomerID=Customers.CustomerID
GROUP BY CompanyName
ORDER BY CompanyName
```

This time I've omitted the Orders.OrderID field from the SELECT list and the GROUP BY clause. This statement will display the total for each customer, since we are not grouping by OrderID:

```
Alfreds Futterkiste                   4272.9999980926514
Ana Trujillo Emparedados y helados    1402.9500007629395
Antonio Moreno Taquería               7023.9775543212891
Around the Horn                       13390.650009155273
Berglunds snabbköp                    24927.57746887207
. . .
```

What we need is a statement that can produce a report of the details with total breaks after each order and each customer, as shown here (I have shortened the product names to fit the lines on the printed page without breaks):

```
Alfreds Futterkiste    10643   Rössle         45.60   15   25    513.00
Alfreds Futterkiste    10643   Chartreuse     18.0    21   25    283.50
Alfreds Futterkiste    10643   Spegesild      12.0     2   25     18.00
                                                                 814.50
Alfreds Futterkiste    10692   Vegie-spread   43.90   20    0    878.00
                                                                 878.00
Alfreds Futterkiste    10702   Aniseed Syrup  10.0     6    0     60.00
Alfreds Futterkiste    10702   Lakkalikööri   18.0    15    0    270.00
                                                                 845.80
Alfreds Futterkiste    10952   Grandma's      25.00   16    5    380.00
Alfreds Futterkiste    10952   Rössle         45.6     2    0     91.20
                                                                 471.20
Alfreds Futterkiste    11011   Escargots      13.25   40    5    503.50
Alfreds Futterkiste    11011   Flotemysost    21.50   20    0    430.00
                                                                 933.50
                                                                4273.00
Ana Trujillo           10308   Gudbrand       28.80    1    0     28.80
Ana Trujillo           10308   Outback        12.00    5    0     60.00
                                                                  88.80
Ana Trujillo           10625   Tofu           23.25    3    0     69.75
Ana Trujillo           10625   Singaporean    14.00    5    0     70.00
Ana Trujillo           10625   Camembert      34.00   10    0    340.00
                                                                 479.75
```

T-SQL provides an elegant solution to this problem with the COMPUTE BY clause. The COMPUTE BY clause calculates aggregate functions (sums, counts, and so on) while a field doesn't change value. This field is specified with the BY keyword. When the field changes value, the total calculated so far is displayed and the aggregate function is reset. To produce the list shown here, you must calculate the sum of line totals (quantity * price – discount) and group the calculations according to OrderID and CustomerID. Listing 7.2 shows the complete statement that produced the list shown earlier:

LISTING 7.2   The OrdersGrouped.sql Query

```
USE NORTHWIND
SELECT CompanyName, Orders.OrderID, ProductName,
    UnitPrice=ROUND([Order Details].UnitPrice, 2),
    Quantity,
    Discount=CONVERT(int, Discount * 100),
    ExtendedPrice=ROUND(CONVERT(money,
                    Quantity * (1 - Discount) *
                    [Order Details].UnitPrice), 2)
FROM Products, [Order Details], Customers, Orders
WHERE [Order Details].ProductID = Products.ProductID And
      [Order Details].OrderID = Orders.OrderID And
      Orders.CustomerID=Customers.CustomerID
ORDER BY Customers.CustomerID, Orders.OrderID
COMPUTE SUM(ROUND(CONVERT(money, Quantity * (1 - Discount) *
            [Order Details].UnitPrice), 2))
            BY Customers.CustomerID, Orders.OrderID
COMPUTE SUM(ROUND(CONVERT(money, Quantity * (1 - Discount) *
            [Order Details].UnitPrice), 2))
            BY Customers.CustomerID
```

The first COMPUTE BY clause groups the invoice line totals by order ID within each customer. The second COMPUTE BY clause groups the same totals by customer, as shown in Figure 7.1. The CONVERT() function converts data types similar to the Format() function of VB, and the ROUND() function rounds a floating point number. Both functions are discussed later in this chapter.

The COMPUTE BY clause can be used with any of the aggregate functions you have seen so far. Listing 7.3 displays the order IDs by customer and calculates the total number of invoices issued to each customer:

FIGURE 7.1:

Using the COMPUTE BY clause to calculate totals on groups

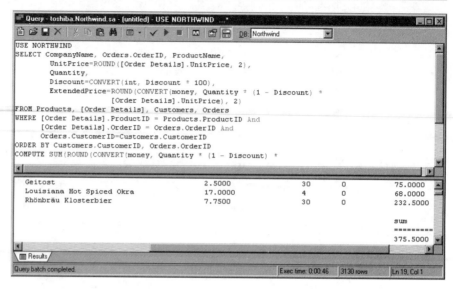

LISTING 7.3   The CountInvoices.sql Query

```
USE NORTHWIND
SELECT Customers.CompanyName, Orders.OrderID
FROM Customers, Orders
WHERE Customers.CustomerID=Orders.CustomerID
ORDER BY Customers.CustomerID
COMPUTE COUNT(Orders.OrderID) BY Customers.CustomerID
```

The SQL engine will count the number of orders while the CustomerID field doesn't change. When it runs into a new customer, the current total is displayed and the counter is reset to zero in anticipation of the next customer. Here's the output produced by the above statement:

```
CompanyName                          OrderID
--------------------  -------

Alfreds Futterkiste                  10643
Alfreds Futterkiste                  10692
Alfreds Futterkiste                  10702
Alfreds Futterkiste                  10835
Alfreds Futterkiste                  10952
Alfreds Futterkiste                  11011
                                     =======
                                     6

Ana Trujillo Emparedados y helados   10308
Ana Trujillo Emparedados y helados   10625
```

```
Ana Trujillo Emparedados y helados      10759
Ana Trujillo Emparedados y helados      10926
                                       =======
                                         4
```

In addition to combining multiple COMPUTE BY clauses in the same statement (as we did in the first example of this section), you can add another COMPUTE statement without the BY clause to display a grand total:

```
USE NORTHWIND
SELECT Customers.CompanyName, Orders.OrderID
FROM Customers, Orders
WHERE Customers.CustomerID=Orders.CustomerID
ORDER BY Customers.CustomerID
COMPUTE COUNT(Orders.OrderID) BY Customers.CustomerID
COMPUTE COUNT(Orders.OrderID)
```

The COMPUTE BY clause requires that the rows are furnished in the proper order, so all the fields following the BY keyword must also appear in an ORDER BY clause. The COMPUTE BY clause will not change the order of the rows to facilitate its calculations. Actually, the SQL engine will refuse to execute a statement that contains a COMPUTE BY clause but not the equivalent ORDER clause; it will abort the statement's execution and display the following error message:

```
A COMPUTE BY item was not found in the ORDER BY list.
All expressions in the COMPUTE BY list must also be
present in the ORDER BY list.
```

Stored Procedures

A *stored procedure* is a routine written in T-SQL that acts on a database's rows. All SQL statements you have seen so far act on selected rows (they select, update, or delete rows), but SQL doesn't provide the means to alter the course of action depending on the values of the fields. There's no support for IF statements and no functions to manipulate strings, formatting functions, and so on. Every DBMS manufacturer extends standard SQL with statements that add the functionality of a programming language. Access queries, for example, recognize the Mid() function, which is identical to the VB function by the same name. It extracts part of a string field and uses it as another field. The equivalent T-SQL function is called SUBSTRING(). In the rest of this chapter, we'll look at the statements and functions of T-SQL.

Stored procedures are attached to SQL Server databases, just like queries are attached to Access databases. The simplest application of stored procedures is to attach complicated queries to the database and call them by name, so that users won't have to enter them more than once. As you will see, stored procedures have many more applications, and they can even be used to build business rules into the database (but more on this in the next chapter).

Syntactical differences aside, the major difference between Access queries and T-SQL stored procedures is that Access queries don't support flow-control statements. The functions recognized by the two DBMSs have mostly different names, but they serve similar purposes. Because Access queries are simpler than T-SQL stored procedures, not to mention that the functions used by Access are identical to those of Visual Basic, we'll start with a quick overview of Access queries and then look into T-SQL's features in depth. Besides, T-SQL is (almost) a programming language and deserves more detailed presentation.

Once a stored procedure has been attached to the database, users and applications can call it as if it were another SQL statement or a built-in statement. Let's say you have written a stored procedure to add a new order to the database. You supply the customer ID and the ordered products' IDs, quantities, and discounts, and the stored procedure does the rest: it creates a new entry in the Orders table, adds the detail lines, and connects them to the order they belong to. The stored procedure makes sure the customer exists, it extracts the product prices from the Products table, and eliminates any chances for errors. Users and applications can call this stored procedure to add a new order and never have to worry about the structure of the tables. If you do change the underlying table structure, you modify this procedure accordingly, and the applications will not even be aware of the changes. I have just described one of the main sample applications used in Chapter 8. But before we get there, we must review Access queries and then discuss the elements of T-SQL.

Writing Access Queries

Access is not nearly as flexible as SQL Server when it comes to stored procedures, but it provides a similar feature, namely queries. A query is an SQL statement attached to the database that can be called by name. Moreover, Access queries are not limited to SQL statements. You can use any VBA function to perform complicated data transformations, comparisons, and so on. However, Access queries do not recognize flow-control statements and are not structured like programs.

Using Parameters with Access Queries

Yet some degree of flexibility can be achieved with parameters. Access queries can accept parameters, which are supplied when the query is executed. If you want to view the customers from specific countries, for example, you don't have to write a different query for each country. You can write a single query that prompts the user for the country name and then uses that name in its WHERE clause to select rows that match the criteria.

Access parameters must be declared with the PARAMETERS keyword before the SQL Statement that uses them. Each parameter has a name and a type. The syntax of the PARAMETERS statement is:

```
PARAMETERS Param_Name Param_Type, Param_Name Para_Type, . . .;
```

You can specify as many parameters as you need for the query. The name of the parameter appears on the title bar of an InputBox that prompts the user for the value of the parameter, so it's more like a prompt rather than a parameter name. Because prompts contain spaces, you must enclose the parameter's name in square brackets. The query that selects customers from a specific country can be written as follows:

```
PARAMETERS [Enter country name] string;
SELECT * FROM Customers
WHERE Country = [Enter country name];
```

The first semicolon at the end of the PARAMETERS statement is required to separate it from the SQL statement that follows. The PARAMETERS statement will prompt the user for the country name with the InputBox shown in Figure 7.2.

FIGURE 7.2:

Supplying parameter values to Access queries

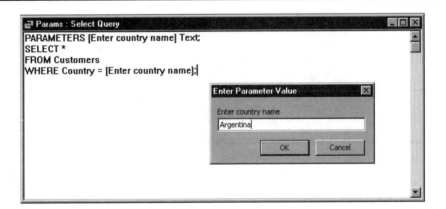

To declare multiple parameters, use commas to separate them. The following Access query will select the orders placed during a user-supplied interval:

```
PARAMETERS [From date] DateTime, [To date] DateTime;
SELECT *
FROM Orders
WHERE OrderDate BETWEEN [From date] AND [To date];
```

When this query is executed, it prompts the user for two dates. Then, it retrieves all the rows from the Orders table whose OrderDate lies between the two supplied dates, including the end dates.

VBA Functions

In addition to parameters, Access queries recognize all the standard VBA functions for manipulating strings, dates and times, and so on. Let's say you want to retrieve the books published by a specific publisher. The obvious criterion is to use the PubID field of the Titles table. To verify this list, you can use the book's ISBN. The second group of digits in the ISBN number are unique to a publisher. Of course, a publisher may have multiple groups. For example, Sybex books have an ISBN of the form 0-7821-XXXX-X. The first digit stands for the country (U.S.), the group 7821 identifies the publisher, and the last digit is a check digit (it's derived from the first nine digits). Sybex can publish up to 9,999 titles before it runs out of ISBNs and requests another group like 7821 from the organization that administers ISBNs worldwide. Sybex has already used up the 8958 group. To select the titles published by Sybex based on the ISBN, you have to isolate the first five digits of the ISBN with the Mid() function and use this substring in your WHERE clause:

```
SELECT * FROM Titles
WHERE Mid(ISBN, 1, 6) = "0-7821" OR Mid(ISBN, 1, 6) = "0-8958"
```

If you execute this query against the Biblio database, you'll find out that the database contains 233 titles from Sybex. You could have used the LIKE operator here, but if the ISBNs didn't contains dashes, then the combinations "7821" and "8958" might appear elsewhere in the ISBN too, so a LIKE operator such as the following might yield incorrect results:

```
SELECT * FROM Titles
WHERE ISBN LIKE "%7821%" OR ISBN LIKE "%8958%"
```

Date and Time Functions

Let's look at a few examples of using some of the date-manipulation functions of Access. The following statement uses the WeekDay() function to extract the day of the week from the OrderDate field and select the orders placed on Mondays:

```
SELECT OrderID, CustomerID
FROM Orders
WHERE (((Weekday([OrderDate]))=2));
```

To make this query a little more complicated, let's count the number of orders placed on the various days of the week. This query can be expressed with the following SQL statement:

```
SELECT Count(OrderID)
FROM Orders
GROUP BY Weekday([OrderDate]);
```

If you run this query, you'll see that the number of orders for each day of the week varies from 164 to 168 (this is a sample database, indeed).

Before we move on to T-SQL, let's look at one last example of an Access query that uses date-manipulation functions. Let's say you want to find out how long it takes the Northwind staff to prepare an order. All the information you need is in the Orders table. You must subtract the Order Date field from the Shipped Date field and calculate the average for all orders, or the average per customer. Listing 7.4 returns the average order preparation span in days.

LISTING 7.4	**The AvgOrderTitle.sql Query**

```
SELECT CompanyName,
       Int(Avg(DateDiff("d", OrderDate, ShippedDate)))
FROM Orders, Customers
WHERE Orders.CustomerID=Customers.CustomerID
GROUP BY CompanyName;
```

The DateDiff() function returns the number of days between the order and shipping dates. Then we take the average per customer (by grouping on the CompanyName field) and finally the integer part of this interval. You can also calculate the average delivery lag per country. This time you must group by country, as shown here:

```
SELECT Country,
       Int(Avg(DateDiff("d", OrderDate, ShippedDate)))
FROM Orders, Customers
WHERE Orders.CustomerID=Customers.CustomerID
GROUP BY Country;
```

Some queries are nearly impossible with Access. Let's say you want to find out the average time span (in days) between successive orders for each customer. To implement this query you would create a new table, move the differences there, calculate averages, and group by customer with the new table's rows. (I may get a message from a reader showing how this is done with a single query, but it will probably be a page-long statement). Queries that involve combinations of successive rows are usually implemented in an application. You retrieve the data you need in a VB application and process them there. With SQL Server's T-SQL, you can implement similar queries on the server, because T-SQL supports not only the date-manipulation functions you need, but the flow-control statements necessary to scan the rows returned by a query.

Writing T-SQL Stored Procedures

The rest of this chapter covers SQL Server stored procedures. In short, a stored procedure does the same calculations as your VB application, only it's executed on the server and uses T-SQL statements. T-SQL is practically a programming language. It doesn't have a user interface, so you can't use it to develop full-blown applications, but when it comes to querying or updating the database and data processing, it can do everything a VB application can do.

You may wonder now, why bother with stored procedures if they don't do more than VB? The answer is that T-SQL is SQL Server's native language, and stored procedures are executed on the server. A stored procedure can scan thousands of records, perform calculations, and return a single number to a VB application. If you perform calculations that involve a large number of rows, you can avoid downloading too much information to the client by writing a stored procedure to do the work on the server instead. Stored procedures are executed faster than the equivalent VB code because they're compiled and they don't move data from the server to the client.

Another good reason for using stored procedures is that once they're defined, they become part of the database and appear to applications as database objects like tables, views, and so on. Earlier I described a stored procedure that adds new orders to a database. This stored procedure is part of the database, and you can set up the database so that users and applications can't modify the Orders table directly. By forcing them to go through a stored procedure, you can be sure that all orders are recorded properly. If you provide a procedure for editing the Orders table, no one can tamper with the integrity of your data. Moreover, if you change the structure of the underlying tables, you can modify the stored procedure, and all VB applications that use the stored procedure will continue as before. You can also implement business rules in the stored procedure (decrease the stock, update a list of best sellers, and so on). By incorporating all this functionality into the stored procedure, you simplify the coding of the client application.

Creating and Executing Stored Procedures

To write, debug, and execute stored procedures against a SQL Server database, you must use the Query Analyzer. In the following chapter you'll find out how you can add stored procedures to a database through your VB application, but let's start with the simpler method.

Enter the definition of the procedure in the Query pane and then press Ctrl+E to execute that definition. This action will attach the procedure to the database, but it will not actually execute it. To execute a procedure that's already been stored to the database, you must use the EXECUTE statement, which is discussed shortly.

To create a new stored procedure and attach it to the current database, use the CREATE PROCEDURE statement. The syntax of the statement is:

```
CREATE PROCEDURE procedure_name
AS
{procedure definition}
```

where *procedure_name* is the name of the new stored procedure, and the block of statement following the AS keyword is the body of the procedure. In its simplest form, a stored procedure is an SQL statement like the ones we have discussed so far. If you think you'll be frequently executing the AllInvoices query (shown in Listing 7.5), you can create a stored procedure containing the SQL statement that retrieves customers, orders, and order details. Every time you need this report, you can call this procedure by name. To create the AllInvoices stored procedure, enter the following lines in the Query pane of the Query Analyzer:

```
CREATE PROCEDURE AllInvoices
AS
```

Then enter the SQL statement shown in Listing 7.5. Because this is not actually an SQL statement, the first time you execute it, it will not return the list of invoices. Instead, it will add the AllInvoices procedure to the current database—so be sure to select the Northwind database in the DB drop-down list, or use the USE keyword to make Northwind the active database:

```
USE NORTHWIND
CREATE PROCEDURE AllInvoices
AS
   … procedure statements …
```

If the procedure exists already, you can't create it again. You must either drop it from the database with the DROP PROCEDURE statement, or modify it with the ALTER PROCEDURE statement. The syntax of the ALTER PROCEDURE statement is identical to that of the CREATE PROCEDURE statement. By replacing the CREATE keyword with the ALTER keyword, you can replace the definition of an existing procedure.

A common approach is to test for the existence of a stored procedure and drop it if it exists. Then, you can add a new procedure with the CREATE PROCEDURE statement. For example, if you are not sure the MyProcedure procedure exists, use the following statements to find and modify it:

```
USE DataBase
IF EXISTS (SELECT name FROM sysobjects
        WHERE name = 'myProcedure')
    DROP PROCEDURE myProcedure
GO

CREATE PROCEDURE myProcedure
AS
. . .
```

The SELECT statement retrieves the name of the desired procedure from the database objects (again, be sure to execute it against the desired database). If a procedure by the name *myProcedure* exists already, EXISTS returns True and drops the procedure definition from the database. Then it proceeds to add the revised definition.

In the last chapter, you saw the SQL statement that retrieves all the orders from the Northwind database. To implement it as a stored procedure, you must insert a few lines that declare a new stored procedure and then append the SQL statement that implements the procedure as is. Listing 7.5 provides the code for the implementation of the AllInvoices batch as a stored procedure:

LISTING 7.5 **The AllInvoices Query Stored Procedure**

```
USE NORTHWIND
IF EXISTS (SELECT name FROM sysobjects
        WHERE name = 'AllInvoices')
    DROP PROCEDURE AllInvoices
GO

CREATE PROCEDURE AllInvoices
AS
SELECT CompanyName, Orders.OrderID, ProductName,
    UnitPrice=ROUND([Order Details].UnitPrice, 2),
    Quantity,
    Discount=CONVERT(int, Discount * 100),
    ExtendedPrice=ROUND(CONVERT(money, Quantity * (1 - Discount) *
                    [Order Details].UnitPrice), 2)
FROM Products, [Order Details], Customers, Orders
WHERE [Order Details].ProductID = Products.ProductID And
      [Order Details].OrderID = Orders.OrderID And
      Orders.CustomerID=Customers.CustomerID
ORDER BY Customers.CustomerID, Orders.OrderID
COMPUTE SUM(ROUND(CONVERT(money, Quantity * (1 - Discount) *
            [Order Details].UnitPrice), 2))
            BY Customers.CustomerID, Orders.OrderID
COMPUTE SUM(ROUND(CONVERT(money, Quantity * (1 - Discount) *
            [Order Details].UnitPrice), 2))
            BY Customers.CustomerID
```

Then press Ctrl+E to execute the procedure's declaration. If you haven't misspelled any keywords, the message "The command(s) completed successfully." will appear in the lower pane of the Query Analyzer's window, as shown in Figure 7.3. You can find the `AllInvoices.sql` file in this chapter's folder on the CD. Load it in Query Analyzer with the File ➤ Open command and then execute it.

FIGURE 7.3:

When you execute a stored procedure's definition, you add it to the database, but the procedure's statements are not executed.

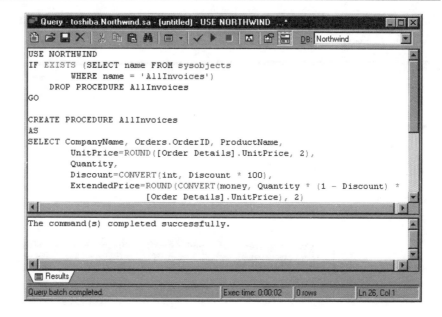

```
USE NORTHWIND
IF EXISTS (SELECT name FROM sysobjects
        WHERE name = 'AllInvoices')
    DROP PROCEDURE AllInvoices
GO

CREATE PROCEDURE AllInvoices
AS
SELECT CompanyName, Orders.OrderID, ProductName,
        UnitPrice=ROUND([Order Details].UnitPrice, 2),
        Quantity,
        Discount=CONVERT(int, Discount * 100),
        ExtendedPrice=ROUND(CONVERT(money, Quantity * (1 - Discount) *
                        [Order Details].UnitPrice), 2)
```

The command(s) completed successfully.

To execute a stored procedure, you must use the EXECUTE statement (or its abbreviation, EXEC) followed by the name of the procedure. Assuming that you have created the AllInvoices procedure, here's how to execute it.

1. First clear the Query pane of Query Analyzer, or open a new window in the Query Analyzer.

2. In the fresh Query pane, type

   ```
   USE Northwind
   EXECUTE AllInvoices
   ```
   and press Ctrl+E. The result of the query will appear in the Results pane of the Query Analyzer, as shown in Figure 7.4.

The first time you execute the procedure, SQL Server will put together an execution plan, so it will take a few seconds. After that, the procedure's execution will start immediately, and the rows will start appearing on the Results pane as soon as they become available.

TIP

If a procedure takes too long to execute, or it returns too many rows, you can interrupt it by pressing the Stop button (a red rectangular button on SQL Server's toolbar). If you execute an unconditional join by mistake, for example, you can stop the execution of the query and not have to wait until all rows arrive.

FIGURE 7.4:

Executing the AllInvoices
stored procedure with the
Query Analyzer

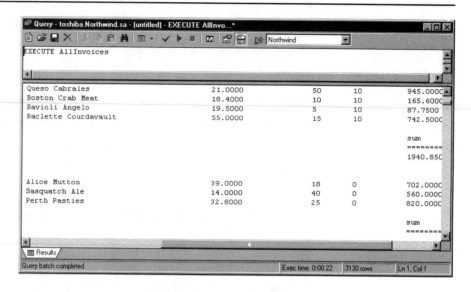

Executing Command Strings

In addition to executing stored procedures, you can use the EXECUTE statement
to execute strings with valid T-SQL statements. If the variable *@TSQLcmd* (all T-SQL
variables must begin with the @ symbol) contains a valid SQL statement, you
can execute it by passing it as an argument to the EXECUTE procedure:

```
EXECUTE (@TSQLcmd)
```

The parentheses are required. If you omit them, SQL Server will attempt to locate
the *@TSQLcmd* stored procedure. Here's a simple example of storing SQL statements into variables and executing them with the EXECUTE method:

```
DECLARE @Country varchar(20)
DECLARE @TSQLcmd varchar(100)
SET @Country='Germany'
SET @TSQLcmd = 'SELECT City FROM Customers
               WHERE Country="' + @Country + '"'
EXECUTE (@TSQLcmd)
```

All T-SQL variables must be declared with the DECLARE statement, have a
valid data type, and be set with the SET statement. You will find more information on the use of variables in the following sections of this chapter.

The EXECUTE statement with a command string is commonly used to build
SQL statements on the fly. You'll see a more practical example of this technique in
the section "Building SQL Statements on the Fly," later in this chapter.

> **WARNING**   Statements that are built dynamically and executed with the help of a command string as explained in this section do not take advantage of the execution plan. Therefore, you should not use this technique frequently. Use it only when you can't write the stored procedure at design time.

Why Use Stored Procedures?

Stored procedures are far more than a programming convenience. When an SQL statement, especially a complicated one, is stored in the database, the database management system can execute it efficiently. To execute an SQL statement, the query engine must analyze it and put together an execution plan. The execution plan is analogous to the compilation of a traditional application. The DBMS translates the statements in the procedure into statements it can execute directly against the database. When the SQL statement is stored in the database as a procedure, its execution plan is designed once and is ready to be used. Moreover, stored procedures can be designed once, tested, and used by many users and applications. If the same stored procedure is used by more than one user, the DBMS keeps only one copy of the procedure in memory, and all users share the same instance of the procedure. This means more efficient memory utilization. Finally, you can limit user access to the database's tables and force users to access the database through stored procedures. This is a simple method of enforcing business rules.

Let's say you have designed a database like Northwind, and you want to update each product's stock, and perhaps customer balances, every time a new invoice is issued. You could write the applications yourself and hope you won't leave out any of these operations, then explain the structure of the database to the programmers and hope they'll follow your instructions. Or you could implement a stored procedure that accepts the customer's ID and the IDs and quantities of the items ordered, then updates all the tables involved in the transaction. Application programmers can call this stored procedure and never have to worry about remembering to update some of the tables. At a later point, you may add a table to the database for storing the best selling products. You can change the stored procedure and the client applications that record new order through this stored procedure need not be changed. Later in this chapter you will see examples of stored procedures that implement business rules.

T-SQL: The Language

The basic elements of T-SQL are the same as those of any other programming language: variables, flow-control statements, and functions. In the following few sections, we'll go quickly through the elements of T-SQL. Since this book is addressed to VB programmers, I will not waste any time explaining what variables are and why they must have a type. I will discuss T-SQL by comparing its elements to the equivalent VB elements and stress the differences in the statements and functions of the two languages.

T-SQL Variables

Unlike Visual Basic, T-SQL is a typed language. Every variable must be declared before it is used, which is quite an adjustment for the average VB programmer. T-SQL supports two types of variables: local and global. Local variables are declared in the stored procedure's code, and their scope is limited in the procedure in which they were declared. The global variables are exposed by the SQL Server, and you can use them without declaring them and from within any procedure.

Local Variables and Data Types

Local variables are declared with the DECLARE statement, and their names must begin with the @ character. The following are valid variable names: @*CustomerTotal*, @*Avg_Discount*, @*i*, @*counter*. To use them, declare them with the DECLARE statement, whose syntax is:

```
DECLARE var_name var_type
```

where *var_name* is the variable's name and *var_type* is the name of a data type supported by SQL Server. Unlike Visual Basic, T-SQL doesn't create variables on the fly. All T-SQL variables must be declared before they can be used. The available data types are listed here:

char, varchar   These variables store characters, and their length can't exceed 8,000 characters. The following statements declare and assign values to char variables:

```
DECLARE @string1 char(20)
DECLARE @string2 varchar(20)
SET @string1 = 'STRING1'
SET @string2 = 'STRING2'
PRINT '[' + @string1 + ']'
PRINT '[' + @string2 + ']'
```

The last two statements print the following:

```
[STRING1            ]
[STRING2]
```

The char variable is padded with spaces to the specified length, while the varchar variable is not. If the actual data exceeds the specified length of the string, both types truncate the string to its declared maximum length (to 20 characters, in this example).

nchar, nvarchar   The nchar and nvarchar types are equivalent to the char and varchar types, but they are used for storing Unicode strings.

int, smallint, tinyint   Use these types to store whole numbers (integers). The int type uses 4 bytes and can store integer values in the range from –2,147,483,648 to 2,147,483,647 (it's equivalent to VB's Long data type). The smallint type is equivalent to Visual Basic's Integer data type and uses 2 bytes. It can store integer values in the range from –32,768 to 32,767. The tinyint type is equivalent to Visual Basic's Byte type and uses 1 byte to store values from 0 to 255.

decimal, numeric   These two types store an integer to the left of the decimal point and a fractional value to the right of the decimal point. The digits allocated to the integer and fractional part of the number are specified in the variable's declaration:

```
DECLARE @DecimalVar decimal(4, 3)
```

The first argument specifies the maximum total number of digits that can be stored to the left and right of the decimal point. Valid values are in the range 1 through 28. The second argument specifies the maximum number of digits that can be stored to the right of the decimal point (the integer part), and its value must be in the range 0 through the specified precision (in other words, the second argument can't be larger than the first argument).

If you store the value 30.25 / 4 to the *@DecimalVar* variable and then print it, it will be displayed as 7.563. If the variable was declared as:

```
DECLARE @DecimalVar DECIMAL(12, 6)
```

the same value will be printed as 7.562500.

datetime, smalldatetime   Use these two types to store date and time values. The datetime type uses 8 bytes: 4 bytes for the date and 4 bytes for the time. The time portion of the datetime type is the number of milliseconds after midnight and is updated every 3.33 milliseconds. The smalldatetime type uses 4 bytes: 2 bytes to store the number of days after January 1, 1900 and 2 bytes to store the number of minutes since midnight.

The following statements demonstrate how to add days, hours, and minutes to variables of the datetime and smalldatetime types:

```
DECLARE @DateVar datetime
DECLARE @smallDateVar smalldatetime
PRINT "datetime type"
SET @DateVar = '1/1/2000 03:02.10'
PRINT @DateVar
```

```
/* Add a day to a datetime variable */
SET @DateVar = @DateVar + 1
PRINT @DateVar
/* Add an hour to a datetime variable */
SET @DateVar = @DateVar + 1.0/24.0
PRINT @DateVar
/* Add a minute to a datetime variable */
SET @DateVar = @DateVar + 1.0/(24.0 * 60.0)
PRINT @DateVar
PRINT "smalldatetime"
SET @smallDateVar = '1/1/2000 03:02.10'
PRINT @smallDateVar
/* Add a day to a smalldatetime variable */
SET @smallDateVar = @smallDateVar + 1
PRINT @smallDateVar
/* Add an hour to a smalldatetime variable */
SET @smallDateVar = @smallDateVar + 1.0/24.0
PRINT @smallDateVar
```

If you enter these lines in the Query pane of the Query Analyzer and execute them, the following output will be produced:

```
datetime type
Jan  1 2000   3:02AM
Jan  2 2000   3:02AM
Jan  2 2000   4:02AM
Jan  2 2000   4:03AM
smalldatetime
Jan  1 2000   3:02AM
Jan  2 2000   3:02AM
Jan  2 2000   4:02AM
```

float, real   The float and real types are known as approximate data types and are used for storing floating-point numbers. These types are known as approximate numeric types, because they store an approximation of the exact value (which is usually the result of a calculation). The approximation is unavoidable because binary and decimal fractional values don't match exactly. The most obvious manifestation of this approximation is that you can't represent the value 0 with a float or real variable. If you perform complicated calculations with floating-point numbers and you want to know whether the result is zero, do not compare it directly to zero, as it may be a very small number but not exactly zero. Use a comparison like the following one:

```
Set @zValue = 1E-20
If Abs(@result) < @zValue
    . . .
```

```
Else
    . . .
End If
```

The LOG() function returns the logarithm of a numeric value. The following two statements return the same value:

```
SET @n1=log(1/0.444009)
SET @n2=-log(0.444009)
```

(the variables *@n1* and *@n2* must be declared as float, or real). If you print the two values with the PRINT statement, the values will be identical. However, the two values are stored differently internally and if you subtract them, their difference will not be zero.

```
PRINT @n1-@n2
```

The result will be the value –4.41415e–008.

money, smallmoney   Use these two types to store dollar amounts. Both types use four fractional digits. The money type uses 8 bytes and can represent amounts in the range –922,337,203,685,477.5807 to 922,337,203,685,377.5807. The small-money type uses 4 bytes and can represent amounts in the range –214,748.3648 to 214,748.3647.

text   The text data type can store non-Unicode data with a maximum length of 2,147,483,647 characters.

image   This date type can store binary data up to 2,147,483,647 bytes in size.

binary, varbinary   These variables store binary values. The two following statements declare two binary variables, one with fixed length and another with variable length:

```
DECLARE @bVar1 Binary(4), @bVar2 varBinary
```

The binary data types can store up to 8,000 bytes. Use binary variables to store the values of binary columns (small images or other unusual bits of information). To assign a value to a binary variable, use the hexadecimal notation:

```
SET @bVar1 = 0x000000F0
```

This statement assigns the decimal value 255 to the *bVar1* variable.

bit   Use the bit data type to represent integer values, which can be either 0 or 1.

timestamp   This data type holds a counter value that's unique to the database—an ever-increasing value that represents the current date and time. Timestamp columns are commonly used to find out whether a row has been changed since it was read. You can't extract date and time information from a timestamp value, but you can compare two timestamp values to find out whether a row was updated since it was read, or the order in which rows were read.

Each table can have only one timestamp column, and this column's values are set by SQL Server each time a row is inserted or updated. However, you can read this value and compare it to the other timestamp values.

uniqueidentifier   This is a globally unique identifier, which is usually assigned to a column with the NEWID() function. These values are extracted from network card identifiers or other machine-related information, and they are used in replication schemes to identify rows.

Global Variables

In addition to the local variables you can declare in your procedures, T-SQL supports a number of global variables, whose names begin with the symbols @@. These values are maintained by the system, and you can read them to retrieve system information.

@@FETCH_STATUS   The @@FETCH_STATUS variable, for example, is zero if the FETCH statement successfully retrieved a row, nonzero otherwise. This variable is set after the execution of a FETCH statement and is commonly used to terminate a WHILE loop that scans a cursor. The global variable @@FETCH_STATUS may also have the value –2, which indicates the row you attempted to retrieve has been deleted since the cursor was created. This value applies to keyset-driven cursors only.

@@CURSOR_ROWS, @@ROWCOUNT   The @@CURSOR_ROWS global variable returns the number of rows in the most recently opened cursor, and the @@ROWCOUNT variable returns the number of rows affected by the action query. The @@ROWCOUNT variable is commonly used with UPDATE and DELETE statements to find out how many rows were affected by the SQL statement. To find out how many rows were affected by an update statement, print the @@ROWCOUNT global variable after executing the SQL statement:

```
UPDATE Customers
    SET PhoneNumber = '030' + PhoneNumber
    WHERE Country = 'Germany'
PRINT @@ROWCOUNT
```

@@ERROR   The @@ERROR variable returns an error number for the last T-SQL statement that was executed. If this variable is zero, then the statement was executed successfully.

@@IDENTITY   The @@IDENTITY global variable returns the most recently used value for an Identity column. As you recall from Chapter 2, Identity columns can't be set; they are assigned a value automatically by the system, each time a new row is added to the table. Applications usually need this information because Identity fields are used as foreign keys into other tables. Let's say you're adding a new order to the Northwind database. First you must add a row to the Orders table. You can specify any field's value, but not the OrderID field's value. When the new row is added to the Orders table, you must add rows with the invoice details to the Order Details table. To do so, you need the value of the OrderID field, which can be retrieved by the @@IDENTITY global variable. In the section "Implementing Business Rules with Stored Procedures," later in this chapter, you'll find examples on how to use the @@IDENTITY variable.

Other Global Variables   Many global variables relate to administrative tasks, and they are listed in Table 7.1. T-SQL exposes more global variables, but the ones listed here are the most common.

TABLE 7.1: Commonly Used T-SQL Global Variables

Variable Name	Description
@@CONNECTIONS	The number of login attempts since SQL Server started for the last time.
@@CPU_BUSY	The number of ticks the CPU spent for the SQL Server since it was started for the last time.
@@IDENTITY	The most recently created IDENTITY value.
@@IDLE	The number of ticks SQL Server has been idle since it was last started.
@@IO_BUSY	The number of ticks SQL Server spent for input/output operations since it was last started.
@@LANGID	The current language ID.
@@LANGUAGE	The current language.
@@LOCK_TIMEOUT	The current lock-out setting in milliseconds.
@@MAX_CONNECTIONS	The maximum number of simultaneous connections that can be made to SQL Server.
@@MAX_PRECISION	The current precision setting for decimal and numeric data types.
@@NESTLEVEL	The number of nested transactions for the current execution. Transactions can be nested up to 16 levels.
@@SERVERNAME	The name of the local SQL Server.
@@TOTAL_ERRORS	The number of total errors since SQL was started for the last time.
@@TOTAL_READ	The number of reads from the disk since SQL Server was started for the last time.
@@TOTAL_WRITE	The number of writes from the disk since SQL Server was started for the last time.
@@TRANCOUNT	The number of active transactions for the current user.
@@SPID	The process ID of the current user process on the server. This number identifies a process, not a user.

You should consult SQL Server's online documentation for more information on the global variables. These variables are used mainly by database administrators, not programmers.

Flow-Control Statements

T-SQL supports the basic flow-control statements that enable you to selectively execute blocks of statements based on the outcome of a comparison. They are similar to the equivalent VB statements and, even though there aren't as many, they are adequate for the purposes of processing rows.

IF ... ELSE

This statement executes a block of statements conditionally, and its syntax is

```
IF condition
    {statement}
ELSE
    {statement}
```

Notice that there's no THEN keyword and that a T-SQL IF block is not delimited with an END IF keyword. To execute more than a single statement in the IF or the ELSE clause, you must use the BEGIN and END keywords to enclose the block of statements:

```
IF condition
    BEGIN
    {multiple statements}
    END
ELSE
    BEGIN
    {multiple statements}
    END
```

Depending on the *condition*, one of the two blocks of statements between the BEGIN and END keywords are executed. Here's an example of the IF statement with statement blocks:

```
IF (SELECT COUNT(*) FROM Customers WHERE Country = 'Germany') > 0
    BEGIN
    {statements to process German customers}
    END
ELSE
    BEGIN
    PRINT "The database contains no customers from Germany."
    END
```

Notice the second pair of BEGIN/END keywords are optional because the ELSE clause is followed by a single statement.

CASE

The CASE statement is equivalent to Visual Basic's SELECT CASE statement. SELECT is a reserved SQL keyword and shouldn't be used with the CASE statement. The CASE statement compares a variable (or field) value against several values and executes a block of statement, depending on which comparison returns a True result.

A car rental company may need to calculate insurance premiums based on a car's category. Instead of multiple IF statements, you can use a CASE structure like the following:

```
CASE @CarCategory
    WHEN 'COMPACT' THEN 25.5
    WHEN 'ECONOMY' THEN 37.5
    WHEN 'LUXURY'  THEN 45.0
END
```

The CASE statement will return a single value: the one that corresponds to the first WHEN clause that's true. Notice this statement is similar to Visual Basic's SELECT CASE statement, but in T-SQL, it's called CASE. The SELECT keyword in the previous line simply tells SQL Server to display the outcome of the CASE statement. If the variable *@CarCategory* is "ECONOMY," then the value 37.5 is printed in the Results pane of the Query Analyzer's window.

To include the value returned by the CASE statement to the result set, you must combine the SELECT and CASE statements as shown here:

```
SELECT @premium=
    CASE @CarCategory
        WHEN 'COMPACT' THEN 25.5
        WHEN 'ECONOMY' THEN 37.5
        WHEN 'LUXURY'  THEN 45.0
    END
```

T-SQL CASE Statement versus VB SELECT CASE Statement

As a VB programmer, sooner or later you'll code a SQL CASE statement as SELECT CASE. The result will not be an error message. The statement will simply select the result of the CASE statement (SELECT is a T-SQL keyword that assigns a value to a variable).

Let's clarify this with an example. The following statements will return the value 7.5. This value will be printed in the Results pane of the Query Analyzer, but you won't be able to use it in the statements following the CASE statement.

Continued on next page

```
DECLARE @state char(2)
SET @state = 'CA'
SELECT CASE @state
    WHEN 'AZ' THEN 5.5
    WHEN 'CA' THEN 7.5
    WHEN 'NY' THEN 8.5
END
```

If you want to store the result to a variable, use the following syntax:

```
DECLARE @state char(2)
DECLARE @stateTAX real
SET @state = 'CA'
SET @stateTAX =
    CASE @state
        WHEN 'AZ' THEN 5.5
        WHEN 'CA' THEN 7.5
        WHEN 'NY' THEN 8.5
    END
PRINT @stateTAX
```

This syntax has no counterpart in Visual Basic. Note that the entire CASE statement is, in effect, embedded into the assignment. The *@stateTAX* variable is set to the value selected by the CASE statement.

WHILE

The WHILE statement repeatedly executes a single statement or a block of T-SQL statements. If you want to repeat multiple statements, enclose them in a pair of BEGIN/END keywords, as explained in the description of the IF statement. The most common use of the WHILE statement is to scan the rows of a cursor, as shown in the following example:

```
FETCH NEXT INTO variable_list
WHILE @@FETCH_STATUS = 0
    BEGIN
    {statements to process the fields of the current row}
    FETCH NEXT INTO variable_list
    END
```

NOTE I'll discuss cursors in the context of T-SQL procedures in Chapter 8.

The FETCH NEXT statement reads the next row of a cursor set and stores its fields' values into the variables specified in the *variable_list*, which is a comma-separated list of variables. The FETCH statement is discussed in the following chapter. For the purposes of this example, you can think of a cursor as a table and FETCH NEXT as the equivalent of the MoveNext method of the Recordset object Finally, @@*FETCH_STATUS* is a global variable that returns 0 while there are more records to be fetched. When we reach the end of the cursor, @@*FETCH_STATUS* returns -1.

CONTINUE and BREAK

These two keywords are used in conjunction with the WHILE statement to alter the flow of execution. The CONTINUE keyword ends the current iteration and forces another one. In other words, the WHILE statement's condition is evaluated and the loop is re-entered. If the condition is False, then the WHILE loop is skipped and execution continues with the line following the END keyword that delimits the loop's body of statements.

The BREAK keyword terminates the loop immediately and branches to the line following the loop's END keyword. The following code segment shows how the two keywords are used in a WHILE loop:

```
WHILE <condition>
    BEGIN
        {read column values into variables}
        IF @balance < 0
            CONTINUE
        IF @balance > 999999
            BREAK
        {process @balance variable and/or other variables}
    END
```

This loop reads the rows of a table or cursor and processes only the ones with a positive balance, less than 1,000,000. If a row with a negative balance is found, the code doesn't process it and continues with the next row. If a row with a balance of 1,000,000 or more is found, the code stops processing the rows by breaking out of the loop.

GOTO and RETURN

These are the last two flow-control statements, and they enable you to alter the flow of execution by branching to another location in the procedure. The GOTO statement branches to a line identified by a label. Here's a simple example of the GOTO statement (in effect, it's a less-elegant method of implementing a WHILE loop):

```
RepeatLoop:
    FETCH NEXT INTO variable_list
    IF @@FETCH_STATUS = 0
        BEGIN
        {process variables}
        GOTO RepeatLoop
    END
```

While more records are in the result set, the GOTO statement branches to the FETCH NEXT statement. The identifier *RepeatLoop* is a label (a name identifying the line to which you want to branch), and it must be followed by a colon. If there are no more records to be fetched and processed, the procedure continues with the statement following the END keyword.

The RETURN statement ends a procedure unconditionally and it, optionally, returns a result. To return a value from within a stored procedure, use a statement like the following:

```
RETURN @error_value
```

@error_value is a local variable, which can be set by the procedure's code. The calling application, which could be another stored procedure, should be aware of the possible values returned by the procedure.

If you don't specify your own error code, SQL Server returns its own error code, which is one of the values shown in Table 7.2.

TABLE 7.2:   RETURN Statement Error Codes

Error Code	Description
−1	Missing object
−2	Data type error
−3	Process involved in deadlock
−4	Permission error
−5	Syntax error
−6	User error
−7	Resource error
−8	Internal problem
−9	System limit reached
−10	Internal inconsistency
−11	Internal inconsistency
−12	Corrupt table or index
−13	Corrupt database
−14	Hardware error

PRINT

The PRINT statement is similar to Visual Basic's Debug.Print method: It prints its argument to the Results pane and is used for debugging purposes. The output of the PRINT statement doesn't become part of the cursor returned by the procedure or T-SQL statement. The syntax of the PRINT statement is:

```
PRINT output_list
```

The *output_list* can be any combination of literals, variables, and functions. To display a message, use a statement like the following one:

```
PRINT "No rows matching your criteria were found in the table."
```

You can also display variable values along with literals, but this requires some conversions. Unlike Visual Basic's PRINT statement, the T-SQL PRINT statement can't print multiple arguments separated with commas. You must format all the information you want to print as strings, concatenate them with the + operator, and then print them. If you want to print a customer name (field CustName) and a total (field CustTotal), you can't use a statement like:

```
PRINT CustName, CustTotal    - WRONG!
```

Instead, you must concatenate the two values and print them as a single string. Since T-SQL is a typed language, you must first convert the numeric field to a string value and concatenate the two:

```
PRINT CustName + CONVERT(char(12), CustTotal)
```

The CONVERT() function converts (casts) a data type to another data type, and it's discussed in the next section of this chapter.

NOTE   Normally, all the output produced by the T-SQL statements forms the result set. This output is usually the data retrieved from the database. To include titles or any other type of information in the result set, use the PRINT statement. When you use the PRINT statement with the Query Analyzer, its output appears in the lower pane of the window. You can't use the PRINT statement to insert additional lines into a cursor.

RAISERROR

Normally, when an error occurs during the execution of a stored procedure, SQL Server displays an error message in the lower pane and aborts the execution. It is possible to raise your own error messages from within your stored procedures with the RAISERROR statement. The syntax of the statement is:

```
RAISERROR errorNum, severity, state
```

The first argument is the error's number, and it must be a value in the range 50,001 to 2,147,483,648. The first 50,000 error codes are reserved for SQL Server. The second argument is the severity of the error and must be a value from 1 to 18 (18 being the most severe custom error). The last argument is an integer in the range 1 to 127, and you can use it to return additional information about the error.

The errors raised by SQL Server have a description, too. To associate a description with your custom errors, use the *sp_addmessage* system stored procedure, whose syntax is:

```
sp_addmessage errorNum, severity, errorDescription
```

This statement adds new error messages to a database and associates them to error numbers. To add a custom error, use a statement like the following one:

```
sp_addmessage 60000, 15, "Can't accept IOU from this customer"
```

Then, every time you run into customers you can't accept IOUs from, raise this error with the RAISERROR statement. Your error message will be handled just like any native SQL Server error message, as shown in Figure 7.5.

FIGURE 7.5:

Raising custom errors from within your stored procedures

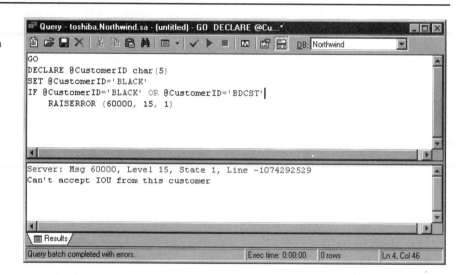

T-SQL Functions

T-SQL supports a number of functions that simplify the processing of the various data types, interacting with the server and implementing the operations you take for granted in application development. In this section we'll discuss the T-SQL functions by comparing them to the equivalent VB functions. Some T-SQL functions have no equivalent in VB, and these functions are discussed in more detail. Notice that the following functions are part of T-SQL, but they can be used outside T-SQL procedures. You can use them in the Query Analyzer's window to process, or format, the output of plain SQL statements.

String Manipulation

T-SQL supports a number of functions for the manipulation of strings, that are similar to the equivalent string functions of Visual Basic, but many of them have different names. The following list summarizes these functions and their arguments.

ASCII(character)   Same as the Asc() function of VB

CHAR(value)   Same as the Chr() function of VB

CHARINDEX(pattern, expression)   Similar to the InStr() function of VB. The CHARINDEX() function returns the position of the first occurrence of the first argument in the second argument.

LEFT(string, len)   Same as the Left() function of VB

RIGHT(string, len)   Same as the Right() function of VB

LEN(string)   Same as the Len() function of VB. It returns the length of a string. The LEN() function will return the length of the string stored in the variable, even if the variable was declared as char.

DATALENGTH(variable)   This function returns the declared length of a variable or field, unlike the LEN() function, which returns the length of the string stored in the variable.

LOWER(string)   Same as the LCase() function of VB

UPPER(string)   Same as the UCase() function of VB

LTRIM(string)   Same as the LTrim() function of VB

RTRIM(string)   Same as the RTrim() function of VB

SPACE(value)   Same as the Space() function of VB

STR(float, length, decimal)   This function converts a float expression to a string, using *length* digits in all and *decimal* digits for the fractional part of the expression. If the numeric value has more fractional digits than specified with the *decimal* argument, the STR() function will round, not simply truncate the numeric value. The function PRINT STR(3.14159, 4, 2) will return the value 3.14, while the expression PRINT STR(3.14159, 5, 3) will return 3.142.

REPLACE(string1, string2, string3)   Same as the Replace() function of VB. It replaces all occurrences of *string2* in *string1* with *string3*.

REPLICATE(char, value)   Same as the String() function of VB. It returns a new string by repeating the *char* character *value* times (notice that the REPLICATE function's arguments appear in reverse order).

REVERSE(string)   Same as the StrReverse() function of VBA. It reverses the order of the characters in the specified string.

SUBSTRING(string, start, length)   Similar to the Mid() function of VB. It returns a segment of a text or binary value. *string* is the variable on which the SUBSTRING() function will act, and *start* and *length* are the starting position and length of the desired segment of the string. The function:

```
SUBSTRING('February 21, 1999',10,2)
```

returns the string 21 (the two characters at the tenth position in the specified string).

NCHAR(value)   Returns the Unicode character whose value is *value*

PATINDEX(pattern, expression)   Similar to the InStr() function of VB and the CHARINDEX() function of T-SQL. It returns the location of the first occurrence of the *pattern* string in the *expression* string.

STUFF(string1, start, length, string2)   This function replaces part of *string1* with *string2*. The part of the first string to be replaced is determined by the position of the first character (*start*) and the *length* to be replaced. If you execute the following lines:

```
DECLARE @a char(30)
SET @a="Database Programming"
SET @a= STUFF(@a, 1, 8, "SQL Server")
PRINT @a
```

the string "SQL Server Programming" will be printed.

QUOTENAME(string, quote_char)   Returns a Unicode string with *quote_char* as the delimiter. The function:

```
QUOTENAME(ContactName, '"')
```

returns the value of the field in a pair of double quotes:

```
"Antonio Morena"
```

You can also use characters that appear in pairs to enclose the string. The function:

```
QUOTENAME(ContactName, "{")
```

returns a string like the following one:

```
{Antonio Morena}
```

SOUNDEX Functions

The following few functions are unique to T-SQL, and they are quite interesting. They're based on the SOUNDEX algorithm, which compares strings based on their sounds. The SOUNDEX algorithm measures how close two words are, rather than whether they are identical or not, and it does so by taking into consideration the first letter of each word, its consonants, and the closeness of the sounds of various letters (such as *p, b, t,* and *d*).

DIFFERENCE(string1, string2)   Returns the difference between two strings as a value between 0 and 4. This function uses the SOUNDEX algorithm to compare sounds, rather than characters. If the two strings match phonetically very well, the DIFFERENCE() function will return the value 4. If they don't resemble each other even remotely, it will return the value 0.

The DIFFERENCE function is commonly used to search with names. Instead of a comparison like

```
WHERE Authors.AuthorName = sAuthor
```

where *sAuthor* is the name supplied by the user, you can use the following comparison:

```
WHERE DIFFERENCE(Authors.AuthorName, sAuthor) = 4
```

The latter comparison will match "Mansfield" with "Mansfeeld", "Petroutsos" with "Petrutsos", and so on.

SOUNDEX(string)   Returns the four-character SOUNDEX code of a word. You can use this value to compare the closeness of two words. The SOUNDEX function converts a string to a four-character code: the first character of the code is the first character of the *string* argument, and the second through fourth characters of the code are numbers that code the consonants in the word (vowels are ignored unless they are the first letter of the string). The strings "Brannon", "Branon", and "Bramon" all have a SOUNDEX value of B655, because the sounds of *n* and *m* are very close. The word "Bradon", however, has a SOUNDEX value of B635 (it differs by a consonant in the middle of the word). The word "Branok" has a SOUNDEX value of B652, since it differs in a consonant at the end.

Conversion Functions

The internal representation of the various columns is not always the most appropriate for reports. T-SQL provides two functions for converting between data types, which are described next.

CONVERT(data_type, variable, style)   The CONVERT() function converts a variable (or column value) to the specified data type. The *data_type* argument can be any valid SQL Server data type. If the data type is nchar, nvarchar, char, varchar, binary, or varbinary, you can specify its length as a numeric value in parentheses.

The *style* argument specifies the desired date format when you convert datetime and smalldatetime variables to character data. Its values are shown in Table 7.3.

TABLE 7.3:   Values of the CONVERT() Function's Style Argument

Value (without Century)	Value (with Century)	Date Format
1	101	mm/dd/yy
2	102	yy.mm.dd
3	103	dd/mm/yy
4	104	dd.mm.yy
5	105	dd-mm-yy
6	106	dd mon yy
7	107	mon dd, yy
8	108	hh:mm:ss
9	109	mon dd yyyy hh:mi:ss:mmmAM (or PM)
10	110	mm-dd-yy
11	111	yy/mm/dd
12	112	yymmdd
13	113	dd mon yyyy hh:mm:ss:mmm(24h)
14	114	hh:mi:ss:mmm(24h)
20	120	yyyy-mm-dd hh:mi:ss(24h)
21	121	yyyy-mm-dd hh:mi:ss.mmm(24h)

Use the CONVERT() function to convert data types before displaying them on the Query Analyzer's window, or to concatenate character and numeric values before passing them to the PRINT statement.

The CompanyName and ContactName columns in the Customers table of the Northwind database have a maximum length of 40 and 30 characters, respectively. If they are included in a query's output, they can nearly overflow the width of the Query Analyzer's window on a typical monitor. You can display them in shorter columns with a statement like the following:

```
USE NORTHWIND
SELECT CONVERT(nchar(30), CompanyName),
       CONVERT(nchar(15), ContactName)
FROM Customers
```

The following statement retrieves the total for all companies and displays it along with the company's name:

```
USE NORTHWIND
SELECT CONVERT(char(25), CompanyName),
       CONVERT(char(10),
               SUM(Quantity * UnitPrice * (1 - Discount)))
FROM [Order Details], Orders, Customers
```

```
WHERE [Order Details].OrderID = Orders.OrderID AND
      Orders.CustomerID = Customers.CustomerID
GROUP BY CompanyName
ORDER BY CompanyName
```

A section of output produced by the above statement is shown here:

```
Around the Horn             13806.8
Berglunds snabbköp          24927.6
Blauer See Delikatessen     3421.95
Blondesddsl père et fils    18534.1
Bólido Comidas preparadas   4232.85
Bon app'                    21963.3
Bottom-Dollar Markets       20801.6
```

If you omit the CONVERT() functions, the company name will be displayed in 40 spaces and the totals with too many fractional digits:

```
Around the Horn                        13806.800003051758
Berglunds snabbköp                     24927.57746887207
Blauer See Delikatessen                3421.9500045776367
```

CAST(variable AS data_type)   The CAST() function converts a variable or column value to the specified data type. This function doesn't do anything more than the CONVERT() function, but it's included for compatibility with the SQL-92 standard.

Date and Time Functions

Like Visual Basic, T-SQL recognizes a number of date and time manipulation functions, which are summarized next.

GETDATE()   Returns the current date and time on the machine that runs SQL Server

DATEADD(interval, number, datetime)   Increments its *datetime* argument by the specified number of intervals. The *interval* argument can be one of the constants shown in Table 7.4.

TABLE 7.4:   Interval Values of the Date and Time Functions

Interval	Value	Range
year	yy, yyyy	1753–9999
quarter	qq, q	1–4
month	mm, m	1–12
dayofyear	dy, y	1–366

Continued on next page

TABLE 7.4 CONTINUED: Interval Values of the Date and Time Functions

Interval	Value	Range
day	dd, d	1–31
week	wk, ww	1–53
weekday	dw	1–7
hour	hh	0–23
minute	mi, n	0–59
second	ss	0–59
millisecond	ms	0–999

DATEDIFF(interval, datetime1, datetime2)   Returns the difference between two datetime arguments in a number of *intervals*, which can be days, hours, months, years, and so on (see Table 7.4). You are going to use this function in a stored procedure that calculates the average time interval between successive orders, in the following chapter.

DATEPART(interval, datetime)   Returns an integer that represents the number of specified parts of a given date

DATENAME(interval, datetime)   Returns the name of a part of a datetime argument. The function DATENAME(month, varDate) returns the name of the month in the *varDate* argument (January, February, and so on) and DATENAME(weekday, varDate) returns the name of the weekday in the *varDate* argument (Monday, Tuesday, and so on). You have seen an Access query that retrieves the number of orders placed on each day of the week. This query uses the Access WeekDay() function to extract the day of the week from the OrderDate field. Here's the equivalent statement in T-SQL:

```
USE NORTHWIND
SELECT DATENAME(weekday, [OrderDate]), Count(OrderID)
FROM Orders
GROUP BY DATENAME(weekday, [OrderDate])
```

If you execute the above statement in the Query Analyzer, you will see the following output:

```
Friday                  164
Monday                  165
Thursday                168
Tuesday                 168
Wednesday               165
```

DAY(), MONTH(), YEAR()   These functions return the weekday, month, and year part of their argument, which must be a datetime value.

Other Functions

T-SQL supports a number of functions that have no equivalent in Visual Basic. These functions are used to manipulate field values and handle Null values, which are unique to databases.

COALESCE(expression, expression, ...)   This function returns the first non-NULL expression in its argument list. The function COALESCE(CompanyName, ContactName) returns the company's name, or the customer's name, should the CompanyName be NULL. Use this function to retrieve alternate information for Null columns in your SELECT statements:

```
SELECT CustomerID, COALESCE(CompanyName, ContactName)
FROM Customers
```

You can also use a literal as the last argument, in case all the values retrieved from the database as Null:

```
SELECT CustomerID, COALESCE(CompanyName, ContactName, "MISSING!")
FROM Customers
```

ISNULL(column, value)   The ISNULL() function is totally different from the IsNull() function of VB. The T-SQL ISNULL() function accepts two arguments, a field or variable name, and a value. If the first argument is not Null, then the function returns its value. If the first argument is Null, then the *value* argument is returned. If certain products haven't been assigned a value, you can still include them in a price list with a zero value:

```
SELECT ProductName, ISNULL(UnitPrice, 0.0)
FROM Products
```

This statement will select all the rows in the Products table along with their prices. Products without prices will appear with a zero value (instead of the "Null" literal).

NULLIF(expression1, expression2)   The NULLIF() function accepts two arguments and returns NULL if they are equal. If not, the first argument is returned. The NULLIF() function is equivalent to the following CASE statement:

```
CASE
    WHEN expression1 = expression2 THEN NULL
    ELSE expression1
END
```

System Functions

Another group of functions enables you to retrieve system information.

SUSER_ID( )   This function accepts the user's login name as an argument and returns the user's ID.

SUSER_NAME( )   This function does the opposite. It accepts the user's ID and returns the user's login name.

USER_ID( ) and USER_NAME( )   These functions are similar, only instead of the login name, they work with the database username and database ID.

USER   This function accepts no arguments and must be called without the parentheses; it returns the current user's database username. If you have logged in as "sa" your database username will most likely be "dbo."

Using Arguments

Stored procedures wouldn't be nearly as useful without the capacity to accept arguments. Stored procedures are implemented as functions: they accept one or more arguments and return one or more values to the caller. Stored procedures also return one or more cursors. A cursor is the equivalent of a VB Recordset. It's the output produced in the Results pane of the Query Analyzer's window when you execute a SELECT statement.

The arguments passed to and from a stored procedure must be declared immediately after the CREATE PROCEDURE statement. They appear as comma-separated lists after the procedure name and before the AS keyword, as shown here:

```
CREATE PROCEDURE procedure_name
@argument1 type1, @argument2 type2, . . .
AS
```

Notice that you don't have to use the DECLARE statement. Other variables declared in the procedure's body must be prefixed with the DECLARE keyword. Listing 7.6 shows a simple stored procedure that accepts two datetime arguments and returns the orders placed in the specified interval (you've seen the equivalent Access query in the section "Writing Access Queries," earlier in this chapter):

LISTING 7.6   **The OrdersByDate Stored Procedure**

```
CREATE PROCEDURE OrdersByDate
@StartDate datetime, @EndDate datetime
AS
SELECT * FROM Orders
WHERE OrderDate BETWEEN @StartDate AND @EndDate
```

To test this procedure, you must first attach it to the Northwind database. Select Northwind in the DB box and then execute the above lines by pressing Ctrl+E. Then open a new query window and execute the following lines:

```
DECLARE @date1 datetime
```

```
DECLARE @date2 datetime
SET @date1='1/1/1997'
SET @date2='3/31/1997'
EXECUTE OrdersByDate @date1, @date2
```

The orders placed in the first quarter of 1997 will appear in the Results pane. Notice that you didn't have to specify the output cursor as an argument; the rows retrieved are returned automatically to the caller. Let's add an output parameter to this stored procedure. This time we'll request the number of orders placed in the same interval. Here's the CountOrdersByDate stored procedure:

```
CREATE PROCEDURE CountOrdersByDate
@StartDate datetime, @EndDate datetime,
@CountOrders int OUTPUT
AS
SELECT @CountOrders = COUNT(OrderID) FROM Orders
WHERE OrderDate BETWEEN @StartDate AND @EndDate
```

The argument that will be returned to the procedure is marked with the OUTPUT keyword. Notice also that it must be assigned a value from within the stored procedure's code. The SELECT statement assigns the values returned by the SELECT query to the *@CountOrders* variable.

To test the new procedure, execute the following lines. The output they'll produce is shown in Figure 7.6.

```
DECLARE @date1 datetime
DECLARE @date2 datetime
SET @date1='1/1/1997'
SET @date2='3/31/1997'
DECLARE @orderCount int
EXECUTE CountOrdersByDate @date1, @date2, @orderCount OUTPUT
PRINT 'There were ' + CONVERT(varchar(5), @orderCount) +
       ' orders placed in the chosen interval'
```

This batch is very similar to the batch we used to test the OrdersByDate procedure, with the exception of the new argument. In addition to declaring the argument, you must specify the OUTPUT keyword to indicate that this argument will be passed back to the caller. You can specify input/output arguments, which pass information to the procedure when it's called and return information back to the caller. The INPUT keyword is the default, so you don't have to specify it explicitly.

There's nothing complicated about arguments. In the next chapter you'll learn how to pass arguments to stored procedures from within your VB code. Before we leave the topic of arguments, let's look at a more complicated stored procedure that uses input arguments and returns a cursor.

FIGURE 7.6:

Testing the CountOrdersBy-
Date with a T-SQL batch

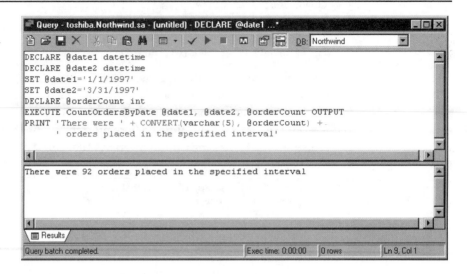

Building SQL Statements on the Fly

The BookSearch procedure searches the Titles table of the Pubs database to locate titles that contain one or more words. It accepts up to five arguments, and it forms the proper SELECT statement based on how many arguments are not empty. The desired SELECT statement should be something like:

```
SELECT Title FROM Titles
WHERE Title LIKE '%keyword1%' AND Title LIKE '%keyword2%'
```

There can be up to five keywords, so you can't use a predefined SQL statement in the procedure. You must build the desired statement on the fly. You must add as many LIKE clauses as there are nonempty arguments. The SearchBooks procedure must be called with five arguments, even if four of them are left empty. After building the SQL statement, it's executed with the EXECUTE statement, and the selected rows are returned to the caller. Listing 7.7 provides the code for the BookSearch procedure.

LISTING 7.7   The BookSearch Stored Procedure

```
USE PUBS
IF EXISTS (SELECT name FROM sysobjects
        WHERE name = 'BookSearch')
    DROP PROCEDURE BookSearch
GO
```

```
CREATE PROCEDURE BookSearch
@Arg1 varchar(99), @Arg2 varchar(99),
@Arg3 varchar(99), @Arg4 varchar(99), @Arg5 varchar(99)
AS
DECLARE @SearchArg varchar(999)
DECLARE @SQLstring varchar(999)

SET @Arg1 = LTRIM(RTRIM(@Arg1))
SET @Arg2 = LTRIM(RTRIM(@Arg2))
SET @Arg3 = LTRIM(RTRIM(@Arg3))
SET @Arg4 = LTRIM(RTRIM(@Arg4))
SET @Arg5 = LTRIM(RTRIM(@Arg5))

SET @SearchArg = "WHERE "
IF LEN(@Arg1) > 0
    SET @SearchArg =
        @SearchArg + "Title LIKE '%" + @Arg1 + "%' AND "
IF LEN(@Arg2) > 0
    SET @SearchArg =
        @SearchArg + "Title LIKE '%" + @Arg2 + "%' AND "
IF LEN(@Arg3) > 0
    SET @SearchArg =
        @SearchArg + "Title LIKE '%" + @Arg3 + "%' AND "
IF LEN(@Arg4) > 0
    SET @SearchArg =
        @SearchArg + "Title LIKE '%" + @Arg4 + "%' AND "
IF LEN(@Arg5) > 0
    SET @SearchArg =
        @SearchArg + "Title LIKE '%" + @Arg5 + "%' AND "
SET @SearchArg = SUBSTRING(@SearchArg, 1, LEN(@SearchArg)-4)
IF LEN(@SearchArg) = 6
    SET @SQLstring = "SELECT Title FROM Titles"
ELSE
    SET @SQLstring = "SELECT Title FROM Titles " + @SearchArg
PRINT @SQLstring
EXECUTE (@SQLstring)
```

To test the BookSearch stored procedure, you must call it with five arguments. Some of them may be empty, but you must declare and pass five variables, as shown here:

```
DECLARE @arg1 varchar(99)
DECLARE @arg2 varchar(99)
DECLARE @arg3 varchar(99)
DECLARE @arg4 varchar(99)
DECLARE @arg5 varchar(99)
SET @arg1 = 'computer'
SET @arg2 = 'stress'
EXECUTE BookSearch @arg1, @arg2, @arg3, @arg4, @arg5
```

If all parameters are empty, then the stored procedure will select all the titles in the database. The BookSearch procedure will return a single title, as well as the SELECT statement it executed (I've included the search argument generated by the stored procedure for testing purposes). If you execute the lines shown above, the following will be printed in the Results pane:

```
SELECT Title FROM Titles WHERE Title
        LIKE '%computer%' AND Title LIKE '%stress%'
Title
----------------------
You Can Combat Computer Stress!
```

Unlike Visual Basic, T-SQL doesn't support a variable number of arguments. If you want to write a stored procedure that accepts an unknown number of arguments, you can create a long string with all the argument values and parse this string in the procedure. You'll see an example of this technique in the section "Implementing Business Rules with Stored Procedures," later in this chapter.

Triggers

You have covered a lot of ground on the topic of stored procedures, and before completing this chapter, I would like to touch on the topic of triggers. *Triggers* are special types of stored procedures, used mostly for administrative tasks. However, they play an important role in SQL Server programming so I won't omit them. A trigger is a procedure that SQL Server invokes automatically when certain actions take place. These actions are to insert, delete, and update a row. In other words, you can define a procedure that's executed automatically every time a table's row is deleted, a new row is inserted into the table, and an existing row is updated. You can think of triggers like VB event handlers for onUpdate, onInsert, and onDelete events.

NOTE   Unlike stored procedures, triggers can't be called directly from within VB applications, but they play a very important role in maintaining SQL Server databases. By incorporating the appropriate triggers in the database itself, you'll simplify many VB programming tasks.

Triggers are commonly used to keep track of changes in the database. If you want to know who's doing what with the company's sensitive data, you can add a few fields in the Orders table and record the user and time information every time a record is added, deleted, or updated. Without triggers, you'd have to implement this feature into every routine that accesses the Orders table for updates. To ensure that every action on the Orders table is recorded, you can create a trigger that's invoked automatically and updates these fields. You can even record this information in another table so that users will not know they are being monitored.

Creating a trigger is similar to creating a stored procedure. You use the CREATE TRIGGER statement, whose syntax is:

```
CREATE TRIGGER trigger_name
ON table
[WITH ENCRYPTION]
FOR [DELETE] [,] [INSERT] [,] [UPDATE]
[NOT FOR REPLICATION]
AS
Block of T-SQL Statements
```

Each trigger has a name and is defined for a specific table and for one or more specific actions (DELETE, INSERT, UPDATE). The [WITH ENCRYPTION] keyword tells SQL Server to store the trigger in encrypted form, so that users can't read it. The [NOT FOR REPLICATION] keyword indicates that the trigger should not be executed when a replication process modifies the table involved in the trigger. Following the AS keyword comes a block of statements that defines the trigger's actions.

As you can see, the same trigger may apply to multiple actions. To distinguish between them, use the statement:

```
IF UPDATE(column)
```

where *column* is a column name. The IF statement will return True if the specified column was inserted or updated. To keep the triggers short, write a separate one for each action.

The CREATE TRIGGER statement is similar to the CREATE PROCEDURE statement. It is followed by the name of the trigger and the keyword ON, which specifies the table on which the trigger will act. The FOR keyword must be followed by the name of an action that invokes the trigger: UPDATE, INSERT, and DELETE. Obviously, if you write a trigger that's invoked every time a row of the Customers table is updated, you should also write a similar trigger that's invoked every time a customer is deleted. If you allow customers to be deleted, you should also remove the orders (and the corresponding details) placed by the specific customers. Following the AS keyword, you specify the T-SQL code to be executed every time the Customers table is updated.

Notice the items *inserted* and *deleted*. These are not variables, but temporary rows that hold the values of the columns. The *inserted* row contains the values you're about to insert into the table, and the *deleted* row contains the original values. You can retrieve any column's value by specifying its name with the FROM keyword, as shown in the example.

Implementing Triggers

Let's add a trigger for each action (insert/update/delete) to the Orders table. The EditOrder and NewOrder triggers will update the fields EditedBy/EditedOn and AddedBy/AddedOn, respectively. EditedBy and EditedOn fields hold the name of the user that edited the order and the date and time; the AddedBy and AddedOn hold the same information but apply to additions of new rows. When a row is deleted, we'll save the same data (the user's name and the date of the action), as well as the order's ID, the customer's ID, and the order's date in a new table. This information will be stored in the Deletions table, which holds information about deleted orders.

Before adding the triggers to the Northwind database, you must add four new fields to the Orders table:

EditedBy   Varchar(20)

EditedOn   Datetime

AddedBy   Varchar(20)

AddedOn   Datetime

You must also add a new table to the database. The structure of the Deletions table is shown here:

DeletedBy   Varchar(20)

DeletedOn   Datetime

DelOrderID   Int

DelCustomerID   Char(5)

DelOrderDate   Datetime

EditOrderTrigger, shown in Listing 7.8, updates the EditedOn and EditedBy fields of the updated row. The GETDATE() function returns the current date, and the USER function returns the name of the current user. Notice how the WHERE statement selects the updated row: It extracts the order's ID from the inserted row. This is a variable maintained by the system, and it contains the columns of the most recently updated or inserted row.

LISTING 7.8   The EditOrder Trigger

```
CREATE TRIGGER EditOrderTrigger ON [Orders]
FOR UPDATE
AS
```

```
DECLARE @OrderID char(5)
SELECT @OrderID = OrderID FROM inserted
UPDATE Orders SET EditedOn=GETDATE(), EditedBy=USER
WHERE Orders.OrderID=@OrderID
```

The NewOrder trigger, shown in Listing 7.9, is identical to the EditOrder trigger.

LISTING 7.9   The NewOrderTrigger

```
CREATE TRIGGER NewOrderTrigger ON [Orders]
FOR INSERT
AS
DECLARE @newOrderID char(5)
SELECT @newOrderID = OrderID FROM inserted
UPDATE Orders SET AddedOn=GETDATE(), AddedBy=USER
WHERE Orders.OrderID=@newOrderID
```

The DeleteOrderTrigger, shown in Listing 7.10, extracts more fields from the deleted variable and inserts their values in a new row of the Deletions table—by the time the DeleteOrderTrigger is invoked, the row has already been removed from the table.

LISTING 7.10   The DeleteOrderTrigger

```
CREATE TRIGGER DeleteOrderTrigger ON [Orders]
FOR DELETE
AS
DECLARE @delOrderID int
DECLARE @delCustID char(5)
DECLARE @delOrderDate datetime

SELECT @delOrderID = OrderID FROM deleted
SELECT @delCustID = CustomerID FROM deleted
SELECT @delOrderDate = OrderDate FROM deleted

INSERT DELETIONS (DeletedOn, DeletedBy,
                  DelOrderID, DelCustomerID, DelOrderDate)
       VALUES (GETDATE(), USER,  @delOrderID,
               @delCustID,  @delOrderDate)
```

To test the triggers, add, update, and delete rows in the Orders table. Notice that you can't delete a row from the Orders table unless the related rows in the Order Details table have already been deleted. You can add a fake row to the Orders table, then edit it and finally delete it. Then open the Orders and Deletions tables to see the rows added by the triggers (a few sample rows are shown in Figure 7.7).

FIGURE 7.7:

Use special fields in your sensitive tables to monitor who's doing what in the database.

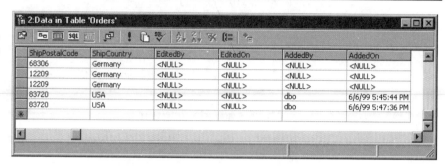

The three triggers shown in this section can also be used to keep track of changes in one or more tables for synchronization purposes. If you need to maintain some degree of synchronization with a different database (it could be a products database in another company that doesn't use SQL Server, for instance), you can keep track of the inserted/updated/deleted rows in a table and then transmit these rows only.

Using Triggers to Implement Cascade Updates and Deletes

Triggers are also used in SQL Server to implement cascaded updates and deletes. As discussed in Chapter 2, Access supports cascaded updates and deletes natively. In effect, you can tell Access to delete all the related lines in the Order Details table every time an order is deleted. Likewise, when a customer is deleted, all related rows in the Orders table will be deleted automatically. As each row in the Orders table is deleted, it takes with it all related rows in the Order Details table.

SQL Server can't cascade updates and deletes automatically, but you can build a trigger to do so. The trigger shown in Listing 7.11 will be fired when a row in the Orders table is deleted. The trigger will delete all the related rows in the Order Details table.

LISTING 7.11   The CascadeOrderDeletes Trigger

```
CREATE TRIGGER CascadeOrderDeletes ON Orders
FOR DELETE
AS
DECLARE @OrderID int
SELECT @OrderID=OrderID FROM deleted
DELETE [Order Details]
FROM [Order Details]
WHERE OrderID=@OrderID
```

To test the trigger, you must first make sure that the relationship between the Orders and Order Details tables is not enforced. To remove the enforcement of the relationship between the two tables, open the Orders table in design mode with SQL Server's Enterprise Manager. Then click the Table and Index Properties button on the toolbar to open the Properties window shown in Figure 7.8.

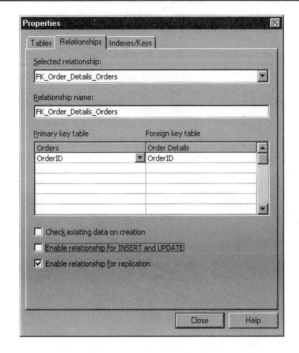

On the Relationships tab, you must select the FK_Order_Details_Orders relationship and clear the option Enable Relationship for INSERT and UPDATE. If you open the Orders table and delete a row, the trigger will delete the related rows in the Order Details table as well. If you enforce the relationship, then you won't be able to remove a row that has dependent rows in the Order Details table.

Removing a row from the Customers table may also impair the integrity of the database, if the specific customer is linked to one or more orders. Listing 7.12 shows the trigger that will remove all the orders linked to the customer you're about to delete.

LISTING 7.12   The CascadeCustomerDeletes Trigger

```
CREATE TRIGGER CascadeCustomerDeletes ON Customers
FOR DELETE
AS
DECLARE @CustID nchar(5)
SELECT @CustID=CustomerID FROM deleted
DELETE FROM Orders WHERE CustomerID=@CustID
```

If you remove a customer, the CascadeCustomerDeletes trigger will be fired. As it deletes the linked rows in the Orders table, the CascadeOrderDeletes trigger is fired, which will remove the detail lines of the order being removed. So, by deleting a single row in the Customers table, you are actually removing several rows from the Orders table and even more rows from the Order Details table. All cascaded deletions take place behind the scenes, thanks to the triggers.

TIP
If you decide to impose the relational integrity of your database by cascading updates and deletes, you must write the appropriate triggers and disable the enforcement of relational integrity for INSERT and UPDATE. Some readers may consider removing the relationships from within a trigger, so that they can cascade the updates and deletions, and then establish them again. It's a good idea, but it doesn't work. You can't remove a relationship from within a trigger.

WARNING
Tampering with a database's referential integrity is a bad idea, in general. Until Microsoft decides to implement cascade updates and deletions in one of the coming versions of SQL Server, you should probably live without this feature. If you *must* change a customer's ID, I would suggest that you write a stored procedure that removes the relationship, updates all related tables, and then re-enforces the relationship. You should not call this stored procedure frequently either, because other users may be editing the database while the referential integrity is not enforced.

Transactions

A *transaction* is a series of database operations that must succeed or fail as a whole. If all operations complete successfully, then the entire transaction succeeds and the changes are committed to the database. If a single operation fails, then the entire transaction fails and no changes are written to the database. If the transaction fails, the changes are removed from the tables and replaced with their original values.

SQL implements transactions with three statements: BEGIN TRANSACTION, COMMIT TRANSACTION, and ROLLBACK TRANSACTION.

BEGIN TRANSACTION

This statement marks the beginning of a transaction. If the transaction fails, the tables will be restored to the state they were at the moment the BEGIN TRANS-

ACTION statement was issued. It is implied here that the database is restored to a previous state with regard to the changes made by your application. Changes made to the database by others are not affected.

COMMIT TRANSACTION

This statement marks the successful end of a transaction. When this statement is executed, all the changes made to the database by your application since the execution of the BEGIN TRANSACTION statement are committed finally and irrevocably to the database. You can undo any of the changes later on, but not as part of the transaction.

ROLLBACK TRANSACTION

This statement marks the end of an unsuccessful transaction. When this statement is executed, the database is restored to the state it was when the BEGIN TRANSACTION statement was executed, as if the statements between the BEGIN TRANSACTION and ROLLBACK TRANSACTION statement were never executed.

The following code segment shows how the transaction-related statements are used in a batch:

```
BEGIN TRANSACTION
{T-SQL statement}
IF @@ERROR <> 0
BEGIN
    ROLLBACK TRANSACTION
    RETURN -100
END
{T-SQL statement}
IF @@ERROR <> 0
BEGIN
    ROLLBACK TRANSACTION
    RETURN -101
END
COMMIT TRANSACTION
{more T-SQL statements}
```

The error codes –100 and –101 identify error conditions. After each operation, you must examine the @@ERROR variable. If it's not zero, then an error occurred, and you must rollback the transaction. If all operations succeed, you can commit the transaction.

The example of the "Adding Orders" section later in this chapter demonstrates how to handle transactions with T-SQL.

Implementing Business Rules with Stored Procedures

A buzzword in modern database applications is the *business rule*. Business rules are the basic rules used by corporations to manipulate their data. A company may have a complicated rule for figuring out volume discounts. Some companies keep track of the current inventory quantities, while others calculate it on the fly by subtracting sales from purchases. So, what's so important about business rules? Modern databases and programming techniques allow you to incorporate these rules either into the database itself, or implement them as special components that can be called, but not altered, by other applications.

In the past, business rules were implemented in the application level. A good deal of the analysis was devoted to the implementation of business rules. If the management changed one of these rules, programmers had to revise their code in several places. A misunderstanding could lead to different implementations of the same rules. A programmer might implement the business rules for the applications used at the cash register, and another programmer might implement the same rules for an ordering system over the Web.

Business rules can be implemented as stored procedures. You can implement stored procedures for all the actions to be performed against the database, embed the business rules in the code, and ask application programmers to act on the database through your procedures. Most programmers need not even understand the business rules. As long as they call stored procedures to update the underlying tables, their applications will obey these rules.

Let's say your corporation wants to enforce these two simple business rules:

- Orders can be cancelled but cannot be altered or removed from the system under any circumstances.

- When items are sold or purchased, the Level field must be updated accordingly, so that the units in stock are available instantly.

If you grant the users, or programmers, of the database write access to the Products or Order Details tables, you can't be sure these rules are enforced. If you implement a stored procedure to add new orders and another stored procedure to cancel orders (a procedure that would mark an order as canceled but would not remove it from the table), you enforce both rules. Applications could enter new orders into the system, but they would never fail to update the Level field, because all the action would take place from within the stored procedure. To make sure they call your stored procedure to delete rows in the Orders table, give them read-only privileges for that table.

The same component can also be used by various tiers. Let's say you decide to go online. Users will place orders through the Web, the data is transmitted to the Web server, and then it is moved to the database server by calling the same stored procedure from within an application that runs on the Web server (most likely an Active Server Page). Not only do you simplify the programming, but you also protect the integrity of the database. Assuming that you can't write every line of code yourself, you can't count on programmers to implement the same operations in different applications and different languages (not to mention what would happen when business rules are revised, or new ones are added).

Another benefit of incorporating business rules into the database is that you can change the rules at any time and applications will keep working. You may decide to record the sales of some special items into separate tables; you may even decide to keep canceled orders in another table and remove their details from the Order Details table. The applications need not be aware of the business rules. You change the stored procedures that implement them and walk away. All the applications that update the database through the stored procedures will automatically comply with the new business rules.

NOTE   Of course, stored procedures are not the only method of implementing business rules. Certain business rules may require too many calculations, and you should not burden the database server with extra work. As you will see in the third part of the book, business rules can also be implemented in VB and packaged as ActiveX components. This alternative is discussed toward the end of the book. For now, use stored procedures to simplify the development of client/server applications.

In this final section of the chapter, you'll build a couple of stored procedures for some of the most common tasks you will perform with a database like Northwind. The first one adds new customers to the Customers table—a straightforward procedure. The second one adds orders and is a fairly complicated stored procedure, because it must update two tables in a transaction.

Adding Customers

We'll start with a simpler example of a stored procedure that implements a business rule: writing a stored procedure to add customers. The stored procedure accepts as arguments all the columns of the Customers table and inserts them into a new row. The addition of the new row is implemented with the INSERT statement. If the insertion completes successfully, the error code zero is returned. If the insertion fails, the procedure returns the error code generated by the INSERT statement. Practically, the only reason this action would fail is because the ID of the customer you attempt to add exists in the Customers table already. The AddCustomer stored procedure doesn't even examine whether a customer with the same ID exists already.

If the customer exists already, the INSERT statement will fail. Besides, there's always a (very slim) chance that, between the test and the actual insertion, another user might add a customer with the same ID. This is a condition that can't be prevented, unless you're willing to lock the entire table for the duration of the insertion operation. The safest approach is to detect the error after the fact and notify the user.

The AddCustomer stored procedure is shown in Listing 7.13. At the beginning it declares all the input arguments. Then it uses these arguments as values in an INSERT statement, which adds a new row to the Customers table. If the INSERT statement encounters an error, the procedure doesn't crash. It examines the value of the @@ERROR global variable. If the @@ERROR variable is not zero, then an error occurred. If the operation completed successfully, the @ERROR variable is zero.

Notice that @@ERROR is stored in a local variable, which is used later in the code. The @@ERROR variable is updated after each line's execution. If you attempt to return the value @@ERROR with the RETURN statement, the calling application will receive an error code that's always zero. That's why you must store the value of @@ERROR after an operation if you want to use it later in your code.

LISTING 7.13   The AddCustomer.sql Stored Procedure

```
USE NORTHWIND
IF EXISTS (SELECT name FROM sysobjects
        WHERE name = 'AddCustomer')
    DROP PROCEDURE AddCustomer
GO

CREATE PROCEDURE AddCustomer
        @custID nchar(5), @custName nvarchar(40),
        @custContact nvarchar(30), @custTitle nvarchar(30),
        @custAddress nvarchar(60), @custcity nvarchar(15),
        @custRegion nvarchar(15), @custPostalCode nvarchar(10),
        @custCountry nvarchar(15),
        @custPhone nvarchar(24), @custFax nvarchar(24)
AS
DECLARE @ErrorCode int
INSERT Customers (CustomerID, CompanyName, ContactName,
                  ContactTitle, Address, City, Region,
                  PostalCode, Country, Phone, Fax)
VALUES (@custID, @custName, @custContact,
        @custTitle, @custAddress,
        @custCity, @custRegion, @custPostalCode, @custCountry,
        @custPhone, @custFax)
SET @ErrorCode=@@ERROR
```

```
IF (@ErrorCode = 0)
    RETURN (0)
ELSE
    RETURN (@ErrorCode)
```

To test the AddCustomer stored procedure, open the `AddCustomer.sql` file with the Query Analyzer and execute it by pressing Ctrl+E. This will attach the stored procedure to your database. Now you can test it by calling it with the appropriate arguments. The `AddACustomer.sql` batch adds a new customer with the ID "SYBEX." Listing 7.14 provides the code for the `AddACustomer.sql` batch.

LISTING 7.14   Adding a New Customer with the AddACustomer Procedure

```
DECLARE @retCode int
DECLARE @custID nchar(5), @custName nvarchar(40)
DECLARE @custContact nvarchar(30)
DECLARE @custTitle nvarchar(30), @custAddress nvarchar(60)
DECLARE @custCity nvarchar(15), @custCountry nvarchar(15)
DECLARE @custPostalCode nvarchar(10), @custRegion nvarchar(15)
DECLARE @custPhone nvarchar(24), @custFax nvarchar(24)
- Set customer data
SET @custID="SYBEX"
SET @custName="Sybex Inc."
SET @custContact="Tobias Smythe"
SET @custTitle="Customer Representative"
SET @custAddress="1000 Marina Village"
SET @custCity="Alameda"
SET @custRegion="CA"
SET @custPostalCode="90900"
SET @custCountry="USA"
SET @custPhone="(714) 5558233"
SET @custFax="(714) 5558233"
- Call stored procedure to add new customer
EXECUTE @retCode = AddCustomer @custID, @custName, @custContact,
                    @custTitle, @custAddress, @custCity,
                    @custRegion, @custPostalCode, @custCountry,
                    @custPhone, @custFax
PRINT @retCode
```

The AddACustomer batch will add a new customer only the first time it's executed. If you execute it again without changing the customer's ID, the error code 2627 will be returned, along with the following error message:

```
Violation of PRIMARY KEY constraint 'PK_Customers'. Cannot insert
duplicate key in object 'Customers'.
The statement has been terminated.
```

You can either change the values passed to the stored procedure, or switch to the Enterprise Manager, open the Customers table, and delete the newly added line.

Adding Orders

The next example is substantially more complicated. This time we'll write a procedure to add a new order. By its nature, this stored procedure must perform many tests, and it may abort the entire operation at various stages of its execution. The NewOrder stored procedure must accept the customer's ID, the employee's ID, the shipper's ID, the shipping address, and the order's details. If the specified customer, employee, or shipper does not exist, the procedure must abort its execution and return an error code to the caller. If any of these tests fail, then the stored procedure exits and returns the appropriate error code (–100 if customer doesn't exist, –101 if employee doesn't exist, and –102 if shipper doesn't exist).

If these tests don't fail, you can safely add the new order to the Orders table. The following operations are implemented as a transaction. If one of them fails, then neither an order nor details will be added to the corresponding tables. The stored procedure must add a new row to the Orders table, insert the current date in the OrderDate field, and then use the OrderID field's value to add the order's lines in the Order Details table. The OrderID field is assigned a value automatically by SQL Server when a row is added to the Orders table. You can find out the ID of the new order by examining the @@IDENTITY variable, which holds the value of the most recently added Identity value for the current connection. This value will be used to add detail rows in the Order Details table.

Then the order's details are added to the Order Details table, one row at a time. Again, if one of them fails, the entire transaction will fail. The most common reason for failure is to submit a non-existing product ID. If you force your application's users to select product IDs from a list and validate the quantity and discount for each product, then none of the operations will fail.

The order details are passed to the AddOrder procedure as a long string, and this part deserves some explanation. Ideally, another stored procedure (or application) should be able to create a cursor and pass it as an argument to the AddOrder procedure. SQL Server 7 stored procedures can't accept cursors as arguments, so another technique for passing an unknown number of arguments has to be used. In this example, I've decided to store the ID, quantity, and discount of each product into a string variable. Each field has a fixed length in this string, so that it can be easily parsed. The product ID is stored as an integer in the first six characters of the string, the quantity as another integer in the next six characters, and the discount in the last six characters. Each order, therefore, takes up 18 characters. If you divide the length of this string by 18, you'll get the number of detail lines. Then, you can call the SUBSTRING() function repeatedly to extract each detail's values and insert them into the Order Details table.

Once the product ID has been extracted from the string variable, you can use it to retrieve the product's price from the Products table. Here are T-SQL statements that retrieve the first product's price and insert it along with the quantity and discount fields into the Order Details table:

```
SET @ProdID = SUBSTRING(@Details, 1, 6)
SET @Qty = SUBSTRING(@Details, 7, 6)
SET @Dscnt = SUBSTRING(@Details, 13, 6)
SELECT @Price=UnitPrice FROM Products
        WHERE ProductID=@ProdID
INSERT [Order Details] (OrderID, ProductID, Quantity,
        UnitPrice, Discount)
        VALUES (@OrderID, @ProdID, @Qty, @Price, @Dscnt)
```

If a product with the specific ID doesn't exist in the Products table, the procedure doesn't take any special action. The INSERT statement will fail to add the detail line because it will violate the COLUMN FOREIGN KEY constraint FK_Order_Details_Products, and the procedure will roll back the transaction and return the error code 547.

Listing 7.15 shows the complete listing of the NewOrder stored procedure. Apart from syntactical differences, it's equivalent to the VB code you would use to add an order to the database.

LISTING 7.15   The NewOrder Stored Procedure

```
USE NORTHWIND
IF EXISTS (SELECT name FROM sysobjects
        WHERE name = 'NewOrder')
    DROP PROCEDURE NewOrder
GO

CREATE PROCEDURE NewOrder
@custID nchar(5), @empID int, @orderDate datetime
@shipperID int, @Details varchar(1000)
AS

DECLARE @ErrorCode int
DECLARE @OrderID int
- Add new row to the Orders table
DECLARE @shipcompany nvarchar(40)
DECLARE @shipAddress nvarchar(60), @shipCity nvarchar(15)
DECLARE @shipRegion nvarchar(15), @shipPCode nvarchar(10)
DECLARE @shipCountry nvarchar(15)
SELECT @shipCompany=CompanyName,
        @shipAddress=Address,
        @shipCity=City,
```

```
                @shipRegion=Region,
                @shipPCode=PostalCode,
                @shipCountry=Country
                FROM Customers
                WHERE CustomerID = @custID
        IF @@ROWCOUNT = 0
            RETURN(-100)     – Invalid Customer!

        SELECT * FROM Employees WHERE EmployeeID = @empID
        IF @@ROWCOUNT = 0
            RETURN(-101)     – Invalid Employee!

        SELECT * FROM Shippers
                WHERE ShipperID = @shipperID
        IF @@ROWCOUNT = 0
            RETURN(-102)     – Invalid Shipper!

        BEGIN TRANSACTION
        INSERT Orders (CustomerID, EmployeeID, OrderDate, ShipVia,
                    ShipName, ShipAddress, ShipCity, ShipRegion,
                    ShipPostalCode, ShipCountry)
        VALUES (@custID, @empID, @orderDate, @ShipperID,
            @shipCompany, @shipAddress, @ShipCity, @ShipRegion,
            @shipPCode, @shipCountry)
        SET @ErrorCode=@@ERROR
        IF (@ErrorCode <> 0)
            BEGIN
            ROLLBACK TRANSACTION
            RETURN (-@ErrorCode)
            END
        SET @OrderID = @@IDENTITY

        – Now add rows to the Order Details table
        – All new rows will have the same OrderID
        DECLARE @TotLines int
        DECLARE @currLine int

        SET @currLine = 0
    – Use the CEILING function because the length of the
    – @Details variable may be less than 18 characters long !!!
        SET @TotLines = Ceiling(Len(@Details)/18)

        DECLARE @Qty smallint, @Dscnt real, @Price money
        DECLARE @ProdID int

        WHILE @currLine <= @TotLines
            BEGIN
            SET @ProdID = SUBSTRING(@Details, @currLine*18 + 1, 6)
            SET @Qty = SUBSTRING(@Details, @currLine*18 + 7, 6)
            SET @Dscnt = SUBSTRING(@Details, @currLine*18 + 13,6)
```

```
      SET @currLine = @currLine + 1
      SELECT @Price=UnitPrice FROM Products WHERE ProductID=@ProdID
      INSERT [Order Details] (OrderID, ProductID, Quantity,
            UnitPrice, Discount)
            VALUES (@OrderID, @ProdID, @Qty, @Price, @Dscnt)
      SET @ErrorCode = @@ERROR
      IF (@ErrorCode <> 0) GOTO DetailError
      END
      COMMIT TRANSACTION
      RETURN (0)
DetailError:
      ROLLBACK TRANSACTION
      RETURN(@ErrorCode)
```

NOTE

Here's the most important reason for using the NewOrder stored procedure. If you allow users and applications to add rows to the Order Details table, it's possible that someone might modify an existing order. This is a highly undesirable situation, and you should make sure it never happens. With the NewOrder procedure, users can't touch existing orders. Each order takes a new ID and all details inherit this ID, eliminating the possibility of altering (even by a programming mistake) an existing order.

Testing the NewOrder Procedure

To test the NewOrder stored procedure, you must declare a number of local variables, assign the desired values to them, and then execute the stored procedure with the EXECUTE statement, passing the variables as arguments. Most arguments represent simple fields, like the ID of the shipper, the customer ID, and so on. The last argument, however, is a long string, with 18 characters per detail line. In each 18-character segment of the string, you must store three fields: the product's ID, the quantity, and the discount. The AddAnOrder batch that exercises the NewOrder procedure is shown in Listing 7.16, and its output is shown in Figure 7.9.

LISTING 7.16   **The AddAnOrder.sql Script**

```
USE Northwind
DECLARE @retCode int
DECLARE @custID nchar(5), @empID int
DECLARE @orderDate datetime, @shipperID int
DECLARE @Details varchar(1000)

SET @shipperID=2
SET @custID='SAVEA'
```

```
SET @empID=4
SET @orderDate = '2/3/2002'
SET @Details="32    10    0.25  47    8     0.20"
SET @Details=@Details + "   75    5    0.05  76   15    0.10"
EXECUTE @retCode = NewOrder @custID, @empID, @orderDate,
                              @shipperID, @Details
PRINT @retCode
..
```

FIGURE 7.9:

Testing the NewOrder stored
procedure with a T-SQL batch

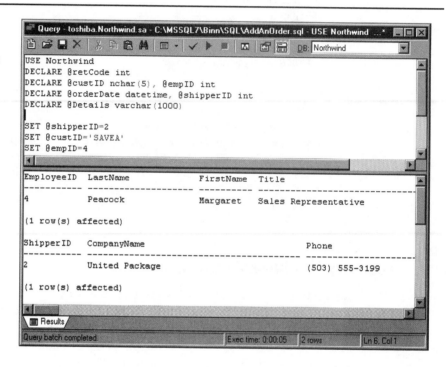

Summary

By now you should have a good understanding of SQL and Transact-SQL and
what stored procedures and triggers can do for you. The next step is to see how
stored procedures can be accessed from within your VB code. In the next chapter,
you will see how to execute stored procedures asynchronously from within your
VB applications, how to create and use cursors in T-SQL, and how to write stored
procedures to perform complicated tasks on the server instead of moving large
amounts of data to the client.

CHAPTER

EIGHT

Making the Most of Stored Procedures

- More methods for executing commands

- Passing parameters to stored procedures

- Executing commands asynchronously

- Implementing business rules with stored procedures

- Working with T-SQL statements

By now you should have a good feel for SQL, T-SQL, and stored procedures. As you dive deeper into database programming with SQL Server, you'll appreciate the usefulness of these tools. However, it's now time to switch back to Visual Basic. In this chapter you'll learn how to use these tools from within your VB applications.

ADO supports many methods for executing SQL statements and stored procedures. Actually, all major objects have a method for executing SQL statements and/or stored procedures, and I discuss them all in the next section. All these methods return a Recordset object containing the rows selected by the SQL statement. Once the rows have been stored in a Recordset variable, you can scan and process them with the methods discussed in Chapter 5.

Methods for Executing SQL Statements and Stored Procedures

Let's start with a summary of each object's methods for executing SQL statements and stored procedures. Then you'll read about the arguments of these methods and see several examples.

> **NOTE**
> All three objects (Connection, Recordset, and Command) can execute stored procedures and SQL statements against a database. You can think of both stored procedures (including Access queries) and SQL statements as *commands*, which are submitted to the DBMS and executed. The DBMS responds by returning a cursor, parameter values, or both.

In short, you can execute commands (SQL statements and stored procedures) against a database using the following methods:

Connection.Execute   The Connection object's Execute method allows you to quickly execute commands against a database. This method can't be used with stored procedures that require parameters. However, it's the simplest method for executing commands asynchronously. (I discuss asynchronous execution later in this chapter, in the section "Asynchronous Command Execution.")

Recordset.Open   The Recordset object's Open method executes a command against a database, or simply opens a table, and retrieves a Recordset object. Use this method if the command requires no parameters and you don't need asynchronous execution. Many programmers use a few Recordset objects in their applications and repopulate them with different cursors in the course of the application.

Command.Execute   The Command object's Execute method is the most flexible method for executing commands against a database, and you already know how to use it to execute SQL statements against the database. With the Command object, you can call stored procedures with input parameters and accept output parameters. You can also use this method to execute commands asynchronously, as you will see later in this chapter.

I discussed the basics of the ADO objects in Chapter 5, but you haven't yet seen how to execute stored procedures with these objects, or how to execute commands asynchronously.

The Connection.Execute Method

The Connection object provides the Execute method, which can execute an SQL statement against a database or invoke a stored procedure. The advantage of using the Connection.Execute method is that you don't have to create any other object. As soon as you establish a connection to a database with the Connection object, you can issue the Execute method and pass the name of the stored procedure, or a string with an SQL statement, as an argument. This method is used to execute action queries against the database too.

The Connection.Execute method returns a cursor, which you would usually assign to a Recordset variable. If, however, you're executing an action query, the Recordset returned by the Execute method will be empty, in which case you need not assign the cursor returned to a Recordset variable. The syntax of this method is:

```
Set RS = Connection.Execute(command, [records], [options])
```

The first argument of the method can be a table name, an SQL statement, or a stored procedure's name. The exact nature of the *command* argument must be specified with the last argument. The other two arguments are optional. The *records* argument is a long variable that returns the number of records affected by an action query. When you execute selection queries, the *records* argument does not return the number of rows selected and you can ignore it. The last argument, *options*, specifies how the server should interpret the command, and it can have one of the values shown in Table 8.1.

TABLE 8.1: The Values of the Execute Method's *options* Argument

Constant	Description
adCmdText	Command is an SQL statement
adCmdStoredProcedure	Command is a stored procedure
adCmdTable	Command is a table name. ADO executes the statement SELECT * FROM <table_name>.
adCmdTableDirect	Opens the table directly
adCmdFile	Command is the name of a file in which a Recordset has been saved
adCmdUnknown	Unknown command type (it's used with Access queries)
adAsyncExecute	Specifies that the command will be executed asynchronously
adAsyncFetch	Specifies that the rows will be fetched asynchronously
adAsyncFetchnonBlocking	Specifies that the rows are fetched asynchronously without blocking subsequent operations
adExecutenoRecords	Executes the command but doesn't return any rows

The items of Table 8.1 can be divided in two categories: the options that specify the *type* of the command (the ones with names starting with *adCmd*) and the options that specify *how* the command will be executed. The two sets of options are not mutually exclusive, and you can combine them with the Or operator, as in the following statement:

```
adCmdText Or adAsyncExecute
```

Normally, stored procedures and SQL statements are executed synchronously, meaning that control isn't returned to your application until the execution of the command completes. It is also possible, however, to execute commands asynchronously: ADO submits the command to the DBMS, but doesn't wait for its completion. Control is relinquished to the VB application, which can proceed with other operations. The calling application will be notified when the command completes its execution. For more information on asynchronous execution of commands, see the section "Asynchronous Command Execution" later in this chapter.

The difference between the constants adCmdTable and adCmdTableDirect is that the first one submits the following query to the DBMS:

```
SELECT * FROM table_name
```

The adCmdTableDirect constant causes ADO to open the specified table directly. Recall that the type of the command must be specified by the final argument. Using Table 8.1, if *command* is an SQL statement, use the option adCmdText. If it's a stored procedure, use the option adCmdStoredProcedure. If it's an Access query, use the option adCmdUnknown. If you omit the last argument, ADO will figure out the type of the command, but this involves an overhead, which you can skip by specifying the command's type.

Using the Connection Object

To execute a command through the Connection object, declare a Connection object with the statement:

```
Dim Conn As ADODB.Connection
```

and then instantiate it with the statement:

```
Set Conn = New ADODB.Connection
```

Assuming that you have already established a connection to the Northwind database with the Conn object, you can:

- Retrieve rows with a selection query:

```
cmd = "SELECT CompanyName, ContactID FROM Customers"
Set RS = Conn.Execute(cmd, , adCmdText)
```

- Execute an action query:

```
cmd = "UPDATE Products SET UnitPrice = 0.85 * UnitPrice"
Conn.Execute cmd, records, adCmdText or _
    adCmdExecuteNoRecords
MsgBox "Your query affected " & records & " records."
```

The adCmdExecuteNoRecords option is not required, but when you know that your query isn't going to return any rows, using this option will improve performance (ADO will not have to figure out whether the query returns a cursor or not). The number of rows affected by the query is returned by the *records* argument.

- Execute a stored procedure

```
cmd = "AllInvoices"
Set RS = Conn.Execute cmd, , adCmdStoredProc
```

If the stored procedure doesn't return a Recordset, use this syntax:

```
cmd = "UpdatePrices"
Conn.Execute cmd, , adCmdStoredProc
```

NOTE   The default Recordset returned by the Execute method of the Connection object is read-only and forward-only. If you need a different type of Recordset, you must first create a Recordset object, set its properties, and then assign the cursor returned by the Connection.Execute method to the Recordset object.

Stored procedures may accept input parameters, or return output parameters. The Connection.Execute method doesn't provide any mechanism for passing parameters back and forth. To execute a procedure that expects or returns parameters, use the Command object, which is described later in this chapter.

The Recordset.Open Method

The Recordset.Open method opens a Recordset based on an SQL statement or stored procedure. Its syntax is shown next:

```
RS.Open source, activeConnection, cursorType, lockType, options
```

The rows returned by the command (if any) are stored in the Recordset object on which you executed the Open method. This method's arguments are all optional—not a strange syntax if you consider that they can be set through the various properties of the Recordset object. The first argument, *source*, is the command (SQL statement, table name, or stored procedure name) you want to execute against the database. The second argument, *activeConnection*, is a Connection object set up to see the desired database. The third argument, *cursorType*, specifies the type of the cursor returned by the Open method, and can have one of the values shown in Table 8.2. For more information on the various cursor types, see the section "Cursor Properties" in Chapter 5.

TABLE 8.2:   The Values of the *CursorType* Argument of the Recordset Object's Open Method

Constant	Description
adOpenForwardOnly	Returns a forward-only cursor
adOpenKeyset	Returns a keyset cursor
adOpenDynamic	Returns a dynamic cursor
adOpenStatic	Returns a static cursor

The *lockType* argument specifies how to lock the records retrieved (or updated) by the command. The topic of locking was discussed in the section, "Concurrency Control" in Chapter 5. The values of the *lockType* argument are repeated here in Table 8.3 for your convenience.

TABLE 8.3:   The Values of the *LockType* Argument of the Recordset Object's Open Method

Constant	Description
adLockReadOnly	The rows can't be updated
adLockPessimistic	The pessimistic locking strategy is applied
adLockOptimistic	The optimistic locking strategy is applied
adLockBatchOptimisitic	The optimistic locking strategy is applied, but changes to the underlying tables are made in batch mode

The last argument of the Open method, *options*, is identical to the last argument of the Connection object's Execute method, discussed in the previous section.

You can omit any of the Open method's arguments as long as you set the Property by the same name. For example, to specify the command that will be executed, use the RecordSource property. To specify the connection to the database, use the ActiveConnection property. To specify the cursor's attributes, use the CursorType and CursorLocation properties, and so on. If you omit the last argument, then the command will be treated as an SQL statement (adCmdText).

TIP

One of the reasons many programmers favor the Recordset object over the other two is that you can break the Recordset into small sections (pages), and you can select any one of these pages from within your application. This technique, which relies on the properties PageCount and PageSize, was described in the section "Paged Output" in Chapter 5. Many programmers use the same Recordset object and populate it with different data in the course of the application.

If a Recordset object has been populated with a cursor, you can't call its Open method again. You must first close the Recordset, and then populate it again by calling the Open method. Here's a sequence of statements that re-populate the RS Recordset variable:

```
CN.ConnectionString = "Provider=Microsoft.Jet.OLEDB.4.0;" & _
                      "Data Source=C:\VB98\Nwind.mdb;"
CN.Open
RS.Open "Customers", CN
If RS.State = adStateOpen Then RS.Close
RS.Open "Categories", CN
```

If you call the Open method on a Recordset object that's already been opened, a runtime error will be generated. Likewise, if you call the Close method on a Recordset object that's not open, you'll get a runtime error as well. That's why you must examine the State property before you attempt to close the Recordset.

The Command.Execute Method

The Command object is the most flexible object for executing queries against a database; therefore, when working with stored procedures that contain many input and output arguments, you should use the Command.Execute method. The reason is that the Command.Execute method is the only one that allows you to pass multiple input parameters to the stored procedure and retrieve multiple output parameters from it. The syntax of this method is:

```
Set RS = Command.Execute([records], [parameters], [options])
```

The Command.Execute method returns a Recordset object with the rows retrieved by the SQL statement or the stored procedure. The *records* argument is set by the Execute method to the number of records affected by an action query. The *parameters* argument is an array of variants that holds the input parameters expected by the stored procedure. (See the section "The Passing Parameters with the Command Object" later in this chapter for more information on setting up and passing parameters to a stored procedure.) The last argument, *options*, specifies how the command will be treated by the database and can have one of the values shown in Table 8.1.

Unlike the other two Execute methods, the Command.Execute method doesn't accept an SQL statement or the name of a stored procedure as argument. You must specify the command to be executed using the CommandText property of the Command object. This property can be set to a valid SQL statement, a table name, or to the name of a stored procedure. Here's an example of how you would execute a command against the database through the Command object. This example calls the Most Wanted Products query. It does not accept any parameters; therefore, the second argument of the Execute method is omitted:

1. Create a new Connection object variable and set it to the Northwind database:

   ```
   Dim Conn As New ADODB.Recordset
   Conn.ConnectionString = . . .
   Conn.Open
   ```

2. Create a Recordset variable to accept the rows returned by the stored procedures:

   ```
   Dim RS As ADODB.Recordset
   ```

3. Create a Command variable that will be used to execute the stored procedure and set its ActiveConnection property to the Connection object you created in step 1:

   ```
   Dim CMD As New ADODB.Command
   CMD.ActiveConnection = Conn
   ```

4. Specify the command to be executed.

   - To execute an SQL statement, assign the statement to the CommandText property and set the CommandType property to adCmdText:

   ```
   CMD.CommandText = "SELECT ContactName, ContactTitle, " & _
                     "Address, City, Region, PostalCode, " & _
                     "Country FROM Customers " & _
                     "WHERE Country = 'Germany'"
   CMD.CommandType = adCmdText
   ```

- To execute a stored procedure, assign its name to the CommandText property and the constant **adCmdStoredProc** to the CommandType property:

```
CMD.CommandText = "[Ten most expensive products]"
CMD.CommandType = adCmdStoredProc
```

NOTE   Stored procedures may require input parameters. The topic of passing parameters back and forth between your VB application and a stored procedure is discussed in detail in the following section.

- If you want to retrieve an entire table, assign its name to the CommandText property and the constant adCmdTable to the CommandType property:

```
CMD.CommandText = "Customers"
CMD.CommandType = "adCmdTable"
```

5. Finally, execute the procedure by calling the Execute method:

```
Set RS = CMD.Execute
```

Calling a Simple Stored Procedure from VB

Let's look at a simple example of calling a stored procedure with the Connection object. Here's the VB code to connect to the Northwind database and retrieve the ten most expensive products (the [Ten most expensive products] stored procedure):

```
Private Sub Command1_Click()
Dim CMD As New ADODB.Command
Dim Conn As New ADODB.Connection
Dim RS As ADODB.Recordset

    Conn.ConnectionString = "Provider=SQLOLEDB.1; " & _
              "Persist Security Info=False;User ID=sa; " & _
              "password=;Initial Catalog=Northwind"
    Conn.Open
    CMD.ActiveConnection = Conn
    CMD.CommandText = "[Ten most expensive products]"
    CMD.CommandType = adCmdStoredProc
    Set RS = CMD.Execute
    List1.Clear
    While Not RS.EOF
        List1.AddItem RS.Fields(0)
        RS.MoveNext
    Wend

    Set RS = Nothing
    Set CMD = Nothing
```

```
        Set Conn = Nothing
    End Sub
```

Note that if you change the connection string to point to the Access version of the same database, you will execute the same query. Since Access doesn't recognize stored procedures, you must also change the CommandType property to adCmdUnknown. Other than that, you needn't touch any other lines in the code. To test this statement use the following connection string:

```
Provider=Microsoft.Jet.OLEDB.4.0;_
Data Source=C:\Program Files\VB98\Nwind.mdb
```

(Make sure you set the Data Source parameter to point to the path of the NWind database on your system.)

Only a small percentage of stored procedures return a single cursor. Most practical stored procedures accept input parameters, and they frequently return parameters to the calling application (sometimes in addition to a standard cursor). In the next section, you'll examine the techniques for passing parameters to and from stored procedures.

Passing Parameters with the Command Object

The Command object exposes a Parameters property, which is a collection. If the stored procedure you execute expects any parameters, you must append the parameter values to the Parameters collection of the Command object. For each parameter of the stored procedure, you must set up a separate object and append it to the Parameters collection.

The Parameters collection is a standard collection, with the usual members, described as follows:

Count Property   The number of parameters in the collection. Each member of the Parameters collection corresponds to a different parameter in the stored procedure.

Item Property   An index to a specific parameter (this index is zero-based). To access the third parameter in the collection, for example, use the expression:

```
CMD.Parameters.Item(2)
```

This is the default property of the Collection, so the previous expression is equivalent to the following one:

```
CMD.Parameters(2)
```

In addition, you can refer to the parameters stored in the Collection with the actual parameter name:

```
CMD.Parameters("@CustName")
```

Append Method   Use this method to add a new parameter to the Collection. To append a parameter to the Collection, you must first create a Parameter object and then call the Append method as shown here:

```
CMD.Parameters.Append Param
```

where *Param* is an object variable declared as ADODB.Parameter.

Delete Method   Use this method to remove a parameter from the Collection. For example, to remove the third parameter, use the statement:

```
CMD.Parameters.Delete 2
```

Refresh Method   This method queries the data provider about the parameters of a specific stored procedure; it's discussed in the section "Retrieving Parameter Information Directly from Stored Procedures" later in this chapter.

The Parameter Object

To pass a parameter to a stored procedure, or to prepare the Command object to accept an output parameter from the stored procedure, you must first create a number of Parameter objects (one for each parameter of the stored procedure). To do this, start as usual by declaring the Parameter object with the statement:

```
Dim Param As New ADODB.Parameter
```

Then you must set the object's properties, which are described in the next few sections. These properties will help ADO match the Parameter objects in your code to the actual stored procedure parameters. The parameters will be passed to the stored procedure when you call the Execute method.

The Type Property   The Type property sets (or returns) the type of the parameter passed to the stored procedure. This property can have one of the values shown in Table 8.4. Notice, however, that not all possible values apply both to Access and to SQL Server.

TABLE 8.4:   Stored Procedures' Parameter Data Types

Constant	SQL Server	Access
adBigInt	int	Long Integer
adBinary	binary	Binary
adBoolean	bit	Yes/No
adChar	char	Text
adCurrency	money, smallmoney	Currency
adDate	datetime	Date/Time

Continued on next page

TABLE 8.4 CONTINUED: Stored Procedures' Parameter Data Types

Constant	SQL Server	Access
adDecimal	decimal	
adDouble		Double
adEmpty		Value
adGUID	ReplicationID	
adInteger	int	Long Integer
adSingle	float	Single
adSmallInt	smallInt	Integer
adTinyInt	tinyInt	Byte
adUserDefined	a user-defined variable	
adVarBinary	image	OLE Object
adVarChar	varchar	Memo

The Size Property   The Size property indicates the maximum size of the parameter in bytes or characters. You should set this property for variable-length data types only, and the specified size should match the number in parentheses following the data type in the parameter's declaration in the stored procedure. For example, if a text parameter is declared in the stored procedure as:

```
DECLARE @CompanyName varchar(40)
```

then the parameter object that corresponds to this parameter must be set up with the following properties:

```
Param.Type = adVarChar
Param.Size = 40
```

The Direction Property   The Direction property specifies whether the parameter represents an input or output parameter (from the stored procedure's point of view). It can have one of the values shown in Table 8.5.

TABLE 8.5:   The Direction Property's Values

Constant	Description
adParamInput	(default) Specifies an input parameter
adParamOutput	Specifies an output parameter
adParamInputOutput	Specifies that the parameter is used both as input and output
adParamReturnValue	Specifies a return value

The last value in the above table corresponds to the procedure's return value. Even if you omit the RETURN statement in a procedure, it will return a value that indicates success (a zero value) or failure (a value greater than zero).

The Value Property   The Value property sets or returns the value of the parameter. Use the Value property to set a parameter value before calling the stored procedure, or read the Value property from within your code to find out the value returned by the procedure. If you don't assign a value to a Parameter object, you can access the corresponding parameter with an index value (0 for the first parameter, 1 for the second parameter, and so on).

The Name Property   Each parameter has a name by which you can refer to it. You can set the Name property to the Parameter's name, or use it to read the parameter's name. The parameter's Name property need not match the actual parameter name as it is declared in the stored procedure.

The NumericScale and Precision Properties   The NumericScale property determines the number of decimal places to which numeric values will be resolved. Use this property to determine how many digits to the right of the decimal point will be used to represent values for the parameter. The Precision property specifies the total number of digits used to represent numeric values. These properties should match the equivalent values specified in the parameter's declaration.

Setting Up Parameter Objects

In this section, I review the process of setting up Parameter objects and passing data back and forth between stored procedures and VB applications. You'll see the code for one of the simplest stored procedures developed so far in this book, the CountOrdersByDate procedure, which accepts two dates as arguments and returns the number of orders placed in the specified interval. Here's the T-SQL code to create the CountOrdersByDate stored procedure:

```
CREATE PROCEDURE CountOrdersByDate
@Fromdate datetime, @Todate datetime,
@OrderCnt int OUTPUT
AS
SELECT @OrderCnt = COUNT(OrderID)
FROM Orders
WHERE OrderDate BETWEEN @Fromdate AND @Todate
```

If you haven't attached the above stored procedure to the Northwind database, do so now by entering the T-SQL statements in a new window of the Query Analyzer. Then execute the procedure by pressing Ctrl+E. Once you have added the stored procedure to the database, let's start with the statements that set up a Command object, and the command to be executed through the object. The code is identical to the code presented earlier to call the Ten Most Expensive Products, except that the name of the stored procedure now changes:

```
Conn.ConnectionString = "Provider=SQLOLEDB.1;" & _
        "User ID=sa;password=;Initial Catalog=Northwind"
```

```
    Conn.Open
Set CMD.ActiveConnection = Conn
CMD.CommandText = "CountOrdersByDate"
CMD.CommandType = adCmdStoredProc
```

The following statements create a Parameter object for the *@StartDate* input parameter and append it to the Command object's Parameters collection:

```
Dim Param As ADODB.Parameter
    Set Param = New ADODB.Parameter
    Param.Name = "Date1"
    Param.Type = adDate
    Param.Value = "4/1/1997"
    Param.Direction = adParamInput
    CMD.Parameters.Append Param
```

After the Parameter object has been appended to the Parameters collection, the *Param* variable is free for use with another parameter. To set up the second input argument and attach it to the same collection, use the following similar statements:

```
Set Param = New ADODB.Parameter
Param.Name = "Date2"
Param.Type = adDate
Param.Value = "6/30/97"
Param.Direction = adParamInput
CMD.Parameters.Append Param
```

Finally, set up an output parameter to accept the value returned by the stored procedure:

```
Set Param = New ADODB.Parameter
Param.Name = "Total Orders"
Param.Type = adInteger
Param.Direction = adParamOutput
CMD.Parameters.Append Param
```

and then execute the stored procedure:

```
CMD.Execute
```

The CountOrdersByDate procedure does not return any rows, so you didn't have to create a Recordset object to accept the output of the procedure. The value of the output parameter is given by the expression:

```
CMD.Parameters("Total Orders").Value
```

Notice that the names of the parameters need not match the actual parameter names, as defined in the stored procedure. The Name property is a convenience for the programmer. Had you not assigned a name to the output parameter, you'd have to access it with an index value, which represents the order in which the parameter was attached to the Parameters collection:

```
CMD.Parameters("2").Value
```

The CMDExecute project on the CD calls the Ten Most Expensive Products stored procedure and the equivalent Access query. Use this project to experiment with simple, cursor-returning procedures. The CMDExecuteParam project on the CD calls the CountOrdersByDate stored procedure and the same Access query. Use this sample project to experiment with stored procedures and Access queries that accept input parameters and return output parameters. You can use all of the sample projects on the CD to experiment with other simple stored procedures. Later in this chapter you'll see more elaborate examples of the Parameters collection.

The CreateParameter Method

The code for setting up Parameter objects is lengthy, so the Command object provides the CreateParameter method. This method can accept all the properties listed above as arguments. The syntax of the CreateParameter method is:

```
Set Param = Command.CreateParameter(Name, Type, _
            Direction, Size, Value)
```

All arguments are optional. You can use the CreateParameter method to generate a new Parameter object (instead of the Set statement) and supply values for all its properties in the same statement. If you don't want to set all the attributes of the Parameter object when you create it with the CreateParameter method, you can still use the Param object's properties to set any of the parameter's attributes. For example, you can create a parameter with the following statements:

```
Dim Param As ADODB.Parameter
Set Param = Command.CreateParameter("MyParam")
```

and set its properties later with statements like the following:

```
Param.Type = adDateTime
Param.Value = Date()
```

Alternatively, you can supply values for the Type and Value properties in the statement that calls the CreateParameter method:

```
Set Param = _
        Command.CreateParameter("MyParam", adDateTime, , , Date())
```

After you have set all the properties of the parameter, you must append the Param object to the Parameters collection with the statement

```
Command.Parameters.Append Param
```

NOTE In the examples in this book I use the more verbose syntax to specify parameter properties, because they are easier to read. In your code you will probably use the shorter notation—just enable the Auto Quick Info feature to let Visual Basic suggest the proper order of the arguments.

Passing Multiple Input Parameters to Procedures

A quick way to pass input parameters to a stored procedure is to use the second argument of the Execute method without setting up a Parameters object. The drawback of this method is that it doesn't report the values of the output arguments.

For example, to pass two dates as input parameters to a stored procedure, use the following statement:

```
Set RS = Command.Execute(, Array("1/2/1997", "3/31/1997")
```

This statement will pass the two dates to the stored procedure that has been specified by the CommandText property of the Command object. The number of elements in the parameter array must match the number of declared arguments in the stored procedure. If the procedure expects another argument between the two, and you don't want to specify its value, make sure you insert an additional separator:

```
Set RS = Command.Execute(, Array("1/2/1997", , "3/31/1997")
```

Calling Access Queries

Let's revise the code to access the same query in the Access NWind database. If you haven't already created the CountOrdersByDate query, do so now. Here's the definition of the query:

```
PARAMETERS [From date] DateTime, [To date] DateTime;
SELECT COUNT(OrderID)
FROM Orders
WHERE OrderDate BETWEEN [From date] AND [To date];
```

NOTE Access queries are not treated by ADO as stored procedures. Their type is adCmdUnknown, and to call them with the Execute method of the Command object, you must change the setting of the CommandType property, as shown here:

```
CMD.CommandType = adCmdUnknown
```

Then change the Connection object's ConnectionString property to point to the NWind database (change the path according to your installation).

```
Conn.ConnectionString = "Provider=Microsoft.Jet.OLEDB.3.51; " & _
                "Data Source=C:\Program Files\VB98\Nwind.mdb"
```

You must also change the values of the two dates. The two databases are not identical; the order dates of the SQL Server Northwind database were moved forward. The orders of 1997 in the Northwind database are the same as the orders of 1995 in the NWind database, so don't be surprised if the same query doesn't retrieve the same rows in the two databases.

The StoredProcedures Project

This section's example, the StoredProcedures project, shown in Figure 8.1, is considerably more complicated than the previous examples. It will, however, allow you to experiment with many data types, input and output parameters, and stored procedures that return parameters, cursors, or both.

When the List Procedures button is clicked, the program extracts the names of all the stored procedures in the Northwind SQL Server database, along with their arguments and descriptions, and displays them on the left pane of the Form. The user can select the name of a stored procedure with the mouse, supply the required argument values in the right-hand list (one argument per line), and then click the Execute Procedure to execute it. If you want to omit the value of an argument, leave a blank line in the list with the arguments. The name of the database is hardwired into the code. It's possible to display the databases on a server and let the user select the desired database (the SQLExecute project of Chapter 4 shows how this is done).

FIGURE 8.1:

The StoredProcedures project demonstrates how to call any stored procedure from within a VB application and supply values to all required parameters.

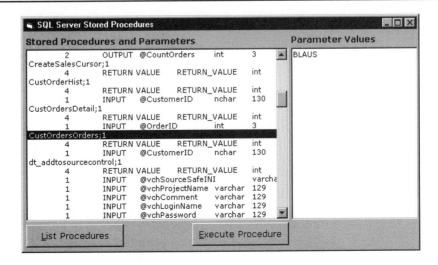

The List Procedures button extracts the definitions of all stored procedures in the database. The code uses the Connection object's OpenSchema to request information about the database's structure. The Form's Load event handler is an example of how to use the OpenSchema method to retrieve the definitions of the stored procedures and their arguments. In Listing 8.1 I'm including the listing of the code that populates the ListBox control on the left, even though this topic hasn't been covered yet. Look up the OpenSchema method in the Appendix for information on how to retrieve information about the tables making up the database, their structure, and so on.

LISTING 8.1   **The Stored Procedures in a Database**

```
Private Sub cmdListProcedures_Click()
Dim ProcedureName As String

    ADOConn.Open "Provider=SQLOLEDB.1;User ID=sa;Initial" & _
                 "Catalog=NorthWind;Data Source=(local)"
    Set AllProcedures = ADOConn.OpenSchema(adSchemaProcedures)
    Set AllParameters = _
                 ADOConn.OpenSchema(adSchemaProcedureParameters)
    Do Until AllProcedures.EOF
        ProcedureName = AllProcedures.Fields(2).Value
        List1.AddItem ProcedureName
        Do While AllParameters!PROCEDURE_NAME = ProcedureName
            Select Case AllParameters!PARAMETER_TYPE
                Case adParamOutput:
                        paramType = "OUTPUT"
                Case adParamInputOutput:
                        paramType = "INPUT/OUTPUT"
                Case adParamInput:
                        paramType = "INPUT"
                Case adParamReturnValue:
                        paramType = "RETURN VALUE"
                Case adParamUnknown:
                        paramType = "UNKNOWN"
                Case Else
                        paramType = "UNKNOWN"
                        ' This is good practice in case the
                        ' ADO spec changes
            End Select
            List1.AddItem vbTab & _
                    AllParameters!PARAMETER_TYPE & vbTab & _
                    paramType & vbTab & _
                    AllParameters!PRAMETER_NAME & vbTab & _
                    AllParameters!TYPE_NAME & vbTab & _
```

```
                AllParameters!DATA_TYPE & vbTab & _
                AllParameters!CHARACTER_MAXIMUM_LENGTH
            AllParameters.MoveNext
            If AllParameters.EOF Then Exit Do
        Loop
        AllProcedures.MoveNext
    Loop
End Sub
```

The Else clause in the long Case statement is included so that the application will work with future versions of ADO, which may support more parameter types.

To execute the selected stored procedure, supply the value for each input parameter in the TextBox control on the right-hand side of the Form, and then click the Execute Procedure button. When the Execute button is clicked, the code sets up a Command object to call the selected stored procedure and pass the user-supplied arguments. After the command is executed, the results are displayed on a grid. You'll see an example of this in the next section.

Each parameter must be entered in a single line. This is not a very convenient method for supplying parameter values, but it's simple and it's meant to demonstrate the topic of calling stored procedures. If you find the functionality of the Stored Procedures application useful, you can build a more elaborate user interface on your own based on Stored Procedures, or you can incorporate its functionality into another application. Don't forget to include the necessary code to validate the types of the user-supplied values against the types of the arguments in the stored procedure.

The code reads the names and types of the parameters directly from the ListBox control, and their values from the TextBox control. It then sets up a number of Parameter objects and attaches them to the Parameters collection of the Command object.

A few words on the contents of the ListBox control. Each parameter is displayed on a separate line, following the stored procedure's name. The first item is the parameter's Direction property. The code displays both a numeric value and a literal. This redundancy enables the program to retrieve the actual value of the parameter's direction quickly, while users need not memorize the meaning of numeric constants—they will read the literal. The third item is the parameter's name, and it's followed by the parameter's type. The type is displayed both as a literal and as a numeric value (again, to simplify the extraction of the parameter's type). The last value in the line is the parameter's length.

The Execute Procedure Button

The complete listing of the Execute Procedure button is shown next. This is a fairly lengthy listing and I will explain briefly how it works.

LISTING 8.2   **Executing Stored Procedures with Input/Output Parameters**

```
Private Sub cmdExecute_Click()
Dim SPResult As New ADODB.Recordset
Dim ADOcmd As ADODB.Command
Dim argumentParts() As String
Dim PValues() As String
Dim records As Long
Dim oParam As ADODB.Parameter

    Set ADOcmd = New ADODB.Command
    Set ADOcmd.ActiveConnection = ADOConn
    If List1.ListIndex = -1 Then Exit Sub
    If Left(List1.Text, 2) = "  " Then Exit Sub
    delim = InStr(List1.Text, ";")
    If delim > 0 Then
        SPName = Left(List1.Text, delim - 1)
    Else
        SPName = List1.Text
    End If
    PValues() = Split(Text1.Text, vbCrLf)
    argPos = List1.ListIndex + 2    ' SKIP RETURN VALUE
    argument = List1.List(argPos)
    i = 0

    Set oParam = ADOcmd.CreateParameter
    oParam.Name = "Return Value"
    oParam.Type = adInteger
    oParam.Direction = adParamReturnValue
    ADOcmd.Parameters.Append oParam
    On Error GoTo ParameterError

    Extract parameter information
    While Left(argument, 1) = vbTab
        argument = Trim(argument)
        argumentParts() = Split(argument, vbTab)
        Set oParam = ADOcmd.CreateParameter
        oParam.Name = argumentParts(3)
        oParam.Type = argumentParts(5)
        oParam.Direction = argumentParts(1)
        If oParam.Direction = 1 Then
            oParam.Value = PValues(i)
```

```
        End If
        If UBound(argumentParts) = 6 Then _
            oParam.Size = argumentParts(5)
        ADOcmd.Parameters.Append oParam
        argPos = argPos + 1
        i = i + 1
        argument = List1.List(argPos)
    Wend
'   Set up Command object to call the stored procedure
    SPName = "[" & SPName & "]"
    ADOcmd.CommandText = SPName
    ADOcmd.CommandType = adCmdStoredProc
    On Error GoTo ExecError
'   Read every parameter's value and append the appropriate
'   Parameter object to the Parameters collection
    For i = 0 To ADOcmd.Parameters.Count - 1
        msg = msg & ADOcmd.Parameters(i).Name & vbTab & _
                ADOcmd.Parameters(i).Value & vbCrLf
    Next
    If Len(msg) > 0 Then
        msg = "Will call " & SPName & _
                "with the following parameters:" & vbCrLf & msg
        MsgBox msg
    End If
'   Execute stored procedure
    Set SPResult = ADOcmd.Execute(records)
    retCode = ADOcmd.Parameters(0).Value
    If retCode <> 0 Then
        MsgBox "The stored procedure returned the error code " _
                    & retCode
    Else
        MsgBox "Command executed successfully"
    End If
'   and display results
    If SPResult.State = adStateClosed Then
        msg = ""
        For i = 0 To ADOcmd.Parameters.Count - 1
            If ADOcmd.Parameters(i).Direction = _
                    adParamInputOutput Or _
                    ADOcmd.Parameters(i).Direction = _
                        adParamOutput Then
                    msg = msg & ADOcmd.Parameters(i).Name & _
                            vbTab & ADOcmd.Parameters(i).Value _
                            & vbCrLf
            End If
        Next
```

```
        If Len(msg) > 0 Then
            msg = "The stored procedure returned the " & _
                    "following parameter values" & vbCrLf & msg
            MsgBox msg
        End If

        Select Case records
            Case 0: Me.Caption = "No records were updated"
                    MsgBox Me.Caption
            Case 1: Me.Caption = "1 record was updated"
                    MsgBox Me.Caption
            Case Is > 0:
                    Me.Caption = records & " record(s) were updated"
                    MsgBox Me.Caption
        End Select
        ResultsForm!MSFlexGrid1.Rows = 0
    Else
        ResultsForm!MSFlexGrid1.Rows = 11
        ResultsForm!MSFlexGrid1.FixedRows = 1
        ResultsForm!MSFlexGrid1.Cols = 2
        ResultsForm!MSFlexGrid1.Cols = SPResult.Fields.Count + 1
        ResultsForm!MSFlexGrid1.Row = 0
        ResultsForm!MSFlexGrid1.ColWidth(0) = TextWidth("99999")
        For iCol = 0 To SPResult.Fields.Count - 1
            ResultsForm!MSFlexGrid1.TextMatrix(0, iCol + 1) = _
                    SPResult.Fields(iCol).Name
            ResultsForm!MSFlexGrid1.ColWidth(iCol + 1) = _
                    SPResult.Fields(iCol).DefinedSize * _
                    TextWidth("A")
            ResultsForm!MSFlexGrid1.Col = iCol + 1
            ResultsForm!MSFlexGrid1.CellFontBold = True
        Next iCol
        iRow = 0
    On Error GoTo DisplayError
        While Not SPResult.EOF
            iRow = iRow + 1
            If iRow = ResultsForm!MSFlexGrid1.Rows Then _
                            ResultsForm!MSFlexGrid1.Rows = _
                    ResultsForm.MSFlexGrid1.Rows + 10
            ResultsForm!MSFlexGrid1.TextMatrix _
                    (iRow, 0) = Format(iRow, "####")
            For iCol = 0 To SPResult.Fields.Count - 1
                If Not IsNull(SPResult.Fields(iCol)) Then
                    ResultsForm!MSFlexGrid1.TextMatrix _
                            (iRow, iCol + 1) = _
                            SPResult.Fields(iCol)
                Else
```

```
                                ResultsForm!MSFlexGrid1.TextMatrix _
                                            (iRow, iCol + 1) = "<NULL>"
                    End If
                Next
                SPResult.MoveNext
            Wend
            ResultsForm.Caption = "Stored Procedure Cursor " & _
                iRow & " record(s) retrieved"
            ResultsForm!MSFlexGrid1.Rows = iRow + 1
            ResultsForm.Show
        End If
        Exit Sub
    ExecError:
        MsgBox "The following error occurred during the " & _
                statement's execution:" & _
                vbCrLf & Err.Description
        Exit Sub
    DisplayError:
        MsgBox "Error in populating the grid with the selected rows"
        Exit Sub
    ParameterError:
        MsgBox "The following error occurred in the " & _
                        "processing of the parameters:" & _
                vbcrfl & Err.Description, vbOKOnly, & _
                "ERROR " & Err.Number
        Exit Sub
    End Sub
```

The code scans each line of the ListBox control following the selected one. All the lines that contain parameters begin with a Tab character. The line

```
argumentParts() = Split(argument, vbTab)
```

splits the parts of the line and stores each part in the *argumentParts()* array. In other words, the current parameter's direction, type, and length are stored in the *argumentParts()* array. These values, along with the user-supplied values, are used to set up the appropriate Parameter object:

```
Set oParam = ADOcmd.CreateParameter
oParam.Name = argumentParts(3)
oParam.Type = argumentParts(5)
oParam.Direction = argumentParts(1)
'   set values for input parameters only
If oParam.Direction = 1 Then
    oParam.Value = PValues(i)
End If
If UBound(argumentParts) = 6 Then oParam.Size = argumentParts(5)
ADOcmd.Parameters.Append oParam
```

Notice that the program sets the values of input parameters only, yet you must leave blank the lines corresponding to output parameters in the TextBox control. After all of the Parameter objects have been set, the stored procedure is executed with the following line:

```
Set SPResult = ADOcmd.Execute(records)
```

The rows returned by the Execute method (if any) are stored in the SPResult Recordset variable. The program scans all the rows of the SPResult Recordset and displays them on a FlexGrid control on a separate Form, as shown in Figure 8.2. You can figure out whether the Recordset contains any rows from within your code by examining its State property. If its value is adStateClosed, then the Recordset is empty. This could be the result of an error during the execution of the stored procedure, or because the stored procedure executed an action query that didn't return any rows. In the latter case, the *records* variable holds the number of rows affected by the action query, and that number is displayed on the Form's title bar.

FIGURE 8.2:

The rows returned by the stored procedure are displayed on a FlexGrid control.

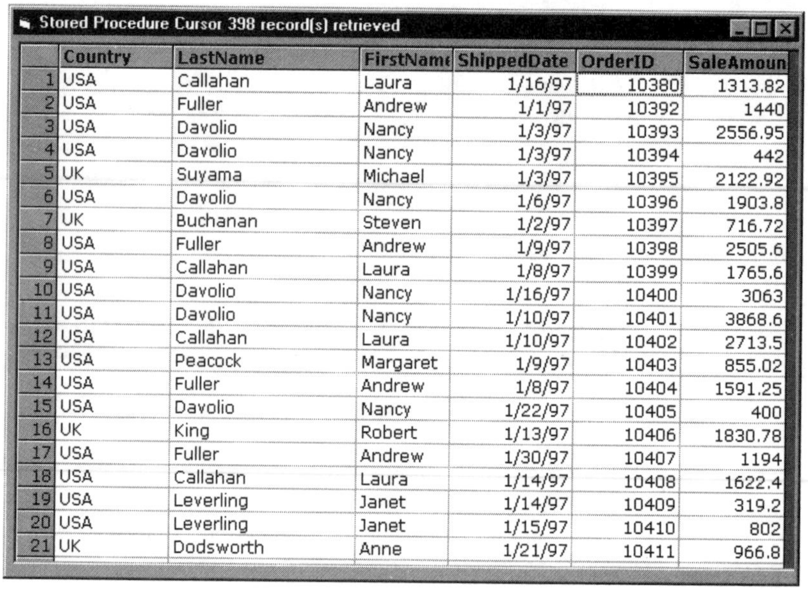

	Country	LastName	FirstName	ShippedDate	OrderID	SaleAmoun
1	USA	Callahan	Laura	1/16/97	10380	1313.82
2	USA	Fuller	Andrew	1/1/97	10392	1440
3	USA	Davolio	Nancy	1/3/97	10393	2556.95
4	USA	Davolio	Nancy	1/3/97	10394	442
5	UK	Suyama	Michael	1/3/97	10395	2122.92
6	USA	Davolio	Nancy	1/6/97	10396	1903.8
7	UK	Buchanan	Steven	1/2/97	10397	716.72
8	USA	Fuller	Andrew	1/9/97	10398	2505.6
9	USA	Callahan	Laura	1/8/97	10399	1765.6
10	USA	Davolio	Nancy	1/16/97	10400	3063
11	USA	Davolio	Nancy	1/10/97	10401	3868.6
12	USA	Callahan	Laura	1/10/97	10402	2713.5
13	USA	Peacock	Margaret	1/9/97	10403	855.02
14	USA	Fuller	Andrew	1/8/97	10404	1591.25
15	USA	Davolio	Nancy	1/22/97	10405	400
16	UK	King	Robert	1/13/97	10406	1830.78
17	USA	Fuller	Andrew	1/30/97	10407	1194
18	USA	Callahan	Laura	1/14/97	10408	1622.4
19	USA	Leverling	Janet	1/14/97	10409	319.2
20	USA	Leverling	Janet	1/15/97	10410	802
21	UK	Dodsworth	Anne	1/21/97	10411	966.8

Stored Procedure Cursor 398 record(s) retrieved

After the execution of the stored procedure, the program creates a list with the output parameters' values and displays them on a Message Box. Finally, it populates the MSFlexGrid control on the ResultsForm and displays the Form.

Retrieving Parameter Information Directly from Stored Procedures

One of the methods of the Parameters collection I haven't discussed so far is the Refresh method, which populates the Parameters collection by requesting information about the parameters from the actual stored procedure. To call the Refresh method, you must first create a Command object, set it to a stored procedure, and then call the ADOCmd.Parameters.Refresh method.

Once the parameter definitions have been read directly from the stored procedure, you can examine their type and direction, prompt the user for the values of the input parameters, and then call the stored procedure. The RefreshMethod project, whose Form is shown in Figure 8.3, demonstrates the use of the Refresh method. First it reads the parameters of the CountOrdersByDate stored procedure, then prompts the user to supply values for the input parameters, and finally calls the stored procedure. If the procedure executes successfully, the values of all parameters (input and output) are displayed on a ListBox control.

FIGURE 8.3:

The RefreshMethod project demonstrates how to retrieve parameter properties directly from a stored procedure.

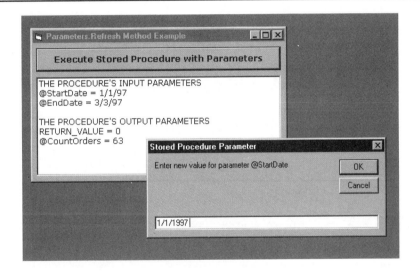

Let me present the code behind the command button "Execute Stored Procedure with Parameters" at the top of the Form, and then I'll discuss briefly the details of the code.

LISTING 8.3   **Calling the Parameters.Refresh Method**

```
Private Sub bttnExecuteProcedure_Click()
    ADOConn.Open "Provider=SQLOLEDB.1;User ID=sa;" & _
        "Initial Catalog=NorthWind;Data Source=(local)"
    Set ADOCmd.ActiveConnection = ADOConn
    ADOCmd.CommandText = "CountOrdersByDate"
    ADOCmd.CommandType = adCmdStoredProc
    ADOCmd.Parameters.Refresh
    On Error GoTo ParameterError
```

```
      For i = 0 To ADOCmd.Parameters.Count - 1
          If ADOCmd.Parameters(i).Direction = adParamInput Or _
          ADOCmd.Parameters(i).Direction = adParamInputOutput Then
              paramName = ADOCmd.Parameters(i).Name
              If Not IsNull(ADOCmd.Parameters(i).Value) Then
                  paramValue = ADOCmd.Parameters(i).Value
                  newvalue = _
                      InputBox("Enter new value for parameter " & _
                          paramName, _
                          "Stored Procedure Parameter", paramValue)
                  If newvalue <> "" Then _
                          ADOCmd.Parameters(i).Value = newvalue
              End If
          End If
      Next
      On Error GoTo ExecutionError
      Set ADORS = ADOCmd.Execute
      On Error GoTo OutputError
      List1.AddItem "THE PROCEDURE'S INPUT PARAMETERS"
      For i = 0 To ADOCmd.Parameters.Count - 1
          If ADOCmd.Parameters(i).Direction = adParamInput Or _
              ADOCmd.Parameters(i).Direction = adParamOutput Then
              List1.AddItem ADOCmd.Parameters(i).Name & " = " & _
                          ADOCmd.Parameters(i).Value
          End If
      Next i
      List1.AddItem " "
      List1.AddItem "THE PROCEDURE'S OUTPUT PARAMETERS"
      For i = 0 To ADOCmd.Parameters.Count - 1
          If ADOCmd.Parameters(i).Direction = _
              adParamInputOutput Or _
              ADOCmd.Parameters(i).Direction = _
              adParamOutput Or _
              ADOCmd.Parameters(i).Direction = _
              adParamReturnValue Then
                  List1.AddItem ADOCmd.Parameters(i).Name & _
                      " = " & ADOCmd.Parameters(i).Value
          End If
      Next i
      Exit Sub
  ParameterError:
      MsgBox "Parameter " & ADOCmd.Parameters(i).Name & _
              vbCrLf & Err.Description
      Exit Sub
  ExecutionError:
```

```
        MsgBox "The following error occurred during the " & _
                "procedure's execution" & vbCrLf & Err.Description
        Exit Sub
    OutputError:
        MsgBox "Error in retrieving Parameter " & _
                ADOCmd.Parameters(i).Name & vbCrLf & Err.Description
        Exit Sub
    End Sub
```

The code sets up a connection to the Northwind database and a Command object to execute the CountOrdersByDate procedure. It then calls the Parameters collection's Refresh method with the following statement in order to populate the members of the Parameters collection with data read directly from the stored procedure:

```
ADOCmd.Parameters.Refresh
```

Once the Parameters collection has been populated, the program scans each parameter, examines its direction, and prompts the user for a new value (for input parameters only). Then, the program calls the stored procedure with the Command object's Execute method, passing the arguments supplied by the user. Finally, the values of both input and output parameter values are displayed on the ListBox control.

Creating and Executing Stored Procedures with VB

The last example in this section is a VB routine that creates a stored procedure, attaches it to the database, and then executes it. The sample application for this section is called CreateExecuteSP, and its Form is shown in Figure 8.4.

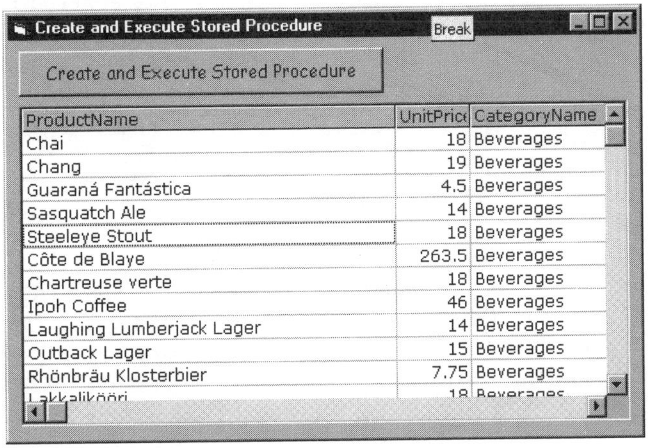

FIGURE 8.4:

The CreateExecuteSP project demonstrates how to create a new stored procedure and execute it from within a VB application.

NOTE	The actual definition of the stored procedure is hardwired in the application's code. I could have read it from a TextBox control, but then you'd have to get the stored procedure's definition correct before testing it. You can easily modify the application so that it reads the definition from a TextBox control and assigns it to the Command object's CommandText property.

As you recall from the discussion of stored procedures in Chapter 6, you always drop the definition of the procedure from the database (if it exists). The code for removing the existing definition of the procedure is executed as a separate command. These lines are usually entered in the Query Analyzer, along with the procedure's definition, and executed together, but this is when dealing with a batch, not a stored procedure. The GO statement you insert between the two segments of the batch does exactly that: It removes the procedure definition, then appends the new one. The GO statement is missing now, because the two segments are executed as separate commands. Here's how the two Command objects are set up and executed:

LISTING 8.4   Creating the Stored Procedure

```
Private Sub CreateSP()
    On Error GoTo ExecError
'    Create command object for stored procedure
    Set Cmd = New Command
    Cmd.CommandType = adCmdText
    Cmd.CommandText = "IF EXISTS (SELECT name FROM sysobjects "
    Cmd.CommandText = Cmd.CommandText & _
                    "WHERE name = 'ProductsCategories') "
    Cmd.CommandText = Cmd.CommandText & _
                    "DROP PROCEDURE ProductsCategories "
    Cmd.Name = "DropSP"
    Set Cmd.ActiveConnection = Conn
    Cmd.Execute
    Set Cmd = Nothing
    Set Cmd = New Command
    Cmd.CommandType = adCmdText
    Cmd.CommandText = "CREATE PROCEDURE ProductsCategories "
    Cmd.CommandText = Cmd.CommandText & "AS "
    Cmd.CommandText = Cmd.CommandText & _
        "SELECT ProductName, Picture, UnitPrice, CategoryName "
    Cmd.CommandText = Cmd.CommandText & _
        "FROM Products, Categories "
    Cmd.CommandText = Cmd.CommandText & _
        "WHERE Products.CategoryID = Categories.CategoryID "
```

```
        Cmd.CommandText = Cmd.CommandText & _
            "ORDER BY CategoryName"
        Cmd.Name = "CreateSP"
        Cmd.ActiveConnection = Conn
        Cmd.Execute
        Set Cmd = Nothing
        Exit Sub
    ExecError:
        MsgBox "Error in creating and executing " & _
                "the stored procedure" & vbCrLf & Err.Description
    End Sub
```

After the procedure's definition has been attached to the database, execute it as usual with the Command object. Here's the code that executes the newly created stored procedure:

LISTING 8.5   **Executing the Stored Procedure with VB**

```
Sub ExecuteSP()
    On Error GoTo ExecError
'   Execute command to add stored procedure
    Set Cmd = New Command
    Cmd.CommandType = adCmdStoredProc
    Cmd.CommandText = "ProductsCategories"
    Cmd.Name = "ExecuteSP"
    Set Cmd.ActiveConnection = Conn
'   Now execute the stored procedure and
'   display the cursor
    RS.CursorLocation = adUseServer
    Set RS = Cmd.Execute
    MSFlexGrid1.Rows = 1
    iCol = 0
    For i = 0 To RS.Fields.Count - 1
        If RS.Fields(i).Type <> adLongVarBinary Then
            MSFlexGrid1.TextMatrix(0, iCol) = RS.Fields(i).Name
            If RS.Fields(i).DefinedSize > 40 Then
                fldSize = 40
            Else
                fldSize = RS.Fields(i).DefinedSize
            End If
            MSFlexGrid1.ColWidth(iCol) = fldSize * TextWidth("A")
            iCol = iCol + 1
        End If
    Next i

    While Not RS.EOF
        LItem = ""
```

```
            For i = 0 To RS.Fields.Count - 1
                If RS.Fields(i).Type <> adLongVarBinary Then
                    LItem = LItem & RS.Fields(i) & Chr(9)
                End If
            Next
            MSFlexGrid1.AddItem LItem
            RS.MoveNext
        Wend
        Exit Sub
    ExecError:
        MsgBox "Error in creating and executing the stored procedure" &
    vbCrLf & Err.Description
    End Sub
```

As you can see, the Command object is very flexible. Every T-SQL statement or batch you can execute in the Query Analyzer can also be executed through the Command object, from within your VB application. The same is true for Access queries, only Access doesn't support multiple output parameters along with a Recordset. In the next section, I move on to a more advanced topic—namely, how to execute commands asynchronously.

Executing Commands Asynchronously

ADO allows the asynchronous execution of SQL statements and stored procedures. In other words, you can initiate the execution of a command and then return to the program immediately. When the asynchronous execution of the command completes, ADO will notify the application by firing the ExecuteComplete event. To execute commands asynchronously, you can use either the Connection object or the Command object. The Recordset object doesn't support asynchronous operations.

The Connection object recognizes the ExecuteComplete event, which is fired when the DBMS completes the execution of the command. The ExecuteComplete event is also fired if the command fails (because of an error in the SQL statement, a timeout, or any other reason). To program the ExecuteComplete event, you must declare the Connection object with the WithEvents keyword:

```
Dim WithEvents Conn As ADODB.Connection
Set Conn = New ADODB.Connection
```

To execute a stored procedure through the Connection object asynchronously, you must specify the adAsyncExecute option in the *options* argument, with a statement like the following:

```
Set RS = Conn.Execute(sProc, records, _
                        adCmdStoredProc Or adAsyncExecute)
```

where *sProc* is the name of the stored procedure, *RS* is a properly declared Recordset variable, and *Conn* is a Connection object. This command submits the request to the DBMS and returns immediately. Your code can continue with other tasks while the request is running. When the *RS* variable is populated, the Conn_ExecuteComplete event will be raised. This is where you must insert the code to process the Recordset returned by a selection query, or examine the number of rows affected by an action query.

The Connection_ExecuteComplete Event

Use the Connection_ExecuteComplete event handler to process the results of a command that was executed asynchronously through the Connection object. The syntax of the ExecuteComplete event is:

```
ExecuteComplete(records, pError, adStatus, _
                pCommand, pRecordset, pConnection)
```

In this syntax, *records* is a long variable that returns the number of rows affected by the query (if it's an action query). The *pError* object describes the error (if any). Use this object to correct the error and repeat the operation, or to notify the users as to what they can do to remedy the situation. Using the *pError* object is not as straightforward as you may think. See the sidebar "Using the pError Object" later in this section.

The *adStatus* argument indicates the status of the execution and can have one of the following values:

TABLE 8.6:   The Values of the *adStatus* Argument of the ExecuteComplete Event

Constant	Description
adStatusErrorsOccurred	The operation completed unsuccessfully
adStatusOK	The operation completed successfully

TIP

The *adStatus* argument's type is EventStatusEnum (see Appendix A for a list of the values of the EventStatusEnum type). This enumerated type contains more values, but they don't apply to the *adStatus* argument of the ExecuteComplete event of the Command object. However, an *adStatus* argument is used by other events, such as the WillConnect event. The WillConnect event's *adStatus* argument can have more values. In fact, you can cancel the connection by setting the *adStatus* argument to `adStatusCancel`. The ExecuteComplete event is fired after the completion of the execution of a command, and it can't be canceled; it will be fired even if the execution of the command fails.

Looking again at the syntax of the ExecuteComplete event, the *pCommand* is an object variable that represents the Command object for which the event took place. If you have started the execution of multiple commands asynchronously, you should examine the *pCommand* object to find out which command has completed its execution. Finally, the *pRecordset* and *pConnection* arguments represent the Recordset and Connection objects on which the Execute method was run.

Using the pError Object

The *pError* object is not set if the command completed successfully. If you attempt to examine the *pError* object in the ExecuteComplete event handler with a statement like the following:

```
Sub Conn_ExecuteComplete(. . .)
'   THIS CODE SEGMENT WILL NOT WORK !
    If pError.Number <> 0 Then
        {handle error}
    Else
        {proces results}
    End If
End Sub
```

you will get an error message indicating that the *pError* object hasn't been set. If the *pError* object isn't set, you can't access its properties. (In effect, you will cause a runtime error if the command is executed successfully!)

If an error occurred during execution, the statements will work as expected. To access the *pError* object, you must first examine the value of the *adStatus* argument. If it's not *adStatusOK*, then an error has occurred and the *pError* object has been set. To access its properties, use the following syntax:

```
If adStatus <> adStatusOK Then
        {examine the properties of the pError object}
    End If
```

The Command.State Property

Oddly, the Command object doesn't recognize any events. The simplest way to find out whether a command that was issued asynchronously completed its execution is to monitor the State property of the Command object on which it was issued. The State property can have one of the values listed in Table 8.7.

TABLE 8.7: The Values of the Command Object's State Property

Constant	Description
adStateClosed	The command is closed.
adStateOpen	The command is open.
adStateExecuting	The command is currently executing.
adStateFetching	The command is fetching rows.

You should add a Timer control to your Form, set its Timer property to one second or so, and use its Timer event to monitor the progress of the asynchronous operation. Here's how you'd program its Timer event:

```
Sub Timer1_Timer()
    If CMD.State <> adStateExecuting Then
        {process results}
    End If
End Sub
```

As you can see, it's simpler to execute commands asynchronously with the Connection object than with the Command object, but the Command object is more flexible when it comes to parameters. Let's put the information of the preceding section together and build a sample application that executes commands asynchronously with the Execute methods of the various ADO objects.

The AsyncExecute Project

The AsyncExecute project, shown in Figure 8.5, demonstrates how to execute commands asynchronously with the Command and Connection objects.

FIGURE 8.5:

The AsyncExecute project demonstrates how to execute commands asynchronously.

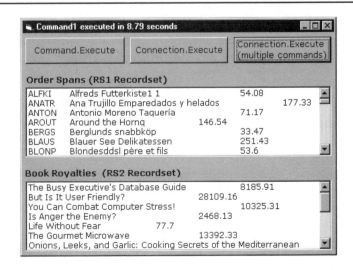

The Command.Execute button executes the OrderSpan stored procedure asynchronously with the Command object. The Connection.Execute button executes the same procedure asynchronously through the Connection object. Finally, the Connection.Execute (multiple commands) button executes the OrderSpan and BookRoyalties stored procedures asynchronously through two different Connection objects. The commands are submitted for execution one after the other. When any of the commands completes, the corresponding Connection object's ExecuteComplete event is fired.

> **NOTE**
>
> I'm using the OrderSpan and BookRoyalties stored procedures because they are the two most complicated procedures presented in this book and they take a few seconds to execute. The OrderSpan procedure is discussed later in this chapter, but for now all you need to know is that it returns a Recordset with two columns: the customer names, and their average order span (time between consecutive orders). The more often a customer places orders, the shorter the order span will be. The BookRoyalties stored procedure calculates the royalties earned by each book in the Pubs database. This stored procedure is also discussed in detail later in this chapter.

To test the AsyncExecute project you must first attach the OrderSpan and Book-Royalties stored procedures to the Northwind database. Before you can use the stored procedures, you must execute the following scripts with the Query Analyzer (in the order shown here): CreateSalesCursor, OrderSpan, MakeTitlesCursor, and BookRoyalties. These files can be found in the TSQL Procedures folder under the Chapter 8 folder on the CD. If you have any problems running the stored procedures, read the section "T-SQL Cursors" later in this chapter, and then run the AsyncExecute project.

The following object variables are declared in the Form's declarations section, so that they are available to all routines. Notice that the Connection objects must be declared outside any procedure (the *WithEvents* keyword has no effect if the corresponding variables are declared in a procedure).

```
Dim WithEvents Conn1 As ADODB.Connection
Dim WithEvents Conn2 As ADODB.Connection
Dim RS1 As New ADODB.Recordset
Dim RS2 As New ADODB.Recordset
Dim StartTime As Long
```

The *StartTime* variable is used in the Visual Basic code to keep track of how long each command takes to execute.

Let's start with the code behind the Command.Execute button, which uses the Command object to execute the command. To find out whether a command's execution has completed, you must monitor the Command object's State property, as discussed previously. While its value is adStateStillExecuting, the command hasn't completed yet.

LISTING 8.6 **Executing Commands Asynchronously with the Command Object**

```
Private Sub Command1_Click()
Dim RS As New ADODB.Recordset
Dim Conn As New ADODB.Connection
Dim CMD As New ADODB.Command

    List1.Clear
    List2.Clear
    Conn.ConnectionString = "Provider=SQLOLEDB.1;" & _
            "User ID=sa;password=;Initial Catalog=Northwind"
    Conn.Open
    CMD.ActiveConnection = Conn
    CMD.CommandText = "OrderSpan"
    CMD.CommandType = adCmdText
    Set RS = CMD.Execute(records, , adAsyncExecute)
    Me.Caption = "Executing ..."
    StartTime = Timer
    While CMD.State = adStateExecuting
        DoEvents
    Wend
    Debug.Print "Command1 executed in " & Timer - StartTime
    List1.Clear
    While Not RS.EOF
        List1.AddItem RS.Fields(0) & vbTab & _
                    RS.Fields(1) & vbTab & vbTab & _
                    Format(RS.Fields(2), "###.##")
        RS.MoveNext
    Wend
    Set CMD = Nothing
    Set RS = Nothing
    Me.Caption = "Asynchronous Execution"
End Sub
```

TIP

The OrderSpan stored procedure took nearly 5 seconds to execute on my system the first time it was invoked (and a little less in subsequent calls). This is unreasonably long, but it's due to the While . . . Wend loop that monitors the Command object's state. You should probably monitor this property from within a Timer control's Timer event and call a subroutine to process the rows. The While . . . Wend loops simulates an application that executes a command asynchronously and carries on with other tasks.

The code behind the Connection.Execute button is shorter, but it relies on the Connection_ExecuteComplete event. The button's code submits the command for execution, and the ExecuteComplete event scans the Recordset variable returned by the stored procedure and displays its rows in the upper ListBox control:

LISTING 8.7   **Executing a Command Asynchronously**

```
Private Sub Command2_Click()
    List1.Clear
    List2.Clear
    Set Conn1 = New ADODB.Connection
    Conn1.ConnectionString = "Provider=SQLOLEDB.1;" & _
            "User ID=sa;password=;Initial Catalog=Northwind"
    Conn1.Open
    StartTime = Timer
    Set RS1 = Conn1.Execute("OrderSpan", records, _
            adCmdStoredProc Or adAsyncExecute)
End Sub
```

LISTING 8.8   **The Conn1 Object's ExecuteComplete Event Handler**

```
Private Sub Conn1_ExecuteComplete(ByVal RecordsAffected As Long,_
            ByVal pError As ADODB.Error, _
            adStatus As ADODB.EventStatusEnum, _
            ByVal pCommand As ADODB.Command, _
            ByVal pRecordset As ADODB.Recordset, _
            ByVal pConnection As ADODB.Connection)
    Debug.Print "Command1 executed in " & _
                Timer - StartTime & " seconds"
    While Not RS1.EOF
        List1.AddItem RS1.Fields(0) & vbTab & _
                    RS1.Fields(1) & vbTab & vbTab & _
                    Format(RS1.Fields(2), "###.##")
        RS1.MoveNext
    Wend

End Sub
```

The Conn2_ExecuteComplete event handler is nearly identical and need not be listed. The last button on the Form submits two commands to the SQL Server, one after the other. The two commands are executed over two different Connection objects, against two different databases: the OrderSpan procedure is executed against the Northwind database, and the BookRoyalties against the PUBS database. (Like the OrderSpan procedure, the BookRoyalties procedure is discussed later in this chapter. The BookRoyalties stored procedure returns a cursor with titles and the royalties they generated.) Here's Listing 8.9, the code behind the third and last button on the Form:

LISTING 8.9   **Executing Two Commands Asynchronously**

```
Private Sub Command3_Click()
    List1.Clear
    List2.Clear
    Set Conn1 = New ADODB.Connection
    Set Conn2 = New ADODB.Connection
    Conn1.ConnectionString = "Provider=SQLOLEDB.1;" & _
            "User ID=sa;password=;Initial Catalog=Northwind"
    Conn1.Open
    Conn2.ConnectionString = "Provider=SQLOLEDB.1;" & _
            "User ID=sa;password=;Initial Catalog=PUBS"
    Conn2.Open
    StartTime = Timer
    Set RS1 = Conn1.Execute("OrderSpan", records, _
                    adCmdStoredProc Or adAsyncExecute)
    Set RS2 = Conn2.Execute("BookRoyalties", records, _
                    adCmdStoredProc Or adAsyncExecute)
End Sub
```

When either Connection's ExecuteComplete event is raised, the corresponding Recordset's rows are displayed on one of the two ListBox controls.

Implementing Business Rules with Stored Procedures

Two of the most practical examples of the last chapter were the stored procedures that implemented business rules. As you recall, you created the procedures Add-Customer and NewOrder to add new customers and new orders to the Northwind database. In this section, you are going to see how these stored procedures can be called from within a VB application.

To turn the AddCustomer and NewOrder stored procedures into real-world business objects, you must first make sure users cannot edit the tables of the database directly. If they can edit or delete orders directly on the database's tables, the two stored procedures will have been practically useless.

Here's a simple method for preventing users from changing the Northwind tables directly. This is the database administrator's job, but I will show you the steps to create a login for the applications and limit its access to the database. Any application that updates the Order and Order Details tables must log on to the SQL Server as "Application." You can create a similar login for the users who are allowed to edit these two tables, so that their additions are managed through the AddCustomer and NewOrder stored procedures. This way, no one will be able to edit the tables at will.

To create a new login, start the Enterprise Manager, open the Logins folder, and right-click the Logins folder. Then, select New Login from the shortcuts menu. Name the new login Application. Set a password for the new login (this is optional, but recommended) and make sure the new login applies to the Northwind database. Then click the OK button to close the Login Properties window.

When you're back to the Enterprise Manager, open the folder of the Northwind database and select the Users folder. Right-click somewhere on the right-hand pane (where the database's users are displayed) and select New Database User. Figure 8.6 shows the New User dialog box. Name the new user Program. To add the new user, all you have to do is select the name of the login you just created from the Login name drop-down list, then click OK. When the user's name appears in the list of users on the Enterprise Manager's left pane, right-click the name and select Permissions.

FIGURE 8.6:

Adding a new user to the Northwind database

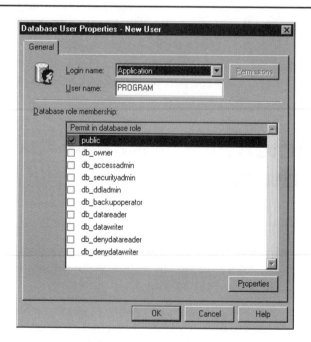

Figure 8.7 shows the permissions of the user Program on the Orders and Order Details tables. Disable the INSERT, UPDATE, and DELETE permissions check boxes on this table by clicking in the corresponding boxes until the red X icon appears. Notice that I didn't change the user's permission to SELECT in the rows for these two tables. Your applications can look up the two tables and retrieve rows, but they can't

edit the tables directly. The Program user must be granted permission to execute the AddCustomer and NewOrder stored procedures, so check their boxes in the column EXEC, also shown in Figure 8.7.

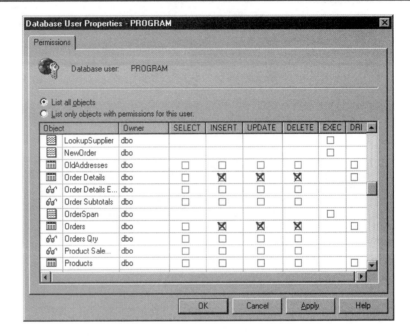

Notice that the triggers you implemented in Chapter 6 will be invoked as expected. You don't have to set any permissions for the triggers. While you're setting the new user's permissions, you should also prevent the new user from even seeing the Deletions table so there are no mishaps with lost information.

Now we are ready to switch to the VB code that calls the AddCustomer and NewOrder stored procedures.

Calling the AddCustomer Procedure from a VB Application

Figure 8.8 shows the AddCustomer.vbp application that allows the user to supply values for all the columns in the Customers table. After these values are supplied, you can add the customer data to the table by clicking the Add Customer button. This button's code reads all the fields on the Form, sets up the appropriate Parameter objects, and calls the AddCustomer stored procedure. Listing 8.10 provides the complete listing of the AddCustomer button's code.

FIGURE 8.8:

The AddCustomer application adds new rows to the Customers table through the AddCustomer stored procedure.

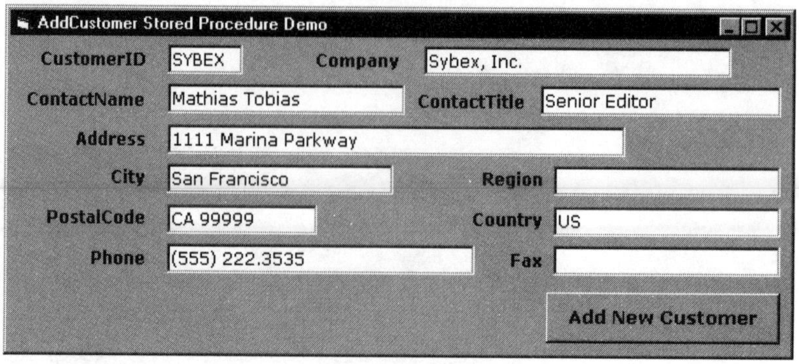

LISTING 8.10   The AddCustomer Command Button

```
Private Sub bttnAddCustomer_Click()
Dim ADOConn As New ADODB.Connection
Dim oParam As ADODB.Parameter
Dim ADOCmd As ADODB.Command
Dim ADOError As ADODB.Error

    ADOConn.Open "Provider=SQLOLEDB.1;User ID=sa;Initial Catalog=North-
Wind;Data Source=(local)"
    Set ADOCmd = New ADODB.Command
    ADOCmd.ActiveConnection = ADOConn

'   The first parameter will hold the
'   stored procedure's return value
    Set oParam = ADOCmd.CreateParameter
    oParam.Name = "RETURN_VALUE"
    oParam.Type = adInteger
    oParam.Direction = adParamReturnValue
    ADOCmd.Parameters.Append oParam

'   CustomerID
    Set oParam = ADOCmd.CreateParameter
    oParam.Name = "CustID"
    oParam.Type = adChar
    oParam.Size = 5
    oParam.Direction = adParamInput
    oParam.Value = txtCustomerID.Text
    ADOCmd.Parameters.Append oParam

'   CompanyName
    Set oParam = ADOCmd.CreateParameter
    oParam.Name = "CustName"
```

```
    oParam.Type = adVarChar
    oParam.Size = 40
    oParam.Direction = adParamInput
    oParam.Value = txtCompanyName.Text
    ADOCmd.Parameters.Append oParam

'   ContactName
    Set oParam = ADOCmd.CreateParameter
    oParam.Name = "custContact"
    oParam.Type = adVarChar
    oParam.Size = 30
    oParam.Direction = adParamInput
    oParam.Value = txtContactName.Text
    ADOCmd.Parameters.Append oParam

'   { more Parameter objects here }

    ADOCmd.CommandText = "AddCustomer"
    ADOCmd.CommandType = adCmdStoredProc
On Error GoTo ExecError
    ADOCmd.Execute
    MsgBox "Customer added successfully!"
    Set ADOCmd = Nothing
    Set ADOConn = Nothing
    Exit Sub
ExecError:
    msg = "Could not add new customer." & vbCrLf & _
            "Error(s) returned by the provider:" & vbCrLf
    msg = msg & ADOConn.Errors(0).Description & vbCrLf
    MsgBox msg
    Set ADOCmd = Nothing
    Set ADOConn = Nothing
End Sub
```

I have omitted the lines that set up most of the parameters, because they are similar to the ones listed here. You can open the project to examine the complete code. If an error occurs during the execution of the stored procedure, it will be intercepted by Visual Basic, which in turn will activate the ExecError error handler. The only thing that could go wrong here is that you might attempt to add a customer with an ID that exists already.

Calling the NewOrder Procedure from a VB Application

Calling the NewOrder stored procedure from VB is a bit more complicated, not only because of the structure of the parameters, but also because the NewOrder procedure returns its own error codes. To call the NewOrder stored procedure, you must first create a Parameter object for each parameter expected by the procedure. The

NewOrder procedure expects the customer and employee IDs, the shipper's ID, and the order's details (a string with the products' IDs, plus their quantities and discounts). To demonstrate how to use this procedure from a VB application, you can use the NewOrder project, whose Form is shown in Figure 8.9.

FIGURE 8.9:

The NewOrder project adds new orders through the NewOrder stored procedure.

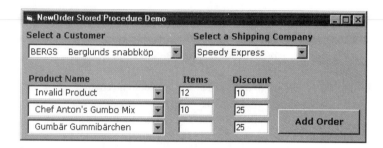

When the Form is loaded, the ComboBox controls containing the customer and shipper names are loaded with data from the corresponding tables. In this case, the customer ID is not a numeric value, and I'm displaying the ID in front of the customer name so that it can be easily retrieved, when the user selects a customer in the list. You can use a more complicated approach to store customer IDs, but with this example I was able to read the customer ID by extracting the five left-most characters of the item selected in the ListBox control. If customer IDs were numeric values (as they are in most databases), you would be able to store each customer's ID in the ItemData property of the ListBox control, making their retrieval even easier.

The shipper IDs are stored in the ItemData array of the ListBox control. At the bottom of the Form, you can select the names of three products and set their quantities and discount percentages. If you expand the Customers ComboBox on the Form, you will notice that the last few customers in the Customers ComboBox, and the last few products in the first Products ComboBox control, are invalid. I've included a few invalid entries so that you can examine the application's behavior with erratic data.

The Add Order Button

After you have specified the order's details, click the Add Order button to update the database. The code behind the Add Order button is lengthy, but only because you need several statements to set up each parameter. The EmployeeID field is set to 4 (presumably, the application knows who's running the application and sets up this field's value automatically). The order's date is also set automatically by the system. The CustomerID and ShipperID values are read from the corresponding boxes. Finally, a For ... Next loop scans the controls at the bottom of the Form and creates the string variable DetLine with the details of the order.

Next, the code calls the stored procedure with the Command object's Execute method and examines the value returned by the stored procedure. A zero value indicates successful execution, in which case the application displays a message and exits. If an error has occurred, the error number is displayed. You can examine the value of the return code and set it to display the appropriate error message. The error code –100 corresponds to an invalid customer code; the error code –101 corresponds to an invalid shipper code; and so on. A positive error code means that an error was raised by the SQL Server during the insertion of a new detail line. In this case, the procedure's return code is the error code returned by the SQL Server.

LISTING 8.11   **The Add Order Command Button**

```
Private Sub bttnNewOrder_Click()
Dim ADOConn As New ADODB.Connection
Dim oParam As ADODB.Parameter
Dim ADOCmd As ADODB.Command
Dim ADOError As ADODB.Error

Dim DetLine As String
Dim item As String * 6

    ADOConn.Open "Provider=SQLOLEDB.1;User ID=sa;Initial Catalog=North-
    Wind;Data Source=(local)"
    Set ADOCmd = New ADODB.Command
    ADOCmd.ActiveConnection = ADOConn

'   The first parameter will hold the
'   stored procedure's return value
    Set oParam = ADOCmd.CreateParameter
    oParam.Name = "RETURN_VALUE"
    oParam.Type = adInteger
    oParam.Direction = adParamReturnValue
    ADOCmd.Parameters.Append oParam

'   CustomerID
    Set oParam = ADOCmd.CreateParameter
    oParam.Name = "@CustID"
    oParam.Type = adChar
    oParam.Size = 5
    oParam.Direction = adParamInput
    oParam.Value = Left(Customers.Text, 5)
    ADOCmd.Parameters.Append oParam

'   EmployeeID
    Set oParam = ADOCmd.CreateParameter
    oParam.Name = "@EmpID"
    oParam.Type = adInteger
```

```
        oParam.Direction = adParamInput
        oParam.Value = 4
        ADOCmd.Parameters.Append oParam

'       Order Date
        Set oParam = ADOCmd.CreateParameter
        oParam.Name = "@OrderDate"
        oParam.Type = adDate
        oParam.Direction = adParamInput
        oParam.Value = Date
        ADOCmd.Parameters.Append oParam

'       Shipper ID
        Set oParam = ADOCmd.CreateParameter
        oParam.Name = "ShipperID"
        oParam.Type = adInteger
        oParam.Direction = adParamInput
        oParam.Value = Shippers.ItemData(Shippers.ListIndex)
        ADOCmd.Parameters.Append oParam

'       Now build string with order details
        For i = 0 To 2
            If Val(Quantities(i).Text) > 0 Then
                LSet item = Products(i).ItemData(Products(i).ListIndex)
                DetLine = DetLine & item
                LSet item = Quantities(i).Text
                DetLine = DetLine & item
                LSet item = Discounts(i).Text
                DetLine = DetLine & item
            End If
        Next

        If Len(DetLine) = 0 Then
            MsgBox "You must specify at least one item!"
            Set ADOCmd = Nothing
            Set ADOConn = Nothing
            Exit Sub
        End If
        Set oParam = ADOCmd.CreateParameter
        oParam.Name = "Details"
        oParam.Type = adVarChar
        oParam.Size = Len(DetLine)
        oParam.Direction = adParamInput
        oParam.Value = DetLine
        ADOCmd.Parameters.Append oParam

        ADOCmd.CommandText = "NewOrder"
        ADOCmd.CommandType = adCmdStoredProc
```

```
On Error GoTo ExecError
    ADOCmd.Execute
    If ADOCmd.Parameters(0).Value <> 0 Then
        MsgBox "Operation failed" & vbCrLf & _
            "The server returned the error # " & ADOCmd
.Parameters(0).Value
    Else
        MsgBox "Order added successfully!"
    End If
    Set ADOCmd = Nothing
    Set ADOConn = Nothing
    Exit Sub
ExecError:
    msg = "Could not add new order." & vbCrLf & _
            "Error(s) returned by the provider:" & vbCrLf
    msg = msg & ADOConn.Errors(0).Description & vbCrLf
    MsgBox msg
    Set ADOCmd = Nothing
    Set ADOConn = Nothing
End Sub
```

Run the NewOrder application, add a few valid orders, and then check out the behavior of the program with invalid data (select an invalid customer, or an invalid product ID in the first item's drop-down list). The NewOrder stored procedure is robust. It will not accept invalid data, and it will not add an order without its details. The transactions are guaranteed to complete (or fail) very quickly, because they take place from within a single stored procedure. If you have implemented the triggers discussed in the previous chapter, you'll see that the appropriate fields are set automatically during each successful transaction.

You have read a lot about stored procedures and have seen how to call them from with your VB code and pass parameters to them. In the last section of this chapter you'll learn how to write stored procedures that actually process the rows of a cursor with T-SQL statements. The material of the following section will also help you understand the similarities and differences between T-SQL cursors and ADO Recordsets.

T-SQL Cursors

As you have probably gathered by now, there is a direct relationship between SQL Server cursors and VB Recordsets. Every time you issue a SELECT statement, SQL Server retrieves the qualifying rows and returns them to the caller, which is a stored procedure or a Visual Basic application. This set of rows is called a cursor. When the cursor is passed to the VB application, it's stored in a Recordset object. In this section, you switch back to T-SQL and see how you can create and process cursors with T-SQL statements. As you will see, both T-SQL statements and the ActiveX Data Objects are not that different. They both access and manipulate databases. In my experience, a basic understanding of T-SQL cursors and the statements for processing them helps VB programmers grasp the concepts on which the various data-access technologies are based.

Cursors versus Recordsets

As you recall from Chapter 4, the difference between cursors and Recordsets is that the cursor contains the information retrieved from the database, the "raw" information. The Recordset object, on the other hand, contains the functionality you need to access these rows in the form of properties and methods. A Recordset is simply an object that references a cursor. It exposes a number of methods and properties you can use to navigate the cursor (not the Recordset) and edit the rows of the underlying cursor. You have probably noticed that some of the Recordset object's properties use the "Cursor" prefix. If, for instance, you want to specify that the rows should reside on the server, you must set the CursorLocation property accordingly. Likewise, the CursorType specifies the type of the cursor. Why aren't these two properties called RecordsetType and RecordsetLocation? These are properties of the cursor object, underlying the Recordset object, so they were named accordingly.

In the examples that follow in this chapter, you will see how to perform the same operations on a cursor with T-SQL statements and on a Recordset with VB statements. You'll learn how to build cursors with T-SQL statements and process them, either from within a stored procedure with T-SQL statements, or by passing them to a VB application and processing them with VB statements.

Cursor Types

Depending on how they store information, there are three types of cursors: static, keyset-driven, and dynamic.

Static Cursors

The static cursor is a shot of the data at the time the cursor was created. Changes made by other users after the cursor was created are not reflected in the cursor; yet, it is possible to update the database through a static cursor.

Keyset-Driven Cursors

A keyset-driven cursor contains a pointer for each row in the result set. When this type of cursor is created, SQL Server creates a list of pointers to the selected rows in the table(s). When a row is requested, SQL Server uses the pointer to fetch the current version of the row. In other words, if another user has changed the row since the cursor was opened, the application will see the latest data changes.

Of course, if new qualifying rows are inserted after the creation of the cursor, these rows will not be seen by the application. This is because there are no pointers for these rows in the keyset. If a row in a keyset-driven cursor is deleted after the creation of the cursor, the application will see a "hole" in its place when it requests this row and will skip to the next valid row.

Dynamic Cursors

Dynamic cursors are the most flexible and expensive of cursors. Dynamic cursors keep track of inserted and deleted rows and are always up-to-date. To maintain a dynamic cursor, SQL Server fetches it from the database every time you land on another row. With dynamic cursors, it is possible that the view will change each time you fetch a row because it is constantly refreshed. If a row has been deleted since the cursor was opened, for example, then the next row will be returned. Likewise, if a row was changed, the application will see the new row the next time you fetch a row. Finally, if a qualifying row was inserted, it will be added to the cursor automatically.

Cursor Navigation

Cursors are also characterized by how they can be navigated. Visual Basic supports a special type of Recordset: the forward-only Recordset. SQL Server doesn't treat the forward-only cursor as another cursor type. Instead, every cursor can be scanned forward-only if it's declared so.

Forward-only cursors are the least flexible ones, but they are most efficient in terms of memory usage (rows that have already been visited need not reside in memory, and SQL Server doesn't have to check the database to see if they have been deleted or altered). Whenever you want to open a cursor and scan its rows sequentially, use forward-only cursors.

Client-Side and Server-Side Cursors

The last categorization for cursors is where they reside. By default, SQL Server cursors reside on the server. Every time your application needs a new row, the row is transmitted from the server to the client. You can also create client-side cursors, which are downloaded to the client computer and are processed there by the application.

Using Cursors

To use a cursor, you must first declare it and open it—just as you must declare a Recordset variable in VB and populate it with the methods you explored in the first half of the chapter. The declaration of the cursor is a bit more complicated than the declaration of a variable. For instance, in addition to the cursor's type, you must also specify its rows. The rows of the cursor are specified with a SELECT statement, so there's nothing new to learn about cursors. Cursors are declared with the DECLARE CURSOR statement, whose syntax is shown next:

```
DECLARE cursorName CURSOR
[FORWARD_ONLY | SCROLL]
[STATIC | DYNAMIC | KEYSET]
[READ_ONLY | SCROLL_LOCKS | OPTIMISTIC]
FOR
SELECT field list
FROM table list
[FOR UPDATE OF column list]
```

Here is a description of the function of each element in this listing:

CursorName This line is a name of your choice and will be used to identify the cursor for the duration of its life. The first keyword following the cursor's declaration (FORWARD_ONLY or SCROLL) tells SQL Server whether the cursor can be scrolled in both directions or forward only. If you don't specify any keyword, then SQL Server will open a forward-only cursor. The forward-only cursor is the most efficient one in terms of resources.

[STATIC | DYNAMIC | KEYSET] This keyword specifies the type of the cursor and is similar to the CursorType property of the Recordset object. Its type must be STATIC (for static cursors), DYNAMIC (for dynamic cursors), or KEYSET (for keyset-driven cursors). If you omit the cursor type, a STATIC cursor is created by default.

[READ_ONLY | SCROLL_LOCKS | OPTIMISTIC] This keyword determines the locking strategy. READ_ONLY cursors can't be updated. Actually, you can change the cursor, but the changes won't be written to the database. The SCROLL_LOCKS option tells SQL Server to lock each row when it's read and release the lock when another row is fetched. The OPTIMISTIC keyword does the opposite. The cursor's rows are not locked, and when an attempt is made to update the database through the cursor, SQL Server examines the fields of the row. If they have not been modified since they were read, the UPDATE or DELETE operation succeeds. If the row has been modified, the operation fails.

FOR This keyword is followed by the cursor's definition. Here you must specify the SELECT statement that reads the desired rows into the cursor.

FOR UPDATE   Using this clause you can specify that only certain columns can be updated through the cursor. If the column list is empty, then all columns can be updated (unless, of course, the cursor's type doesn't allow updates, or the READ_ONLY keyword has been specified).

The following statement retrieves all product names and IDs from the Northwind Products table and stores them in the AllProducts cursor:

```
DECLARE AllProducts CURSOR
    FOR SELECT ProductName, ProductID
        FROM Products
```

To use this cursor from within a stored procedure or a T-SQL batch, you must first open it with the OPEN statement, whose syntax is:

```
OPEN [GLOBAL|LOCAL] cursor_name
```

The GLOBAL or LOCAL keywords specify the scope of the cursor. Local cursors are visible only in the stored procedure where they were declared, and they cease to exist when the stored procedure terminates. Global cursors, on the other hand, are visible from within any procedure. By default, cursors are opened as Local.

Finally, when you no longer need the cursor, you can close it with the CLOSE statement:

```
CLOSE cursor_name
```

Closing a cursor doesn't destroy its definition. You can later reopen the cursor by executing the OPEN statement again. When you close a static or keyset cursor, the data structures that hold the data (or the keys) are released.

To release the resources allocated to the cursor and actually destroy it, use the DEALLOCATE statement:

```
DEALLOCATE cursor_name
```

Once a cursor is deallocated, you can no longer open it. You must declare it again with the DECLARE statement, and then open it.

Scanning a Cursor

There are two basic operations you can perform on a cursor: scan its rows, and update the underlying tables. Scanning a cursor with T-SQL is similar to scanning a Recordset's rows with VB. You keep reading rows until there are no more rows left. To update the underlying tables, you simply assign new values to the columns of the current row.

After a cursor has been opened, you can examine the @@CURSOR_ROWS global variable to find out how many rows were returned into the cursor. If you execute the following statements, the number of contacts (or companies) in the Customers table will appear in the lower pane of Query Analyzer:

```
USE Northwind
DECLARE AllContacts CURSOR
    KEYSET
    FOR
    SELECT CompanyName, ContactName, ContactTitle
    FROM Customers
OPEN AllContacts
PRINT @@CURSOR_ROWS
```

Notice that the @@CURSOR_ROWS variable may return the value −1. This means that the cursor has not been completely populated yet. Even if the @@CURSOR _ROWS variable returns a positive value, this value reflects the number of rows currently in the cursor and may not be the total number of rows in the cursor. If the cursor contains too many rows, SQL Server may return only a fraction of the qualifying rows. To read all the rows of a cursor, you should set up a WHILE loop, which keeps reading its rows with the FETCH NEXT statement until the @@FETCH _STATUS variable returns −1.

The FETCH Statement

To read a row from an open cursor, use the FETCH statements, which are equivalent to the Move methods of the Recordset object. The syntax of the FETCH statement is:

```
FETCH [FIRST | PREVIOUS | NEXT | LAST]
FROM cursor name
INTO variable list
```

FETCH FIRST and FETCH LAST read the first and last row in the cursor respectively. FETCH NEXT and FETCH PREVIOUS read the next and previous rows in the cursor. If the cursor is forward-only (the default type of cursor created by SQL Server), then only the FETCH NEXT and FETCH LAST statements can be used.

In addition, you can use the ABSOLUTE and RELATIVE keywords to read a row by number, or a row relative to the current one. The ABSOLUTE FETCH statement must be followed by the row's number. For example, the statement:

```
ABSOLUTE FETCH 3 FROM Authors
```

will fetch the third row of the cursor. If you know a row's position with respect to the last row of the cursor, use a negative value. For instance, the statement:

```
ABSOLUTE FETCH -1 FROM Authors
```

will fetch the second to last row in the cursor.

The columns read by the FETCH statement are displayed in the lower pane of the Query Analyzer's Query window. To process the column values, you must first store them into local variables using the INTO keyword. The INTO keyword must be followed by a comma-delimited list of variables. The first column is stored in the first variable in the list, the second column in the second variable, and so on. The following statement reads the columns of the current row in the variables *@var1*, *@var2*, and so on:

```
FETCH NEXT INTO @var1, @var2, . . .
```

The local variables must be declared with the same type as the column that will be stored in them.

Listing 8.12 is a short T-SQL segment that creates a cursor, and then opens it and reads its rows one at a time. This code segment doesn't process the columns: It simply prints them in the Query Analyzer's Query window, as shown in Figure 8.10.

LISTING 8.12   The ScanCursor.sql Batch

```
USE Northwind
DECLARE AllContacts CURSOR
    KEYSET
    FOR
    SELECT CompanyName, ContactName, ContactTitle
    FROM Customers
GO
OPEN AllContacts
PRINT 'The cursor contains ' +
        CONVERT(char(3), @@CURSOR_ROWS) + ' rows'
DECLARE @Company varchar(40)
DECLARE @Contact varchar(40)
DECLARE @Title varchar(40)

FETCH FIRST FROM AllContacts INTO @Company, @Contact, @Title
WHILE @@FETCH_STATUS = 0
BEGIN
    PRINT CONVERT(char(30), @Company) +
        CONVERT(char(25), @Contact) +
        CONVERT(char(20), @Title)
    FETCH NEXT FROM AllContacts INTO @Company, @Contact, @Title
END
CLOSE AllContacts
DEALLOCATE AllContacts
```

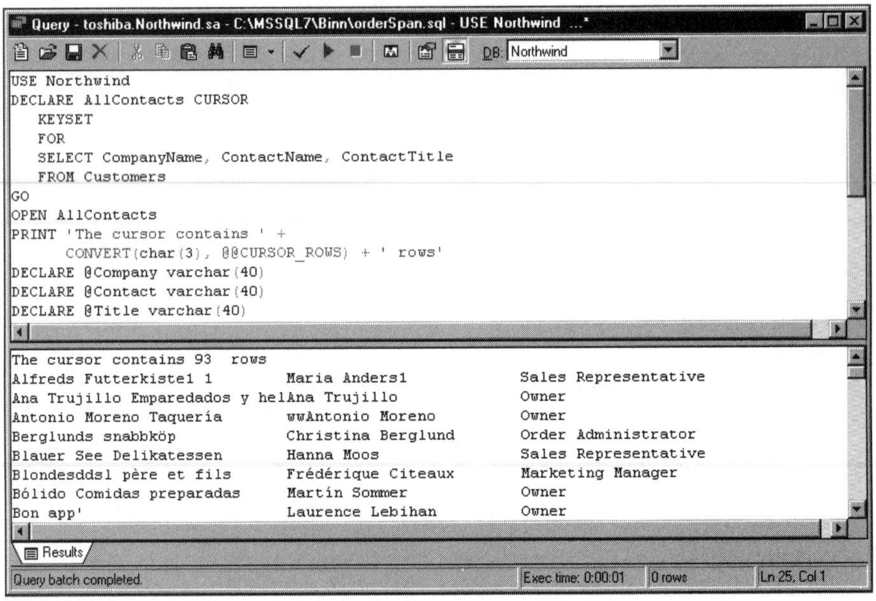

FIGURE 8.10:

Scanning a cursor with T-SQL statements in the Query Analyzer's Query window

You will see several examples of creating and scanning cursors with T-SQL statements in the following sections of this chapter. Cursors are used a lot in programming the SQL Server because there is no way to directly access the rows of a table. Cursors are the equivalent of Visual Basic's Recordsets, and they are just as useful.

Cursor Updating

As mentioned already, the default cursor returned by SQL Server is a forward-only, read-only cursor. If you specify a different type of cursor, you can update the underlying table(s), just as you can update rows through the Recordset object. Updating a cursor is very similar to updating rows with the SQL UPDATE statement. The following UPDATE WHERE statement updates a single row, which is specified with the WHERE clause:

```
UPDATE Products SET UnitPrice = 1.10 * UnitPrice
    WHERE ProductID = 34
```

If the product IDs and prices are stored in a cursor, you must execute a so-called "positional update." In other words, you can't issue a WHERE clause as usual. You can only update the current cursor row with the clause WHERE CURRENT OF. To update the current row of the AllProducts cursor, use the statement:

```
UPDATE Products SET UnitPrice = 1.10 * UnitPrice
    WHERE CURRENT OF AllProducts
```

The same clause applies to the DELETE statement. To delete the current row in the cursor, use the statement:

```
DELETE FROM AllProducts WHERE CURRENT OF AllProducts
```

Notice that you can't insert new rows to a cursor. You must issue the INSERT statement directly against a table in the database.

Examples

As you have seen in this and the last chapter, T-SQL combines the non-procedural nature of SQL with traditional programming elements. You can query the database with the ease of SQL and then process the results as you would with a VB application. In this section, you'll find some practical, non-trivial examples of stored procedures and how to call them from within VB applications.

> **NOTE**
>
> The examples of this section involve T-SQL scripts and VB applications. The T-SQL code can be found in the "TSQL Procedures" folder, under the Chapter 8 folder on the CD. The VB projects are stored in their own folders, as usual.

Before looking at the examples, however, I should explain why you use T-SQL to process the results, and not Visual Basic. When a stored procedure is added to the database, SQL Server prepares an execution plan, which is equivalent to compiling the statements. Stored procedures are executed very efficiently on the server, and they free the client. Another good reason for using stored procedures is to minimize the amount of data moved from the server to the client. Let's say you wanted to calculate the author royalties in the PUBS database. Without stored procedures, you would have to read the rows of the authors table, the royalty schedule table (which contains each author's royalty break points), and the sales for each author to the client. Once the required data was on the client, you would have to process it with Visual Basic to produce a list of authors and amounts. Imagine if you only needed the average royalty for all authors, or the number of books that have covered their advances!

Stored procedures are also used to implement business rules, so that client applications will not access the database directly.

Calculating Order Spans

The following example, the AvgOrderSpan stored procedure, is an advanced stored procedure that manipulates cursors. The procedure performs some calculations on the rows of the Orders table that simply are not possible with straight SQL. Let's say you want to know the average time between orders for the Northwind customers. The information you need is the average interval between consecutive orders.

The type of information you need can't be retrieved from the database with straight SQL statements, because it involves calculations between successive rows of the Orders table. Most programmers would download the entire table to the client and scan its rows there to calculate the differences between successive order dates. From there, they would compute the average order span. Since this book is addressed to VB programmers, I'll show you on the CD the VB code that calculates the average order span for each customer.

The AvgOrderSpan project shows you how to calculate the average order span for each customer in VB and T-SQL. Run the project and click the Order Spans (VB) button to see the titles and the royalties they generate (Figure 8.11). You can examine the VB code to see how it compares order dates in successive rows to calculate the average order span.

FIGURE 8.11:

The AvgOrderSpan project demonstrates how to perform the same task with VB and T-SQL statements.

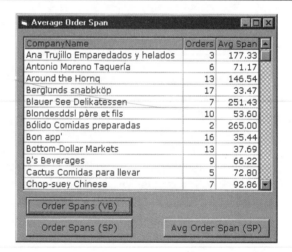

The AvgOrderSpan T-SQL procedure works just like its VB counterpart. It scans the rows of the Orders table, calculates the distance in days between successive orders of the same customer, and then takes the average. This operation can't be carried out with a simple SQL statement. To calculate the average order span, you must first create a cursor with the information you need. This cursor should contain the columns OrderID, CustomerID, and OrderDate of the Orders table. For the purposes of the report's appearance, you'll include the CompanyName field as well. Since this information isn't static, it must be retrieved from the database every time it's needed. Therefore, you will create a stored procedure to create this cursor. Here's the CreateSalesCursor procedure that creates the Sales cursor (you'll see shortly how this cursor will be used).

LISTING 8.13   **The CreateSalesCursor Stored Procedure**

```
CREATE PROCEDURE CreateSalesCursor
AS
DECLARE Sales CURSOR FOR
SELECT Customers.CompanyName, Customers.CustomerID,  Orders.OrderID,
Orders.OrderDate
FROM Customers, Orders
WHERE Orders.CustomerID=Customers.CustomerID
ORDER BY Customers.CustomerID, Orders.OrderID
```

This cursor contains all the information you need to calculate the average order span for all customers in the Northwind database. The query involves calculations between successive rows of the cursor. Here's a simple T-SQL code segment for scanning the entire cursor:

```
EXECUTE CreateSalesCursor
OPEN Sales
FETCH NEXT FROM Sales
WHILE @@FETCH_STATUS=0
    FETCH NEXT FROM SALES
```

If you enter these lines into the Query Analyzer's Query window and execute them, you'll see a list of customers and their orders. Each row will have a header, which makes the list hard to read. Don't worry about the appearance of the data; it will be read by another stored procedure, and no user will ever see it.

All you have to do now is store the values of the CustomerID and OrderDate fields into two local variables. At each iteration of the loop, these two variables will contain the CustomerID and OrderDate fields of the previous record. While the CustomerID is the same, the program must calculate the difference between the two orders in days (with the DateDiff() function) and add the result to a counter variable. When you hit the last row for the specific customer, you can calculate the average order span and zero the counter variable in preparation for the next customer's orders.

The actual code, shown below in Listing 8.14, is a bit lengthy, but straightforward. It reads the first line from the cursor and saves its fields to local variables. It then reads the next row and compares the new customer's ID to the ID of the previous customer. If the IDs are the same, it subtracts the old order's date from the current order's data and adds the difference to the *@TotalDays* local variable. It then stores the current row's fields to a set of local variables so that they'll become the previous row's field when the next row is read.

When the orders of the current customer are exhausted, the average order span for this customer is added to the *@avgDiff* local variable. The *@TotalDays* and other global variables that are used to calculate the customer's average order span are reset, and the process is repeated for all the orders. The final result is assigned to the variable *@avgOrderSpan*, which is the value returned by the stored procedure to the caller. Here's the AvgOrderSpan procedure's code:

LISTING 8.14 **The AvgOrderSpan Stored Procedure**

```
IF EXISTS (SELECT name FROM sysobjects
        WHERE name = 'AvgOrderSpan')
    DROP PROCEDURE AvgOrderSpan
GO

CREATE PROCEDURE AvgOrderSpan
@avgOrderSpan float OUTPUT
AS

EXECUTE CreateSalesCursor

OPEN Sales
    DECLARE @customer nvarchar(40), @customerID nchar(5)
    DECLARE @order int, @date datetime
    DECLARE @currentCustomer varchar(40)
    DECLARE @currentCustomerID nchar(5)
    DECLARE @previousDate datetime, @Days int, @TotalDays int
    DECLARE @Customers int
    DECLARE @Orders int
    DECLARE @AvgDiff float

    FETCH NEXT FROM Sales
                INTO @customer, @customerID, @order, @date
    SET @currentCustomer = @customer
    SET @currentCustomerID = @customerID
    SET @previousDate = @date
    SET @TotalDays = 0
    SET @Orders = 0
    SET @AvgDiff = 0
    SET @Customers = 0
```

```
        WHILE @@FETCH_STATUS = 0
        BEGIN
            FETCH NEXT FROM Sales
                    INTO @customer, @customerID, @order, @date
                IF @customer = @currentCustomer
                BEGIN
                    SET @Days = DATEDIFF(day, @previousDate, @date)
                    SET @TotalDays = @TotalDays + @Days
                    SET @Orders = @Orders + 1
                    SET @previousDate = @date
                END
                ELSE
                BEGIN
                    IF @Orders > 0
                        SET @AvgDiff = @AvgDiff +
                            CONVERT(float, @TotalDays) /
                            CONVERT(float, @Orders)
                    SET @currentCustomer = @Customer
                    SET @currentCustomerID = @CustomerID
                    SET @previousDate = @Date
                        SET @TotalDays = 0
                SET @Orders = 0
                SET @Customers = @Customers + 1
                END
        END
    CLOSE Sales
    DEALLOCATE Sales
    SELECT @avgOrderSpan = @AvgDiff / @Customers
```

Testing the AvgOrderSpan

To test the AvgOrderSpan procedure, open a new query window in the Query Analyzer and execute the following lines (don't forget to execute the stored procedure's definition first; the AvgOrderSpan procedure hasn't been attached to your copy of the database yet):

```
DECLARE @result decimal(4,2)
EXEC AvgOrderSpan    @result OUTPUT
PRINT "The average order span is " + CONVERT(char(5), @result)
```

The @result variable (see Figure 8.12) was declared as decimal to avoid a large number of fractional digits and the need to format them for display.

The following VB code is all that is necessary to set up a Connection object and call the AvgOrderSpan stored procedure. It establishes a connection to the database with a Connection object as usual, then sets up a Parameter object to hold the value that the procedure will return. Finally, it executes the procedure:

FIGURE 8.12:

Executing the AvgOrderSpan procedure in the Query Analyzer

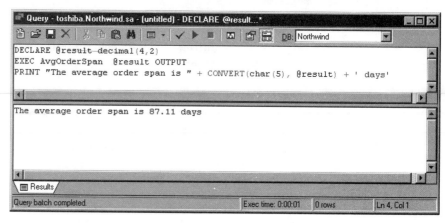

LISTING 8.15   Calling the AvgOrderSpan Procedure from VB

```
Set ADOConn = New ADODB.Connection
ADOConn.ConnectionString = "Provider=SQLOLEDB;"
                "Persist Security Info=True;User ID=sa; "
                "Initial Catalog=Northwind;Data Source=(local)"
ADOConn.Open
Set ADOcmd.ActiveConnection = ADOConn
ADOcmd.CommandText = "AvgOrderSpan"
ADOcmd.CommandType = adCmdStoredProc
'    Prepare the output parameter
ADOParam.Name = "averageOrderSpan"
ADOParam.Type = adSingle
ADOParam.Direction = adParamOutput
ADOcmd.Parameters.Append ADOParam
'    Execute the stored procedure
 ADOcmd.Execute
```

Calculating Order Spans for Each Customer

Let's revise the AvgOrderSpan so that it returns a new cursor instead of a single value. The OrderSpan procedure will return a cursor with each customer's average order span. This procedure is similar to the one you looked at already, but it's not as straightforward as you might think. The problem is that each customer's average order span is calculated separately. If you use the SELECT statement to select the current company and its average order span in the output cursor, T-SQL will create a separate cursor for each title. In other words, the stored procedure will return multiple cursors. (To read the output of a stored procedure that returns multiple

Recordsets, you must use the NextRecordset method, which is discussed in the last section of this chapter).

Since you know that all the rows you'll return to the caller have the same structure, you should be able to fit them into a single cursor. This is exactly what you are going to do, but the required code is not trivial. To create a single cursor, you will create a temporary table and store the results there. When all the titles and their royalties are available, you can retrieve all the rows of the temporary table with a single SELECT statement.

To create a temporary table from within a T-SQL stored procedure, use the following statements:

```
CREATE TABLE #tmpTable
    (
    fld_CustID nchar(5),
    fld_CustName nvarchar(40),
    fld_AvgDiff float
    )
```

The pound sign in front of the table's name denotes that this is a temporary table that will be removed automatically at the end of the session. Do not look for this table's name in the database either.

The code then calculates each customer's order span; only, instead of using the SELECT statement, it inserts a new row in the #tmpTable table with the statement:

```
INSERT #tmpTable VALUES
            (@currentCustomerID, @currentCustomer, @AvgDiff)
```

At the end of the stored procedure, you gather all the rows of the #tmpTable table into a single cursor using the following statement:

```
SELECT * FROM #tmpTable
```

Other than that, the AvgOrderSpan stored procedure is the implementation of the equivalent VB code with T-SQL statements. Here's the OrderSpan stored procedure's complete listing:

LISTING 8.16   **The OrderSpan.sql Stored Procedure**

```
IF EXISTS (SELECT name FROM sysobjects
        WHERE name = 'OrderSpan')
    DROP PROCEDURE OrderSpan
GO

CREATE PROCEDURE OrderSpan
AS
SET NOCOUNT ON
```

```
EXECUTE CreateSalesCursor
CREATE TABLE #tmpTable
    (
     fld_CustID nchar(5),
     fld_CustName nvarchar(40),
     fld_AvgDiff float
    )
OPEN Sales
    DECLARE @customer nvarchar(40), @customerID nchar(5)
    DECLARE @order int, @date datetime
    DECLARE @currentCustomer varchar(40),
    DECLARE @currentCustomerID nchar(5)
    DECLARE @previousDate datetime, @Days int,
    DECLARE @TotalDays int

    DECLARE @Orders int
    DECLARE @AvgDiff float

    FETCH NEXT FROM Sales
            INTO @customer, @customerID, @order, @date
    SET @currentCustomer = @customer
    SET @currentCustomerID = @customerID
    SET @previousDate = @date
    SET @TotalDays = 0
    SET @Orders = 0

    WHILE @@FETCH_STATUS = 0
    BEGIN
        FETCH NEXT FROM Sales
                INTO @customer, @customerID, @order, @date
            IF @customer = @currentCustomer
            BEGIN
                SET @Days = DATEDIFF(day, @previousDate, @date)
                SET @TotalDays = @TotalDays + @Days
                SET @Orders = @Orders + 1
                SET @previousDate = @date
            END
            ELSE
            BEGIN
                IF @Orders <> 0
                    SET @AvgDiff = CONVERT(float, @TotalDays) /
                                CONVERT(float, @Orders)
                    ELSE
                    SET @AvgDiff = 0
                INSERT #tmpTable VALUES
                (@currentCustomerID, @currentCustomer, @AvgDiff)
```

```
                    SET @currentCustomer = @Customer
                    SET @currentCustomerID = @CustomerID
                    SET @TotalDays = 0
                    SET @Orders = 0
                    SET @previousDate = @Date
                END
        END
    CLOSE Sales
    SELECT * FROM #tmpTable
    DEALLOCATE Sales
```

The Order Span (SP) button calls the OrderSpan stored procedure with the Command.Execute method. There are no input parameters to pass to the procedure, nor output parameters to be returned, so the code is quite short:

```
ADOConn.ConnectionString = "Provider=SQLOLEDB; " & _
                " Persist Security Info=True;User ID=sa; " & _
                "Initial Catalog=Northwind;Data Source=(local)"
ADOConn.Open
Set ADOcmd.ActiveConnection = ADOConn
ADOcmd.CommandText = "OrderSpan"
ADOcmd.CommandType = adCmdStoredProc
Set ADORS = ADOcmd.Execute
```

The rest of the code displays the rows of the ADORS Recordset on a FlexGrid control. You can open the OrderSpan project to examine its code.

Calculating Book Royalties

The last example of this section is an even more complicated stored procedure that combines multiple tables in its calculations. The BookRoyalties stored procedure calculates the royalties generated by each title in the PUBS sample database. Each book earns royalties according to its sales. According to a royalty schedule consisting of break points and percentages, the percentage earned by the author(s) becomes more generous as sales increase. The first 1,000 books may bring to the author 10%, the next 3,000 books will bring in 12%, and so on. The royalty schedule for the titles of the PUBS database is stored in the roysched table. The title with ID = PC1035 earns the following (quite generous) royalties:

Copies Sold			Royalty
0	to	2,000	10%
2,001	to	3,000	12%
3,001	to	4,000	14%
4,001	to	10,000	16%
10,001	to	50,000	18%

This royalty schedule corresponds to lines 3 through 7 of the roysched table, shown in Figure 8.13.

FIGURE 8.13:

The royalty schedule table of the PUBS database

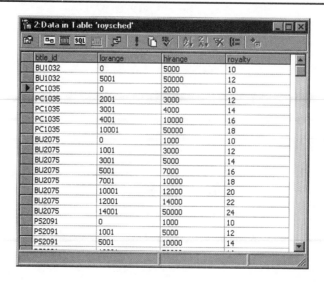

The titles table contains information about the books in the database, including the number of copies sold by each title so far. (Actually, it contains the year-to-date sales, but you'll assume this figure represents the book's total sales.) From the titles table, you can see that the title with ID = PC1035 has sold 8,780 copies, and its royalties are calculated as follows:

```
2000 * 22.95 * 0.10 +
1000 * 22.95 * 0.12 +
1000 * 22.95 * 0.14 +
4780 * 22.95 * 0.16
```

The total is $28,079. To calculate the royalties earned by each title, you must take into consideration the multiple percentages and breaks of the roysched table. This can't be done with a single SQL statement. So, you'll either download all the information you need to the client and write a VB application that calculates royalties, or write a stored procedure that does it on the server and returns the book titles and their royalties. To calculate the royalties on the client, you must download the entire titles and roysched tables. The VB code that scans the rows of the titles table and calculates the royalties is shown here in Listing 8.17:

LISTING 8.17   Calculating Book Royalties with VB

```
Private Sub BookRoyaltiesVB_Click()
    Set CN = New ADODB.Connection
    CN.ConnectionString = "Provider=SQLOLEDB;Password=;" &_
            "Persist Security Info=True;User ID=sa;" & _
            "Initial Catalog=PUBS;Data Source=(local)"
```

```
CN.Open
Set Books = New ADODB.Recordset
Set Books.ActiveConnection = CN
SQLcmd = "SELECT Title, ytd_sales, price, "
SQLcmd = SQLcmd & " lorange, hirange, Roysched.royalty "
SQLcmd = SQLcmd & " FROM Titles, Roysched "
SQLcmd = SQLcmd & " WHERE Titles.title_id=Roysched.title_id"
SQLcmd = SQLcmd & " ORDER BY Title, Roysched.royalty"
Books.Open SQLcmd, , adOpenStatic, adLockReadOnly
Screen.MousePointer = vbHourglass
prevTitle = Books.Fields("Title")
MSFlexGrid1.Rows = 1
While Not Books.EOF
    If Books.Fields("Title") <> prevTitle Then
        MSFlexGrid1.AddItem prevTitle & Chr(9) & _
                Format(BookRoyalty, "###.00")
        TotRoyalties = TotRoyalties + BookRoyalty
        TitleCount = TitleCount + 1
        prevTitle = Books.Fields("title")
        BookRoyalty = 0
        prevBreak = 0
    End If
    If Books.Fields("ytd_sales")<Books.Fields("hirange") Then
        If Books.Fields("lorange") <= _
            Books.Fields("ytd_sales") Then
            BookRoyalty = BookRoyalty + _
            (Books.Fields("ytd_sales") - prevBreak) * _
            Books.Fields("price") * _
            Books.Fields("royalty") / 100#
        End If
    Else
        BookRoyalty = BookRoyalty + _
        (Books.Fields("hirange") - prevBreak) * _
        Books.Fields("price") * _
        Books.Fields("royalty") / 100#
        prevBreak = Books.Fields("hirange")
    End If
    Books.MoveNext
Wend
MSFlexGrid1.AddItem prevTitle & Chr(9) & _
            Format(BookRoyalty, "###.00")
TotRoyalties = TotRoyalties + BookRoyalty
TitleCount = TitleCount + 1
Screen.MousePointer = vbDefault
MsgBox "The average royalty generate by all books is " & _
```

```
                    Format(TotRoyalties / TitleCount, "###.##")
        Set RS = Nothing
        Set CN = Nothing
    End Sub
```

This code segment is part of the BookRoyalties project, which is shown in Figure 8.14. The code executes an SQL statement that retrieves all titles along with their royalty schedules. Each title is repeated in the query's Recordset as many times as there are royalty breaks. Then the code scans the rows of the Books Recordset. While the title doesn't change, the code calculates the escalating royalties of the current title.

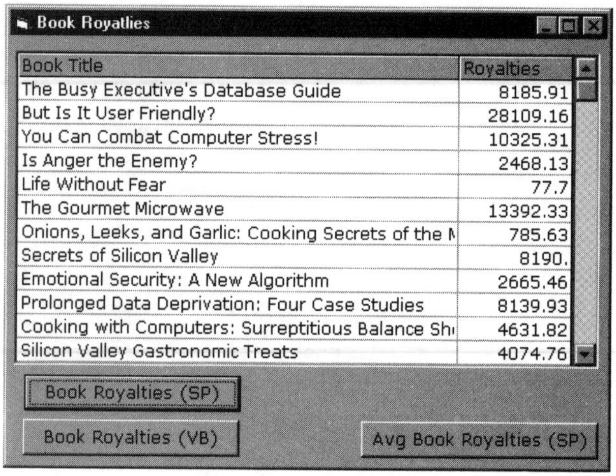

FIGURE 8.14:

The BookRoyalties application demonstrates how to calculate a book's royalties with VB code, as well as how to call the BookRoyalties stored procedure to retrieve a Recordset with the titles and their total royalties.

The other two buttons on the BookRoyalties Form calculate the royalties for each title and the average royalties generated by all titles. The BookRoyalties (SP) button calls the BookRoyalties stored procedure, and the Avg Book Royalties (SP) button calls the AvgBookRoyalties procedures.

The BookRoyalties procedure doesn't require any input parameters, nor does it return any values. The VB code calls this procedure with the Connection object's Execute method. This method returns a cursor, which is assigned to the Books Recordset. The rows of the Books Recordset are then displayed on a Grid control. The code behind the BookRoyalties (SP) button is shown next, in Listing 8.18:

LISTING 8.18   **Calling a Stored Procedure with the Connection.Execute method**

```
Private Sub BookRoyaltiesSP_Click()
    Screen.MousePointer = vbHourglass
    Set CN = New ADODB.Connection
```

```
        CN.ConnectionString = "Provider=SQLOLEDB;Password=;" & _
                "Persist Security Info=True;User ID=sa;" & _
                "Initial Catalog=PUBS;Data Source=(local)"
    CN.Open
    ProcName = "BookRoyalties"
    Set Books = CN.Execute(ProcName)
    MSFlexGrid1.Rows = 1
    While Not Books.EOF
        MSFlexGrid1.AddItem Books.Fields(0) & Chr(9) & _
                    Format(Books.Fields(1), "###.##")
        Sum = Sum + Books.Fields(1)
        Books.MoveNext
    Wend
    Screen.MousePointer = vbDefault
    MsgBox "The average royalty for all books is " & _
            Format(Sum / (MSFlexGrid1.Rows - 1), "###.##")
    Set Books = Nothing
    Set Conn = Nothing
End Sub
```

The MakeTitlesCursor procedure extracts the information you need in order to calculate the royalties from the database (book titles, prices, units sold, and royalty schedule) and stores it into the Sales cursor. Here's the cursor created by the Make-TitlesCursor procedure:

BookID	Sales	Price	Low	Hi	Percent
BU2075	18722	2.99	0	1,000	10
BU2075	18722	2.99	1,001	3,000	12
BU2075	18722	2.99	3,001	5,000	14
BU2075	18722	2.99	5,001	7,000	16
BU2075	18722	2.99	7,001	9,000	18
BU2075	18722	2.99	10,001	12,000	20
BU2075	18722	2.99	12,001	14,000	22
BU2075	18722	2.99	14,001	50,000	24
PS2091	2045	10.95	0	1,000	10
PS2091	2045	10.95	1,001	5,000	12
PS2091	2045	10.95	5,001	10,000	14
PS2091	2045	10.95	10,001	50,000	16
PS2106	111	7.00	0	2,000	10
PS2106	111	7.00	2,001	5,000	12
PS2106	111	7.00	5,001	10,000	14
PS2106	111	7.00	10,001	50,000	16
MC3021	22246	2.99	0	1,000	10
MC3021	22246	2.99	1,001	2,000	12
MC3021	22246	2.99	2,001	4,000	14
MC3021	22246	2.99	4,001	6,000	16
MC3021	22246	2.99	6,001	8,000	18

MC3021	22246	2.99	8,001	10,000	20
MC3021	22246	2.99	10,001	12,000	22
MC3021	22246	2.99	12,001	50,000	24

The following T-SQL batch will attach the cursor's definition to the database so that other stored procedures can open it. Enter the lines in Listing 8.19 in the Query Analyzer (or open the `MakeTitlesCursor.sql` file on the CD), and then execute it by pressing Ctrl+E. The stored procedure will be attached to the database, but it will not be executed.

LISTING 8.19   The MakeTitlesCursor Procedure

```
IF EXISTS (SELECT name FROM sysobjects
        WHERE name = 'MakeTitlesCursor')
    DROP PROCEDURE MakeTitlesCursor
GO

CREATE PROCEDURE MakeTitlesCursor
AS
DECLARE Sales CURSOR
FORWARD_ONLY STATIC FOR
    SELECT Titles.title_id, Titles.Title,
        Titles.ytd_sales, Titles.price,
        roysched.lorange, roysched.hirange,
        roysched.royalty
    FROM Titles, roysched
    WHERE titles.title_id=roysched.title_id
```

The BookRoyalties procedure calls the MakeTitlesCursor procedure to create the Sales cursor. It then opens the Sales cursor and scans its rows. At each iteration, it compares the total number of copies sold to the royalty breaks. If the total sales exceed the break point, then the entire quantity of the corresponding break is multiplied by the percentage. If not, then the difference of total copies sold minus the last royalty break is multiplied by the appropriate percentage. The listing of the BookRoyalties procedure is shown next, in Listing 8.20. It's fairly long, but that's because T-SQL is verbose compared to VB. The procedure's structure is identical to the structure of the VB code segment shown earlier.

LISTING 8.20   The BookRoyalties Stored Procedure

```
IF EXISTS (SELECT name FROM sysobjects
        WHERE name = 'BookRoyalties')
    DROP PROCEDURE BookRoyalties
GO

CREATE PROCEDURE BookRoyalties
```

```
AS
SET NOCOUNT ON
EXECUTE MakeTitlesCursor

CREATE TABLE #tmpTable
    (
    fld_TitleID char(6),
    fld_Title varchar(80),
    fld_TotRoys money
    )
OPEN Sales
    DECLARE @TitleID char(6), @Title char(80),
    DECLARE @TitlePrice float, @TitleSales int
    DECLARE @Low int, @Hi int, @Royalty int
    DECLARE @currentTitleID varchar(6)
    DECLARE @previousLow int
    DECLARE @BookRoyalties float

    FETCH NEXT FROM Sales INTO @TitleID,
                @Title, @TitleSales, @TitlePrice,
                @Low, @Hi, @Royalty
    SET @currentTitleID = @TitleID
    SET @previousLow = 0
    IF @TitleSales < @Hi
        SET @BookRoyalties =
                @TitleSales * @TitlePrice * @Royalty /100
     ELSE
        SET @BookRoyalties =
                @Hi * @TitlePrice * @Royalty / 100
    WHILE @@FETCH_STATUS = 0
    BEGIN
        FETCH NEXT FROM Sales INTO @TitleID,
                    @Title, @TitleSales, @TitlePrice,
                    @Low, @Hi, @Royalty
        IF @TitleID = @currentTitleID
        BEGIN
            IF @TitleSales > @hi
                SET @BookRoyalties =
                    @BookRoyalties + @TitlePrice *
                    (@Hi - @Low + 1)* @Royalty / 100
            ELSE
            BEGIN
                    IF @TitleSales > @Low
                    SET @BookRoyalties =
                        @BookRoyalties + @TitlePrice *
                        (@TitleSales - @previousLow) *
                        @Royalty / 100
```

```
                END
                SET @previousLow = @Hi
            END
            ELSE
            BEGIN
                INSERT #tmpTable VALUES
                        (@currentTitleID, @Title, @BookRoyalties)
                SET @currentTitleID = @TitleID
                SET @previousLow = @Low
                IF @TitleSales < @Hi
                    SET @BookRoyalties =
                        @TitleSales * @TitlePrice * @Royalty /100
                ELSE
                    SET @BookRoyalties =
                        @Hi * @TitlePrice * @Royalty / 100
            END
        END
    CLOSE Sales
    SELECT * FROM #tmpTable
    DEALLOCATE Sales
```

To test the AuthorRoyalties stored procedure, open the MakeTitlesCursor file in the Query Analyzer and execute it. The Sales cursor's definition will be added to the database. Then open the AuthorRoyalties procedure and execute it to add the stored procedure to the database. To see the royalties earned by each title, enter the following line in the Query window and execute it:

```
EXECUTE BookRoyalties
```

The BookRoyalties Project

The BookRoyalties project demonstrates how to call the BookRoyalties procedure from within your VB code. The button Book Royalties (SP) calculates the book royalties by calling the BookRoyalties stored procedure. The code behind this button is shown next, in Listing 8.21.

LISTING 8.21   **Calling the BookRoyalties Stored Procedure**

```
Private Sub BookRoyaltiesSP_Click()
    Screen.MousePointer = vbHourglass
    Set CN = New ADODB.Connection
    CN.ConnectionString = "Provider=SQLOLEDB;Password=;" & _
            "Persist Security Info=True;User ID=sa;" & _
        "Initial Catalog=PUBS;Data Source=(local)"
    CN.Open
    ProcName = "BookRoyalties"
```

```
        Set Books = CN.Execute(ProcName)
        MSFlexGrid1.Rows = 1
        While Not Books.EOF
            MSFlexGrid1.AddItem Books.Fields(0) & _
                    Chr(9) & Format(Books.Fields(1), "###.##")
            Sum = Sum + Books.Fields(1)
            Books.MoveNext
        Wend
        Screen.MousePointer = vbDefault
        MsgBox "The average royalty for all books is " & _
                Format(Sum / (MSFlexGrid1.Rows - 1), "###.##")
        Set Books = Nothing
        Set Conn = Nothing
    End Sub
```

The code is straightforward. It uses a Connection object to establish a connection to the PUBS database and then uses this object's Execute method to retrieve the cursor with the titles and the corresponding royalties. This cursor is assigned to a Recordset object, which is scanned as usual. The results are displayed on a FlexGrid control. The VB code calculates the average royalty for all the books by keeping track of the sum of royalties and the count of books.

The third button on the Form calls the AvgBookRoyalties stored procedure, which is a variation of the BookRoyalties procedure. This procedure returns a single value, which is the average royalty for all titles. You can find the AvgBookRoyalties stored procedure in the Chapter 8 folder on the CD. To test the AvgBookRoyalties procedure in the Query Analyzer, open the AvgBookRoyalties.sql file and execute it. Then run the stored procedure by executing the following T-SQL statements in a new window in the Query Analyzer:

```
DECLARE @avgRoyalty float
EXECUTE AvgBookRoyalties @avgRoyalty OUTPUT
PRINT @avgRoyalty
```

You can open the BookRoyalties project in the Visual Basic IDE and examine the code that calls the AvgBookRoyalties stored procedure.

Multiple Recordsets

As you recall from the discussion of T-SQL batches and stored procedures, every value selected using the SELECT statement becomes part of the return cursor. Each SELECT statement returns a separate cursor. The following statement, containing two SELECT statements, returns two cursors: one with the customers from Germany, and a second with the customers from Argentina:

```
SELECT * FROM Customers
WHERE Country = 'Germany'
SELECT * FROM Customers
WHERE Country = 'Argentina'
```

The rows of both cursors have the same structure, but SQL Server doesn't know this while it's processing the statement. Because two SELECT statements may select different columns, it creates a separate cursor for each statement.

TIP
Every SELECT statement in a T-SQL batch or stored procedure generates a separate cursor, even if this cursor contains a single value.

ADO handles these multiple cursors a bit differently than regular cursors. If you assign the cursor returned by the above statement to a Recordset object and then scan its rows, you'll see that it contains the customers from Germany only. To read all the customers from Germany and Argentina, use the following statements:

```
RS.Open ("Customers2", Conn1)
While Not RS.EOF          ' Customers in Germany
    {process current row}
    RS.MoveNext
Wend
Set RS = RS.NextRecordset
While Not RS.EOF          ' Customers in Argentina
    {process current row}
    RS.MoveNext
Wend
```

When multiple SQL statements are executed, ADO executes the first statement only and returns the corresponding cursor. When the NextRecordset method is called, the second statement is executed and another cursor is returned. You can keep opening Recordsets and compare them to Nothing. When a Nothing Recordset arrives, you know that there are no more statements to be executed (Listing 8.22, in the next section, shows how to iterate through multiple Recordsets).

TIP
Do not rely on a Recordset's EOF property being True to find out whether the command will return more Recordsets or not. One of the statements might not return any rows, but this is not an indication that all Recordsets have been exhausted. It is possible for a Recordset to have both its EOF and BOF properties set to True. This does not mean that you've reached the last Recordset. It simply means that the current Recordset did not return any rows.

Non-Uniform Recordsets

It is also possible to create non-uniform Recordsets, and this is a fairly common situation. You have seen how you can group rows according to a column and calculate group totals. One of the first SQL statements examined in Chapter 7 was the following one, which returns the details for all orders and calculates the totals per order, and per customer. The statement is repeated here for your convenience:

```
USE NORTHWIND
SELECT CompanyName, Orders.OrderID, ProductName,
     UnitPrice=ROUND([Order Details].UnitPrice, 2),
     Quantity,
     Discount=CONVERT(int, Discount * 100),
     ExtendedPrice=ROUND(CONVERT(money, Quantity * (1 - Discount) *
                     [Order Details].UnitPrice), 2)
FROM Products, [Order Details], Customers, Orders
WHERE [Order Details].ProductID = Products.ProductID And
     [Order Details].OrderID = Orders.OrderID And
     Orders.CustomerID=Customers.CustomerID
ORDER BY Customers.CustomerID, Orders.OrderID
COMPUTE SUM(ROUND(CONVERT(money, Quantity * (1 - Discount) *
          [Order Details].UnitPrice), 2))
          BY Customers.CustomerID, Orders.OrderID
COMPUTE SUM(ROUND(CONVERT(money, Quantity * (1 - Discount) *
          [Order Details].UnitPrice), 2))
          BY Customers.CustomerID
```

If you look at the structure of the cursor returned by this statement, you'll see that its rows don't have a uniform structure. The rows produced by the COMPUTE BY statements contain a single value only, while the SELECT statement returns the customer name along with the order's details. Each group of lines forms a separate cursor and must be accessed with a different Recordset object.

Figure 8.15 shows the output of the MutipleCursors project. You can see the last few orders of the Familia Arquibaldo company. Following the total of the last order, you can see the total of all the orders placed by the specific company.

The MultipleCursors project demonstrates how to scan cursors with totals. The rule for scanning non-uniform Recordsets is the same: Each group of rows generated by the same SELECT or COMPUTE BY statement is a different cursor, which must be read with the NextRecordset method. Listing 8.22 is the core of the MultipleCursors project's code:

FIGURE 8.15:

The MultipleCursors project demonstrates how to scan Recordsets with multiple, non-uniform Recordsets.

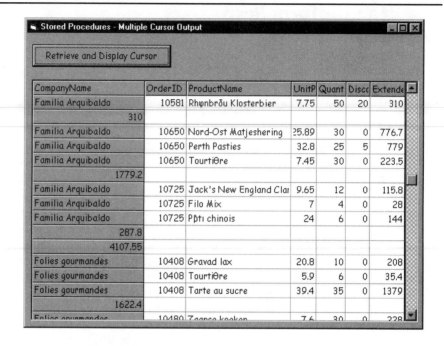

LISTING 8.22   **Scanning Multiple Recordsets**

```
Set RS = New ADODB.Recordset
Set Cmd = New Command
Cmd.CommandType = adCmdStoredProc
Cmd.CommandText = "AllInvoices"
Cmd.ActiveConnection = Conn
Set RS = Cmd.Execute
iCounter = 1
    While Not RS.EOF
        LItem = ""
        For i = 0 To RS.Fields.Count - 1
            If RS.Fields(i).Type = adDouble Then
                LItem = LItem & _
                    Format(RS.Fields(i), "#0.00") & Chr(9)
            Else
                LItem = LItem & RS.Fields(i) & Chr(9)
            End If
        Next
        MSFlexGrid1.AddItem LItem
        iCounter = iCounter + 1
        RS.MoveNext
```

```
        DoEvents
        If RS.EOF Then
            Set RS = RS.NextRecordset
            If RS Is Nothing Then
                Screen.MousePointer = vbDefault
                Exit Sub
            End If
            iCounter = 1
        End If
    Wend
```

This is a generic procedure that will scan all types of multiple Recordsets. That's why it doesn't place the totals in the appropriate cells. If you know the structure of the records, you can place them in the appropriate cells; for example, the totals will appear under the cells with the values being totaled.

Non-uniform cursors are convenient in situations where a single stored procedure must return many different values from the database. There's another type of non-uniform Recordsets, the *shaped* Recordsets. The main characteristic of these Recordsets is that they are structured hierarchically. Hierarchical cursors are implemented with the SHAPE command, and the techniques for creating and scanning hierarchical Recordsets are discussed in Chapter 10, "Shaping Your Data."

Summary

In this chapter, you have learned how to access databases from within your code indirectly with the help of stored procedures, as well as how to manipulate non-uniform Recordsets. Stored procedures allow you to implement business rules on the server and simplify the programming of the client applications. You have also learned how to create cursors from within your stored procedures, and how to pass these cursors to a VB application as Recordsets.

In the next chapter, I discuss a few more advanced ADO topics, including error handling and concurrency control. These are very important (and frequently overlooked) topics in database programming.

CHAPTER
NINE

More ADO Programming

- Choosing the right cursor type

- ADO error handling

- Multiuser considerations

- ADO events

In this chapter, we'll continue exploring how to program ADO with Visual Basic. The last chapter focused on programming client-side cursors with ADO, and the examples were fairly simple. As you will notice, nearly all of the sample applications and examples in the ADO documentation are limited to client-side cursors and optimistic locking. The assumption behind optimistic locking is that no two users will access the same row at the same time. While this assumption is valid most of the time, inevitably there will be situations where your application will attempt to save the changes in a row that has been edited, or even deleted, by another user since you last read it. Your application, therefore, must be able to cope with unusual situations. As the name of the locking mechanism implies, it's based on a best-case, not real-life, assumption.

The Data Form Wizard, for example, doesn't generate code to deal with unusual situations. Moreover, the code generated by the Data Form Wizard can't handle server-side cursors, which seriously limits its usefulness. The most robust and professional database applications use server-side cursors. Real databases are quite large, and you simply can't afford to transfer volumes of data to the client. To avoid concurrency problems, they use stored procedures to manipulate the tables. The ADO Data Control (or the DataEnvironment object), along with the data-bound and data-aware controls, can simplify your code, but they can't handle concurrency. You must provide your own code to handle concurrency.

This chapter is about cursors and how to handle them from within your VB code. Different cursors have different characteristics, and you can't write an application that will work with all types of cursors. You must first evaluate your options, then choose the best cursor for the job and finally start coding. This chapter starts with an overview of cursor types and then we'll build a simple data-entry application using different types of cursors. Instead of showing you the code and explaining how it works, I will guide you through the problems you'll encounter, explain why cursors behave the way they do (especially when it's not obvious why), and then suggest coding techniques.

Choosing the Right Cursor Type

You've probably read or heard more than you care to about cursors, but there's even more. Different types of cursors behave differently, and you should know what to expect when you code database applications. In fact, the first step in designing a database application is using the proper cursor type. The danger is that if you choose the wrong type of cursor, the problems will not surface immediately. Problems like network congestion and server overload will appear only after the database has grown quite large, and by then the problem will be far more difficult to fix.

Let's start with the cursor's location. A client-side cursor resides on the client, while a server-side resides on the server. In terms of resources and performance, this means:

- Client-side cursors must be transmitted to the client. Network bandwidth is always an issue, and you shouldn't upload to the client more information than necessary. Once the data is on the client you don't need additional trips to the server, but you can't be sure you're viewing the most recent data.

- Server-side cursors do not simply consume memory on the server machine (which is not insignificant, but we'll ignore it). SQL Server actually maintains server-side cursors and transmits the rows requested by the application to the client as needed. This is extra work for the server, and the more work you ask it to do, the less performance you'll get.

Client-side cursors are, by definition, static. You won't get an error if you specify a dynamic client-side cursor, but you won't get a dynamic cursor either. Selecting a client-side cursor means that you don't need to see the changes made by others since you've opened the cursor. You can refresh it from time to time, but this entails moving all the rows from the server to the client.

A feature that's unique to static cursors is that you can request the number of qualifying rows. Only static Recordsets can return their number of rows. All other types of Recordsets return the value "–1." ADO is basically telling you that it doesn't know or doesn't care about the number of rows. In a forward-only cursor, ADO doesn't know the number of rows, because it sees one row at a time. In a dynamic cursor, ADO doesn't care about the number of rows, because this number can change at any time. The membership is not fixed, so the number of rows may change the very moment you have requested it. Keyset cursors have a fixed membership, so they also report the correct number of rows. If you're using non-static cursors, you shouldn't care about the number of rows. Your application should not rely on the actual number of rows in the cursor.

Let's say you're writing an application to maintain titles, like the ones in the Biblio database. If you build this application using the ADO Data Control, chances are you will use a client-side cursor. You'll test the application, you'll train the users, and everything will look fine. You will have practically forgotten the details of the application when users start complaining about the speed. The application will be slow, and will even tend to slow down other applications! The database you previously tested with a few thousand titles will have grown to 50,000 titles, and your application that opens the Titles table through an ADO Data Control downloads the *entire* cursor to each client.

Ideally, you shouldn't create large client-side cursors. An application that edits titles should force users to specify as much as possible the titles they're interested in, and then move only the information requested to the client. For example, you could require that users specify a publisher and work with the selected publisher's books. Are there situations when you must create a large cursor and upload it to the client? The truth is that you never have to use large cursors on the client. We all do from time to time, but there's no need. Just think about it. What can the user do with as few as a few hundred rows? Nothing. If a user needs more than just a few rows, then he probably needs to see some summary information, not every row.

You may be thinking, "But I want to populate a data-aware control, so that my users can select the desired row with the mouse!" Why don't you require that users specify some selection criteria? If they want to view customers, give them the option to select a small fraction of the table's rows by specifying a state, the first few characters in the company name, and so on. You can even generate more complicated criteria, such as customers that have placed three or more orders in the last month. If you understand how the users of the application want to browse the database, you'll be able to limit the size of the cursors you load to the client. An application that displays invoices and allows users to calculate all types of totals is a prime candidate for using client-side cursors. Invoices don't change, and a few new invoices aren't going to change the current trends, so you can download all the data to the client and process it there. The table with the invoices, however, is quite large. To make the best use of the network bandwidth as well as of the computing power of the client, select the invoices needed by the user and download them to the client.

You should also make sure that the user needs all the information. If he needs totals by customers and dates, make sure you select the totals only, and not details.

Cursors and Data-Aware Controls

A data-aware control can't be populated with a server-side cursor. To populate a DataCombo control with the names of the publishers, you have to move all publisher names to the client. If the RecordSource for the Recordset you're using to populate the control resides on the server, then the data-aware control will not be populated. The reason is that a server-side cursor is transmitted to the client a few rows at time, as needed. To populate the DataCombo control, you must transmit the entire cursor to the client.

"OK," you might say, "I'll use server-side cursors for everything else, but I'll use client-side cursors to populate my data-aware controls." Even so, the population of a data-aware control is not a license to transmit huge cursors to the client. What good is it to be able to locate the desired title among a million titles with the mouse? Users will end up entering a good segment of the title, so why not ask them to supply this information first, then grab the (few) qualifying rows and send them to the client?

The bottom line is that client-side cursors have to be small. A large cursor on the client means that most of its rows will never be seen by the user or utilized in any way. If you end up using very large client-side cursors, reconsider your application's design. You're probably biting off more than you can chew. Design a new interface that limits the number of rows in the cursor before you actually create it.

Also, do not use data-aware controls to store long lists of values. Storing the names of the publishers in a title-browsing application is reasonable. Storing the titles in a data-aware control is quite unreasonable. Make a good estimate of the number of rows a table will have in its final form and then decide whether it can be stored on a data-aware control. If you think users would locate items in this control with the mouse rather than typing, then go ahead and use a data-aware control. "Features" that are not utilized by the users overload the application and consume valuable bandwidth.

Even after you apply some selection criteria, the resulting Recordset may be quite large. You can still limit the number of rows transmitted to the client by providing a Next Page and a Previous Page button (a technique that's used routinely on the Web). The user may not know that he has selected 200 or 2,000 rows. Your application can retrieve the first 20 or 50 rows from the database (use the TOP N predicate in your SQL statement) and populate a control on the Form. When the Next Page button is clicked, transmit the next batch of rows by including restrictions in the WHERE clause of your SQL statement.

The following code assumes you're displaying company names alphabetically, and it retrieves the next 20 rows from the database:

```
RSCustomers.MoveLast
lastName = RSCustomers.Fields("CompanyName")
SQLcmd = "SELECT TOP 20 * FROM Customers " & _
    "WHERE CompanyName > '" & lastName & "%'" & _
    "ORDER BY CompanyName"
```

We go to the last line of the Recordset on the client, extract the name of the last company, and use it to build a SELECT statement that retrieves the 20 rows whose CompanyName field comes after the name of the company already on the client. This code will work only if the rows are retrieved alphabetically by company name. Exactly how you'll express the restriction in the SQL statement depends on the application and the nature of the data, but there will always be a method to retrieve a small number of rows at a time.

Avoid Wide Cursors

Cursors do not grow in length only. If you want to display order numbers and dates, don't specify the Orders table, or a statement like:

```
SELECT * FROM Orders
WHERE OrderData Between '1/1/1998' AND '1/31/1998'
```

This statement will move a lot of information to the client that your application doesn't need. Shipping addresses, for example, are rarely needed, but if you include them with the * operator, you'll double the size of the client-side cursor for no reason at all.

Short of data-entry applications, you'll rarely have to download rows in their entirety to the client. Most applications require only a few of the table's columns.

Of course, you must take into consideration any data-bound controls on the Form. Let's say you want to populate a DataCombo control with the names of the publishers. When the user selects a publisher name in the control, the publisher's address and phone number should appear on two data-bound TextBox controls on the same Form. The following SQL statement retrieves all the information you need to populate the DataCombo control:

```
SELECT PubID, CompanyName
FROM Publishers
```

However, it doesn't retrieve the information needed to bind the TextBox controls to the Address and Phone fields. Use the following statement instead:

```
SELECT PubID, CompanyName, Address, Phone
FROM Publishers
```

If you want to bind too many fields, it may be better to request their values as needed, at run time. Let's return to the titles-browsing application, which displays the publisher names on a DataCombo control. If you want to display additional information about publishers, place a button on the Form. When this button is clicked, you can make a trip to the database, read all the fields, and display them on a separate Form.

Data-Aware Controls Are Not Perfect

While we're at the topic of data-aware controls, I should state a few thoughts on these controls. At first, they seem great. They can link tables behind the scenes without a single line of code, and they're great as lookup tools. After you use them for a while, you'll try to program them like the regular ListBox and Combo-Box controls; and you will find out that they do not support the basic properties of their plain counterparts. For instance, you can't find out the number of items in a DataList control with the ListCount property, even though the membership doesn't change. You must use the RecordCount property of the Recordset object you used to populate them.

Another limitation is that you can't step through their elements with the List property. You can't allow users to select multiple items (only one row at a time), and you can't select an item from within your code. These limitations aren't the result of poorly designed controls. Keep in mind that data-aware controls are meant to work with Recordsets, and a fundamental concept in manipulating the rows of a Recordset is that of the all-accessible current row. At any given time you can access the fields of the current row in the Recordset. To access the fields of another row, you must first move to that row.

This may explain the behavior of data-aware controls, but it's not going to help you if you need the features of a regular ListBox control in your application. You can implement data-aware controls using the plain ListBox and ComboBox control as long as you're willing to provide your own code. The trick in duplicating the function of a data-aware control from within a regular ListBox or ComboBox control is to use integers for primary keys. The Publishers table in the Biblio database uses an integer primary key, and you can store these values in control's ItemData property while populating it with the names of the publishers. Each time a new item is selected in the list, you must program the control's Change, or Click, event to perform the lookup operation that the data-aware control would perform automatically. (You can also design a custom ActiveX control based on the ListBox control to encapsulate the ListBox control's functionality and bind it to a data source with the appropriate code.)

This is a small price to pay, considering the flexibility of the regular ListBox control. For example, you can display all the publishers and let the user select one or more names, and then retrieve the titles of the selected publishers. The Selected-Products project discussed below demonstrates how to bind manually the regular ListBox control to the Northwind database and use it in your user interface.

The SelectedProducts Projects   The SelectedProducts project, whose main Form is shown in Figure 9.1, demonstrates how you can use ListBox controls as part of the user interface of applications that access databases. The two controls are populated from within the application's code. The user can select multiple categories or suppliers and retrieve the products that belong to the selected categories, or are purchased from the selected suppliers. The SQL statement is generated on the fly and executed against the database. Finally, the qualifying rows are displayed on a DataGrid control.

FIGURE 9.1:

The SelectedProducts project populates two ListBox controls with key fields as part of the interface of a database-accessing application.

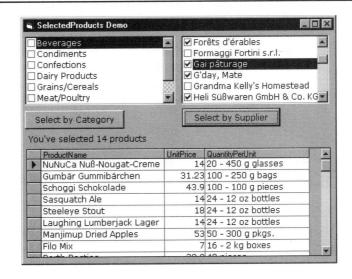

The SelectedProducts project uses a DataEnvironment object to connect to the database and retrieve the names of the categories and suppliers. They are the All-Categories and AllSuppliers objects, which are set to the Categories and Suppliers tables of the Northwind database respectively. Their cursors reside on the client and are read-only. Here are the SQL statements that retrieve the desired rows from the two tables:

AllSuppliers Object
```
SELECT SupplierID, CompanyName
FROM Suppliers
```

AllCategories Object
```
SELECT CategoryID, CategoryName
FROM Categories
```

These two objects will create the rsAllSuppliers and rsAllCategories Record-sets, which are used to populate the two ListBox controls in the Form's Load event, shown in Listing 9.1.

LISTING 9.1   Populating the ListBox Controls

```
Private Sub Form_Load()
DataEnvironment1.AllCategories
While Not DataEnvironment1.rsAllCategories.EOF
    List1.AddItem _
        DataEnvironment1.rsAllCategories.Fields("CategoryName")
    List1.ItemData(List1.NewIndex) = _
        DataEnvironment1.rsAllCategories.Fields("CategoryID")
    DataEnvironment1.rsAllCategories.MoveNext
Wend
DataEnvironment1.AllSuppliers
While Not DataEnvironment1.rsAllSuppliers.EOF
    List2.AddItem _
        DataEnvironment1.rsAllSuppliers.Fields("CompanyName")
    List2.ItemData(List2.NewIndex) = _
        DataEnvironment1.rsAllSuppliers.Fields("SupplierID")
    DataEnvironment1.rsAllSuppliers.MoveNext
Wend
End Sub
```

When the user selects one or more items in either list and clicks the corresponding button, the program builds an SQL statement to retrieve the products in the selected categories (or by the selected suppliers). This SQL statement is used to build the SelProducts Recordset, as shown in Listing 9.2. After the rsSelProducts Recordset has been created, it is used to populate the DataGrid control.

LISTING 9.2   **Building an SQL Statement on the Fly**

```
Private Sub bySupplier_Click()
If List2.SelCount = 0 Then
    MsgBox "Please select one or more suppliers first"
    Exit Sub
End If
For i = 0 To List2.ListCount - 1
    If List2.Selected(i) Then
        selSuppliers = selSuppliers & List2.ItemData(i) & ", "
    End If
Next i
selSuppliers = Left(selSuppliers, Len(selSuppliers) - 2)
SQLcmd = "SELECT ProductName, UnitPrice, QuantityPerUnit " & _
        "FROM Products " & _
        "WHERE SupplierID IN (" & selSuppliers & ")"
DataEnvironment1.Commands(3).CommandText = SQLcmd
DataEnvironment1.Commands(3).CommandType = adCmdText
Set SelProducts = DataEnvironment1.Commands(3).Execute
PopulateDGrid
End Sub
```

The PopulateGrid() subroutine populates the DataGrid control and sets the width of the various columns. You can open the project in the Visual Basic IDE and examine the code (it's worth taking a look at the code, which uses the Columns collection to access individual columns and set their properties).

ADO Error Handling

Error handling is one of the most important topics of any language, and I'm assuming you're familiar with Visual Basic's error handling capabilities (error trapping). ADO, however, is a database access component, and it sits between your application and a provider. The provider is a driver (a program); different databases come with different drivers. Each database has different capabilities, and ADO's role is to make all databases look the same to your application. This is especially difficult because each provider raises different errors. In addition to provider-specific errors, ADO itself can raise errors. This means that there are two types of errors you must handle: ADO errors and provider-specific errors. ADO errors are reported to Visual Basic and generate runtime errors, which you can trap in your VB code and handle as usual. Provider-specific errors are stored in the Errors collection of the Connection object. This means that as you code, you should know which operations cause ADO errors and which ones cause provider-specific errors. This is especially important since not all provider-specific errors raise runtime errors in VB. Most provider-specific errors cause VB runtime errors, but the Err object contains information about the most recent error, whereas the Errors collection of the Connection object may contain multiple errors raised by the same operation. Most ADO errors are handled through Visual Basic's Err object and the error-trapping mechanism built into the language. In complicated situations you may have to examine the Errors collection to find out exactly what has happened.

Let's start with the ADO error codes and their descriptions. Table 9.1 summarizes the errors that ADO passes to Visual Basic. These are runtime errors, which you can trap from within your VB code, and you'll see how to handle them in the second half of this chapter.

TABLE 9.1: The ADO Error Codes and Descriptions

Constant	Error Number	Description
adErrInvalidArgument	3001	The application is using arguments that are of the wrong type, are out of acceptable range, or are in conflict with one another.
adErrNoCurrentRecord	3021	Either BOF or EOF is True; or the current record has been deleted; or the operation requested by the application requires a current record.
adErrIllegalOperation	3219	The operation requested by the application is not allowed in this context.
adErrInTransaction	3246	The application cannot explicitly close a Connection object while in the middle of a transaction.
adErrFeatureNotAvailable	3251	The operation requested by the application is not supported by the provider.
adErrItemNotFound	3265	ADO could not find the object in the collection corresponding to the name or ordinal reference requested by the application.
adErrObjectInCollection	3367	Can't append. The object is already in the collection.
adErrObjectNotSet	3420	The object referenced by the application no longer points to a valid object.
adErrDataConversion	3421	The application is using a value of the wrong type for the current operation.
adErrObjectClosed	3704	The operation requested by the application is not allowed if the object is closed.
adErrObjectOpen	3705	The operation requested by the application is not allowed if the object is open.
adErrProviderNotFound	3706	ADO could not find the specified provider.
adErrBoundToCommand	3707	The application cannot change the ActiveConnection property of a Recordset object with a Command object as its source.
adErrInvalidParamInfo	3708	The application has improperly defined a Parameter object.
adErrInvalidConnection	3709	The application requested an operation on an object with a reference to a closed or invalid Connection object.

The descriptions of the errors are quite thorough. The two errors you'll be getting most often are the errors 3704 and 3705. `Error 3704` occurs when you attempt to access a Recordset that hasn't been set yet. `Error 3705` occurs when you attempt to change the data source of a Recordset. You must first close the Recordset, then change its data source. To handle ADO errors, insert an `On Error Goto` statement to redirect program control to an error handler.

To handle provider-specific errors, use the `On Error Resume Next` statement and examine the Connection.Errors collection after each operation that could have raised a provider-specific error. The Errors collection is made up of Error objects, which display the properties listed in Table 9.2.

TABLE 9.2:   The properties of the Error Object

Property	Description
Description	This property returns the description of the error and it's set either by ADO or a provider. Providers are responsible for passing specific error text to ADO. ADO adds an Error object to the Errors collection for each provider error or warning it receives.
HelpContext, HelpFile	Indicates the help file and topic associated with an Error object. HelpContextID returns a context ID, as a Long value, for a topic in a Help file. HelpFile is the path to a Help file.
NativeError	This property returns the provider-specific error's number. Consult the documentation of the provider for information on specific error codes.
Number	This is the provider-specific error number and you can use it in your error-handling routine to determine the error that has occurred.
Source	Indicates the name of the object or application that originally generated an error. Use the Source property on an Error object to determine the name of the object or application that originally generated an error. For ADO errors, this property value will be ADODB.ObjectName, where ObjectName is the name of the object that triggered the error.
SQLState	This property indicates the SQL state for a given Error object and it returns a five-character string that follows the ANSI SQL standard. Use the SQLState property to read the five-character error code that the provider returns when an error occurs during the processing of an SQL statement.

To find out all the errors in the Errors collection, use a loop like the following one:

```
For Each objError In CN.Errors
    Debug.Print "Number " & objError.Number
    Debug.Print "Decription " & objError.Description
    Debug.Print "Source " & objError.Source
    Debug.Print "Native Error " & objError.NativeError
    Debug.Print "SQLState " & objError.SQLState
Next
```

The Errors collection is cleared every time an operation causes a new provider-specific error. Operations that complete successfully do not clear the Errors collection.

Multiuser Considerations

In this section you are going to explore the behavior of different types of cursors when you program them from within your VB application. All cursors are update-able. It doesn't make any difference if it resides on the client or the server, or whether it's a dynamic, keyset, static, or forward-only cursor. If it's not a read-only cursor, it can be used to update the underlying tables.

Updating the underlying tables through a cursor is not trivial. When many users are accessing the same tables, any of the following may happen:

- One user edits a row and wants to commit the changes to the database. Does the application know that another user has already modified the same row since it was last read? And if the application detects it, what should it do? In most cases we go ahead and overwrite other people's changes. But there are situations, as in reservation applications, where this is not an option. You should be able to find out whether someone else has touched the row we edited since we read it last. If another user has already changed the same row, the application should be able to warn the user and offer a few options.

- While one user is editing a row, another user might actually delete the very same row. This is an even more difficult situation, although quite rare. Why would a user edit a row in a table, when another user thinks that the row shouldn't even be there? Rare as this case is, your application should be able to handle this extreme situation. Ideally, you should offer users the option to add the row that was deleted by someone else. While a user thinks he's updating a row, your code is actually inserting a new one. At the very least, the application should let the user know what happened and cancel the operation.

Let's see how ADO updates tables through the various types of cursors. We are going to use the Customers application we developed in the Customers project of Chapter 6, "Programming with the ADO Objects." We'll simply change the type and location of the cursor, then see the error messages we get back from the server and the code to handle them. We'll use SQL Server in the examples of this chapter to see what happens in a real client/server environment.

Working with Client-Side Cursors

Let's start our exploration of the various types of cursors with an application we developed earlier in the book. Open the Customers application (it's in the folder of Chapter 6 on the CD). Open the DataEnvironment Designer and right-click the All-Customers object. Switch to the Advanced tab of its property pages and make sure the Cursor Location is set to client-side, and the Lock Type is set to Optimistic, as shown in Figure 9.2.

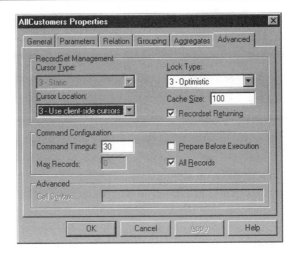

FIGURE 9.2:

The CursorLocation and Lock-Type properties are the two most important properties of a Recordset.

Deleting Rows

Let's see how the basic operations are performed through this type of Recordset. Run the application and delete a customer. Because customers can't be removed from the Customers table (they are linked to the Orders table), you'll get the following error message:

```
DELETE statement conflicted with COLUMN REFERENCE constraint
'FK_Orders_Customers'. The conflict occurred in database 'Northwind',
table 'Orders', column 'CustomerID'.
```

This error's number is 3604 (actually, it's a large negative value, from which you must subtract the constant vbObjectError). Your application should trap this error, display the appropriate message to the user, and abort the operation. To abort the operation, you must call the CancelUpdate method of the Recordset object. If you don't, the Recordset's current row will be a deleted one, and you'll get the same error message as soon as you attempt to call one of the navigational methods. Listing 9.3 shows the code behind the Delete button.

LISTING 9.3   Deleting a Row in a Client-Side Cursor

```
Private Sub bttnDelete_Click()
    reply = MsgBox("Record will be deleted permanently. Proceed?",
vbYesNo)
    If reply = vbYes Then
        On Error Resume Next
        DataEnvironment1.rsAllCustomers.Delete
        If Err.Number <> 0 Then
```

```
            MsgBox "Could not delete record" & vbCrLf & _
                "ERROR # " & Err.Number - vbObjectError & _
                vbCrLf & Err.Description
            DataEnvironment1.rsAllCustomers.CancelUpdate
        End If
    End If
End Sub
```

Now we'll examine what happens when you attempt to delete a row that has already been deleted by another user. Since all customers in this application are linked to one or more invoices, we must add a new customer that we can delete later. Add a new customer by clicking the Add Customer button. Specify a valid customer (a unique ID and a company name). Then switch to the SQL Enterprise Manager, open the Customers table (you may have to click the Run button to refresh the grid with the customers), and locate the new customer. Delete it by pressing the Del button; this action mimics deletion by another user. Click the Run button to make sure that the row is gone, and then return to the VB application. Click the Delete Customer button to delete the new customer, pretending we don't know it has already been deleted. After confirming your desire to delete the current customer, you will get the following runtime error:

```
The specified row could not be located for updating: Some values may
have been changed since it was last read.
```

This is error number 3640. If you ignore this error, you won't be able to move to another row. You must call the CancelUpdate method to cancel the pending operation, as shown in the previous listing.

Add a few new customers and then delete them directly from your VB application (no need to experiment with the SQL Enterprise Manager any longer. The VB program can handle deletions on its own). If you attempt to navigate through the rows of the Customers table with the Next and Previous buttons, you'll realize that sometimes the navigational buttons don't take you to the previous/next row. This happens when the next and previous rows have been deleted. When you move to the next row, for example, and this row has been deleted, ADO "parks" on the current row. Actually, it moves to the deleted row, but it's smart enough not to bind the controls to the deleted row. Keep moving in the same direction. After you have gone through all the deleted rows in the direction of the navigation, you will see the fields of the first valid row it lands on.

The short version of the story is that rows are not actually removed from client-side cursors. They are marked as deleted so that you can no longer land on them, but they are still part of the cursors. (In case you're wondering, no, you can't restore the deleted rows from the cursor).

Since you can't remove them from the cursors, there should be a way to skip them and land on the first valid row in the direction of the movement. The simplest method is to keep calling the same navigational method (MoveNext or MovePrevious) while the current row is deleted. To find out whether a row in a client-side cursor has been deleted, examine its Status property. If its value is adRecDBDeleted, it means the row is invalid. Listing 9.4 shows the revised code for the Next button.

LISTING 9.4   Skipping Deleted Rows during Navigation

```
Private Sub bttnNext_Click()
    DataEnvironment1.rsAllCustomers.MoveNext
    While _
        DataEnvironment1.rsAllCustomers.Status = adRecDBDeleted _
        And Not DataEnvironment1.rsAllCustomers.EOF
            DataEnvironment1.rsAllCustomers.MoveNext
    Wend
    If DataEnvironment1.rsAllCustomers.EOF Then
        DataEnvironment1.rsAllCustomers.MoveLast
    End If
End Sub
```

Updating Rows

If you edit a customer, then the changes will be committed to the database as soon as the Update method of the Recordset object is called. But let's interfere with the edit process. Click the Edit Customer button, change a field's value, and then switch to the SQL Enterprise Manager. Open the Customers table, locate the same row you're editing in your application, edit one of the fields you have already changed in the VB application, and move to another row. The changes have been committed to the database.

Now switch back to the VB application and click the OK button. This time you'll get the following error message:

```
The specified row could not be located for updating: Some values may
have been changed since it was last read.
```

The error number is 3640 again. Here's what happened. On the VB Form, you're editing the TextBoxes. Even though they are bound to the database, they do not reflect the actual values in the underlying table, because the cursor resides on the client. That's why you can't see the latest values of the fields on the Form. What you see are the values of the fields when the cursor was read—which is when the Form was loaded. Therefore, when ADO attempted to save the edited row, it found out that the original values of certain fields were no longer the same as they were when the row was read from the table. This caused it to generate the error message.

TIP

If you change some fields from within the VB application and different ones from within SQL Server's Enterprise Manager, then the update operation will not fail. SQL Server compares each field's original value to the value in the cursor to determine whether it can update it or not. If the two values match, it means that the field hasn't been changed. If not, then someone has changed the field since it was read into the cursor and it doesn't update it.

To commit the changes, you must call the Update method. If the update fails, then you must call the CancelUpdate method to abort the operation. Listing 9.5 shows the code behind the OK button.

LISTING 9.5   **Updating a Row in a Client-Side Cursor**

```
Private Sub bttnOK_Click()
    On Error Resume Next
    DataEnvironment1.rsAllCustomers.Update
    If Err.Number <> 0 Then
        If DataEnvironment1.rsAllCustomers.EditMode = _
                adEditAdd Then
            MsgBox "Could not add record" & vbCrLf & _
                    Err.Description
        Else
            MsgBox "Could not save changes." & _
                    vbCrLf & Err.Description
        End If
        DataEnvironment1.rsAllCustomers.CancelUpdate
        DataEnvironment1.rsAllCustomers.Move 0
    Else
        DataEnvironment1.rsAllCustomers.Resync adAffectCurrent
    End If
    ShowButtons
End Sub
```

In the previous listing, notice that the OK button is used to end both the addition of a new row and the editing of an existing one. The program simply displays a different message for each, but it handles both operations by calling the CancelUpdate method. To see why you must call the CancelUpdate method, comment it out temporarily (insert an apostrophe at the beginning of the line), as well as the following line that calls the Move method. Edit a record in the VB Form, then edit the same field(s) of the same row in SQL Server's Enterprise Manager. Then, return to the VB application. Click OK to commit the changes. ADO will generate an error message indicating that it couldn't update the row, but the application will not crash.

If you attempt to move to another row with the navigational keys, you'll get an error message again. An update operation hasn't completed successfully. Because of this pending operation on the current row, ADO refuses to move to another row. The line that cancels the operation is actually required. As you saw in Chapter 6, the Data Form Wizard doesn't insert this line. It simply takes for granted the assumption of the optimistic locking mechanism—namely, that no two users will attempt to update the same row at the same time. This is a reasonable assumption, but it's only an assumption. The locking mechanism doesn't guarantee that two users will not attempt to update the database at once—it *assumes* that this will not happen. You must take action from within your code, or else a runtime error will be generated eventually.

If the Update method terminates successfully, the following line synchronizes the Recordset with the underlying row:

```
DataEnvironment1.rsAllCustomers.Resync adAffectCurrent
```

Why do we need this line? Let's say you've changed one field in the table and another user has changed another field. Your update will not fail. Yet, the user will see the new values of the fields that were edited on the client, but the old values of the remaining fields. To make sure users view the latest version of the row after an update, call the Resync method for the specific row.

You will probably claim that this is a client-side cursor, and as such, we know that it won't always be up-to-date. Then again, when a row is modified, users expect to see the current field values, so it's not a bad idea to synchronize the row. Notice that we're not synchronizing the entire cursor, just a single line. This is what the adAffectCurrent argument does: it synchronizes the current row only. Had we synchronized the entire cursor, we would defeat the purpose of the client-side cursor.

Updating the Data-Bound Controls

You will probably be surprised to know that the controls on the Form aren't updated at this point. The client-side cursor has been updated, but the data-bound control displays the old values. To see that this is true, let's print the values of the fields in the cursor so that we will have them in front of us to compare once we edit the rows. To do this, insert the following lines after the line that calls the Resync method:

```
For i = 0 To DataEnvironment1.rsAllCustomers.Fields.Count - 1
    Debug.Print DataEnvironment1.rsAllCustomers.Fields(i).Value
Next
```

Now, run the program again, edit the same row from within both the VB application and SQL Server's Enterprise Manager, then read the values of the fields both on the Form's data-bound controls and on the Immediate window. They will be different, as shown in Figure 9.3. I've changed the Region field from "OR" to "OREGON" in the Enterprise Manager. The result is the annoying discrepancy shown in the figure.

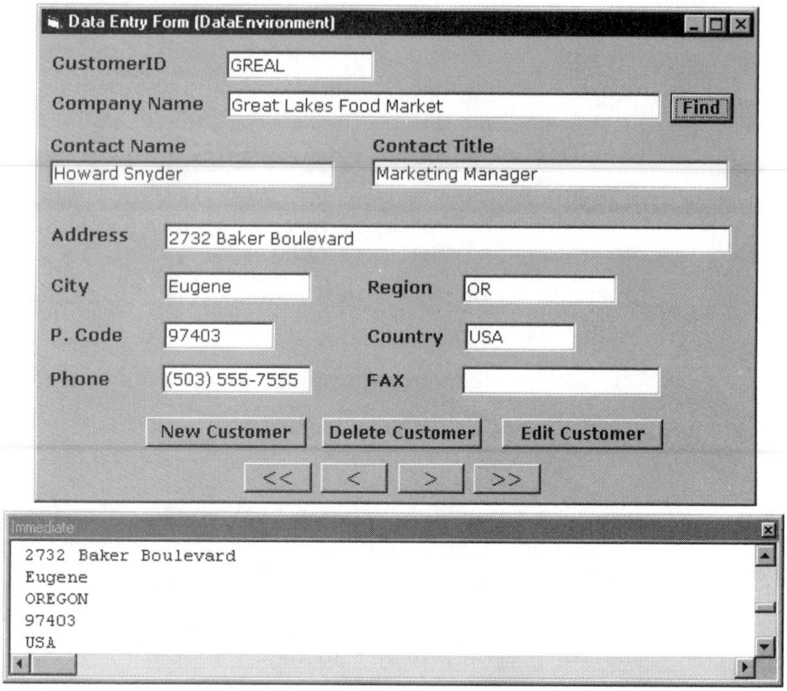

FIGURE 9.3:

Data-bound controls are not refreshed automatically when you call the Recordset object's Resync method.

To force a data-bound control to read its value from the underlying cursor, you must set one of its data-binding properties. The following lines set the DataField property of the data-bound controls on the Form:

```
txtCustID.DataField = "CustomerID"
txtCustName.DataField = "CompanyName"
txtContactName.DataField = "ContactName"
```

You should place these lines in a subroutine, say the ReBind() subroutine, and call it after each call to the Resync method. You can actually rebind the controls by setting their DataSource property too. There's a more elegant method to set the DataField property of all TextBox controls on the Form, which is shown next:

```
Dim ctrl As Control
For Each ctrl In Me.Controls
    If ctrl.Tag = "TextBox" Then
        Set ctrl.DataSource = DataEnvironment1.rsAllCustomers
    End If
Next
```

For this code to work, you must set the Tag property of each data-bound TextBox control to the string TextBox (or any other string that uniquely identifies the data-bound controls on the Form).

Update Anyway!

What do you do when your application can't update a row because someone else has changed one of its fields already? If you attempt to update the table again, you'll keep getting the same error message. As long as the underlying field values are different than the ones you read, you won't be able to update the table. Most users would like to have the option "Update Anyway!" on their Forms. To update the table regardless of the differences in the underlying fields, you must:

1. Store the new values into local variables.

2. Read the row again.

3. Move the values you have stored from the variables to the cursor.

4. Update the table again.

Fairly complicated, isn't it? ADO should provide a method to update a row unconditionally, but it doesn't. If it did, I bet it would be the most abused method. Still, you *can* use the Resync method to synchronize only the underlying values. The Resync method, whose syntax is shown next, accepts an argument that determines which values will be synchronized to the database fields:

```
ADODC1.Resync affectRecords, resyncValues
```

By default, the Resync method synchronizes the Recordset's values with the actual field values in the database by reading the rows again from the database. The default value of the *resyncValues* argument is adResyncAllValues. The underlying values are also synchronized.

The other value of the *resyncValues* argument is adResyncUnderlyingValues. It causes the Resync method to synchronize only the UnderlyingValue properties of the Recordset's rows. The practical value of this form of the Resync method is that you can make ADO think that your changes are the most recent ones, in which case they'll be committed to the database successfully.

Here's why this trick works. When you call the Update method, ADO compares the UnderlyingValue property of all the fields in the current row to the actual field values in the database. If they are the same, it means no other user has touched the row since your application read it and ADO can commit the changes. If they differ, it means that someone else has modified the row since your application read it, and ADO refuses to update the row. Actually, it generates the runtime error 3640, as you saw previously. By synchronizing the UnderlyingValue properties, you fool ADO into thinking that you have just read the row and edited it instantly. In most cases, your changes will be committed successfully to the database.

This technique is most useful with disconnected Recordsets, and we'll discuss it in more detail in Chapter 11, "Disconnected Recordsets and Remote Data

Access." You will also find an example of this technique in action in the same chapter.

Adding Rows

Let's add a new row with the New Customer button. When this button is clicked, all data-bound controls on the Form are cleared in preparation of the new customer's data. If you fail to specify a company name, you'll get the error message 3604:

```
Cannot insert the value NULL into column 'CompanyName', table 'North-
wind.dbo.Customers'; column does not allow nulls. INSERT fails.
```

A similar error will be generated for all field values that violate a constraint. If you specify an ID that exists already, you'll get the same error number, but with the following description:

```
Violation of PRIMARY KEY constraint 'PK_Customers'. Cannot insert
duplicate key in object 'Customers'.
```

It's rather confusing to have to handle the same error number with different descriptions. You should simply display a message indicating that the operation can't be completed, followed by the message returned by ADO (the average user will not understand what this message says, so you may opt to display a custom message).

Both errors can be handled easily. The user must terminate the Add operation and return to the edit mode. The user can either change the value of the field that caused the problem and update the table again, or cancel the operation. Before you exit, though, you must call the CancelUpdate method to discard the new row that was created by the AddNew method (see the OK button's code in Listing 9.3).

Refreshing the Cursor

If your application is using a client-side cursor, you should probably provide a Refresh button. A user may keep the cursor open for editing for extended periods of time. In the meantime, the underlying data may undergo numerous changes. If the application has a Refresh button, the user can retrieve the most up-to-date values from the table.

You may be thinking, "Isn't this button going to confuse the users?" I will agree, users need not be concerned with cursor locations and cursor types; but sometimes you'll have to explain a few basic capabilities of your application.

To refresh the entire Recordset, call the Resync method, specifying the adAffect-All argument, which causes ADO to refresh the entire Recordset. The code behind the Refresh button is shown next:

```
Private Sub bttnRefresh_Click()
    DataEnvironment1.rsAllCustomers.Resync adAffectAll
End Sub
```

Working with Server-Side Cursors

Now we'll explore the behavior of a server-side cursor under the same circumstances discussed in the preceding sections. As you should expect, server-side cursors behave differently because they reside on the same machine as the SQL Server and they can access the tables immediately.

Deleting Rows

Let's start with the deletion of a row that's linked to the Orders table and can't be removed from the table. If you attempt to remove a row from the Customers table, you'll get error 3617 with the following (hardly descriptive) message:

    Errors occurred

We can cancel the deletion of a row that can't be removed because it violates a primary/foreign key constraint using the CancelUpdate method. After canceling a deletion operation, you can use the navigational keys to move to another row. If you attempt to add a new row immediately after canceling the deletion of a row, you'll get the VB error message shown in Figure 9.4. This error message simply tells you that there's a row pending deletion. Unless this row is removed, you won't be able to add new row.

FIGURE 9.4:

This error message will be generated if you don't call the CancelUpdate method after the unsuccessful deletion of a row.

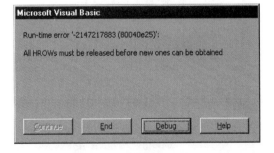

If you delete a row from this Recordset, it will be removed from the cursor too. Therefore, you need not insert the loop that skips the deleted records in the Next and Previous buttons. If the deletion fails, we must call the CancelUpdate method to restore the row that has been marked for deletion.

Updating Rows

Editing a row generally poses no problem. If the edit operation fails, however, it means someone else has edited the same row since we last read it. In this case, we should be able to retrieve the latest version of the row and display it on the Form. Unfortunately, dynamic cursors don't support the Resync method. The

Move 0 method will not force the row to be refreshed. The row will be read from the cache, and we'll get the values of the fields as they were before we started editing them, not the current values of the fields. You must try to move to the next or previous row and then back to the current one using the following syntax:

```
DataEnvironment1.rsAllCustomers.CancelUpdate
DataEnvironment1.rsAllCustomers.MoveNext
DataEnvironment1.rsAllCustomers.MovePrevious
```

This is a dynamic cursor, and it should fetch each row from the table. This looks like a neat trick, but it won't work. Can you guess why not? It won't work because the default cache size for the rsAllCustomers Recordset is 100 rows. Unless you're on the first row in the cache and you call the MovePrevious method (or you're on the last row and you call the MoveNext method), ADO isn't going to read rows from the actual table. The solution is to change the size of the cache. Open the DataEnvironment Designer's window, right-click the rsAllCustomers object and select Properties. In the Advanced tab of its property pages, set the cache size to 1 row. If you run the application again, it will work as intended. Every time an edit operation fails, it will display the row's current field values in the table. The complete listing of the OK button's Click event handler is shown next in Listing 9.6.

LISTING 9.6   **Updating a Row in a Server-Side Cursor**

```
Private Sub bttnOK_Click()
    On Error Resume Next
    DataEnvironment1.rsAllCustomers.Update
    If Err.Number <> 0 Then
        If DataEnvironment1.rsAllCustomers.EditMode = _
                adEditAdd Then
            MsgBox "Could not add record" & vbCrLf & _
                Err.Description
        Else
            MsgBox "Could not save changes." & _
                vbCrLf & Err.Description
        End If
        DataEnvironment1.rsAllCustomers.CancelUpdate
        DataEnvironment1.rsAllCustomers.MoveNext
        DataEnvironment1.rsAllCustomers.MovePrevious
    End If
    ShowButtons
    LockFields
End Sub
```

Specifying a cache size of 1 row defeats the purpose of the cache, right? The most efficient solution to the problem of updating server-side cursors is to use stored procedures, or execute an action query that inserts a new row directly against the database. If you want to use data-bound controls with a server-side cursor, you should set the cursor's cache size to 1.

Let's check out what happens when an edit operation fails because the current row has been removed from the table. Add a new customer, then edit it. Switch to the SQL Enterprise Manager and delete the new customer from the Customers table. Then switch back to the application and click OK to commit the changes. As expected, you'll get an error message. Then, the MoveNext/MovePrevious methods will be called. The MoveNext will take you to the next row momentarily. The MovePrevious method will return to the previous valid row, which obviously is not the one just deleted.

The MoveNext/MovePrevious combination may fail if you're on the last row. In this case you should call the two methods in reverse order. Insert the appropriate error-trapping code to make sure you always land on a valid row.

Adding Rows

Adding rows to a server-side cursor is fairly simple. The AddNew method creates an empty Recordset in the table, and you edit it live. When the Update method is called, the new row is committed to the database. Only one of two things can go wrong at this point: either one or more fields might be invalid (they violate a constraint, for example), or you might specify an invalid key. If your application generates primary keys, you will probably search the table for the new key and commit the new row only if this key does not already exist. Even then it is possible (although very unlikely) that another user will have added a row with the same key after you have verified that your key is not being used, and before you call the Update method. The only approach that will work in all cases is to call the Update method anyway and see whether ADO returns an error message about duplicate keys. If it does, the primary key you've chosen already exists in the database.

This will not happen if you let the DBMS generate keys for you (an Identity field in SQL Server, or an AutoNumber field in Access). These keys, which are called surrogate keys, are totally meaningless, but they are very convenient. Primary keys are used to link tables, and we're never interested in their actual values. Sometimes the entity stored in a table may have a primary key of its own. Books, for example, have ISBNs, which are unique by definition. Of course users make mistakes, and the "unique" value may already have been used. So, to make your application totally failsafe, you must still verify that an ISBN value has not already been used by mistake with another book.

As with client-side cursors, a new row is automatically committed to the database as soon as the application moves to another row (by calling a navigational method, or the Find method, for example). It is strongly suggested that you disable the navigational keys while a row is being added or edited.

How About the ADO Data Control?

The application we used in this section is based on the DataEnvironment objects. Most developers will use the Connection and Command objects of the DataEnvironment object to build database applications. If you want to use the ADO Data Control instead, the same techniques will work as described. You can place an ADO Data Control on the Form, set it up to see the Customers table in the Northwind database, and then replace all the instances of:

```
DataEnvironment1.rsAllCustomers
```

in the code with the following expression:

```
ADODC1.Recordset
```

This is the only change required, and the new project that's based on the ADO Data Control will work as before. The two expressions evaluate to a Recordset object, and they support the same properties and methods. There is one difference I should mention, however. Remember the loop that skips the deleted rows in the navigational buttons? This loop is not needed when you use the ADO Data Control. The control will skip the deleted rows automatically, and it will land on the first valid row in the direction of navigation in the Recordset.

You may choose to use the ADO Data Control to simplify the testing of an application, but manipulate the Recordset via VB code. In the production version of the application, you should hide the Data controls by setting their Visible property to False.

ADO Events

It is also possible to program the ADO objects and the ADO Data Control using events. Both objects support several events with which you can simplify certain programming tasks. Like the properties and methods, the ADO objects and ADO Data Control share the same events, which are discussed here. These events can be categorized according to the object that fires them:

- The Connection object events, which are fired when you establish asynchronous connections, or execute commands asynchronously

- The Recordset object events, which are fired when the current row changes (because a Move method has been called, for example), or when the underlying Recordset is about to be updated

NOTE   The Command object does not raise any events. To execute commands asynchronously, use the Connection object's Execute method, as described in Chapter 10, "Making the Most of Stored Procedures."

You will find the complete list of events later in this section, but the Connection object and Recordset object events have common characteristics that I will discuss first. Many of the ADO events are paired. One of the events in the pair is fired right before an action takes place, and the other event is fired when the action has completed. The events fired prior to the action begin with the prefix "Will," and the events fired upon completion end with the suffix "Complete." The events WillChangeRecord and RecordChangeComplete are an example.

Another common characteristic of the ADO events is that they accept a large number of arguments, which complicate their coding a little (and sometimes considerably). If you have programmed the ADO Data Control's events, you know that the ADO objects support the same events. They are also equivalent to the DAO (the older Data Access Objects component) events—only ADO recognizes more events and offers finer control over the actions it performs on the database.

To take advantage of the ADO events in your code, you must declare variables that represent the Recordset and Connection events with the WithEvents keywords. If the following declaration appears in the Form's declarations section, then its name will appear in the Code window's Object list and you can select the event you want to program in the window's Events list, as shown in Figure 9.5.

FIGURE 9.5:

The ADO Recordset object's events

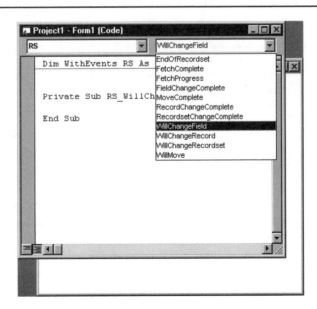

Using ADO Events

We have not used events in the examples of this book, with the exception of asynchronous operations. The ADO events are available and you can use them in programming your applications, but most developers don't use them extensively. As I explained already, there's no reason to code the WillChangeField or WillChangeRecordset event to validate the data. Validate your data with your own subroutine, when the user clicks the OK button to commit the changes. If you're using the ADO Data Control and allow users to add new records by setting the EOFAction property to adDoAddNew, then you must use the Will events to find out when certain actions will take place. Other than monitoring the progress of asynchronous operations, the ADO events are not used extensively in database programming, especially if you consider that databases are usually updated through stored procedures.

The Will and Complete Events

In general, the Will events let you examine what's about to happen and, optionally, cancel the operation from within the event's handler. The Complete events notify your application that the operation completed, and you can examine the error code returned by the event (if any).

The most confusing aspect of the Will and Complete events is that the same events may be fired more than once for the same operation. Each time this happens they are being called for a different reason, which means you must examine the adReason argument to find out why they were called and insert the appropriate code for each reason. Another potentially confusing situation is that an operation you cancel may still fire events. If you decide to cancel an update from within the WillChangeField event handler, the FieldChangeComplete event will still be fired to indicate that the operation has completed (unsuccessfully, but it has completed anyway).

Let's consider for a moment the WillChangeField and FieldChangeComplete events. Some programmers go as far as programming the WillChangeField event to examine whether the field should be changed or not. I think you should design your application so that it knows when a field can change or not. When a field shouldn't change, turn on the Locked property of the control to which the field is bound. For example, you should use an Edit button on the Form so that the user will signal his intention to start editing a record. If a field's value depends on the contents of other controls on the Form, use its Change or LostFocus events to determine whether the user can change its value. The benefit of this approach is that you can take immediate action, instead of deferring all validation until the moment when the user is ready to commit the changes to the database.

Some Common Event Arguments

In this section we are going to discuss some arguments that are used by a number of different events. These arguments apply to many operations and we can discuss them before we look at each event's description.

The adStatus Argument

When the event handler routine is called, the *adStatus* parameter is set to one of the informational values presented in Table 9.3.

TABLE 9.3: Values of the adStatus Argument on Input

Constant	Description
adStatusOK	This value indicates that the operation that caused the event completed successfully.
adStatusErrorsOccurred	This value indicates that the operation that caused the event did not complete successfully, or the operation was cancelled from within a Will event's code.
adStatusCantDeny	A Will event cannot request cancellation of the operation about to occur.

The *adStatus* parameter can also be set from within the event handler to pass information to back to the ADO. You can set the *adStatus* parameter to one of the values presented in Table 9.4.

TABLE 9.4: Values of the adStatus Argument on Output

Constant	Description
adStatusUnwantedEvent	Requests that this event handler will receive no further notifications.
adStatusCancel	Requests cancellation of the operation that is about to occur.

The pError Argument

The *pError* argument is a reference to an ADO Error object containing details about why the operation failed if the status parameter equals adStatusErrorsOccurred. If an operation has completed successfully, the *pError* argument is not set and you should not access it from within your code. If you do, you'll get a runtime VB error because you've attempted to access an object that hasn't been set.

```
If status = adStatusErrorsOccurred Then
    {process pError}
End If
```

The Object Argument

This argument is an object variable representing the Connection or Recordset object to which the operation applies. Use this parameter to identify the specific object that raised the event, in case multiple objects fire the same event. If you have initiated two asynchronous connections, for example, you will receive two Connect-Complete events, one for each object. Use the event's object parameter to find out which connections has been established.

The adReason Argument

A number of actions can fire the same event. The WillChangeRecord event, for example, is fired when the current record is edited, as well as when it's deleted. To find out why an event was fired, use the *adReason* argument. Notice that events with an *adReason* parameter may be called several times for the same operation, but for a different reason each time.

The WillChangeRecord event handler, for instance, is called for operations that are about to do or undo the insertion, deletion, or modification of a record. Use the *adReason* argument to find out the operation that fired the event. You must return adStatusUnwantedEvent in the *adStatus* argument to request that an event handler without an *adReason* argument stop receiving event notifications. However, an event handler with an *adReason* argument may receive several notifications, each for a different reason. Therefore, you must return adStatusUnwantedEvent for each notification caused by a different reason.

For example, assume you have a WillChangeRecord event handler in your code. If you don't want to receive any further notifications whatsoever, simply code the following:

```
Set adStatus = adStatusUnwantedEvent
```

However, if you want to process events where the row is about to be deleted, but cancel notifications for all other reasons, then code the following:

```
if (adReason = adRsnDelete)
' Process an event for this reason.
...
else
' Stop receiving events for any other reason.
Set adStatus = adStatusUnwantedEvent
```

Table 9.5 summarizes the values of the *adReason* argument.

TABLE 9.5: The adReason Argument's Values

Constant	Description
adRsnAddNew	The AddNew method was called
adRsnClose	The Close method was called
adRsnDelete	The Delete method was called
adRsnFirstChange	The current row was changes for the first time
adRsnMove	The Move method was called
adRsnMoveFirst	The MoveFirst method was called
adRsnMoveLast	The MoveLast method was called
adRsnMoveNext	The MoveNext method was called
adRsnMovePrevious	The MovePrevious method was called
adRsnRequery	The Requery method was called
adRsnResync	The Resync method was called
adRsnUndoAddNew	The Cancel method was called after a call to the AddNew method
adRsnUndoDelete	The Delete method was called, and then cancelled with a call to the CancelUpdate or CancelBatch method
adRsnUndoUpdate	An Update method was called, and then cancelled with a call to the CancelUpdate or CancelBatch method
adRsnUpdate	The Update method was called

You may be wondering when you will receive an event notification with a parameter of adRsnUndoDelete or adRsnUndoAddNew. You may call the AddNew to add a new row. To commit the new record to the database, you must call the Update method. This method will fire a WillChangeRecordset event. Even though you have issued the Update method, the information passed back by the arguments of the WillChangeRecordset event handler may necessitate the abortion of the AddNew operation. Even so late in the process, you can abort the operation by calling the CancelUpdate method. If you do so, the RecordsetChangeComplete event will be fired, to notify your application that the original operation was cancelled. The *adReason* argument's value will be adRsnUndoAddNew.

Now we can examine the individual ADO events and their arguments in detail. In the following sections the events are grouped according to the operation that fires them.

Transaction Events

The following events are fired when you implement multiple actions as a transaction:

```
BeginTransComplete(TransactionLevel As Long, _
            pError As Error, adStatus As EventStatusEnum, _
            pConnection As Connection)
```

This event is fired to indicate that the BeginTransaction method has completed (in effect ADO started processing the transaction). *pConnection* is a reference to the Connection object that initiated the transaction. The *pError* and *adStatus* arguments were discussed earlier. The *TransactionLevel* argument, finally, indicates the transaction's depth when multiple transactions are nested.

```
CommitTransComplete(pError As Error, _
                adStatus As EventStatusEnum, _
                pConnection As Connection)
```

This event simply notifies your application that the transaction you initiated on the pConnection object was committed. The *adStatus* argument tells you whether the transaction was committed successfully and, if not, the *pError* Error object gives more information about the error.

You probably want to know how it's possible for a transaction to be committed unsuccessfully. The CommitTransComplete event simply tells your application that SQL Server has processed the transaction; even though the transaction itself may have failed. The CommitTransComplete event is raised in response to the Commit-Trans method, which signals your intention to commit the transaction. The transaction may fail because it violates a constraint in one of the tables involved. SQL Server will not process the transaction before you call the CommitTransaction method. The CommitTransComplete event notifies your code that the Commit-Transaction method has been processed, and it reports whether the transaction was successful or not.

```
RollbackTransComplete(pError As Error, _
            adStatus As EventStatusEnum, pConnection As Connection)
```

The RollbackTransComplete event is analogous to the CommitTransComplete event, but it's fired when a transaction is rolled back. Its arguments are the same as with the CommitTransComplete event.

Connection Events

The events of this section are fired when you establish and abort connections through the Connection object, or when you execute a command through the same object.

```
WillConnect(ConnectionString As String, UserID As String, _
            Password As String, Options As Long, _
            adStatus As EventStatusEnum, _
            pConnection As Connection)
```

This event is fired in response to the Connect method and notifies your application that a new connection is about to be established. The *ConnectionString*, *UserID*, and *Password* arguments contain all the information required to establish the connection, and *pConnection* is a reference to the Connection object whose Connect method you have called. This event isn't programmed frequently.

```
ConnectComplete(pError As Error, _
            adStatus As EventStatusEnum, _
            pConnection As Connection)
```

The ConnectComplete event is used in establishing asynchronous connections, as discussed in Chapter 10, "Making the Most of Stored Procedures." It notifies your code that a connection attempt has completed. Use the *adStatus* argument to find out whether the connection attempt was successful or not. If ADO wasn't able to connect successfully, you will find more information about the error in the *pError* argument.

```
Event Disconnect(adStatus As EventStatusEnum, _
            pConnection As Connection)
```

The Disconnect event is fired when a connection is closed with the Close method. The *pConnection* argument is a reference to the corresponding Connection object, and *adStatus* reports the success or failure of the Close Method.

```
WillExecute(Source As String, CursorType As CursorTypeEnum, _
            LockType As LockTypeEnum, Options As Long, _
            adStatus As EventStatusEnum, pCommand As Command, _
            pRecordset As Recordset, pConnection As Connection)
```

The WillExecute method is fired before a Command object is executed. The ExecuteComplete event is fired when the command's execution completes and is used in executing commands asynchronously.

The WillExecute event recognizes a number of arguments. The *CursorType* and *LockType* arguments are the values of the Recordset's CursorType and LockType properties. *pCommand* is a reference to the Command object on which you will execute the command; *pConnection* is a reference to the Connection object that's used for the execution of the command; and *pRecordset* is a Recordset object where the results of a query will be stored.

The *Source* argument is an SQL statement that is the name of a stored procedure or table. It specifies how the command will act on the database. Finally, *adStatus* returns information about the success or failure of the operation.

Recordset Events

The following events are fired while you're editing the fields of the current row in a Recordset object. The first group of Recordset events are the navigational events that are fired in response to Move methods, as well as when the end of the

Recordset is reached. The second group of Recordset events is fired in response to operations that update the tables.

```
WillMove(adReason As EventReasonEnum, _
        adStatus As EventStatusEnum, pRecordset As Recordset)
```

The *adReason* and *adStatus* arguments were explained earlier. The *pRecordset* is a reference to the Recordset object that fired the event.

```
MoveComplete(adReason As EventReasonEnum, pError As Error, _
        adStatus As EventStatusEnum, pRecordset As Recordset)
```

A WillMove or MoveComplete event is not fired only when you call one of the Recordset object's Move methods. It may also be fired by the following methods: Open, Bookmark, AddNew, and Requery. Setting any of the following properties will also fire these events, because they may cause the current row to change: Filter, Index, AbsolutePage, and AbsolutePosition.

```
EndOfRecordset(fMoreData As Boolean, _
        adStatus As EventStatusEnum, pRecordset As Recordset)
```

The EndOfRecordset event is fired when the end of the Recordset identified by the last argument has been reached. The *adStatus* event indicates whether the operation that fired the event completed successfully. The first argument emulates the behavior of the ADO Data Control's EOFAction property. Set the *fMoreData* argument to True to append a new empty row to the end of the Recordset (in effect, you'll move the end of the Recordset by one row).

A number of events are fired in pairs and are related to Field, Record, and Recordset changes. The WillChangeField and ChangeFieldComplete events are fired before and after ADO changes a field's value.

```
WillChangeField(cFields As Long, Fields, _
        adStatus As EventStatusEnum, pRecordset As Recordset)
```

```
FieldChangeComplete(cFields As Long, Fields, pError As Error, _
        adStatus As EventStatusEnum, pRecordset As Recordset)
```

In the above event, *cFields* represents the number of fields that will change value (or the number of fields that changed value in the FieldChangeComplete event). ADO raises a single event, regardless of how many fields you change in the current row. If you're changing multiple rows, then a pair of WillChangeField and FieldChangeComplete events will be fired for each row.

Likewise, the WillChangeRecord and RecordChangeComplete events are fired before and after one or more rows in the Recordset are changed. The WillChangeRecordset event is fired after the FieldChangeComplete event. If no field has been

changed by the operation (an Update operation, for example), then the WillChange-
eRecord and RecordChangeComplete events are not fired.

```
WillChangeRecord(adReason As EventReasonEnum, _
          cRecords As Long, adStatus As EventStatusEnum, _
          pRecordset As Recordset)

RecordChangeComplete(adReason As EventReasonEnum, _
          cRecords As Long, pError As Error, _
          adStatus As EventStatusEnum, pRecordset As Recordset)
```

The *adReason* argument indicates what action caused the row change. *cRecords* is the
number of records that will change (or the number of records that were changed in
the RecordChangeComplete event).

The WillChangeRecordset and RecordsetChangeComplete events are fired when
the Recordset changes. A Recordset can change when new rows are added to it or
deleted, not when individual rows are changed. When you Refresh a Recordset
object, for example, these two events should be fired once. If the Recordset's size
exceeds the size specified with the CacheSize property, then these events will be
fired each time a new group of rows is read from the cache. The smaller the Cache-
Size property, the more often these events are fired.

```
WillChangeRecordset(adReason As EventReasonEnum, _
          adStatus As EventStatusEnum, pRecordset As Recordset)

RecordsetChangeComplete(adReason As EventReasonEnum, _
          pError As Error, adStatus As EventStatusEnum, _
          pRecordset As Recordset)
```

The *adReason* argument specified the action that caused the Recordset to be
changed and can have one of the following values: *adRsnRequery*, *adRsnResync*,
adRsnClose, and *adRsnOpen*.

Asynchronous Operations' Events

The following events are fired by asynchronous operations, and you can use them
to monitor the progress of the operations.

```
Event FetchProgress(Progress As Long, MaxProgress As Long, _
          adStatus As EventStatusEnum, pRecordset As Recordset)
```

The Event FetchProgress is fired periodically during a lengthy asynchronous
operation to report how many more rows have been retrieved so far into the
Recordset represented by the *pRecordset* parameter. The number of rows is given
by the *Progress* argument, and the (anticipated) total number of rows in the Recordset is *MaxProgress*. You can express the progress of the operation with the fraction

Progress / MaxProgress, as long as *MaxProgress* is not zero. The *adStatus* argument should be adStatusFetching.

```
Event FetchComplete(pError As Error, _
            adStatus As EventStatusEnum, pRecordset As Recordset)
```

This Event FetchComplete event is fired when an asynchronous operation completes. The *pError* argument indicates a possible error, and you should examine it only if the *adStatus* argument is adStatusErrorsOccurred.

Worked Examples

This is the last of the basic ADO programming chapters in the book. In the second part of the book we'll cover a few advanced ADO topics, including hierarchical Recordsets and custom data-bound controls.

Before you move on to the second part of the book, you might want to read Part 4 (Chapters 17 and 18). Those chapters contain applications that combine many of the topics discussed in this book. I have designed a couple of projects that demonstrate not only how to use ADO in your applications, but also how to design data-browsing and -editing applications. The tutorial is written as a chapter, but it contains long code segments, so we've decided to move these examples in the last part of the book.

The first project is called DataEntryDemo.vbp, and it's a data-entry Form for the Biblio database. This application allows you to select rows by their title or ISBN. ISBNs are unique, and you can use them to select a single book's row. Searching with titles is substantially more complicated, because you can't expect users to enter the exact title of a book. Even then, you may face difficulties, as there are books with identical titles. The program retrieves all the titles that match the user-supplied criteria and displays them on a list. The user can then select a title with the mouse, see its details on the Form and, optionally, edit it. The same example demonstrates how to update multiple tables from within your application, as each book's information is distributed in four different tables (Titles, Authors, Publishers, and Title Author). You must manipulate all four tables each time the user edits an existing title or adds a new one.

The DataEntryDemo project demonstrates how to build a functional user interface without having to count on the limited navigational capabilities of the ADO Data Control. Figure 9.6 shows the main Form of the project with the list of titles that begin with the word "Mastering." After the user selects the desired title, the list contracts and the data-bound controls of the Form become visible.

Continued on next page

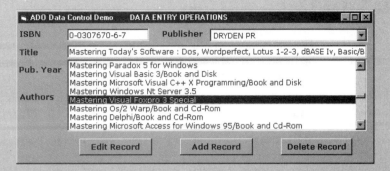

FIGURE 9.6:

Selecting a title in the DataEntryDemo project's main Form

The second example is an invoicing application, the Invoices project, that adds invoices to the Northwind database. The program's user interface is fairly simple, but as explained in the text, invoicing applications should be simple. (Can you imagine a clerk selecting product names with the mouse at a cash register?) The program assumes that the product IDs are available at the time the invoice is issued, and the only additional piece of information required is the quantity (and, optionally, the discount). In a real-world application, the product IDs would be entered with a bar-code scanner. The main Form of the Invoices project is shown Figure 9.7.

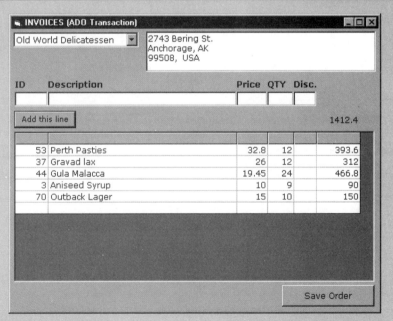

FIGURE 9.7:

Placing an invoice with in the Northwind database

The application must update two tables in the Northwind database, the Orders and Order Details tables. These two actions must be performed as a transaction: They must both succeed or they must both fail. You will see how to implement the transaction both with ADO, and by calling a stored procedure.

Summary

This chapter concludes the second part of the book. So far, you've learned how to manipulate databases through the ADO interface and to develop database applications. If you need to look up the ADO members, consult the Appendix on the companion CD. This appendix summarizes all ADO properties and methods and their syntax.

The next part of the book covers some advanced ADO topics, such as hierarchical Recordsets and custom data-bound controls. In this part of the book, you will learn how to write Classes that encapsulate the data-access operations, and custom data-bound controls, which will simplify the development of client applications. You will also learn how to access databases remotely, through the Remote Data Services (RDS) component.

PART II

Advanced Data-Access Techniques

CHAPTER

TEN

Shaping Your Data

- Designing hierarchical Recordsets

- The SHAPE command

- Using the MSHFlexGrid control

- Nested hierarchies

- Using parameterized commands

- Scanning hierarchical Recordsets

- Building forms with hierarchical Recordsets

The Recordsets you have explored so far in this book are flat and uniform: they contain the same number of columns in each row, and all columns are single-valued. A single-valued (or scalar) column contains a value with the same type (a numeric value, a string, date, image and so on). As you will see, it is possible for a column to contain an entire Recordset. This type of Recordset is called *hierarchical*, or *shaped*, and it allows you to store complex structured data. Well, you don't exactly store data in a hierarchical Recordset directly. You retrieve data from multiple tables in your database and store them in a hierarchical Recordset along with their structure.

Let's say you want to retrieve all the orders placed with the Northwind corporation. Retrieving Order IDs from the Orders table is of very little use—you won't see who placed the order (just the customer's ID), nor will you see the order's details. What you need is a list of customers, the orders for each customer, and the details of each order. You've examined the SQL statement that retrieves this information from the Northwind database in Chapter 5, but I repeat it here for your convenience:

```
USE NORTHWIND
SELECT CompanyName, Orders.OrderID, ProductName,
    UnitPrice=ROUND([Order Details].UnitPrice, 2),
    Quantity,
    Discount=CONVERT(int, Discount * 100),
    ExtendedPrice=ROUND(CONVERT(money, Quantity *
                (1 - Discount) * [Order Details].UnitPrice), 2)
FROM Products, [Order Details], Customers, Orders
WHERE [Order Details].ProductID = Products.ProductID And
        [Order Details].OrderID = Orders.OrderID And
        Orders.CustomerID=Customers.CustomerID
ORDER BY Customers.CustomerID, Orders.OrderID
```

This statement will return a Recordset with a uniform structure, which is shown here (I've copied the first few lines of the cursor returned by the query and have abbreviated the product names to fit each row on a single line of the printed page):

```
B's Beverages   10289   Aniseed Syrup    8.00   30   0   240.00
B's Beverages   10289   Wimmers Sem...   26.60   9   0   239.40
B's Beverages   10471   Organic ...      24.00   30   0   720.00
B's Beverages   10471   Gnocchi di ...   30.40   20   0   608.00
B's Beverages   10484   Sir Rodney's...   8.00   14   0   112.00
B's Beverages   10484   Boston Crab ...  14.70   10   0   147.00
B's Beverages   10484   Manjimup ...     42.40    3   0   127.20
B's Beverages   10538   Outback Lager    15.00    7   0   105.00
B's Beverages   10538   Mozzarella ...   34.80    1   0    34.80
B's Beverages   10539   Konbu             6.00    8   0    48.00
B's Beverages   10539   Sir Rodney's...  10.00   15   0   150.00
B's Beverages   10539   Geitost           2.50   15   0    37.50
B's Beverages   10539   Maxilaku         20.00    6   0   120.00
```

This cursor contains all the information you're interested in, but it also contains a lot of redundant information. The customer's name will be repeated along with each order and each detail line. Order IDs will also be repeated along with each detail line. The order 10289, for example, contains two detail lines, and the order 10484 contains three detail lines. The order's number need not be transmitted with each row.

The cursor returned by the above statement is too large for the information it contains, and it needn't be. Moreover, the structure of this cursor doesn't reflect the structure of the data you requested. You need a cursor with the structure of a Tree-View control, where each customer name will appear once. Under a customer's node, you should be able to see the orders, and under each order's nodes, you should be able to see the order's details. A TreeView control can map the structure of the data very efficiently. Here's the equivalent hierarchical Recordset with the same information:

```
B's Beverages
        10289
                Aniseed Syrup    8.00    30    0    240.00
                Wimmers Sem...  26.60     9    0    239.40
        10471
                Organic ...     24.00    30    0    720.00
                Gnocchi di ...  30.40    20    0    608.00
        10484
                Sir Rodney's...  8.00    14    0    112.00
                Boston Crab ... 14.70    10    0    147.00
                Manjimup ...    42.40     3    0    127.20
        10538
                Outback Lager   15.00     7    0    105.00
                Mozzarella ...  34.80     1    0     34.80
        10539
                Konbu            6.00     8    0     48.00
                Sir Rodney's... 10.00    15    0    150.00
                Geitost          2.50    15    0     37.50
                Maxilaku        20.00     6    0    120.00
```

(I have copied the lines of the last listing and deleted the information that's repeated.) This cursor looks better, and it reflects the actual structure of the data you requested.

Now that you have a general understanding of hierarchical Recordsets, the remainder of this chapter explores how they are designed and how you can manipulate them from within your code. The key concept is that hierarchical Recordsets are made up of multiple Recordsets with parent/child relationships between them.

The top-level Recordset in this example is the Recordset with the customers, within which:

- The orders of each customer form a separate Recordset, which is a child of the Recordset with the customers.

- The Recordset with the details is a child of the Recordset with the orders.

Designing Hierarchical Recordsets

In Chapter 6, "Programming with ADO," you learned how to build Connection and Command objects with the DataEnvironment Designer (DE Designer). You saw how to create multiple Command objects and attach them to a single Connection object. The DataEnvironment Designer also allows you to build hierarchies of Command objects.

The DE Designer allows you to build command hierarchies with point-and-click operations. However, designing command hierarchies with the DE Designer is a little more involved than designing multiple Commands, because in a command hierarchy, each Command object is a child of another Command object. Thus you must specify the parent-child relationship.

Specifying Parent-Child Relationships

In a parent-child relationship, the first Command object is placed under the Connection object as usual. However, unlike multiple commands, parent-child relationships require that additional Command objects are appended to an existing Command object with the Add Child command. You can nest as many child commands as your application dictates. However, rarely will you build a command hierarchy with more than half a dozen child commands.

A child command is related to its parent command with a common field, similar to the relationship between primary and foreign keys (see Chapter 2, "Basic Concepts of Relational Databases"). In most cases, the fields you'll be using to establish parent-child relationships are, in fact, the primary and foreign keys of the key fields of the various tables involved. If you prefer to think in terms of SQL statements, the common field is the same field you would use in a SELECT statement's WHERE or JOIN clause to connect two tables. If the parent command contains the rows of the Customers table and the child command contains the rows of the Orders table, you must relate the two Command objects with the CustomerID field.

In addition to relating parent and child commands, you can specify aggregates on the child commands. These aggregates become new fields of the parent command. For example, you can use the COUNT function to count the OrderIDs under each customer, or the SUM function to calculate the sum of an order's details or the sum of all orders for a customer. The result, which is the number of orders placed by a customer or the customer total, becomes a new field for the parent Command object.

NOTE   The topic of building command hierarchies with aggregates is discussed in detail later in this chapter.

Building a Command Hierarchy

Let's follow the steps of building a command hierarchy with the Northwind database data. You're going to build a DataEnvironment object with all the customers, their orders, and the detail lines.

To begin, start a new Data Project and open the DataEnvironment (DE) Designer by double-clicking its name in the Project window. When the Designer's window appears, select the Connection object. Then follow these steps to build a command hierarchy with the customers, their orders, and the order details:

1. Rename the Connection object to NWConnection.

2. Open the object's Data Link Properties window and establish a connection to the Northwind SQL Server database. (This process is explained in detail in Chapter 3.)

3. Add a new Command object under the NWConnection Connection object. Right-click the NWConnection object and select Add Command from the shortcut menu. The new Command object will be named Command1 by default, and you should change its name to AllCustomers. This object will host the cursor with the Customers table's rows.

4. Open the Property Pages of the AllCustomers command (right-click and select Properties) and set its Data Source to the Customers table. Close the Properties dialog box by clicking the OK button.

Now that you've created a Command object with the customers, you're ready to create a new Command object with the rows of the Orders table and connect each order to the customer that placed the order. To do so, follow these steps:

1. Right-click the AllCustomers object, and from the shortcut menu select Add Child Command. The new Command object will be placed under the

AllCustomers object, not under the Connection object. If you've clicked the wrong object, delete the new object and repeat this step. Rename the new Command object to AllOrders. Your DataEnvironment window should look like the one shown here:

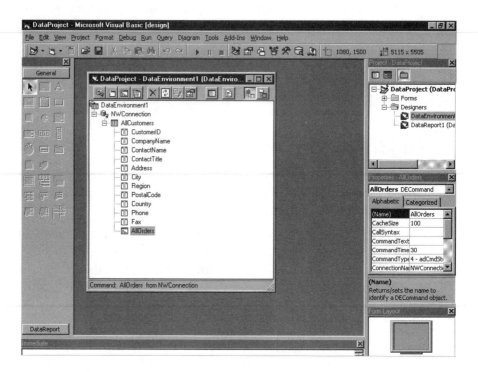

2. Right-click the AllOrders object and open its Properties window. Set its Data Source to the Orders table of the Northwind database. Do not close the Properties window yet.

3. Now you'll connect the child object to its parent object. Switch to the Relation tab of the Properties window. This tab should look like the one shown in Figure 10.1. DE Designer suggests that this object is related to the AllCustomers object (an obvious guess), and the relation should be based on the CustomerID field (since this is the only field name common to both tables). To activate this relation, click the Add button. Doing so will place a new line in the large List-Box control at the bottom of the Form (this line is not shown in Figure 10.1).

NOTE   Don't forget to click the Add button. Many users see the suggested relation and then click the OK button.

---

4. Click OK to close the Properties window. Now you're going to add yet another child command with the order's detail lines. Back in the DE Designer window,

select the AllOrders command with the mouse, right-click its name, and select Add Child Command.

5. Set the new Command object's Data Source to the Order Details table. Switch to the Relation tab again and relate the AllDetails object to its parent object (AllOrders) with the OrderID field. Again, the DE Designer will suggest the proper fields, so all you have to do is click the Add button to activate the relation and then click the OK button to return to the DE Designer window.

FIGURE 10.1:

Establishing a relationship between a parent and a child Command object

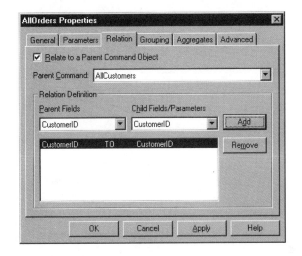

So you just created your command hierarchy—and it was quite simple, too. Now you need to confirm that the DE Designer has created a command hierarchy. Right-click the AllCustomers object and select the Hierarchy Info command. A small window like the one shown in Figure 10.2 will appear. This is a strange command indeed. It looks a lot like an SQL statement, but most of the keywords are new to you. It's a SHAPE command—an extension to standard SQL for generating hierarchical Recordset. Fortunately, it was generated automatically for you, and you don't need to learn the SHAPE command and write command hierarchies from scratch.

NOTE   The SHAPE command is discussed later in this chapter. Eventually, you'll have to edit the statements generated by the DE Designer, or create SHAPE commands from within your code.

If you check the View ADO Hierarchy check box in this dialog box, you will see a picture of the hierarchy (see Figure 10.3). The AllDetails object is a child of the AllOrders object, which in turn is a child of the AllCustomers object. Close the Hierarchy Information window to return to your project.

FIGURE 10.2:

The DataEnvironment Designer generated a SHAPE statement that reflects the command hierarchy you specified with point-and-click operations.

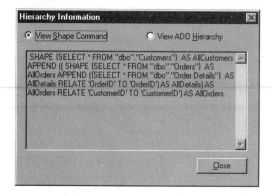

FIGURE 10.3:

The ADO Hierarchy of the SHAPE statement shown in Figure 10.2

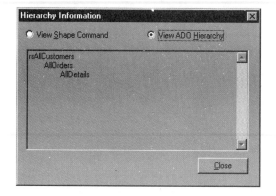

The command hierarchy is of very little use without being able to map it on a control and visualize it. As you can guess, the ideal control for visualizing a command hierarchy is the TreeView control. Populating a TreeView control with the rows of a command hierarchy requires quite a bit of code (and you'll see how this is done later in the chapter). Visual Basic 6 comes with an ActiveX control that was designed to map command hierarchies. This is the MSHFlexGrid control, which is discussed next.

The MSHFlexGrid Control

The MSHFlexGrid (Microsoft Hierarchical FlexGrid) control is added automatically to the Toolbox when you open a Data Project. (You can also add it to the Toolbox of another project type through the Components dialog box.) This control can read a hierarchy of commands directly off the DE Designer and display their data along with their structure. Figure 10.4 shows the MSHFlexGrid control that displays the command hierarchy you created in the last section. Some of the orders have a plus sign in front of them, which means that they have not been expanded.

The minus sign indicates that the order's details are expanded, and you shrink them again by clicking this icon.

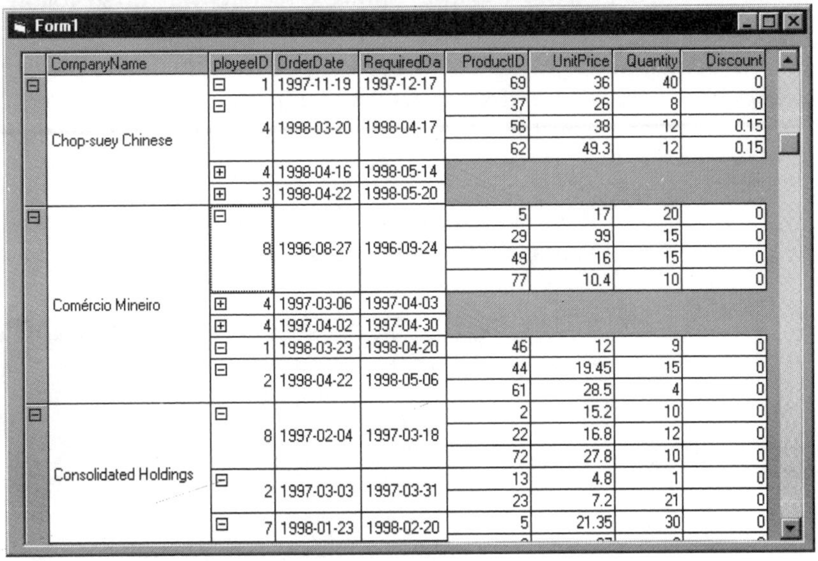

FIGURE 10.4:

Mapping the command hierarchy of Figure 10.3 on a hierarchical MSHFlexGrid control

To view the MSHFlexGrid's properties, place an instance of the control on the project's Form, make it large enough to hold all the information, and then switch to its Properties window. You will see that this control has only two data-binding properties. You'll use these properties to bind the control to a command hierarchy, just as you bind a DataGrid control to a single Command object. The data-binding properties of the MSHFlexGrid control are:

DataSource   The name of a DataEnvironment object or an ADO Data Control with a SHAPE command

DataMember   The name of a command object in the DataSource property that contains the definition of the Recordset to be mapped on the control

Mapping a Command Hierarchy to the MSHFlexGrid Control

To display the rows of the command hierarchy on the MSHFlexGrid control, you must first set the value of the DataSource property to DataEnvironment1 and the value of the DataMember property to AllCustomers. By setting the DataMember property to a child command, you can map a segment of the hierarchy to the MSH-FlexGrid control. For this example, you'll map the entire hierarchy.

When you switch to the project's Form, you won't see any field names on the MSHFlexGrid control. The MSHFlexGrid control is not a simple data-bound control like the ones you examined in Chapter 6, and you need to set a few more properties before it can display a command hierarchy. To do so, follow these steps:

1. Right-click the MSHFlexGrid control on the Form and, from the shortcut menu, select the Retrieve Structure command. This command will read the structure of the hierarchical Recordset you specified with the DataSource and DataMember properties and map it to the control.

2. Right-click the control again and select Properties. The control's Property Pages window will appear on the screen:

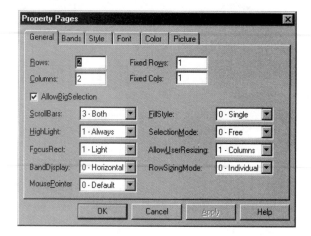

3. The General tab contains fields for setting the control's operational parameters (number of rows and columns, whether the user can resize cells, how the various bands will be displayed, and so on). The Style, Font, Color, and Picture tabs let you adjust the appearance of the controls. There's nothing new on these tabs.

4. Switch to the Bands tab to specify which fields will be displayed on the control. Each Command's Recordset is displayed on the control as a separate band (a segment of the control). Bands are expandable, so you can show or hide the child Recordsets at run time. Select a Command object's name in the Band drop-down list, and you will see the names of the fields in the corresponding Recordset at the bottom of the Form, as shown here:

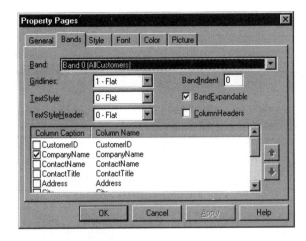

In this list, you can clear the check boxes in front of the names of the fields you don't want to view on the grid control.

5. Clear all fields of the AllCutomers band except for the CompanyName field.

6. Select the AllOrders band and clear all fields except for the OrderID and OrderDate fields.

7. Switch to the AllDetails band and view its fields. Keep all the fields in this band except for the OrderID field.

You're done setting up the MSHFlexGrid control for displaying the AllCustomers command hierarchy. Press F5 to run the program, and you will see the MSHFlex-Grid control in action. Your Form should look like the one shown in Figure 10.4.

The MSHFlexGrid control is quite powerful. It has mapped the structure of the Recordset, and you can view or hide any customer or order (including its details) by clicking the plus and minus signs in front of their names. The columns of the grid control are not sized correctly, so you'll have to change the AllowUserResizing property, so that columns and/or rows can be resized at run time by the user.

The MSHFlexGrid control resembles the TreeView control, in that it can organize hierarchical information. The MSHFlexGrid control, however, can handle Recordsets only; you can't assign arbitrary structured data to this control as an alternative to the TreeView control. In the next section, you will see how to map a hierarchical Recordset on a TreeView control.

Like the regular MSFlexGrid control, the MSHFlexGrid control doesn't allow editing of its cells. Yet it recognizes some events, that you can program to enable the editing of the cells. They are the EnterCell and LeaveCell events, which are triggered when the user selects or leaves a cell respectively. You can program these events to enable direct editing of the control's cells.

TIP

I suggest you do not allow your users to edit the fields of a hierarchical Recordset. The MSHFlexGrid control is not an editing tool. If you use it to display titles, for example, you would like to be able to change a book's publisher by picking the new publisher from a drop-down list. The hierarchical FlexGrid control doesn't permit look-up operations.

The MSHFlexGrid control is very handy for quickly visualizing the structure of a hierarchical Recordset, but I don't find it very convenient as a user interface. It offers too much information and very little control over its appearance, and it's more difficult to program than the more traditional data-bound controls. I really look forward to a new control for displaying command hierarchies, like the grid used by Access to display tables and related rows.

Using Aggregates

Let's return to the AllCustomers example. In the previous section, you retrieved all the details from the database, but how about the totals? You still don't know each detail line's subtotal, or an order's total. In this section we'll revise the definition of the hierarchical Recordset by adding aggregate fields.

To define an aggregate function, follow these steps:

1.   Open a Command object and switch to the Aggregates tab of the Command object's Property Pages, shown in Figure 10.5.

2.   To add an aggregate to a Command object, select the aggregate in the left column and click the Add button; the controls on the right side of the tab will be enabled.

3.   Each aggregate is calculated on the rows of a child Recordset and becomes a new field in the parent Recordset. As such, it must have a name, which you enter in the Name box.

4.   In the Function box, select the type of the aggregate to be calculated (Any, Average, Count, Maximum, Minimum, Standard Deviation, or Sum).

5.   In the Aggregate On drop-down list, select the child Recordset on which the aggregate will be calculated.

6.   In the Field box, select the child Recordset's field that the calculations will be based.

7.   When you have finished selecting the aggregate settings, click Apply.

The Invoices aggregate in Figure 10.5 calculates the total number of invoices placed by a customer. To do so, it uses the COUNT() aggregate function to count the OrderID fields of the Orders child Recordset.

FIGURE 10.5:

Specifying an aggregate for a
Command object

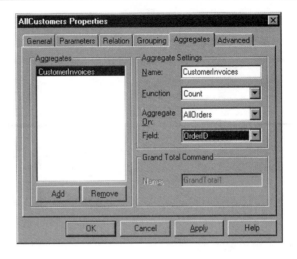

The CustomerSales Project

The CustomerSales project on this book's companion CD demonstrates how to
build a hierarchical Recordset with totals. To make the example a little more interesting, I've used SQL statements to select a small number of columns from each
table only. Figure 10.6 shows the DE Designer window after the specification of
the Connection object and the nested Command objects. When you run the project, you will see a hierarchical Recordset of customers, orders, and order details
on a hierarchical FlexGrid control, as shown in Figure 10.7.

FIGURE 10.6:

The CustomerSales project's
DE Designer window

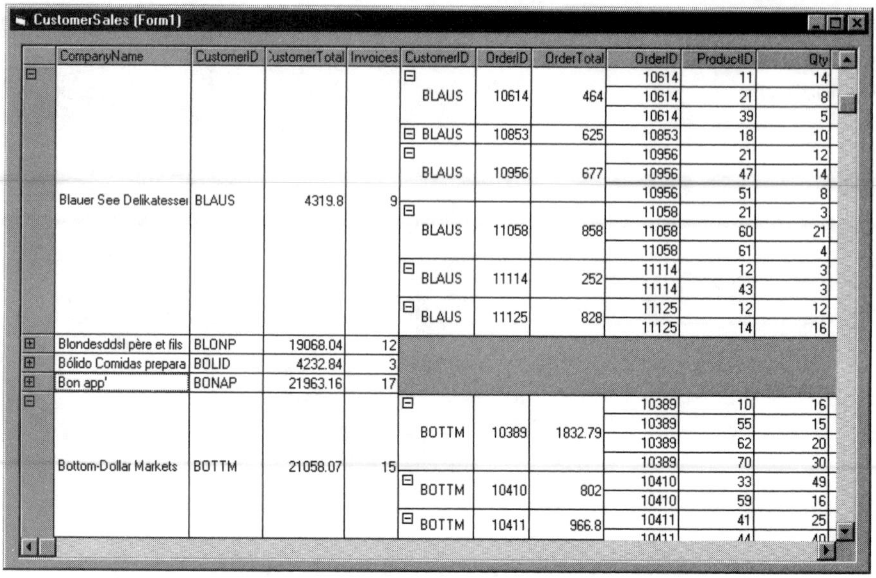

FIGURE 10.7:

Running the CustomerSales project

To build the DataEnvironment object of the CustomerSales project (which is the core of the project), follow these steps:

1. Start a new Data Project and double-click its DataEnvironment Designer to open it in design view. Rename the Connection object to SALESConnection and add a new Command object.

2. Rename the Command object to Customers and then open its Property Pages. In the General tab, set the object's data source to the following SQL statement:

    ```
    SELECT CompanyName, CustomerID FROM Customers
    ```

3. When you return to the DE Designer window, add a Child Command under the Customers object and rename it to Orders. Open its Property Pages and set its Data Source to the following SQL statement:

    ```
    SELECT CustomerID, OrderID FROM Orders
    ```

4. Click the OK button to return to the DE Designer window. Then add another child Command under the Orders object. Rename it to Details and set its Data Source to the following SQL statement:

    ```
    SELECT OrderID, ProductID, Quantity AS [Qty],
          UnitPrice AS [Price], Discount AS [Disc.],
          ROUND(Quantity * UnitPrice * (1 - Discount), 2, 1)
               AS LineTotal
    FROM [Order Details]
    ```

5. When you return to the DE Designer window, you will see the names of the fields of the Order Details object, as well as the Line Total field. This is the detail line's subtotal. You'll use this field to build an aggregate on each order (the order's total) and another aggregate on each customer (the customer's total).

6. To add a few aggregates to your DataEnvironment object, begin by right-clicking the Orders object and select Properties.

7. Select the Aggregates tab (see Figure 10.8). To add a new aggregate, click the Add button.

8. In the Aggregate Settings section on the right side of the box, set the Aggregate Name to OrderTotal.

9. Set the Function field to Sum (you are going to sum the LineTotal fields of the Details Recordset). The fields will be totaled within each order, and the aggregate will be the order's total.

10. Set the AggregateOn field to Details (you'll total a field in the Details Recordset) and the Field to LineTotal (the field to be summed). The OrderTotal aggregate will become a new field in the parent Recordset (it couldn't possibly belong to the Recordset on which the aggregate is defined).

11. When you're done, click the OK button to return to the DE Designer window. So far, you've added a new field to the Orders command, which is the total of each order.

FIGURE 10.8:

Specifying aggregates in a command hierarchy with the DE Designer

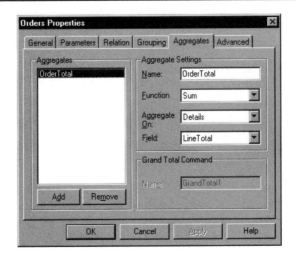

Now you must add a total of the orders placed by each customer, as well as the count of the orders placed by each customer. Open the Properties window

of the Customers object, switch to the Aggregates tab and add two aggregates: the customer's total sales (CustomerTotal) and the number of orders placed by the customer (Invoices). Add the CustomerTotal and Invoices aggregates by clicking the Add button and setting their properties as shown in Figure 10.9.

FIGURE 10.9:

The properties of the
a) CustomerTotal and
b) Invoices aggregates

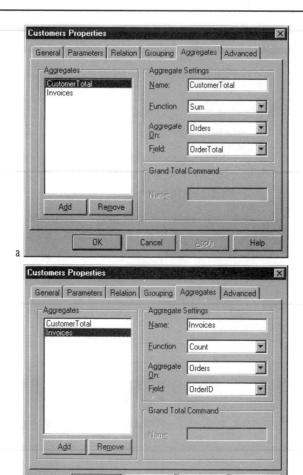

When you close the Customer Properties window and return to the DE Designer window, you will see that the CustomerTotal and Invoices aggregates have become two new fields in the Customers object. Mapping the hierarchical Recordset on an MSHFlexGrid control is a straightforward process, which I will not repeat here. Just place an MSHFlexGrid control on the Form and map on it the structure of the Customers object.

You'll return to this project later in this chapter and you'll map its Recordsets to three different data-bound controls. You'll also add the code so that when a customer is clicked, the corresponding orders are displayed. Likewise, when an order is clicked, the corresponding details are displayed.

Grouping

In the Properties window of the Customers object, notice the Grouping tab. Use this tab to specify the grouping of the Recordset's rows. For each grouping you specify, a new column is added to the corresponding Command object. This column holds the values of the field on which the grouping was based. For example, if you group all customers by country, a new column will be added automatically to the top-level parent Recordset with the country names. All customers within a country will be grouped together, and you can create aggregates on the column of the grouping.

To group customers by country and calculate the total for all customers in a country, switch to the Grouping tab on the Properties window of the AllCustomers Command object. Then specify a new grouping on the Country field, as shown in Figure 10.10.

FIGURE 10.10:

Grouping the rows of the All-Customers Command object according to country

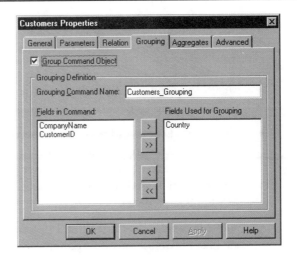

The SHAPE Command

The SHAPE command is not part of the SQL standard—if you attempt to execute a SHAPE command with the Query Analyzer, you will get an error message. The SHAPE command is implemented with the MSDataShape provider, which is

Microsoft-specific. The data are retrieved by the OLE DB provider, but before they are presented to the application, they are passed to the MSDataShape provider. The MSDataShape provider is part of ADO, not a component of OLE DB.

If you want to create hierarchical Recordsets in your project, you must specify the MSDataShape provider in the Connection object. The provider blends the SHAPE statement with regular SQL statements so smoothly that the statements for generating shaped Recordsets look and feel like SQL statements.

The simplest syntax of the SHAPE command is as follows:

```
SHAPE {parent_command} [AS parent_alias]
APPEND ({child_command} [AS child_alias]
RELATE parent_col TO child_col) [AS col_alias]
```

The basic operation of the SHAPE command is to create two (or more) Command objects and relate their Recordsets based on the value of a common field. This is reflected on the statement's syntax.

NOTE   As a reminder, the square brackets are not part of the statement's syntax. They indicate optional parts of the statement. The curly brackets, however, are part of the statement's syntax.

The elements of the SHAPE command are as follows:

- *parent_command* is a SELECT statement that specifies the first Recordset. You can opt to assign a name to this command.

- The APPEND keyword specifies the second Recordset and how it relates to the parent command. The arguments of the APPEND keyword are enclosed in a pair of parentheses. The placement of the parentheses becomes very important in nested shaped Recordsets (which are defined with multiple APPEND keywords).

- *child_command* is another SELECT statement that specifies the second Recordset. Like the definition of the parent command, this statement is also enclosed in a pair of curly brackets, and it may have a (optional) name.

- The RELATE keyword specifies the names of the matching columns in the two Recordsets.

Let's look at the SHAPE command that returns a shaped Recordset with the customers of the Northwind database and their orders and the equivalent SQL statement that retrieves the same information in a flat, uniform Recordset:

```
SHAPE {SELECT * FROM "dbo"."Customers"}  AS AllCustomers
```

```
APPEND ({SELECT * FROM "dbo"."Orders"}  AS AllOrders
  RELATE 'CustomerID' TO 'CustomerID') AS AllOrders
```

The first SELECT statement selects all the rows of the Customers table, and the second SELECT statement selects all the rows of the Orders table. The last line relates the two Recordsets with the CustomerID fields. All the rows of the child Recordset whose CustomerID field is the same as the CustomerID field of the parent command are inserted after the customer row.

The equivalent SQL statement is shown next:

```
SELECT * FROM Customers, Orders
WHERE Customers.CustomerID = Orders.CustomerID
```

There are quite a few similarities between this and the SHAPE command's RELATE statement; the RELATE statement is identical to the plain SQL statement's WHERE clause. Yet in the RELATE statement, you don't have to specify the tables to which the fields belong. The reason is that the RELATE statement requires that the first field belongs to the parent command and the second one to the child command. The SELECT clauses of the SHAPE and SQL statement are also similar, but in the SHAPE command each table must have its own SELECT statement.

Multiple Child Recordsets

A shaped Recordset may have one parent Recordset and multiple child Recordsets. Each customer, for example, could have its own set of payments. If the Northwind database had a Payments table, then you could append two child Recordsets after each customer: one with the orders, as before, and another one with the payments. The two child Recordsets are equal in stature and independent of each other. They do relate to their common parent Recordset, however, with the CustomerID field. Here's a SHAPE command that creates a shaped Recordset with two child Recordsets:

```
SHAPE   {SELECT * FROM "dbo"."Customers"} AS AllCustomers
APPEND ({SELECT * FROM "dbo"."Orders"} AS AllOrders
          RELATE CustomerID TO CustomerID) AS AllOrders,
        ({SELECT * FROM "dbo"."Payments"} AS AllPayments
          RELATE CustomerID TO CustomerID) AS AllPayments
```

Notice that multiple child commands are separated with a comma. The general syntax of a SHAPE command with multiple child Recordsets is shown here:

```
SHAPE   {parent_command} [AS parent_alias]
APPEND ({child1_command} [AS child1_alias]
          RELATE parent_col TO child_col) [AS col1_alias],
        ({child2_command} [AS child1_alias]
          RELATE parent_col TO child_col) [AS col2_alias]
```

Nested Hierarchies

As you have seen already, the DE Designer can create shaped Recordsets with multiple nested commands (child commands that have their own child commands). The Recordset with the order details can't be appended directly to the parent command (Customers). It's a child of the Orders Recordset, and it must be appended to the first child command. Here's the SHAPE command generated by the DE Designer for the customers/orders/order details hierarchical Recordset:

LISTING 10.1   The Customers/Orders/Order Details Command

```
SHAPE {SELECT CompanyName, CustomerID FROM Customers}
    AS Customers
   APPEND (( SHAPE {SELECT CustomerID, OrderID
                    FROM Orders }  AS Orders
   APPEND ({SELECT OrderID, ProductID, Quantity AS [Qty],
           UnitPrice AS [Price], Discount AS [Disc.],
           ROUND(Quantity * UnitPrice * (1 - Discount), 2, 1)
           AS LineTotal
           FROM [Order Details]}  AS Details
RELATE 'OrderID' TO 'OrderID') AS Details,
    SUM(Details.'LineTotal') AS OrderTotal) AS Orders
RELATE 'CustomerID' TO 'CustomerID') AS Orders,
    SUM(Orders.'OrderTotal') AS CustomerTotal,
    COUNT(Orders.'OrderID') AS Invoices
```

The syntax of a SHAPE command with multiple nested child commands is:

```
SHAPE   {parent_command} [AS parent_alias]
APPEND (( SHAPE {nested_child1_command} [AS child1_alias]
    APPEND ({nested_child2_command} [AS child2_alias]
    RELATE child2_col1 TO child1_col1) [AS col1_alias])
RELATE parent_col2 TO child1_col2) [AS col2_alias]
```

In this syntax, the first APPEND statement contains a new SHAPE command where a SELECT statement would normally appear. You can nest more child commands by inserting additional SHAPE commands. Just insert additional opening and closing parentheses, as shown in the above statement. My suggestion is to use the DE Designer to generate the SHAPE command, then copy and paste it into your code—unless, of course, you must generate the command at run time, in which case you must prepare an outline of the command and replace its parts with the appropriate SQL statements and column names.

Using Parameterized Commands

There are situations in which you want to be able to use parameters in the expressions that select the desired rows from the table(s). In the previous examples, you have used expressions like the following one in the RELATION statement:

```
RELATE (OrderID TO OrderID)
```

This expression assumes that both the parent and child Recordsets contain an OrderID field. While it's fine to include the OrderID field in the parent Recordset (presumably, the Orders Recordset), why repeat this information in every line of the child Recordset (the Details Recordset)? Instead of including the OrderID field in both Recordsets, you could use a more complicated SELECT statement like the following one, that uses parameters:

```
SHAPE {SELECT OrderID FROM Orders WHERE CustomerID=?}
        AS Orders
APPEND ({SELECT ProductID, Quantity,
        [Order Details].UnitPrice, Discount,
        Quantity * [Order Details].UnitPrice * (1 - Discount)
            AS LineTotal
        FROM [Order Details], Products
        WHERE OrderID=?} AS [Order Total]
RELATE OrderID TO PARAMETER 0) AS [Order Total]
```

This command uses a SELECT statement to retrieve the details of a specific order, which is identified by its ID. The SELECT statement includes a WHERE clause, which specifies that only the details of a specific order be retrieved. The OrderID field is not part of the child command's Recordset. Since you can't specify a value for the OrderID field at design time, set it to a parameter (the question mark), which will be resolved at run time. The RELATE statement relates the two Recordsets by requesting that the child Recordset's parameter be set to the OrderID of the current order.

You may still wonder why or when to use this technique. You'll return to the topic of parameterized SHAPE commands in the section "The AnyShape Project," later in this chapter, where you'll see a few examples of this technique in action.

Using Stored Procedures with the SHAPE Command

The APPEND statement recognizes stored procedures in addition to SQL statements. Let's say you've built a stored procedure that retrieves the orders of a specific customer, specified by its ID. If the name of the stored procedure is called

GetCustomerOrders, here's how you would use it to create a hierarchical Record-set with customers and their orders:

```
SHAPE  {SELECT * FROM customer}
   APPEND {CALL GetCustomerOrders cust_id (?) }
   RELATE (cust_id TO PARAMETER 0)
```

The stored procedure has taken the place of a SELECT statement, and it's called with a single parameter (the customer's ID). This parameter is specified later, in the RELATE statement. The RELATE statement uses the expression PARAMETER 0 to identify the first parameter of the stored procedure.

Executing SHAPE Commands

To execute a SHAPE command through your code, you store it into a string variable and execute it against the database as usual. Just keep in mind that SHAPE commands are not like regular SQL statements and can't be executed by the native SQL engine. As mentioned earlier, SHAPE statements are executed by the MSDataShape provider, so you must include this information in your connection string. The following VB statements will execute the SHAPE command that retrieves all the customers and their orders from the Northwind database:

```
SHAPEcmd = "SHAPE {SELECT * FROM Customers}  AS AllCustomers "
SHAPEcmd = SHAPEcmd & _
            "APPEND ({SELECT * FROM Orders}  AS AllOrders "
SHAPEcmd = SHAPEcmd & _
            "RELATE CustomerID TO CustomerID) AS AllOrders "
CN.Provider = "MSDataShape"
CN.ConnectionString = _
    "Data Provider=SQLOLEDB;" & _
    "Persist Security Info=False;" & _
    "User ID=sa;" & _
    "Initial Catalog=Northwind;" & _
    "Data Source=EXPERTNEW"
CN.Open
HRS.ActiveConnection = CN
HRS.Open SHAPEcmd
```

The object variables *CN* and *HRS* represent a Connection and a hierarchical Record-set, respectively, and they must be declared with the following statements:

```
Dim CN As New ADODB.Connection
Dim HRS As New ADODB.Recordset
```

The AnyShape Project

Figure 10.11 shows the AnyShape project, which demonstrates how to execute SHAPE commands against a SQL Server database through the Connection object. You can also use this project to experiment with SHAPE commands on your own. Simply enter a SHAPE command in the TextBox control at the top and click the Execute SHAPE Command button to execute it. If the command was executed successfully, the hierarchical Recordset will be displayed in the lower pane of the Form. If not, the error message returned by the MSDataShape provider will be displayed on a message box.

FIGURE 10.11:

Use the AnyShape project to execute SHAPE commands against the Northwind database.

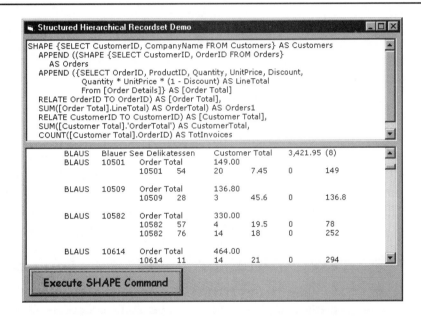

The following statements declare the Connection object that's used to establish a connection to the database and the Recordset object that's returned by the MSDataShape provider:

```
Dim CN As New ADODB.Connection
Dim HRS As New ADODB.Recordset
```

The Command button's Click event handler sets up the connection and executes the SHAPE command with the Recordset's Open method.

LISTING 10.2   Executing a SHAPE Command

```
Private Sub Command1_Click()
    SHAPEcmd = Text1.Text
    On Error GoTo SHAPEError
```

```
        CN.Provider = "MSDataShape.1"
        CN.ConnectionString = "Data Provider=SQLOLEDB.1;" & _
                "Persist Security Info=False;User ID=sa; " & _
                "Initial Catalog=Northwind;Data Source=EXPERTNEW"
        CN.Open
        HRS.ActiveConnection = CN
        HRS.Open SHAPEcmd
        Screen.MousePointer = vbHourglass
        Me.Caption = "Populating ListBox control"
        ScanRecordset HRS
        Screen.MousePointer = vbDefault
        Me.Caption = "Structured Hierarchical Recordset Demo"
        Set HRS = Nothing
        Set CN = Nothing
        Exit Sub
    SHAPEError:
        MsgBox Err.Description
        Set HRS = Nothing
        Set CN = Nothing
    End Sub
```

Notice that the Connection object requires both a Provider and a Data Provider. The Provider is set to MSDataShape, and the Data Provider is set to the name of the OLE DB provider, as usual. To display the hierarchical Recordset, the code calls the ScanRecordset() subroutine passing the hierarchical Recordset itself. The ScanRecordset() subroutine is discussed in the following section.

Executing Parameterized SHAPE Commands

Let's use the AnyShape project to experiment with parameterized SHAPE commands. The default SHAPE command that appears in the upper pane of the project's window creates the ubiquitous customers/orders/order details hierarchy. Figure 10.11 shows the data returned by this command.

As you can see, the IDs of customer and orders are repeated unnecessarily. This happens because, in order to relate child Recordsets to their parents, you must select the CustomerID and OrderID fields in the corresponding SELECT statements. The SHAPE command contains the following RELATE clauses:

```
RELATE OrderID TO OrderID
RELATE CustomerID TO CustomerID
```

The hierarchical Recordset returned by this command has the following shortcomings:

- The details include product IDs instead of product names. Clearly, you must adjust your SELECT statement so that it replaces product IDs with the actual product names (all you need is a WHERE clause to match the IDs to product names in the Products table).

- The ID of the order is repeated with each detail line. Here, you need another WHERE clause that will connect the OrderID field of the detail line to the OrderID of the parent Recordset, which contains the orders.

- The ID of the customer is repeated with each order. As you can guess, you'll add yet another WHERE clause that will connect the CustomerID field of the order to the CustomerID field of the parent Recordset, which contains the customers.

Following is the SHAPE statement that displays the same hierarchy, only it doesn't repeat the IDs by using parameterized SELECT statements. The parameters are resolved at run time. The current customer's ID in the outer Recordset (the one with the customer information) is passed to the child SHAPE command as a parameter. The first child SHAPE command selects the orders of the current customer. The same happens with the second nested SHAPE command: The current order's ID is passed to the inner-most SHAPE command. This SHAPE command selects the details of the current order.

LISTING 10.3   A SHAPE Command with Parameters

```
SHAPE {SELECT CustomerID, CompanyName FROM Customers} AS Customers
    APPEND ((SHAPE {SELECT OrderID FROM Orders WHERE CustomerID=?}
        AS Orders
    APPEND ({SELECT ProductName, Quantity,
                [Order Details].UnitPrice, Discount,
                Quantity * [Order Details].UnitPrice *
                (1 - Discount) AS LineTotal
                    FROM [Order Details], Products
                    WHERE [Order Details].ProductID =
                        Products.ProductID AND
                        OrderID=?} AS [Order Total]
    RELATE OrderID TO PARAMETER 0) AS [Order Total],
    SUM([Order Total].LineTotal) AS OrderTotal) AS Orders1
    RELATE CustomerID TO PARAMETER 0) AS [Customer Total],
    SUM([Customer Total].'OrderTotal') AS CustomerTotal,
    COUNT([Customer Total].OrderID) AS TotInvoices
```

The output produced by this statement is shown in Figure 10.12. Examine the differences in the last two SHAPE commands and the output they produced (Figures 10.11 and 10.12). As you can see, it pays to write a longer SHAPE statement with parameterized SELECT statements.

FIGURE 10.12:

A revised SHAPE command for generating the same hierarchy as the one of Figure 10.11

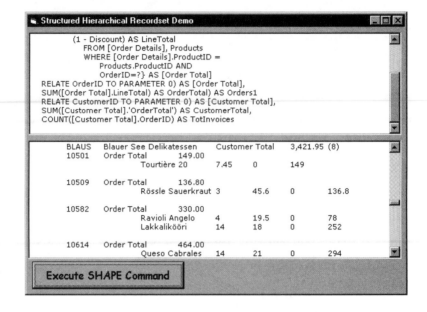

Scanning Hierarchical Recordsets

So far, you've seen how to create hierarchical Recordsets, either through the DE Designer, or with SHAPE commands. How about scanning the Recordset's rows? The difference between flat and hierarchical Recordsets is that in a hierarchical Recordset, some fields are entire Recordsets. The process of scanning a hierarchical Recordset is similar to the process of scanning a folder. Most of the entries in the folder are filenames, which you can print immediately. Some of the entries, however, are folders themselves, and they may contain nested folders, as well. Thus, to scan a folder, you have to use a recursive routine. Here's the pseudo-code for scanning the HRS hierarchical Recordset:

```
Sub ScanRecordSet(Hrecordset As Recordset)
While Not HRecordset.EOF
    For Each field in the Recordset
        If current field Is Recordset Then
            ScanRecordSet(current field)
        Else
            {process current field}
        End If
    Next
    HRecordset.MoveNext
Wend
```

The ScanRecordSset() subroutine is called with a Recordset object as argument. It starts by scanning all the rows of the Recordset with a While ... Wend loop, and at each iteration it processes every field of the current row. If a field is a Recordset, then the subroutine calls itself, passing the field (which is a Recordset variable) as argument. This process continues until all the rows of the original Recordset are exhausted.

To find out whether a field is a Recordset or not, examine its Type property. For single-valued fields, this property's value is a constant that corresponds to one of the data types supported by ADO. The values of the Type property are discussed in Chapter 4. One of these values is adChapter, which indicates that the field is a Recordset. Here's the listing of the ScanRecordset() subroutine:

LISTING 10.4   **The ScanRecordset Subroutine**

```
Sub ScanRecordset(RS As ADODB.Recordset)
IndentDepth = IndentDepth + 1
While Not RS.EOF
    For i = 0 To RS.Fields.Count - 1
        If RS.Fields(i).Type <> adChapter Then
            If RS.Fields(i).Type = adDouble Then
                ListLine = ListLine & Chr(9) & _
                            Format(RS.Fields(i), "#,###.00")
            Else
                If RS.Fields(i).Name = "TotInvoices" Then
                    ListLine = ListLine & Chr(9) & "(" & _
                                RS.Fields(i) & ")"
                Else
                    ListLine = ListLine & Chr(9) & RS.Fields(i)
                End If
            End If
        Else
            ListLine = ListLine & Chr(9) & RS.Fields(i).Name
        End If
    Next

    For j = 0 To RS.Fields.Count - 1
        If RS.Fields(j).Type = adChapter Then
            List1.AddItem ListLine
            ListLine = ""
            ScanRecordset RS.Fields(j).Value
        End If
    Next
    List1.AddItem String(IndentDepth - 1, Chr(9)) & ListLine
    ListLine = ""
    RS.MoveNext
Wend
IndentDepth = IndentDepth - 1
End Sub
```

The program displays the hierarchical Recordset on a ListBox control, using a different indentation for the child Recordsets. It builds each row by appending fields to the *ListLine* string variable, with the tab character between them.

After all scalar fields of the current row have been scanned, the program continues with the child Recordsets, and it does so by calling itself and passing the Value of the current field as argument. Since the expression RS.Fields(i).Value is a Recordset, it is scanned just like its parent Recordset. Its fields are indented appropriately with the help of the *InDepth* variable, which is increased by one every time the subroutine is invoked and decreased by one every time the subroutine exits.

TIP

To experiment with the code for scanning hierarchical Recordsets, you can use the ScanHRecordset project on the CD, which uses the ScanRecordset() subroutine to populate a ListBox control with the rows of a hierarchical Recordset.

Mapping Hierarchical Recordsets to TreeView Controls

Short of the MSHFlexGrid control, the most appropriate ActiveX control for displaying hierarchical Recordsets is the TreeView control. Each node of the control stores a Recordset, nested nodes store nested child Recordsets, and the leaves of the control store single-valued fields. Figure 10.13 shows the customers/order/order details hierarchical Recordset mapped to a TreeView control. The Form shown is the main Form of the TVShape application.

FIGURE 10.13:

Mapping a hierarchical Recordset to a TreeView control

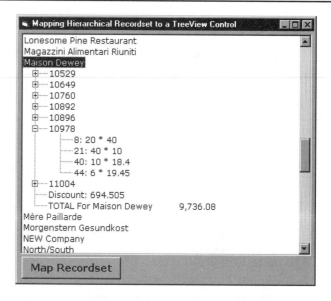

The TreeView control doesn't support any methods that will allow you to automatically map the Command objects of the DE Designer to its nodes. Instead, you must scan the Recordsets from within your code and append its rows as nodes to the control.

You know how to scan hierarchical Recordsets already. This time, instead of displaying the rows of the Recordset on a ListBox control, you'll be creating nodes (nested, if needed) on a TreeView control. Here's the outline of the subroutine that maps the Recordset to a TreeView control:

1. Scan the Recordset as usual with While … Wend loop. The structure of this loop is not new to you:

```
While Not RS.EOF
     {process current row}
   RS.MoveNext
Wend
```

2. At each iteration, do the following:

   - Append a new node to the TreeView control. This node represents a parent record. If the parent Recordset contains the customers, create a new node for the current customer.

   - For each child record, create a new node under the parent node (the customer node). If the child Recordset contains the customer's orders, append a node for each order.

   - If the child record contains its own child Recordset, append yet another node. If the Recordset with the orders contains a child Recordset with the order's details, append a new node for each detail line under the node that represents the order.

This process is repeated until all child records are exhausted. You could have written a recursive process to scan the hierarchical Recordset, but I've chosen a simpler approach for this example. When the structure of the Recordset in known in advance and doesn't have too many nested Recordsets, the explicit approach of this example is simpler. Besides, you can name the nodes from within your code— if you were using a recursive procedure to scan any hierarchical Recordset, you'd have to use the field (or generic) names to label the tree's nodes. Following is the subroutine that implements the algorithm outlined earlier.

LISTING 10.5   **Mapping a Shaped Recordset to a TreeView Control**

```
Private Sub MapRS2Tree_Click()
Dim OrderTotal As Currency
Dim CustomerTotal As Currency
Dim OrderDiscount As Currency
```

```
TreeView1.Sorted = True
DataEnvironment1.rsCommand1.Open
Set Customers = DataEnvironment1.rsCommand1
Screen.MousePointer = vbHourglass
While Not Customers.EOF
    TreeView1.Nodes.Add , tvwFirst, _
                            Customers.Fields("CustomerID"), _
                            Customers.Fields("CompanyName")
        Set Orders = Customers("Command2").Value
        While Not Orders.EOF
            pKey = Customers.Fields("CustomerID")
            TreeView1.Nodes.Add pKey, tvwChild, "K" & _
                            Orders.Fields("OrderID"), _
                            Orders.Fields("OrderID")
            Set Details = Orders("Command3").Value
            While Not Details.EOF
                pKey = "K" & Orders.Fields("OrderID")
                TreeView1.Nodes.Add pKey, tvwChild, , _
                        Details.Fields("ProductID") & ": " & _
                        Details.Fields("Quantity") & _
                        " * " & Details.Fields("UnitPrice")
                OrderDiscount = OrderDiscount + _
                        Details.Fields("Quantity") * _
                        Details.Fields("UnitPrice") * _
                        Details.Fields("Discount")
                OrderTotal = OrderTotal + _
                        Details.Fields("Quantity") * _
                        Details.Fields("UnitPrice")
            Details.MoveNext
        Wend
        CustomerTotal = CustomerTotal + _
                        OrderTotal - OrderDiscount
        CustomerDiscount = CustomerDiscount + OrderDiscount
        OrderTotal = 0
        OrderDiscount = 0
        Orders.MoveNext
    Wend
    cKey = Customers.Fields("CustomerID")
    TreeView1.Nodes.Add cKey, tvwChild, , _
            "Discount: " & CustomerDiscount
    TreeView1.Nodes.Add cKey, tvwChild, , "TOTAL For " & _
            Customers.Fields("CompanyName") & Space(10) & _
            Format(CustomerTotal, "#,###.00")
    CustomerTotal = 0
    CustomerDiscount = 0
    Customers.MoveNext
    DoEvents
```

```
    Wend
    Set Customers = Nothing
    Set Orders = Nothing
    Set Details = Nothing
    DataEnvironment1.rsCommand1.Close
    Screen.MousePointer = vbDefault
End Sub
```

Notice how the code constructs each node's key. The Customers table uses a string as primary key, which can be used as a key value as is. The Orders table uses a numeric value as primary key, which can't be used as node key. The program prefixes the numeric value with the "K" character, and it uses this string as a key. The order with ID of 10248, for example, will be appended as a new node to the TreeView control with the key "K10248."

Building Forms with Hierarchical Recordsets

As you recall from Chapter 6, when you drop the parent Command object on a Form, the DE Designer creates all the data-bound controls needed to display (and optionally edit) the fields of the parent object. To see how it handles a hierarchical Recordset's fields when you place them on a Form, add a new Form to the Customer-Sales project and open it in design mode. Make sure you see both the DataEnvironment window and the Form on your screen. Then drop the AllCustomers object on the Form. The DE Designer will place simple data-bound controls on the Form, where the fields of the top parent Recordset will be displayed (see Figure 10.14). The child Recordsets are displayed on a MSHFlexGrid control, since each row in the parent Recordset has many matching rows in the child Recordset.

FIGURE 10.14:

This Form was created by the DE Designer when a hierarchical Recordset was dropped on the Form.

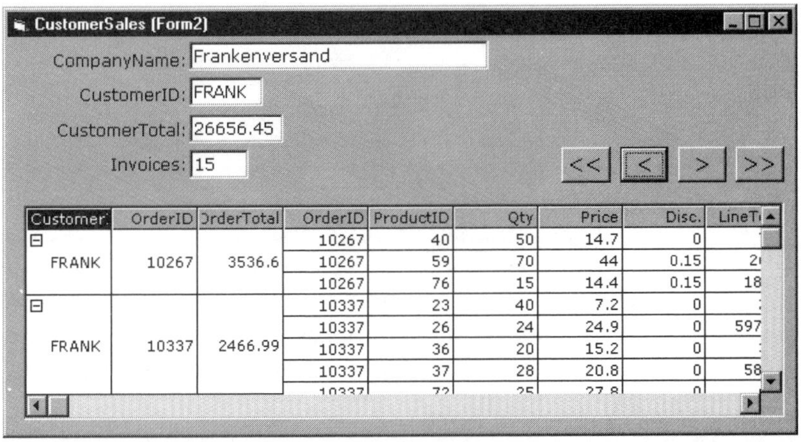

NOTE   The Form shown in Figure 10.14 is the CustomerSales2 Form of the project on this book's companion CD. To see this Form, open the CustomerSales Form, set its startup Form to CustomerSales2, and then run the project.

The code behind the four navigational buttons uses the Move methods of the AllCustomers object. Use these buttons to navigate through the customers. As you move to another customer, the contents of the MSHFlexGrid control are updated with the orders and details of the selected customer.

The PopulateShape Project

The last project in this chapter demonstrates how to display hierarchical Recordsets on traditional data-bound controls and in specific on DataGrid controls. The PopulateShape project displays each Recordset on a separate DataGrid control, as shown in Figure 10.15. Each time the user selects a customer by clicking in a row of the control, the customer's orders are displayed in the second DataGrid control. Likewise, each time the user selects an order on the control, the order's details are displayed on the third DataGrid control.

FIGURE 10.15:

The PopulateShape project's Form

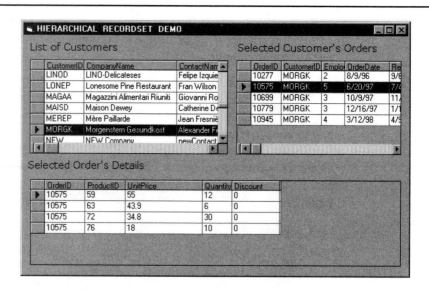

I will not discuss the DataEnvironment object that creates the three Recordsets. If you want to see the definitions of the three Command objects, open the project and view the objects' properties. The interesting part of the application is the code that monitors the user's selections and populates the DataGrid controls appropriately.

The project's Form contains three DataGrid controls. The DataGrid with the customers is populated when the Form is loaded with the following statements:

```
Private Sub Form_Load()
    DataEnvironment1.rsCommand1.Open
    Set Customers = DataEnvironment1.rsCommand1
    Set DataGrid1.DataSource = DataEnvironment1.rsCommand1
End Sub
```

When the user moves to another row in the control, the RowColChange event is fired. From within this event's handler, you must populate the second DataGrid control with the orders of the selected customer (the rows of the second Command object). Here's the code that populates the DataGrid control with the selected customer's orders:

```
Private Sub DataGrid1_RowColChange(LastRow As Variant, _
            ByVal LastCol As Integer)
    Customers.Bookmark = DataGrid1.Bookmark
    Set Orders = Customers("Command2").Value
    Set DataGrid2.DataSource = Orders
End Sub
```

Command2 is the name of the Command object that retrieves the orders of the currently selected customer in the parent Recordset. Notice the line that sets the Customers Recordset's Bookmark property. The child Recordset will be populated when you call the property Customers("Command2").Value. For this to happen, it needs to know the current row of the parent Recordset. The Command2 object will return a Recordset with the orders of the selected customer, so you must make sure that the row selected by the user on the first DataGrid control is the Customers Recordset's current row. This is what the first statement does.

Finally, a similar code segment is executed when the user selects a new row in the DataGrid control with the orders to populate the third control on the Form:

```
Private Sub DataGrid2_RowColChange(LastRow As Variant, _
            ByVal LastCol As Integer)
    Orders.Bookmark = DataGrid2.Bookmark
    Set Details = Orders("Command3").Value
    Set DataGrid3.DataSource = Details
End Sub
```

The code is quite simple, and the DataGrid controls are easier to program than the MSHFlexGrid control. You can set the width of their columns, hide certain columns by reducing their width to one pixel, and so on. The PopulateShape project uses three very simple Command objects, which retrieve an entire table each. As an exercise, you can replace the DataEnvironment of the project with the Data-Environment of the CustomerSales project (discussed earlier in this chapter). This

DataEnvironment object uses SQL statements to retrieve the data you want to see on the Form, rather than the entire table. Do you want to avoid the duplication of the customer and order IDs on the Form? Then write SQL statements (or stored procedures) that accept parameters, as explained in the section "Executing Parameterized SHAPE Commands," earlier in this chapter.

Summary

Hierarchical Recordsets were the first of the advanced topics covered in this part of the book. In the following chapter you'll learn how to access databases remotely, through the Internet. You will see how you can write Web pages with data-bound HTML controls, similar to VB Forms with data-bound controls. The Remote Data Services and Remote Data Control allow you to bind HTML control to the fields of a remote database. The techniques discussed in Chapter 11 apply to Internet Explorer only. You will find more on accessing databases remotely in Part III, which shows you how to build Web applications that interact with databases.

CHAPTER

ELEVEN

Remote Data Access

- Custom Recordsets

- Disconnected Recordsets

- Handling update conflicts

- Remote Data Services

- ADO Remote

11

This chapter discusses several topics with a common theme: how to get data from a database, then disconnect from the server and process the rows locally on the client. In other words, how to work with a Recordset without maintaining a connection to the database at all times. After processing the data, we should be able to update the database, and you will see how this is done.

The first question I must answer is why we should be able to disconnect from our data source. Ideally, we shouldn't need to; we should use notebooks, be constantly connected to the Net over high-speed links, and never have to install applications on our own machines. Ideally, we should have access to everything, at all times and at very low cost, may I add. Practically, however, we have to deal with numerous limitations, one of them being that we can't be constantly connected to the Internet. Even when we're connected to the Internet, every time we click a hyperlink we can see how seriously limited (and precious) bandwidth is.

Local area networks operate at a wider bandwidth, but then applications that run on local area networks are far more demanding. In short, there's never enough bandwidth. The more bandwidth you give to developers, the more data they want to move between servers and clients. So, the practical value of the topics discussed in this chapter is that you can develop client applications that retrieve all the information they need and process it locally, without many trips to the server. This type of client application can be useful in enterprise applications that run on many workstations in a local area network, as well as in Web applications that are deployed on corporate intranets.

The most interesting application of disconnected Recordsets is that they can be stored on the client's disk. When a Recordset is stored on disk, it is *persisted*. As you may recall from Chapter 5, it is possible to create Recordsets in code—that is, you can have Recordsets without a database. If you think about it, this is an ideal data-storage mechanism for complicated data structures. Why deploy a multidimensional array in your application when you can create a Recordset from within your code? The Recordset can be sorted and filtered automatically, displayed on data-bound control, and persisted to disk with the Save method. You can even use more traditional database tools in your applications, like the DataGrid control. Setting up a Recordset takes a few lines of code, but it pays off when it comes to manipulating data.

Custom Recordsets

Let's say you need a structure to store information about cities (names, population, average temperature, and so on). You can create a multidimensional array to store this information, but then you must provide your own code to sort the array. If you want to isolate a segment of the array, you must extract the desired elements yourself. If you choose to store the information into a custom Recordset, you can use the Recordset object's Sort method to sort the rows and its Filter method to isolate the desired rows. The most important advantage of this approach is that you can save all the information to disk by calling the Recordset object's Save method (to read the same information from the disk, use the Open method). If you consider how much code it takes to store an arbitrary multidimensional array to disk, you'll realize that the Save and Open methods alone will justify the use of custom, disconnected Recordsets in simple applications that don't justify the overhead of a database.

Creating Custom Recordsets

Although this topic is not directly related to database programming, I would like to show you how to create a custom Recordset, populate it, and then persist it on disk. First, you must add a reference to the Active Data Objects Library to your project. Then, you'll be able to declare a Recordset variable with the following statement:

```
Dim RS As ADODB.Recordset
```

RS is a variable that can hold any Recordset. The exact structure of the Recordset is determined when you assign an actual cursor to the variable. Since you aren't going to assign a cursor to the variable, you must define its structure in your code. You must declare the fields of the custom Recordset and then add them to the Recordset's structure using the Append method of the Fields collection. The syntax of the Append method is:

```
RS.Fields.Append fld_name, fld_type, [fld_size], [fld_attributes]
```

fld_name and *fld_type* are the field's name and type respectively. The field's type must be one of the data type constants recognized by ADO (see Table 5.8 in Chapter 5 for a list of all data types recognized by ADO). The *fld_size* argument is optional and it's the field's size in characters or bytes (it applies to character or binary fields only). If the field's type is varchar, then *fld_size* is not optional. The last argument, *fld_attributes*, can have one of the values from Table 5.7, also in Chapter 5. Notice that not all of the data types can be used with custom Recordsets. The adChapter is one of these types, as you can't build custom Recordsets with ADO 2.5.

The following statements will create a Recordset for storing various pieces of information about cities:

```
RS.Fields.Append "CityName", adVarChar, 20
RS.Fields.Append "Population", adInteger
RS.Fields.Append "AvgTemperature", adFloat
```

To use the Recordset, you must first open it. Since it's not connected to a database, you must call the Open method without any arguments:

```
RS.Open
```

Then, you can call the usual methods of the Recordset object to populate it. To add a new row to the Recordset call the AddNew method and then assign values with the new row's fields through the Fields collection:

```
RS.AddNew
RS.Fields("CityName") = "Raleigh"
RS.Fields("Population") = 241500
RS.Fields("AvgTemperature") = 59.04
```

Finally, you can commit the changes to the Recordset with the Update method:

```
RS.Update
```

The Fields collection is the Recordset's default property, so the previous lines could have been written as follows:

```
RS.AddNew
RS(0) = "Raleigh"
RS(1) = 241500
RS(2) = 59.04
RS.Update
```

You can also pass two arrays to the AddNew method, one with the names of the fields you want to set and another with the matching values:

```
RS.AddNew Array("CityName", "Population", "AvgTemperature"), _
          Array("Raleigh", 241500, 59.04)
```

Updating a row is also simple. Just set the new field value(s) and then call the Update method:

```
RS.Fields("Population") = 260000
RS.Update
```

To delete a row, just move to the row you want to delete and then call the Delete method:

```
RS.Delete
```

There are no arguments to the Delete method, and you need not call the Update method to commit the changes.

Persisting Custom Recordsets

No matter how you populate or process the custom Recordset, eventually you will have to store it on disk. Do so by calling the Save method, passing the adPersistADTG constant:

```
RS.Save file_name, adPersistADTG
```

You can also use the adPersistXML constant, in which case ADO will store the information in XML format. The benefit of XML representation is that it maintains the structure of the Recordset as well, but custom Recordsets can't be hierarchical.

To read a custom Recordset that has already been stored to disk, call the Open method, whose syntax is:

```
RS.Open source, activeConnection, cursorType, lockType
```

The *source* argument can be an SQL statement, the name of a stored procedure, or the name of a file with the persisted Recordset. When you specify a file as the source of the Open method, you don't need to specify a Connection.

Once you create a custom Recordset in your code, you can use any of the ADO methods discussed in Chapters 5 and 6 to manipulate its rows. Since custom Recordsets are local to each application, you don't have to deal with concurrency issues.

Creating and Managing Disconnected Recordsets

In this section you'll learn how to work with disconnected Recordsets. A disconnected Recordset is nothing but a plain Recordset, like the ones you've been using so far, except it doesn't maintain a live connection to the database. To create a disconnected Recordset, you create a client-side Recordset and then break the connection to the database. The Recordset exists on the client computer, where it can be edited as usual. To write the changes back to the underlying table(s), you must establish a new connection to the database and call the Recordset's UpdateBatch method. Notice that the disconnected Recordset's LockType property must be set either to adLockReadOnly (if you don't plan to change its rows) or to adLockBatchOptimistic (if you want to be able to write the changes back to the database with the UpdateBatch method).

The following statements create a Recordset on the client computer and then disconnect it by setting its ActiveConnection property to Nothing. The *CN* variable that represents the connection is released, as it won't be needed until the user decides to update the database.

```
CN.ConnectionString = "Provider=SQLOLEDB.1;" & _
        "User ID=sa;Initial Catalog=Northwind"
CN.Open
RS.CursorLocation = adUseClient
RS.CursorType = adOpenStatic
RS.LockType = adLockBatchOptimistic
```

```
RS.Open "SELECT * FROM Customers", CN, _
            adOpenStatic, adLockBatchOptimistic
Set RS.ActiveConnection = Nothing
Set CN = Nothing
```

To manipulate the Recordset on the client, use all the properties and methods of the Recordset object. Just keep in mind that it's a client-side Recordset. All the changes affect the local copy of the Recordset, and they are not reflected in the underlying table(s) until you call the UpdateBatch method. The only issue worth discussing here is how to commit the changes you have made to the disconnected Recordset back to the database.

Batch Updating a Disconnected Recordset

The UpdateBatch method will attempt to write all the changes made to the Recordset back to the database. First, it will make sure that a row can be updated and then it will update it. If the row has been changed after it was read into the disconnected Recordset, it will not be updated, and this is where your problems begin. The Recordset object provides a few mechanisms to simplify the handling of rows that can't be updated, but exactly how you will handle the conflicts depends on the application, and you must provide some code.

TIP

Ideally, all edited rows of the disconnected Recordset should be updated. Rows that are updated frequently and by many users should not belong to a disconnected Recordset. You must weigh the benefits of a disconnected Recordset against the burden of handling many conflicts between the rows in the disconnected Recordset and the same rows in the database. If a manager wants to review sales information, you can move all the information you may need to the client, even if this means multiple Recordsets, and then disconnect. This is the best scenario for disconnected Recordsets. If the rows needed by the application are likely to be edited by other users as well, then try to avoid disconnected Recordsets. If you can't (because the manager wants to edit the same information on a plane), then you should be ready to handle massive conflicts between the rows of the disconnected Recordset and the database rows.

Let's say you have set up a Connection object in your code, the *CN* object. To read a Recordset through the *CN* object, use the following statements:

```
RS.ActiveConnection = CN
RS.Open SQL_statement
```

where *SQL_statement* is the SELECT statement that retrieves the desired rows from the database. After the *RS* variable has been populated with the qualifying rows, you can break the connection to the database with the following statement:

```
Set RS.ActiveConnection = Nothing
```

After processing the Recordset on the client computer, you must establish a new connection to the database and commit the changes through this connection. Set up a Connection object with the same properties as the one you created to read the rows, and assign it to the disconnected Recordset's ActiveConnection property:

```
RS.ActiveConnection = CN
```

At this point, the Recordset has been connected to its source and you can commit the changes to the database. If you want to discard the changes, you can call the CancelBatch method to cancel the changes and refresh the Recordset with "fresh" data from the database. If the user decides to commit the changes to the database, call the UpdateBatch method:

```
RS.UpdateBatch
```

If one or more rows can't be updated, you can find the conflicting records by setting the Recordset's Filter property to *adFilterConflictingRecords*. The rows that were successfully updated will be removed temporarily, and you can iterate through the rows of the filtered Recordset to examine the rows that were not updated.

Now you must handle the conflicting rows. This process can't be automated, as different applications must handle these rows differently. You don't have many options, however. You can either overwrite the conflicting rows in the database, or ignore the changes in the disconnected Recordset for the conflicting rows. You should try to take care of the conflicts without user intervention. Users always think they have the highest priority. Besides, if a user takes even a few seconds to react, another user may change the row in question. Try to establish rules to resolve conflicts. The most common rule is that the last person to change the row wins. You could store the name of the user who changed each row last, as well as when this action took place, and then compare time stamps and/or user names. If you end up discarding any changes made in the disconnected Recordset, make sure you let the user know.

To understand how you can handle the conflicts, you must understand a few properties and methods of the Recordset object, which are discussed next.

The Value, OriginalValue, and UnderlyingValue Properties

These are properties of the Field object. The Value property, which is the Field object's default property, is the current value of the field. Even if the Recordset is not disconnected, the Value property may not be the same as the actual field value in the database. This is the case if another user has changed the row after it was read into the Recordset.

The OriginalValue property is the value that was read from the database when the row was fetched into the Recordset. You can't change this value by editing a row. It will change only if you call the Update method, which will move the values from the Recordset to the database. The Update method will also change the OriginalValue property of the fields in the Recordset.

The UnderlyingValue property is the field's most current value. If the Recordset is not disconnected, when you call the UnderlyingValue property, ADO goes to the database and reads the value of the corresponding field. In a disconnected Recordset, the UnderlyingValue and OriginalValue properties have the same value.

The Resync Method

The Resync method updates the Value and/or UnderlyingValue properties of the involved rows. If Resync is called without an argument, it reads the values of the fields in the database and copies them into the Recordset's rows. It updates both the Value and UnderlyingValue properties. If it's called with the *adResyncUnderlyingValues* argument, it reads the values of the fields from the database and copies them into the UnderlyingValue properties, but it will not affect the Value properties. The statement

```
RS.Resync, adResyncUnderlyingValues
```

will copy the field values from the database into the UnderlyingValue properties of the fields in the Recordset.

Handling Update Conflicts

To update the database with the values of a disconnected Recordset, call the UpdateBatch method. The UpdateBatch method will update as many rows as it can and will flag the rows that could not be updated. You can find the conflicting records by setting the control's Filter property to *adFilterConflictingRecords*. This will eliminate (temporarily) the records that were updated successfully. At this point, you can either handle each conflicting record separately (which we rarely do) or overwrite all the values in the database.

To update all conflicting records unconditionally, you must change the UnderlyingValue property of the fields in the conflicting rows, because this is how ADO figures out whether it can update a row or not. If the UnderlyingValue of all fields in the row are the same as the field values in the database, it updates the table row. If not, it adds the row to the collection of conflicting rows. If you call the Resync method with the *adResyncUnderlyingValues* argument, the UnderlyingValue properties will become the same as the field values in the database. The Value properties will not change; they will hold the edited values. If you call the UpdateBatch method again, this time it should be able to update all rows. It may still fail, as it is possible for another user to change one or more rows after you have resynced the Recordset and before you call the UpdateBatch method for the second time. To handle even this rather unlikely situation, you can call the Resync and Update-Batch methods from within a loop:

```
While Not (RS.EOF And RS.BOF)
    RS.UpdateBatch
    RS.Resync, ad ResyncUnderlyingValues
    RS.Filter = adFilterConflictingRecords
Wend
```

This loop will keep resyncing and updating the Recordset until all rows have been copied to the database and have overwritten the field values in the database.

WARNING   The UpdateBatch method will report as conflicting all the rows that could not be updated because they changed since they were read into the Recordset. Some rows may fail to update the database not because of conflicts, but because their new values violate a constraint. Nothing will stop you from removing a row with related rows in another table from a disconnected Recordset. When you attempt to update the Recordset, however, this row will not be marked as conflicting; instead, it will raise a runtime error. To complicate matters even more, ADO will not raise a runtime error for each row it can't update; it will raise a runtime error for the first row it can't update and will ignore the remaining ones. How do you handle errors (and, while you're at it, conflicts)? My suggestion is to iterate through the disconnected Recordset's rows and update one row at a time. If you can insert the appropriate validation code to make sure that only valid data are transmitted to the database, then you'll minimize the chance of update failures caused by constraint violations. But if the code for updating disconnected Recordsets gets too complicated, chances are you shouldn't be using them.

Data-Browsing and -Editing with Disconnected Recordsets

In this section you'll design a data-browsing and -editing application for rows of the Customers table in the Northwind database. This will be based on the Customers project of Chapter 4, "A First Look at ADO," but this time you're going to use a disconnected Recordset. All the information will be downloaded to the client at once, where it will be edited locally through the interface shown in Figure 11.1. The changes will be committed to the database at once with the UpdateBatch method. The interesting part of this project is how to handle conflicts between the local Recordset and the rows in the database.

FIGURE 11.1:

The DisconnectedRS project demonstrates the use of disconnected Recordsets in a VB application.

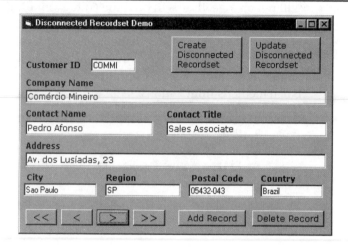

To create a disconnected Recordset, you need a Recordset and a Connection object. Both objects must be available to multiple procedures, so insert the following declarations at the beginning of the Code module and outside any procedure.

```
Dim RS As New ADOR.Recordset
Dim CN As New ADODB.Connection
```

The Create Disconnected Recordset button reads the Recordset to the client and then disconnects from the database. The code behind this button is straightforward, and the properties of the Recordset are mandatory. Disconnected Recordsets are obviously client-side Recordsets and, as such, they are static. Their LockType property must be set to adLockBatchOptimistic; any other setting will cause the Recordset to expire as soon as its connection to the database is broken (unless it's a read-only Recordset, of course).

LISTING 11.1   The Create Disconnected Recordset Button

```
Private Sub Command1_Click()
    CN.ConnectionString = "Provider=SQLOLEDB.1; " & _
            " User ID=sa;" & _
            " Initial Catalog=Northwind"
    CN.Open
    RS.CursorLocation = adUseClient
    RS.CursorType = adOpenStatic
    RS.LockType = adLockBatchOptimistic
    RS.Open "SELECT * FROM Customers", CN, _
            adOpenStatic, adLockBatchOptimistic
    Set RS.ActiveConnection = Nothing
    CN.Close
```

```
        Set CN = Nothing
        BindTextBoxes
        EnableControls
    End Sub
```

The BindTextBoxes procedure binds the TextBox controls on the Form to the RS Recordset's fields by setting the controls' DataSource and DataField properties. You can also use an ADO Data control to bind the controls to the fields by placing an ADO Data control on the Form and then setting its Recordset property to the *RS* variable. The code of the BindTextBoxes subroutine is straightforward.

LISTING 11.2   **The BindTextBoxes Procedure**

```
Sub BindTextBoxes()
    Set txtCompany.DataSource = RS
    txtCompany.DataField = "CompanyName"
    Set txtContactName.DataSource = RS
    txtContactName.DataField = "ContactName"
    Set txtContactTitle.DataSource = RS
    txtContactTitle.DataField = "ContactTitle"
    Set txtAddress.DataSource = RS
    txtAddress.DataField = "Address"
    Set txtCity.DataSource = RS
    txtCity.DataField = "City"
    Set txtRegion.DataSource = RS
    txtRegion.DataField = "Region"
    Set txtPCode.DataSource = RS
    txtPCode.DataField = "PostalCode"
    Set txtCountry.DataSource = RS
    txtCountry.DataField = "Country"
End Sub
```

The code behind the navigational buttons calls the corresponding Move methods of the *RS* variable. The Add Record and Delete Record buttons call the AddNew and Delete methods of the *RS.Recordset* variable, respectively. While a row is being added or edited, you should disable the navigational buttons and display the usual OK and Cancel buttons. I have not included this functionality in the application because you have seen it in several sample applications already.

Let's look at the code that commits all changes in the local Recordset to the database. The code starts by examining the number of pending rows (these are the rows that must be updated). It does so by setting the Recordset's Filter property to adFilterPendingRecords. If there are no pending rows, the program doesn't even attempt to commit the changes. If there are pending rows, it calls the UpdateBatch method to commit the changes.

If some of the rows can't be updated because they violate constraints, a runtime error is generated. When you delete a row, it is removed immediately from the local Recordset. When you commit the changes to the database, ADO may discover that some of the deleted rows can't be actually removed, because they're related to rows in other tables and their removal would violate the integrity of the database. These rows are not conflicts; they will generate runtime errors. They simply can't be removed from the database and you must refresh the disconnected Recordset to synchronize it with the actual rows in the database.

The same is true for rows with invalid keys, Null fields, and so on. All these rows will be ignored. Notice that ADO will generate a single runtime error for the first row it can't commit to the database. Subsequent rows that violate constraints or the integrity of the database will be discarded silently.

In addition to the rows that are discarded, there may be conflicting rows as well. Conflicting rows are simpler to handle. In this example, the code prompts the user as to whether he wants to update the rows in the database unconditionally. If the user agrees, the program synchronizes the Underlying values of the conflicting rows and then calls the UpdateBatch method again. Because the Recordset has been filtered, only the conflicting rows will be transmitted to the database.

LISTING 11.3   **The Update Disconnected Recordset Button**

```
Private Sub bttnSubmit_click()
    CN.ConnectionString = "Provider=SQLOLEDB.1; " & _
              "User ID=sa;Initial Catalog=Northwind"
    CN.Open
    Set RS.ActiveConnection = CN

    RS.Filter = adFilterPendingRecords
    If RS.RecordCount = 0 Then
        MsgBox "There are no records to be updated."
    Else
        On Error Resume Next
        RS.UpdateBatch
        If Err.Number <> 0 Then
            MsgBox Err.Description
            RS.Filter = adFilterConflictingRecords
            If RS.EOF And RS.BOF Then
                MsgBox "All changes successfully committed"
            Else
                reply = MsgBox("There were conflicts " & _
                        "in updating the table" & vbCrLf & _
```

```
                        " Commit changes anyway?", vbYesNo)
            If reply = vbYes Then
                On Error GoTo 0
                RS.Resync adAffectGroup, & _
                        adResyncUnderlyingValues
                RS.UpdateBatch
            End If
        End If
    End If
End If
RS.Filter = ""
Set RS.ActiveConnection = Nothing
Set CN = Nothing
Set RS = Nothing
DisableControls
End Sub
```

The rows that violate the integrity of the database were discarded; however, you can't tell which rows these were. The current version of ADO (I'm using an early beta version that comes with the Beta 3 version of Windows 2000) does not support a filtering operation that removes the rows that were not updated successfully. If you want to know which rows failed to update the database, you must monitor all the changes with the help of the Recordset object's events, and specifically the RecordChangeComplete event. This event is fired when a record is changed and it reports the action that caused it. You can monitor the first argument of the method, the *adReason* argument, and keep track of the additions, modifications, and deletions, probably in a custom Recordset. When the original Recordset is refreshed, you can compare the two Recordsets and find out which rows failed to update the database. This is probably too much work and cancels all the benefits of using disconnected Recordsets. Disconnected Recordsets are meant to simplify the development of certain types of applications, and they cannot replace regular client-side Recordsets.

WARNING   Many programmers who are new to ADO attempt to locate all the rows that failed to update the database in the conflicting rows collection. The conflicting rows are the ones that were changed by other users since you (or the application) read them. ADO doesn't update these rows as a courtesy to you, the programmer, and not because it can't.

The Remote Data Services

The Remote Data Services (RDS) is another data-access component, designed to work with ADO. RDS is not a superset or subset of ADO; it complements ADO. Where ADO assumes you have a connection to a database and you retrieve rows through this connection, RDS allows you to retrieve Recordsets from remote databases.

RDS has a simple object model, consisting of three components. The *RDSDataControl* object is equivalent to a Data Control; it binds the controls on a Web page to the fields of a Recordset. The *RDSDataSpace* object is a component that allows the client application to contact components on the Web server over the HTTP protocol. These first two objects reside on the client and are installed by Internet Explorer. The *RDSDataFactory* component runs off the Web server and allows you to create Recordsets and transmit them to the client via HTTP. The RDSDataFactory is the least useful object and is not discussed in this book. The other two components are discussed in detail and demonstrated with examples.

The RDSDataControl object binds controls on a Web page to database fields. The RDSDataControl is an ActiveX control that's used only with Web pages (there's no need to use this control with a client application written in VB); it's equivalent to the ADO Data Control of Visual Basic.

The RDSDataSpace object creates COM objects on the Web server and returns references to these objects to the client application. A COM object is a Class: a component that can be accessed through properties and methods it exposes. ADO is a COM object. It has no visible interface but can be accessed through the members it exposes. To use ADO in a project, you must add a reference to the ADO component. Visual Basic loads the DLL that implements ADO and executes it in the same memory space as the VB application. COM components are loaded along with an application, and the two communicate with each other as if they were a single application.

The catch is that COM objects packaged as DLLs must be loaded in the same memory space as the application that uses them. This is the case with VB applications that use Classes. When the application creates an instance of a Class with the CreateObject() function, the DLL that implements the Class is loaded in the same memory space as the application and executed there. When the client application is running on a remote computer, however, it can't communicate directly with a Class. This is where the DataSpace comes in. The DataSpace object is a proxy for the components that reside on the server. A Web application may need to access a component on the Web server. Where a VB application would call the CreateObject() function to create an instance of a Class and then use it, the Web application must call the CreateObject method of the DataSpace object.

The RDSDataSpace object has no equivalent object in VB, so don't worry if you don't quite understand how it works or how to use it in your code. You are going to see what it can do for your application and how to use it on a Web page to support the RDSDataControl.

Using the RDSDataControl on the Web

The RDSDataControl is a lightweight data control, designed for use on Web pages. It has no visible user interface, but it's an ActiveX control that can be placed on a Web page with the <OBJECT> tag. Its function is to connect to a database through the HTTP protocol and retrieve a Recordset. Once the Recordset is on the client computer, the connection is automatically dropped and the rows live on the client, where they can be processed. In effect, the Recordset maintained on the client by the RDSDataControl is a disconnected Recordset. You can update the Recordset on the client and then submit the changes back to the server in Batch mode.

The RDSDataControl is also a data source, and you can bind DHTML controls to the RDS control. As you move through the rows of the Recordset with the control's Move methods, the DHTML controls are automatically updated. If you edit them, the new values overwrite the original values in the Recordset. The RDSDataControl exposes the usual navigational methods, as well as methods for sorting and filtering rows of the Recordset. These methods are similar to the equivalent methods of the ADO Recordset, but the Recordset of the RDSDataControl does not support all the features of the ADO Recordset. Let's start by reviewing the process of using the RDSDataControl on a Web page.

Placing an RDSDataControl on a Web Page

To place an instance of the control on a Web page, use the following tag:

```
<OBJECT CLASSID="clsid:BD96C556-65A3-11D0-983A-00C04FC29E33"
ID="RDSDC">
</OBJECT>
```

The long *CLASSID* string is the control's programmatic ID. This is how the control is known to the system, and you can find this value in the Registry. The control is installed along with Internet Explorer (version 4 or higher), so this approach works only in Internet Explorer clients.

Retrieving a Recordset

To retrieve a Recordset from a server, you must set the control's Connect, Server, and SQL properties. These properties can be set in the <OBJECT> tag, or they can be set in the Window_onLoad event, which is fired when a Web page is loaded and before it's drawn. If you want to specify the Recordset in the <OBJECT> tag, use the following parameters between the <OBJECT> and </OBJECT> tags:

```
<OBJECT CLASSID="clsid:BD96C556-65A3-11D0-983A-00C04FC29E33"
ID="RDSDC">
<PARAM NAME="Connect" VALUE="DSN=NWIND;UID=username;PWD=password;>
<PARAM NAME="Server" VALUE="http://servername">
<PARAM NAME="SQL" VALUE="SELECT * FROM Customers">
</OBJECT>
```

The Server property specifies the server where the data will come from. If you're using a single computer as server and client, you can use the URL 127.0.0.1 or leave the Server property blank. The Connect property determines the DSN of the database you want to connect to. (If you don't know how to set up a DSN for a database, see the section "DSN-Based Connections" in Chapter 5.) Notice that this must be a System DSN and not a User DSN. Finally, the SQL property is set to a SELECT statement that will retrieve the desired rows from one or more tables.

If you'd rather load the Recordset from within your code, you must still place the <OBJECT> tag of the control on the page (without the parameters) and then insert the following lines in the page's Window_onLoad event handler:

```
Sub Window_onLoad()
    RDSDC.Connect = "DSN=NWIND;UID=username;PWD=password;"
    RDSDC.Server= "http://servername"
    RDSDC.SQL="SELECT * FROM Customers"
    RDSDC.Refresh
End Sub
```

Notice that you call the Refresh method to actually assign the Recordset to the control. The advantage of this method is that you can reload a new Recordset from within the page's script, by placing the same lines in a button's onClick event handler.

Binding DHTML Controls to the RDSDataControl

The last step is to bind DHTML elements to the control's Recordset. This is done with the help of the DATASRC and DATAFLD attributes of the DHTML element. To bind a Text element to the CompanyName field, use the following tag:

```
<INPUT Type=Text Name=txtCompany DATASRC="#RDSDC"
DATAFLD="CompanyName">
```

Notice the # sign in front of the control's name in the DATASRC attribute. This is required to indicate that the element is bound to a Recordset that resides on the client. The Text control is a regular HTML control, but when you specify the DATASRC and DATAFLD it becomes a DHTML control.

In addition to intrinsic controls, you can bind more complicated objects to a RDS-DataControl. To bind a table to a Recordset, use the following table definition:

```
<TABLE ID="Products" BORDER="1">
<THEAD BGCOLOR=#cceecc>
<TD><B>Product Name</B><TD ALIGN=center><B>Price</B>
</THEAD>
<TR>
<TD><SPAN ID=ProductName></SPAN>
<TD ALIGN=right><SPAN ID=ProductPrice></SPAN>
</TABLE>
```

This is an odd table definition for HTML, but then again this is not HTML; it's DHTML and will only work with Internet Explorer. Internet Explorer will create as many rows as necessary to append all the rows of the Recordset to the table. As you can see, the contents of the columns are not specified; you insert a placeholder <SPAN> tag. To bind the table's columns to database fields, you must set the DATASRC and DATAFLD properties of the SPAN attribute. To do so, you must execute the following statements from within a script:

```
Products.DATASRC="#RDSDC1"
ProductName.DATAFLD="ProductName"
ProductPrice.DATAFLD="UnitPrice"
```

The following HTML page will display a table whose cells are bound to the ProductName and UnitPrice fields of the Products table in the Northwind database. Change the value of the DSN to match the DSN of the Northwind database on your system. The same code will work with both the Jet and SQL Server version of the database. The document is called SimpleRDSTable.htm and you'll find it in this chapter's folder on the CD.

LISTING 11.4   The SimpleRDSTable.htm Page

```
<HTML>
<HEAD>

<OBJECT ID=RDSDC1 WIDTH=1 HEIGHT=1
CLASSID="CLSID:BD96C556-65A3-11D0-983A-00C04FC29E33">
</OBJECT>

<SCRIPT Language=VBScript>
Sub Window_OnLoad()
'    Set up the RDSDataControl for Categories
     RDSDC1.Server = ""
     RDSDC1.Connect = "DSN=NWINDDB"
     RDSDC1.SQL = "SELECT ProductName, UnitPrice FROM Products"
     RDSDC1.Refresh
     Products.DATASRC="#RDSDC1"
```

```
        ProductName.DATAFLD="ProductName"
        ProductPrice.DATAFLD="UnitPrice"
End Sub

</SCRIPT>
</HEAD>

<BODY>
<CENTER>
<TABLE ID="Products" BORDER="1">
<THEAD BGCOLOR=#cceecc>
<TD><B>Product Name</B><TD ALIGN=center><B>Price</B>
</THEAD>
<TR>
<TD><SPAN ID=ProductName></SPAN>
<TD ALIGN=right><SPAN ID=ProductPrice></SPAN>
</TABLE>
</CENTER>
</BODY>
</HTML>
```

For a more advanced and practical example of binding DHTML tables to database fields, see the section "The RDSTable.htm Page" later in this chapter. As you can understand, binding DHTML elements to the fields of a database would be extremely useful if we could edit the table through the controls on a Web page. This is exactly what the RDSTable page demonstrates.

The RDSDataControl's Members

The most important properties of the RDSDataControl are the Connect, Server, and SQL properties, discussed in the previous section. Even if you use the RDS-DataControl to bind DHTML elements to database fields, these are the properties you must set. In addition, the control supports several properties and methods, which are discussed here.

The ReadyState Property   The ReadyState property indicates the status of the control while it fetches data from the database; its value is one of the following constants:

Constant	Description
adcReadyStateComplete	The Recordset has been fetched and is ready to be used by the application.

adcReadyStateInteractive	The Recordset is being fetched, but some rows are available for use.
adcReadyStateLoaded	The Recordset has not been fetched yet and no rows are available to the application.

If an error occurs and no data can be loaded, the ReadyState property will be set to adcReadyStateLoaded. In addition, each time the ReadyState property changes value, the onReadyStateChange event is fired.

The Recordset Property   The Recordset property allows you to access the rows of the Recordset downloaded to the client through the RDSDataControl. This property is an ADOR (ADO Remote) Recordset object, and it exposes many of the members of the ADODB.Recordset object. You can use the MoveFirst, Move-Last, MovePrevious, and MoveNext methods to navigate through the Recordset (the Move method is not supported), use the RecordCount property to find the number of rows in the Recordset, and so on.

The FilterColumn, FilterCriterion, and FilterValue Properties   These properties allow you to filter the disconnected Recordset. The ADOR.Recordset doesn't support the Filter method, unlike the ADODB.Recordset. You must specify a column name with the FilterColumn property, a relational operator with the FilterCriterion property, and the desired value with the FilterValue property. To isolate the customer whose ID is "ALFKI," use the following statements:

```
RDSDC.FilterColumn = "CustomerID"
RDSDC.FilterCriterion = "="
RDSDC.FilterValue = "ALFKI"
```

To apply the filter, call the Reset method, which is described next.

The Reset Method   The relational operators you can use with the FilterCriterion property are =, <>, <= and >=. The ADOR.Recordset object's filtering capabilities are quite limited when compared to the Filter property of the ADODB .Recordset object. However, you can apply multiple filters by calling the Reset method with the True argument.

Normally, the Reset method filters the original Recordset. If you want to apply a new filter to an already filtered Recordset, call the Reset method as follows:

```
RDSDC.Reset True
```

To isolate the products with an ID in the range from 1 to 10, use the following statements:

```
RDSDC.FilterColumn = "ProductID"
RDSDC.FilterCriterion = ">="
RDSDC.FilterValue = "1"
```

```
RDSDC.Reset
RDSDC.FilterColumn = "ProductID"
RDSDC.FilterCriterion = "<="
RDSDC.FilterValue = "10"
RDSDC.Reset True
```

The FilterColumn, FilterCriterion, and FilterValue are properties of the RDS-DataControl object. So is the Reset method. Oddly, the ADOR.Recordset object supports the Recordset Filter property, in a limited way. You can set the Recordset .Filter property to one of the following values to isolate rows according to their status:

Value	Action
adFilterConflictingRecords	Filters out all rows except conflicts
adFilterPendingRecords	Filters out all rows except those pending
adFilterNone	Resets the current filter and repopulates the Recordset with all its rows

The Refresh Method   The Refresh method updates the RDSDataControl's Recordset by reading its rows from the database. This method causes all the rows of the Recordset to be moved from the server to the client, and the remote Recordset is overwritten without any warnings.

The SubmitChanges and CancelUpdate Methods   The SubmitChanges method sends the rows that have been changed since the last time the disconnected Recordset was refreshed. The SubmitChanges method is equivalent to the UpdateBatch of the ADODB.Recordset object. However, the SubmitChanges method may not update the rows in the database. If at least one row fails to update, then the SubmitChanges method will not update any row in the database. You will see how the SubmitChanges method is used on a Web page in the next section.

Asynchronous Operations   The RDSDataControl can fetch and refresh Recordsets asynchronously. By default, both operations are performed asynchronously, which is what you want in a Web application. To specify that the rows of a Recordset must be fetched synchronously, set the FetchOptions property to adcFetchUpfront:

```
RDSDC.FetchOptions = adcFetchUpfront
```

(The other valid setting for this property is adcFetchBackground.)

To specify that the Recordset must be refreshed synchronously, set the ExecuteOptions to adExecSync.

A Data-Browsing and -Editing Web Page

Figure 11.2 shows an example of a Web page that allows you to retrieve a Recordset to the client, edit it, and then submit the changes to the database by establishing a new connection. The RDSDemo page displays the fields of the Customers table and allows you to edit them, or add new ones, from Internet Explorer. All you need is a connection to your corporate Web server.

FIGURE 11.2:

The RDSDemo page uses a disconnected Recordset to edit the rows of the Customers table through a Web interface.

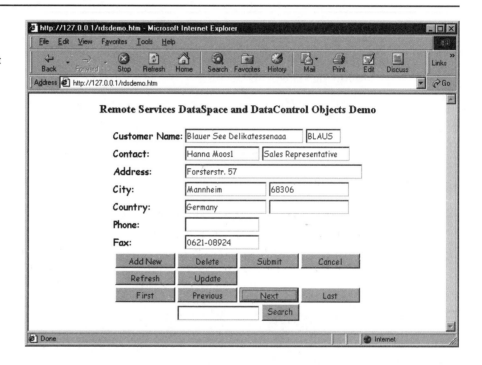

This page uses a client-side script, which reacts to the Click event of the various buttons. The script is written in VBScript, and the event handlers for the buttons on the Form are specified in the tags that insert the buttons on the Form. Here are the definitions for the first few buttons on the Form:

```
<INPUT Type=button Value="Add New" Width = 150 Name=bttnAdd
        OnClick=AddNew() style="HEIGHT: 24px; WIDTH: 100px">
<INPUT Type=button Value=Delete Width = 150 Name=bttnDelete
        OnClick=Delete() style="HEIGHT: 24px; WIDTH: 100px">
<INPUT Type=button Value=Submit Width = 150 Name=bttnSubmit
        OnClick=Submit() style="HEIGHT: 24px; WIDTH: 100px">
<INPUT Type=button Value=Cancel Width = 150 Name=bttnCancel
        OnClick=Cancel() style="HEIGHT: 24px; WIDTH: 100px">
```

The style attribute is a DHTML attribute that determines the appearance of the control on the Form. These definitions will work with Internet Explorer only.

The RDSDemo page contains a RDSDataControl and several DHTML controls that are bound to the RDSDataControl. The RDSDataControl was placed on the page with the following tag:

```
<OBJECT ID=RDSDC WIDTH=1 HEIGHT=1
CLASSID="CLSID:BD96C556-65A3-11D0-983A-00C04FC29E33">
</OBJECT>
```

The RDSDC (RDSDataControl) binds all the controls on the Form to the fields of the Customers table. The first few Text controls were placed on the page with the following statements:

```
<TD height=10 ><FONT FACE='Comic Sans MS'>Customer Name:</FONT>
<TD>
<INPUT name=txtCustomer DataSrc=#RDSDC DataFld=CompanyName
        style="HEIGHT: 24px; WIDTH: 200px">
<TR>
<TD height=10><FONT FACE='Comic Sans MS'>Contact: </FONT>
<TD>
<INPUT name=txtContact DataSrc=#RDSDC DataFld=ContactName
        style="HEIGHT: 24px; WIDTH: 150px">
```

The actual binding takes place when the Form is loaded with the following statements:

```
Sub Window_OnLoad()
    RDSDC.Server = "http:/PROTOSERVER"
    RDSDC.Connect = "DSN=SQLNWIND;UID=sa"
    RDSDC.SQL = "SELECT * From Customers"
    RDSDC.Refresh
End Sub
```

Don't forget to change the name of the server and the DSN to match the corresponding names on your installation. The RDSDemo.htm file you will find on the CD uses an empty string as the Connect property, so that it will work on the local system. You could have specified the values of the Server, Connect, and SQL parameters in the <OBJECT> tag as well.

The Add New button calls the Recordset's AddNew method and moves the focus to the first Text control on the Form:

```
Sub AddNew()
        RDSDC.Recordset.AddNew
        txtCustomer.Select
End Sub
```

To commit the changes to the Recordset, you must click the Update button. The script calls the Update method and then moves to the next row:

```
Sub UpdateRecord()
    RDSDC.Recordset.Update
    RDSDC.Recordset.MoveNext
End Sub
```

The most interesting procedure is the Submit() subroutine, which is called every time the user wants to post the changes to the database. The script calls the SubmitChanges method of the disconnected Recordset to transmit all the rows that were edited to the Web server. The script starts by counting the number of pending rows, to make sure there are rows to be updated. If so, the SubmitChanges method is called. If some of the changes violate the integrity of the database, no rows will be updated. Unfortunately, the RDSDataControl doesn't support a Resync method. In the last section of this chapter, you will see how to use business objects from within your Web page to edit individual rows in the database.

LISTING 11.5   **Updating the Database with the Submit Method**

```
Sub Submit()
    RDSDC.Recordset.Filter = adFilterPendingRecords
    On Error Resume Next
    If RDSDC.Recordset.RecordCount = 0 Then
        MsgBox "There are no records to be updated."
        RDSDC.Recordset.Filter = adFilterNone
    Else
        RDSDC.SubmitChanges
        If Err.Number <> 0 then
            MsgBox Err.Description
        End If
    End If
    RDSDC.Recordset.Filter = adFilterNone
End Sub
```

The last two controls on the page allow you to locate rows based on their Contact-Name field. Enter the first few characters of the desired row's contact name and then click the Search button. The RDSDataControl doesn't support a Find method, so you must use the Filter properties. Since you can't use a LIKE operator, use this trick: filter out all the rows with a contact name less than the supplied value followed by a space and greater than the same value followed by a z. Here's the script that implements the Search feature:

```
Sub Search()
    RDSDC.FilterColumn="ContactName"
    RDSDC.FilterCriterion=">="
```

```
        RDSDC.FilterValue=Trim(txtSearch.Value) & " "
        RDSDC.Reset

        RDSDC.FilterCriterion="<="
        RDSDC.FilterValue=Trim(txtSearch.Value) & "Z"
        RDSDC.Reset(TRUE)

        If RDSDC.Recordset.Recordcount = 0 Then RDSDC.Refresh
    End Sub
```

The RDSTable.htm Page

The page shown in Figure 11.3 contains two DHTML tables. The table on the left displays the rows of the Categories table in the Northwind database. This table's contents don't change. Each time the user clicks a category name, the products belonging to this category are displayed on the second table. This is an interesting trick that allows you to use tables as navigational tools within a Recordset. The same page can display different sets of information without additional trips to the server. It downloads the Categories and Products tables and manipulates them locally, from within a client-side script.

FIGURE 11.3:

The RDSTable.htm page

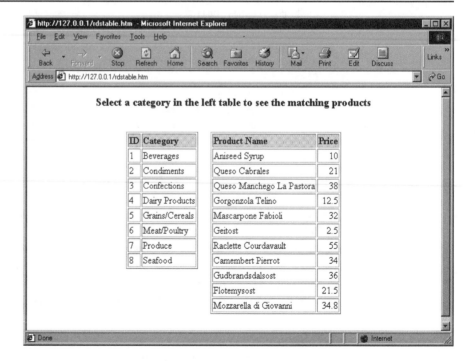

```
<TABLE BORDER= "1" ID="Categories">
<THEAD BGCOLOR=#cceecc>
<TD><B>ID</B><TD><B>Category</B>
</THEAD>
<TR onClick=GetRowID()>
<TD><SPAN ID=CategoryID></SPAN>
<TD><SPAN ID=CategoryName></SPAN>
</TABLE>
```

This table contains two columns and many rows. The exact number of rows is determined by the number of rows in the first RDSDataControl. As you can see, the name of the control doesn't appear in the table's definition. You can populate the table at any time from within your script by setting the two <SPAN> sections of the table with statements like these:

```
Categories.DATASRC="#RDSDC1"
CategoryID.DATAFLD="CategoryID"
CategoryName.DATAFLD="CategoryName"
```

These lines are typical of DHTML tables. They set the table's DATASRC property to the name of the RDSDataControl with the desired Recordset. Once done, set the DATAFLD property of each SPAN section of the table to the appropriate field name. The table is resized automatically to accommodate all the rows in the Recordset.

Another interesting procedure in this script is the GetRowID function, which retrieves the ID of the row that was clicked. To find out which row in the left table was clicked, use the following expression:

```
window.event.srcelement.recordNumber
```

This expression returns the index of the selected row. The index of the first row is 1. The script skips all the previous rows and, when it hits the selected one, uses the category ID as the FilterValue for the second Recordset. It filters out the products that don't belong to the selected category and displays the rows of the selected category on the second table.

The script could have retrieved the ID of the selected category faster if it took advantage of the fact that the ID is the same as the row number, but this technique doesn't work with all tables. It just happens to work with the Categories table, because the categories are numbered sequentially. The Customers table, for example, doesn't use consecutive numeric keys, so the row number wouldn't be the same as the customer's key. Here's the complete listing of the RDSTable .htm page.

LISTING 11.6   **The RDSTable.htm Page**

```
<HTML>
<HEAD>

<OBJECT ID=RDSDC1 WIDTH=1 HEIGHT=1
CLASSID="CLSID:BD96C556-65A3-11D0-983A-00C04FC29E33">
</OBJECT>

<OBJECT ID=RDSDC2 WIDTH=1 HEIGHT=1
CLASSID="CLSID:BD96C556-65A3-11D0-983A-00C04FC29E33">
</OBJECT>

<SCRIPT Language=VBScript>
Sub Window_OnLoad()
'    Set up the RDSDataControl for Categories
    RDSDC1.Server = ""
    RDSDC1.Connect = "DSN=SQLNWIND;UID=sa"
    RDSDC1.SQL = "SELECT CategoryID, CategoryName FROM Categories"
    RDSDC1.Refresh
    Categories.DATASRC="#RDSDC1"
    CategoryID.DATAFLD="CategoryID"
    CategoryName.DATAFLD="CategoryName"
'    Set up the RDSDataControl for Products
    RDSDC2.Server = ""
    RDSDC2.Connect = "DSN=SQLNWIND;UID=sa"
    RDSDC2.SQL =
    "SELECT CategoryID, ProductName, UnitPrice FROM Products"
    RDSDC2.Refresh
    Products.DATASRC="#RDSDC2"
    ProductName.DATAFLD="ProductName"
    ProductPrice.DATAFLD="UnitPrice"
End Sub

Sub GetRowID()
'    Get selected row's number
    RowID = window.event.srcelement.recordNumber
'    and then scan rows sequentially to reach
'    the selected line
    RDSDC1.Recordset.MoveFirst
    For iRow = 1 To RowID - 1
        RDSDC1.Recordset.MoveNext
```

```
      Next
'     Reset the filter of the 2nd RDSDataControl
      RDSDC2.FilterColumn=""
      RDSDC2.Reset
'     and set a new filter (the selected category ID)
      RDSDC2.FilterColumn="CategoryID"
      RDSDC2.FilterCriterion="="
      RDSDC2.FilterValue=RDSDC1.Recordset.Fields(0)
      RDSDC2.Reset
End Sub

</SCRIPT>
</HEAD>

<BODY>
<CENTER>
<H3>Select a category in the left table to see the matching
    products</H3>
<TABLE CELLSPACING=20>
<TR>
<TD VALIGN=TOP>
<TABLE BORDER= "1" ID="Categories">
<THEAD BGCOLOR=#cceecc>
<TD><B>ID</B><TD><B>Category</B>
</THEAD>
<TR onClick=GetRowID()>
<TD><SPAN ID=CategoryID></SPAN>
<TD><SPAN ID=CategoryName></SPAN>
</TABLE>
<TD VALIGN=top>
<TABLE ID="Products" BORDER="1">
<THEAD BGCOLOR=#cceecc>
<TD><B>Product Name</B><TD ALIGN=center><B>Price</B>
</THEAD>
<TR>
<TD><SPAN ID=ProductName></SPAN>
<TD ALIGN=right><SPAN ID=ProductPrice></SPAN>
</TABLE>
</TABLE>
</CENTER>
</BODY>
</HTML>
```

The DataSpace Object

You're probably tired of reading that client applications shouldn't contact the database directly. You should implement a middle tier that exposes all the methods you need to access and modify the tables. RDS-based applications shouldn't be different. The data-bound approach presented in the previous examples is too simple to be practical. The client application should be able to call the methods of a Class on the server. In a VB application, this is almost trivial. You add a reference to the Class in your project, create an instance of the Class, and call its members to access the database. This works on a LAN because the DLL that implements the Class can be downloaded to the client and executed there. Things are quite different on the Web. You just can't expect that all the clients will download and install the required DLLs. You can't contact the remote DLL either, because DCOM can't get through firewalls. We need a method to contact a remote DLL through the HTTP protocol.

The following statement will create an instance of the clsCustomer Class in a VB application by calling the CreateObject() function. The following statement will create an instance of the specified Class when executed from within VB:

```
Set myObject = CreateObject("Project.Class")
```

This function will work in VB and VBScript, as long as the client application is running on the same computer as the Class. If the Class is registered on another computer on the LAN, then you must use the following form of the same function:

```
Set myObject = CreateObject("Project.Class", "server_name")
```

(If the Class is configured on the client machine to run via DCOM, then you don't have to specify the *server_name* argument. You can call it as if it were installed on the local machine.) What do you think will happen if the client is Internet Explorer and the Class resides on a Web server? To answer this question, you should know that a Class's code (a DLL) must be executed in the same memory space as the application that uses it. An application can't communicate with the DLL over the HTTP protocol. So, the CreateObject() function will not work over the Web.

The answer to this problem is DCOM (Distributed COM). DCOM allows two remote processes to communicate with each other. DCOM is something like a telephone. Since you can't shout loud enough to be heard in another town, you use a mechanism to transfer your voice to the other end (and vice versa). The telephone is a proxy: a mechanism that makes each person involved in the conversation feel as though they are in close proximity to the other person. (If you didn't know how the telephone works, you'd probably think you're talking to a person the same room, or at least the same house.)

To return to DCOM, the proxy is a component that runs on the client and acts as an intermediary between the COM component on the server (the Class) and the client application. The client application thinks it's talking directly to the Class, while in reality it goes through a proxy. On the server's end, there's another component, called a *stub*. The server stub communicates with the client's proxy on one end and the actual COM component on the other end. These two components enable the client application to contact a component on the server. DCOM is the cornerstone of Microsoft's DNA (Distributed interNet Architecture) and enables remote applications to use COM components on the server over the HTTP protocol. Theoretically, you should be able to write applications that work over the Internet, just as they do on a LAN. Practically, it's not that simple. We will get there someday, for sure, but the vehicle may not be DCOM. If you're a Microsoft shop, DCOM is the only way to build clients that contact components on the Web server.

FIGURE 11.4:

Proxies and stubs impersonate client and server components and allow them to communicate through the HTTP protocol.

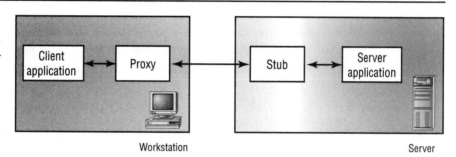

Workstation

Server

This information is not really useful to you, the VB developer, because you won't have to write proxies or stubs yourself. However, you must follow certain rules to make your Web application talk to COM objects on the Web server. You must also change a few settings in the server computer's Registry. The entire process is not totally transparent to you, but it sure is simpler that writing your own proxy mechanism.

The RDSDataSpace object is the client proxy. If you want to contact a component on the server through the HTTP protocol, you must place an instance of the RDSDataSpace object on the page and use its CreateObject method to create an instance of the component on the server:

```
objRDSDS = CreateObject("RDS.DataSpace")
Set myObj = objRDSDS.CreateObject("Project.Class")
```

In the following section, we'll build a Web page that calls the methods of a business component on the Web server to manipulate the rows of the Customers table. First, you must build the Class. Not from scratch—instead, you will revise the CustomerClass you built in an earlier chapter so that it can be called remotely.

Building Classes for RDS

Building Classes is not new to you. Any of the Classes you have built so far can be called remotely from a client machine through the Remote Data Services (RDS). However, there are a few things you should have in mind, including a few simple rules. Before getting into the details of building Classes for RDS, let me explain when you should use Classes remotely.

A Web page that uses RDS (the RDSDataControl or RDSDataSpace components) can only be viewed with Internet Explorer. This is a serious drawback, and pages based on RDS should be used in intranet environments. If you plan to develop a Web application and deploy it on the Internet, forget the RDS components.

ADOR Recordsets

The main functionality of RDS is to maintain a local Recordset on the client and update a database on a remote computer on demand. This local Recordset is similar to the ADODB.Recordset, but not quite the same. If you want to experiment with the RDS.Recordset object in a VB project (to see its members in the Object Browser window), you must add a reference to the component Microsoft ActiveX Data Objects Recordset Library. Then, you'll be able to access the ADOR component from within your code. ADOR exposes a single property, which is the Recordset object. The ADOR.Recordset is a subset of the ADODB.Recordset and exposes the basic functionality of a Recordset to the remote client. Both Recordsets expose the same members in the Visual Basic IDE, but some of the properties and methods are not available in the browser environment. For example, you can't read or set the ActiveConnection property, because the browser doesn't maintain a connection to the database (it doesn't even maintain a connection to the Web server, which explains why it's so difficult to maintain state in a Web application).

As such, the RDS.Recordset is a disconnected Recordset. This means it's a static, client-side Recordset, and its properties must be set to account for this. Even if your Class creates ADODB.Recordsets, they are automatically translated into ADOR .Recordsets before they are transmitted to the client. It is imperative to set the CursorType, CursorLocation, and LockType properties to these values:

Property Name	Setting
CursorType	adOpenStatic
CursorLocation	adUseClient
LockType	adLockBatchOptimisitc

If you fail to use these settings, your browser will eventually crash with an "unexpected error." Even if you don't plan to update the Recordset, you can't set its LockType to read-only. Setting this property to adLockBatchOptimistic is the only way for VB to figure out that this is a disconnected Recordset.

The Revised clsCustomers Class

In the last example of this chapter, you are going to revise the RDSDemo page. With the RDSDataControl, we rely on a data control to bind the controls on the page to the appropriate database field and take care of actions such as editing the controls and updating the database. It's what the ADO Data Control and the data-bound controls do on a VB Form, only this time the Form is a Web page. The revised application will use business objects on the Web server to contact the database, and you'll use the ClassCustomers Class to contact the database. This Class exposes methods for editing/deleting existing customers and adding new ones. It's one of the sample applications you'll develop in Chapter 12. If you are not familiar with Classes, you should read Chapter 12 first, and then return to complete this section's example. You'll change the code a little, and then you'll design a new Web page to display the fields of the current row in the Customers table.

The first step is to revise the clsCustomers Class. Open the project Customers from Chapter 12 and save it in a new folder (you will find the revised project in the RemoteCustomers folder in this chapter's folder on the CD). Before you save the project, rename the ClassCustomers project to RemoteCustomers (no need to rename the test project). If you don't rename the project, when the revised Class is registered it will replace the original.

Change the declarations of the Class's methods. By default, Visual Basic passes parameters by reference. The calling application passes a pointer to the location where the information is stored. The pointer is valid in the context of the client computer's memory space, but the Class has no access to the client's memory, so all arguments must be passed by value. (You can pass arguments by reference, but the marshalling process is slower and wastes bandwidth, because the actual values of the arguments are marshalled back to the client.) To pass arguments by value, insert the keyword ByVal in front of every argument in the function's argument list. The revised declarations of the functions that implement the various methods look like this:

```
Public Function addCustomer(ByVal CustomerID, _
                ByVal CompanyName, ByVal ContactName, _
                ByVal ContactTitle, ByVal Address, _
```

```
                                ByVal City, ByVal Region, ByVal PCode, _
                                ByVal Country, ByVal Phone, _
                                ByVal Fax) As Boolean

Public Function updateCustomer(ByVal CustomerID, _
                        ByVal CompanyName, ByVal ContactName, _
                        ByVal ContactTitle, ByVal Address, _
                        ByVal City, ByVal Region, ByVal PCode, _
                        ByVal Country, ByVal Phone, _
                        ByVal Fax) As Boolean

Public Function deleteCustomer(ByVal CustomerID) As Boolean
```

Even better, declare the actual type of each argument (but you don't have to). The GetCustomers() function returns a Recordset, not a simple variable like the other functions. Change its declaration to the following, which specifies the data type it returns:

```
Public Function GetCustomers(Optional _
            ByVal CustomerID As String) As ADODB.Recordset
```

The method returns an ADODB.Recordset, which will be automatically translated in an ADOR.Recordset variable before it's returned to the client. This will be taken care of by the proxy on the Web server. Don't change the function's type to ADOR.Recordset, because you want to be able to test it with the test project, locally. As mentioned already, the default Recordset created by ADO won't work for a remote client application. You must specify the cursor and lock type properties. Here's the revised GetCustomers() function:

LISTING 11.7   **The Revised GetCustomers() Method**

```
Public Function GetCustomers(Optional _
            ByVal CustomerID As String) As ADODB.Recordset
Dim RS As New ADODB.Recordset

    On Error GoTo SelectError
    If Trim(CustomerID) = "" Then
        SQLselect = "SELECT * FROM Customers"
    Else
        SQLselect = _
                "SELECT * FROM Customers WHERE CustomerID='" & _
                CustomerID & "'"
    End If
    RS.CursorLocation = adUseClient
    RS.CursorType = adOpenStatic
```

```
    RS.LockType = adLockBatchOptimistic
    RS.Open SQLselect, CN
    Set GetCustomers = RS
    Exit Function
SelectError:
    Set GetCustomers = Nothing
End Function
```

The test project works as is, because it calls stored procedures. If the original project was accessing the database directly through ADO, you'd have to edit the test project heavily too.

Using the RemoteClass

The test page for the RemoteClass component shown in Figure 11.5 is called RDSClassDemo.htm and can be found in this chapter's folder on the CD. I'll discuss the page's code, but don't open it with Internet Explorer yet. This project won't work before you change some settings in the Registry. This process will be described shortly, but let's start with the VBScript code that runs on the client.

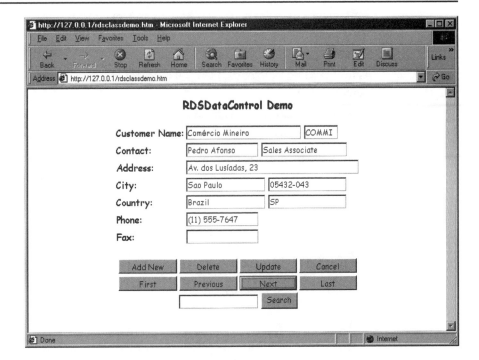

To use the RemoteClass on a Web page, you must create an instance of the RDS-DataSpace object and then use this object to create an instance of the RemoteClass .clsCustomers Class. Here's the code you must insert in the page's Window_onLoad event handler:

LISTING 11.8   **Contacting the RemoteCustomers.clsCustomers Class**

```
Sub Window_onLoad()
    Set ObjDS = CreateObject("RDS.DataSpace")
    Set objCustomers = _
            ObjDS.CreateObject("RemoteCustomers.clsCustomers", "")
    Set RS=ObjCustomers.GetCustomers
    RDSDC.SourceRecordset = RS
End Sub
```

After the execution of the above code, the RDSDataControl will bind the DHTML controls on the Form to the data source (the RS Recordset). The remaining code must be changed, because we want to update the database through the Class's methods, not through the RDSDataControl. The RDSCOM.htm page, which is the client example, is a bit rough around the edges, but it demonstrates how to contact the Class. I will discuss how to improve the example after we look at the basic code.

The tags for placing the data-bound DHTML controls on the Form are the same as for the RDSDemo page. Here's the tag for the Text control that displays the CompanyName field:

```
<INPUT name=txtCustomer DataSrc=#RDSDC
DataFld=CompanyName style="HEIGHT: 24px; WIDTH: 200px">
```

The code behind the navigational buttons is the same. The navigation takes place through the RDSDataControl. The Delete button calls the customerDelete method, passing the current row's ID to the deleteCustomer method:

LISTING 11.9   **Deleting the Current Customer**

```
Sub Delete()
    If objCustomers.deleteCustomer(CStr(txtCustomerID.Value)) Then
        RDSDC.Recordset.Delete
    End If
End Sub
```

When the Add button is clicked, the following code calls the AddNew method of the Recordset object. Notice that this method prepares the *local* Recordset for the addition of a new row. The new row will be added to the Customers table in the database later, when you'll call the addCustomer method:

```
Sub AddNew()
    RDSDC.Recordset.AddNew
End Sub
```

To edit the current row, the user doesn't have to click a button first; this is one of the areas in the code you should improve. The user can click on the fields of the current row and change their values. To commit the changes to the database, the user must click the Update button (or the Cancel button to discard the changes). If they click one of the navigational buttons instead, the local Recordset will be updated, but the changes won't be reflected to the database. You should provide an Edit button, which will disable all other buttons on the Form and display the Update and Cancel buttons only. While this task is trivial with a VB Form, it's not as simple on a HTML page, because it's not easy to overlap controls. Conceptually, it is probably simpler to change the captions of the buttons, but this requires quite a bit of code. Anyway, this feature has not been implemented in the sample application and it's the first area of the application you should improve.

The Update button must commit the current row to the database. However, it must distinguish between an edit and an add operation, so that it can call the appropriate method. Here's the Update button's handler for the Click event:

LISTING 11.10   The Update Button's Code

```
Sub UpdateRecord()
    custID=txtCustomerID.Value
    custCompany=txtCustomer.Value
    custContactName=txtContactName.Value
    custContactTitle=txtContactTitle.Value
    custAddress=txtAddress.Value
    custCity=txtCity.Value
    custRegion=txtRegion.Value
    custPCode=txtPCode.Value
    custCountry=txtCountry.Value
    custPhone=txtPhone.Value
    custFAX=txtFAX.Value
    '   Are we adding a record?
    If RDSDC.Recordset.EditMode=adEditAdd Then
        If objCustomers.addCustomer(custID, _
                custCompany, custContactName, _
                custContactTitle, custAddress, _
                custCity, custRegion, custPCode, _
                custCountry, custPhone, custFAX) Then
```

```
                RDSDC.Recordset.Update
            Else
                MsgBox "Unable to add record"
            End If
'       Are we editing a record?
        Else
            If objCustomers.updateCustomer(custID, _
                    custCompany, custContactName, _
                    custContactTitle, custAddress, _
                    custCity, custRegion, custPCode, _
                    custCountry, custPhone, custFAX) Then
                RDSDC.Recordset.Update
            Else
                MsgBox "Unable to update record"
            End If
        End If
End Sub
```

The script attempts to update (or add) the row in the database by calling the Updatecustomer (or Addcustomer) method. If the method succeeds, then it calls the RDSDataControl's Update method to update the local Recordset as well. The complete listing of the RDSClassDemo.htm page follows.

LISTING 11.11   The RDSClassDemo.htm Page

```
<HTML>
<HEAD>

<OBJECT ID=RDSDC WIDTH=1 HEIGHT=1
CLASSID="CLSID:BD96C556-65A3-11D0-983A-00C04FC29E33">
</OBJECT>

<OBJECT ID=RDSDS WIDTH=1 HEIGHT=1
CLASSID="CLSID:BD96C556-65A3-11D0-983A-00C04FC29E36">
</OBJECT>

<SCRIPT Language=VBScript>
Const adEditAdd = 2
Dim objDS
Dim objCustomers

Sub Window_onLoad()
    Set ObjDS = CreateObject("RDS.DataSpace")
    Set objCustomers = _
        ObjDS.CreateObject("ClassCustomers.clsCustomers", "")
    Set RS=ObjCustomers.GetCustomers
    RDSDC.SourceRecordset = RS
End Sub
```

```
Sub Search()
    RDSDC.FilterColumn="ContactName"
    RDSDC.FilterCriterion=">="
    RDSDC.FilterValue=Trim(txtSearch.Value) & " "
    RDSDC.Reset

    RDSDC.FilterCriterion="<="
    RDSDC.FilterValue=Trim(txtSearch.Value) & "Z"
    RDSDC.Reset(TRUE)

    If RDSDC.Recordset.Recordcount = 0 Then
        RDSDC.SourceRecordset=objCustomers.GetCustomers
    End If
End Sub

Sub Cancel()
    RDSDC.Recordset.CancelUpdate
End Sub

Sub AddNew()
    RDSDC.Recordset.AddNew
End Sub

Sub Delete()
    If objCustomers.deleteCustomer(CStr(txtCustomerID.Value)) Then
        RDSDC.Recordset.Delete
    End If
End Sub

Sub MoveFirst()
    RDSDC.Recordset.MoveFirst
End Sub

Sub MovePrevious()
    RDSDC.Recordset.MovePrevious
    If RDSDC.Recordset.BOF Then RDSDC.Recordset.MoveFirst
End Sub

Sub MoveNext()
    RDSDC.Recordset.MoveNext
    If RDSDC.Recordset.EOF Then RDSDC.Recordset.MoveLast
End Sub

Sub MoveLast()
    RDSDC.Recordset.MoveLast
End Sub

Sub UpdateRecord()
    custID=txtCustomerID.Value
    custCompany=txtCustomer.Value
```

```
            custContactName=txtContactName.Value
            custContactTitle=txtContactTitle.Value
            custAddress=txtAddress.Value
            custCity=txtCity.Value
            custRegion=txtRegion.Value
            custPCode=txtPCode.Value
            custCountry=txtCountry.Value
            custPhone=txtPhone.Value
            custFAX=txtFAX.Value
        ' Are we adding a record?
        If RDSDC.Recordset.EditMode=adEditAdd Then
            If objCustomers.addCustomer(custID, custCompany, _
                    custContactName, custContactTitle, _
                    custAddress, custCity, custRegion, _
                    custPCode, custCountry, custPhone, custFAX) Then
                RDSDC.Recordset.Update
            Else
                MsgBox "Unable to add record"
            End If
        ' Are we editing a record?
        Else
            If objCustomers.updateCustomer(custID, custCompany, _
                    custContactName, custContactTitle, _
                    custAddress, custCity, custRegion, _
                    custPCode, custCountry, custPhone, custFAX) Then
                RDSDC.Recordset.Update
            Else
                MsgBox "Unable to update record"
            End If
        End If
    End Sub
</SCRIPT>
</HEAD>

<BODY>
<CENTER>
<FONT FACE='Comic Sans MS'>
<H3>Remote Services DataSpace and DataControl Objects Demo</H3>
<TABLE FRAME=all cellPadding=1 cellSpacing=1>
<TR>
<TD height=10 ><FONT FACE='Comic Sans MS'>Customer Name:</FONT>
<TD>
<INPUT name=txtCustomer   DataSrc=#RDSDC DataFld=CompanyName
        style="HEIGHT: 24px; WIDTH: 200px">
<INPUT name=txtCustomerID DataSrc=#RDSDC DataFld=CustomerID
        style="HEIGHT: 24px; WIDTH: 60px">
```

```
<TR>
<TD height=10><FONT FACE='Comic Sans MS'>Contact: </FONT>
<TD>
<INPUT name=txtContactName  DataSrc=#RDSDC DataFld=ContactName
       style="HEIGHT: 24px; WIDTH: 125px">
<INPUT name=txtContactTitle DataSrc=#RDSDC DataFld=ContactTitle
       style="HEIGHT: 24px; WIDTH: 150px">
<TR>
<TD height=10><FONT FACE='Comic Sans MS'>Address: </FONT>
<TD>
<INPUT name=txtAddress DataSrc=#RDSDC DataFld=Address
       style="HEIGHT: 24px; WIDTH: 300px">
<TR>
<TD height=10><FONT FACE='Comic Sans MS'>City: </FONT>
<TD>
<INPUT name=txtCity  DataSrc=#RDSDC DataFld=City >
<INPUT name=txtPCode DataSrc=#RDSDC DataFld=PostalCode >
<TR>
<TD height=10><FONT FACE='Comic Sans MS'>Country: </FONT>
<TD>
<INPUT name=txtCountry DataSrc=#RDSDC DataFld=Country >
<INPUT name=txtRegion  DataSrc=#RDSDC  DataFld=Region >
<TR>
<TD height=10><FONT FACE='Comic Sans MS'>Phone: </FONT>
<TD>
<INPUT name=txtPhone DataSrc=#RDSDC DataFld=Phone
       style="HEIGHT: 24px; WIDTH: 125px">
<TR>
<TD height=10><FONT FACE='Comic Sans MS'>Fax: </FONT>
<TD>
<INPUT name=txtFax DataSrc=#RDSDC DataFld=Fax
       style="HEIGHT: 24px; WIDTH: 125px">
</TABLE>
<P>
<TABLE border=0>
<TR>
    <TD><INPUT Type=button Value="Add New" Width = 150 Name=bttnAdd
        OnClick=AddNew() style="HEIGHT: 24px; WIDTH: 100px">
    <TD><INPUT Type=button Value=Delete Width = 150 Name=bttnDelete
        OnClick=Delete() style="HEIGHT: 24px; WIDTH: 100px">
    <TD><INPUT Type=button Value=Update Width = 150 Name=bttnUpdate
        OnClick=UpdateRecord() style="HEIGHT: 24px; WIDTH: 100px">
    <TD><INPUT Type=button Value=Cancel Width = 150 Name=bttnCancel
        OnClick=Cancel() style="HEIGHT: 24px; WIDTH: 100px">
<TR>
```

```
    <TD><INPUT Type=Button Value=First Width=150 NAME=bttnFirst
        OnClick=MoveFirst() style="HEIGHT: 24px; WIDTH: 100px">
    <TD><INPUT Type=Button Value=Previous Width=150
        NAME=bttnPrevious OnClick=MovePrevious()
        style="HEIGHT: 24px; WIDTH: 100px">
    <TD><INPUT Type=Button Value=Next Width=150 NAME=bttnNext
        OnClick=MoveNext() style="HEIGHT: 24px; WIDTH: 100px">
    <TD><INPUT Type=Button Value=Last Width=150 NAME=bttnLast
        OnClick=MoveLast() style="HEIGHT: 24px; WIDTH: 100px">
</TABLE>
<INPUT Type=text NAME=txtSearch>
<INPUT Type=button Value="Search" Width = 150
    Name=bttnSearch OnClick=Search()>
</CENTER>
</BODY>
</HTML>
```

The next few sections describe the steps you must perform on the Web server to make the project work. I have tested the project with Windows 98 and Windows 2000. The same steps will work with Windows NT, provided you have installed Service Pack 3, and it will probably work with Windows 95 (although I don't think any readers will actually use RDS with Windows 95).

Register the DLL in the Web Server   The first step is to register the component. To register an ActiveX DLL, use the REGSVR32.EXE utility, as explained in the section "Registering a Class" of Chapter 12, "Data-Aware Classes." The Remote-Customers Class can be registered with the following command (open an MS-DOS Prompt window, switch to the folder where the RemoteCustomers.dll file is stored):

```
C:\Windows\System\REGSVR32 RemoteCustomers.dll
```

Most users have a special folder where they store their custom components, such as the \COMponents. This folder can be anywhere, as long as it can be loaded by applications when needed.

After registering the custom component, your Registry Editor window should look like the one shown in Figure 11.6. The following key corresponds to the newly registered component:

```
My Computer\HKEY_CLASSES_ROOT\RemoteCustomers
```

The programmatic ID of the Class is listed in the left pane (this is the name you use to access the component from within your VB code), and the long string in the right pane is the Class's ID.

FIGURE 11.6:

All registered components on your computer appear in the My Computer\HKEY_CLASSES_ROOT branch of the Registry.

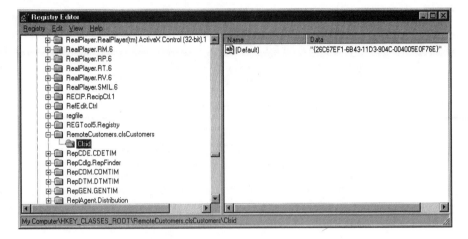

Enabling Execution of Components   The custom component is implemented as a DLL. DCOM, however, can't invoke DLLs; it works with EXE files only. Therefore, you need an EXE file that can invoke the members of a Class stored in a DLL. This EXE file, which is an impersonator for a DLL executable, exists already—it's the DLLHOST.EXE file. However, you must specify that the custom components can be executed locally through the DLLHOST.EXE file. To do so, open the Registry with the RegEdit utility (Start ➣ Run ➣ RegEdit) and locate the custom component by name (RemoteCustomers.clsCustomers). RegEdit will locate the entry for the custom Class in the branch My Computer\HKEY_LOCAL_MACHINE\SOFTWARE\Classes\CLSID, as shown in Figure 11.7. If you expand this entry, you will see several keys that were created automatically when the Class was registered. Add the key LocalServer and then set its (Default) value to the path of the DLLHOST.EXE application.

FIGURE 11.7:

Specifying a local host for the custom COM component

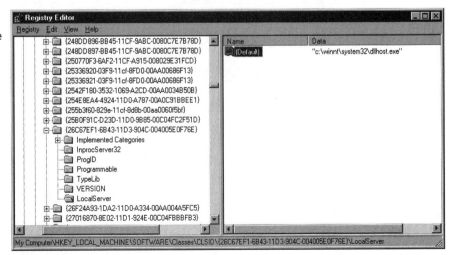

Security Considerations   The Web server will not create an instance of a Class just because a client has made a request. The Web server will contact a Class and create an instance of it only if it has been told that it's safe to do so. To tell your Web server (whether it's Internet Information Server or the Personal Web Server) that it can contact a Class and create an instance of it, you must add the name of the Class to the specific branch of the Registry.

Open the Registry with the RegEdit utility (Start ➤ Run ➤ RegEdit). Move down the following path:

```
My Computer\HKEY_LOCAL_MACHINE\System\
CurrentControlSet\Services\W3SVC\Parameters\ADCLaunch
```

This branch of the Registry contains the names of the components that can be invoked by the Web server. Just add the key RemoteCustomers.clsCustomers. After the addition of the new key, your RegEdit window should look like the one shown in Figure 11.8.

FIGURE 11.8:

Giving permission to the Web server to run a custom component

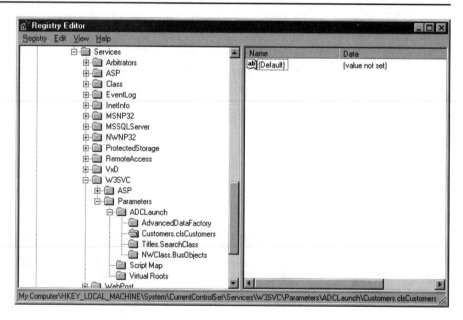

Summary

In this chapter you've learned how to access databases remotely, through the Remote Data Services. You will find more information on accessing databases through the Web in the third part of the book. The techniques we'll discuss in the third part of the book can be used with any browser, as opposed to the techniques of this chapter, which require Internet Explorer.

In the next chapter we'll discuss middle-tier components. You'll learn how to build custom Classes to implement business objects and how these components can simplify the development of client applications. Then, you'll learn how to build custom ActiveX controls to standardize the user interface of your client applications.

Data-Aware Classes

- ■ Middle-tier components

- ■ Implementing a Class

- ■ Implementing business rules

If you are not familiar with object programming, you probably think this is an advanced chapter. Classes and their cousins, ActiveX controls, are your means of implementing custom components in Visual Basic. The ADO component is implemented as a Class, and you know how a Class is used in an application. You add a reference to the Microsoft ActiveX Data Objects Library, and you can access all the objects exposed by ADO. A Recordset object is declared as an ADODB.Recordset variable; you can use this variable's members to access all the properties and methods of the Recordset object.

Now, you'll learn how to build your own components. The benefit of working with components (database components in this case) is that they isolate the front-end application from the database. You saw how to use ADO to access both Access and SQL Server databases. After you connect to the appropriate database, you don't have to worry about low-level details. ADO knows how to access the various databases, and you use high-level operations to access the tables. To update a row, you set the values of the Fields collection of the Recordset object and then call the Update method. This approach works with any database you can access through ADO (that is, every database that can be accessed through OLE DB drivers).

Nowadays, no application accesses databases directly and only a relatively small number of applications use the native API functions to access databases. Most VB developers use components such as DAO or ADO, which hide many details and allow the developers to view any database as a collection of tables, indexes, cursors, and other objects. We say that ADO is an abstraction layer. Although it knows how to access a database (a very complicated task), it presents a simpler view of the same object to the programmer.

Your custom components can do the same with advanced database operations. As you recall from Chapter 8, "Making the Most of Stored Procedures," placing a new order requires that multiple tables be updated and all actions be performed as a transaction. You implemented this operation in Chapter 8 as a stored procedure, and you saw how to add an order by calling the AddOrder stored procedure. The AddOrder stored procedure adds another abstraction layer. The application programmer doesn't have to know how you store data in your database; just how to call the AddOrder stored procedure. The AddOrder stored procedure can be called by multiple applications, too.

ADO is a very general interface, which you use to access any database. For a specific database, you can develop custom components that add a layer of abstraction that's unique to the database and your application.

Let's say you've written a component that searches a database in many different ways. The client application need not be concerned with the structure of the tables nor with the SQL statements that retrieve the desired rows. The client application calls the custom component passing the search criteria as arguments and retrieves the result of the search as a Recordset object. The code for searching the database may get quite complicated, but the client application doesn't see that complexity. The same component can also be used by a Web application that searches the database.

To call a stored procedure, you have to set up a Command object and a number of parameters. This is not a trivial task. You can add another layer that abstracts the details of calling the stored procedure. In other words, you can write a VB procedure that accepts all the information in the form of arguments, sets up the Command object, and then calls the stored procedure. This procedure must be incorporated into every application that needs to add orders to the database. This approach has a drawback. If you decide to change the procedure, you must redistribute the source code to many programmers and have them recompile their applications.

If you implement this procedure as a Class, however, you can change it as often as you like. All you have to do is install the new component on the network; all applications that use it will automatically see the new procedure. Of course, if you change the interface of the Class (in other words, you change the number of the order of the arguments), then you must change the applications and recompile them. Let's return to the custom search component we developed earlier. At some point, you may wish to add SOUNDEX capabilities to the search component (make it locate words that sound like the ones specified by the user, instead of exact matches only). The client application will still call the same method, only this time it will retrieve more rows. All you have to do is recompile the component, not the applications that use it. Of course, you must not change the interface. If you add more arguments to the method that performs the search, then you must edit the client application and recompile it.

As you know, it is possible to write your own Classes and add them to any project. I'm not suggesting that you build something like ADO, but you can write Classes that incorporate the functionality of ADO and perform very specific tasks. For example, you can write a Class that exposes a number of properties for accessing a specific table. In a way, it is similar to writing stored procedures, but Classes can hide the specifics of ADO, as well as the structure of the database, and allow you to perform all the tasks you need to perform on a database by calling methods of the Class and setting properties. In addition to Classes, you'll learn how to build data-bound ActiveX controls, which can be reused in many applications to shorten development time (this topic is discussed in the Chapter 13, "Data-Aware Controls"). Classes simplify the application logic, whereas ActiveX controls simplify the presentation logic.

The major advantage of Classes is that they sit somewhere between the client application and the database. In effect, they implement the third tier. The three-tier architecture was discussed in the first chapter of the book, but you'll look at this model in more detail in the following section.

The Third Tier

Before you look at data-aware Classes and how they can simplify your applications, let's review the three-tier model. A three-tiered application is not the answer to all your data access problems. No, the third tier is not needed for many types of applications, and I expect the majority of this book's readers to develop two-tier applications with the ADO component. However, if you want to build scalable applications or develop data-aware applications for the Web, you should be aware of the benefits of this architecture.

If you work as a member of a team, then you will have to get used to working with Classes. Even if you don't design them, someone else will design Classes that you will use in your projects. Let's say you work on developing a large project. Many of the modules that will be developed will access a database with sales information, similar to the Northwind database. Without Classes, every programmer must understand the structure of the database and write SQL statements to retrieve data or the code to update the database. If you develop a Class that exposes members, such as `GetOrders(customerID)` and `GetOrderDetails(orderID)`, every programmer can retrieve a customer's orders and a specific order's details by simply calling these methods. If you implement a method for each action you want to perform against the database, you can think of your Class as a custom ADO component. Whereas ADO exposes the members you need to access any database, the custom component exposes the members you need to access the specific database. The custom Class isolates the client application from the data access layer and simplifies the development of the client applications.

Figure 12.1 is a simple diagram of a three-tier architecture. The client application is what the user sees. The basic responsibility of the client application is to present the data to the user, accept user input and pass it to the server. In a two-tier model the client application communicates directly with the database server. As you recall from the previous chapters, the client application should use stored procedures to access the tables. In the three-tier model, the client application calls the methods of the Class and lets the Class access the actual tables.

FIGURE 12.1:

The three-tiered application model

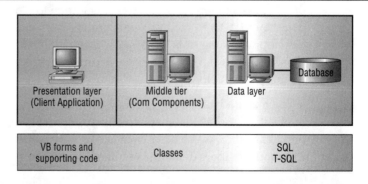

Presentation layer (Client Application)	Middle tier (Com Components)	Data layer
VB forms and supporting code	Classes	SQL T-SQL

Why introduce another layer? The reasoning behind the two-tier model is that we want the client to get as much work off the database server as possible, and to let the server focus on data retrieval and update tasks (which is what it does best). So, we split the application into two parts: the data access part (the code that's executed on the server) and the rest (the code that's executed on the client). The "rest" is quite a bit: It includes the presentation logic and the application logic. The presentation logic is the code that presents data to the user. This part must reside on the client. The application logic is the code that processes the data and implements the so-called business rules. So, there's a third layer, the middle tier, which is not part of either the presentation layer or the data access layer.

Business rules are ways in which your corporation processes the data. The application layer consists of all the procedures that do not access the tables in the database and do not display data on the client application's Form. The validation of credit cards and the calculation of insurance premiums are typical examples of business rules that are best implemented in the middle tier. The rules that apply to your corporation need not be implemented on the server. The validation of a credit card is a typical example. It's quite clear that the database server should not have to validate credit cards because the client could easily validate them. Consider, however, that large networks may have dozens of computers taking orders, so credit card validation begins to pose some challenging problems. Will all clients contact the organization that validates credit cards? Wouldn't it be better to deploy a separate component that does just that? Well, this component belongs to the middle tier. The clients pass credit card information and the amount to be charged to the middle-tier component, and they receive a yes/no answer.

You may consider changing the validation method. You could use a different organization for credit reports, to add new credit cards, and so on. If the credit card validation component were on the client, you'd have to update the application on all clients. In a large corporation, this is a major headache. By isolating it from both the presentation and data access layers, you can modify it any way you like and at any time. As long as the client can call this component by passing credit card information and the amount to be charged, the client application does not need to be modified and the data access layer does not need to be changed.

Let's say you need to retrieve the names of the customers who have placed at least one order in the last six months. Normally, you'd have to write a fairly complicated SQL statement to get the names of these customers. Alternatively, you can build a Class that exposes a method, with a name such as `CustomersWithRecentOrders` or `Customers6Mos`, which retrieves these names and returns them to the client. All the programmer needs to know is the name of the method.

How would you implement the `GoodCustomers` method (a method that returns a Recordset with the names of the "good" customers)? Or the `BestCustomers` method? These definitions are business rules, and the corporation may change the rules every other week. If your client application retrieves the good and best customers with a SQL statement, you'll have to change the client application and distribute it to all the workstations every time the rule changes. If you isolate the business logic from the presentation logic, you will be able to change the rule in one place, the middle tier, and all clients will see the changes through the existing code.

> **NOTE**
>
> Many programmers implement business rules as stored procedures, which is fine. Classes, however, are more flexible. You can use VB code to implement complicated validation rules, which would be a serious burden to the database server.

The Web's Three Tiers

The typical example of a three-tier application is a Web application. The browser is the client. Unlike desktop applications, the browser has its own built-in mechanism for displaying data, and you can't change it. You must supply HTML documents with the information you want to present to the viewer. The browser's task is to process an HTML document and display it. The application logic resides on the Web server (the machine that supplies the requested pages to the client). The application logic determines the structure of the information that will be presented to the client. For example, you may build a series of pages that enable the user to locate the desired information (the item to be purchased, for example) by drilling down into hierarchically structured categories. Or, you may present a single page, in which the user can enter search arguments.

The data presented to the user reside in a database; the pages on the Web server must access the database and retrieve the desired information. The client doesn't change—it's Internet Explorer or Netscape Navigator. The database doesn't change either—it's usually a machine running SQL Server. The middle layer, however, can be changed at will. If you don't like the look of your Web site, you can redesign the pages and present the same information in any number of different ways, but you don't have to change either the client application or the database.

> **NOTE**
>
> If you are not familiar with Web applications, the application layer is a series of Active Server Pages, programs written in VBScript. Here's what they do: receive data from the client (usually search arguments), use the data to query the database, format the results as HTML documents, and pass them to the client. For more information on Active Server Pages and how they interact with the client and the server, see Chapter 14, "Accessing Databases over the Web."

OK, I'm not interested in building Web applications. Do I still have to learn about the three tiers? I suggest you understand how the third tier is implemented and what problems you will run into if you decide to scale your application. The reason for implementing a third layer in your applications is scalability. As you recall from the examples, two-tiered applications establish a connection to a database and keep it open for as long as they need it. Establishing a connection is a very expensive operation, and too many Connection objects will have a very serious impact on the database server. In a two-tier application that's being used within a small company, this is not a big issue. Things are quite different when you move to the Web. A Web server may serve hundreds of users at once, and you simply can't afford to maintain a connection for each user.

Let's discuss this connection "bottleneck" a little. The ASP page on the Web server must contact the database server, request some data (always a small cursor because it can't download hundreds of rows to the client), and then transmit an HTML document with the data to the client. The connection is no longer needed and can be released. Because it will be awhile before the same user request another page, ASP pages create connections to access the data requested and then release these objects. As mentioned already, creating a connection is a time-consuming process, however. One of the reasons for using a middle tier is because middle-tier components can pool connections. They maintain a pool of connections and reuse them as needed. You simply can't pool connections from within your applications, and you should be thankful that VB does it for you. The bad news is that the process is not totally transparent to you. You must deploy the Microsoft Transaction Server (MTS), but this topic is discussed in Chapter 16.

Most readers will probably never program for MTS. Even if you build Web applications, you probably use a tool such as Site Server, which takes care of crucial details like connection pooling. However, you should understand what MTS does and how you can make your Classes work with MTS. This is an advanced topic, which you can safely ignore until you're ready to build an enterprise application. In the meantime, you can use Classes to simplify the development of client applications. To implement a Class, you must think about the requirements of the application, design the procedures to implement the business rules, and finally build the Class and the client application. After the Class is in place, the development of the client application is greatly simplified.

Implementing a Class

A Class is a special type of program that has no user interface. A program without a user interface is a peculiar type of program called a *component*. A component exposes its functionality through properties and methods that constitute the component's interface. As you can guess, a component doesn't function on its own; it needs an application to invoke it and request its services. To access the functionality of a Class, you must add to your application a reference to the Class. You do so by declaring one or more object variables and using their members to access the functionality of the Class. These object variables represent *instances* of the Class.

The code that implements the Class (usually a DLL) need not reside on the same computer as the application that uses it. In other words, you can install the Class on a single machine on the network and have all clients on the network access it through a properly declared variable . If your Class contains a public function named the Best-Customers method, all client applications will be able to retrieve the names of the best customers. They don't need to know the rules that classify customers.

The first example we'll develop in this chapter is a client application for browsing and editing the rows of the Customers table. It's a very simple example, but you don't want a very complicated Class. As you will see, building and testing a Class is not a simple task. If you're familiar with building ActiveX components with Visual Basic, you will find it very easy to follow the example. However, I will present all the steps in building the sample application for the benefit of users who have not built their own Classes in the past.

Figure 12.2 shows the sample application, which is called ClassCustomers (you can find it in this chapter's folder on the CD). The rows of the Customers table are displayed on an MSFlexGrid control at the top of the Form. The user can select a customer to edit or delete by clicking its row. When a row in the grid is clicked, the corresponding row's fields are displayed in the TextBox controls at the bottom of the Form. The user can edit the current row through the TextBox controls.

FIGURE 12.2:

The ClassCustomers project demonstrates how a client application accesses a database through the members of the clsCustomers Class.

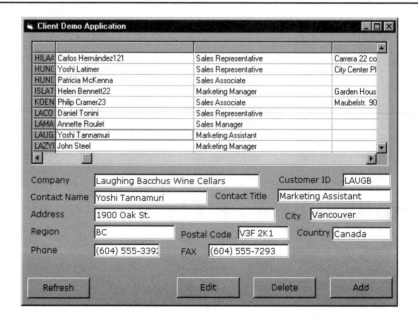

When you edit a row, the application sends the new information to the database by calling the appropriate members of the Class. If an update operation succeeds, it also posts the new values on the grid control. This approach is safe because you update the information displayed on the client only when you get a confirmation from the middle-tier component. However, it's even safer to retrieve the row from the original table and only then post it on the grid. To see the new Recordset after you add or update a row, click the Refresh button at the bottom of the Form. You can change the application on your own, whenever you like.

The clsCustomers Class

Let's build a Class that exposes the methods we need to access the Customers table. These methods are the addCustomer, updateCustomer, and deleteCustomer methods that are implemented in the clsCustomers Class. Start a new ActiveX DLL project, rename the Class module to **clsCustomers**, and rename the project's name to **ClassCustomers**. Figure 12.3 shows the Project window after renaming the Class module and adding the test project.

FIGURE 12.3:

Add a test project to every ActiveX DLL project to test the custom component in the same VB project

The clsCustomers Class Module's Properties

If you select the clsCustomers component in the Project window, you will see its properties in the Properties window:

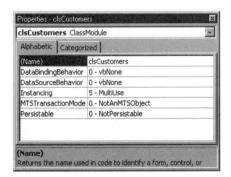

The Class module exposes the following properties.

Name   This is the name of the Class. Choose a meaningful Class name because this is the way your Class will appear in the References dialog box when you attempt to add a reference to the Class in another project.

DataBindingBehavior, DataSourceBehavior   The DataBindingBehavior property allows you to make the Class data-bound, and it can have one of the following values:

> **vbNone**   The Class isn't data bound.
>
> **vbSimpleBound**   The Class is bound to a single row.
>
> **vbComplexBound**   The Class is bound to a Recordset.

The DataSourceBehavior property allows you to build a Class that acts as a Data Source, and it can have one of the following values:

> **vbNone**   The Class is not a Data Source.
>
> **vbDataSource**   The Class is a Data Source.

You are not going to build data-bound Classes, but you will see how to build data-bound controls in the next chapter. The custom Classes you are going to build are *data-aware*. You're going to provide all the code to connect to the database and manipulate the tables instead of relying on VB to bind certain members of the Class to database fields. In general, it makes more sense to build data-bound ActiveX controls because controls have a visible interface. After you bind a field to a member of the control, the field values display on the control's interface.

Instancing   The Instancing property determines whether (and how) other applications can create instances of the Class. This property can have one of the following values:

> **Private**   Private objects can be accessed only by components in the same application. If you are developing a Class that can't be used in other projects or you don't want to make it available to other developers, set its Instancing property to Private.
>
> **MutliUse**   This setting, which is the opposite of Private, allows a single instance of the Class to provide as many objects as required by the client applications. This is the default value of the Instancing property, and you shouldn't change it, especially for components that access databases.
>
> **GlobalMultiUse**   The objects exposed by GlobalMultiUse component are available to the entire system and can be accessed by an application, as if they were system components. Visual Basic provides its system-wide objects,

which are called *global objects*. The Screen and Printer objects, for example, are global objects because you need not add a reference to them in the applications that use them. If you think you have an object that's so important for the rest of the system (and not just the application that needs it) to know about, set its Instancing property to GlobalMultiUse.

PublicNotCreatable   The objects of a Class with this setting can be accessed by other applications, but can't be created. Now, what good is this? The objects of a PublicNotCreatable Class must be first created by another component in the same Class and accessed through the Class' members. For example, let's say you have a Class that implements database operations. One of the objects exposed by the Class represents the database. Another Class object represents a Table of the database. If you allow the developer to access the second object directly, there's a chance he may attempt to open a Table without first opening the database. If you make the Class that exposes the Database object public, but you make the Class that exposes the Table object PrivateNotCreatable, and then you create a reference to the object that represents the table as soon as the database is opened, the developer can access the Table object directly, but only after it has been created.

Coding the Class' Members

Now, switch to the Class' Code window and select the Initialize event of the Class object. Each Class has an Initialize event and a Terminate event. These two events are fired when an application creates a new instance of the Class and when this instance is terminated, respectively. In the Initialize event, you must create a Connection object that will be used to access the database. In the Terminate event, you must release this object.

The Connection object will be maintained for the duration of the Class's life. In this chapter, I will assume that you're developing applications that will run on a local area network. With an application that will be used on a vary large network or on the Web, you may have hundreds or thousands of Connection objects alive. Alternatively, you can create Connection objects as you need them, contact the database, and then release them as soon as possible.

The Connection object is an ADO object, so you must add a reference to the ADO Object Library. Open the Project menu, select References; in the References window, click the Microsoft ActiveX Data Objects 2.1 Library (version 2.5 should be available by the time you read this book). Then, insert the following declaration in the Class' code outside any procedure:

```
Dim CN As ADODB.Connection
```

Then, enter the appropriate code to create and release a Connection object in the two events of the Class. Listing 12.1 shows some sample code that does this.

LISTING 12.1   **The Class' Initialize and Terminate Events**

```
Private Sub Class_Initialize()
    Set CN = New ADODB.Connection
    CN.ConnectionString = "Provider=SQLOLEDB.1; " & _
            "User Id=sa;Initial Catalog=Northwind"
    CN.Open
End Sub

Private Sub Class_Terminate()
    CN.Close
    Set CN = Nothing
End Sub
```

The *CN* object variable can be used from within any procedure to access the Northwind database. You must decide what actions the client application should perform against the database and implement them as methods of the clsCustomers Class. A method is nothing more than a public function. By the way, the *CN* variable is not accessible by the applications that use the services of the clsCustomers Class. The *CN* variable is private to the Class.

Next, you must implement all the actions you want to perform against the database as public functions. Every public function will be exposed as a method of the ActiveX component. You can also create public Property Let and Property Get procedures to add properties to the Class. The clsCustomers Class exposes a single property for demonstration purposes only. It's the DatabaseName property, which returns the name of the database. This property is read-only, so you must implement its Property Get procedure only:

```
Public Property Get DatabaseName()
    DatabaseName = "NORTHWIND"
End Property
```

NOTE

If you're familiar with building custom ActiveX controls, you already know how to implement properties. This book isn't about building ActiveX components, and you should probably review the process of building ActiveX components before you develop custom components for your applications.

Let's return to the data-manipulating functions. The `addCustomer`, `updateCustomer`, and `deleteCustomer` functions add, update, and delete a row, respectively, in the Customers table. All three functions build the appropriate SQL statement, which they execute against the database. Here's the listing of the addCustomer member:

LISTING 12.2   The addCustomer Member

```
Public Function addCustomer(CustomerID, CompanyName, _
             ContactName, ContactTitle, Address, City, _
             Region, PCode, Country, Phone, Fax) As Boolean
Dim SQLInsert As String

    On Error GoTo AddError
    SQLInsert = "INSERT INTO Customers " & _
             "(CustomerID, CompanyName, ContactName, " & _
             " ContacTtitle, " & _
             " Address, City, Region, PostalCode, " & _
             " Country, Phone, Fax)" & _
             " VALUES (" & "'" & CustomerID & _
             "', '" & CompanyName & _
             "', '" & ContactName & _
             "', '" & ContactTitle & _
             "', '" & Address & _
             "', '" & City & _
             "', '" & Region & _
             "', '" & PCode & _
             "', '" & Country & _
             "', '" & Phone & _
             "', '" & Fax & "')"
             Debug.Print SQLInsert
    CN.Execute SQLInsert
    addCustomer = True
    Exit Function
AddError:
    addCustomer = False
End Function
```

The updateCustomer member is quite similar. The only difference is that the updateCustomer doesn't set the CustomerID field. Instead, it uses it to specify the row to be changed in the statement's WHERE clause. Here's the updateCustomer member:

LISTING 12.3   The updateCustomer Member

```
Public Function updateCustomer(CustomerID, CompanyName, _
             ContactName, ContactTitle, Address, City, _
             Region, PCode, Country, Phone, Fax) As Boolean
```

```
Dim SQLUpdate As String

    On Error GoTo UpdateError
    SQLUpdate = "UPDATE Customers  " & _
                "SET CompanyName ='" & CompanyName & "'," & _
                "    ContactName ='" & ContactName & "'," & _
                "    ContactTitle='" & ContactTitle & "'," & _
                "    Address     ='" & Address & "'," & _
                "    City        ='" & City & "'," & _
                "    Region      ='" & Region & "'," & _
                "    PostalCode  ='" & PCode & "'," & _
                "    Country     ='" & Country & "'," & _
                "    Phone       ='" & Phone & "'," & _
                "    Fax         ='" & Fax & "'" & _
                " WHERE CustomerID='" & CustomerID & "'"
    CN.Execute SQLUpdate
    updateCustomer = True
    Exit Function
UpdateError:
    updateCustomer = False
End Function
```

Finally, the deleteCustomer function builds a simple DELETE statement, passing only the customer's ID as argument:

LISTING 12.4   **The deleteCustomer Member**

```
Public Function deleteCustomer(CustomerID) As Boolean
Dim SQLDelete As String

    On Error GoTo DeleteError
    SQLDelete = "DELETE FROM Customers  " & _
                " WHERE CustomerID='" & CustomerID & "'"
    CN.Execute SQLDelete
    deleteCustomer = True
    Exit Function
DeleteError:
    deleteCustomer = False
End Function
```

As you can see, all three functions build the appropriate SQL statement and execute it against the database through the CN object. If the SQL statement is executed successfully, the corresponding function returns a True value. If not, it returns False to indicate that the operation failed. You can return the Err object itself or a string with the error's description. You'll see how to return an Err object from a Class in the next example.

Normally, you implement a Class so that it raises errors through the Err object. To raise a run-time error, use the Raise method, whose syntax is

```
Err.Raise number, source, description, helpfile, helpcontext
```

- *number* is a long integer in the range 513 to 65535 that identifies the error. The error numbers up to 512 are reserved for system errors. You must also add the constant vbObjectError to the custom error number. To raise the error 999, you must use the expression `999 + vbObjectError`.

- *source* is a string that identifies the object or application that raises the error. For errors raised by custom objects this string should be the name of the project followed by the name of the Class: programName.ClassName.

- *description* is another string that provides textual information about the error. The last two arguments, *helpfile* and *helpcontext*, are the name of a help file and the context ID of a topic in the help file, respectively.

You have all the members for updating the database, but how about retrieving its rows? You need another function that will return a Recordset to the client application. This function should be able to return either all the rows or a selected row in the table. To retrieve a specific row, you should pass the ID of the desired customer as argument. If you call the function without arguments, then it should return all the rows of the table.

LISTING 12.5   The GetCustomers Member

```
Public Function GetCustomers(Optional CustomerID As String)_
      As ADODB.Recordset
   On Error GoTo SelectError
   If Trim(CustomerID) = "" Then
       SQLselect = "SELECT * FROM Customers"
   Else
       SQLselect = "SELECT * FROM Customers WHERE " & _
                    "CustomerID='" & CustomerID & "'"
   End If
   Set GetCustomers = CN.Execute(SQLselect)
   Exit Function
SelectError:
   Set GetCustomers = Nothing
End Function
```

Notice that the function's argument is optional. If you omit it, it will return all the rows of the table. This contradicts everything I've been saying about keeping the size of the cursors you pass to the client as small as possible, but the Customers table is not very large. If this were a table with 100,000 rows, you'd have to come up with a different user interface. Obviously, you wouldn't be able to move all the rows to the client and display them on a grid control. On the other hand, you shouldn't force users to select customers by their IDs. You would have to filter the customers and move small chunks of the table at once. For example, you could select customers based on country, the first few characters in the company name, the number of orders they have placed, and so on. If you have no idea about the size of the cursor that a SELECT statement will create, use the TOP N clause, which limits the size of the cursor.

This is all the code of the clsCustomers Class. You're ready to test the Class by calling the members it exposes from within a VB application. As you can guess, the client application need not set up its own Connection and Command objects; and build and execute SQL statements against the database, not even the name of the database. It allows the user to browse and edit the Customers table by calling the members of the clsCustomers Class with the proper arguments.

Testing the clsCustomers Class

Testing a Class is different from testing standard applications. You must create a test project, instantiate the Class through an object variable, and call its members to manipulate the Customers table. The new Class must also be registered to the system, so that any application can reference it. Every time you change the Class' code, you must register the component and test it.

While you're testing the project, VB will register the component for you. If you plan to use the component on another machine, you must register it manually. See the sidebar "Registering a New Class," later in this section.

To simplify the process of testing custom components, Visual Basic allows you to create a project group. If you add a test project to the Class project, you'll be able to edit and test the Class from within the same VB project. If you haven't done so already, add a new Standard EXE project with the File ➤ Add Project command. Rename the new project to TestProject and its Form to TestForm. You'll use the TestProject's Form to test the clsCustomers Class. When you run the project, Visual Basic should execute the test project. Right-click the name of the test project in the Project window and select the Set As Startup command from the shortcut menu.

Next, switch to the test project, open the Form, and place the controls shown in Figure 12.2 on the test form. The project can be found in the CustomersClass folder on the CD, under this chapter's folder.

To access the members of the clsCustomers Class from within another application, you must add a reference to this component. Open the project menu, select References, and check the item ClassCustomers (VB should have it pre-selected for you because it belongs to the same project group). Although the Class' name is clsCustomers, Visual Basic displays the name of the project in the References dialog box. While you have the References dialog box in front of you, check the ADO Object Library as well. No, you won't use ADO to access the database, but you need a Recordset object, where you'll store the rows moved to the client. The References dialog box should look like the one shown in Figure 12.4.

You can also create an instance of the clsCustomers Class with the CreateObject function. To do so, you must declare a variable with the following statement:

```
Dim cClass As Object
```

FIGURE 12.4:

Adding a reference to the ClassCustomers to the current project

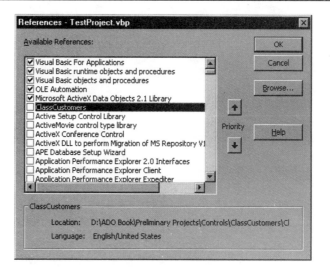

Then, in the Form's Load event, call the CreateObject method, passing the Class' name as argument. You must specify the complete Class' name, as follows:

```
Set cClass = CreateObject("ClassCustomers.clsCustomers")
```

The *cClass* variable's type is Object, and it's late bound (yet, it's better than a variant). Because the project doesn't contain a reference to the Class, you can't declare a proper variable.

Some languages, including VBScript, don't use typed variables and they don't support variable declarations. To use the Class from within a script, you must create an instance of the Class with the CreateObject method. For more information about using a custom Class from within a script, see the section "Build More Flexible Applications with Classes," later in this chapter.

Registering a New Class

To use this component from within another application, you don't have to include the Class itself in the project. The new component is private to the project, and it can't be accessed from within other applications. To make the component available to every application on the system, you must register the component.

The first method to register the Class is to simply create the Class' DLL file. Select the Class module in the Project window, open the File menu, and click the command Make class_name.DLL, where class_name is the Class's name. This command creates a DLL file in the folder you specify, and it also registers the new component to the system.

If you want to distribute the component to another computer, you can copy the DLL file to a folder in the target computer (DLLs are usually placed in the Windows/System folder) and register it with the REGSVR32 utility. To register a DLL with the REGSVR32 utility, use a command like the following one:

```
C:\WINDOW\SYSTEM\REGSVR32 class_name.dll
```

where *class_name.dll* is the name of the DLL you want to register. This is a DOS command and must be executed from within a DOS Prompt window.

The target computer will add the new component to the list of available components, and any application can use it. The DLL is executable code that's loaded in the same memory segment as the host application, and it's executed as if it were part of the application. If you change the Class' code and recompile it, the applications will see the new version of the component. There's no need to re-register the component or recompile the application that uses it (unless you change the component's interface, as mentioned earlier in the chapter).

Since the DLL was compiled with VB, the VB runtime DLL is also required. This DLL will be installed when you install the application on the target computer with the appropriate setup application.

Now you can create the *cClass* object variable with the following declaration:

```
Dim cClass As New ClassCustomers.clsCustomers
```

As soon as you type the New keyword, you see a list of components available to your project. Notice that the complete name of the component is made up of the name of the project, followed by the name of the Class with a period between them.

As you can guess, all the action will take place through the *cClass* object variable. You'll use it to access the methods exposed by the custom Class. When the Form is loaded, you move the rows of the Customers table to the client. To access the members of the clsCustomer Class, you must create an object variable to represent the Class in the application's code:

```
Dim cClass As New ClassCustomers.clsCustomers
```

All the members of the Class can be accessed through the *cClass* variable. To retrieve the row that corresponds to the customer ALFKI, use the following statement:

```
Set RS = cClass.GetCustomers("ALFKI")
```

The loadCustomers() subroutine retrieves all the rows by calling the GetCustomers member of the Class without an argument. Then, it populates the MSFlexGrid control. The code (Listing 12.6) is straightforward.

LISTING 12.6   **Populating the Grid Control with Customer Data**

```
Sub loadCustomers()
Dim RS As ADODB.Recordset
    Set RS = cClass.GetCustomers
    If RS Is Nothing Then
        MsgBox "Could not read customer information"
        MSFlexGrid1.Rows = 1
        Exit Sub
    Else
        MSFlexGrid1.Rows = 1
        MSFlexGrid1.Cols = RS.Fields.Count
        For i = 0 To RS.Fields.Count - 1
            MSFlexGrid1.ColWidth(i) = _
                TextWidth("A") * RS.Fields(i).DefinedSize
        Next
        While Not RS.EOF
            MSFlexGrid1.Rows = MSFlexGrid1.Rows + 1
            For iCol = 0 To RS.Fields.Count - 1
                If IsNull(RS.Fields(iCol)) Then
                    MSFlexGrid1.TextMatrix _
                        (MSFlexGrid1.Rows - 1, iCol) = "<NULL>"
                Else
                    MSFlexGrid1.TextMatrix _
                        (MSFlexGrid1.Rows - 1, iCol) = _
                        RS.Fields(iCol)
                End If
            Next
            RS.MoveNext
        Wend
    End If
End Sub
```

The loadCustomers subroutine is called from within the Form's Load event, as well as from within the Refresh button's Click event handler. The procedure is general enough to accommodate any Recordset. You can copy this procedure to your own projects to populate an MSFlexGrid control with the rows of a Recordset.

The user can select a customer by clicking anywhere on the grid. The selected customer's fields will appear in the TextBox controls at the lower half of the Form. The lower half of the Form is a simple data entry application, which is identical to the other data entry applications you have built in earlier chapters. The difference is how you navigate through the rows of the Customers table.

The editing buttons on the Form control the usual operations. The TextBox controls are normally locked, unless you're editing the current row. The test Form's code is not new to you. When the Add or Edit button is clicked, all editing buttons are hidden and in their place, the OK and Cancel buttons appear. The user can commit the changes to the database or cancel them by clicking the appropriate button. While editing a row, the user is not allowed to select another row in the grid. The editing operation must end with a click of the OK or Cancel button. At this point, the usual editing buttons will be enabled and the user will be allowed to browse the customers on the grid.

Another feature of this project is that the user is not allowed to change an existing customer's ID. The CustomerID field is displayed on a TextBox control that's locked during editing, but it's unlocked when a new row is added. When the Add and Edit buttons are clicked, the following code is executed:

LISTING 12.7   **The Add Button's Code**

```
Private Sub bttnAdd_Click()
    txtCustomerID.Locked = False
    HideEditButtons
    UnlockFields
    ClearControls
End Sub
```

LISTING 12.8   **The Edit Button's Code**

```
Private Sub bttnEdit_Click()
    HideEditButtons
    UnlockFields
End Sub
```

When the OK button is clicked, the following code commits the changes to the database. The code uses the Locked property of the txtCustomerID TextBox control to find out which action has ended and calls the appropriate method.

LISTING 12.9   **The OK Button's Code**

```
Private Sub bttnOK_Click()
Dim success As Boolean
    If Trim(txtCustomerID.Text) = "" Then
```

```
                    MsgBox "Can't add a customer without a unique ID"
                    Exit Sub
                End If
            If Trim(txtCompany.Text) = "" Then
                    MsgBox "The Company Name field can't be Null"
                    Exit Sub
            Else
                If txtCustomerID.Locked Then
                    success = _
                        cClass.updateCustomer(txtCustomerID.Text, _
                        txtCompany.Text, txtContactName.Text, _
                        txtContactTitle.Text, txtAddress.Text, _
                        txtCity.Text, txtRegion.Text, _
                        txtPCode.Text, txtCountry.Text, _
                        txtPhone.Text, txtFAX.Text)
                    If Not success Then
                        MsgBox "There was an error in " & _
                                "updating the customer"
                    Else
                        UpdateGrid
                    End If
                Else
                    success = _
                        cClass.addCustomer(txtCustomerID.Text, _
                        txtCompany.Text, txtContactName.Text, _
                        txtContactTitle.Text, txtAddress.Text, _
                        txtCity.Text, txtRegion.Text, _
                        txtPCode.Text, txtCountry.Text, _
                        txtPhone.Text, txtFAX.Text)
                    If Not success Then
                        MsgBox "There was an error in " & _
                                "updating the customer"
                    Else
                        AddToGrid
                    End If
                End If
            End If
            ShowEditButtons
            LockFields
        End Sub
```

One last remark about this application. The changes are posted to the database through UPDATE and INSERT statements. What do you think will happen if another user already changed the row you're editing since you last read it? Your changes will be committed to the database unconditionally because the updates are not submitted to the server by ADO. Unless the row has been removed or locked by another user, your changes will be committed to the database.

If this were a reservation application, you'd have to make sure that the row hadn't already been changed by another user since you read it. The only way to find out whether the row has changed is to add a timestamp column to the table. You should read the current value of this column and compare it to the equivalent value you read from the table when the row was retrieved. If the two values match, then you can go ahead and update the row. If not, you should cancel the update and notify the user. The course of action depends on the nature of the application, but you should allow the user to see the latest data. Of course, these actions must be performed from within a stored procedure. Time is of the essence and you should make sure that the update will take place immediately after the comparison, or someone else might get a chance to change the row.

In most practical situations, the last user to update a row wins. Why would two different users change the address or fax number of the same customer? Even when this happens, they're probably making identical changes, so you can unconditionally commit the changes with a stored procedure such as the updateCustomer one.

If you test this application carefully, you'll discover the following bug: the client application doesn't send Null values to the middle tier. If you leave a TextBox control empty, the program will write a zero-length string to the database. This value is not the same as a Null value. Obviously, the user didn't intend to store this (meaningless) value to the database. A blank field should be mapped to a Null value before it's sent to the database. The client application doesn't map zero-length strings to Nulls, and neither does the middle tier. This type of validation could take place either on the client or on the server, but I would rather leave it to the middle tier. Leaving a field blank is not a user's mistake, and you aren't going to display any messages on the client computer. It's a trivial conversion that can take place on the middle tier.

WARNING This is one of the most common mistakes in database programming. Many people will pass the values of the controls to the database (either through ADO or through stored procedures) without converting blank strings to Null values. You should always convert blank strings to Null before writing to the database and always check for Null values when you assign field values to VB controls. If you attempt to assign a Null value to the Text property of a TextBox control, for example, you'll get a runtime error. To avoid this error, use a few statements such as the following:

```
txtAddress.Text = ""
If Not IsNull(RS.Fields("Address")) Then _
        txtAddress.Text = RS.Fields("Address")
```

More Business Rules

You can experiment with middle layers with this application. Let's say you want to keep information about old addresses when a customer changes address. This task belongs to the application logic. Clearly, it has nothing to do with the presentation layer. If you're using SQL Server, you can either implement this rule in the middle-tier or add a trigger to the Customers table that does it automatically.

You should probably create another table, which is an exact copy of the original Customers table (well, you could omit the contact information). Then, you can change the updateCustomer procedure so that when it detects a difference in the address, it stores the old address to the copy of the Customers table and then updates the Customers table.

The client application is not aware of the changes. It still calls the same member of the clsCustomer Class and passes the same parameters. The middle-tier functions, however, perform additional tasks that are of no interest to the client application. If you think about it, why should it care about the old address? The client application is a front end for browsing and editing the Customers table. The less we require from the client application, the swifter it is and the easier it is to maintain. The client application may be ported to a thin client. By keeping everything that doesn't directly relate to the presentation layer in the middle tier, the easier it will be to port the client application to a thin client.

Another task for the middle tier is the validation of the data. Simple validation must take place on the client, but there are applications that require complicated validation techniques. The validation may involve a lot of calculations, looking up multiple arrays, and so on. Calculating insurance premiums involves large arrays and quite a few calculations. Without the middle layer, you'd have to either move large tables to every client, or burden the server with the calculations. One approach is to load the tables to the middle tier and have all clients request the calculation of premiums from one or more components that reside in the middle component. This approach makes sense if the middle-tier component is running on a separate machine on the network. As you realize, any advanced example that would really convince you for the necessity of the middle tier is absolutely beyond the scope of this book. However, you will know that an application calls for a middle tier when you run into one.

TIP   You may find it hard to decide whether an operation belongs to the middle tier or whether it should be implemented as a stored procedure. Many programmers are biased toward stored procedures because they're fairly easy to code and they can become part of the database. A good rule to follow is that business rules that involve database operations (such as searching related tables) should be implemented as stored procedures. If the operations involve many calculations or complex control-flow statements, then they should be implemented as Classes.

Build More Flexible Applications with Classes

A Class such as clsCustomers is one of the simplest Classes you can build. Yet, it has simplified the design of the front-end application. It can do more than that. If you expose the loadCustomers and addCustomer members to other applications, users can take advantage of these members to access some of the functionality of your application programmatically. Let's consider two corporations that merge. One of the first changes in the new corporation is to combine the MIS departments (and then get rid of half of the programmers). Each corporation has its own Customers table, but the two tables must be merged. If your application exposes only a visible interface, there's no way to automate the merging of the two tables (short of writing T-SQL batch files to merge the two tables). If other programs can access the clsCustomers table, they can easily add the new customers to the database. Even an XLS file with contact information can be entered into the Customers table. All you have to do is iterate through the rows of the spreadsheet; extract the values expected by the addCustomer method; and then call the method from within VBA, VBScript, or any other language.

As another example, consider an order that arrives in electronic form. After executing the order, you must invoice the customer. Issuing an invoice means that someone has to type the details (product IDs and quantities). If the application exposes a method such as issueInvoice, you can turn the document with the order's details into an invoice. As you can see, building with Classes is not a fancier method of coding; it's a practical method to develop flexible, scalable applications.

If you are familiar with VBScript you already know that you can access the clsCustomers Class from within a script. The following script adds a new customer to the database. The code is nearly identical to the VB code you use in an application, with the exception that VBScript is a type-less language (you can't declare variables) and its error handling capabilities are quite limited.

LISTING 12.10   The addCustomer Script

```
On Error Resume Next
Set CClass=CreateObject("ClassCustomers.clsCustomers")
If Err.Number <> 0 Then
    MsgBox "Could not contact clsCustomers Class"
    WScript.Quit
End If
ret = CClass.addCustomer("NEW", "newContact","NEW Company",_
        "newContactTitle", "newAddress", "newCity", _
        "newPCode", "newRegion", "newCountry", _
        "newPhone", "newFAX")
```

```
If Err.Number <> 0 Then
    MsgBox Err.Description
    WScript.Quit
End If
If ret=True Then
    MsgBox "New customer successfully added"
Else
    MsgBox "Could not add customer"
End If
```

NOTE   If you're not familiar with Windows scripts, they are the equivalent of the DOS batch files. Place the code of Listing 12.10 in a text file with extension VBS, and then you can double-click its icon to execute it. Scripts require that the Windows Scripting Host be installed on your system. If you're running Windows 95, you can download the Windows Scripting Host from the Microsoft Web site.

In short, Classes are not limited to Web applications. Every application can benefit from Classes and you should try to implement the basic data-access and manipulation routines of your applications as methods of a Class, so that any other application can perform these operations against the database. At the very least, the same Class can be reused by multiple applications that perform the same operations.

The SearchTitles Class

In this section, you will build a Class that retrieves titles from the Biblio database based on user-supplied keywords. The keywords could be title words or author names. As you will see, the SQL statements for retrieving the qualifying rows are anything but trivial. By implementing the search operation in the middle tier, you free the client from having to build complicated SQL statements. Moreover, the same component can be used by multiple applications. You can change the actual implementation of the search method, recompile the Class, and all applications will use the new code. You will use the same Class in a desktop application, as well as in a Web application. The client, a VB application in the first case and an ASP page in the case of the Web, is a very simple application that calls the GetTitles method of the Class to retrieve the qualifying rows. All the work is done in the middle tier. This is exactly what the Class will buy you: All client applications that must search the Biblio database will go through the custom component and developers need not be concerned with the structure of the database, SQL optimization issues, and so on.

Your custom component is called SearchTitles, and it searches the Biblio database for titles with one or more keywords or author names. The Web is flooded with on-line bookstores, so a custom search component should be of interest to many readers. The SearchTitles Class exposes the GetTitles method, which can search the database in three distinct ways:

- With one or more title words

- With one or more author names

- With one or more title keywords and one or more author names

The GetTitles method builds the appropriate SQL statement (a non-trivial statement), executes it against the database, and returns a Recordset with the qualifying rows to the client application. The method is implemented as a function that returns a Variant. The reason for returning a generic type is that you want to be able to return errors as well. If the SQL statement can't be executed successfully, the method will return an Err object, which the calling application will handle.

The first two search modes are straightforward. They're based on a SELECT statement that selects the titles that contain all the keywords or all author names, respectively. The third method is quite interesting, and I'll discuss its implementation shortly.

The GetTitles method builds the appropriate SQL statement by calling the MakeSQLStatement function and passing to it the arguments it received from the calling application. The MakeSQLStatement function returns a string with the SQL statement that will retrieve the desired titles. Then, it executes the SQL statement by calling the ExecuteSQLStatement function. The implementation of the GetTitles function is shown in Listing 12.11.

LISTING 12.11   The GetTitles Method

```
Public Function GetTitles(searchArgument As String, _
              searchMode As Integer) As Variant
Dim SQLStatement As String
    SQLStatement = MakeSQLStatement(searchArgument, searchMode)
    Set GetTitles = ExecuteSQLStatement(SQLStatement)
End Function
```

The GetTitles function is the only public function in the Class. The other two functions called from within the GetTitles function's code are private to the Class, and can't be called from external applications. Let's look at the implementation of the two functions.

The MakeSQLStatement is responsible for building a SQL statement that retrieves the titles according to the user-supplied keywords. The first argument, *search-Argument*, contains one or more keywords. They can be title words or author names. The second argument, *searchMode*, determines how the database will be searched. It can have one of the following values:

0   Searches book titles only

1   Searches author names

2   Searches both titles and authors

The first two search modes are straightforward. The program builds a SELECT statement that combines all the keywords with the AND operator. The more keywords you specify, the fewer titles you will retrieve. The third search mode is more complicated. Basically, it's the "quick search" mode you find in just about any on-line bookstore. If the keywords are title words or author names, the Get-Titles method should return the same titles as with the first or second search mode. If the keyword is "Homer," for example, you assume that the user wants all the works of Homer or books about Homer. Here's the SQL statement that returns these titles:

```
SELECT Titles.ISBN, Title, Author FROM
    ((Titles LEFT JOIN [Title Author] ON
    [Title Author].ISBN = Titles.ISBN)
    LEFT JOIN Authors ON [Title Author].Au_ID = Authors.Au_ID)
    WHERE Titles.ISBN IN
        (SELECT Titles.ISBN FROM Titles, [Title Author], Authors
        WHERE Titles.ISBN=[Title Author].ISBN AND
        [Title Author].Au_ID=Authors.Au_ID AND
        (Authors.Author LIKE 'HOMER%' OR
        Titles.Title LIKE '%HOMER%') )
    ORDER BY Titles.Title
```

The interesting part of the SQL statement is the inner WHERE clause. Here, you select the ISBNs of the books that contain the word "Homer" in their titles or that have Homer as their author. Notice that you can't use a clause such as the following:

```
WHERE Authors.Author LIKE 'HOME%'
```

If you do, the statement will return the qualifying titles, but with a minor problem: Only the specified author will be returned with each title, even if some of the books have multiple authors.

If you specify two keywords, such as "Visual" and "Mansfield," the Class doesn't know that "Visual" is a title keyword and "Mansfield" is a name. It will attempt to locate all titles that contain at least one of the keywords. You want to make sure that if both keywords are title words, they must appear together in the title. Likewise, if they're both author names, you want to retrieve titles written by both authors. Finally, if one of them is a title word and the other one is an author name, you want the titles that contain one of the keywords in their title and the other one as the title's author. This is the SQL statement produced by the GetTitles method for the keywords "Visual" and "Mansfield:"

```
SELECT Titles.ISBN, Title, Author FROM
    ((Titles LEFT JOIN [Title Author] ON
    [Title Author].ISBN =  Titles.ISBN)
    LEFT JOIN Authors ON [Title Author].Au_ID = Authors.Au_ID)
    WHERE Titles.ISBN IN
        (SELECT Titles.ISBN FROM Titles, [Title Author], Authors
         WHERE Titles.ISBN=[Title Author].ISBN AND
        [Title Author].Au_ID=Authors.Au_ID AND
        (Authors.Author LIKE 'VISUAL%' OR
        Titles.Title LIKE '%VISUAL%') AND
        (Authors.Author LIKE 'MANSFIELD%' OR
        Titles.Title LIKE '%MANSFIELD%'))
    ORDER BY Titles.Title
```

You can experiment with more complicated searches to see how the program handles them. The SQL statements produced by the GetTitles method are interesting examples and you should take a closer look at them.

These lengthy statements are not simple to write, but as you will see, you build it one clause at a time. Each keyword must appear either in the title or in the book's authors. These clauses are then combined with the AND operator. The AND operator is required because the more keywords you specify, the fewer titles you expect to retrieve. In other words, the more specific you are about the desired titles, the fewer titles will qualify. Here's how the MakeSQLStatement function builds the proper SQL statement:

LISTING 12.13   **The MakeSQLStatement Function**

```
Private Function MakeSQLStatement(AllArgs As String, _
                searchMode As Integer) As String
Dim i As Integer
Dim arguments As Integer
Dim args() As String
Dim SQLStatement As String

    If (Left(AllArgs, 1) = Chr(34) And _
                    Right(AllArgs, 1) = Chr(34)) Or _
            (Left(AllArgs, 1) = Chr(39) And _
            Right(AllArgs, 1) = Chr(39)) Then
```

```
        AllArgs = Replace(AllArgs, Chr(34), "")
        AllArgs = Replace(AllArgs, Chr(39), "")
        SQLStatement = "SELECT Titles.ISBN, Title, Author" & _
                    " FROM Titles, Authors, [Title Author] "
        SQLStatement = SQLStatement & _
                    "WHERE Titles.Title LIKE " & "'" & _
                    "%" & AllArgs & "%" & "'"
        SQLStatement = SQLStatement & _
                    "AND [Title Author].Au_ID" &_
                    " =  Authors.Au_ID "
        SQLStatement = SQLStatement & _
                    "AND Titles.ISBN = [Title Author].ISBN "
        SQLStatement = SQLStatement & _
                    "AND Titles.ISBN=[Title Author].ISBN"

    Exit Function
End If
' remove commas (,)
While InStr(AllArgs, ",") > 0
    AllArgs = Replace(AllArgs, ",", " ")
Wend
' remove period(s)
While InStr(AllArgs, ".") > 0
    AllArgs = Replace(AllArgs, ".", "")
Wend
' remove multiple spaces
While InStr(AllArgs, "  ") > 0
    AllArgs = Replace(AllArgs, "  ", " ")
Wend
' and convert them to upper case
AllArgs = UCase(AllArgs)
' extract individual words from search argument
args() = Split(AllArgs, " ")
arguments = UBound(args())
' BUILD SQL STATEMENT
Select Case searchMode
    Case 0:     ' TITLE ONLY
      SQLStatement = "SELECT Titles.ISBN, Title, Author FROM "
      SQLStatement = SQLStatement & _
        "((Titles LEFT JOIN [Title Author] " & _
        "ON  [Title Author].ISBN = Titles.ISBN) " & _
        "LEFT JOIN Authors ON [Title Author].Au_ID = " & _
        "Authors.Au_ID) "
      SQLStatement = SQLStatement & "WHERE "
      For i = 0 To arguments
```

```
                SQLStatement = SQLStatement & _
                        "Titles.Title LIKE " & "'" & "%" & _
                        args(i) & "%" & "'" & " and "
            Next
            SQLStatement = _
                    Left(SQLStatement, Len(SQLStatement) - 4)
            SQLStatement = _
                    SQLStatement & " ORDER BY Titles.ISBN"

        Case 1:      ' AUTHOR ONLY
            SQLStatement = "SELECT Titles.ISBN, Title, " & _
                    "Author FROM "
            SQLStatement = SQLStatement & _
                "((Titles LEFT JOIN [Title Author] ON " &_
                "[Title Author].ISBN =  Titles.ISBN) " & _
                "LEFT JOIN Authors ON " & _
                "[Title Author].Au_ID = Authors.Au_ID) "
            SQLStatement = SQLStatement & _
                "WHERE Titles.ISBN IN " & _
                "(SELECT Titles.ISBN FROM Titles, "  & _
                " [Title Author], Authors WHERE " & _
                " Titles.ISBN=[Title Author].ISBN AND "  & _
                " [Title Author].Au_ID=Authors.Au_ID AND "
            For i = 0 To arguments
                SQLStatement = SQLStatement & _
                        "Authors.Author LIKE " & "'" & _
                        args(i) & "%" & "'" & " AND "
            Next
            SQLStatement = _
                    Left(SQLStatement, Len(SQLStatement) - 4)
            SQLStatement = _
                    SQLStatement & ") ORDER BY Titles.ISBN"

        Case 2:      'BOTH Title And AUTHOR
            SQLStatement = "SELECT Titles.ISBN, Title, " & _
                    "Author FROM "
            SQLStatement = SQLStatement & _
                    "((Titles LEFT JOIN [Title Author] ON " &_
                    "[Title Author].ISBN =  Titles.ISBN) " &_
                    "LEFT JOIN Authors ON " & _
                    "[Title Author].Au_ID = Authors.Au_ID) "
            SQLStatement = SQLStatement & _
                    "WHERE Titles.ISBN IN " & _
                    "(SELECT Titles.ISBN FROM Titles, " & _
                    "[Title Author], Authors WHERE " & _
                    "Titles.ISBN=[Title Author].ISBN AND " & _
                    "[Title Author].Au_ID=Authors.Au_ID AND "
```

```
                    For i = 0 To arguments
                        SQLStatement = SQLStatement & _
                            "(Authors.Author LIKE " & "'" & _
                            args(i) & "%" & "'" & _
                            " OR Titles.Title LIKE " & "'" & _
                            "%" & args(i) & "%" & "'" & ") AND "
                    Next
                    SQLStatement = _
                            Left(SQLStatement, Len(SQLStatement) - 4)
                    SQLStatement = _
                            SQLStatement & ") ORDER BY Titles.ISBN"
                End Select
                MakeSQLStatement = SQLStatement
            End Function
```

At the beginning, the code massages the string with the keywords. It removes multiple spaces, and it replaces commas and periods with single spaces. Then, it extracts the individual keywords into the args() array with the Split function. Once the proper SQL statement has been built, you can execute it with a Connection object's Execute command. The ExecuteSQLStatment function does just that, as follows:

LISTING 12.14   The ExecuteSQLStatement Function

```
        Private Function ExecuteSQLStatement(SQLStatement As String) _
                        As Variant
        Dim SQLcmd As String
            SQLcmd = Replace(SQLStatement, Chr(13), "")
            SQLcmd = Replace(SQLcmd, Chr(10), "")
            SQLcmd = Trim(SQLcmd)
            On Error Resume Next
            ADOResult.CursorType = adOpenStatic
            ADOResult.CursorLocation = adUseServer
            Set ADOResult = ADOConn.Execute(SQLcmd)
            If Err.Number <> 0 Then
                Set ExecuteSQLStatement = Err
            Else
                Set ExecuteSQLStatement = ADOResult
            End If
        End Function
```

This is all the code in the TitleSearch Class (I have omitted the Class' initialization and termination code, but this should be rather trivial by now). There's certainly room for improvement, but this is a good starting point. You can add the code to handle quotes, spaces, and other special symbols that may throw off the

SQL engine. For example, the code can't handle keywords that consist of multiple words, such as "Visual Basic" or "Object oriented." You can revise the code so that it doesn't split words placed in double quotes.

Testing the TitleSearch Class

To test the new custom Class, add a test project as usual. The project's test Form is shown in Figure 12.5. The MSFlexGrid control at the top of the Form is where the qualifying titles are displayed. The TextBox and ComboBox controls at the bottom of the Form allow you to specify the search arguments and the search mode. Enter the desired keywords in the TextBox control using the space (or comma) to separate multiple keywords. Then, click the Search Now button to retrieve the qualifying rows and display them on the grid.

FIGURE 12.5:

The TitleSearch Class's Test Form

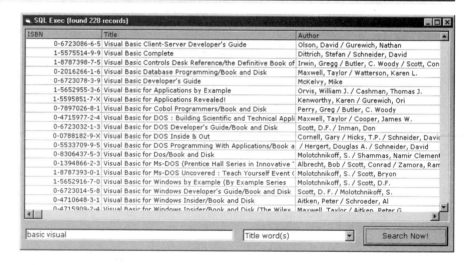

The Recordset returned by the GetTitles method may contain multiple rows with the same title, but with different authors. A book written by three different authors will be returned in three rows, each one having a different author. Clearly, a hierarchical Recordset would be a better choice, but the code shown here is simpler. You should edit the project's code so that it returns a hierarchical Recordset. The example you will find on the CD scans the Recordset; although the book's ID is the same, it appends the new author to a string, using the slash character as separator. After all rows of the same book have been scanned, the title along with its authors is displayed on the grid.

To test your custom Class, place the control you see in Figure 12.6 on the test Form. You must be able to access the custom Class from within the test project's code, so you must add a reference to the SearchTitles Class. Open the Project menu and select References. You will see the References window for your project. The SearchTitles component will appear right after the components that have been added to the test project already, as shown in Figure 12.6. Check this component to add it to the current project. While you're at it, check the Microsoft ActiveX Data Objects Library. As with the test project of the previous project, you are not going to access the tables of the Biblio database directly through ADO, but you must declare a Recordset object to receive the rows returned by the GetTitles method.

The ComboBox control is populated at design time with the following options:

0 Title keyword(s)

1 Author Name(s)

2 Title Keyword(s) and Author Name(s)

FIGURE 12.6:

To use the Titles Class in a project, you must first add a reference to the custom component through the References dialog box.

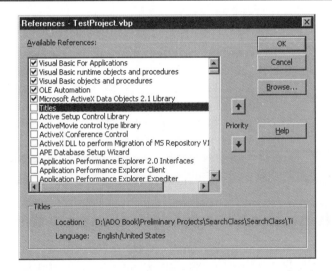

When the Search Now button is clicked, the program calls the GetTitles method. The test Form's code doesn't process the arguments; it passes the keywords as entered in the first TextBox, and the index of the selected item in the ComboBox control.

If the search was successful, the program calls the PopulateGrid subroutine, which populates the MSFlexGrid control with the Recordset returned by the Get-Titles method. If an error occurred during the execution of the statement, the GetTitles method returns an Err object, with the error's number and its description.

That's why the GetTitles method returns a generic object. If the return value's type is ErrObject, you treat it as an Err object. If not, it's a Recordset, and you process it accordingly.

LISTING 12.15 **The Search Now Button's Code**

```
Private Sub Command1_Click()
Dim rs As New ADODB.Recordset
Dim TitlesClass As New Titles.TitleSearchClass
Dim obj As Object
    Set obj = TitlesClass.GetTitles(txtArgs.Text, _
                                cmbMode.ListIndex)
    If TypeName(obj) = "ErrObject" Then
        MsgBox "failure"
    Else
        Set rs = obj
        PopulateGrid rs
    End If
End Sub
```

The PopulateGrid subroutine's code is straightforward, and you can find it on the CD. As you can see, the client application deals exclusively with the presentation of the data to the user. It calls the GetTitle method to access the database and then displays the results. The dirty work is done by the Class, which is another black box to the developer. In the following section, you'll see another client application, which uses the same component to search the Biblio database—this time the client is Internet Explorer and the middle tier is an ASP page on the Web Server, which calls the same method.

Using the SearchTitles Class on the Web

Let's test our custom Class with a Web site. The page you see in Figure 12.7 is a page that allows the user to supply keywords and submit them to a Web Server. The request is processed on the Web Server by an ASP page, which uses the SearchTitles Class to access the Biblio database. The ASP page doesn't have to know anything about the Biblio database. It calls the GetTitles method, formats the Recordset returned by the method as a HTML table, and passes it to the browser. Each title displayed on the table should be a hyperlink to the corresponding book. You'll find more elaborate techniques for presenting information to the browser in the next part of the book. This is a simple example that demonstrates how to middle-tier components in the Web.

FIGURE 12.7:

This page submits the user-supplied keywords to the GetTitles.asp page on the server.

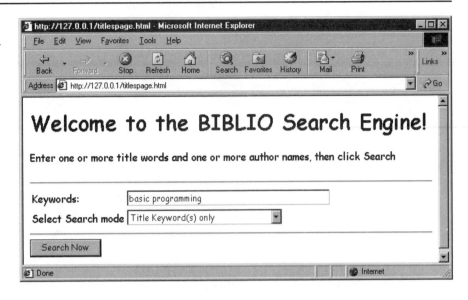

The page shown in Figure 12.7 was generated by the following HTML file.

LISTING 12.16   The TitlesPage.html File

```
<HTML>
<FONT FACE='Comic Sans MS'>
<H1>Welcome to the BIBLIO Seach Engine!</H1>
Enter one or more title words and one or more author names, then click
Search
<P>
<FORM ACTION='GetTitles.asp' METHOD=POST>
<HR>
<TABLE>
<TR><TD>Keywords:
<TD><INPUT TYPE=Text NAME='SearchArguments' SIZE=50>
<TR>
<TD>
Select Search mode
<TD>
<SELECT NAME='SearchMode' SIZE=1>
<OPTION VALUE=0>Title Keyword(s) only</OPTION>
<OPTION VALUE=1>Author Name(s) only</OPTION>
<OPTION VALUE=2>Title Keyword(s) and Author Names</OPTION>
</SELECT>
</TABLE>
<HR>
<INPUT TYPE=SUBMIT VALUE="Search Now">
```

When the Search Now button is clicked, the GetTitles.asp script on the server is invoked. The browser sends a string to the Web server that contains the name of the application and the values of the controls on the Form. All you have to do is specify the names of the application that will process the request with the ACTION keyword of the FORM tag.

NOTE
For more information on calling scripts on the Web server and transmitting information to the server see Chapters 14 and 15.

The GetTitles.asp is a small program written in VBScript that reads the parameters passed by the browser and uses them as arguments to the GetTitles method. Then, it formats the rows returned by the Class and formats them as an HTML table, which can be viewed on the client. Here's the listing of the GetTitles.asp script:

LISTING 12.17   The GetTitles.asp Script

```
<%
searchFor=Request.Form("SearchArguments")
searchBy=Request.Form("SearchMode")
Response.Write "<FONT FACE='Comic Sans MS'>"
Response.Write "<H2>Your search for <I>" & searchFor & _
               "</I> returned the following titles</H2>"
Set TClass=CreateObject("Titles.TitleSearch")
Set RS=TClass.GetTitles(CStr(searchFor), CInt(searchBy))
Response.Write "<TABLE>"
Response.Write "<TR>"
Response.Write "<TD WIDTH=150 VALIGN=top>" & _
               RS.Fields(0) & "<TD VALIGN=top>" & RS.Fields(1)
Response.Write "<TR>"
If Not IsNull(RS.Fields(2)) Then
    Response.Write "<TD><TD><FONT SIZE=-1>" & RS.Fields(2)
    Response.Write "<TR>"
End If
thisID=RS.Fields(0)
If Not RS.EOF Then RS.MoveNext
While Not RS.EOF
    If RS.Fields(0) <> thisID Then
        Response.Write _
            "<FONT SIZE=+1><TD WIDTH=150 VALIGN=top>" & _
            RS.Fields(0) & "<TD VALIGN=top>" & _
            RS.Fields(1) & "<TD>"
        Response.Write "<TR>"
        Response.Write "<TD><TD><FONT SIZE=-1>" & RS.Fields(2)
```

```
                    Response.Write "<TR>"
            Else
                    Response.Write "<TD><TD><FONT SIZE=-1>" & RS.Fields(2)
                    Response.Write "<TR>"
            End If
            thisID=RS.Fields(0)
            RS.MoveNext
    Wend
    Response.Write "</TABLE>"
    %>
```

The script receives parameters from the Web page and passes them to the Get-Titles method of the TitleSearch Class. Notice that the code uses the Server object to retrieve the values on the Form's controls. Then, it converts them to the appropriate type before passing them to the GetTitles method as arguments. VBScript is a typeless language and all its variables are variants. The GetTitles method, however, expects one string and one integer argument, so you can't pass two variants. The CStr() and CInt() functions convert their argument to a string and integer type, respectively.

The GetTitles method returns a Recordset, which the script scans, one row at a time, and generates the table shown in Figure 12.8. The code that generates the table is similar to the code of the PopulateGrid subroutine that displays the same information on an MSFlexGrid control.

FIGURE 12.8:

Output of the GetTitles.asp script

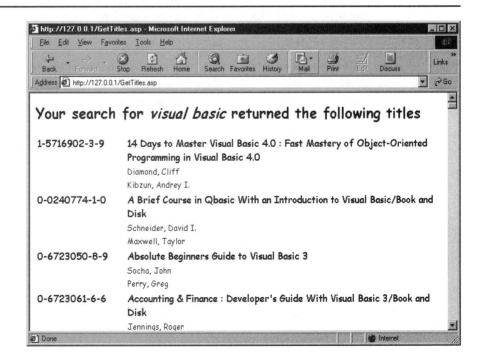

You will notice that the *RS* variable is not declared or initialized. Its type is determined the moment it's assigned the result of the GetTitles method. Then, you can call the usual members of the Recordset object to access the rows stored in it.

To summarize, Classes allow you to build middle-tier components that isolate front-end applications from the data access layer. The benefits of building and using custom Classes in your applications is that Classes do the following:

- Simplify the coding of the client applications. You don't have to access the database directly through ADO objects, and you don't have to set up Command objects to execute SQL statements and stored procedures against the database.

- Expose much of the functionality of the application to other applications (thus, making your application programmable). External applications can manipulate the database through the methods you choose to make public.

- Implement middle-tier components that can run under MTS. This topic is discussed in detail in Chapter 16.

Summary

Data-aware Classes allow you to separate the business logic, or application logic, from the presentation and data layers. The client application doesn't directly see the database. Instead, it sees methods that are tailored for accessing a specific database. In the following chapter, you'll see how to do something similar for the presentation layer. You'll learn how to build custom controls for your applications and to standardize many of the data presentation operations of the client application through the use of custom ActiveX controls.

CHAPTER

THIRTEEN

Data-Aware Controls

- ◼ Building data-bound controls

- ◼ Building data source controls

- ◼ The DataRepeater control

- ◼ Using the Data Object Wizard

In the previous chapter, you learned how to simplify the coding of client applications by building custom Classes. A custom Class exposes methods that abstract many of the operations you perform against a database. The second major aspect of client applications is how they present data to and interact with the user. To simplify this aspect of client applications, VB provides a number of data-bound and data-aware controls. Just as you build custom Classes for a specific database, you can build custom ActiveX controls to simplify the user interface of the client application. The custom ActiveX controls you'll design will be used on many Forms, and the client's interface will have a consistent look.

In this chapter, you'll learn how to build data-bound ActiveX controls, which can be reused in many applications and can shorten development time. As you will see, Visual Basic comes with a wizard for generating data objects (Classes and ActiveX controls), which should make the development of these components quite trivial. Like all other wizards, however, the Data Object wizard is not a tool to be trusted completely. I'll discuss its shortcomings; you can then decide how far you will go with this tool.

Custom ActiveX controls simplify the programming by embedding much of the functionality you need on the presentation layer into custom components. If you're familiar with building custom ActiveX controls, you'll see how to turn any ActiveX control into a data-bound control. You'll also learn how to build custom ActiveX controls that act as data sources. In specific, you will see how to build a custom Data control with richer navigational capabilities than the ADO Data Control.

Finally, you will see how to use the Data Object Wizard (DOW) to streamline the process of building custom ActiveX controls for a specific application. The Data Object Wizard can't build controls that can be used with any application, like the ones that come with VB. The DOW generated control bind to specific fields in the database, and you can't change the bindings at design time. Even so, DOW can build data-bound controls in seconds. You could build Forms that duplicate the functionality of these controls, but it's not nearly as simple as using the Data Object Wizard.

The first time you open the projects of this chapter, you'll get an error message to the effect that an ActiveX control couldn't be located. This happens because you have the control's code, but the control itself hasn't been installed on your system yet. Continue loading the project and when you run the project, the custom control will be registered and you'll be able to use it. The error message will not appear the next time you load the same project.

Building Data-Bound Controls

If you're familiar with the process of building custom ActiveX controls (basically, if you know how to use the ActiveX Control Interface Wizard), you already know how to build a data-bound ActiveX control. The process is very simple, but I will go through an example briefly for the benefit of readers who haven't built data-bound controls yet. If you have not designed a custom ActiveX control, you should review the process briefly. In the last section of this chapter, you'll see how you can build data-bound ActiveX controls with the Data Object Wizard, and you should be able to understand the code generated by the wizard. I'm assuming that you're familiar with the process of building ActiveX controls. If not, you can still use the custom controls generated by the DOW, but you won't be able to tweak the code produced by the wizard to achieve the functionality you require.

To build a data-bound control, just put together a UserControl object with one or more constituent controls. You don't even have to implement any members at all. Use the ActiveX Control Interface Wizard to build the control, and then specify the control's data-bound properties. For example, you could design a custom control that's based on a TextBox constituent control. This is the simplest control you can create. Just place a TextBox control on the UserControl object and map the control's members to the equivalent members of the TextBox control (your custom control's Text property to the Text property of the TextBox control, the custom control's Font property to the TextBox control's Font property, and so on). To make your custom ActiveX control data-bound, you must specify which of the control's properties will be mapped to the DataField property. Visual Basic will add the required data-binding properties so that you can bind the control to a data source at design time. Let's demonstrate the process by building a very simple data-bound control.

The DBControl Project

The data-bound control you'll build in this section duplicates the functionality of the TextBox control and can be bound to a data source (the DataEnvironment object or the ADO Data Control). This control doesn't do anything more than the regular TextBox control when bound to field; it's meant to demonstrate how to bind its Text property to a field in the data source. The data-bound property, called *Display-Field*, is delegated to the Text property of a TextBox constituent control. In addition to the main data-bound property, the DBControl exposes the *PrimaryKey* property, which is the current row's primary key value. The PrimaryKey property must be set by the developer at design time to the table's primary key field. As you will see, this property doesn't appear in the control's Properties window. It's a member of the DataBindings collection and it must be set from within the DataBindings window. You can use this property from within your code to look up related rows in other tables (publisher names, product categories, and so on).

To design the control, start a new ActiveX project and rename it DBControl-Project. Then, rename the UserControl object to DBControl. ActiveX controls can't exist on their own; they must reside on a Form. Therefore, you need a Form on which to place the control before you can test it. It's a good idea to add the test project as early as possible, so add a new project to the current project with the File ➤ Add Project command. Name the new project TestProject, and then name its Form TestForm.

Now, you can open the UserControl object in design mode and place a TextBox control on it. The UserControl object that's placed automatically by VB in the Project window of an ActiveX control project is the control's "Form." The control's user interface will be drawn on this object, just as you draw a regular Form's interface by placing controls on it. The size and placement of the TextBox control on the UserControl object doesn't matter. You want the TextBox to be as large as the control, and you'll provide the appropriate code in the UserControl object's Resize event handler. The visible interface of the control is as simple as it gets. Now, you must design the programmatic interface of the control. This interface consists of the properties and methods exposed by the custom control, as well as of the events recognized by the control.

Using the ActiveX Control Interface Wizard

To build the control's code you'll use the ActiveX Control Interface Wizard. This is Visual Basic's most useful and most complete wizard. It can build robust controls, which you can use immediately in your projects. To use the wizard, you must add it to the Add-Ins menu. Select Add-Ins ➤ Add-In Manager; when the Add-Ins dialog box appears, double-click the item VB6 ActiveX Control Interface Wizard. Then, close the dialog box and open the Add-Ins menu. The entry VB6 Control Interface Wizard has been added to the menu, and you can start the wizard by selecting the newly added command in the Add-Ins menu. To be able to build data-bound custom ActiveX controls, you should be familiar with the process of building ActiveX controls. However, I will present the various steps of the wizard for the readers who have not built ActiveX controls in the past.

The first window of the wizard is a welcome window, which you can disable for future runs. Click Next to see the Select Interface Members window, in which you can select the standard members of the interface (see Figure 13.1).

This window contains the Available Names list, which contains the names of the members of the constituent control(s) and the UserControl object. The wizard knows how to implement all these members, and you can select any of the members you want to add to your control. Just select them in the left list, and click the button with the arrow to the right. Let's not add too many features to this sample control. Keep the members proposed by the wizard, except for the Text property (you'll map the DisplayField custom property to the Text property of the TextBox constituent control).

FIGURE 13.1:

Select Interface Members
window

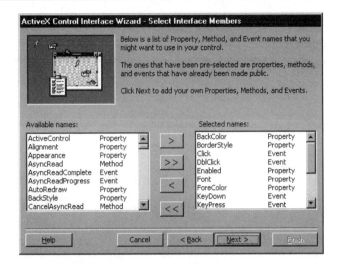

Click Next and you will see the Create Custom Interface Members window of the wizard (see Figure 13.2). Here, you can add your custom members to the new control. As discussed already, you'll add the DisplayField property and the Primary-Key property.

FIGURE 13.2:

Create Custom Interface
Members window

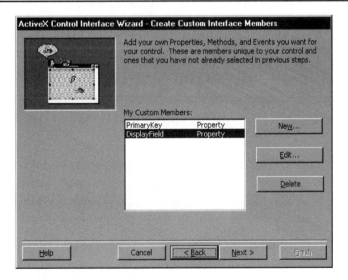

Click the New button and you'll be prompted to enter the names of the custom members and their types. Enter PrimaryKey in the Name box and check the option Property. This tells the wizard that the PrimaryKey member is a property. Then, click New again, enter the name DisplayField, and check the option Property. You can add as many members as you wish to the custom control. The wizard doesn't know how to implement custom members and it will generate just the declarations of the various members. Then, you must step in and add the appropriate code. Click Next again to see the Set Mapping window (see Figure 13.3).

Your custom control consists of a UserControl object and a constituent control, the TextBox control. Many of the control's members can be mapped to the members of the constituent control(s) or the UserControl object, and this is where you define the mappings.

FIGURE 13.3:

Set Mapping window

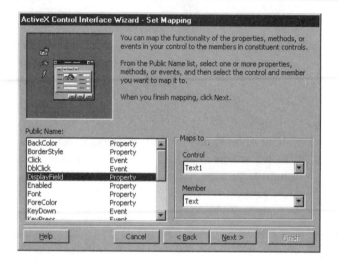

All of the members are mapped to the equivalent member of the Text1 constituent control, with the exception of the PrimaryKey property. The PrimaryKey property isn't mapped to an existing member. The DisplayField property is mapped to the Text property of the Text1 control. Select the member you want to map in the left box, and set the mapping in the Map box. To map a custom member to a constituent control's member, select the name of the constituent control in the Control box and the member of the constituent control to which the custom member is mapped. Map all the control's members to the equivalent members of the Text1 control, except for the PrimaryKey property. The DisplayField property of the control must be mapped to the Text property of the Text1 constituent control. Then, click Next to see the Set Attributes window (see Figure 13.4).

On this window, you must specify the various attributes of the members that have not been mapped already. Select the PrimaryKey member in the Public Names list and set its Data Type to String. This property has no default value, so leave the Default Value box empty. Then, click the Next button, and click Finish on the last window to generate the custom ActiveX control.

FIGURE 13.4:

Set Attributes window

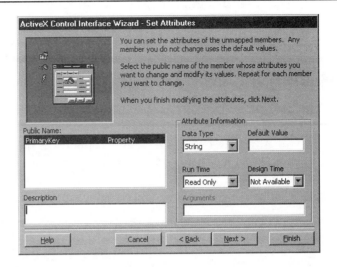

If you examine the code generated by the wizard, you'll see that the wizard delegates the control's members to the equivalent members of the constituent controls. For the PrimaryKey property, it inserted the following lines:

Listing 13.1   The Implementation of the PrimaryKey Property

```
Public Property Get PrimaryKey() As String
    PrimaryKey = m_PrimaryKey
End Property

Public Property Let PrimaryKey(ByVal New_PrimaryKey As String)
    m_PrimaryKey = New_PrimaryKey
    PropertyChanged "PrimaryKey"
End Property
```

The Property Get procedure is called when the application reads the PrimaryKey property of the control, whereas the Property Let procedure is called when the application sets the property's value. The code maintains a local variable, the *m_PrimaryKey* variable, with the property's value.

The wizard will generate all the code for you, but there's still one procedure you must code yourself. This is the UserControl's Resize event handler, in which you make sure that the TextBox control is resized to match the size of the control on the Form. Here's the UserControl object's Resize event handler:

LISTING 13.2   The UserControl's Resize Event Handler

```
Private Sub UserControl_Resize()
    Text1.Left = 0
    Text1.Top = 0
```

```
        Text1.Width = UserControl.Width
        Text1.Height = UserControl.Height
    End Sub
```

Making the Control Data-Bound

To make the control data-bound, you must open the Procedure Attributes dialog box (in the Tools menu). When the Procedure Attributes dialog box appears, click the Advanced button to see all the options, as shown in Figure 13.5. In the Name box, select the DisplayField property. Then check the "Property is data bound" option at the bottom of the Form. When you check this option, four options will be enabled. Check the first option in this group, "This property binds to DataField."

FIGURE 13.5:

The Procedure Attributes
dialog box

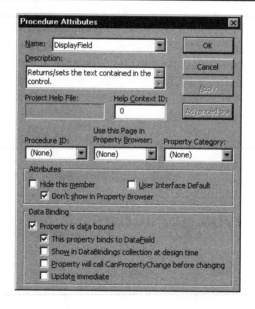

When the option "This property binds to DataField" is checked, the following properties will be added to the control: DataSource, DataMember, and DataField. You don't have to add any code for these properties; they'll be added to the control automatically. This means that you can bind the control to a data source through the DataSource property (and optionally through the DataMember property). The DataField property's box in the Properties window will be populated with the names of the data source's fields, and you can select the field to which the Text property of the control will be bound.

Select the name of the DisplayField property in the Name box of the Procedure Attributes window and check the option "This property binds to DataField." Visual Basic will bind the constituent control's Text property to the field specified in the control's DataField property. The custom control may bind more than a single property. These properties must be bound to different fields of the same row. Moreover, they can be displayed on other constituent controls, or you can simply expose them as properties of the control. The PrimaryKey property will be exposed as a property because the primary key of a table doesn't change.

Select the PrimaryKey property in the Name box of the Procedure Attributes window, and then check the options "Property is data bound" and "Show in Data-Bindings collection at design time." You must also check the option "Don't show in Property Browser" because primary keys don't change. Then, click OK to close the Procedure Attributes window, and you're ready to use the new control in your projects.

If you used the custom data-bound control on a Form at this point, the control would display the value of the field that it's bound to, but you wouldn't be able to edit the field through the control. When a property changes value, you must call the PropertyChanged method, passing the name of the property that changed value as an argument. This statement is executed from within the Property Let procedure, which is invoked every time the control lands on another row of the Recordset. The same method must be called when the field value is edited on the control. This action is signaled by the Change event of the Text1 control, so you must insert the following lines in the control's code:

```
Private Sub Text1_Change()
    PropertyChanged "Text"
End Sub
```

Testing the DBControl

To test the new control, switch to the test project and open its Form. Make sure that all the windows of the custom control (its design and code windows) are closed. On the Toolbox, you see a new icon, which represents the control you just designed (you can change the control's default icon by setting its ToolboxBitmap property to a file with an icon—an .ICO file).

Place an instance of the new control on the Form, size it accordingly, and then open its Properties window. The control has quite a few properties, although I've added only half a dozen properties. Notice the data-binding properties. Visual Basic has added the DataSource and DataMember properties to specify the control's data source, the Data Field property, and the DataBindings collection. All these properties were added because the control's DataBindingBehavior property was set to vbSimpleBound. Indeed, it's that simple to build a data-bound control.

Then, place an ADO Data Control on the Form and set it to the Titles table of the Biblio database. Use the Microsoft Jet OLE DB Provider to connect to the database. Select the DBControl on the test Form and set its DataSource property to the ADO

Data Control and its DataField property to the Title field. Open the DataBindings collection (select DataBindings in the control's Properties window, and click the button with the ellipsis to see the window shown in Figure 13.6). The DataBindings window displays the names of the data-bound properties except for the one that binds to the DataField property (the Text property). In this example, only the PrimaryKey property will appear in the list.

FIGURE 13.6:

The Data Bindings window for the DBControl

You must specify the field to which the selected property will be bound in the boxes to the right of the list with the property names. The data source must be the same as the one you used for the DataField property. Expand the Data Source box and select ADODC1. The Data Member box must be set only if you use a Data-Environment object as the data source, so leave it empty. Then, set the Data Field property to the name of the field the PrimaryKey property binds to (the ISBN field). Click OK to close the window and run the test project.

WARNING   Your project group contains two projects: an ActiveX control project and a standard EXE project. Only the second project can be executed by pressing F5. You must set the TestProject as the project group's Startup Object. Right-click the test project's name in the Project window and select Set as Startup. Then, press F5 to run the test project.

The first title in the database appears in the DBControl. As you move through the rows of the Titles table with the ADO Data Control's navigational buttons, the current title displays on the custom control. If you edit the title, the changes will be committed to the database as soon as you leave the current row.

The PrimaryKey is not used. This property will be accessed usually from within your code to look up fields in other tables (publisher names, for example). You can add a Label control on the test Form, as shown in Figure 13.7, and display on it the book's ISBN from within your code. Program the ADO Data Control's Move-Complete event as follows:

```
Private Sub Adodc1_MoveComplete(ByVal adReason As _
        ADODB.EventReasonEnum, ByVal pError As ADODB.Error,_
        adStatus As ADODB.EventStatusEnum, _
        ByVal pRecordset As ADODB.Recordset)
    Label1.Caption = DBControl1.PrimaryKey
End Sub
```

Every time the user moves to a new row, the program retrieves the current row's ISBN and displays it on a Label control.

FIGURE 13.7:

The DBControl's test Form

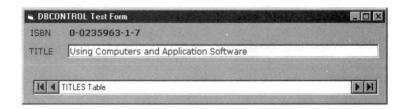

If you want to experiment with building data-bound controls, you can modify the DataBound control so that it automatically displays the primary key on a Label control. You must modify the design of the control by adding a Label control on it. Run the ActiveX Control Interface wizard again to create a new control and set the attributes of the new property through the Procedure Attributes window.

> **NOTE**
>
> If you have designed custom ActiveX controls in the past, you'll probably wonder why we haven't made the PrimaryKey property read-only at run time. Obviously, users shouldn't be allowed to change the table's primary key. If you attempt to make this property read-only, the control will not work because the PrimaryKey property must be set to the current row's primary key. You don't have to provide the code for this action, but VB updates the property's value automatically for you. If you make a data-bound property read-only, then VB won't be able to bind it to a field at run time.

The control built in this section is a simple data-bound control. You rely on VB to associate one of its properties to the DataField property, and one or more properties to the DataBinding collection. This is the simplest type of control you can design with VB. In addition to simple data-bound controls, you can build complex data-bound controls, which bind to an entire Recordset and not to a single row. The DataList control is an example of a complex data-bound control.

As you can guess, you can't create complex data-bound controls by setting a few attributes. You must actually use the ADO component and the objects it exposes from within the control's code to retrieve the desired Recordset and then display it on the control. This is a fairly complicated design, but you can use the Data Object Wizard to design complex data-bound controls, as you will see shortly. This wizard is quite different from the ActiveX Control Interface Wizard (it's discussed in the section "The Data Object Wizard," later in this chapter). In the meantime, let's look at a different type of data-aware control, one that can act as a data source (something like a custom data control).

Building a Data Source Control

A data-bound control is straightforward to build. It's difficult to come up with a data-bound control that brings extra functionality not found in the data-bound (and data-aware) controls of Visual Basic. The data-bound control doesn't "see" the database directly. Instead, it relies on a data control to bind it to a specific field and simply displays the value of the field.

To bring new functionality to your application, you must build a custom ActiveX control that acts as a data source to data-bound controls. This control has direct access to the database, and you get really creative with data controls. Figure 13.8 shows the custom data control you're going to build in this section. The FilterData-Control exposes the usual navigational buttons as the ADO Data Control, but it also allows users to filter the Recordset based on any field. By applying the appropriate filter, you can shorten the Recordset considerably so that it can be scanned with the Move methods. This control demonstrates how to manipulate a Recordset from within your control's code, and you can use the ideas discussed here to build more elaborate data source controls.

FIGURE 13.8:

The FilterDataControl in action

To design the custom control, start a new ActiveX Control project as usual. Change the default name of the UserControl object in the Project window to FilterDataControl and rename the project to FilterProject. Before you do anything else, add a test project. Open the File menu and select Add Project. Visual Basic will add a new project, and the current project will become a project group. The reason for creating a project group is to simplify the testing and debugging of the custom ActiveX control. An ActiveX control project can't be executed like a regular VB project. To test the control, you must place it on a Form of another project, set its properties at design time, and then run the project to test the behavior of the control. To simplify the process of testing and debugging the custom control, you can add a new project to the ActiveX control project and create a project group. The test project is the group's startup object, so that when you press F5 the test project is placed in run mode. You can break the execution of the test project, switch to the ActiveX control, edit the code, and resume execution. Finally, you must set the User Control object's DataSourceBehavior property to vbData Source.

The FilterDataControl's Interface

The FilterDataControl is similar to the ADO Data Control. It supports the same navigational methods, but it enables the user to filter the Recordset according to any field. The ComboBox control on the left is populated with the names of all the fields (column names) in the current Recordset. Every time the user selects another field, the second ComboBox control is populated with the unique values for this field. If you select the Country field in the first ListBox, for example, all country names in the table will appear in the second ComboBox control. If you select a country name in the second list, then the Recordset will be filtered automatically, and only the customers in the selected country will appear on the control.

Designing the Control

Designing a custom ActiveX control has much in common with designing a Form. All the action takes place on a UserControl object, which is the equivalent of a VB Form object. You place the controls that comprise the control's interface on the User-Control object and then you program them. The controls that make up your custom control's visible interface are called constituent controls, and many of the properties of the custom control are delegated to the constituent controls. This is what you did in the last example. The new custom control doesn't delegate any properties to constituent controls. Instead, it manipulates the rows of the Recordset and it exposes the fields of the current row to the host application. You must maintain a Recordset variable from within your code and program all the methods and properties of the control.

Place the controls on the UserControl object, as shown in Figure 13.9. You can rearrange them on the control, as you like. The UserControl object, which is the "Form" of the custom control, should be large enough to hold the controls.

FIGURE 13.9:

The UserControl object's constituent controls

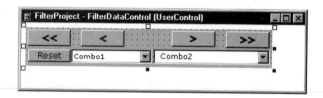

Run the ActiveX Control Interface Wizard. Do not select any of the standard members proposed by the wizard in the Select Interface Members window. Click the button with the two arrows to the left to remove all items from the Selected Names list. Then click Next to open the Create Custom Interface Members window. Here, you must specify the control's custom members. This is a data control; it must expose the usual navigational methods, as well as the underlying Recordset. Add the following custom members:

    Methods   MoveFirst, MovePrevious, MoveNext, MoveLast

    Properties   ConnectionString, RecordSource, Recordset

    Events   Repositioned, AtEOF, AtBOF

These are the very basic members of a data control, with the exception of the events. Your custom control will fire the Repositioned event when it lands on a new row (it's equivalent to the MoveComplete event), and will fire the AtEOF and AtBOF events when it reaches the two ends of its Recordset.

Click Next to move to the Set Mapping window, in which you need not supply any information. None of the members are mapped to a constituent control. On the next window (Set Attributes), you must set the types of the various properties. Set the ConnectionString and RecordSource property types to String and the Recordset property's type to ADODB.Recordset.

The wizard generates very little code—mostly placeholders, in which you must insert the actual code. The first piece of code you must provide is the GetData-Member subroutine. This subroutine is invoked automatically when the control is placed in run mode, and it's responsible for establishing a connection to the database and retrieving the specified Recordset. The GetDataMember must take into consideration the settings of the ConnectionString and RecordSource properties. Here's the implementation of the GetDataMember procedure:

LISTING 13.3   **The UserControl Object's GetDataMember Procedure**

```
Private Sub UserControl_GetDataMember(DataMember As String, _
                                      Data As Object)
Dim conn As String
```

```
On Error GoTo GetDataMemberError
    If rs Is Nothing Or cn Is Nothing Then
        ' make sure various properties have been set
        If Trim$(m_ConnectionString) = "" Then
            MsgBox "No ConnectionString Specified!", _
                    vbInformation, Ambient.DisplayName
            Exit Sub
        End If
        If Trim$(m_RecordSource) = "" Then
            MsgBox "No RecordSource Specified!", _
                vbInformation, Ambient.DisplayName
            Exit Sub
        End If
        If Trim$(m_ConnectionString) <> "" Then
            ' Create a Connection object and establish
            ' a connection.
            Set cn = New ADODB.Connection
            cn.ConnectionString = m_ConnectionString
            cn.Open

            ' Create a RecordSet object.
            Set rs = New ADODB.Recordset
            rs.CursorLocation = adUseClient
            rs.CursorType = adOpenStatic
            rs.Open m_RecordSource, cn, , adLockOptimistic
        Else
            Set cn = Nothing
            Set rs = Nothing
        End If
    End If
    Set Data = rs
    Combo1.AddItem "Select a field"
    For i = 0 To rs.Fields.Count - 1
        Combo1.AddItem rs.Fields(i).Name
    Next
    Combo1.ListIndex = 0
    Set rsFilter = New ADODB.Recordset
    Exit Sub

GetDataMemberError:
    MsgBox "Error: " & CStr(Err.Number) & vbCrLf & vbCrLf & _
        Err.Description, vbOKOnly, Ambient.DisplayName
    Exit Sub

End Sub
```

Most of the code of the GetDataMember will be the same for all custom data controls you develop. You must insert the lines that are specific to the unique functions of the control at the end. In this example, you're loading the field names to the DataCombo1 control. You will replace these lines with the code that initializes the constituent controls on the UserControl object.

The *rsFilter* Recordset variable is declared outside any procedure, and it holds the distinct values of the selected field. In other words, I use this Recordset to populate the second ComboBox control on the Form.

Filtering the Recordset

The basic operation of the custom control is the filtering of the Recordset. The Combo1 control is populated when you set control's DataMamber property. This ComboBox control holds the names of the fields. When a new field name is selected, the control's code goes out to the database and retrieves all the values of the specific field. If the selected field is the Country field, the second ComboBox control will be populated with the names of the countries in the Customers table (there will be no duplicates, of course). Here's the code that's executed when a new selection is made in the first ComboBox control:

LISTING 13.4   **Retrieving the Distinct Field Values**

```
Private Sub Combo1_click()
    If Combo1.Text = "Select a field" Then Exit Sub
    If rsFilter.State = adStateOpen Then rsFilter.Close
    RecSource = "SELECT DISTINCT TOP 100 " & _
                Combo1.Text & " FROM " & RecordSource & " "
    rsFilter.Open RecSource, cn, adOpenKeyset, adLockPessimistic
    Combo2.Clear
    Combo2.AddItem "Select a value"
    While Not rsFilter.EOF
        If Not IsNull(rsFilter.Fields(0)) Then _
                Combo2.AddItem rsFilter.Fields(0)
        rsFilter.MoveNext
    Wend
    Combo2.ListIndex = 0
End Sub
```

The action of selecting a field name doesn't filter the Recordset. You must select an item in the list with the values to actually filter the Recordset. Once the filter is applied, the Recordset is reset to the first row. The navigational methods apply to the filtered rows. The code that filters the Recordset is invoked from within the ComboBox control's Click event, which is shown in Listing 13.5.

LISTING 13.5	**Filtering the Recordset**

```
Private Sub Combo2_Click()
    On Error GoTo FilterError
    If Combo2.Text = "Select a value" Then Exit Sub
    rs.Filter = Combo1.Text & " LIKE '" & Combo2.Text & "%'"
    If rs Is Nothing Then
        rs.Filter = ""
    Else
        On Error Resume Next
        rs.MoveFirst
        If Err.Number <> 0 Then
            MsgBox "No records match the filter specification"
            Combo1.ListIndex = 0
            Combo2.ListIndex = 0
        End If
    End If
    Exit Sub

FilterError:
    MsgBox Err.Description
    rs.Filter = ""
End Sub
```

The FilterDataControl could potentially move large amounts of data to the client. You should probably use the TOP N clause to limit the number of rows retrieved. You can also add a property to the control that determines the number of unique values for the second ComboBox control. The country and the contact's title are meaningful filters because these columns have a small set of possible values. If you attempt to filter the rows by the company name, you'll end up moving a large number of rows. If the table doesn't contain too many company names, you can use the filter to actually locate company names in a ComboBox control. You can also execute an SQL statement with the COUNT function to find out the number of rows that must be moved to the client and move them only if they don't exceed a given threshold. If the number of distinct values is too many to be moved to the client, you should let the user specify a value and then filter the rows according to this value. If the user selects the column Company Name in the left list, you need not load all possible values to the client. Instead, you can let the user enter a value in the second ComboBox control and then retrieve the rows with company names starting with the user-supplied string. The filter expression would be the same, but the user would have to enter the value instead of selecting an existing one.

Finally, the FilterDataControl allows you to return to the original Recordset by clicking the Reset button, which sets the Filter property to adFilterNone.

The complete listing of the control can be found on the CD. You can use it as a template for building your own data controls. Just delete the parts that are specific to this control and replace them with appropriate code for your own control. You should copy the GetDataMember subroutine and add the rest of the code yourself. Each data source control is unique and you must provide the code that implements the unique features.

Testing the FilterDataControl

To test the custom control, switch to the test Form and place an instance of the FilterDataControl on the Form. Then place a few TextBox controls on the Form, where the fields of the current row will be displayed, as shown in Figure 13.8. Set up the control to see the Northwind database (you can use either the Jet or SQL Server version of the database). Do so by assigning the proper value to the ConnectionString property and the "Customers" string to the RecordSource property. Unfortunately, you can't invoke the Data Link Properties dialog box to set up the control's data source automatically.

To bind the TextBox controls on the Form to the custom data source control, select each TextBox control and set its DataSource property to FilterDataControl1 (the name will appear automatically in the list of valid values) and its DataField property to the name of the field to which you want to bind the control. Once the DataSource property has been set, the names of the columns in the data source (the Customers table) will appear automatically in the DataField drop-down list. All you have to do is select the proper column name for each data-bound TextBox control, and you can use the FilterDataControl to navigate through the rows of the Customers table. The test Form doesn't contain a single line of code.

The DataRepeater Control

The section explores a data-aware control that's very different from all other controls discussed in this book. It's the DataRepeater control, which is a container for custom data-bound controls, and it can host multiple instances of the same control. It's a handy tool for creating a data-bound control with a functionality that is similar to that of the DataGrid control. Figure 13.10 shows a DataRepeater control with multiple instances of a custom control that displays the basic fields of each title in the Titles table. You can use the DataRepeater's scrollbars to locate the desired title. As far as editing the rows displayed on the DataRepeater control, see the sidebar "Does the DataRepeater Control Update Tables?" later in this section.

FIGURE 13.10:

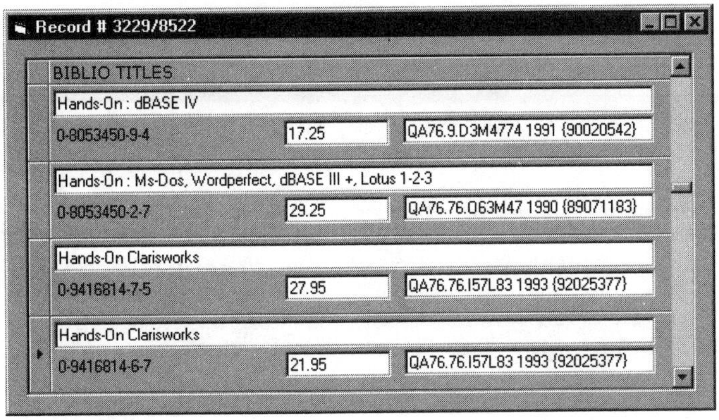

Using the DataRepeater control with a custom control

The DataRepeater control can be used as an alternative to the DataGrid control when you want to arrange the fields vertically on the control (on the DataGrid control, each row's fields appear next to each other), or include CheckBox and Image controls. The DataRepeater control is not used frequently, but I think it's a very flexible method for displaying multiple fields of small Recordsets. You can use it to display rows with many Yes/No (or True/False) fields, and allow the user to compare multiple rows.

To use the DataRepeater control, you must first design a custom control. You can't place the standard data-bound controls on the DataRepeater control (this functionality is readily available with the DataList or DataGrid control). The Title-Control project that you'll use in this section can be found in the DataRepeater folder. This project uses the TitleControl custom ActiveX control to populate the DataRepeater control on the test project's Form. The TitleControl displays four fields of the Titles table: Title, ISBN, Description, and Comments. The Description field's value is the book's call number (a value used to catalogue books in libraries), and the Comments field holds the book's price, so I named the two properties CallNum and Price.

The TitleControl's visible interface consists of four constituent controls: three TextBox controls and one Label control. The Label control is used to display the book's ISBN because this field shouldn't be edited. The control exposes only a few custom properties, which correspond to the four fields bound to the constituent controls. The control's custom properties are the following:

fldTITLE   The book's title. This property binds to the DataField property.

fldISBN   The book's ISBN. This property appears in the DataBindings collection, and it should be bound to the ISBN field.

fldCALLNUM   The book's call number. This property appears in the DataBindings collection, and it should be bound to the Comments field.

fldPRICE   The book's price. This property appears in the DataBindings collection, and it should be bound to the Description field.

The control's code was generated by the ActiveX Control Interface Wizard. You will probably add a call to the PropertyChanged method in the Change event of the various TextBox controls, so that users can edit the underlying fields through the control. Other than that, you don't have to modify the code produced by the wizard. I'm inserting the entire listing here. The listing is quite short (considering that it implements a custom ActiveX control) and straightforward.

LISTING 13.6   **The TitleControl's Code**

```
Public Property Get fldTITLE() As String
    fldTITLE = fTITLE.Text
End Property

Public Property Let fldTITLE(ByVal New_fldTITLE As String)
    fTITLE.Text() = New_fldTITLE
    PropertyChanged "fldTITLE"
End Property

Public Property Get fldISBN() As String
    fldISBN = fISBN.Caption
End Property

Public Property Let fldISBN(ByVal New_fldISBN As String)
    fISBN.Caption() = New_fldISBN
    PropertyChanged "fldISBN"
End Property

Public Property Get fldPRICE() As String
    fldPRICE = fPRICE.Text
End Property

Public Property Let fldPRICE(ByVal New_fldPRICE As String)
    fPRICE.Text() = New_fldPRICE
    PropertyChanged "fldPRICE"
End Property

Public Property Get fldCALLNUM() As String
    fldCALLNUM = fCALLNUM.Text
End Property

Public Property Let fldCALLNUM(ByVal New_fldCALLNUM As String)
    fCALLNUM.Text() = New_fldCALLNUM
    PropertyChanged "fldCALLNUM"
End Property

Private Sub fCALLNUM_Change()
    PropertyChanged "fldCALLNUM"
```

```
End Sub

Private Sub fPRICE_Change()
    PropertyChanged "fldPRICE"
End Sub

Private Sub fTITLE_Change()
    PropertyChanged "fldTITLE"
End Sub

Private Sub UserControl_ReadProperties(PropBag As PropertyBag)
    fTITLE.Text = PropBag.ReadProperty("fldTITLE", "")
    fISBN.Caption = PropBag.ReadProperty("fldISBN", "")
    fPRICE.Text = PropBag.ReadProperty("fldPRICE", "")
    fCALLNUM.Text = PropBag.ReadProperty("fldCALLNUM", "")
End Sub

Private Sub UserControl_WriteProperties(PropBag As PropertyBag)
    Call PropBag.WriteProperty("fldTITLE", fTITLE.Text, "")
    Call PropBag.WriteProperty("fldISBN", fISBN.Caption, "")
    Call PropBag.WriteProperty("fldPRICE", fPRICE.Text, "")
    Call PropBag.WriteProperty("fldCALLNUM", fCALLNUM.Text, "")
End Sub
```

The control produced by the wizard is not data-bound. To specify how the properties will be bound to database fields, you must set the attributes of the properties in the Procedure Attributes dialog box. The fldTITLE property is the one that binds to the control's DataField property. All other properties appear in the DataBindings collection.

The design of the control is really trivial. You can test it by placing an instance of the control on a new Form and bind it to a data source. The project's test Form uses the TitleControl to populate a DataRepeater control, as shown in Figure 13.10. Place a DataRepeater control on the project's test Form and then locate its Repeated-ControlName in the Properties window. You will see a list of all custom controls installed on your system. The new control will not yet appear in this list. Visual Basic displays all registered controls in this drop-down list.

TIP   To use a new ActiveX control with the DataRepeater control, you must first register it. Select the TitleControl object in the Project window and then open the File menu. Select the command "Make TitleControl.ocx," and you'll be prompted for the location of the OCX file. You can create the control's OCX file in the same folder as the project, or the System folder. Save the new OCX file in the project's folder. When VB compiles the custom control into an OCX file, it also registers it. Thus, the next time you expand the RepeatedControlName drop-down list, you will see the name of the new custom control: TitlesControlProject.TitlesControl.

Set the RepeatedControlName property to the name of the control you just created. Then, locate the DataRepeater control's DataSource and DataMember properties. Set them to an ADO Data Control or a DataEnvironment object that points to the Titles table of the Biblio database. For the purposes of this project, I created a DataEnvironment object with a Connection object (the BIBLIO object) to the Biblio database and a Command object (the BIBLIOTitles object) that retrieves the titles with the following SQL statement:

```
SELECT * FROM Titles
ORDER BY Title
```

The DataRepeater control DataSource property must be set to BIBLIO and its DataMember to BIBLIOTitles. You specified where the DataRepeater control will pump its data from. The data will end up on the TitleControl, not on the DataRepeater control. So, you must specify the bindings of each data-bound property of the custom control. Right-click the DataRepeater control and select Properties. You will see the control's Property Pages, shown in Figure 13.11.

FIGURE 13.11:

Specifying the Repeated-Control's data bindings through the DataRepeater control's Property Pages

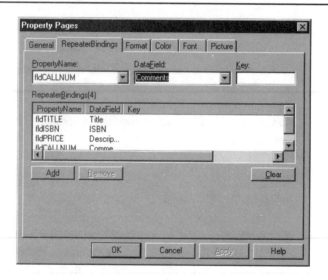

Switch to the RepeaterBindings tab and set the bindings of each data bound property. Select the property name in the PropertyName box and the name of the property in the DataField box. Then click the Add button to add the new binding to the collection. The control's properties are bound as follows:

PropertyName	DataField
fldTITLE	Title
fldISBN	ISBN

fldPRICE	Description
fldCALLNUM	Comments

Close the Property Pages dialog box and then run the project. The DataRepeater control will be populated by all the titles in the Biblio database. The titles appear in alphabetical order, and you can quickly locate the desired title with the help of the vertical scrollbar.

Does the DataRepeater Control Update Tables?

The DataRepeater control is not a problem-free control. Even if the data-bound control you use to populate it may be capable of updating the underlying table(s) in its data source, when placed on a the DataRepeater control, it exhibits the following annoying behavior: It lets you change the displayed field values, but it doesn't change the underlying tables. I've spent quite a bit of time trying to figure out a workaround, but I haven't come up with an elegant solution so far. If you absolutely want to update the underlying tables from within a DataRepeater control, place another instance of the data-bound control on the Form. Then, use the DataRepeater control to select the desired row and the individual copy of the data-bound control to edit the fields.

This approach almost works. The problem with it is that users may edit the fields on the DataRepeater control and expect that the database is also updated.

The DataRepeater control fires the DataUpdate event if one or more fields have been changed. This event is fired when you leave the repeated control you're editing, and not when you move from one field to another. Moreover, this event is fired once for each field that has changed value, and it reports the name of the field that was changed. To update the database, read the values of the fields that were changed from the repeated control and update the current row. The simplest method to update the underlying table is to copy the values from the repeated control on another instance of the same control, which is placed directly on the Form. You can keep this instance of the control invisible, so that users will think they're editing the fields on the DataRepeater control.

The Data Object Wizard

The Data Object Wizard (DOW) is one of the add-ins that come with VB, and it generates data-aware Classes and ActiveX controls. In the last section, you learned how to build custom ActiveX control with the ActiveX Control Interface Wizard. This is a tool that helps you develop any type of custom ActiveX control, data-bound or not. The DOW generates a few types of custom controls that are bound to a specific

Recordset, and they work in the context of a specific application. The control's visible interface is also generated by the wizard. You simply select the control's type and the wizard puts the appropriate constituent controls on the UserControl object.

The DOW can generate two types of objects: data-aware Classes and data-bound controls. The data-aware Classes are not meant to be used as middle-tier components, however. They are created only as the foundation on which the data-bound controls are built. It shouldn't surprise you that the documentation doesn't contain a single example that shows how to use the DOW in building middle-tier components. The purpose of a DOW-generated Class is to serve as the foundation of data-bound ActiveX controls. Before we actually build a few controls with the DOW, let's see how it builds custom data-bound controls.

Setting Up a DataEnvironment Object for DOW

As you will see, the DOW-generated custom ActiveX controls do not access the database directly. You must create a DataEnvironment object with the Command objects for reading, updating, and deleting the rows of the cursor. If the cursor contains foreign keys to other tables, you must also create Command objects that look up the values of the foreign keys. For example, if you're building a control for the Products table, as you'll do in the following sections, you should build a Command object that looks up category IDs in the Categories table. Once the lookup command is in place, the custom control will automatically translate the CategoryID field into a category name and display the string in the place of the ID. So, before you even start the DOW, you must design the Command objects for accessing the database and perform the necessary lookup operations.

Write Your Data-Manipulation Stored Procedures

The DOW-generated ActiveX controls access the database through stored procedures, which you must create ahead of time. If you want to display data only, but not edit them on the control, you must create a Command object that retrieves the desired cursor. If you want the control to be editable (and update the database), you must create three stored procedures: one for adding a row, another one for deleting, and third one for updating the underlying table(s).

Write Your Lookup Stored Procedures

The DOW-generated ActiveX controls include lookup fields. If you build a custom ActiveX control to display the rows of the Titles table in the Biblio database, you can specify that the publisher's name displays in the place of the PubID field. The control will update the table by inserting IDs (numeric values), but the user will see publisher names and will be able to specify a new publisher by selecting a name from a ComboBox control.

Creating Classes with DOW

In this section, you're going to build a Class whose members access the Products table of the Northwind database. This Class will be generated by DOW, and it will be used later to build a custom ActiveX control to browse and edit the same table. Remember, you must build a number of stored procedures for accessing the table's rows, inserting new rows, and editing/deleting existing rows, as well as two stored procedures for looking up product categories and suppliers. The lookup stored procedures are quite simple, really. They do not actually perform the lookup; they return pairs of IDs and strings, and the ActiveX control will do the lookup.

Let's build an ActiveX control for displaying the products of the Northwind database. Start a new Data Project and set the DataEnvironment object Connection object to the Northwind database. Then, add a new Command object, rename it AllProducts, and set its data source to the Products table. The controls you'll build will be based on this Command object, which returns the rows of the Products table.

The next step is to create the stored procedures AddProduct, DeleteProduct, and UpdateProduct to the Northwind database. The stored procedures must be defined in the SQL Enterprise Manager or the Query Analyzer. Here are the definitions of the three stored procedures:

LISTING 13.7   **The AddProduct Stored Procedure**

```
REATE PROCEDURE AddProduct
@ProductName nvarchar(40),
@SupplierID int,
@CategoryID int,
@QuantityPerUnit nvarchar(20),
@UnitPrice money

AS
DECLARE @ErrorCode int
INSERT Products (ProductName, SupplierID, CategoryID,
        QuantityPerUnit, UnitPrice)
VALUES (@ProductName, @SupplierID, @CategoryID,
        @QuantityPerUnit, @UnitPrice)
SET @ErrorCode=@@ERROR
IF (@ErrorCode = 0)
    RETURN (@@Identity)
ELSE
    RETURN (-@ErrorCode)
```

The AddProduct procedure returns the ID of the newly added product. This ID is generated automatically by SQL Server. If an error occurred, the error code generated by SQL Server is returned with a negative sign (to distinguish the error codes from valid product IDs).

LISTING 13.8   **The UpdateProduct Stored Procedure**

```
CREATE PROCEDURE UpdateProduct
@ProductID int,
@ProductName nvarchar(40),
@SupplierID int,
@CategoryID int,
@QuantityPerUnit nvarchar(20),
@UnitPrice money
AS
DECLARE @ErrorCode int
UPDATE Products SET
            ProductName = @ProductName,
            SupplierID=@SupplierID,
            CategoryID=@CategoryID,
            QuantityPerUnit=@QuantityPerUnit,
            UnitPrice=@UnitPrice
WHERE ProductID=@ProductID

SET @ErrorCode=@@ERROR
IF (@ErrorCode = 0)
   RETURN (0)
ELSE
   RETURN (@ErrorCode)
```

LISTING 13.9   **The UpdateProduct Stored Procedure**

```
CREATE PROCEDURE DeleteProduct
@ProductID int
AS
DELETE FROM Products WHERE ProductID=@ProductID
```

Finally, you must create two more stored procedures that will be used by the controls for looking up the values of the SupplierID and CategoryID fields. These two fields in the Products table store numeric values, which correspond to actual company names and category names in the Suppliers and Categories tables. The lookup is performed as follows: You supply a stored procedure that returns the pairs of IDs and strings to be used in the place of the IDs. The two stored procedures we need to look up the category IDs and supplier IDs are shown next:

LISTING 13.10   **The LookupSupplier and LookupCategory Procedures**

```
CREATE PROCEDURE LookupSupplier AS
SELECT SupplierID, CompanyName
FROM Suppliers
```

```
CREATE PROCEDURE LookupCategory AS
SELECT CategoryID, CategoryName
FROM Categories
```

Now you're ready to run the DOW to generate custom ActiveX controls for the Northwind database. First, you must create a Class that encapsulates all the functions you want to include in your controls. Attach the VB6 Data Object Wizard to your Add-Ins menu, if it's not already there. Then, select the VB6 Data Object Wizard command from the Add-Ins menu to start the wizard. The first window is a splash screen you can disable for future runs. Click Next to see the Create Object window. On this window, you can select the type of object you want to create, and you have two options: either a Class or a User Control. A User Control is always based on an existing Class, so start by checking the Class option. Then, click Next to see the Select Data Environment Command window:

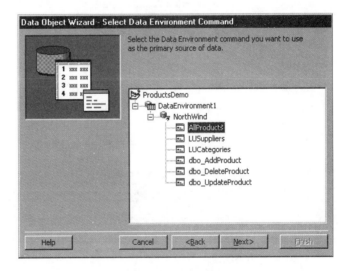

On the Select DataEnvironment window, you see all the objects in the project's DataEnvironment window. You must select the Command object on which the Class will be based. This is a command that returns the cursor with the data you want to view or edit; in the case of this example, it is the AllProducts Command object. The Class returns all the rows of the Products table and the custom ActiveX controls you will build later will be populated with the rows of the same table. Select the AllProducts item and click Next to see the Define Class Field Information window.

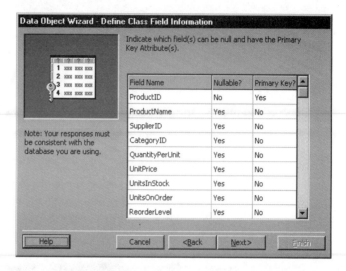

This window displays the names of all fields returned by the AllProducts command object and two columns, in which you can specify which fields are allowed to have Null values and which one is the primary key. The wizard should have been able to pick up this information from the database, but it didn't. Be sure that the information you supply on this window doesn't conflict the definition of the table in the database. For the AllProducts command, the ProductID field can't be Null and it's the primary key. Click Next, and you will see the Define Lookup Table Information window:

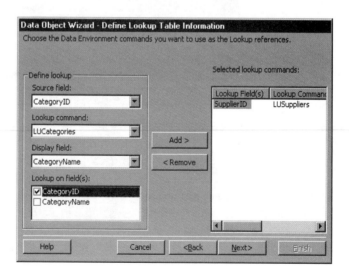

On this window, you can specify the lookup operations. To define a lookup, you must set the values of the fields in the left section of the window and click the Add button to add the specified lookup to the list of lookup commands.

Let's specify the lookup of the CategoryID field. Expand the Source field list, which contains the names of all the fields in the AllProducts cursor. Select the field to be looked up, which is the Category ID field. Then, expand the Lookup command list, which contains the names of all the Command objects in the DataEnvironment window. Select the LUCategories command, which corresponds to the Lookup-Categories stored procedure. After you specify the Lookup command field, the Display field and Lookup on field(s) will be populated with the names of the fields returned by the LookupCategories stored procedure. The Display field is the CategoryName (the descriptive field) and the Lookup on field(s) is the CategoryID (the primary key). The wizard will generate the code to replace every instance of the CategoryID field with the matching value of the CategoryName field, so that the control that will be based on this Class never sees the CategoryID field. Click the Add button to add the newly defined lookup to the list of Selected Lookup Commands. Then, define a lookup for the SupplierID field with the following settings:

Field Name	Field Value
Source Field	SupplierID
Lookup Command	LUSuppliers
DisplayName	CompanyName
Lookup on Fields	CategoryID

The Map Lookup Fields Window   Click the Next button to see the Map Lookup Fields window. For each lookup you have defined, you will see a window displaying the mapping between the Source Command Field and the Lookup Command Field. Just make sure that the mapping is correct and click Next to go through all the Map Lookup Fields windows. Then you will see the Define and Map Insert Data Command window.

The Define and Map Insert Data Command Window   This window maps the Source fields (the names of the fields in the AllProducts cursor) to parameters of the addProduct stored procedure. If the names of the parameters are the same as the name of the fields they map to (with the @ symbol in front of their names), then the wizard will map them properly. If you have used different parameter names in the stored procedure, you must map them on this window. Select a field in the left column and the name of the parameter it corresponds to in the right column. Just make sure that the names of the parameters are the same as the names of the fields they correspond to, and the wizard will populate this window on its own.

The Define and Map Update Data Command Window   This window maps the Source fields (the names of the fields in the AllProducts cursor) to parameters of the updateProduct stored procedure. The same comments about parameter names as in the previous paragraph apply here as well.

The Define and Map Delete Data Command Window   This window maps the Source fields (the names of the fields in the AllProducts cursor) to parameters of the deleteProduct stored procedure. The same comments about parameter names as in the previous paragraph apply here as well. Click Next for the last time to see the last window that prompts you to click Finish to generate the Class's code.

The wizard will create two Classes: the clsDOW Class, which contains the definition of an enumerated type; and the rsclsNWProducts, which is the Class with the members for accessing the actual data. The rsclsNWProducts exposes the members listed next. The various members are classified according to their function and only the non-trivial ones are explained:

Properties

AbsolutePosition, BOF, EOF   These are standard Recordset properties you will need from within the application's code to determine the current row.

SaveMode   This property lets you specify whether the control will update rows immediately or in batch mode. See the section "The SaveMode Property" for more information.

CategoryID, Discontinued, ProductID, ProductName, QuantityPerUnit, ReorderLevel, SupplierID, UnitsInStock, UnitPrice, UnitsOnOrder   For each field in the Command object on which the control is based, the wizard generates a property by the same name that corresponds to a column in the current row.

LUCategoriesCategoryName, LUSuppliersCompanyName, rsLUCategories, rsLUSuppliers   These properties relate to the lookup operations. The properties whose name begins with LU return the lookup name of the corresponding property. The other two properties are Recordsets with two columns: the IDs and the names of the fields being looked up.

Methods

AddRecord   This method adds a new record. It expects the values of the fields as arguments.

Delete   This method deletes a row based on a primary key value.

Move, MoveFirst, MovePrevious, MoveLast   These are usual navigational methods.

MoveToPK   This is another navigational method that allows you to move fast to the row with a specific primary key value (see the "The MoveToPK Method" section for more information).

ResyncRow   This method refreshes the current row by reading it from the database.

rsUpdate   This method updates the entire Recordset on which the Class is based.

Update   This method updates the current row in the underlying table.

UpdateBatch   This method updates all changed rows in batch mode.

Events

ClassError   This event is raised when an error occurs in the Class.

DeleteRecordComplete   This event signals the completion of a deletion operation.

rsMoveComplete   This event signals the completion of a navigational operation.

rsUpdateComplete   This event signals the completion of an update operation.

Validate   This event is fired when you move to another row, and it gives you a chance to validate the current row's fields. It accepts a single argument, the Cancel argument, which is of the Boolean type. Set the Cancel argument to True to cancel the changes.

The rsclsNWProducts Class will be used by DOW for the creation of a custom ActiveX control. DOW-generated Classes are hardly useful as middle-tier components, and they're never used on their own. They are the foundation of custom ActiveX control, and the next section describes how DOW uses them to build a control.

Creating Custom ActiveX Controls with DOW

Generating a custom ActiveX control with the DOW is a very simple process because all the information has been defined in the Class on which the control will be based. All you have to do is tell the wizard which Class you want to base your control on and the type of control you want. The wizard will generate the control, and you can use it on your data browsing and editing Forms.

TIP The custom ActiveX controls generated by the DOW are specific to a Recordset; they're specific to the Recordset generated by the Class. In general, an ActiveX control is not tied to a specific application. You can use it with any application by setting its data-binding properties accordingly. Even the DBControl we developed earlier in this chapter can be used with any database. The ActiveX controls we'll explore in this section are specific to a Recordset and can only accommodate a specific application. However, they can be used in many Forms, as long as they all have similar data-access requirements.

ActiveX Control Types

The DOW can generate four types of data-bound controls:

Single Record Control   This control is basically a Form for editing and browsing tables. It contains one data-bound control for each field (this is usually a TextBox control for most fields or a CheckBox control for True/False fields).

DataGrid Control   This control displays the entire cursor on a DataGrid control. You can make the DataGrid control editable, so that you can manipulate the underlying tables from within your application.

DataList Control   This control displays the first column in the Recordset on a DataList control. This type of control is used as lookup control and it's similar to the DataList control. However, it exposes the values of the other columns in the selected row as properties.

DataCombo Control   Another form of lookup control, similar to the previous one. The DataCombo control takes up less space on the form.

The members exposed by the various types of DOW-generated ActiveX controls are the same (with a few exceptions), and they're all based on the same Class.

To build a custom data-bound control with DOW, open the Add-Ins menu and select the Data Object Wizard add-in. The first screen is the same as before, except this time you must check the option "A User Control object bound to an existing Class object." The existing Class object is the Class you created earlier. Click Next, and you'll see another window with all the components of the DataEnvironment object. Here, you must select the rsclsNWProducts component. Click Next again to see the Select User Control Type window, shown in Figure 13.12. Here, you must select the type of control you want to create by checking the appropriate radio button.

FIGURE 13.12:

The Select User Control Type
window

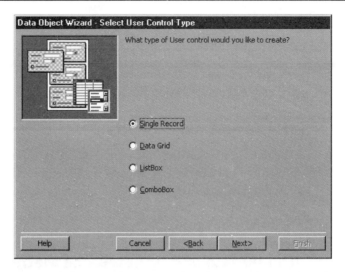

Leave the option Single Record checked and click Next. The next window lets you change the type of control that will be used to display each field. The wizard picks up the information from the Class and suggests the proper type of control for each field, as you can see here:

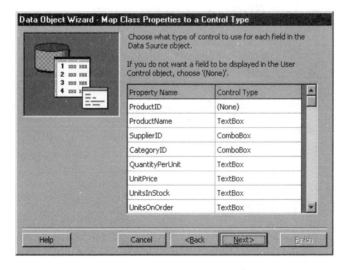

Click Next again, and you'll see the last window of the wizard, where you can specify the name of the custom control. Enter NWProducts and click the Finish button to build the control.

DOW will generate a control with a TextBox control for each field, and it will name it uctNWProductsSingleRecord. Had you selected a custom control based on the DataGrid control, it would have been named uctNWProductsDataGrid, and so on. While you're at it, build all four types of custom controls. We will explore each control type later in this section. First, I'll discuss briefly some unique members of the DOW-generated controls.

The SaveMode Property

The data-bound controls generated by DOW can update the database immediately or in batch mode. To specify that the underlying table(s) must be updated in batch mode, you must set the control's SaveMode property to adSaveBatch. Of course, you must include a Command button or other mechanism for calling the UpdateBatch method.

The Update and UpdateBatch Methods

To save changes made to the current row, you can call the Update method. The changes will also be committed to the database when you move to another row. If you're working in batch mode, however, you must call the UpdateBatch method.

The GridEditable Property

This property applies to custom controls based on the DataGrid control and makes the control editable when set to True. In effect, it's equivalent to setting the Data-Grid control's AllowAddNew, AllowEdit, and AllowDelete properties to True.

The ResyncRow Method

This method refreshes the current row by reading its fields from the database. Use this method to display the most up-to-date field values or to discard any changes made to the current row.

The Navigational Methods

All DOW-generated controls support the usual navigational methods (except for the controls based on the DataGrid object, of course). In addition to the Move methods, they support a MoveToPK method, which allows you to specify the current row by its primary key. The syntax of the MoveToPK method is

```
MoveToPK(primary_key)
```

where *primary_key* is the value of the desired row's primary key.

TIP

Notice that the ActiveX controls produced by the DOW work with client-side cursors only. If you set the CusrorLocation property of the AllCustomers Command object to server-side, the controls will not even be populated at run time.

Testing the DOW-Generated Controls

You have seen the process of generating ActiveX controls with the Data Object Wizard. You should create three versions of the same basic control, all in the same project. Create three controls: a single record control, a DataGrid control, and a DataList control. You can find the project used in this section in the DOWAXControls folder in this chapter's folder on the CD (the ProductsDemo project).

NOTE

If you open the ProductsDemo project from the CD, you'll get the usual warning that the custom controls can't be found on your system. Ignore this message and continue loading. When you run the project for the first time, VB will register the custom controls, and you'll be able to use them on the test Form.

All three controls are based on the rsclsNWProducts Class; and they are named uctNWProductsSingleRecord, uctNWProductsDatagrid, and uctNWProductsList-Box. The test project of the DOWControl project group contains three Forms that demonstrate the use of each custom control.

NOTE

To test the individual custom controls, you must change the project's Startup Form. To set a different start-up Form, open the Project Properties dialog box (Project ➤ Project Properties), and select another Form in the Startup object drop-down list.

The three test Forms of the project are shown in the figures of the following sections. You'll see how each type of control is used in a project, and then I'll discuss briefly some of the problems with the automatically generated controls.

The ProductDataGridForm

This Form of the test project, shown in Figure 13.13, uses the custom control based on the DataGrid control. To enable the user to edit the rows of the cursor, you must set the GridEditable property to True. I have also set the control's SaveMode to adBatch, so that changes are committed to the database only when the user clicks the Update Database button on the Form. This button calls the UpdateBatch method.

FIGURE 13.13:

The ProductDataGrid
test Form

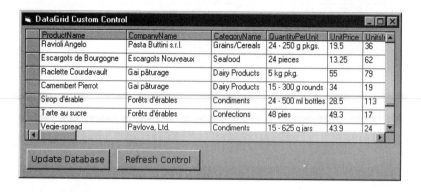

If the user changes his mind and wants to cancel the changes on the grid, he can click the Refresh Cursor button to re-read the data from the table and populate the control from scratch. Any changes made in the meantime by others will appear on the control, while changes made on this Form will be discarded. The code behind the two buttons on the Form is shown next.

LISTING 13.11   The Refresh and Save Buttons

```
Private Sub bttnRefresh_Click()
    uctNWProductsDataGrid1.InitNWProducts
End Sub

Private Sub bttnSave_Click()
    uctNWProductsDataGrid1.UpdateBatch
End Sub
```

You should examine the code generated by the wizard and see how the control combines the DataGrid control with a regular ComboBox control, which acts as a lookup tool for the columns whose values are being looked up in other tables. The code populates the ComboBox control and places it exactly over the cell you're editing. You can copy this code (it's the ShowFloatingControl procedure) and use it with your own projects. This code can be used with any project that relies on the DataGrid control and requires lookup operations.

The ProductLookupForm

The ProductLookup test Form demonstrates how to use two custom controls on the same Form as navigational tools, as shown in Figure 13.14. The control that's based on the ListBox control acts as a lookup tool, whereas the Single Record control displays the details of the selected title.

The ProductLookup Test Form

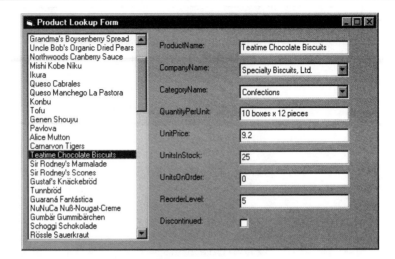

The custom control with the list of products (the uctNWProductsListBox1 control) recognizes the ListBoxClick event. This event reports the primary key's value as argument, which you can use from within your code to retrieve the row selected in the list. Here's the code in the uctNWProductsListBox1 control's Click event handler:

LISTING 13.12   Programming the ListBox_Click Event

```
Private Sub uctNWProductsListBox1_ListBoxClick _
        (ProductID As Variant)
    uctNWProductsSingleRecord1.MoveToPK ProductID
End Sub
```

If you run the test project with the ProductLookupForm as its startup object, you'll notice that as you move from title to title, the Category and Supplier field go through a lot of values before the final (and correct) value is displayed. It seems as if the control's code scans the rows of the lookup tables until it finds the category name (and supplier name) that match the IDs in the two fields of the current row. Indeed, this is how the lookup operation works! It seems contradictory to put so much effort into making the cursors as small as possible and writing stored procedures to speed up the updates, and then have a control that iterates through the rows of a cursor to find a match.

If you examine the code of the ActiveX control, you will find the following subroutine. The GetSurKeyLUCategories function locates the row with the CategoryID value you're looking up with a loop, which is the least efficient method. It's not trivial to fix this behavior—you'll have to change the code in many more places, outside of this function as well. Even if you decide to fix the code that performs the lookup operation, you will have to repeat the changes every time you run the wizard.

LISTING 13.13 **The GetSurKeyLUCategories Function**

```
Private Function GetSurKeyLUCategories(categoryid) As Integer
'================================================================
'Name: GetSurKeyLUCategories
'
'Author: Microsoft Data Object Wizard
'
'Date: 08/21/1999 11:44
'
'Description: Moves the RecordSet class to the
'AbsolutePosition value of the Foreign Key parameters.
'
'Comment:
'================================================================
    If IsNull(categoryid) Then
        GetSurKeyLUCategories = -1
        Exit Function
    End If
    oNWProducts.rsLUCategories.MoveFirst
    ' Loop through each record in the Foreign Key RecordSet
    ' class until we find the actual Foreign Key values
    While Not oNWProducts.rsLUCategories.EOF
        'If the Foreign Key RecordSet field value(s) equal the
        'Select Foreign Key field values,
        'then get the Surrogate Key (AbsolutePosition) value.
        If _
            oNWProducts.rsLUCategories("categoryid").Value = _
                    Val(categoryid) Then
            'Get the Surrogate Key (AbsolutePosition) value.
            GetSurKeyLUCategories = _
                    oNWProducts.rsLUCategories.AbsolutePosition
            Exit Function
        End If
        oNWProducts.rsLUCategories.MoveNext
    Wend

    'If the Surrogate Key (AbsolutePosition) value is not found,
    'set the function to the first Recordset item
    GetSurKeyLUCategories = 1
End Function
```

This inefficiency is due to the fact that the DOW can't make any assumptions as to the type of the primary key. If you're using integer primary keys, you'll be able to come up with a technique to quickly locate the matching item in the ComboBox control's list. It would also be very convenient if the Seek method worked with client-side cursors.

The ProductSingleRecord Form

The custom control that displays one row at a time is quite robust. All the controls on the Form in Figure 13.15 (with the exception of the navigational buttons at the bottom) belong to the uctNWProductsSingleRecord control. They display the fields of the current row in the Products table.

The buttons at the bottom of the Form allow you to navigate through the rows of the Recordset on which the control is based. The code behind the navigational buttons calls the navigational methods exposed by the control.

FIGURE 13.15:

The ProductSingleRecord
Test Form

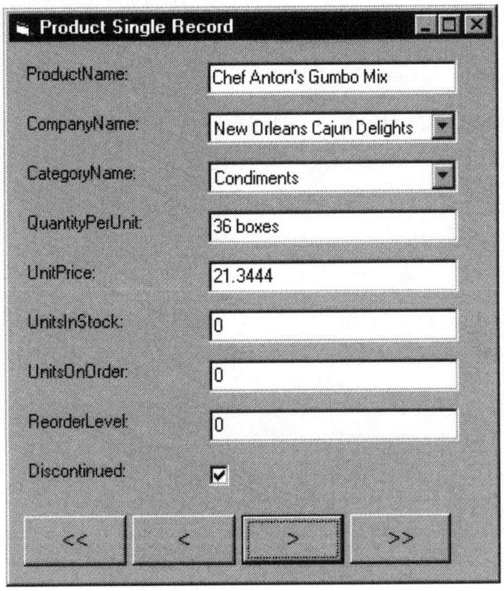

LISTING 13.14   The Code of the Form's Navigational Buttons

```
Private Sub bttnFirst_Click()
    uctNWProductsSingleRecord1.MoveFirst
End Sub

Private Sub bttnLast_Click()
    uctNWProductsSingleRecord1.MoveLast
End Sub

Private Sub bttnNext_Click()
    uctNWProductsSingleRecord1.MoveNext
End Sub

Private Sub bttnPrevious_Click()
    uctNWProductsSingleRecord1.MovePrevious
End Sub
```

If you want to access the values of the fields in the current row, you'll realize that the control doesn't expose them as properties—even if the Class on which the control is based exposes the fields as properties. In the following section, you'll see how to expose the entire Recordset underlying the custom control to the application that hosts the control.

Tweaking Your Custom Data-Bound Controls

As I mentioned earlier, the Data Object Wizard is one of Visual Basic's tools that can stand substantial improvement. A major shortcoming is that you can't access the values of the individual fields displayed on the control. Switch back to the ProductSingleRecordForm Form of the ProductsDemo project. Other than navigating through the Recordset with the usual Move methods (which are exposed by the control) and editing the fields on the control's TextBoxes, there's nothing else you can do. You can't even access the values of the current row's fields. Consider the MoveToPK method, which allows you to move a row with a specific primary key value. What good is this method if you can't access the primary keys of the records? After a few futile attempts to build interfaces based on custom ActiveX controls generated by the DOW, I had to give up. Then, I decided to give this tool another chance because I had access to the code it produces. How difficult is it to modify the code to incorporate the functionality I need? Sometimes it's quite simple; sometimes it's not.

> **TIP**
>
> By the way, even if you decide that the functionality of the DOW-generated controls is limited for your applications, it's a good idea to examine the code produced by the wizard and even experiment with it.

It's not my intention to write a book on how to modify the code produced by the DOW and how you can tweak it. However, I will show you some simple workarounds. Some problems are deeply rooted into the design of the code generator. Obviously, you're not expected to step in and fix all the problems. Again, I insist on the DOW because I think it will be heavily revised for the next version of the language and it will become a real developer's tool. Even in its current implementation, the Data Object Wizard is a useful tool for generating data-bound controls for manipulating client-side Recordsets.

To expose the fields of the current row, open the control's Code window and look for the declaration of the *rsclsNWProducts* object. This is the data source of the Class on which the control is based.

```
Private WithEvents oNWProducts As rsclsNWProducts
```

Change the Private keyword to Public and you can access the data source of your custom control. Here are some of the properties it exposes:

AbsolutePosition   This is current row's position in the cursor. DOW works with client cursors only, so you can safely access this property.

Field Names   The control exposes the values of the current row's fields as properties with names that are identical to the names of the cursor's fields (ProductID, ProductName, and so on).

Field values after Lookup   Some properties expose the values of the fields after lookup. The LUCategoriesCategoryName is the name of the current product's category name, and LUSuppliersSupplierName is the name of the current product's supplier name. In other words, you can access the product's CategoryID with the expression:

```
uctNWProductsSingleRecord1.oNWProducts.CategoryID
```

This expression will return an integer (the category ID). The following expression, however, will return the name of the product's category:

```
uctNWProductsSingleRecord1.oNWProducts.LUCategoriesCategoryName
```

Lookup tables   You can also access the entire table returned by the lookup stored procedures. The following loop scans all the pairs of category IDs, and names and prints them on the Immediate window:

```
rsLookup.MoveFirst
While Not rsLookup.EOF
    For i = 0 To rsLookup.Fields.Count - 1
        Debug.Print rsLookup.Fields(i) & "    ";
    Next
    Debug.Print
    rsLookup.MoveNext
Wend
```

Summary

This chapter concludes our discussion of data-bound objects. In the next chapter, you will build a three-tier application that combines many of the topics discussed in the last few chapters. You will see how the same middle-tier components can be used both on a local area network and on the Web, and how these components simplify the development of the front end.

PART III

Databases on the Web

CHAPTER
FOURTEEN

Accessing Databases over the Web

- The structure of Web applications

- HTML tags and Forms

- VBScript

- The ASP object model

- Using cookies

- Making queries with ASP files

- Accessing databases with ADO

In this chapter, you will find all the information you need to access your database over the Web. You will learn how to create Web pages that can query and/or update a database, request registration information from viewers, accept orders through a Web site, and perform related operations. This chapter shows you how to apply your knowledge of Visual Basic and the ADO component to build Web applications.

The Web is by its nature a client/server environment. The browser is the client whose task is to present the information, and the Web server's task is to provide the documents requested by the client. Elaborate Web sites use multiple tiers as well. The Web server is the first tier on the server's side, and it provides the HTML documents to the client. If a page requires data that reside on a database, as is the case with online stores, there's an additional tier: the database server. As you will see, the Web server can't access databases directly. It uses the ADO component to access the database server. If the site incorporates business rules, it may require a third tier, which provides the ActiveX components that implement these rules.

The various tiers of the server may be running on the same or different machines. The tiers are distinguished according to the functionality they provide, not the machine they run on. You can start with a single machine that runs both IIS and SQL Server. When the number of visitors outgrows your Web server, you can move the SQL Server to a different machine. You may also develop ActiveX components that can be called by the Web server, but reside on a third machine. A bank's site, for example, may use a single machine to verify the user, but retrieve the customer's data from a different server (depending on the customer's branch or state).

The picture of the Web as a three-tier environment is depicted in Figure 14.1. The principles behind the operation of the Web are quite simple. In order to build Web applications, however, you must understand how these tiers are implemented. If browsers could execute VB code, building Web applications would be very simple. Unfortunately, browsers can't handle anything but HTML and JavaScript. (Sure, Internet Explorer can execute VBScript code too, but Netscape can't.) At this point, Web applications rely heavily on the server, rather than the client, and you must learn how to write applications that access databases on one end and interact with the client on the other end.

FIGURE 14.1:

The tiers of the Web

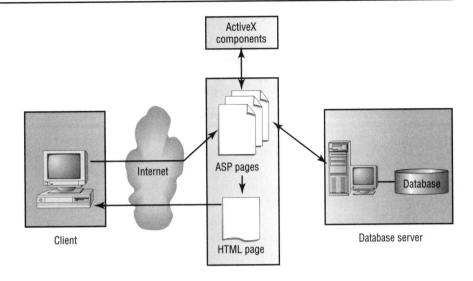

FIGURE 14.1:

The tiers of the Web

Web Applications

This chapter is about Web applications. I do not intend to show you how to write HTML pages or how to download ActiveX components or Java Classes to the client, where they can be executed. No, Web applications are not games you play over the Internet. They are plain old HTML pages that interact with the server.

Web pages are by definition interactive. Clients make requests and servers respond by providing the requested documents. Although this model of interaction has proved to be so functional and so efficient that it took the world by storm, it doesn't take into consideration the need for the client to pass any significant amount of information to the server. The Web was based on the premise that clients request new documents from the server. This was a reasonable assumption for the early days of the World Wide Web, but the unexpected adoption of this technology led very quickly to the need for a more elaborate scheme of information flow between clients and servers.

People are no longer interested in simply requesting documents from a server; they need up-to-date, live information. That type of information can't be stored in HTML documents; instead, it must be retrieved from a database the moment it's requested. In effect, you would like to be able to interact with the servers through an interface comprising cute boxes, buttons, and any of the controls we use in building Windows applications. It's too late for that, however. The Web interface was adopted because it was simple, and it was implemented on just about every operating system. If it weren't for its simplicity, it's doubtful that the Web would have grown as rapidly. Some companies have actually tried to make Web pages look more like Forms, but these attempts have failed.

To allow for better two-way communication between clients and servers, the HTML standard was enhanced with Forms and controls. A Form is a section of a page into which users can enter information (enter text in Text controls, select an option from a drop-down list, or check a radio button). The controls are the items that present or accept information on the Form. The values of the controls are sent to the server by the browser and processed there. HTML Forms and controls are quite rudimentary when compared to VB Forms and controls, but they are the only means of interaction between clients and servers (excluding the click of the mouse on a hyperlink).

Therefore, if you want to build a Web application, you must limit yourself to these controls. Your page may not look quite like a VB Form, but this is something you must live with, and it doesn't seem it's going to change any time soon. Yet, these controls coupled with hyperlinks are adequate for building applications that run over the Internet.

NOTE   Technically, you're not limited to the standard HTML controls. You can create custom ActiveX controls to use on your HTML pages. However, these custom controls must first be downloaded and installed on the client computer before your pages can use them. Most users wouldn't allow third-party controls to be installed on their systems, so using ActiveX controls means your page won't look as intended and won't even function as designed. That's why very few sites ask you to download custom ActiveX controls. If you develop Web applications to be used on an intranet in which IE has been adopted as the standard browser, however, you can use any ActiveX control on your pages.

Another limitation had to be overcome. Browsers are designed to communicate with Web servers in a very simple manner. They request documents by submitting a string known as a URL (Uniform Resource Locator). URLs are the addresses of HTML documents on the Web. The URL of the desired document is usually the destination of a hyperlink in the document itself. The browser knows how to extract the destination of the selected hyperlink and request the document. Alternatively, you can specify the URL of the desired document by entering its name in the browser's address box.

To interact with the server, browsers should be able to pass more than a document's URL to the server. Sometimes, they have to pass a lot of information back to the server, such as query criteria, registration information, and so on. This problem was solved by allowing the client to attach all the information that must be passed to the server along with the destination's URL. The destination need not be an HTML document. It can be the name of an application that runs on the server and knows how to process the parameter values passed by the browser.

Figure 14.2 shows what happens when you use the AltaVista search engine to locate articles on database programming. The search argument is "+database +programming", and the browser passes the following URL to the server:

```
http://www.altavista.com/cgi-
    bin/query?pg=q&kl=XX&q=%2Bdatabase+%2Bprogramming
```

This is not a common URL. The first part is the URL of an application that runs on the server. It's the query application in the `cgi-bin` folder under the Web server's root folder. The question mark separates the name of the application from its arguments. The query application accepts three arguments: *pg*, *kl*, and *q*. The first two arguments are of no interest to you. The last argument is the search string. The symbol "+" was replaced by the string %2B (the hexadecimal representation of the plus character). The query application will read the information passed by the client, query the database with the specified keywords, and return another HTML document with the results of the query. The question mark in this URL separates the name of the application from the arguments. The ampersand symbol separates multiple arguments.

FIGURE 14.2:

Invoking a server application and passing arguments to it from within the browser

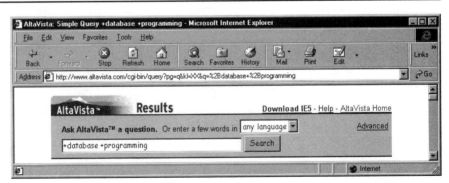

In effect, we fool the browser into thinking that the destination document has a really long URL. The Web server will figure out what the browser is about to do and it will invoke the query application and pass the specified parameters to it.

A Web application is a site with multiple HTML pages and server programs that interact with each other. HTML pages call server applications and pass parameters to them. These applications, which are called *scripts*, are executed on the server, process the values submitted by the client, format the results as HTML documents, and send them to the client. In all honesty, Web applications shouldn't even be called applications, but we shouldn't be so critical. Just think of the fact that a single machine can serve thousands of clients, make sales for your company, and allow people to interact with their company's database across the country or across the globe.

Typical Web Applications

Let's look at a few typical Web applications and analyze their requirements. Most corporations have a Web site already for "a presence on the Web," as they claim. A simple Web site with static pages is of no interest to you (but it's the starting point for any corporation ready to do business on the Web).

The most common Web applications are online stores. An online store uses an intuitive interface that allows users to browse through products, locate and select the ones they're interested in, and order them. Even companies that do not sell online, like automobile companies, have set up online stores where users can compare prices, customize a car, and then look up dealer names in their area.

Of all types of online stores, bookstores are the most common and most popular ones. Every major bookstore is also selling through the Web, not to mention a few bookstores that operate exclusively through the Web. Computer manufacturers also have a dynamic presence on the Web. Nearly every mail-order company selling computers and peripherals is also selling on the Web. The common characteristic of all these stores is that they don't focus on intensive searches. Instead, they allow you to build a custom system (by selecting the amount of RAM, hard disk size, and other options) and then calculate the price of your dream machine. I could go on and on, but I will end this list with a third form of online store, one that sells through bids. They advertise new or used products, accept bids, and sell to the highest bidder(s). Bids take place in real time, usually in a very short period. Airlines will frequently offer tickets at reduced prices through a bidding process. You can see the bids as other viewers place them and either continue or give up.

The information presented in this chapter applies to all types of Web sites, but I will focus on the components of accessing databases over the Web. After all, a database can be found behind every application. An online store has two basic requirements:

- The products database is accessed through the controls on a Form. A component on the server must read the data entered by the user on the Form, select the appropriate rows from the database, and format them as an HTML document that can be displayed on the client.

- It accepts orders. To accept an order, the online store must read user-supplied information (including sensitive information such as credit card numbers), validate it, and store it in a database. This information will be used later to materialize the order.

A site that's used for user registration and online support has similar requirements. This type of Web application is used to provide support to registered users. The first time you connect to a site like this, you provide some data, and you specify a username and password. After that, you can connect to the site, visit areas that are limited to registered users, and browse the site as usual. In most cases, users are allowed to search a database with keywords and related articles of interest.

For the purposes of this chapter, I assume that you are familiar with HTML. The examples in this section do not use elaborate Web pages, just text, hyperlinks, and tables. And HTML controls, of course. The HTML controls are stripped-down versions of the intrinsic Visual Basic controls and are discussed in the section "HTML Forms and Controls." You'll start by exploring the structure of a Web application and its special requirements. An overview of VBScript and HTML controls follows. The majority of the chapter discusses the objects of the Active Server Pages, and especially how to use the ADO component to access databases from within server scripts.

The Structure of Web Applications

Web applications have a special requirement. The various Forms of an application are mapped to HTML pages. In a VB application, there are many options for its Forms to communicate with one another. They can use public variables, they can read directly the values of the controls on any page, and they can set each other's properties. The situation is different on the Web. Each page is a separate entity, and it can't interact directly with another page of the same site—not to mention the fact that users can bookmark any page and jump to this page directly.

A Web application is a site that works like a VB application. You enter information on a Form, this information is transmitted to the server, and the result of the processing returns to the client as another document. The processing that takes place on the server is (in 99% of the cases) a database search. The results of the search are then furnished back to the client in the form of another HTML page.

Here's the first main difference between a VB interactive application and a Web application: the Forms of the VB application can remain open on the desktop, and users can switch from one to the other with a mouse-click. This is not true with a Web application. A Web application can display only one Form (page) at a time. In order to switch to another page, you must either select a link on the current page, or click the Back button to view a page you already visited.

How about running multiple instances of Internet Explorer, so that you can view multiple pages of the same site at once? That's the worst thing you can do. It will confuse the server, which in turn will confuse you.

Let's say you're looking for VB titles on the Sybex site. Imagine that you opened two windows of IE: one with the search Form and another one with the results. If this were a VB application, every time you changed the search criteria on the first page and clicked on a button, the second Form would be populated with the results. This isn't going to happen on the Web. The server doesn't keep track of how many and which pages you have opened on your computer. As far as the server is concerned, you are viewing a single page at a time.

HTML pages cannot easily communicate with one another like VB Forms. When a Form's controls are submitted to the server, the script running on the server must store all the parameter values to local variables and use them to prepare the next page. After the page has been prepared and transmitted to the client, the information is lost forever—unless the server stores it into a local file or database, or on the client computer as a cookie.

HTML Forms and Controls

To interact with the viewer, besides the ubiquitous hyperlinks, HTML recognizes a few special tags that insert controls on a Form. HTML controls are stripped-down versions of common controls from Windows that you're used to using in VB. You can use controls to collect information from the user for registration purposes, take orders over the Internet, or let the user specify selection criteria for record retrieval from databases. HTML provides the following controls:

TABLE 14.1: The HTML Controls

Control Name	Description
CheckBox	A box that can be checked or cleared to indicate that an option is selected.
RadioButton	A circular button that can be checked or cleared to indicate one of multiple options. This control is similar to Visual Basic's Option control.
Text	A box that accepts a single line of text, similar to Visual Basic's default TextBox control.
Password	A text control that doesn't display the characters as they are typed; it displays a * instead.
TextArea	A box that accepts multiple lines of text, similar to a TextBox control with its MultiLine property set to True.
Selection	A list of options from which the user can select one or more, similar to Visual Basic's ListBox or combo box controls.
Button	A usual button that can trigger various actions, similar to Visual Basic's Command-Button control.

Before you place any controls on a page, you must create a Form with the <FORM> tag. All controls must appear within a pair of <FORM> tags (you can place the controls anywhere in the HTML file, but the simplest method of transmitting the values entered by the viewer on the controls is to place all controls in a Form section):

```
<FORM NAME = "myForm">
{your Controls go here}
</FORM>
```

The NAME attribute is optional, but it's a good practice to name Forms. Beyond the NAME attribute, the <FORM> tag accepts two more attributes, METHOD and ACTION, which determine how the data will be submitted to the server and how they'll be processed there. The METHOD attribute can have one of two values, POST and GET. These two attributes are discussed in detail in the section "The GET and POST Methods" later in this chapter.

The <FORM> tag recognizes the ID attribute as well. The ID is similar to the NAME attribute, but it can be used in programming the Form from within a client-side script. This is also true for the controls. If you want to be able to program the controls on the Form from within a script on the client, use the ID attribute with various control tags, which are discussed in the following sections.

The CheckBox Control

The CheckBox control is a little square with an optional check mark. Figure 14.3 shows a typical situation that calls for CheckBox controls. The check mark is a toggle that turns on and off every time the user clicks on the control. It is used to present a list of options, from which the user can select none, one, or more. When the check mark is turned on, the CheckBox is said to be checked; when it's turned off, the control is said to be *cleared*. The user may check any number of options, from none to all.

FIGURE 14.3:

CheckBox controls are used to present to users a list of options, from which they can check none, one, or more.

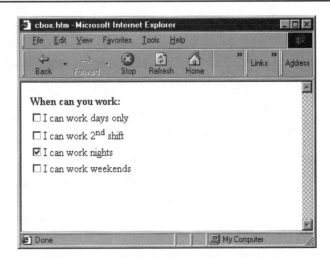

The CheckBox control can be inserted in a document with the following tag:

```
<INPUT TYPE = CHECKBOX NAME = "Check1">
```

where *Check1* is the control's name. You'll use it later to find out whether the control is marked or not, for instance. By default, a CheckBox is cleared. To make a CheckBox checked initially, you use the CHECKED option in its <INPUT> tag:

```
<INPUT TYPE = CHECKBOX NAME = "Check1" CHECKED>
```

The RadioButton Control

The RadioButton control is similar to the CheckBox control except that it's round and, instead of a check mark, a solid round mark appears in the center of a checked RadioButton. RadioButton controls are used to present a list of options, similar to a group of CheckBox controls, but only one option can be selected in a group of RadioButtons. Figure 14.4 shows a typical arrangement of several RadioButtons. Notice that the options are mutually exclusive and only one of them can be checked. Not only that, but the responsibility of clearing the previously checked button lies on the control itself; there's nothing you must do in your code to clear the checked button every time the user makes a new selection.

FIGURE 14.4:

RadioButtons are used to display mutually exclusive options, and only one of them can be active.

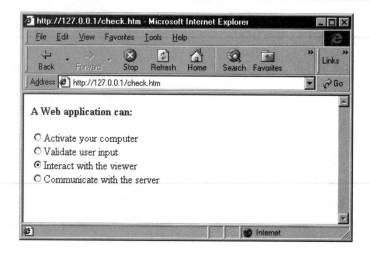

To insert a RadioButton in a document, use a line similar to the one for the CheckBox, only this time enter the type of the Control type as RADIO:

```
<INPUT TYPE = RADIO NAME = "Radio1">
```

Although each CheckBox on a Form has its own name, you can have several RadioButtons with the same name. All RadioButtons with the same name form a group and only one member of the group can be checked at a time. Every time the user clicks on a RadioButton to check it, the previously checked one is cleared automatically. To initially check a RadioButton, use the CHECKED attribute, which works similarly to the attribute with the same name of the CheckBox control.

Because several RadioButton controls may belong to the same group but only one of them can be checked, they must also share the same name. The group of RadioButton controls on the page in Figure 14.4 was created with the following lines:

```
<B>A Web application can:</B>
<P>
<INPUT TYPE=RADIO NAME="Q" VALUE=1>Activate your computer<BR>
<INPUT TYPE=RADIO NAME="Q" VALUE=2>Validate user input<BR>
<INPUT TYPE=RADIO NAME="Q" VALUE=3>Interact with the viewer<BR>
<INPUT TYPE=RADIO NAME="Q" VALUE=4>Communicate with the server<BR>
```

The Text Control

The Text control is a box that can accept user input. It is used for entering items such as names, addresses, and any form of free text. Figure 14.5 is a Form that contains several Text controls.

FIGURE 14.5:

The Text control accepts user input on a single line.

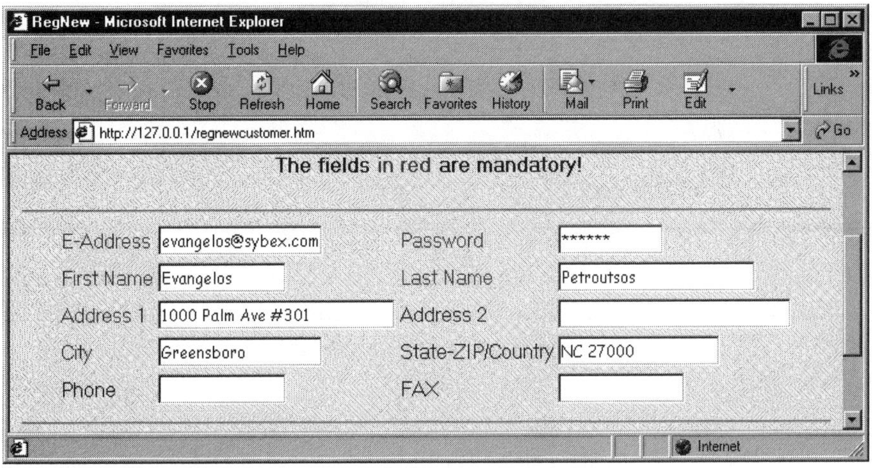

To insert a Text control on a page, use the <INPUT> tag and set the TYPE attribute to TEXT. The line will display a Text control on the page, with the string "Sybex" in it:

```
<INPUT TYPE = TEXT NAME = "Publisher" VALUE = "Sybex">
```

The viewer can enter any string by overwriting the existing one or appending more text at its end. The usual text editing and navigational keys (Home key, arrow keys, the DEL and INS keys) will work with the Text control. However, you can't format the text in a Text control by using different fonts, or even font attributes such as bold and italic.

Finally, you can specify the size of the control on the page with the SIZE attribute, and you can specify the maximum amount of text it can accept with the MAXLENGTH attribute. For example, the Text control defined as the following can accept user input up to 100 characters, whereas its length on the page corresponds to the average length of 40 characters in the current font:

```
<INPUT TYPE = TEXT NAME = "Publisher" SIZE = 40
    MAXLENGTH = 100 VALUE = "Sybex">
```

The Password Control

The Password control is a variation on the Text control. Its behavior is identical to that of the Text control, but the characters entered are not displayed. In their places, the user sees asterisks instead. It's meant for input that should be kept private. To create a Password control, you use an input tag similar to that for a Text control, but specify the PASSWORD type:

```
<INPUT TYPE = PASSWORD NAME = "Secret Box"
    SIZE = 20 MAXLENGTH = 20>
```

Other than a different TYPE attribute, Password controls are identical to Text controls.

The TextArea Control

You can also provide your users with a control that accepts multiple lines of text. The operation of the TextArea control is quite similar to that of a Visual Basic TextBox control that has its MultiLine property set to True (this handles the carriage-return character and causes it to add a new line). All navigational and editing keys will work with the TextArea control as well. To place a TextArea control on a Form, use the <TEXTAREA> tag:

```
<TEXTAREA NAME = COMMENTS ROWS = 10 COLS = 50></TEXTAREA>
```

This tag creates a box on the page, whose dimensions are 10 rows of text with 50 characters per line. The ROWS and COLS tags specify the dimensions of the control on the page (in units of the current font).

Besides its attributes, another difference between the TextArea control and the other controls you've seen so far is that the TextArea control must end with the </TEXTAREA> tag. The reason for this is that the TextArea control may contain a lengthy, multiple-line default text that must be enclosed between the two tags and can't be assigned to an attribute:

```
<TEXTAREA NAME = COMMENTS ROWS = 10 COLS = 50>
This is the greatest Web site I've seen in years!
Congratulations!!!
</TEXTAREA>
```

The text between the two <TEXTAREA> tags is displayed initially in the box. In the unlikely event that the user is less than excited about your pages, he can overwrite your initial comments. Notice that all line breaks in the text will be preserved. There's no need to use paragraph or line break tags to format the initial text of a TextArea control. (If you do include HTML tags in the text, they will be displayed in the Text box as you typed them.) If the text can't fit in the space provided, the appropriate scrollbars will automatically be added to the control.

Figure 14.6 shows a Form with two TextArea controls of different sizes. The first TextArea control and its contents were defined with the following lines. Notice the lack of any HTML formatting tags in the text. The line breaks are preserved, but the control isn't going to process any HTML tags:

```
<TEXTAREA NAME=INGREDIENTS ROWS = 10 COLS = 40 MAXLENGTH = 2000>
2   pounds lamb, no bones
1   lt white wine
4   large white onions
12  teaspoons curry
1   tablespoons cooking oil
2   large bananas
1   fresh pineapple
</TEXTAREA>
```

FIGURE 14.6:

A Form with two TextArea controls, one that displays information and one that allows new information to be entered

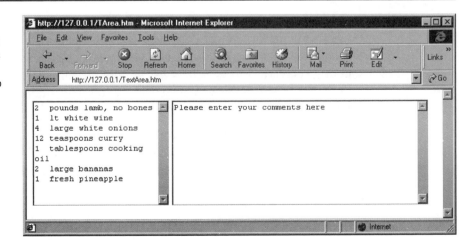

The second TextArea control was defined and filled with text with a similar pair of tags. Remember that the TextArea control doesn't insert line breaks on its own, so you must try not to exceed the maximum line length (as defined with the ROW attribute) if you want the contents of the control to be entirely visible along each line.

The Selection Control

The Selection control is a control that presents a list of options to the viewer, and lets him or her select none, one, or more of them. The tag for the Selection control is <SELECT>, and it must be followed by a matching </SELECT> tag. The attributes that may appear in a <SELECT> tag are NAME (the control's name), SIZE (which specifies how many options will be visible), and MULTIPLE (which specifies whether the user may chose multiple items or not). To place a Selection control on your Form, use the following tag:

```
<SELECT NAME = "UserOptions" SIZE = 4 MULTIPLE = MULTIPLE>
</SELECT>
```

Between the two <SELECT> tags, you can place the options that make up the list, each one in a pair of <OPTION> tags:

```
<SELECT NAME = "UserOptions" SIZE = 6 MULTIPLE = MULTIPLE>
<OPTION>Computer</OPTION>
<OPTION>Monitor</OPTION>
<OPTION>Printer</OPTION>
<OPTION>Modem</OPTION>
<OPTION>Speakers</OPTION>
<OPTION>Microphone</OPTION>
<OPTION>Mouse</OPTION>
</SELECT>
```

This Selection control is shown in Figure 14.7, along with two more lists. Although the control contains seven options, only six of them are visible. The SIZE attribute will help you save space on your pages when you have a long list of options to present to the user. The user can also select multiple options (with the Shift and Control keys), even if some of them are not visible. To disable multiple selections, omit the MULTIPLE attribute.

To minimize the Selection control's size on the Form, omit the MULTIPLE attribute (if possible), and don't specify how many items will be visible. The result will be a list with just one visible element. If the user clicks on the arrow, the list will expand and all its elements will become visible until the user makes a selection. Then, the list collapses back to a single item.

FIGURE 14.7:

The Selection control lets you
present lists of options, from
which viewers can select one
or more.

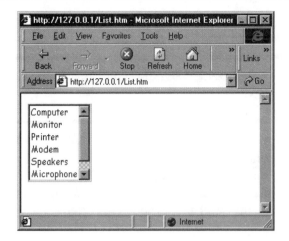

The <OPTION> tag has a VALUE attribute, too. This attribute specifies the string(s) that will be sent back to the server when the user submits the Form with that option selected. In other words, it is possible to display one string in the list, but send another value to the server. Here's a modified version of the previous list:

```
<SELECT NAME = "UserOptions" SIZE = 6 MULTIPLE = MULTIPLE>
<OPTION VALUE=1>Computer</OPTION>
<OPTION VALUE=2>Monitor</OPTION>
<OPTION VALUE=3>Printer</OPTION>
<OPTION VALUE=4>Modem</OPTION>
<OPTION VALUE=5>Speakers</OPTION>
<OPTION VALUE=6>Microphone</OPTION>
<OPTION VALUE=7>Mouse</OPTION>
</SELECT>
```

When the selection on this list is submitted to the server, instead of the actual string the server sees a number, which corresponds to the viewer's selection.

The Button Control

The Button is a control that can be clicked to trigger certain actions. Buttons are used to trigger two actions: submit the data to the server, or reset all controls on the Form to their original values. With VBScript, Buttons can be used to trigger any actions you can program in your pages with VBScript statements that are executed on the client. However, I am not going to discuss client-side scripting in this book (not all browsers support VBScript).

You can place two types of Buttons on a Form. The most important one is the SUBMIT Button; it transmits the contents of all controls on the Form to the server. The RESET Button clears the controls on the Form (or resets them to their initial values) and doesn't submit anything.

These two types of Buttons can be placed on a Form with the following <INPUT> tags:

```
<INPUT TYPE = SUBMIT VALUE = "Send Data">
<INPUT TYPE = RESET VALUE = "Reset Values">
```

where VALUE is the caption that appears on the Button. Each Form should contain at least a SUBMIT Button to transmit the information entered by the user to the server. (If the page contains a script, then you can submit the data to the server via the script and you don't have to include a SUBMIT Button.)

VBScript

VBScript is a scripting language that is based, obviously, on Visual Basic. The first application of VBScript was to program Web pages and activate the client. Microsoft pushed VBScript as the language of the Web, but other browsers didn't follow. Today, only Internet Explorer supports VBScript natively, and JavaScript has become the de facto standard of client languages. The situation is quite different on the server, however.

Microsoft moved VBScript from the client to the server. Whereas older Web servers used Perl or other peculiar languages to interact with the client, Microsoft added support for VBScript in its IIS, and simplified the development of server-side scripts. Today, VBScript is used as a general scripting language by applications such as Outlook, and it can be easily incorporated into VB applications with the Scripting control. VBScript may not have activated the Web as Microsoft promised, but it's a major scripting language.

I will not spend any time discussing VBScript. It's a core language without a user interface, which manipulates objects exposed by the Web server. The structure of the language is identical to that of Visual Basic: it supports all the math, string, date, and time functions; it supports the same flow-control statements; and it recognizes the same data types as Visual Basic. VBScript, however, is a type-less language. Its variables are variants, and you don't have the option to declare variables of any other type. However, you can cast variants to specific data types with the type-conversion functions.

The great benefit of VBScript is its simplicity. In addition to support for VBScript, Microsoft designed several components for handling client requests on the Web server. These components, along with server-side VBScript, are known as Active

Server Pages (ASPs). An Active Server Page is a script on the server that corresponds to an HTML page. Traditionally, Web pages contained text, images, and hyperlinks to other HTML documents. Every time a hyperlink in a Web document is activated, a request for a new HTML document is made. ASP documents are HTML documents, interspersed with VBScript statements. An HTML document may contain any number of VBScript statements, anywhere. The only requirement is that they are enclosed in a pair of <% and %> tags. Everything that appears between these two tags is treated as VBScript code and executed on the server. The output it produces replaces the original VBScript code.

Instead of a trivial example, let me start with one of the examples that I'll use later in this chapter. The following is a script that displays the customers of the Northwind database. It's a mixture of HTML and VBScript statements (the VBScript statements are enclosed by the <% %> tags):

LISTING 14.1   **The AllCustomers.asp Script**

```
<HTML>
<H1>Query Results</H1>
<TABLE>
<%
Set DBObj = Server.CreateObject("ADODB.Connection")
DBObj.Open "NWindDB"
SQLQuery = "SELECT Country, CompanyName, ContactName,
            ContactTitle FROM Customers ORDER BY Country"
Set RSCustomers = DBObj.Execute(SQLQuery)
Do While Not RSCustomers.EOF
%>
  <TR>
    <TD> <FONT FACE="Verdana" SIZE=2>
    <% = RSCustomers.Fields("Country") %>
    </FONT></TD>
    <TD> <FONT FACE="Verdana" SIZE=2>
     <% = RSCustomers.Fields("ContactName") & " (" &
          RSCustomers.Fields("ContactTitle") & ")"  %>
    </FONT></TD>
    <TD><FONT FACE="Verdana" SIZE=2>
      <% = RSCustomers.Fields("CompanyName") %>
    </FONT></TD>
  </TR>
<%
RSCustomers.MoveNext
Loop
%>
</HTML>
```

The first three lines are plain HTML tags that start a new page and open a table. Then comes some VBScript code that sets up a connection to the Northwind database and opens the RSCustomers Recordset, which holds all the rows of the Customers table. The last statement in this first group of VBScript statements starts a loop that iterates through the rows of the RSCustomers Recordset. Notice that the groups of VBScript statements is delimited with the tags <% and %>.

The script starts with a few plain HTML tags (they add a new row to the table). The loop's body consists mostly of HTML tags with a few embedded VBScript statements. The following statement returns the value of the Country field of the current row in the Recordset:

```
<% = RSCustomers.Fields("Country") %>
```

When this script is processed on the server, the above expression will be replaced by the actual field value. A few more VBScript statements at the end of the script terminate the loop and close the HTML document.

To test this script, store it in a text file with extension ASP (it's the AllCustomers .asp file in this chapter's folder on the CD). Place the file in the Web server's root folder (or a virtual folder). Then connect to your Web site and open it. If the Web server is running on the same machine that you're using to test the projects, use the address

```
http://127.0.0.1/allcustomers.asp
```

You can test ASP files with both Internet Information Server (IIS) and the Personal Web Server. You will see a page like the one shown in Figure 14.8.

FIGURE 14.8:

The output of the AllCustomers.asp script

If you double-click the ASP file's icon, you will not see the page in Figure 14.8. The ASP file must be processed by the server. Only then will the VBScript statements be replaced by the output they produce. The Web server executes the script as follows:

1. Text outside the special tags <% and %> is sent to the client as is (it's considered to be HTML code that will be processed by the client).

2. VBScript statements are executed and replaced by the output they produce. Some statements, such as the WHILE and WEND statements, do not produce any output at all. They are needed to control the flow of the script. To understand how ASP scripts are executed on the server, open the AllCustomers .asp file with a text editor and then view the document's source code with the browser's View ➤ Source command, which is shown below. As you can see, the document sent to the client doesn't contain a single VBScript statement, only HTML code.

LISTING 14.2   **The Output Produced by the AllCustomers.asp Script**

```
<HTML>
<H1>Query Results</H1>
<TABLE>

  <TR>
    <TD> <FONT FACE="Verdana" SIZE=2>
    Argentina
    </FONT></TD>
    <TD> <FONT FACE="Verdana" SIZE=2>
     Sergio Gutiérrez (Sales Representative)
    </FONT></TD>
    <TD><FONT FACE="Verdana" SIZE=2>
      Rancho grande
    </FONT></TD>
  </TR>

  <TR>
    <TD> <FONT FACE="Verdana" SIZE=2>
    Argentina
    </FONT></TD>
    <TD> <FONT FACE="Verdana" SIZE=2>
     Yvonne Moncada (Sales Agent)
    </FONT></TD>
    <TD><FONT FACE="Verdana" SIZE=2>
      Océano Atlántico Ltda.
    </FONT></TD>
  </TR>
```

```
<TR>
  <TD> <FONT FACE="Verdana" SIZE=2>
  Argentina
  </FONT></TD>
  <TD> <FONT FACE="Verdana" SIZE=2>
   Patricio Simpson (Sales Agent)
  </FONT></TD>
  <TD><FONT FACE="Verdana" SIZE=2>
    Cactus Comidas para llevar
  </FONT></TD>
</TR>
{more lines with the same structure follow}
```

The ASP Object Model

Server-side VBScript and Active Server Pages support several built-in objects, which I will discuss here and demonstrate with examples. I'll start by listing these objects and their descriptions. In the following sections, you will see examples that demonstrate how to use these objects in ASP scripts to accomplish practical and useful tasks.

As always, it's quite easy to understand and use the objects exposed by a component, if you understand what the component was designed to do. ASP was designed to simplify the development of Web server applications: programs that run on the server and interact with the client. Therefore, ASP should provide the following functionality:

- Prepare output to be downloaded to the client. This is done with the Response object, which represents the output stream that will be transmitted to the client. The Response object's Write method, for example, sends a string to the client and the Response.Cookie() method sends a cookie to the client computer.

- Accept the parameter values submitted to the server by the client. This is done with the Request object. The Request.Cookie() method, for example, returns the value of a cookie on the client computer.

- Access other components on the server. VBScript is the core of a programming language. On its own, it can do very little. The Server object allows VBScript to contact COM components on the server. With the Server object, VBScript can create ADO objects and view databases. Most scripts retrieve information from a database with the help of the Server object, encode it in HTML format, and return it to the client with the Response object.

- Maintain information about each client on the server via server-side scripts. When a user logs into a site with a user name and password, ASP should keep this information on the server so that the user won't have to submit it every time he or she jumps to another page of the same site. This is done with the Session object.

- Maintain information about the state of the current Web site, such as the number of hits it has taken. This is done with the Application object.

The Response, Request, Server, Session, and Application objects are the five basic objects that nearly every Web application uses. There are other optional components, but they are not discussed in this book. You'll use these five objects to write server applications that interact with the clients and focus on applications that access databases over the Web.

I will start with a discussion of these objects, and then move on to show you how to access databases from within your server-side scripts. The ASP objects covered in this chapter are not nearly as complicated as the ADO object.

The Application Object

This object represents an ASP application, which is the collection of all ASP files in the virtual folder and its subfolders. You can use the Application object to share information among all users of an ASP application. The Application object has two methods, which are the Lock and Unlock methods. The Lock method prevents other clients from modifying any of the Application object's properties. The Unlock method allows other clients to modify these properties.

The Application object also supports two events: the Application_onStart event, which is triggered when the application starts; and the Application_onEnd event, which is triggered when the application ends. Use these events to execute initialization code or cleanup code, respectively.

The purpose of the Application object is to store values that can be shared among the clients. This is especially useful in intranet environments, in which the users of the ASP application have a common goal. You can also use the Application object on pages that are posted on the Internet. To create a new variable or change the value of an existing variable in the Application object, use statements like the following ones:

```
<%
    Application("WelcomeMessage") = "Happy Valentine's Day!"
    Application("MaxScore") = 254000
%>
```

WelcomeMessage is a string variable; and *MaxScore* is a numeric one. Of course, *WelcomeMessage* must be changed on February 14. To make sure that no other client is attempting to set (or read) the same variable at the time the scripts accesses it, first lock the Application object, then change the variable, and finally unlock the object, as shown here:

```
<%
    Application.Lock
    Application("WelcomeMessage") = "Happy Valentine's Day!"
    Application("MaxScore") = 254000
    Application.Unlock
%>
```

You can use the Application object to build a simple visitor counter, by keeping track of a variable:

```
<%
    Application.Lock
    Application("Visitors") = Application("Visitors") + 1
    Application.Unlock
%>
```

These commands must be executed in the home page of your site, which is displayed the first time a user connects to your site. You can then display the value of the *Visitors* variable on your Web page with a line like the following one:

```
You are visitor # <% = Application("Visitors") %>
```

To make sure that this variable maintains its value, you must save it in a local file and retrieve it, update it, and save it again. See the description of the Text-Stream object later in this chapter for a discussion on how to access files on the server through the server-side script. The *Visitors* variable must be initialized when the home page of the application is first loaded, an action that is signaled by the Application_onStart event. As long as the server is up and running, the application maintains the values of its variables.

The Session Object

This object represents an ASP session. Each time a new user connects to the site by opening its main page, a new session object is created for that viewer. You can use the Session object to store information that's specific to the viewer. Like the Application object, the Session object supports two events: the Session_onStart event, which is triggered when the session starts; and the Session_onEnd event, which is triggered when the session ends. The following statement stores a variable in the Session object:

```
Session("ViewerName") = "Charles Brannon"
```

This variable will live for the duration of the current session and will automatically be released when the session ends. The next time the same user connects to the same site, a new Session object will be created and the previous statement must be executed again (you'll probably prompt the user for his or her name).

Use the Session object to store information you want to share among the application's pages. HTTP is a stateless protocol, and maintaining state between the pages of the application is something you can't take for granted. You can use the Session object to store "global" variables (variables that can be shared by all the pages of the site). However, you should not store object variables in the Session object. This is just about the worst thing you can do for your Web application.

If you want to store information that persists between sessions, you can't store them in the Session object. Use cookies instead. Cookies are stored on the client computer and your application can read them again when the same client connects to the site. This is how shopping baskets work with most sites. Some sites store the orders in the database and don't use cookies (some viewers may turn off cookies), but this requires that viewers identify themselves every time they connect to the site.

The Request Object

The Request object retrieves the values (query parameters) that the client passes to the server during an HTTP request, the values of the cookies stored on the client computer through the Response object, and server variables. The Request object exposes the collections shown in Table 14.2:

TABLE 14.2:   The Collections Exposed by the Request Object

Collection Name	Description
ClientCertificate	The values of fields stored in the client certificate that is sent in the HTTP request
Cookies	The values of cookies sent in the HTTP request
Form	The values of form elements in the HTTP request body
QueryString	The values of variables in the HTTP query string
ServerVariables	The values of predetermined environment variables

The QueryString collection is the most important one because it retrieves the values of the parameters in the HTTP query string, that is, the values encoded after the question mark in the HTTP request. These are the values of the Form's elements passed by the client using the GET method. You can also pass parameter values to the Web server by creating a URL from within a client script. The syntax of the QueryString collection is

```
Request.QueryString(variable)
```

where *variable* is the name of the variable in the HTTP query string to retrieve. If a client calls the `TestPage.asp` file as

```
/ASPages/TestPage.asp?Name=Joe+Doe&EMail=JDoe@local.net
```

the query string is

```
Name=Joe+Doe&EMail=JDoe@local.net
```

Name and *EMail* are the names of two controls where the viewer has entered some information. To retrieve the values of the two parameters, use the statements

```
Request.QueryString("Name")
```

which will return the string "Joe Doe," and

```
Request.QueryString("EMail")
```

which will return the string "Jdoe@local.net."

If you retrieve the value of the property Request.QueryString without any parameters, it will return the entire query string. See the section "Making Queries with ASP Files" later in this chapter for examples on the Request method. The section "Using Cookies" shows how to retrieve the cookies stored on the client computer through the Request.Cookies collection.

The Response Object

The Response object represents the output stream that's sent to the client. All the information you want to send to the client must be submitted through the Response object's Write method. In addition to textual information, which can be sent to the client with the Response object's Write method, you can also send cookie values to the client with the Cookies collection of the Response object.

The Cookies collection of the Response object contains all the cookies stored on the client computer by your site, and their values. You can create new cookies by adding more members to the Collection, or read the values of existing ones. The syntax of the Cookies collection of the Response object is

```
Response.Cookies(cookie)(key).attribute = value
```

where *cookie* is the name of the cookie. To specify a simple cookie and its value, use a statement like the following one:

```
Response.Cookies("ServerName")="www.myserver.com"
```

key is an optional argument indicating that the cookie is a dictionary (an array of name value pairs). To read the value of the ServerName cookie use the following expression:

```
SNname = Response.Cookies("ServerName")
```

To create a cookie with a key, use statements such as the following:

```
<%
Response.Cookies("Preferences")("ForeColor") = "Blue"
Response.Cookies("Preferences")("BackColor") = "lightyellow"
%>
```

The ForeColor and BackColor cookies are attributes of the Preferences key. When you request the value of a cookie from within a script on the server (this is done through the Response object's properties), you can determine whether a cookie has keys with the following statement:

```
<%= Response.Cookies("Preferences").HasKeys %>
```

If Preferences is a cookie dictionary, the preceding expression evaluates to True. Otherwise, it evaluates to False. The following statements create a cookie on the client and set various attributes:

```
<%
Response.Cookies("Favorites") = "Century"
Response.Cookies("Favorites").Expires = "December 31, 2000"
Response.Cookies("Favorites").Domain = "myserver.com"
Response.Cookies("Favorites").Path = "/Dates"
Response.Cookies("Favorites").Secure = FALSE
%>
```

The first line sets the Favorites cookie value to "Century." The remaining lines set the various attributes of the cookie. The cookie expires at the end of the millennium, is not secure, and is sent to the virtual folder `Dates` only. Scripts that are executed from within another virtual folder on the server can't access this cookie.

The *attribute* argument specifies information about the cookie itself and can have one of the following values, shown in Table 14.3:

TABLE 14.3: Cookie Attributes and Their Meaning

Attribute	Description
Expires	The date on which the cookie expires
Domain	If specified, the cookie is sent only to requests to this domain
Path	If specified, the cookie is sent only to requests to this path, and not to every page in the virtual folder
Secure	Specifies whether the cookie is secure
HasKeys	Specifies whether the cookie contains keys (in other words, it's a dictionary)

All arguments are write-only, except for the *HasKeys* argument, which is read-only.

Finally, the *value* argument specifies the value to be assigned to the key or an attribute.

If you have placed orders online, you already know that the IDs of the products you select are stored on the client computer (your computer) as cookies. They remain in your basket until you either order them or empty the basket. Shopping baskets are usually implemented as cookies. There are other methods for implementing a shopping basket, but cookies are the simplest and most convenient.

Let's say you want to implement an online bookstore, and you decide to store the IDs (ISBNs) of the books chosen by the user on the client computer, in the form of cookies. Instead of using cookie names such as "0-310-943917," you can create a directory of cookies and access them with an index value:

```
Response.Cookies("ISBN")(1)
Response.Cookies("ISBN")(2)
```

The name of the first cookie in this Collection is the ISBN of the first book (0-310-943917, for example), and its value is the number of copies ordered. The following few sections discuss the Response object's methods: the Write, Clear, and End methods.

The Write Method

The Write method writes a string to the current HTTP output. Its syntax is

```
<% Response.Write string %>
```

where *string* is the data to write. This argument is a variant; it can contain text, numeric values, or dates. However, it can't contain the combination "%>". To display the delimiter, use the escape sequence "%\>".

TIP The longest string you can you can pass to the Response.Write method with a literal argument can't exceed 1,022 characters (VBScript limits static strings to 1,022
bytes). If the string is stored in a variable, you can specify longer strings.

The Write method of the Response object is used to create any output you want
to send to the client. The following statement will cause the value of the Address
field of the current row of the Recordset object to be sent to the client:

```
<% Response.Write RS.Fields("Address") %>
```

The following example sends a customer name, but formats it as a hyperlink:

```
<% Response.Write "<A HREF=ShowCustomer.asp?ID='>" &
      RS.Fields("CustomerID") & "'>" &
      RS.Fields("CompanyName") &  "</A>" %>
```

This statement will display the company name as a hyperlink to the ShowCustomer
.asp script on the server and passes the company's ID as a parameter. This technique is used in the AllCountries example, later in this chapter.

You will use the Response object in several examples in later sections of this
chapter. The advantage of using the Write method over mixing HTML tags and
VBScript commands is that scripts that use the Write method don't contain too
many delimiters and the resulting server-side script is easier to read.

The Clear Method

The Clear method erases any buffered HTML output. You can use this method
before sending output to the client with the Write method, or to handle errors.
The Clear method will work only if the Response.Buffer property has been set to
False; its syntax is

```
Response.Clear
```

Let's say you're creating an HTML table and populating it with field values
read from a Recordset. If an error occurs in the process, you can clear any information you have written to the output stream by calling the Response object's
Clear method. As you may have guessed, the Buffer property prevents the server
from sending any information to the client before the End method is called. Normally, the server doesn't wait for the script to close the Response object before it
transmits the information to the client. Whatever information you wrote to the
output stream through the Response object can be sent to the client at any time.
To change this default behavior, set the Buffer property to False.

The Flush Method

The output generated by the Write method is stored in a buffer, and the Web server transmits it to the client when it gets a chance. That's why you don't have to wait for the entire page to arrive when you connect to a URL. You can force the buffer to be transmitted to the client by calling the Flush method. If the script takes a long time to execute, you can flush the output every now and then, so that the viewer won't think that the Web server is not responding. To use the Flush method, you must first set the Response object's Buffer property to True, as shown in the following code segment:

```
Response.Buffer = True
{ Response.Write <text>
  Response.Write <text> }
Response.Flush
```

When buffering is on, the Web server doesn't send any output to the client, unless you call the Flush method.

The End Method

The End method causes the Web server to stop processing the script and return the current result. The remaining contents of the file are not processed and its syntax is

```
Response.End
```

The Server Object

The Server object provides access to methods and properties on the server. It has a single property, the ScriptTimeOut property, which sets a time limit for a script's execution, and several methods.

The ScriptTimeOut Property

The ScriptTimeout property specifies the maximum amount of time a script can run before it is terminated. Its default value is 90 seconds. The timeout will not take effect while a server component is processing (for example, an operation on a database that takes awhile to complete won't be timed out).

The MapPath Method

The MapPath method maps a specified relative or virtual path to the corresponding physical directory on the server. It must be used when opening files for input or output with the TextStream object, discussed later in the chapter. Its syntax is

```
Server.MapPath( path )
```

where *path* is the relative or virtual path to be mapped to a physical directory. If path starts with either a backward or forward slash (either / or \), the MapPath method assumes that the path argument is a virtual path. If path doesn't start with a slash, the MapPath method assumes that the path is relative to the directory of the ASP file being processed.

Normally, your script shouldn't care about the actual value returned by the Map-Path method because it's passed as argument to another method, usually the Create-TextFile or OpenTextFile method, which creates or opens a file, respectively. These methods are discussed in the section "The File Access Component" later in the chapter.

The CreateObject Method

The CreateObject method creates an instance of a server component, similar to the CreateObject() function of Visual Basic. A server component is an application on the server computer that can be contacted through the methods and properties it exposes. After a server component is created, you can call its methods and properties from within a server-side script. A typical example of a server component that can be called from within a script is the ADO component, which you can use to access databases on the server.

There are also a few components, installed along with the Active Server Pages, which can be accessed through the CreateObject method. The server components that you will explore in this chapter are the ActiveX Data Objects component (ADO), which allows your script to access databases on the server; the FileSystem component, which allows your script to access files on the server; and the Browser Capabilities component, which lets your script know the capabilities of the browser used to view a page.

The syntax of the CreateObject method is

```
Server.CreateObject( progID )
```

where *progID* is the type of object to create. The value of the progID argument for any given server can be found in the Registry or in Visual Basic's Object Browser. This method returns an object variable, through which you can access the server component's methods and properties, just as you do with Visual Basic. In the section "Using the SearchTitles Class on the Web," in Chapter 12, you saw how to use the CreateObject() method to call COM components on the Web server.

The URLEncode Method

The URLEncode method applies URL encoding rules to a string. Its syntax is

```
Server.URLEncode(text)
```

where *text* is the string to be URL encoded. Use this method to prepare URLs with parameters. The statement

```
<%= Server.URLEncode("Function name 4-cos(X/3)") %>
```

will pass the client the following string:

```
Function name 4%252Dcos(X%252F3)
```

All characters that are not letters or numeric digits are replaced with their hexadecimal values, prefixed with the % symbol.

The HTMLEncode Method

The HTMLEncode method applies HTML encoding to a string. Its syntax is

```
Server.HTMLEncode(text)
```

where *text* is the string to be HTML-encoded. Use this method to place HTML listings on the page. The statement below will display the following string on the browser's window:

```
<%= Server.HTMLEncode("The <IMG> tag doesn't
                        have a matching </IMG> tag") %>

The &lt;IMG&gt; tag doesn't have a matching &lt;/IMG&gt; tag
```

Using Cookies

A *cookie* is a fancy term for a value that's sent by the HTTP server to the client. The browser extracts this value from the HTML file's header and stores it on the local computer. Cookies are binary values that are stored by the browser into a special folder—this means they can't harm your computer. If you want to see the cookie values left by the various HTTP servers on your computer, open the Windows/Cookie folder. You'll probably find quite a few cookies there.

As you already know, the HTTP protocol is stateless. In other words, the Web server doesn't remember what computers have connected to it. Every time a client requests a document, the server establishes a connection, furnishes the document, and closes the connection. As a result, it's not easy to maintain state between sessions. When you select a few items in an online store, they are placed in a basket. How does the server know the items selected by each client? The answer is that it doesn't! The IDs of the selected products are stored on the client computer, and the server reads them from the client when it needs them.

The ISBNCookies Example

This is a slightly more complicated example, which stores a directory of cookies on the client. Let's say you're building an online bookstore (as you will do in Chapter 18), and you decide to store the shopping basket's contents on the client computer in the Form of cookies. (This approach assumes that the client hasn't disabled cookies on the client computer, but most people don't. That's why some of the most popular electronic stores leave cookies on the client.)

The other alternative is to store the basket's contents on the server. This means additional storage requirements, more work for the server, and less convenience for the viewer. Some sites require that you place an order before you abandon the current session. If you leave the store, your basket is empty the next time you connect. Even if the basket isn't emptied between sessions, you must identify yourself in order to view your basket. This process isn't repeated every time you open the basket, only the first time in each session. Even so, it's not the ultimate in user-friendliness.

Maintaining state between sessions is a sore point in Web applications (I'll return to this topic in later chapters as well). If every user had a unique IP address, similar to one's electronic address (or phone number, for that matter), things would be significantly simpler. Unfortunately, IP addresses are typically assigned to users as they connect to the Internet, and you can't assume that a user's current IP will belong to the same user in another session.

For each order, you want to store the book's ID (its ISBN) and the corresponding quantity on the client computer. Because you don't know how many books a user may select, it's best to create an array of ISBN and quantity cookies. Every time the user selects a new title, you must search for the specific ISBN in the cookies collection. If the ISBN has been ordered already, you will increase the quantity by one (and notify users that they have selected this title already). If it has not been selected already, then a new cookie must be added to the cookies collection of your Web site to the client.

One of the sample documents for this chapter on the CD is the ISBNCOOKIES.HTM document. Place this document in your Web server's root folder and open it with your browser. In the browser's Address box, enter

```
http://127.0.0.1/ISBNCOOKIES.HTM
```

If the Web server is running, you will see the page shown in Figure 14.9. This is a very simple document that contains two hyperlinks to the SAVECOOKIES.ASP and READCOOKIES ASP files. The SAVECOOKIES.ASP file creates three cookies on the client computer: they are three ISBNs, and their values are integers (number of items).

FIGURE 14.9:

The ISBNCOOKIES.HTM page

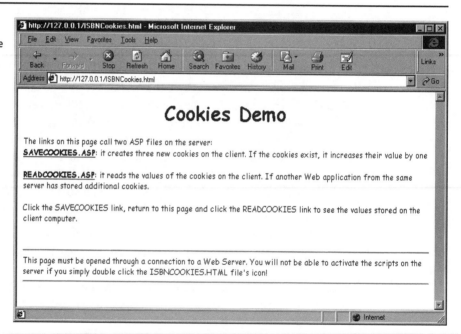

The SAVECOOKIES.ASP script is shown in Listing 14.3.

LISTING 14.3   **The SAVECOOKIES.ASP Script**

```
<%
    OrderISBN="0-300-999991"
    CurQuantity = Request.Cookies("BasketItem")(OrderISBN)
    If CurQuantity = 0 Then
        Response.Cookies("BasketItem")(OrderISBN) = "1"
        BookFound = False
```

```
Else
    Response.Cookies("BasketItem")(OrderISBN) =
            Request.Cookies("BasketItem")(OrderISBN)+1
   BookFound = True
End If
Response.Cookies("BasketItem").Expires = Date + 365

OrderISBN="0-300-999992"
CurQuantity = Request.Cookies("BasketItem")(OrderISBN)
If CurQuantity = 0 Then
    Response.Cookies("BasketItem")(OrderISBN) = "1"
    BookFound = False
Else
    Response.Cookies("BasketItem")(OrderISBN) =
            Request.Cookies("BasketItem")(OrderISBN)+1
 BookFound = True
End If
Response.Cookies("BasketItem").Expires = Date + 365
OrderISBN="0-300-999993"
CurQuantity = Request.Cookies("BasketItem")(OrderISBN)
If CurQuantity = 0 Then
    Response.Cookies("BasketItem")(OrderISBN) = "1"
    BookFound = False
Else
    Response.Cookies("BasketItem")(OrderISBN) =
            Request.Cookies("BasketItem")(OrderISBN)+1
      BookFound = True
End If
Response.Cookies("BasketItem").Expires = Date + 365
Response.Write "<HTML><FONT FACE='Comic Sans MS'>"
Response.Write "<H3>SAVECOOKIES Script</H3>"
Response.Write "This script increased the values of the
                following product IDs (ISBNs)"
Response.Write "<BR>0-300-999991, 0-300-999992, 0-300-999993"
%>
```

This script reads the first cookie's value in the *BasketItem* collection with the following expression:

```
Request.Cookies("BasketItem")(OrderISBN)
```

If the cookie exists, the script increases its value by one and then writes it back to the client:

```
Response.Cookies("BasketItem")(OrderISBN) =
            Request.Cookies("BasketItem")(OrderISBN)+1
```

If the cookie does not exist, the value 1 is written to the client with a similar expression. The same process is repeated for the other two cookies (ISBNs). The output of the script is shown in Figure 14.10.

FIGURE 14.10:

The output produced by the SAVECOOKIES.ASP script

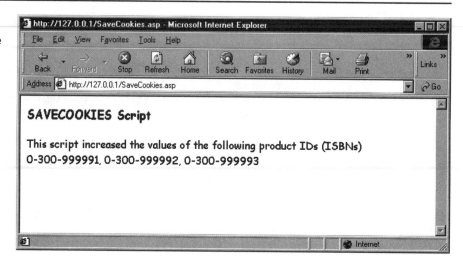

The READCOOKIES.ASP script (Listing 14.4) reads the three cookies from the client computer and displays their names (ISBN numbers) and values (quantities) on a new page, which is shown in Figure 14.11. This script uses a For … Next loop to scan the members of the BasketItem cookie:

FIGURE 14.11:

The output produced by the READCOOKIES.ASP script

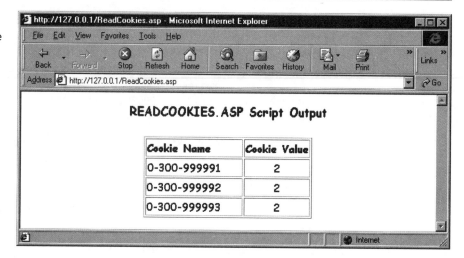

LISTING 14.4   **The READCOOKIES.ASP Script**

```
<%
    Response.Write "<HTML><FONT FACE='Comic Sans MS'>"
    Response.Write "<CENTER>"
    Response.Write "<H3>READCOOKIES.ASP Script Output<BR><BR>"
    Response.Write "<TABLE BORDER=ALL>"
    Response.Write "<TR><TD><B>Cookie Name</B>"
    Response.Write "<TD><B>Cookie Value</B>"
    For Each cookie in Request.Cookies("BasketItem")
        Response.Write "<TR>"
        Response.Write "<TD ALIGN=CENTER>" & cookie &
                        "      "
        Response.Write "<TD ALIGN=CENTER> "
        Response.Write Request.Cookies("BasketItem")(cookie)
    Next
    Response.Write "</TABLE>"
    Response.Write "</HTML>"
%>
```

Making Queries with ASP Files

ASP scripts accept query parameters from the client computer and process them. Before you can process the values submitted by the client, however, you must read them. In the early days of the Web, the process of extracting the values submitted from the client was difficult, and Web developers were using languages such as Perl to write server scripts. VBScript changed all that. As you recall from the discussion of the <FORM> tag, there are two methods of submitting parameter values to the server: the GET and the POST methods. They are both specified with the METHOD attributes of the <FORM> tag.

The GET and POST Methods

The main difference between the two methods is the way data are sent to the server. The GET method appends all parameter values to the URL of the client script, producing a very long URL. In addition, there's a limit of 2Kb on the number of characters that can be returned to the server, and all the information is visible to the user in the Address box of the browser. The POST method can transmit longer parameter strings, and it doesn't display them on the browser's Address box along with the URL of the script. The POST method, however, can return values that have been entered on a Form's controls to the server.

The two methods are handled differently on the server, too. To extract the values submitted with the POST method, you must use the Form collection of the Request object. To extract the values submitted with the GET method, you must use the QueryString collection of the Request object. The following two examples demonstrate the two methods for submitting parameter values to the server.

The Form Collection (Use with POST Method)

The Form collection contains a member for each control on the Form. The value of the first control on the Form is the following:

```
Request.Form(0).Value
```

To access all the control values, you can use a loop like the following one:

```
For Each ctrl In Request.Form
    {process value Request.Form(ctrl)}
Next
```

If you use the above structure to access the parameters, keep in mind that *ctrl* is the name of the parameter and *Request.Form(ctrl)* is the parameter's value.

If the script knows the name of the control, you can access a value by name. If the Form contains a control named *Email*, you can read this control's value with this statement:

```
CustEmail = Request.Form("Email")
```

To retrieve the entire string submitted to the server, use the Form property of the Request object without an index:

```
Request.Form
```

The QueryString Collection (Use with GET Method)

The QueryString collection contains a member for each parameter passed to the server in the URL. To access the first parameter in the collection use the following expression:

```
Request.QueryString(0)
```

If you know the name of the parameter, you can access it by name:

```
Request.QueryString("Email")
```

The Request object also exposes a QueryString property, which contains the entire string returned by the client.

The BOXESGET and BOXESPOST Pages

The BOXESGET.HTM and BOXESPOST.HTM pages demonstrate the GET and POST methods. The pages are identical when viewed with a browser (see Figure 14.12). The page displays a Form with six Text controls on it. You could use this arrangement to accept product codes and quantities, for example. The three long Text controls are members of the BOX array, and the other three Text controls are members of the QTY array. Both pages use identical statements to display the Form:

```
<INPUT TYPE=TEXT SIZE=40 NAME=Box><INPUT TYPE=TEXT SIZE=5 NAME=QTY>
<BR>
<INPUT TYPE=TEXT SIZE=40 NAME=Box><INPUT TYPE=TEXT SIZE=5 NAME=QTY>
<BR>
<INPUT TYPE=TEXT SIZE=40 NAME=Box><INPUT TYPE=TEXT SIZE=5 NAME=QTY>
<INPUT TYPE=SUBMIT>
```

FIGURE 14.12:

The BoxesGET.HTM and BoxesPOST.HTM pages display the same Form, but they use different methods to submit the parameter values to the server.

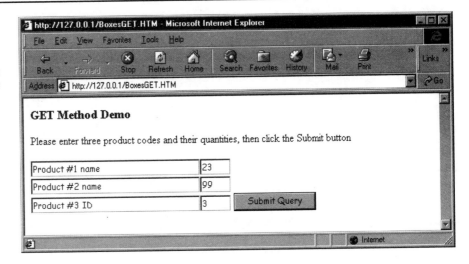

The data supplied by the user are submitted to the server with the GET and POST methods, respectively. Here are the <FORM> tags for both files:

BoxesGET.HTM

```
<FORM ACTION=ReadGET.asp METHOD=GET>
```

BoxesPOST.HTM

```
<FORM ACTION=ReadPOST.asp METHOD=POST>
```

To open the Boxesget.ASP page with your browser, enter the address

```
http://127.0.0.1/Boxesget.HTM
```

in the Address box. Enter a few values and submit the Form to the Web server by clicking the Submit button. The page will call the ReadGET.asp script on the server with the following URL:

```
http://127.0.0.1/ReadGET.asp?
    Box=Box1&QTY=Q1&Box=Box2&QTY=Q2&Box=Box3&QTY=Q3
```

The GET method passes the parameter values to the server along with the URL of the script. To process the parameter values on the server, the ReadGET.asp script uses the QueryString property of the Request object. The ReadGET.asp script displays the entire string passed by the client, as well as the values of the individual fields. Here's the script's listing:

```
<%
Response.Write "<HTML>"
Response.Write "<BODY BGCOLOR=#F0F0F0>"
Response.Write "<H2>Passing Parameters with the GET Method</H2>"
Response.Write "<FONT SIZE=+1>"
Response.write "The following parameter string was passed to the _
    server: "
Response.Write "<BR><KBD>" & request.QueryString & "</KBD>"
Response.Write "<BR><BR>"
Response.Write "The individual field names and values are:"
Response.Write "<TABLE BORDER>"
Response.Write "<TR><TD>" & UCase(request.QueryString("Box")(1)) & _
    "<TD>" & Request.QueryString("QTY")(1)
Response.Write "<TR><TD>" & UCase(request.QueryString("Box")(2)) & _
    "<TD>" & Request.QueryString("QTY")(2)
Response.Write "<TR><TD>" & UCase(request.QueryString("Box")(3)) & _
    "<TD>" & Request.QueryString("QTY")(3)
Response.Write "</TABLE>"
Response.Write "</BODY>"
Response.write "</HTML>"
%>
```

To open the BoxesPOST.ASP page with your browser, enter the address

```
http://127.0.0.1/BoxesPOST.HTM
```

in the Address box. Enter a few values and submit the Form to the Web server by clicking the Submit button. The page will call the readPOST.asp script on the server with the URL

```
http://127.0.0.1/readPOST.asp
```

The POST method doesn't pass the parameter values to the server along with the URL of the script. The first advantage of this method is that viewers don't see what information you pass from the client to the server.

To process the parameter values on the server, the readPOST.asp script uses the Form property of the Request object. The readPOST.asp script displays the entire string passed by the client, as well as the values of the individual fields. Here's the script's listing:

```
<%
Response.Write "<HTML>"
Response.Write "<BODY BGCOLOR=#F0F0F0>"
Response.Write "<H2>Passing Parameters with the POST Method</H2>"
Response.Write "<FONT SIZE=+1>"
Response.write "The following parameter string was passed
               to the server: "
Response.Write "<BR><KBD>" & request.Form & "</KBD>"
Response.Write "<BR><BR>"
Response.Write "The individual field names and values are:"
Response.Write "<TABLE BORDER>"
Response.Write "<TR><TD>" & UCase(request.Form("Box")(1)) & "<TD>" & _
    Request.Form("QTY")(1)
Response.Write "<TR><TD>" & UCase(request.Form("Box")(2)) & "<TD>" & _
    Request.Form("QTY")(2)
Response.Write "<TR><TD>" & UCase(request.Form("Box")(3)) & "<TD>" & _
    Request.Form("QTY")(3)
Response.Write "</TABLE>"
Response.Write "</BODY>"
Response.write "</HTML>"
%>
```

Figure 14.13 shows how the two pages call the appropriate script on the server.

FIGURE 14.13:

Passing the same parameter values with the (a) GET and (b) POST methods

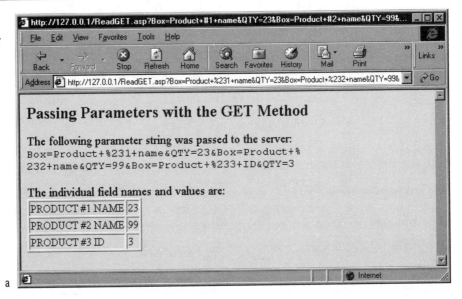

FIGURE 14.13 (CONTINUED):

Passing the same parameter values with the (a) GET and (b) POST methods

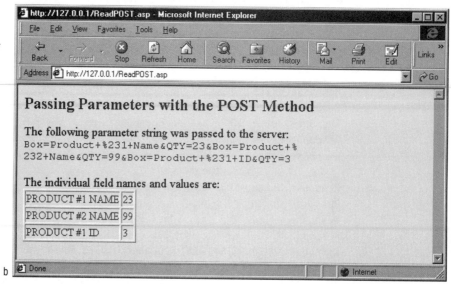

b

The Apply.asp Example

The next example uses an actual Form to submit its contents to the server with the Form's Submit method. The page with the Form is shown in Figure 14.14. In this section, you will submit the Form to the server, where an ASP page will process it (it will actually display its values). After you extract the values of the parameters, you can process them any way you like—Save them to a database, create a report, and so on.

The page with the Form shown in Figure 14.14 is called `Apply.htm`. It contains the following controls:

- A SELECT control (POSITION), where the user selects the desired position
- Five TEXT controls (LNAME, FNAME, ADDRESS, TEL, FAX), where the user enters first and last name, address, and phone and fax numbers
- A group of three RADIO controls (DGREE1, DGREE2, DGREE3), used to specify the applicant's education
- A group of CHECKBOX controls (DAYS, NIGHTS, SHIFT, WEEKEND), used to specify when the applicant can work
- Another group of CHECKBOX controls (MARRIED, MINORITY, CITIZEN), used to specify the applicant's status

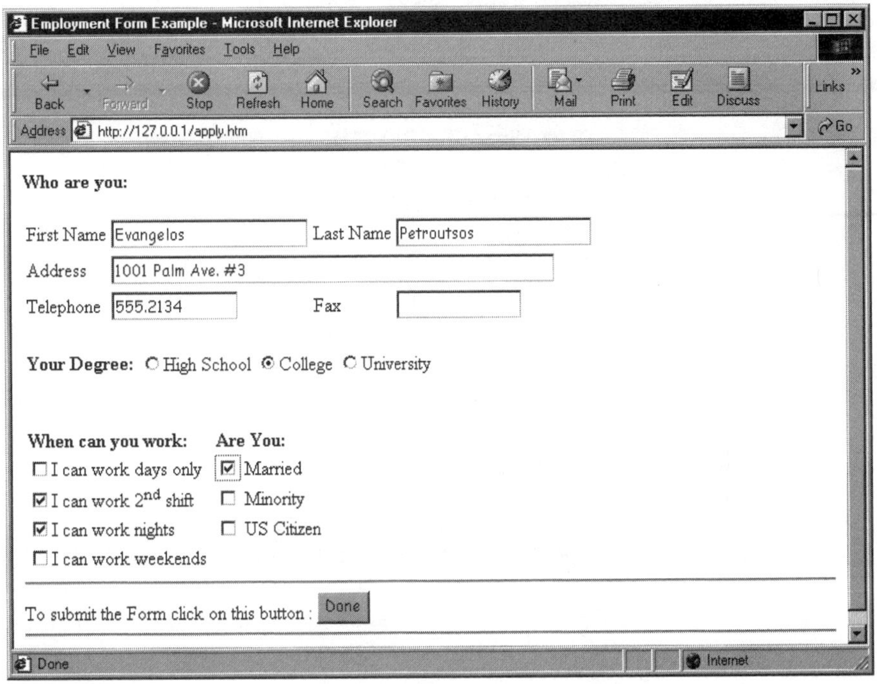

FIGURE 14.14:

The apply.htm page contains a Form with the HTML intrinsic controls.

Here's the apply.htm document's listing. The Form on the Apply page contains all the HTML controls you can use to interact with the viewers from within your Web applications. The ASP script that processes this page demonstrates how to read the values of all the controls on the Web server.

LISTING 14.5   The apply.htm Page

```
<HTML>
<HEAD>
<TITLE>Employment Form Example</TITLE>
</HEAD>

<BODY>
<FORM name=APPFORM ACTION=APPLY.ASP METHOD=GET>
<P><B>Who are you:</B>
<P>
<TABLE>
  <TBODY>
  <TR>
    <TD>First Name</TD>
```

```
            <TD><INPUT maxLength=25 name=FNAME size=25> </TD>
            <TD>Last Name</TD>
            <TD><INPUT maxLength=25 name=LNAME size=25> </TD></TR>
         <TR>
            <TD>Address</TD>
            <TD colSpan=3><INPUT maxLength=60 name=ADDRESS size=60> </TD></TR>
         <TR>
            <TD>Telephone</TD>
            <TD><INPUT maxLength=15 name=TEL size=15> </TD>
            <TD>Fax</TD>
            <TD><INPUT maxLength=15 name=FAX size=15>
             </TD></TR></TBODY></TABLE>
<P>
<P>
<TABLE>
  <TBODY>
  <TR>
    <TD><B>Your Degree:</B></TD>
    <TD><INPUT name=DGREE1 type=radio value=HighSchool>High School</TD>
    <TD><INPUT name=DGREE2 type=radio value=College>College</TD>
    <TD><INPUT name=DGREE3 type=radio value=University>University</TD>
    </TR></TBODY></TABLE>
<P><BR>
<P>
<TABLE>
  <TBODY>
  <TR>
    <TD><B>When can you work:</B></TD>
    <TD></TD>
    <TD><B>Are You:</B></TD>
  <TR>
    <TD><INPUT name=DAYS type=checkbox>I can work days only</TD>
    <TD></TD>
    <TD><INPUT name=MARRIED type=checkbox value=MARRIED> Married </TD>
  <TR>
    <TD><INPUT name=SHIFT type=checkbox>I can work 2<SUP>nd</SUP>
        shift</TD>
    <TD></TD>
    <TD><INPUT name=MINORITY type=checkbox value=MINORITY>
        Minority</TD>
  <TR>
    <TD><INPUT name=NIGHTS type=checkbox>I can work nights</TD>
```

```
      <TD></TD>
      <TD><INPUT name=CITIZEN type=checkbox value=CITIZEN>
          US Citizen</TD>
   <TR>
      <TD><INPUT name=WEEKEND type=checkbox>I can work weekends</TD>
      <TD></TD>
      <TD></TD></TR></TBODY></TABLE>
  <HR>
  To submit the Form click on this button : <INPUT type=SUBMIT
      value=Done>
  <HR>
  </FORM>
  </BODY>
  </HTML>
```

Notice that the RADIO controls aren't called DEGREE1, DEGREE2, and DEGREE3. There is an interesting HTML-related problem here, which you will discover only by testing the page. Because the various parameters in the query string are separated by the ampersand character, somewhere the following character combination will appear:

```
&DEGREE=some+value
```

To HTML, &DEG is the symbol for degrees (a small, raised circle) and the name of this parameter on the server will no longer be DEGREE. The characters &DEG will be substituted with the symbols for degrees. They will create serious problems when parsing the string at the server. The & symbol will disappear, joining the name of the control with the name of the previous control in the string.

The control's contents are submitted to the server with the Form's Submit button. The <FORM> tag contains the name of the application on the server that will handle this request:

```
<FORM NAME=APPFORM ACTION="/ASPages/Apply.asp" METHOD=GET>
```

The Apply.asp page on the server uses the Request.QueryString property to display the entire query string. Then, it uses the same property with the names of the various controls as indexes to extract the individual values of the controls and display them. Notice that only the checked CHECKBOX and RADIO controls are transmitted. That's why the script on the server examines all possible values. If a given CHECKBOX or RADIO control's value is empty, it means that the control hasn't been checked (or selected). The output produced by the Apply.asp page for the document from Figure 14.14 is shown in Figure 14.15.

FIGURE 14.15:

The output of the Apply.asp page for the data submitted with the Form of the Apply.htm page shown in Figure 14.14

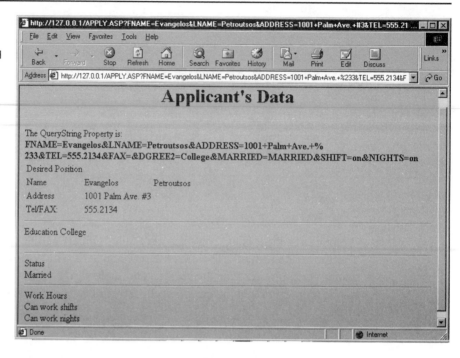

The `Apply.asp` file used to produce the response shown in Figure 14.14 is detailed in Listing 14.6.

LISTING 14.6   The Apply.asp Script

```
<HTML>
<BODY BGCOLOR=silver>
<FONT FACE=Verdana SIZE=2>
<CENTER>
<H1>Applicant's Data</H1>
</CENTER>
<BR>
<BR>
<SCRIPT LANGUAGE=VBScript RUNAT=Server>
    Response.write "The QueryString Property is: <BR>"
    Response.write "<B>" & Request.QueryString & "</B>"
    Response.write "<TABLE>"
    Response.write "<TD> Desired Position <TD>" & _
    Request.QueryString("POSITION")
    Response.write "<TR>"
    Response.write "<TD>Name <TD>" & Request.QueryString("FNAME")
```

```
       Response.write "<TD>" & Request.QueryString("LNAME")
       Response.write "<TR>"
       Response.write "<TD> Address <TD>" & Request.QueryString("ADDRESS")
       Response.write "<TR>"
       Response.write "<TD> Tel/FAX: <TD>" & Request.QueryString("TEL")
       Response.write "<TD>" & Request.QueryString("FAX")
       Response.write "</TABLE>"
       Response.write "<HR>Education"
'      NOW EXAMINE EACH DEGREE RADIO BUTTON'S VALUE
       If Request.QueryString("DGREE1") <>"" Then
           Response.Write "High School<P>"
       End If
       If Request.QueryString("DGREE2") <>"" Then
           Response.Write "College<P>"
       End If
       If Request.QueryString("DGREE3") <>"" Then
           Response.Write "University<P>"
       End If
'      NOW EXAMINE THE MARRIED CHECKBOX
       Response.write "<HR>Status"
       If Request.QueryString("MARRIED") <>"" Then
           Response.Write "<BR>Married"
       End If
'      NOW EXAMINE THE MINORITY CHECKBOX
       If Request.QueryString("MINORITY") <>"" Then
           Response.Write "<BR>Minority"
       End If
'      NOW EXAMINE THE CITIZEN CHECKBOX
       If Request.QueryString("CITIZEN") <>"" Then
           Response.Write "<BR>US Citizen"
       End If
'      NOW EXAMINE THE LAST GROUP OF CHECKBOXES ON THE FORM
       Response.write "<HR>Work Hours"
       If Request.QueryString("DAYS") <>"" Then
           Response.Write "<BR>Can work days"
       End If
       If Request.QueryString("SHIFT") <>"" Then
           Response.Write "<BR>Can work shifts"
       End If
       If Request.QueryString("NIGHTS") <>"" Then
           Response.Write "<BR>Can work nights"
       End If
       If Request.QueryString("WEEKEND") <>"" Then
               Response.Write "<BR>Can work weekends"
       End If
```

```
      Response.Write "</CENTER>"
      Response.End
   </SCRIPT>
   </BODY>
   </HTML>
```

To test the `Apply.asp` example, copy the `Apply.*` files from the CD into the Web server's root folder. Then, start Internet Explorer, connect to the local HTTP server, and invoke the file `apply.htm` by entering the following URL in the Address box:

```
   http://127.0.0.1/apply.htm
```

Notice the RUNAT attribute of the <SCRIPT> tag. This is an alternative to the <% and %> tags; it instructs the Web server to treat the entire script as a server-side script.

Accessing Databases with ASP

The most important applications you will build with ASP are applications that extract data from databases on the server, format them with HTML tags, and return them as new HTML pages to the client. With Active Server Pages, you can use the ActiveX Data Objects (ADO) of the Database component to access the database, possibly process the data, and then format them as HTML tables. The ADO uses the ODBC drivers, and can access all databases supported by ODBC.

To use the ADO, you can create a Data Source Name (DSN) for the database you want to access, or specify the connection string in the script. In this chapter's examples we are going to use the NWind database, which comes with Visual Basic. I'm assuming you have set up a DSN for the Northwind database, and you've named it NWINDDB (the process is outlined in Chapter 5). You can use either the SQL Server or the Jet version of the database. To use the ADO object, you must create an object variable with the CreateObject method, whose syntax is

```
   <%
   Set DBObj = Server.CreateObject("ADODB.Connection")
   %>
```

The *DBObj* object variable is your gateway to the ODBC databases installed on the server. To actually open a database, call the Open method of the *DBObj* object variable, as shown here:

```
   <%
   DBObj.Open "NWINDDB"
   %>
```

NWindDB is the name I used as the System Data Source for the NWind database on my system. You may have to change the name of the database accordingly on your system. For the examples in this book, I set up two DSNs: the NWINDDB DSN for the Northwind database and the BIBLIO DSN for the Biblio database.

Querying Databases

After connecting to the database, you can use the Execute method of the *DBObj* object to execute SQL commands and retrieve records from the database represented by the DSN. Let's say you want to create a Recordset variable with the names of all customers in the Northwind database.

First, create a string variable with the SQL statement

```
SQLQuery = "SELECT Country, CompanyName, ContactName, "
SQLQuery = SQLQuery & " ContactTitle FROM Customers "
SQLQuery = SQLQuery & " ORDER BY Country"
```

This SQL statement retrieves a few fields of all the rows from the Customers table and sorts them according to the Country field. To actually create the Recordset with the customers, call the Execute method of the *DBObj* object and pass the *SQLQuery* string as parameter:

```
Set RSCustomers = DBObj.Execute(SQLQuery)
```

RSCustomers is the name of a Recordset variable, which you can manipulate through your code. When the Recordset is first created, the pointer is located at the first record, and you can read the field values with the Fields collection. To display the company name of the first record on the page, use the following statement:

```
<% = RSCustomers.Fields("CompanyName") %>
```

To scan the entire Recordset, use a Do loop to examine the Recordset's EOF property. Although it's not True, it moves to the next record with the MoveNext method. Here's the structure of a loop that scans the entire Recordset:

```
<% Do While Not RSCustomers.EOF %>
    { statements to process the current record }
<% RSCustomers.MoveNext
Loop %>
```

The AllCustomers.asp Example

Let's look at an example that uses the methods and properties of the ADO objects to retrieve all the customers in the Northwind database and display them on a Web page. The AllCustomers.asp page uses the ADO component to open the

Northwind database and create a Recordset with the SQL statement presented earlier. Then, it scans all the rows of the Recordset and displays them in HTML format. Here's the complete listing of the AllCustomers.asp page:

LISTING 14.7   **The AllCustomers.asp Page**

```
<HTML>
<%
Set DBObj = Server.CreateObject("ADODB.Connection")
DBObj.Open "NWindDB"
SQLQuery = "SELECT Country, CompanyName, ContactName, "
SQLQuery = SQLQuery & "ContactTitle FROM Customers "
SQLQuery = SQLQuery & "ORDER BY Country"
Set RSCustomers = DBObj.Execute(SQLQuery)
%>
<H1>Query Results</H1>
<% Do While Not RSCustomers.EOF %>
  <TR>
    <TD> <FONT FACE="Verdana" SIZE=2>
    <% = RSCustomers("Country") %>
    </FONT></TD>
    <TD> <FONT FACE="Verdana" SIZE=2>
      <% = RSCustomers("ContactName") & " (" %>
      <% = RSCustomers("ContactTitle") & ")" %>
    </FONT></TD>
    <TD><FONT FACE="Verdana" SIZE=2>
      <% = RSCustomers("CompanyName") %>
    </FONT></TD>
  </TR>
<%
RSCustomers.MoveNext
Loop
%>
</HTML>
```

The AllCustomers.asp file's code is straightforward. It extracts the values of the fields using the Fields collection of a Recordset variable (*RSCustomers*). The output of the AllCustomers.asp page is shown in Figure 14.16. There's an even simpler method to produce an HTML page based on a Recordset. As you recall from Chapter 4, the GetString method of the Recordset object can retrieve and then format the Recordset using the delimiter you supply to this method as arguments.

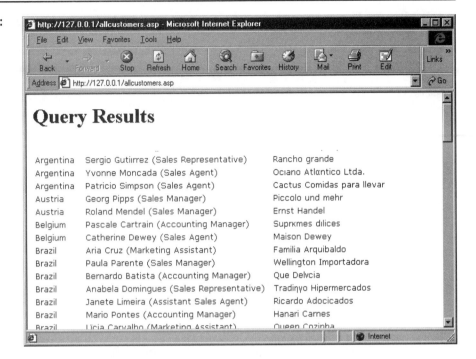

The AllCountries Example

In the next example, you will use a more complicated SQL statement to allow the user to select a country and then display the customers from the selected country. Although you could prompt the user to enter the country name, you will do something more interesting. You'll create a page with all country names, making each country name a hyperlink. When a hyperlink is clicked, you will call an ASP page on the server, passing the hyperlink's name as parameter.

To test the project, open the AllCountries.asp file and click a country name. Each country name is a hyperlink to another ASP file that displays the names of the companies (and their contact) of the selected country on a new page. The AllCountries.asp page displays the names of the countries, as shown in Figure 14.17.

FIGURE 14.17:

The AllCountries.asp file displays the names of the countries in the Customers table as hyperlinks. Clicking a country name displays the customers from the selected country.

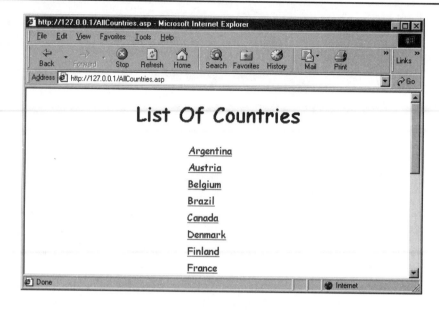

The AllCountries.asp page is quite similar to the AllCustomers.asp page, but it uses a different SQL statement. The following statements open the database and create the Recordset with the country names:

```
<%
Set DBObj = Server.CreateObject("ADODB.Connection")
DBObj.Open "NWindDB"
SQLQuery = "SELECT DISTINCT country
            FROM Customers ORDER BY Country"
Set RSCustomers = DBObj.Execute(SQLQuery)
%>
```

The remaining lines display the names of the countries (the Recordset contains a single field) and format them as hyperlinks. The following statement would display the country name on the page:

```
<% = RSCustomers.Fields("Country") %>
```

If you enclose this expression in pair of <A> tags and supply a URL, the names of the countries can become hyperlinks on the page:

```
<A HREF="/ASPages/CountryCustomersH.asp?COUNTRY=
<% = RSCustomers.Fields("Country") %> ">
<% = RSCustomers.Fields("Country") %> </A>
```

The hyperlink's destination is the CountryCustomers.asp file, which is similar to the AllCustomers.asp page. Instead of displaying all the customers in the database, the CountryCustomers.asp page uses a different SQL statement, which extracts customers from a specific country only. If the user clicks on the Brazil hyperlink, the expression `<% = CustCountry %>` is replaced with the string "Brazil", and the hyperlink becomes the following:

```
<A HREF="/ASPages/CountryCustomers.asp?COUNTRY=Brazil">Brazil</A>
```

This is a hyperlink to the `CountryCustomers.asp` file, followed by the parameters string "COUNTRY=Brazil". The `CountryCustomers.asp` page retrieves the COUNTRY parameter's value with the statement:

```
ReqCountry=Request.QueryString("COUNTRY")
```

It then uses the ReqCountry variable to build the SQL statement that retrieves the customers from the specified country:

```
SQLQuery = "SELECT CompanyName, ContactName, ContactTitle " & _
           "FROM Customers WHERE Country = '" & _
           ReqCountry & "' ORDER BY ContactName"
Set RSCustomers = DBObj.Execute(SQLQuery)
```

Then, the program proceeds to display the customers from the specified country with the following loop:

```
<% Do While Not RSCustomers.EOF %>
  <TR>
  <TD> <FONT FACE="Verdana" SIZE=2>
  <% =RSCustomers("ContactName")&" (" &
     RSCustomers("ContactTitle") & ")"  %>
     </FONT>
  </TD>
  <TD><FONT FACE="Verdana" SIZE=2>
  <% = RSCustomers("CompanyName") %>
     </FONT>
  </TD>
  </TR>
<%
RSCustomers.MoveNext
Loop
%>
```

Let's revise the `CountryCustomers.asp` script, so that instead of simply displaying the company names as text, it formats them as hyperlinks, as shown in Figure 14.18. The destination of each hyperlink will be the `Customer.asp` script, which will display all the information about a customer on a new page.

The revised script is different only in the segment that displays the customers. The script creates hyperlinks using the CustomerID field as parameter:

```
<A HREF= /AXPages/Customer.asp?CUSTOMERID=
        <% =RSCustomers("CustomerID") %> </A>
        <% =RSCustomers("CompanyName") %>
```

Notice that the code is using the CustomerID field as parameter because this field is an index field and the SQL engine will locate the desired customer more quickly. The CustomerID field is retrieved from the database by the CountryCustomers.asp script, but it's not displayed anywhere. It's passed as parameter to the Customer .asp script.

FIGURE 14.18:

The output of the Country-Customers.asp page

The Customer.asp page uses the value of the query parameter to locate a specific customer and then displays the customer's complete data. The code of the Customer.asp file is shown next:

LISTING 14.8   The Customer.asp Script

```
<HTML>
<%
ReqCustomer=Request.QueryString("CUSTOMERID")
Set DBObj = Server.CreateObject("ADODB.Connection")
DBObj.Open "NWindDB"
SQLQuery = "SELECT * FROM Customers WHERE CustomerID = '" &
           ReqCustomer & "'"
Set RSCustomers = DBObj.Execute(SQLQuery)
%>
<CENTER>
<H1>Query Results</H1>
<H3>Customer Data (CustomerID = <% = ReqCustomer %>)</H3>
</CENTER>
```

```
<FONT FACE="Verdana">
<CENTER>
<TABLE>
<TR>
<TD><B>Company Name <TD> <% = RSCustomers("CompanyName") %>
<TR>
<TD><B>Contact Name <TD> <% = RSCustomers("ContactName") %>, _
<% = RSCustomers("ContactTitle") %>
<TR>
<TD><B>Address <TD> <% = RSCustomers("Address") %>
<TR>
<TD><B>City <TD> <% = RSCustomers("City") %>
<TR>
<TD><B>Region <TD> <% = RSCustomers("Region") %>
<TR>
<TD><B>Postal Code <TD> <% = RSCustomers("PostalCode") %>
<TR>
<TD><B>Country <TD> <% = RSCustomers("Country") %>
<TR>
<TD><B>Phone <TD> <% = RSCustomers("Phone") %>
<TR>
<TD><B>Fax <TD> <% = RSCustomers("Fax") %>
</TABLE>
</CENTER>
</HTML>
```

This file was omitted from the CD by mistake. Please enter the code in a text file and save it with the extension ASP.

Taking an Order

The last example in this section demonstrates how to build a Web application for entering order data and how to read and validate the values entered by the user with a server-side script. The Place Order page, shown in Figure 14.19, allows the user to enter a series of Product IDs and quantities (to a maximum of 20 lines per order). The Order page contains a Form with 40 Textbox controls: 20 for entering product codes and 20 more for entering quantities. This is not the most user-friendly interface for placing orders, but it's intended for business-to-business orders. When you visit an online store on the Web, you spend your time browsing and occasionally placing an order. Businesses know what they need (often their inventory applications generate lists of purchases), and they don't need to browse the products, just order them. A Form with a TextArea control in which users could paste a list of product IDs and quantities, with one pair of items per line, might work even better.

FIGURE 14.19:

The GetOrder.asp page

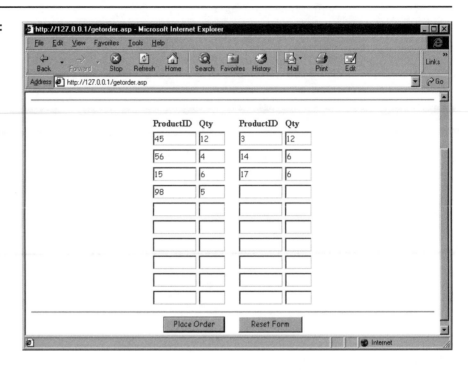

The controls you see on the Form of Figure 14.19 were not placed there by 40 <INPUT> tags. The page was generated by the following server-side script:

```
<%
For i=1 to 10
    Response.Write "<TR><TD><INPUT TYPE=TEXT SIZE=10 _
            NAME=ProdID><TD><INPUT TYPE=TEXT SIZE=5 NAME=QTY>"
    Response.Write "<TD><TD><INPUT TYPE=TEXT SIZE=10 _
            NAME=ProdID><TD><INPUT TYPE=TEXT SIZE=5 NAME=QTY>"
Next
%>
```

(The underscore characters used here to break the long lines are not valid in HTML and ASP files. They are used here to indicate that multiple text lines should be entered as a single line.)

Notice that all the controls for entering product IDs are named *ProdID*, and all the controls for entering quantities are named *QTY*. By using the same name for a group of controls, you automatically create an array of controls. Individual controls can be accessed by an index value.

The <FORM> tag's ACTION attribute specifies the name of the script on the server, the ConfirmOrder.asp script, which will process the order placed by the user. This script reads the product IDs and the quantities entered by the client, looks them up in the Products table of the Northwind database, and displays a confirmation page (shown in Figure 14.20). In this section, you'll build a simple script that displays the product names, quantities, and subtotals.

FIGURE 14.20:

The ConfirmOrder.asp script confirms the order placed through the GetOrder.asp page.

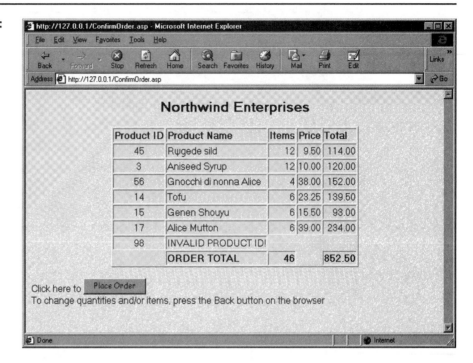

Here's the listing of the GetOrder.asp script:

LISTING 14.9   **The GetOrder.asp Script**

```
<HTML>
<CENTER>
<H1>Northwind Enterprises</H1>
<H2>Web Order Form</H2>
<HR>
<FORM ACTION="ConfirmOrder.asp" METHOD=POST>
<TABLE>
<TR>
<TD><B>ProductID</B>
<TD><B>Qty</B>
<TD>    
<TD><B>ProductID</B>
```

```
<TD><B>Qty</B>
<%
For i=1 to 10
    Response.Write "<TR><TD><INPUT TYPE=TEXT SIZE=10 _
            NAME=ProdID><TD><INPUT TYPE=TEXT SIZE=5 NAME=QTY>"
    Response.Write "<TD><TD><INPUT TYPE=TEXT SIZE=10 _
            NAME=ProdID><TD><INPUT TYPE=TEXT SIZE=5 NAME=QTY>"
Next
%>
</TABLE>
<HR>
<INPUT TYPE=SUBMIT VALUE="Place Order">
    
<INPUT TYPE=RESET  VALUE=" Reset Form ">
</FORM>
</CENTER>
</HTML>
```

The interesting part of this application is the ConfirmOrder.asp script (List-ing 14.10), which looks up the product IDs in the Northwind database and retrieves their prices and names.

LISTING 14.10   The ConfirmOrder.asp Script

```
<%
    AllProducts = Request.Form
    ProductList = "(" & Request.Form("ProdID")(1)
    For i=2 to 20
        currID = Trim(Request.Form("ProdID")(i))
        If Len(currID) > 0 And IsNumeric(currID) Then
            ProductList = ProductList & ", " & _
                            Request.Form("ProdID")(i)
        End IF
    Next
    ProductList=ProductList & ")"
    Set DBConnection=Server.CreateObject("ADODB.Connection")
    DBConnection.Open "NWINDDB"
    SQLArgument = "SELECT ProductID, ProductName, UnitPrice "
    SQLArgument = SQLArgument & "FROM Products WHERE ProductID "
    SQLArgument = SQLArgument & "IN " & ProductList
    Set SelProducts = Server.CreateObject("ADODB.Recordset")
    SelProducts.Open SQLArgument, DBConnection, 2
    HTMLOut = "<BODY BGCOLOR=lightyellow>"
    HTMLOut = HTMLOut & "<FONT FACE='MS Sans Serif'>"
    HTMLOut = HTMLOut & "<CENTER>"
    HTMLOut = HTMLOut & "<H2>Northwind Enterprises</H2>"
```

```
HTMLOut = HTMLOut & "<TABLE BORDER=FRAME BGCOLOR=lightcyan>"
HTMLOut = HTMLOut & "<TR><TD><B>Product ID</B>"
HTMLOut = HTMLOut & "<TD><B>Product Name</B>"
HTMLOut = HTMLOut & "<TD><B>Items</B><TD><B>Price</B>"
HTMLOut = HTMLOut & "<TD><B>Total</B>"
HTMLOut = HTMLOut & "<TR>"
iProd=1
HLine=""
For iProd=1 to 20
    ProdID=Request.Form("ProdID")(iProd)
    Items=Request.Form("QTY")(iProd)
    SelProducts.MoveFirst
    If IsNumeric(ProdID) And Len(ProdID) > 0 _
                        And IsNumeric(Items) Then
        If Items > 0 Then
            SelProducts.Find "ProductID=" & ProdID
            Cells=Cells+1
            If SelProducts.EOF Then
                HTMLOut = HTMLOut & "<TD ALIGN=CENTER>" & _
                ProdID & "<TD> INVALID PRODUCT ID!<TD><TD>"
            Else
                Price=SelProducts.Fields("UnitPrice")
                HTMLOut = HTMLOut & "<TD ALIGN=CENTER>" & _
                SelProducts.Fields("ProductID") & "    " & _
                "<TD>" & SelProducts.Fields("ProductName") & _
                "    " & "<TD ALIGN=RIGHT>" & Items & _
                "<TD ALIGN=RIGHT>" & _
                 FormatNumber(Price, 2) &  _
                "<TD ALIGN=RIGHT>" & _
                FormatNumber(Price * Items, 2)
                HLine=HLine & ProdID & Space(6-Len(ProdID))
                HLine=HLine & Price & Space(6-Len(Price))
                HLine=HLine & Items & Space(6-Len(Items))
                OrderTotal = OrderTotal + Price * Items
                OrderItems = OrderItems + CInt(Items)
            End If
            HTMLOut = HTMLOut & "<TR>"
        End If
    End If
Next
HTMLOut = HTMLOut & "<TD><TD><B>ORDER TOTAL</B>"
HTMLOut = HTMLOut & "<TD ALIGN=RIGHT><B>" & OrderItems
HTMLOut = HTMLOut & "</B><TD><TD ALIGN=RIGHT><B>"
HTMLOut = HTMLOut & "FormatNumber(OrderTotal, 2) & "</B>"
HTMLOut = HTMLOut & "</TABLE>"
HTMLOut = HTMLOut & "</CENTER>"
```

```
HTMLOut = HTMLOut & "<FORM ACTION='AcceptOrder.asp' _
                          METHOD='POST'>"
HTMLOut = HTMLOut & "<INPUT TYPE=HIDDEN NAME=All VALUE=" & _
                          Server.URLEncode(HLine) & ">"
HTMLOut = HTMLOut & "Click here to "
HTMLOut = HTMLOut & _
            "<INPUT TYPE=SUBMIT VALUE='Place Order'><BR>"
HTMLOut = HTMLOut & "To change quantities and/or items, _
            press the Back button on the browser"
HTMLOut = HTMLOut & "</FORM>"
Response.Write HTMLOut
%>
```

This script doesn't iterate through the product IDs and look up each one. To avoid the execution of many commands against the database, it generates a comma-separated list of Product IDs and then uses this list with the IN clause of a SELECT statement. The Recordset returned by this statement contains the names and the prices of all the products specified on the Form of the GetOrder.asp page. Product IDs without quantities are ignored. The script can then process the Recordset locally, without any additional database queries.

The ConfirmOrder script doesn't place orders; it simply confirms them. If the viewer wants to change the products and/or quantities, he must click the Back button to return to the GetOrder page. To actually place the order, the user must click the Place Order button at the bottom of the Form. This button calls the Accept-Order script on the server (you'll see how this script handles the order later in the chapter). The ConfirmOrder script must also pass the list of product IDs and quantities to the AcceptOrder script. It does so by building a long string with the Product IDs, prices, and quantities, and placing it on a Hidden control. The user never sees this control (and can't change it, of course). When the Place Order button is clicked, the control's contents are submitted to the server.

Each order line has a length of 18 characters and contains three fields of six characters: one each for the product's ID, the price, and the quantity of the specific product. As you may recall from Chapter 7, you used the same technique to build a long string and then pass it as argument to the NewOrder stored procedure. This technique enabled you to add rows to multiple tables of the Northwind database with a single command. You'll see how the order will be added to the database later in this chapter.

The Form with the Hidden control and the Button is inserted at the bottom of the ConfirmOrder script with a <FORM> tag. Here are the statements that insert the <FORM> tag:

```
HTMLOut = HTMLOut & "<FORM ACTION='AcceptOrder.asp' _
                          METHOD='POST'>"
```

```
HTMLOut = HTMLOut & "<INPUT TYPE=HIDDEN NAME=All VALUE=" & _
                    Server.URLEncode(HLine) & ">"
HTMLOut = HTMLOut & "Click here to "
HTMLOut = HTMLOut & _
         "<INPUT TYPE=SUBMIT VALUE='Place Order'><BR>"
HTMLOut = HTMLOut & "To change quantities and/or items, _
         press the Back button on the browser"
HTMLOut = HTMLOut & "</FORM>"
```

To place the long string with the order's information on the Hidden control, the script encodes it as a URL string with the URLEncode method, so that it can be transmitted to the server with the POST method. Here's what the <FORM> tags look like on the client:

```
<FORM ACTION='AcceptOrder.asp' METHOD='POST'>
<INPUT TYPE=HIDDEN NAME=All
VALUE=45++++9%2E5+++12++++3+++++10++++12++++56++++38++++4+++++14++++23%
    2E25+6+++++15++++15%2E5++6+++++17++++39++++6+++++>
Click here to <INPUT TYPE=SUBMIT VALUE='Place Order'>
<BR>
To change quantities and/or items, press the Back button on the browser
</FORM>
```

The `AcceptOrder.asp` script can be found on the CD. This script retrieves the single parameter value and replaces the plus signs with spaces before processing it. Notice that the decimal point is encoded as %2E. The script must also replace all instances of the string %2E with a period before breaking up the string into its components, and then process the order. Of course, you don't need to confirm the order. You could retrieve the order's details from within the `ConfirmOrder.asp` script. It's actually simpler to do so, but I've chosen to include the `AcceptOrder.asp` script to show you how to pass information to a server-side script from within a page's code, without user interaction.

Updating a Database

The second basic requirement of an online store is to store orders to a database. To update a database from within an ASP file, you can use the ADO component, just as you would do from within your VB applications. The simpler method is to call the AddNew method and then use the Recordset object's Fields collection to assign the values passed by the browser to the appropriate fields. You can also create an INSERT statement with the appropriate arguments from within the ASP script and execute it against the database with the Command object.

As usual, you must validate the data supplied by the client. First, you should make sure that the non-nullable fields have valid values. If they don't, you must display another page, prompting the user to correct any errors and resubmit the page. To view the Form, the user must click the browser's Back button. After the initial validation, you must make sure that the new record will not be rejected by the database. The usual approach is to attempt to locate the record with same key field(s). If such a record exists, you must prompt the user again. If everything goes well, you can add the new record with the AddNew method, assign values to the fields, and finally commit the new record with the Update method. Let's look at an example of adding new records to the database. The example of this section allows users to register through the Web.

A Customer Registration Form

The Form shown in Figure 14.21 allows the viewer to enter information for the purposes of an online registration. If you open the RegNewCustomer.htm page with your browser, you will see that the mandatory fields are displayed in red. After entering the required data on the Form's controls, the user can submit the Form to the server by clicking the Submit button.

FIGURE 14.21:

The RegNewCustomer.htm page accepts registration information from the viewer and submits it to the server.

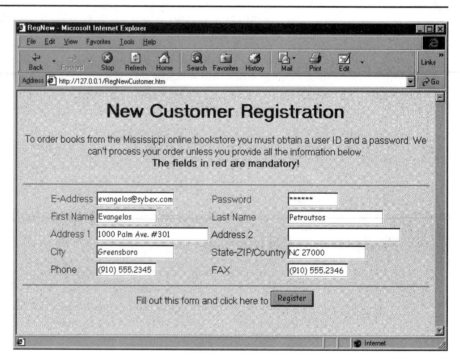

The HTML source of the RegNewCustomer.htm page is shown next. The Form on this page submits the control values to the RegisterNew.asp script using the GET method.

LISTING 14.11   The RegNewCustomer.htm Page

```
<HTML><FONT FACE='MS Sans Serif'>
<HEAD>
<meta http-equiv="Content-Type"
content="text/html">
<TITLE>RegNew</TITLE>
</HEAD>
<BODY BGCOLOR=#F0F0B0>
<CENTER>
<FONT SIZE="6"><B>New Customer Registration</B></FONT>

<P>To order books from the Mississippi online bookstore
you must obtain a user ID and a password.
We can't process your order unless you provide all the information below.
BR>
<B>The fields <FONT COLOR=red>in red</FONT> are mandatory!</B>
<P>
<FORM NAME=RegNew ACTION=/ASPages/RegisterNew.ASP METHOD="GET">
<HR>
<TABLE BORDER="0">
    <TR>
        <TD><FONT COLOR=red>E-Address
        <TD><input type="text" size="20" name="EMail">
        <TD><FONT COLOR=red>Password
        <TD><input type="text" size="12" name="Password">
    <TR>
        <TD><FONT COLOR=red>First Name
        <TD><input type="text" size="15" name="FName">
        <TD><FONT COLOR=red>Last Name
        <TD><input type="text" size="25" name="LName">
    <TR>
        <TD><FONT COLOR=red>Address 1
        <TD><input type="text" size="30" name="Address1">
        <TD>Address 2
        <TD><input type="text" size="30" name="Address2">
    <TR>
        <TD><FONT COLOR=red>City
        <TD><input type="text" size="20" name="City">
        <TD>State-ZIP/Country
        <TD><input type="text" size="20" name="ZIP">
    <TR>
        <TD><FONT>Phone
        <TD><INPUT TYPE="text" size="15" name="Phone">
        <TD>FAX
        <TD><input type="text" size="15" name="FAX">
```

```
      <TR>
</TABLE>
<HR>
Fill out this form and click here to <INPUT TYPE=SUBMIT VALUE="Register">
</FORM>
</BODY>
</HTML>
```

To test this page, you need a database with a table in which new registrations will be entered. I have created a new database with a single table, the RegCustomers table. In Chapter 18, where you'll build an online bookstore, you'll be asked to add this table to the Biblio database, so you might as well do it now. Here are the fields of the RegCustomers table:

EMail	char(20)
Password	char(12)
FName	char(15)
LName	char(25)
Address1	char(30)
Address2	char(30)
City	char(20)
StateZip	char(20)
Phone	char(15)

The ASP script assumes that the DSN for the database with the RegCustomers table is WEBOrders. If you use a different name, modify the `RegisterNew.asp` script accordingly. Let's look at the script that processes the registration data. The `RegisterNew.asp` script extracts the parameters values submitted to the server through the Request.QueryString object. First, it validates the data; in the case of an error, it redirects the viewer to an `InvalidRegData.htm` page with the following statements:

```
If CustEmail = "" Or CustPassword = "" Or _
   CustFName = "" Or   CustLName = "" Then
       Response.Redirect "InvalidRegData.htm"
       Response.End
End If
```

The `InvalidRegData.htm` file should contain a message indicating that all required data was not supplied and should prompt the user to click the Back button to return to the previous page.

Then, it displays the data on a new page (this is a debugging aid so you don't really need to display the control values). Before committing any data to the database, the script attempts to locate a record with the same e-mail and password. If such a record doesn't exist, this is a first-time customer who is then registered. If the record exists, the script welcomes the user. This application is not very elaborate. It requires that the e-mail and password combination be unique. Usually, each customer is identified by a single field. If the e-mail field exists in the database, but the password is incorrect, the script should not register the user. Most likely, the user has mistyped the password and the script should not register a customer with the same e-mail twice.

Here's the listing of the ASP script that processes the registration data on the server:

LISTING 14.12   The RegisterNew.asp Script

```
<%
    CustEMail = Request.QueryString("EMail")
    CustPassword = Request.QueryString("Password")
    CustFName = Request.QueryString("FName")
    CustLName = Request.QueryString("LName")
    CustAddr1 = Request.QueryString("Address1")
    CustAddr2 = Request.QueryString("Address2")
    CustCity = Request.QueryString("City")
    CustZIP = Request.QueryString("ZIP")
    CustPhone = Request.QueryString("Phone")
    CustFAX = Request.QueryString("FAX")
    CustMyAddress = Request.QueryString("MyAddress")
    CustMailPromo = Request.QueryString("MailPromo")

    If CustEmail = "" Or CustPassword = "" Or CustFName = "" Or
    CustLName = "" Then
        Response.Redirect "InvalidRegData.htm"
        Response.End
    End If

    Response.Write "<HTML><FONT FACE='MS Sans Serif'>"
    Response.Write "<BODY BGCOLOR=#F0F0B0>"
    Response.Write "<HR>"
    Response.Write CustEMail & "      "
    Response.Write CustPassword & "<BR>"
    Response.Write CustLName & ", "
    Response.Write CustFName & "<BR>"
    Response.Write CustAddr1 & "<BR>"
    Response.Write CustAddr2 & "<BR>"
```

```
Response.Write CustCity & "      "
Response.Write CustZIP & "<BR>"
Response.Write CustPhone & "      "
Response.Write CustFAX & "<BR>"
Response.Write "<HR>"

SQLArgument = "SELECT * FROM RegCustomers WHERE EMail='" &
UCase(CustEMail) & "'" & " AND Password='" & CustPassword & "'"
connectString="DSN=WEBOrders;User ID=sa;password="
adOpenKeyset = 1
adUseServer = 2
adLockOptimistic=3
Set SelTitles=Server.CreateObject("ADODB.Recordset")
SelTitles.CursorLocation=adUseServer
SelTitles.Open SQLArgument, connectString, adOpenDynamic,
adLockOptimistic
If SelTitles.EOF Then
    SelTitles.AddNew
    SelTitles.Fields("EMail")=CustEMail
    SelTitles.Fields("Password")=CustPassword
    SelTitles.Fields("LName")=CustLName
    SelTitles.Fields("FName")=CustFName
    SelTitles.Fields("Address1")=CustAddr1
    SelTitles.Fields("Address2")=CustAddr2
    SelTitles.Fields("City")=CustCity
    SelTitles.Fields("StateZIP")=CustZIP
    SelTitles.Fields("Phone")=CustPhone
    SelTitles.Fields("FAX")=CustFAX
    SelTitles.Update
    Response.Write "<FONT SIZE=+2>You were successfully
registered!</FONT>"
Else
    SelTitles.MoveFirst
    Response.Write "<FONT SIZE=+2>Welcome back " & CustFName &
    CustLName & "</FONT>"
End If
SelTitles.Close
Set SelTitles=Nothing
%>
```

You can explore this project on your own and modify the script so that it registers users by their e-mail address only. If an existing address is specified with a different password, the script should display a page, explaining that the e-mail address is already assigned and giving the user a chance to correct the password and try again. As you understand, I'm using the e-mail address as user ID because this is a unique string and people don't forget it.

The File Access Component

The File Access component consists of two objects that give your scripts access to text files: the FileSystemObject object and the TextStream object, which were introduced with VBScript 2.0. The FileSystemObject object gives your script access to the server computer's file system, and the TextStream object lets your script open, read from, and write to text files. These objects can't be used with binary files, because this would make VBScript unsafe even on the server.

The FileSystemObject Object

The FileSystemObject object gives your script access to the server computer's file system and is available only with the server-side VBScript. To gain access to server's file system, you must create a FileSystemObject variable with the CreateObject method:

```
Set fs = CreateObject("Scripting.FileSystemObject")
```

The *fs* variable represents the file system. You can use the FileSystemObject object to access text files on the server computer's disk with the methods described next.

CreateTextFile Method

The first method of the FileSystemObject object creates a text file that returns a TextStream object that can be used to read from or write to the file. The syntax of the CreateTextFile method is

```
fs.CreateTextFile(filename, overwrite, unicode)
```

The *filename* argument specifies the name of the file to be created and is the only required argument. *overwrite* is a Boolean value that indicates whether you can overwrite an existing file (if True) or not (if False). If the overwrite argument is omitted, existing files are not overwritten. The last argument, *unicode*, indicates whether the file is created as a Unicode or ASCII file. If the *unicode* argument is True, the new file will be created as a Unicode file; otherwise, it will be created as an ASCII file. If omitted, an ASCII file is assumed.

To create a new text file, you must first create a FileSystemObject object variable and then call its CreateTextFile method as follows:

```
Set fs = CreateObject("Scripting.FileSystemObject")
Set TStream = fs.CreateTextFile("c:\testfile.txt", True)
```

The *TStream* variable represents a TextStream object, whose methods allow you to write to or read from the specified file.

OpenTextFile Method

In addition to creating a new text file, you can open an existing file with the OpenTextFile method, whose syntax is

```
Set TStream = fs.OpenTextFile(filename, iomode, create, format)
```

The OpenTextFile method opens the specified file and returns a TextStream object that can be used to read from or write to the file.

The *filename* argument is the only required one. Of the remaining optional arguments, *iomode* can be one of the constants:

ForReading   The file is opened for reading data.

ForAppending   The file is opened for appending data.

The *create* optional argument is a Boolean value that indicates whether a new file can be created if the specified filename doesn't exist. The last argument, *format*, is also optional. It can have one of the following values, which indicate the format of the opened file. If the format argument is True, the file is opened in Unicode mode; if it's False, the file is opened in ASCII mode. If omitted, the file is opened using the system default (ASCII).

To open a TextStream object for reading, use the following statements:

```
Set fs = CreateObject("Scripting.FileSystemObject")
Set TStream = fs.OpenTextFile("c:\testfile.txt", ForReading)
```

Like the CreateTextFile method, the OpenTextFile method returns a TextStream object, whose methods allow you to write to or read from the specified file.

The TextStream Object's Methods

After a TextStream object is created with the CreateTextFile or the OpenTextFile method, you can use the following methods to read from and write to the file:

Read   The Read method reads a specified number of characters from a TextStream object. Its syntax is

```
TStream.Read(characters)
```

where *characters* is the number of characters to be read from.

ReadAll   The ReadAll method reads an entire TextStream (text file) and returns the resulting string. Its syntax is simply the following:

```
TStream.ReadAll
```

ReadLine   The ReadLine method reads one line of text at a time (up to, but not including, the new-line character) from a TextStream file and returns the resulting string. Its syntax is

```
TStream.ReadLine
```

Skip Method   This method skips a specified number of characters when reading a TextStream file. Its syntax is

```
TStream.Skip(characters)
```

where *characters* is the number of characters to be skipped.

SkipLine   The SkipLine method skips the next line when reading from a TextStream and its syntax is

```
TStream.SkipLine
```

The characters of the skipped lines are discarded, up to and including the next new-line character.

Write   The Write method writes the specified string to a TextStream file. Its syntax is

```
TStream.Write(string)
```

where *string* is the string (literal or variable) to be written to the file. Strings are written to the file with no intervening spaces or characters between each string. Use the WriteLine method to write a new-line character or a string that ends with a new-line character.

WriteLine   This method writes the specified string followed by a new-line character to the file. Its syntax is

```
TStream.WriteLine(string)
```

where *string* is the text you want to write to the file. If you call the WriteLine method without an argument, a new-line character is written to the file.

WriteBlankLines   This method writes a specified number of blank lines (new-line characters) to the file. Its syntax is

```
TStream.WriteBlankLines(lines)
```

where *lines* is the number of blank lines to be inserted in the file.

The TextStream Object's Properties

The TextStream object provides several properties that allow your code to know where the pointer is in the current TextStream. These properties are:

AtEndOfLine   This is a read-only property that returns True if the file pointer is at the end of a line in the TextStream object; otherwise, it returns False. The AtEndOfLine property applies to files that are open for reading. You can use this property to read a line of characters, one at a time, with a loop similar to the following one:

```
Do While TSream.AtEndOfLine =False
    newChar = TStream.Read(1)
    {process character}
Loop
```

AtEndOfStream   This is another read-only property that returns True if the file pointer is at the end of the TextStream object. The AtEndOfStream property applies only to TextStream files that are open for reading. You can use this property to read an entire file, one line at a time, with a loop like the following one:

```
Do While TStream.AtEndOfStream = False
    newChar = TStream.ReadLine
    {process line}
Loop
```

Column   This is another read-only property that returns the column number of the current character in a TextStream line. The first character in a line is in column 1. Use this property to read data arranged in columns, without tab or other delimiters between them.

Line   This is a read-only property that returns the current line number in the TextStream. The Line property of the first line in a TextStream object is 1.

Using the TextStream Object

The TextFile.asp page demonstrates several of the TextStream object's methods. When this file is called, it creates a text file on the server computer and writes a few lines in it. Then, it opens the file, reads its lines, and displays them on an HTML page (shown in Figure 14.22), which is returned to the client computer. As you will see, it uses the Write method of the Response object to send its output to the client.

FIGURE 14.22:

The output of the TextFile.asp page, which reads the lines of a text file on the server and displays them on the browser's window on the client.

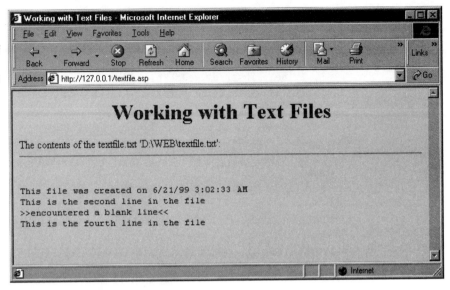

LISTING 14.13   The TextFile.asp Script

```
<HTML>
<HEAD>
<TITLE>Working with Text Files</TITLE>
</HEAD>
<BODY BGCOLOR=#E0E0E0>
<CENTER>
<H1>Working with Text Files</H1>
</CENTER>
<%
  Set FileObj = Server.CreateObject("Scripting.FileSystemObject")
  TestFile = Server.MapPath ("/ASPages/textfile.txt")
  Set OutStream= FileObj.CreateTextFile (TestFile, True, False)
  str1 = "This file was created on " & Now()
  OutStream.WriteLine Str1
  OutStream.WriteLine "This is the second line in the file"
  OutStream.WriteBlankLines(1)
  OutStream.WriteLine "This is the fourth line in the file"
  Set OutStream = Nothing
  Response.Write "The contents of the textfile.txt '" & _
                    TestFile & "':<BR>"
  Response.Write "<HR>"
  Set InStream= FileObj.OpenTextFile _
                (TestFile, 1, False, False)
```

```
%>
  <PRE>
<%
  Response.Write Instream.Readline & "<BR>"
  While InStream.AtEndOfStream = False
     TLine = Instream.ReadLine
     If Trim(TLine) <> "" Then
            Response.Write TLine & "<BR>"
        Else
            Response.Write ">>encountered a blank line<<" & "<BR>"
        End If
  Wend
  Set Instream=Nothing
%>
</PRE>
</BODY>
</HTML>
```

The Server object's CreateObject method is used to create a FileSystemObject object, through which the script can access the server's hard disk. Then, it calls the MapPath method, to map a virtual folder to the actual folder name and specify a full path name. OutStream is a TextStream object, whose Write method you use to write to the file. After the desired lines are written to the file, you set the Text-Stream object variable to Nothing to release the resources it occupied.

In the second half of the script, you create another TextStream object to read the lines of the same file. The file's lines are read with a While ... Wend loop, which examines the value of the TextStream object's AtEndOfStream property to find out how many lines to read from the file:

```
While InStream.AtEndOfStream = False
   TLine = Instream.ReadLine
   {process Tline text line}
Wend
```

The output is formatted with the <CODE> tag to display them as a listing. Notice that the use of the Response object minimized the need for <% and %> delimiter tags.

Summary

In this chapter, you've learned the structure of Web applications, how to build server-side scripts that use the ASP objects, and how to maintain state among the various pages of a Web site. The tool we used to build the examples is the simplest one there is: NotePad. You won't find many developers building Web sites from scratch. There are many tools that automate the design and programming of a site, one of them being the Visual InterDev. Before you can use any tool to design a Web application, however, you must understand the ASP objects and server-side scripting. Now that you can write server-side scripts with NotePad, things can only get easier.

VB itself comes with a tool for building Web applications. The tool is actually a new project type, the IIS Application project type, and it's discussed in the following chapter. This is not a designer's tool, it's a programmer's tool. An IIS application allows you to connect the various events that may take place on a Web page to VB events, which you can program as usual.

CHAPTER
FIFTEEN

15

Building IIS Applications

- WebClasses

- Building IIS applications

- Processing client requests

- Connecting Events to WebClasses

This chapter explores a new type of project introduced with Visual Basic 6, the Internet Information Server (IIS) project. As you can understand by its name, this project's type applies to Web applications. An IIS project is a VB project that runs on the server and services client requests. It's a Web application like the ones you've learned to build in the previous chapter: a series of HTML pages that interact with the server with the help of Active Server Pages and VBScript. There are no new objects to introduce in this chapter, and no new statements to learn.

It sounds like a rerun of the previous chapter, but it's not. Where Chapter 14 introduced Active Server Pages and client-side VBScript, this chapter shows you how to build Web applications from within Visual Basic's IDE. The starting point is a set of HTML pages. These pages contain hyperlinks and/or HTML controls and they can collect information at the client (the browser). This information is sent to the Web server, where a script processes it. An IIS project is similar to a VB project, in the sense that it uses HTML pages instead of Forms and it translates client requests to events. Every hyperlink, or button, on the application's pages can be mapped to an event. The project receives this event and processes it, by calling a handler to which the event is connected. Basically, an IIS project is a way of mapping Web applications to VB applications. IIS is meant to help VB developers use the tools they're familiar with to the Web. Unlike NotePad, the VB editor is more productive and its Intellisense features speed up the coding.

However, you can't design an HTML page with drag-and-drop operations. HTML pages must be prepared outside the VB IDE (preferably with NotePad). The IIS project type isn't going to help you with the presentation layer. Once a request is made by the client to your Web application, however, you have at your disposal all of Visual Basic's tools, including Classes and ActiveX Data Objects. Let's start by examining the basic component of an IIS project, the WebClass, which allows you to connect events on the client to procedures in the client application.

Understanding WebClasses

A WebClass is the basic item of an IIS application. In the last chapter you learned how to develop ASP scripts that run on the server and communicate with the client. An ASP script on its own can't do much. It can read the values of the parameters passed by the client and generate output in HTML format, which is automatically sent to the client. This is a lot, considering how easy it is to access the parameter values with the Request object and generate HTML code on the fly with the Response object. Yet, in order to access databases and use business objects, you must use the ADO library and create customer components.

A WebClass replaces the custom component. You must still write the code using Visual Basic, but you don't have to package it as a DLL and then use it with the script. You can develop the procedures you need in VB and test them in the browser. When an error occurs, you're taken back to the Visual Basic IDE to fix it and then continue (if possible). A WebClass lets you combine VB code with the objects of the ASP component to create HTML files. There's nothing new here. We'll do the same thing we did in the previous chapter, only this time we'll use WebClasses and Visual Basic's IDE instead of NotePad.

Let's say you're writing a Web application that accesses a database. You know how to extract information from the database and how to update the tables of the database. Once you get the parameters passed from the client (which can be search arguments, or field values), you can use plain VB code as you did in the previous chapters. The only difference is that the final cursor (if any) must be formatted as an HTML document before it's transmitted to the client. As you will see, there are ways to automate this step as well, by building HTML templates. If the parameters passed by a client must be processed by a script that involves many calculations, you can use VB code to process the data and then pass the results as another HTML document.

Another way to look at WebClasses is the following. Web pages contact ASP scripts. When you design IIS applications with Visual Basic, WebClasses are the equivalent of an ASP file. The Web page passes the URL of the WebClass to the server, along with parameter values. The Web server passes the parameter values to the WebClass, which processes the request and sends the appropriate output to the client. Behind the scenes, Visual Basic will create the appropriate ASP file(s) on the server and the Web page will actually see this ASP file. The developer, however, need not deal with the details of creating the Web site, moving the files there, and maintaining the site. VB takes care of these details for you.

Building an IIS Application

Start a new IIS Application project. Figure 15.1 shows the Visual Basic IDE for the IIS Application project. The folder Designers contains a WebClass item and this item's designer appears in the middle of the window. The WebClass item may contain HTML Template WebItems and Custom WebItems. So, at the heart of an IIS Application you'll find the WebItems. A WebItem is like a Class; it contains procedures (including event handlers) that a Web page can request.

FIGURE 15.1:

The default components of an
IIS application

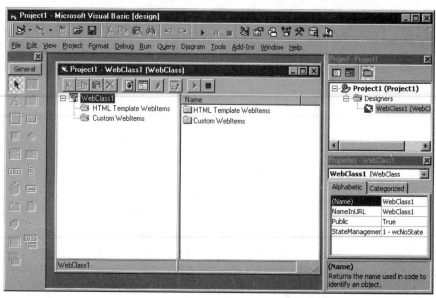

An HTML template file is an HTML page that is associated with the application and can be downloaded to the client as is. The HTML template may also contain replacement sections, which the WebClass will replace with specific HTML elements (text, images, tags) before sending the file to the client.

As you recall from the last chapter, the server component (the ASP script) can create an HTML page on the fly with the Response.Write method. The HTML template simplifies the task of generating Web pages on the fly. The template contains the structure of the page: its title, some text that's always the same, the background, and so on. The parts of the page that change from client to client and from request to request are inserted by the WebClass, as the page is transmitted to the client. You must mark them in the template file with special tags and then instruct the WebClass object to process these tags before sending the file to the client. Usually, we replace these tags with the columns of a Recordset.

HTML templates allow you to separate the content from the logic of a Web site. A Web author will create the template, which involves mostly visual design and artistic work. The programmer will supply the script, or the parts of the page that must be generated programmatically. This is probably the most compelling reason for creating IIS applications in the Visual Basic environment. You'll see shortly how this is done with an example.

Let's return to the IIS project's Designer window and see how the WebClass object interacts with the client. Click the View Code button on the Project Explorer to see the code inserted automatically by Visual Basic:

LISTING 15.1 **The Default WebClass_Start Event Handler**

```
Option Explicit
Option Compare Text

Private Sub WebClass_Start()

    'Write a reply to the user
    With Response
        .Write "<html>"
        .Write "<body>"
        .Write "<h1><font face=""Arial"">WebClass1's Starting _
            Page</font></h1>"
        .Write "<p>This response was created in the Start event of _
            WebClass1.</p>"
        .Write "</body>"
        .Write "</html>"
    End With

End Sub
```

The Start event of the WebClass is fired when the application starts. This is not a Visual Basic application, however. It's an IIS application that starts when a client contacts the URL of the WebClass. In the Start event, you can insert the code to create a Web page on the fly, or you can request that an HTML template be displayed when the application starts:

```
Private Sub WebClass_Start()
    'Write a reply to the user
    Template1.WriteTemplate
End Sub
```

Template1 is the name of an HTML file that holds the first page of the application. This file needs be processed before it's transmitted to the client.

If you run the project now by pressing F5, the Debugging Properties tab of the Project Properties dialog box will appear, as shown in Figure 15.2. Since an IIS project is implemented as a DLL, you must specify what will happen when the application starts.

Visual Basic suggests that the project start with the WebClass1 component. It will start Internet Explorer using the URL of the IIS application, which is

```
http://localhost/WebTest1/WebClass1.ASP
```

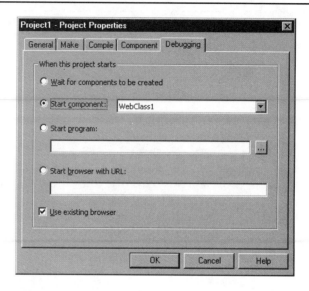

As you can see, the project was tested with the local Web server (IIS or Personal Web Server) running on the same computer; if the Web server is installed on another machine, the *localhost* part of the URL will be different. Visual Basic has created an ASP file, the WebClass1.ASP file, which invokes the WebClass component of the application. When the WebClass object is invoked, the WebClass_Start event is fired. We have programmed this event to respond by writing something to the output.

The ASP file resides in the WebTest1 virtual folder of the Web server. This virtual folder was created automatically by Visual Basic. Normally, you should create this virtual folder yourself, map it to the application's folder, assign the appropriate rights, and so on. An IIS project takes care of setting up the Web for you. The document that will be displayed on the browser is quite simple (see Figure 15.3).

Let's display an initial page that contains a hyperlink. The destination of the hyperlink will be another page on the same Web. Let's say you've created a second HTML file, the Template2 component, and added it to the project. The following script will display a very simple page as before, only this time the page contains a hyperlink to another document in the same site. Listing 15.2 shows the revised code of the WebClass's Start event.

FIGURE 15.3:

The sample page created by
the default IIS application

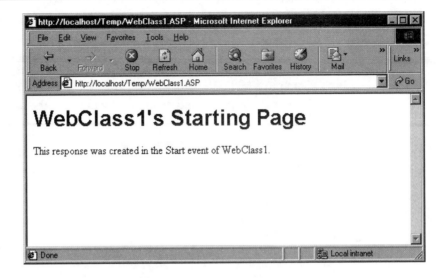

LISTING 15.2   Displaying an HTML Page with a Hyperlink

```
Private Sub WebClass_Start()
    'Write a reply to the user
    With Response
        .Write "<html>"
        .Write "<body>"
        .Write "<h1><font face=""Arial"">
                WebClass1's Starting Page</font></h1>"
        .Write "<p>This response was created in the
                Start event of WebClass1.</p>"
        .Write "<p>Click <A HREF="" & URLFor(Template2) &
                   "">here</A> to see another document"
        .Write "</body>"
        .Write "</html>"
    End With
End Sub
```

The code is straightforward, except for the code that generates the hyperlink.
The URLFor function will return the URL of another document in the same Web.
Now, we can create the Template1 HTML Template.

Creating HTML Templates

Switch to the Designer window and right-click the item WebClass1. From the
shortcut menu select Add HTML Template. Visual Basic will display a message
box, indicating that the project must first be saved, before an HTML template is

added. Save the project's components to a new folder (you can find the project in the IISDemo1 folder on the CD). Invoke the Add HTML Template command again and you'll see the File Open dialog box, where you must select an existing HTML file. Visual Basic doesn't come with a built-in HTML editor that would allow you to create an HTML file in the same environment. Click Cancel to close the dialog box, switch to a text editor (use NotePad for a simple HTML file like the one we'll use in this example) and create a new file with the following contents:

LISTING 15.3   The HTMLForm.htm Page

```
<HTML>
<FORM >
Search Arguments:
<INPUT TYPE=Input NAME="Args" VALUE="Programming">
Search Mode:
<SELECT NAME="Mode">
<OPTION VALUE="0">Title Keywords</OPTION>
<OPTION VALUE="1">Author Name</OPTION>
<OPTION VALUE="2">Title and Author</OPTION>
</SELECT>
<INPUT TYPE=submit NAME="BttnSend" value="Submit Query">
</FORM>
</HTML>
```

This is a simple HTML file that contains a Form with two controls: a Text control and a List control. As you recall from Chapter 11, this Form allows the user to enter the search criteria and then perform a search in the BIBLIO database. Save this file as HTMLForm.htm in the same folder as the project. Make sure it's saved with the extension HTM, and not with extension TXT. Return to the IIS project and add a new HTML template. Right-click the WebClass1 item in the left pane and from the shortcut menu select the Add HTML Template command. A File Open dialog box will appear, where you can select the file you just created.

When the template is added to the project, you'll receive a warning to the effect that an HTML tag on the Form has not been connected to a WebItem yet, as shown in Figure 15.4. As you will see, each Submit button (or hyperlink) on a Form can be connected to a WebItem and each time the button (or the hyperlink) is clicked, the corresponding WebItem's Respond event will be fired. This is where you'll insert the code to respond to the client request. Ignore this message and click OK.

If you run this project now, you will see the page shown in Figure 15.5. You can enter one or more keywords in the Text control and select the Search mode in the list. When the Search Now button is clicked, the controls' contents are submitted to the server. Of course, the server isn't going to react because we haven't programmed it yet. We'll do so in the next section.

FIGURE 15.4:

This message tells you that the Form on the HTML page isn't connected to a WebItem in the project.

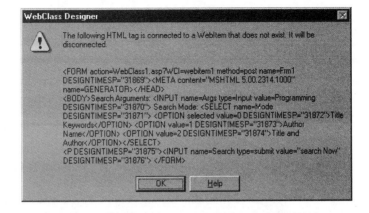

FIGURE 15.5:

The HTMLForm.htm page

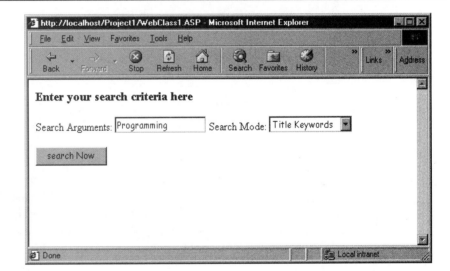

Processing Client Requests

We are going to create a component to process the client request. This component is a WebItem. Right-click the WebClass1 entry in the Designer window and select Add Custom WebItem. The new WebItem will be named by default WebItem1. Don't change the name.

If you open the Code window and select WebItem1 in the Objects list, you'll see that the WebItem recognizes three events:

> **ProcessTag**   This event takes place when the HTML template is read and gives the WebItem a chance to modify it before sending the HTML code to

the client. Use this event to replace specific areas of the HTML Template with HTML code (text and tags).

Respond   This event is fired every time the WebItem is contacted by the client.

UserEvent   This event is fired every time the client raises a custom event (you'll see shortly how you can fire custom events).

The event we're interested in is the Respond event of WebItem1. This event will be fired when the HTMLForm.htm page requests the WebItem1 object on the server. The HTML file will pass the values of the two controls on the Form, which are named *Args* and *Mode*. The event handler must extract these values, process them, and pass an HTML document back to the client. You know already that the parameter values must be read with the Request.Form property and the output must be generated with the Response.Write method. WebItem2 should respond to the request with the following code:

```
Private Sub WebItem1_Respond()
    Response.Write "WEBITEM1_RESPOND invoked "
    Response.Write "with the following values<P>"
    Response.Write Request.Form("Args") & "<P>"
    Response.Write Request.Form("Mode") & "<P>"
End Sub
```

Finally, we must specify that the Form's Submit button be linked to the Web-Item object. Select the Template1 item in the left pane of the Designer window and the components of the document will appear in the right pane. Right-click the Frm1 item and from the shortcut menu select Connect to WebItem. A window with all the components of the project will appear. Select the WebItem1 component and click OK. The Form's Submit button is now linked to the WebItem1 object.

At this point, your project contains a WebClass, which in turns contains an HTML template (Template1) and a custom WebItem (WebItem1). The Submit button on the Form has been linked to WebItem1 and the WebItem1_Respond event will be fired when the user clicks the Search Now button on the Form. Here's the project's code:

LISTING 15.4   **The IISDemo2 Project's Code**

```
Option Explicit
Option Compare Text

Private Sub WebClass_Start()
    'Write a reply to the user
    Template1.WriteTemplate
End Sub
```

```
Private Sub WebItem1_Respond()
    Response.Write "WEBITEM1_RESPOND invoked "
    Response.Write "with the following values<P>"
    Response.Write Request.Form("Args") & "<P>"
    Response.Write Request.Form("Mode") & "<P>"
End Sub
```

IISDemo2 is a simple IIS application that demonstrates the basic functions of Web-Classes and WebItems. We are going to look at a more complicated example, but first let's summarize three key items in writing code for a WebClass.

URLFor Function   Use this method to insert the URL of any component. Visual Basic will generate the proper URL and you don't have to worry about absolute or relative URLs and what will happen when the application is moved to another computer or folder.

Respond Event   Every time the client contacts a WebItem, the WebItem's Respond event is triggered automatically. All you have to do is code this event.

WriteTemplate Method   Use this method to send an HTML file to the client as is. You can also process the HTML file, using the ProcessTag event (discussed in the next section).

Connecting Events to WebClasses

Let's return our attention to the <FORM> tag of the HTMLForm.htm file, which is repeated here:

```
<FORM NAME=Frm1 ACTION="WebClass1.asp?WCI=webitem1" METHOD=post>
```

We didn't insert the ACTION and METHOD attributes in the <FORM> tag. VB did it for us, when we connected the Frm1 element of the Form to WebItem1. The ACTION attribute is the URL of the server application (or server script in the case of Active Server Pages). The application's name is WebClass1.asp and there's nothing peculiar so far. But the name of the server application is followed by a parameter, the WCI parameter. As you can see, the name of the WebItem that will process the request on the server is passed as parameter. Obviously, any additional parameters will be appended to this URL by the browser automatically. WCI stands for WebItem and this is how you specify the name of a WebItem in the application's WebClass.

The WebItem1_Respond event is fired when the user clicks the Form's Submit button. This is the event where we inserted the code to display the values of the parameters passed by the browser to the server in the previous example. We're now going to contact the TitleSearch Class to retrieve the Biblio database's titles that match the specified criteria. The Web application doesn't need to know how we search the database and it's not going to build a SELECT statement. It will simply call a business object on the Web server.

You can edit an existing template from within the Visual Basic IDE. To do so, right-click the name of the template in the left pane and select Edit HTML Template from the shortcut menu. Your designated HTML editor will start with the Template1 HTML file. You can specify the HTML editor of your choice through the Advanced tab of the Options dialog box (Tools ➤ Options). Figure 15.6 shows my favorite HTML editor.

FIGURE 15.6:

Use the Advanced tab to specify the HTML editor to be invoked by Visual Basic when you select to edit an HTML Template.

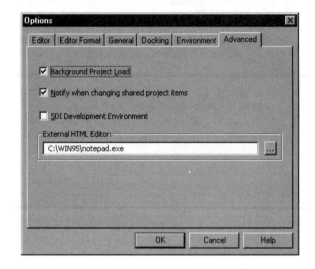

If you save the changes to the HTM file and return to the Visual Basic IDE, you'll be prompted to refresh the HTML template. So, it's safer to edit the template from within the Visual Basic IDE, to make sure that the changes will take effect immediately.

Assuming that you have removed the ACTION attribute from the HTML template, open the WebClass Designer and select the template that contains the hyperlink (or any other tag) you want to connect to WebItem1. In the right pane of the Designer you will see the elements of the template. Template1 contains a <BODY> and a <FORM> tag. The FORM is named Frm1 and there is no action associated with it. To specify an action, right-click the Frm1 item in the right pane of the Designer. In the shortcut menu select Connect to WebItem and you will see the Connect to WebItem dialog box. This dialog box contains all the components in the project. Click the WebItem1 entry and click the OK button. When the dialog box is closed, the ACTION for the Frm1 item in the right pane of the Designer will be set to WebItem1. You have just connected the Form's ACTION attribute to the WebItem1 component.

If you open the `HTMLForm.htm` file you will see that the Designer has modified its contents. The new <FORM> tag is:

```
<FORM NAME=Frm1 _
    ACTION="WebClass1.ASP?WCI=WebItem1&amp;WCU" METHOD=post>
```

To disconnect the attribute from the WebItem, you can right-click Frm1 item in the right pane of the Designer and select Disconnect from the shortcut menu. The WCU keyword is explained in the following section.

In addition to invoking WebItems on the server, an element on the Web page can also call a custom event of the Template1 WebItem on the server. To do so, select the Template1 entry in the left pane of the Designer and right-click the Frm1 item in the right pane. From the shortcut menu select Connect to Custom Event. An event will be automatically added to the Template1 entry in the right pane of the Designer window. The event's name is by default the same as the Template's element name (Frm1). Change the name of the custom event to Frm1Event. Visual Basic will modify the <FORM> tag in the `HTMLForm.htm` file automatically. The new <FORM> tag is shown next:

```
<FORM NAME=Frm1
    ACTION="WebClass1.ASP?WCI=Template1&amp;WCE=Frm1Event&amp;WCU"
    METHOD=post>
```

The WCE keyword specifies the name of the event to be invoked. The WebItem to which the event will be reported is specified with the WCI keyword.

When the user clicks the Submit button on the Form, the Template1 WebItem's custom event will be fired. Therefore, we must add another event handler to the project, which will process the parameters submitted by the HTML page. This event handler is very similar to the WebItem1_Respond event handler.

```
Private Sub Template1_FRM1Event()
    Response.Write "TEMPLATE1_FRM1EVENT invoked "
    Response.Write "with the following values<P>"
    Response.Write Request.Form("Args") & "<P>"
    Response.Write Request.Form("Mode") & "<P>"
End Sub
```

The revised project, in which the HTML page invokes a custom event of the Template1 WebItem, can be found in the `EventDemo` folder under the `IISDemo` folder.

There's a third way to contact a procedure on the server, namely by invoking an event of a custom WebItem. First, you must add a custom event to the WebItem.

Right-click the entry WebItem1 in the right pane of the Designer and from the shortcut menu select Add Custom Event. Rename the custom event to WebEvent. Then edit the HTML template and change the <FORM> tag to:

```
<FORM NAME=Frm1
    ACTION="WebClass1.ASP?WCI=WebItem1&amp;WCU=WebEvent&amp" _
        METHOD=post>
```

Then open the Code window and enter the following code in the custom event's handler:

```
Private Sub WebItem1_WebEvent()
    Response.Write "WEBITEM1_WEBEVENT invoked "
    Response.Write "with the following values<P>"
    Response.Write Request.Form("Text1") & "<P>"
    Response.Write Request.Form("Text2") & "<P>"
End Sub
```

This project is identical to the IISDemo project, only it contacts a custom event of the WebItem1 object on the server. The revised project can be found in the UEvent-Demo under the IISDemo folder on the CD.

In the following section we are going to build an IIS application that demonstrates the separation of the application's content and logic. The sample application will show you how to process HTML Templates before they are sent to the client and how to contact other server components (the Active Data Objects, in specific).

Calling a Component

Now we'll add a few lines of code in the WebItem_Respond event to do something useful with this page. We'll call the GetTitles method of the Titles component to retrieve the titles that match search criteria supplied by the viewer on the HTMLForm page as shown in Figure 15.7.

The first step is to add a reference to the Titles component to the project. While the Components dialog box is open, add a reference to the ActiveX Data Object Library. We are not going to contact the database directly from within the Class's code, but we need a Recordset variable to store the rows returned by the GetTitles method. Now we can create an instance of the SearchTitles component from within the WebClass object and call the GetTitles method:

```
Private Sub WebItem1_Respond()
Dim SearchFor As String
Dim SearchBy As Integer
Dim objTitles As Titles.TitleSearchClass
Dim RS As Recordset
Dim currTitle As String
```

```
            SearchFor = CStr(Request.Form("Args"))
            SearchBy = CInt(Request.Form("Mode"))
            Set objTitles = New Titles.TitleSearchClass
            Set RS = objTitles.GetTitles(SearchFor, SearchBy)
            Response.Write "<H4>Your search for " & SearchFor & _
                    " returned the following titles</H4>"
            Response.Write "<TABLE>"
            Response.Write "<TR><TD VALIGN=top WIDTH=120><B>" & _
                    RS.Fields("ISBN") & _
                    "</B><TD VALIGN=top>" & _
                    "<A HREF='" & URLFor(WebItem2) & "&ISBN=" & _
                    RS.Fields("ISBN") & "'>" & _
                    RS.Fields("Title") & "</A>"
        currTitle = RS.Fields("ISBN")
        While Not RS.EOF
            If RS.Fields("ISBN") <> currTitle Then
                Response.Write _
                    "<TR><TD VALIGN=top WIDTH=120><B>" & _
                    RS.Fields("ISBN") & "</B><TD VALIGN=top>" & _
                    "<A HREF='" & URLFor(WebItem2) & "&ISBN=" & _
                    RS.Fields("ISBN") & "'>" & _
                    RS.Fields("Title") & "</A>"
                currTitle = RS.Fields("ISBN")
            Else
                If Not IsNull(RS.Fields("Author")) Then
                    Response.Write "<TR><TD><TD><I>" & _
                    RS.Fields("Author") & "</I>"
                End If
            End If
            RS.MoveNext
        Wend
    End Sub
```

The WCDemo Project

The example in this section is an IIS application that uses the ADO library to retrieve records from the NWIND database and present them to the client. This example will also demonstrate how to separate the site's content from its logic (not in a dramatic way, unfortunately; this could only be demonstrated clearly with a large-scale project, which can't be presented in this book). Let's start by looking at the various pages of the application.

When the user connects to the IIS application's home page, they see a list with the names of the product categories in the NWIND database. The user can select a category in the list and click the Show Products button to see the products in the selected category, as shown in Figure 15.8.

FIGURE 15.7:

The selected titles as displayed from within the WebItem's Respond event

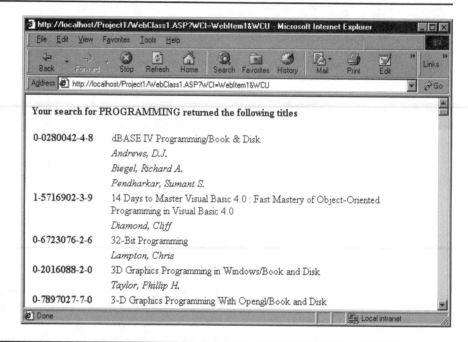

FIGURE 15.8:

The home page of the WCDemo IIS application

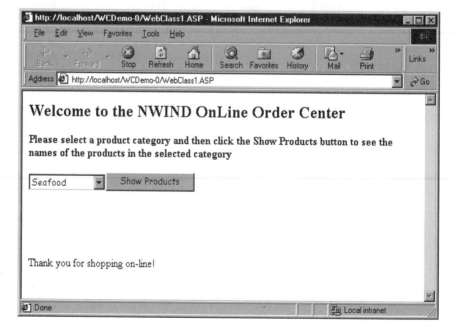

The next window, shown in Figure 15.9, displays the products in the selected category, along with their prices and a check box. To select a product, the user must check the box in front of its name. After the desired products have been selected, the user can click the Order button to submit the order to the server.

FIGURE 15.9:

The Selected Products page

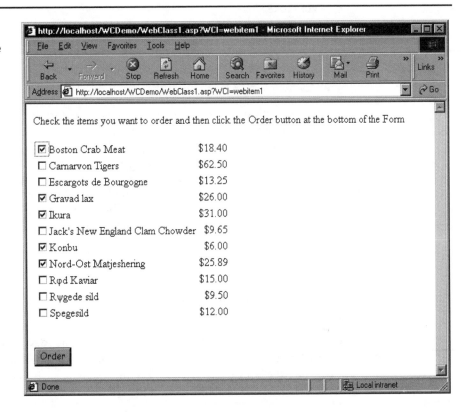

The application on the server confirms the order by displaying a page with the IDs of the selected products. The WCDemo application is incomplete, but once the application that processes the order on the server has the IDs of the selected products, it can update the database, issue invoices, and so on.

The WCDemo application demonstrates the separation of the application's project from its logic. The initial page of the application doesn't contain the list box with the categories. Instead, it contains a specially marked section, which is replaced with the appropriate <SELECT> tag when the page is downloaded. Here's the listing of the HTML page that displays the product categories:

```
<BODY><H2>Welcome to the NWIND OnLine Order Center</H2>
<B>Please select a product category and then click the Show Products
button to see the names of the products in the selected category</B>
```

```
<P>
<WC@OPTIONS>
PLS ENTER AN OPTION CONTROL HERE
<BR>
AND A  SUBMIT BUTTON
</WC@OPTIONS>
<P>
<BR><BR><BR><BR>
Thank you for shopping on-line!
</BODY>
</HTML>
```

Notice the section of the document enclosed by the <WC@OPTIONS> and </WC@OPTIONS> tags. This section of the page will not appear on the browser; the Web author inserts it there as a reminder to a VB developer. The developer must replace these lines with the appropriate tags.

The WCDemo application consists of an HTML Template WebItem (the CategoriesPage) and two custom WebItems. When the application starts, the WebClass_Start event is fired. From within the Start event's handler we must display the CategoriesPage template:

```
Private Sub WebClass_Start()
    'send a Web page to the user
    CategoriesPage.WriteTemplate
End Sub
```

As the CategoriesPage template is read and downloaded to the client computer, the WebClass must replace the specially marked section with the tags that will produce the list of categories. This action must take place in the template's ProcessTag event handler. This event is fired before an HTML template is downloaded to the client.

LISTING 15.5   **The ProcessTag Event Handler**

```
Private Sub CategoriesPage_ProcessTag(ByVal TagName As String, _
    TagContents As String, SendTags As Boolean)
If TagName = "WC@OPTIONS" Then
    TagContents = "<FORM NAME=Frm1 ACTION="" & _
        "WebClass1.asp?WCI=webitem1"" & " METHOD=post>" & vbCrLf
    TagContents = TagContents & "<SELECT NAME=Categories SIZE=1>" & _
        vbCrLf
    TagContents = TagContents & "<OPTION SELECTED VALUE='1'> _
        Beverages</OPTION>" & vbCrLf
```

```
    TagContents = TagContents & _
       "<OPTION SELECTED VALUE='2'>Condiments</OPTION>" & vbCrLf
    TagContents = TagContents & _
       "<OPTION SELECTED VALUE='3'>Confections</OPTION>" & vbCrLf
    TagContents = TagContents & _
       "<OPTION SELECTED VALUE='4'>Dairy Products</OPTION>" & vbCrLf
    TagContents = TagContents & _
       "<OPTION SELECTED VALUE='5'>Grains/Cereals</OPTION>" & vbCrLf
    TagContents = TagContents & _
       "<OPTION SELECTED VALUE='6'>Meat/Poultry</OPTION>" & vbCrLf
    TagContents = TagContents & _
       "<OPTION SELECTED VALUE='7'>Produce</OPTION>" & vbCrLf
    TagContents = TagContents & "<OPTION SELECTED
VALUE='8'>Seafood</OPTION>" & vbCrLf
    TagContents = TagContents & "</SELECT>"
    TagContents = TagContents & "<INPUT TYPE=Submit VALUE="" & _
       "Show Products" & "">" & vbCrLf
    TagContents = TagContents & "</FORM>"
End If
End Sub
```

The code is straightforward. We don't even read the categories from the database (assuming that the categories don't change frequently). This is how you modify HTML templates on the fly. The TagContents argument contains the text that will replace the section of the HTML file enclosed in the <CW@> tags. The template may contain multiple sections to be replaced, as long as they have different names. The Web author, or designer, can add as much content as they like to the page, as long as they know roughly how much space is needed for the display of the categories. Placing a Form with the appropriate controls on the page is the responsibility of the VB developer.

The Form's ACTION attribute is straightforward. It calls the WebItem1 component of the WCDemo.asp application. Right-click the Custom WebItems entry in the Designer's left pane and select Add Custom WebItem. The new WebItem will be named WebItem1.

WebItem1 will be called when the user clicks the Show Products button. Thus, we must program its Respond event to generate another HTML file on the fly. This time we are going to open the NWIND database and retrieve the selected products directly from the database. The code uses the ADO component to open the NWIND database. The same statement would have been used in a VB application to retrieve the Recordset with the desired products. Here's the WebItem1_ Respond event handler:

LISTING 15.6   **The WebItem1_Respond Event Handler**

```
Private Sub WebItem1_Respond()
Dim selectedCategory As Integer
Dim SQLQuery As String
Dim DBConnection As ADODB.Connection
Dim RSProducts As ADODB.Recordset

    selectedCategory = Request.Form("Categories")
    Set DBConnection = Server.CreateObject("ADODB.Connection")
    DBConnection.Open "NWINDDB"
    SQLQuery = "SELECT ProductID, ProductName, UnitPrice " & _
               "FROM Products " WHERE CategoryID=" & _
                  selectedCategory & " ORDER BY ProductName"
    Set RSProducts = DBConnection.Execute(SQLQuery)
    Response.Write "Check the items you want to order and _
                then click the Order button at the bottom of the Form"
    Response.Write "<FORM NAME=ORDERFORM ACTION="" & _
                "WebClass1.asp?WCI=webitem2"" & "METHOD=POST>"
    Response.Write "<TABLE>"
    While Not RSProducts.EOF
       Response.Write "<TR>" & vbCrLf
       Response.Write "<TD><INPUT TYPE=Checkbox NAME=SelProduct _
          VALUE=PROD" & RSProducts.Fields("ProductID") & vbCrLf
       Response.Write "<TD>" & _
                   RSProducts.Fields("ProductName") & _
                   "<TD ALIGN=right>" & _
                   FormatCurrency(RSProducts.Fields("UnitPrice"), 2)
        Response.Write "</TR>"
        RSProducts.MoveNext
    Wend
    Response.Write "</TABLE>" & vbCrLf
    Response.Write "<BR><BR>"
    Response.Write "<INPUT TYPE=SUBMIT VALUE=Order>"
    Response.Write "</FORM>"
    Set RSProducts = Nothing
    Set DBConnection = Nothing
  End Sub
```

The user will select the desired products by checking the boxes in front of the names. To avoid keeping the Recordset open, we store the products' IDs in the page itself. The names of the CheckBox controls are formed by concatenating the string "PROD" and the product's ID. If the product codes were not numeric values, we could have named the CheckBoxes after these IDs. When the Order button on this page is clicked, the names of the selected CheckBoxes will be passed to another component of the server application, which can use them to prepare the order (issue the invoice, update the stock and so on; these operations are not shown in this example).

As you can see in the <FORM> tag, the parameters will be passed to WebItem2. The WebItem2_Respond event handler of the WCDemo application creates another page with the names of the selected product codes. We don't process the data passed back to the server at all, but this is all the information you need in order to process the order. For example, you can store the selected product codes and names to an array, design pages that allow the user to review the selected items (and possibly drop some of them), add products from multiple categories, and finally place the order.

Summary

In the last two chapters you've learned how to build Web applications. The next chapter, which is the last one in this part of the book, discusses the Microsoft Transaction Server. This topic is of interest only to those who plan to develop Web applications, or client applications that will be used in very large networks. MTS maintains a pool of connections, and you will see how you can exploit this feature of MTS to build highly scalable applications.

CHAPTER
SIXTEEN

Microsoft Transaction Server

- Microsoft Transaction Server

- Connection and object pooling

- The ObjectContext object

- Building MTS packages

- Exporting MTS packages

Microsoft Transaction Server is a service that simplifies some of the most difficult tasks of deploying DCOM components in a distributed environment. MTS's functionality is diverse and can be used in just about any distributed application. As far as your VB applications are concerned, you'll be using MTS to manage your objects and connections to the database.

Since we're talking about transactions, let's look at the basic properties of transactions. As you recall from previous chapters, a transaction consists of multiple actions that must take place as a whole: they must all succeed, or fail. It is possible, however, for a transaction to involve only a single action. It sounds odd, but MTS works by monitoring such generic transactions. When an action completes (successfully or otherwise), MTS can release its resources or use them in another process. Every transaction has the following characteristics, which are collectively known as the *ACID requirements*:

Atomicity A transaction is atomic because all its parts must complete successfully. If one of them fails, then all actions in the transaction must also fail. If a transaction can be broken into smaller actions, then we have two (or more) transactions. In other words, if one or more of the actions can fail without leaving the database in an inconsistent state, these actions shouldn't be part of the same transaction.

Consistency A transaction is consistent if it doesn't violate the integrity of the database. Whether the transaction succeeds or fails, it should leave the database in a consistent state. If a transaction fails, it must undo all temporary changes and leave the database in the state it was in before the transaction started.

Isolation A transaction must be isolated from all other actions. A transaction that debits one account and credits another should be totally transparent. When it's done, it must update the database at once. For example, if another user requests the balance of the accounts involved in the transaction, there shouldn't be missing amounts. The transaction must first update both accounts, then make the changes visible to the other applications. This means that the transaction will have to lock certain rows for a few milliseconds.

Durability A transaction must also be durable. If all actions succeed, then it must write the modified data back to the disk. However, it must take into consideration possible media failures. In other words, it's not enough to make sure that the transaction is valid and all changes *can* be committed. The transaction must see that the changes are indeed committed before it completes.

It makes sense, therefore, to treat isolated actions as transactions. If any circumstances prevent the successful completion of the action, then the transaction must be rolled back (or, in MTS's terminology, be *abandoned*).

MTS was initially designed as a distributed transaction coordinator. Sounds complicated, and it is, but this isn't a topic of this book. Distributed transactions are probably the last thing you will do as an (accomplished) programmer. Most of us will never write code to handle distributed transactions, but we will use other features of MTS.

A distributed transaction is a transaction that takes place across multiple databases or servers. When you request that money be transferred from your account to another account in another bank, a distributed transaction must take place. When you withdraw money from another bank's ATM, a distributed transaction must also take place. The bank whose ATM you're using should not record the transaction but fail to notify your bank! If you've ever used your ATM card overseas, you may have noticed that withdrawals may take a few days to be posted to your account. This means that distributed transactions are not being used everywhere they should.

So, a distributed transaction must update at least two, possibly remote, databases. This is quite a task, but to you, the developer, it can be as simple as a local transaction—if you're using MTS, that is.

In addition to being a distributed transaction coordinator, MTS exposes additional functionality, such as object management. This is what we want to use MTS for in this chapter. Let's see what object management can do for your application. Imagine that you've written a Web application that uses a middle tier on the Web server. Thousands of viewers hit your pages daily, or hourly. This may translate into dozens of concurrent connections to the database and dozens of requests for the same object. It's not unlikely that a hundred viewers may call the TitlesSearch component at once. As you can understand, the Web server will be overwhelmed. It will hardly have time to initiate and release instances of the TitlesSearch Class. The database server will be overwhelmed by requests as well, and each request must be serviced by a different connection (provided it runs on a different machine, because if it's running on the same machine as the Web server you should consider shutting down the server). Creating a new Connection object is a resource-intensive operation and should be avoided. So how do we scale up our application?

The solution is to use a pool of objects and connections and reuse them. But this pooling (or *brokering*, as it's sometimes called) of objects is not a trivial task—not even for C++ programmers, and it's certainly beyond VB programmers. So we need a mechanism that will pool connections and objects automatically for us. This mechanism is Microsoft Transaction Server, and this is how we'll use MTS in this chapter—as an object manager. It will do so much for your application, in this capacity alone, that you can ignore its other features.

Using MTS as Object Manager

Fortunately, using MTS as an object manager is quite easy. You'll add a few lines of code to our Classes, set a few properties, and then install the Class to run under MTS. The process isn't quite transparent, but it's as simple as it gets.

To MTS-enable your Classes, you must add a reference to the Microsoft Transaction Server Type Library. Then you must insert a few statements to tell MTS when a transaction starts and when it ends. This is how MTS knows when to assign an existing Connection to your application and when to take it back and use it with another instance of the application. Each transaction is delimited with the methods of the ObjectContext object, which is exposed by the MTS Type Library. Finally, we must set a Class property to tell MTS that the Class can be executed under MTS control. The same property can be set from within the MTS Explorer (I'll show you later how this is done). Making a Class MTS-enabled (or MTS-friendly) is only half the job; you must also tell MTS that the Class must be executed under its control. The second phase doesn't involve any code, but there are a few steps you must follow. There is a wizard that will take you through the process, as you will see in the section "Creating MTS Packages," later in this chapter.

Building MTS Components

As I mentioned earlier, building MTS-enabled components is straightforward, but it requires some extra code. MTS-enabled components make use of two interfaces, the ObjectContext and ObjectControl interfaces. Both interfaces expose methods, which you must use in your code. The ObjectControl interface is optional, and we will not use it in the examples. The ObjectContext interface, however, must be used.

The ObjectContext Interface

The ObjectContext interface maintains context information about an object. This information includes the object's creator, information about the environment in which the object's code is running, transactional information, and so on.

The object's context has nothing to do with its state. When we talk about a component's state, we mean variables that maintain their values between calls. A business object designed to run under MTS must be stateless; this type of object is referred to as MTS-friendly. As mentioned already, the reason for executing objects under MTS control is that we want MTS to take care of reusing them. As soon an object is no longer needed by the application that created it, MTS can use it with another client application (or another instance of the same client application). If you attempt to store state information in a global variable, the component won't crash, but one application's state may be used in another application. The result is an application that can't be debugged.

Always keep in mind that MTS-enabled components are stateless. You can maintain state in the calling application and pass arguments with state information to the methods that need it. (In a VB application, you can use global variables to store state information. In a Web application, you can use cookies, or you can use the Session object to store the values of selected variables.) We want MTS components to be stateless because otherwise MTS can't reuse the component. The application server must maintain the state for every object instantiated by all clients. Imagine a component that maintains a Connection object. If this component is used by a few hundred clients, the application server must maintain one connection per client—and each client will use this connection for a tiny fraction of the component's lifetime.

As far as your VB code goes, the ObjectContext object stores information about the context of the object and exposes the following methods:

CreateInstance   This method creates an MTS object, similar to the CreateObject() function of Visual Basic. The CreateObject() function, however, always creates a new context for the object. MTS-enabled components must be created and released from within a transaction, so they must be created with the CreateInstance method and not with the CreateObject() function.

SetComplete   This method tells MTS that a transaction running under its control has successfully completed. MTS can commit the transaction and then deactivate the object and reuse its resources.

SetAbort   This method tells MTS that a transaction running under its control has completed unsuccessfully. MTS can abort the transaction and then deactivate the object and reuse its resources.

IsInTransaction   This method returns a True/False result based on whether the object is executing within a transaction.

DisableCommit   This method allows you to temporarily disable the commitment of a transaction. The DisableCommit method disables the SetComplete and SetAbort methods. After a call to the DisableCommit method, MTS can reuse the object's resources.

EnableCommit   This method enables the commitment of a transaction. You can reactivate the SetComplete and SetAbort methods with the EnableCommit method.

The ObjectControl Interface

This is another interface, which must be implemented in your VB application with the Implements statement:

```
Implements ObjectControl
```

This object is optional, but if used it adds three more methods to the application:

> **Activate**   This is a placeholder for any code you want to execute when the Class is activated
>
> **Deactivate**   This is a placeholder for any code you want to execute when the Class is deactivated
>
> **CanBePooled**   Set this property to False to prevent the object from being pooled by MTS.

You'll see how these methods are used in developing MTS-enabled components in the examples of the following sections.

MTS-Enabling a Component

Now we can build an MTS-enabled component. You'll start with an existing component, (the TitleSearch component) and MTS-enable it. Then, you'll configure the component to run under MTS. In Chapter 11, you used this component to build a VB client application. The TitleSearch Class works fine with a client application. It establishes a connection to the server and maintains it in the course of its execution. Then we tested the component on a Web page. We showed that it works, but this page shouldn't be deployed on the Internet. Can you imagine what will happen when hundreds or thousands of clients search the database? For every request, the Web server (or the server where the business object is running) will have to establish a new connection to the database.

In this section you'll rewrite the code of the Class so that it can run under MTS. In effect, MTS will create a pool of Connection objects and use the first available one each time a new request is made by a client.

Your first step is to rewrite all members of the Class, so that they will run as transactions. The process is simple: add a few statements at the beginning of each member's code to initiate a context and start an MTS transaction, and a few statements at the end of each member's code to complete, or abort, the transaction. The start and end of the transaction delimit the interval during which the component requires a connection to the database. After the completion of the transaction, the connection can be reused by another component.

Open the Titles project and save it in a different folder. You will find the revised TitleSearch Class in the MTSTitles folder under this chapter's folder on the CD. The first step is to rename the Class, so that it won't clash with the existing one. Rename the Class to MTSTitleSearch. Then add a reference to the component Microsoft Transaction Server Type Library to the project. Select References from the Project menu and check the corresponding component in the Components dialog box, as shown in Figure 16.1. A reference to the MTXAS.DLL will be added to the project, and you can access the MTS services through this component.

FIGURE 16.1:

A MTS-enabled Class must contain a reference to the Microsoft Transaction Server Type Library.

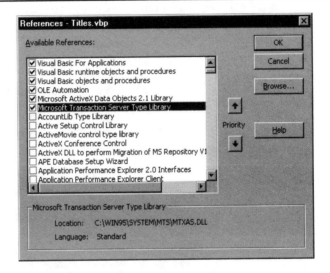

Then open the Properties window of the Class and set its MTSTransactionMode property to 2 (Requires Transaction). This property is new in VB6 ActiveX DLL projects and allows you specify whether and how the Class will run under MTS control. Here are the settings for this property:

0 – NotAnMTSObject   This setting tells VB that the Class is not going to run under MTS control; it's the default setting for the property. All other settings apply to MTS-enabled components.

1 – NoTransactions   This setting tells MTS to run the component without a transaction. Use this setting for components that are called infrequently and do not use a Connection object.

2 – RequiresTransaction   This is the default setting for components written to run under MTS control. It tells MTS that the component must run as a transaction, but not necessarily as a new one. If the calling object has initiated a transaction, then the component will be executed within the same transaction. Obviously, if the inner transaction fails, the outer one will also fail (see the last setting for an alternative setting).

3 – UsesTransaction This setting tells MTS that the component must run under a transaction only if the calling component is in a transaction. If not, then the called component will run without a transaction

4 – RequiresNewTransaction This setting tells MTS that the component must be executed from within a new transaction, even if the client application that created the object is already in a transaction. This will prevent an inner transaction from affecting the success of an outer transaction. If you use this setting routinely, you'll offset the benefit of MTS's object brokerage and connection pooling capabilities.

The Project's Properties

This is a good point to review the project's properties and make sure you've set them correctly. Select the Class in the Project window, open the Project menu, and select Project Properties. The window shown in Figure 16.2 will appear on your screen.

FIGURE 16.2:

The Project Properties for an MTS-enabled component

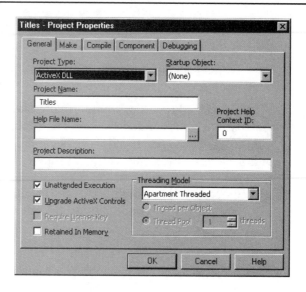

The project's type must be ActiveX DLL. Any component that must be executed under MTS must be implemented as a DLL. You know that all components that are not executed in the same memory space as the client application must be

implemented as ActiveX EXE servers, but MTS is a totally different story. (Actually, MTS uses an EXE that allows DLLs to run in a different memory space from your application).

The Threading Model of the component must be Apartment Threaded. With this model, each member of the component is executed on its own thread. Therefore, you can have multiple instances of the same component running at once without interfering with each other.

The Unattended Execution option tells Visual Basic that your component won't attempt to interact with the user (by displaying message boxes, for example). Even if your code attempts to interact with the user, VB will suppress the corresponding statements, if the Unattended Execution option is checked. The component will be executed on a server, which is attended only in the case of hardware failures.

Then switch to the Component tab of the Project Properties Pages and check the Binary Compatibility option. This is the safest compatibility setting. If the Class's interface hasn't changed—that is, if you haven't added a new member or the arguments of a method, but only the implementation of the method—VB won't generate a new GUID for the component. The GUID is a long string by which the component is known to the rest of the system, and it's stored in the Registry when you register a component.

The No Compatibility setting creates a new GUID every time you compile the Class. This means no backward compatibility of the existing projects that use the component. You must open them, remove the reference to the old component, and add a reference to the new component.

The Project Compatibility setting is the default selection and maintains compatibility during the testing and debugging of the component.

Changing the Class's Code

First, you must get rid of the Connection object that's created when the Class is initiated and released when the Class is terminated. With MTS, connections should be used briefly and then released so that they can be reused by other applications. In traditional client/server applications, we connect as early as possible and release the connection as late as possible (that is, we maintain a single connection throughout the session). But MTS-enabled components should create a connection as late as possible and release them as early as possible, so you must remove the statements that create a global connection. Instead, establish a connection just before you need it and release it as soon as you execute a command and retrieve the results (if any).

Start by removing the Form declarations and the Initialize and Terminate event handlers from the project. Here are the statements you must remove:

```
Dim ADOConn As New adodb.Connection
Dim ADOCommand As New adodb.Command
Dim ADOResult As New adodb.Recordset
```

```
Private Sub Class_Initialize()
    ADOConn.ConnectionString = _
        "Provider=Microsoft.Jet.OLEDB.4.0; " & _
        "Persist Security Info=False; " & _
        "Data Source=C:\Program Files\VB98\Biblio.mdb"
    ADOConn.Open
End Sub

Private Sub Class_Terminate()
    ADOConn.Close
    Set ADOConn = Nothing
    Set ADOResult = Nothing
End Sub
```

Then locate the lines that execute a command against the database and insert the following lines to establish a connection to the database:

```
ADOConn.ConnectionString = _
        "Provider=Microsoft.Jet.OLEDB.4.0; " & _
        "Persist Security Info=False; " & _
        "Data Source=C:\Program Files\VB98\Biblio.mdb"
ADOConn.Open
```

Repeat this step for every statement that executes a command against the database. The connection must be released after the command's execution with the following statement:

```
Set ADOConn = Nothing
```

So far, you've edited the code so that connections are created as late as possible and released as early as possible.

Next, you must initiate each member as a transaction. You must tell MTS to start a transaction at the beginning of the function's code and terminate it before exiting the function. Insert the following lines at the beginning of the code:

```
Dim oContext As ObjectContext
On Error GoTo ContextError
Set oContext = GetObjectContext()
```

The GetObjectContext() method initiates an MTS transaction, which must be terminated with one of the SetComplete/SetAbort methods.

The ContextError error handler must abort the transaction with the following statements:

```
ContextError:
    oContext.SetAbort
    Err.Raise Err.Number, "GetTitle", Err.Description
```

The transaction ends with the SetAbort method. It's not necessary to raise errors, but it's a good practice to pass error information to the client with the Err.Raise method.

You're almost done. The last step is to terminate the transaction successfully. After the execution of the SQL statement that retrieves the desired titles, enter the following statements to terminate the transaction and release the Connection and Recordset objects:

```
oContext.SetComplete
ADOConn.Close
Set ADOConn = Nothing
```

What you've done so far was insert a few lines at the beginning and the end of the function's code to make the member MTS-enabled. You must do the same for all the members of the Class. Here's the complete listing of the TitleSearch Class:

LISTING 16.1   The TitleSearch Class as an MTS-Enabled Component

```
Public Function GetTitles(searchArgument As String, _
                searchMode As Integer) As Variant
Dim SQLStatement As String

Dim oContext As ObjectContext
On Error GoTo ContextError
Set oContext = GetObjectContext()

    SQLStatement = MakeSQLStatement(searchArgument, searchMode)
    Set GetTitles = ExecuteSQLStatement(SQLStatement)
    oContext.SetComplete
    Exit Function
ContextError:
    Err.Raise Err.Number, "GetBook", Err.Description
    If Not oContext Is Nothing Then oContext.SetAbort
End Function
```

```
Public Function GetBook(ISBN As String) As adodb.Recordset
Dim oContext As ObjectContext
Set oContext = GetObjectContext()

On Error GoTo ContextError

    SQLcmd = "SELECT * FROM Titles WHERE ISBN = '" & ISBN & "'"
    ADOConn.ConnectionString = _
            "Provider=Microsoft.Jet.OLEDB.4.0; " & _
            "Persist Security Info=False; " & _
            "Data Source=C:\Program Files\VB98\Biblio.mdb"
    ADOConn.Open
    ADOResult.CursorType = adOpenStatic
    ADOResult.CursorLocation = adUseClient
    Set ADOResult = ADOConn.Execute(SQLcmd)
    Set GetBook = ADOResult
    oContext.SetComplete
    On Error Goto 0
    ADOConn.Close
    Set ADOResult = Nothing
    Set ADOConn = Nothing
    Exit Function
ContextError:
    Err.Raise Err.Number, "GetBook", Err.Description
    If Not oContext Is Nothing Then oContext.SetAbort
End Function
```

Notice the If statement in the error handlers. This statement makes sure the oContext object was successfully created, before it attempts to call any of its methods.

The function MakeSQLStatement need not be changed. This function is private to the GetTitles function and can't be called from client applications. The ExecuteSQLStatement is MTS-enabled however, even though it's private to the Class. The reason is that ExecuteSQLStatement uses a Connection object, which will come from MTS's pool of connections.

Create the new DLL (File ➤ Make Titles.dll). VB will register the component on the local computer. As you will see, we are going to register the new custom component under MTS, so you must unregister the component on the local computer. Before running the test project, or calling the members of the new custom component from within a Web page, you must tell Microsoft Transaction Server that there's a new component to be executed under its control.

Creating MTS Packages

The last step before deploying the MTS-enabled component is to install it under MTS, so that each time an application needs an instance of the component, MTS will use an existing instance if one exists. To deploy a component under MTS, you must create an MTS package, which is a group of components that run in the same process and form a single unit. Any component that runs under MTS must belong to a package. This is how MTS can administer the components, monitor transactions, and pool objects. Let's create an MTS package for the Titles component.

Start Transaction Server Explorer. In the first window, you will see a list of all the servers on your network. Select the local server and double-click its icon. The next window contains several icons, one of them being the Packages Installed folder. If you open the Packages Installed folder now, you'll see the sample packages already installed, as shown in Figure 16.3.

FIGURE 16.3:

The Transaction Server Explorer, showing the installed packages

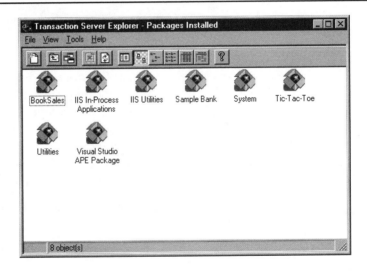

This folder contains all the packages already installed on the selected computer. We must add a new package for the new component we just developed (the revised Titles component). Right-click somewhere on the window and, from the shortcut menu, select New (or select the New command from the File menu).

The New command will start the Package Wizard, which will take you through the steps of installing the new package. The first window (Figure 16.4) provides two large buttons, one for installing a pre-built package and another one for creating a new package.

FIGURE 16.4:

The first window of the MTS Package Wizard

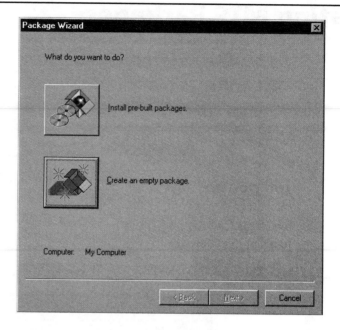

The first button installs a package that has already been installed. We'll use this option later to move the package to the production machine. The first time you create a new object, click the button Create an Empty Package and you will see the Create Empty Package window, where you must supply a name for the package. Let's call the new package TITLES. Enter the package's name and click Finish to create the new, empty, package. When you return to the MTS Explorer window, you will see that the TITLES package has been added to the list of installed packages.

The Wizard will add a key for the TITLES package to the Registry (Figure 16.5). The path of the new key is

```
My Computer\HKEY_LOCAL_MACHINE\Software\Microsoft\
Transaction Server\Packages
```

Now you must set the properties of the empty package—basically, you must add one or more components to the package. When you add a component to an MTS package, the Registry entry for this component is modified, so that any calls to the specific component will be routed through MTS. Your applications will be able to call the members of these components, but MTS will intercept the calls and run them in the context of a transaction. In other words, this step will make the whole process of connection pooling transparent to the application that calls the component.

FIGURE 16.5:

The new package's entry in the Registry

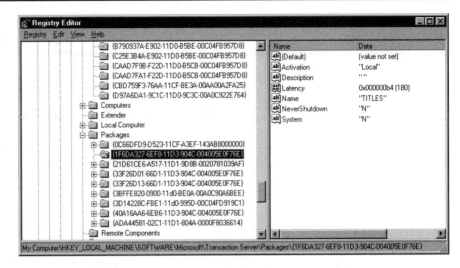

Setting the Properties of a Package

In the MTS Explorer window, right-click the TITLES package and, from the shortcut menu, select Properties. The Properties Pages of the package consist of three tabs:

The General Tab

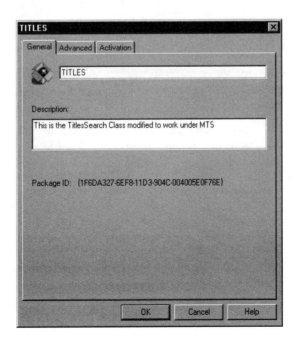

This is where you can change the name of the package and enter a short description. The package's GUID is also displayed on this page (this is the ID inserted into the Registry by MTS's Package Wizard).

The Advanced Tab

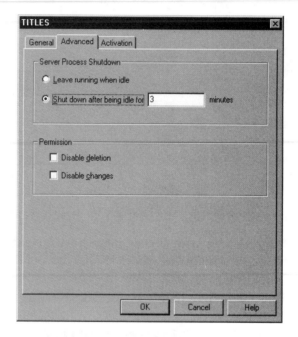

This tab contains the settings of two properties:

> **Server Process Shutdown Property**   This option allows you to leave the component (server process) running while no one is accessing a component, or force it to shut down after a specified interval. By default, MTS will shut down the component if it's been idle for more than 3 minutes. If MTS needs the component's resources, it should be able to deactivate it immediately.
>
> Leave the default value of 3 minutes, unless the component is only used occasionally, in which case you should make it even shorter. If a component is accessed by many client applications, all the time, check the option "Leave running when idle."
>
> **Permission Property**   This property allows you to protect components in the MTS environment. Check the Disable deletion option to prevent anyone from removing components from the MTS. You can also prevent the editing of components by checking the Disable changes option.

These settings have nothing to do with user privileges and how users will be accessing components; they are meant to protect components from accidental removal. Even then, you can add components to the package.

The Activation Tab

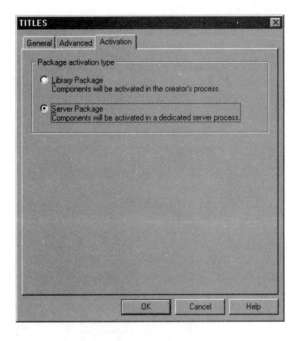

MTS components can be activated in two methods:

Library Package   A Library package runs in the memory space of the client application that created it. As you can understand, this method can't be used with Web applications. For example, you can't use roles with this method.

Server Package   This is the default method and you shouldn't change this setting. The package runs in its own process on the server (the computer on which it was installed). When a component runs out-of-process, it must be implemented as an ActiveX EXE. This is how VB works, not an MTS requirement. MTS, however, requires that the component be packaged as an ActiveX DLL (and as far as I know, this is the only situation where an ActiveX DLL is executed out-of-process). The component runs under the control of MTS, so it makes sense to think of it as running in the process of the MTS.

Adding Components to a Package

It's now time to add the MTSSearchTitles component to the package. Double-click the icon of the TITLES package and you will see its Components folder on the MTS Explorer window. Open the Components folder by double-clicking its icon. You will see an empty window, which normally contains all the installed components. Right-click somewhere on this window, select New from the shortcut menu (or select the File ➤ New command), and you will see the first window of the Component Wizard.

FIGURE 16.6:

The Component Wizard's initial window

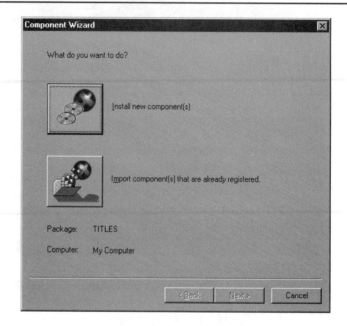

The first button, "Install new component(s)," is used to add components that have not been registered on the local machine—that is, components that do not exist in a package. If you haven't registered the TITLES.DLL yet, use this button. The other option applies to components that have already been registered in the local machine's Registry. If you have processed the TITLES.DLL component with the REGSRV32 utility, click the button "Install component(s) that are already registered."

Click the top button on the Component Wizard window and you will see the Install Components window. Here, at last, you can add components to the TITLES package. Click the Add Files button and a File Open dialog box will prompt you to select the folder where the desired DLL(s) reside. Most users have a single folder where they place their components. Assuming you have created the TITLES.DLL component in the COMponents folder, navigate to this folder and double-click that file. The path of the selected component will be added in the upper list and the name of the component in the DLL file will be added to the lower list, as shown in Figure 16.7. Click Finish to close the wizard and add the component to the TITLES Package.

FIGURE 16.7:

The Install Components window of the MTS Components Wizard

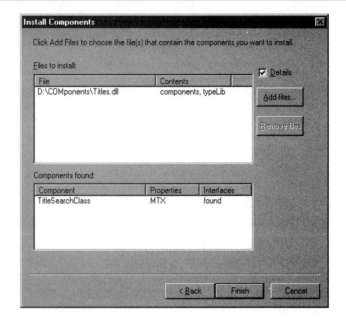

When you return to the MTS Explorer window, you will see the icon of the new component. The Titles.TitleSearchClass icon will appear in the Components folder under the component's name. Just double-click the icon of the Class and then double-click the Components icon. You will see the interfaces folder; double-click again and you'll see the Class's interface, whose name is _TitleSearchClass. Double-click this icon and this time you'll see a folder named Methods. If the component exposed properties, there would be a Properties folder as well. Double-click the Methods folder and you'll see, as in Figure 16.8, the names of the methods exposed by the custom component.

The two methods we're interested in are the GetTitles and GetBook methods. These are the two methods you've implemented in the Class. The other methods are used by MTS to create and release instances of the Class. The QueryInterface method, for example, contains all the information needed by MTS to query the members of the Class and make sure the client application calls the Class's methods with their proper names and passes the correct arguments. VB programmers don't need the additional members, and you can safely ignore them.

FIGURE 16.8:

The TitleSearchClass component's methods

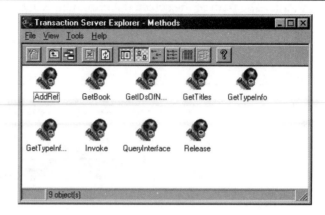

Exporting MTS Packages

You have created a new MTS package for your custom component, most likely in
the same machine as the one you used to develop the Class. The package will be
deployed on another computer, so you must export the package you created to a
production server. Right-click the new package and select Export in the shortcut
menu. In the following prompt, select the PAK file. The wizard will create a PAK
file, which you must copy to the production server. On the production server, you
must install a new package, only this time you'll specify that you're installing a
prebuilt package. Locate the PAK file you exported and MTS will create a new
package on the production server.

For Web applications, the production server is usually the Web server. The ASP
scripts that call the component are executed on this machine. If you want to deploy
the application to a LAN, you must do one more thing: You must register the DLL
you have already installed under MTS. If not, VB won't be able to locate the
component, because it's not registered. When your VB application calls the Create-
Object method, the local machine should access the component on the application
server. What you need is an entry in the local Registry telling Windows that the
component must be accessed via DCOM. To register the remote component to a
workstation, you must run an executable file that has the same name as the PAK
file and resides in the same folder. This will configure the local workstation to
access a component that runs under MTS via DCOM.

Summary

In this chapter you were introduced to the Microsoft Transaction Server, which is useful for developing Web applications, or client applications for very large networks. The final two chapters provide worked examples of the concepts covered throughout this book. There are no new objects to learn, or new concepts to master. The applications, however, are non-trivial; they're quite lengthy. This is the reason we've decided to present them at the end of the book, so that they wouldn't interrupt the flow of the text. You have probably read Chapter 17 after you were through the first part of the book, but if you haven't done so, this is a good time to explore a few 'real-world' applications. Chapter 18 is an online bookstore and demonstrates how to contact databases through Web pages.

PART IV

Putting Your Knowledge to Work

CHAPTER

SEVENTEEN

Building an Invoicing Application

- A data-entry application

- An invoicing application (ADO only)

- An invoicing application (ADO + stored procedures)

So far you've learned just about every property and method of the ADO objects. You've seen quite a few examples, but they were all rather short, meant to demonstrate a single topic. It's time now to look at two fairly complicated projects that manipulate several tables in a database. The projects are not really complicated, but they are quite practical and represent some of the most common types of database applications you will have to develop: elaborate user interfaces to browse and edit multiple linked tables and transactional processing.

The first example, DataEntryDemo, demonstrates how to edit the titles of the Biblio database. This is not a simple application, like an application that edits customers, because each title has a publisher and multiple authors. This is a typical data-entry and browsing application that manipulates multiple tables at once. Another important aspect of this application is the user interface. The navigational methods of the ADO Recordset object are severely limited, and you must come up with a design that's both simple and functional. The DataEntryDemo application demonstrates a flexible technique for retrieving a small number of rows from the database at a time. You could probably download all the rows of the Titles table to the client, but if the database grows from 8,000 titles to 800,000 titles, this is no longer an option.

The second example, Invoices, demonstrates how to issue invoices. This application poses two problems: First, invoices involve updates in multiple tables, and these updates must be implemented as transactions. You can't add a new row in the Orders table without adding the detail lines to the Order Details table. Moreover, the design of the application poses an interesting problem. Its user interface must be extremely simple. Invoicing is a sensitive operation and shouldn't rely on special actions by the user.

The DataEntryDemo Project

The first project is an application for browsing and editing the titles of the Biblio database. The main purpose of this project is to demonstrate how to manipulate multiple related tables as well as some flexible navigational techniques. Each title's information is stored in several tables, and you will see how to connect all these tables. You have already seen how to connect titles and publishers, but the link between titles and authors is a bit more complicated. It involves an intermediate table, the Title Author table, as you recall from the discussion of the Biblio database. This table was introduced to resolve the many-to-many relationship between titles and authors. If you are not familiar with the structure of this database, this is a good point to review it by once again examining its relational diagram (Figure 17.1).

FIGURE 17.1:

The relational diagram of the Biblio database

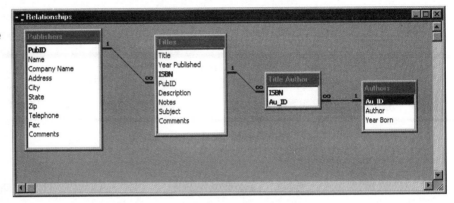

Editing the authors of a title entails changes in the Authors and Title Author tables. This will complicate the code a little, but before you start thinking about the code, there's another issue you must deal with—namely, when the related tables will be changed. The user may remove an author and add two new authors to an existing title. The application should not update any tables while the row is being edited, because the user might cancel the operation. You should store the information about the new authors in some variables and commit it to the database only if the user signals his intention to commit the changes by clicking an OK button.

The DataEntry project uses the Access version of the Biblio database. If you have ported the Biblio database to SQL Server, then the same code will work with the SQL Server version of the database. The program uses ADO Data Controls to store the Recordsets required for its operation. It makes extensive use of data-bound and data-aware controls, as well as client-side cursors. A major goal in the design of the application was the minimization of information that must be moved from the server to the client. The sure method to minimize the size of the client-cursors is to force users select the title they want to view with their ISBN. ISBNs are unique, so you'll be able to retrieve one title at a time from the database—a very convenient approach for programmers, but the least-convenient interface for the user. Users should also be able to locate the desired book(s) by title, and you will see how this is done in the following section.

Flexible Navigational Techniques

Let's start with a discussion of the navigational techniques. Some of you may have better ideas in mind, but I'm sure you won't object to the ones described here. Most users would locate titles either with the book's ISBN or its title. ISBNs are unique. When an ISBN is entered in the appropriate TextBox on the Form and the user presses the Enter key, the program will either locate the book and display its fields on the Form, or prompt the user to enter a new title.

Locating records by title is a bit more complicated. Titles are not unique. Two books may have the exact same title, or they may differ in the last few characters of the title (the book's edition, for example). Moreover, you shouldn't force users to enter the entire title. The program should locate all the titles that match the partial title description entered in the title's TextBox control. These titles can be displayed on a DataList control, as shown in Figure 17.2, where users will locate a title with their mouse or the arrow keys. Once a title is selected in this list, the corresponding record's fields will appear on the Form's data-bound controls and the list of books will disappear, as shown in Figure 17.3.

FIGURE 17.2:

The list of titles that match the beginning of the title entered in the Title box

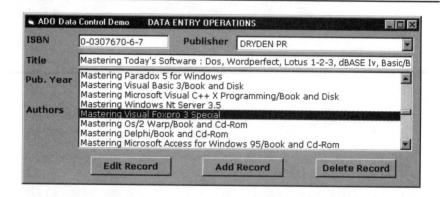

FIGURE 17.3:

Once a title has been selected, the list of partial matches retracts and the selected title's fields are displayed on the Form.

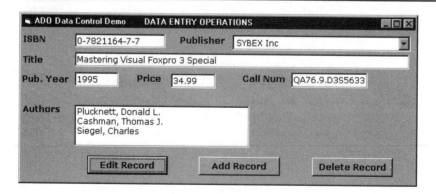

NOTE

The program requires that the partial description of the title consists of the first few words in the title. In other words, you can't enter keywords and expect the application to locate any title that contains them. It's not difficult to modify the code and perform more complicated searches, but keep in mind that this program will be used by data-entry operators, and not by customers. The operators of the application maintain the database; they don't browse it. In other words, they're looking for specific titles, not for titles on "programming" or "cooking."

Let's outline the basic operations of the application and the code to implement them. You will find step-by-step instructions in later sections, but it's important to know where you want to arrive before you start writing.

1. You need three ADO Data Controls on your Form: one for titles (the SelTitles data control), one for publishers (the Publishers data control), and one for authors (the Authors data control). The SelTitles data control will be used for storing the selected titles (the titles that match the partial description of the title) and not the entire Titles table.

2. You also need some data-bound controls to display the current record's fields. Most fields will be mapped to TextBox controls, with the exception of the publisher. You're going to display a list of publishers in a DataCombo control, so that the user can select a publisher with the mouse.

3. The authors of the current title will be displayed on a ListBox control. This control is populated with the title's authors each time you move to another row.

The ADO Data Controls on the Form will be invisible. You don't want the user to navigate though the titles with the data controls; instead, you want the application to be in control. You'll provide two navigation methods:

By ISBN   When the user enters an ISBN in the appropriate TextBox and then presses Enter, the application will locate the title (it's guaranteed to be a unique title) and display its fields. If the ISBN isn't found, then a new record is created and the user must supply values for the fields.

By Title   When the user enters a title in the appropriate TextBox and then presses Enter, the application will locate all the titles that match the description with a LIKE operator:

```
WHERE Title LIKE txtTitle.Text & "%"
```

Chances are that this operation will retrieve more than one title. The titles will be displayed on a ListBox control, where the user can select one with the mouse. Once the desired record has been selected, the ListBox control with the titles will become invisible. The selected title's fields will appear on the various controls, where they can be edited.

Now comes a very important aspect of the application's user interface. The controls on the Form will be locked, so that users can't edit them by mistake. Data-bound controls appear very convenient at the beginning, but once you start using them to build real-world applications, you'll discover their shortcomings. Data-entry operators want to know when they're just viewing a row and when they're editing it, so your application should have an Edit button to signal the user's intention to edit the current record. You shouldn't let users edit fields any time they see a record. Unless the user has indicated his or her intention to edit a field, the data-bound controls on the Form should remain locked. Likewise, while a title is being edited, you must disable the navigational buttons on the Form. Unless a user explicitly accepts or rejects the changes, they shouldn't be allowed to move to another row.

Besides retrieving records by ISBN or Title, the user can add new records or delete existing ones. Provide two buttons, Add New and Delete, that must be clicked to signal the user's intention to the application. To add a new record, you must call the AddNew method; to complete the addition of a new record, you must call the Update method. Although the changes will be committed to the database as soon as the user moves to another record, you'll prohibit navigation during editing of an existing or new record. To do so, you'll hide the usual editing buttons and display an OK and a Cancel button. When the OK button is clicked, changes must be committed to the database with the Update method. When the Cancel button is clicked, the current record must be restored to its original status with the CancelUpdate method.

Let's start by designing the Form. Later on you'll implement the details discussed here by inserting the appropriate code.

Designing the Form

The design of the DataEntryDemo application's main Form is straightforward. Most of the fields displayed on the Form are mapped to data-bound TextBox controls, and they "see" the database through the appropriate ADO Data Controls. You can see only one table through a data control, so you must place three of them on the Form: one for titles, another for publishers, and a third for authors. The properties of the ADO Data Controls must be set as follows:

Control Name	CursorLocation	CursorType
SelTitles	adUseClient	adOpenStatic
Publishers	adUseClient	adOpenStatic
Authors	adUseClient	adOpenStatic

The ConnectionString property for all three controls is the same:

```
Provider=Microsoft.Jet.OLEDB.4.0; _
    Data Source=C:\Program Files\VB98\Biblio.mdb
```

As you can see, all ADO Data Controls represent static, client-server cursors, so it's imperative to keep the size of their cursors as small as possible. There's nothing you can do about the Publishers cursor, because you need all the publisher names to populate the AllPublishers DataCombo control. However, the Recordsets of the other two controls should store a small number of rows.

The Publisher ADO Data Control's RecordSource property is the following SQL statement (it retrieves the IDs and names of all publishers):

```
SELECT [Company Name], PubID FROM Publishers
ORDER BY [Company Name]
```

The SelTitles ADO Data Control is populated at run time with an SQL statement that retrieves the titles that match the partial description entered by the user in the Title TextBox control on the Form. The titles are needed to populate a DataList control on the Form, so they must be moved to the client. The more specific that users can be about the desired title, the fewer partial matches there will be and the fewer rows will be moved to the client.

The Authors ADO Data Control's RecordSource property is also set at run time with an SQL statement that retrieves the names of the authors of the selected title:

```
SELECT Author FROM Authors, [Title Author]
WHERE Authors.Au_ID = [Title Author].Au_ID AND
      [Title Author].ISBN= currentISBN
```

currentISBN is a variable that holds the current title's ISBN.

Next, place all the Label controls that hold the field names and the TextBox controls that hold the field values. Use a DataCombo control for the publishers (the AllPublishers control) and set its properties as follows:

Property	Setting
RowSource	Publishers (the name of the ADO Data Control)
ListField	Company Name
DataSource	SelTitles
DataField	PubID
BoundColumn	PubID

The DataCombo control displays the names of the publishers, and it's bound to the SelTitles control's Recordset. When the current row in this Recordset changes, the selected title's publisher is displayed on the DataCombo control.

Programming the Controls

Let's start by looking at the KeyPress event handler of the txtTitle TextBox, which displays the book's title. When the Enter key is pressed, the program retrieves all rows from the Titles table that start with the specified string. It picks up the TextBox control's string, uses it to build the appropriate SQL statement, and uses the resulting Recordset to populate the DataList control, as shown in the following listing.

LISTING 17.1   **Retrieving Partial Matches**

```
Private Sub txtTitle_KeyPress(KeyAscii As Integer)
    If bttnOK.Visible Then Exit Sub
    If KeyAscii = vbKeyReturn Then
        SelTitles.RecordSource = _
                        "SELECT * FROM Titles WHERE " & _
                        "Title LIKE '" & Trim(txtTitle.Text) & "%'"
        SelTitles.Refresh
        RefreshAuthors
        If SelTitles.Recordset.RecordCount = 0 Then
            reply = _
                MsgBox("Did not find the requested title." & _
                        "Add it?", vbYesNo)
            If reply = vbYes Then
                HideEditButtons
                UnlockFields
                SelTitles.Recordset.AddNew
            Else
                SelTitles.RecordSource = _
                            "SELECT * FROM Titles " & _
                            WHERE ISBN='" & lastISBN & "'"
                SelTitles.Refresh
            End If
        ElseIf SelTitles.Recordset.RecordCount > 1 Then
            DataList2.ListField = "Title"
            DataList2.Visible = True
            DataList2.SetFocus
        End If
        KeyAscii = 0
    End If
End Sub
```

If the program is in the midst of adding or editing a row, it exits immediately (the Enter key is not used in entering a title). If the program is not in edit mode, the code populates the SelTitles ADO Data Control with the titles that start with the characters already in the txtTitle control. The control is populated by setting its RecordSource property to the appropriate SQL statement. This is a client-side Recordset (it's needed to populated a DataList control), so you can examine its Record-Count property. If the SelTitles object's cursor contains exactly one record, you need not populate, or even display, the DataList control. The selected title's fields are displayed on the Form automatically, because they're bound to the database through the SelTitles control.

If the SELECT statement retrieves more than one row, you must populate the DataList control and then make it visible. Also, you must set the Focus to the

DataList control, so that the user can select a title with the arrow keys. (I haven't included any code to prevent the user from clicking any of the buttons, but you may wish to do so.)

To select a title, the user must either press Enter or double-click an item on the list. In either case, the code calls the SelectTitle subroutine, which displays the fields of the selected title and hides the list with the titles.

LISTING 17.2   Selecting a Title on the DataList Control

```
Sub SelectTitle()
    If IsNull(DataList2.SelectedItem) Then
        Beep
        Exit Sub
    End If
    SelTitles.Recordset.Bookmark = DataList2.SelectedItem
    RefreshAuthors
    DataList2.Visible = False
End Sub
```

Notice that the selected title becomes the current row of the SelTitles control's cursor. Don't change the control's Recordset, because this would require another trip to the server. If you don't change the current row (and we won't), it's quite indifferent whether the control's cursor contains other rows in addition to the selected one.

A similar process takes place when the user presses Enter while the txtISBN TextBox has the focus. When a title is selected by its ISBN, though, the application will either locate the desired title or establish that the title does not exist and prepare the Form for the addition of a new row. If you think it makes sense to search with a partial ISBN, then modify the code accordingly (use the code of Listings 17.1 and 17.2 as a guide).

All data-bound controls on the Form are bound to the corresponding field in the database through the SelTitles controls, so you need not set them explicitly. They'll be set as soon as the current row changes. The authors, however, are displayed on a ListBox control, which won't be automatically updated. You have to populate it with the RefreshAuthors subroutine, which is shown next:

LISTING 17.3   Retrieving a Title's Author Names

```
Public Sub RefreshAuthors()
    Authors.RecordSource = _
            "SELECT Author, Authors.Au_ID FROM Authors, " & _
            "[Title Author] WHERE " & _
            "Authors.Au_ID=[Title Author].Au_ID AND " & _
            "[Title Author].ISBN='" & _
            SelTitles.Recordset.Fields("ISBN") & "'"
```

```
        Authors.Refresh
        AuthorList.Clear
        tmpAuthorList.Clear
        While Not Authors.Recordset.EOF
            AuthorList.AddItem Authors.Recordset.Fields("Author")
            AuthorList.ItemData(AuthorList.NewIndex) = _
                            Authors.Recordset.Fields("Au_ID")
            tmpAuthorList.AddItem Authors.Recordset.Fields("Author")
            tmpAuthorList.ItemData(tmpAuthorList.NewIndex) = _
                            Authors.Recordset.Fields("Au_ID")
            Authors.Recordset.MoveNext
        Wend
    End Sub
```

This long statement retrieves the names of the current title's authors in the Authors control's cursor. This cursor is used to populate the ListBox control with the authors' names.

As you can see, the code populates another ListBox control, the tmpAuthorList control. The tmpAuthorList holds the author names as they were read from the database, in case the user decides to cancel the edit operation after they have added or removed one or more authors. If the user clicks the Cancel button, the contents of the tmpAuthorList control are copied to the AuthorList control.

Editing the Current Title

To edit the current row on the Form, the user must click the Edit Record button. As you know by now, you must hide the usual editing buttons, display the OK and Cancel buttons (so that the user can end the editing process), and unlock the controls on the Form. If the EOF property is True, it means there's no row to be edited and the program aborts the operation. Here's the code behind the Edit Record button.

LISTING 17.4   Preparing to Edit a Row

```
    Private Sub bttnEdit_Click()
        If SelTitles.Recordset.EOF Then
            MsgBox "Please select a title to edit!"
            Exit Sub
        End If
        HideEditButtons
        UnlockFields
    End Sub
```

The code behind the Add Record button is quite similar. It calls the HideEdit-Buttons and UnlockFields subroutines, but it also calls the AddNew method of the SelTitles.Recordset object to append a new blank row. Here's the code of the Add Record button's Click event:

LISTING 17.5   **Preparing to Add a Row**

```
Private Sub bttnAdd_Click()
    HideEditButtons
    ClearFields
    UnlockFields
    SelTitles.Recordset.AddNew
End Sub
```

The editing process can be terminated with the OK button, which commits the changes to the database, or the Cancel button, which restores the original field values (if editing) or aborts the addition of a new record (if adding). The canceling operation is simpler. You call the CancelUpdate method to abort the changes (or the addition of the new row), then read the original values from the cursor by calling the Resync method. The Resync method reads the current values of the row from the database. To display the new field values, you must set one of the data-binding properties of the controls on the Form.

The user may have canceled the addition of a new row, and in this case the Resync method will fail, because there's no underlying row. To avoid this runtime error, we test the EOF property of the SelTitles Recordset. If the user has canceled the addition of a new row, the Recordset's EOF property will be set to True. If the user has canceled the addition of a new row, we simply clear the fields on the Form and then display the usual editing buttons.

LISTING 17.6   **Canceling an Edit Operation**

```
Private Sub bttnCancel_Click()
    SelTitles.Recordset.CancelUpdate
    If SelTitles.Recordset.EOF Then ' User has canceled
                                    ' the addition of a new row
        ClearFields
    Else                            ' User has canceled the
                                    ' editing of an existing row
        SelTitles.Recordset.Resync adAffectCurrent
        RebindControls
        AllPublishers.BoundText = _
                SelTitles.Recordset.Fields("PubID")
        RefreshAuthors
    End If
    ShowEditButtons
    LockFields
End Sub
```

To commit the changes, call the Update method. First, the code validates the ISBN and Title fields. (You should probably add some more validation code for the publication year and the price.) Then, it removes the title's original authors by removing the corresponding rows from the Title Author table. Once the original authors are removed, the code updates the current row and adds the new authors with the UpdateAuthors subroutine. The UpdateAuthors subroutine adds the appropriate ISBN/AuthorID pairs in the Title Author table. Here's the code of the OK button:

LISTING 17.7   **Committing the Changes to the Database**

```
Private Sub bttnOK_Click()
Dim bkISBN As String

    If txtISBN.Text = "" Then
        MsgBox "Can't add a book without a valid ISBN"
        Exit Sub
    End If
    If txtTitle.Text = "" Then
        MsgBox "Can't add a book without title"
        Exit Sub
    End If

    bkISBN = SelTitles.Recordset.Fields("ISBN")
    Authors.RecordSource = _
            "SELECT * FROM [Title Author] WHERE ISBN='" & _
            bkISBN & "'"
    Authors.Refresh
    While Not Authors.Recordset.EOF
        Authors.Recordset.Delete adAffectCurrent
        Authors.Recordset.Update
        Authors.Recordset.MoveNext
    Wend
    SelTitles.Recordset.Fields("PubID") = AllPublishers.BoundText
    On Error GoTo UpdateError
    SelTitles.Recordset.Update
    On Error Goto AuthorUpdateError
    bkISBN = SelTitles.Recordset.Fields("ISBN")
    UpdateAuthors bkISBN
ExitHere:
    ShowEditButtons
    LockFields
    Exit Sub
UpdateError:
    SelTitles.Recordset.CancelUpdate
    SelTitles.Recordset.Resync adAffectCurrent
    MsgBox "An error occurred during update. " & _
            " Please make sure your data are valid for each field"
    RebindControls
```

```
        RefreshAuthors
        GoTo ExitHere
    AuthorUpdateError:
        Authors.Recordset.CancelUpdate
        MsgBox "An error occurred while updating the title's authors"
        RebindControls
        RefreshAuthors
        GoTo ExitHere
    End Sub
```

Notice the error handlers of this procedure. We must notify the user as to what went wrong, and there are two possible operations that might fail: the update of the Titles table, or the addition of the new authors. These operations could have been implemented as a transaction, so that we'll never end up with an incomplete title. A transaction is not really a requirement in this application. You'll see how to implement transactions in the next example.

To delete the current row, call the Recordset object's Delete method:

LISTING 17.8   **Deleting the Current Row**

```
Private Sub bttnDelete_Click()
Dim delISBN As String

    reply = MsgBox("The record will be deleted permanently. " & _
                    "Proceed?", vbYesNo)
    If reply = vbYes Then
        delISBN = SelTitles.Recordset.Fields("ISBN")
        SelTitles.Recordset.Delete
        DeleteAuthors delISBN
        AuthorList.Clear
        tmpAuthorList.Clear
        ClearFields
        txtTitle.SetFocus
    End If
End Sub
```

The DeleteAuthors subroutine deletes the rows of the Title Author table that correspond to the ISBN being deleted.

Manipulating a Title's Authors

This is all the code you need to edit all of the fields, with the exception of the authors. Adding and removing authors is not as simple, as it must take place on another Form. Because you can't force users to enter the exact name of each author, you should allow them to select the desired author's name from the Authors table. Figure 17.4 shows this Form.

FIGURE 17.4:

The NewAuthors Form

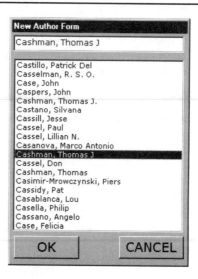

To add an author to the title, you must right-click the Authors box on the main Form. A shortcut menu will pop up with two options, one for adding a new author and another for deleting the selected author. You can add two more buttons on the Form, Add Author and Delete Author. Even better, assign two hotkeys to the options of the pop-up menu, so that users won't have to reach for the mouse. The following KeyUp event handler shows how to use the F4 key to delete the selected author and the F8 key to add a new author (you will see shortly how the AddAuthor and DelAuthor procedures work):

```
Private Sub AuthorList_KeyUp(KeyCode As Integer, Shift As Integer)
    If KeyCode = vbKeyF8 Then
        AddAuthor_Click
    End If
    If KeyCode = vbKeyF4 Then
        DelAuthor_Click
    End If
End Sub
```

When the New Author Form shows up, you can enter the first few characters of the author's name in the upper box and press Enter. The program will locate all the authors that match the description and display them on the DataList control, as shown in Figure 17.4. If you enter an author name that doesn't exist, it will be automatically added to the Authors table. Perhaps you'd like to request a confirmation from the user before committing the new author name to the database. Or, you could open yet another Form, where the user can enter more information about the author (address, phone number, and so on).

When the names matching your description appear on the DataList control, you will be able to select one with the mouse or the arrow keys. The program will move the focus to the DataList control, so that you select a name without reaching for the mouse. When you've located the desired name, press Enter to add it to the list of authors of the selected title.

Let's follow the code that adds a new author to a title. The current title's authors are displayed on the TitleAuthors control. When the user right-clicks this control, the following code is executed:

LISTING 17.9   Invoking the NewAuthor Form

```
Private Sub AuthorList_MouseUp(Button As Integer, Shift As _
                Integer, x As Single, y As Single)
    If Not bttnOK.Visible Then Exit Sub
    If Button = vbRightButton Then
        PopupMenu au_Menu
    End If
End Sub
```

The *au_Menu* pop-up menu contains two commands, the Add Author and Delete Selected Author commands. When the Add Author command is selected, the AddAuthor subroutine is executed, which simply displays the NewAuthorForm:

```
Private Sub AddAuthor_Click()
    NewAuthorForm.Show vbModal
End Sub
```

When the NewAuthorForm is activated, it clears the TextBox control at the top in preparation for some user input:

```
Private Sub Form_Activate()
    Text1.Text = ""
    Text1.SetFocus
End Sub
```

When the Enter key is pressed, the program goes out to the database, retrieves all the author names that match the description on the TextBox control on the Form, and displays them on the DataList control.

LISTING 17.10   Selecting Authors by Name

```
Private Sub Text1_KeyUp(KeyCode As Integer, Shift As Integer)
If KeyCode = vbKeyReturn Then
    If Trim(Text1.Text) = "" Then Exit Sub
    AuName = Text1.Text
    If InStr(AuName, "'") Then
        MsgBox "Invalid author name! Names can't contain successive quotes"
```

```
            Exit Sub
        End If
        AuName = Replace(AuName, "'", "''")
        Authors.CommandType = adCmdText
        Authors.CursorLocation = adUseClient
        Authors.RecordSource = _
                    "SELECT Author, Au_ID FROM Authors WHERE " & _
                    "Author LIKE '" & AuName & "%'"
        Authors.Refresh
        If Authors.Recordset.RecordCount = 0 Then
            Authors.Recordset.AddNew
            Authors.Recordset.Fields("Author") = Text1.Text
            Authors.Recordset.Update
            Authors.RecordSource = "SELECT Author, Au_ID " & _
                        "FROM Authors WHERE Author LIKE '" & _
                        AuName & "%'"
            Authors.Refresh
        End If
        Set DataList1.RowSource = Authors
        DataList1.ListField = "Author"
        DataList1.SetFocus
    End If
End Sub
```

The code builds a SELECT statement that retrieves all author names starting with the specified string and stores them in the cursor of the Authors ADO Data Control. This is a client-side cursor, because it must populate a data-aware control (the DataList1 control). The more specific users are about the author's name, the fewer rows will have to be moved to the client. The DataList control is populated by simply assigning the Authors Recordset to its RowSource property.

Finally, when the desired author has been selected, the user must click the OK button or press the Enter key. This action will add the selected author to the AuthorList control on the application's main Form and then hide the NewAuthor Form. Here's the code behind the NewAuthor Form's OK button:

LISTING 17.11   Adding a New Author to the Current Title

```
Private Sub Command1_Click()
Dim newAuthorID As Long
Dim newAuthorName As String

'   First, we must make sure the selected author's name
'   is not already linked to the title
    For i = 0 To DataEntryForm.AuthorList.ListCount - 1
        If DataEntryForm.AuthorList.List(i) = DataList1.Text Then
            MsgBox "You can't add the same author twice"
```

```
            Me.Hide
            Exit Sub
        End If
    Next

'   Get the author's ID
    newAuthorID = Authors.Recordset.Fields("Au_ID")
    newAuthorName = Authors.Recordset.Fields("Author")
    DataEntryForm.AuthorList.AddItem newAuthorName
    DataEntryForm.AuthorList.ItemData( _
            DataEntryForm.AuthorList.NewIndex) = newAuthorID
    Me.Hide
End Sub
```

The DataEntry application demonstrates how to browse and edit large databases using moderately sized cursors. The application has a user-friendly interface, yet it doesn't download more data to the client than it needs. Examine the code of the project, and enhance the application by adding the proper tab order to the controls and shortcut keys to move to any field (so that the user need not press the Tab key repeatedly). You should also control the Form's caption from within your code to reflect the current action (add/edit/browse). You will discover a few minor problems in the code, but the error-trapping code would have obscured the code that performs the basic operations.

You can also add features that are specific to a corporation. For example, you can provide a button that allows users to work with a specific publisher's titles, or allow users to select titles without a price or author(s), so that they can fix those entries.

An Invoicing Application

The second application is quite different and considerably more demanding. It's an invoicing application that allows the user to select the customer that placed the order and enter the items ordered. The program must insert the appropriate rows in the Orders and Order Details tables. Moreover, it must correctly update both tables. If one of the updates fails, then no changes should be made to the database. Therefore, the updates to the database must be performed as a transaction. A transaction involves multiple actions (updates) on the tables of the database. If all actions complete successfully, then the transaction is committed. If one of them fails, then the transaction must be rolled back and the database will be left in the state it was in before the transaction started (bar the changes made by other users at the same time, of course).

Implementing Transactions with ADO

Open the Invoices project (this project can be found in the InvoicesSP folder on the CD). Figure 17.5 shows the window that appears. In this chapter, you will see two versions of the Invoices application, one that uses ADO objects and another that uses the NewOrder stored procedure.

FIGURE 17.5:

The Invoices project

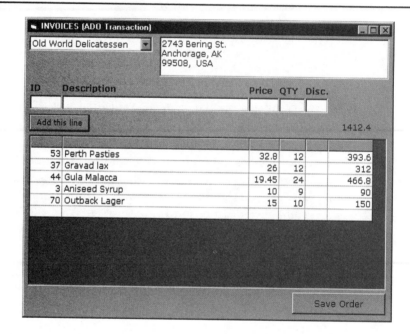

When the Form is loaded, you must populate the DataCombo control with the names of the customers (company names). You'll do so by creating a client-side cursor, the RSCustomers Recordset. Every time a company name is selected on the list, you want to display the company's address on a TextBox control, so grab some additional information along with the names of the companies to the client. You also need information about the products (IDs, names, and prices). This information is stored in the RSProducts Recordset and is not displayed on any control. You'll use the information later from within your code to find the description and price of a product, as the user enters its ID on the Form.

The two client-side Recordsets are populated from within the Form's Load event handler, which is shown next.

LISTING 17.12   **Retrieving Customer and Product Information**

```
Private Sub Form_Load()
    NWConnection.ConnectionString = "Provider=SQLOLEDB.1; " & _
```

```
                    "Persist Security Info=False;User ID=sa; " & _
                    "Initial Catalog=Northwind"
        NWConnection.Open
        RSProducts.ActiveConnection = NWConnection
        RSProducts.CursorType = adOpenStatic
        RSProducts.CursorLocation = adUseClient
        RSProducts.Open "SELECT ProductID, ProductName, " & _
                    "UnitPrice FROM Products"
        RSCustomers.ActiveConnection = NWConnection
        RSCustomers.CursorType = adOpenStatic
        RSCustomers.CursorLocation = adUseClient
        RSCustomers.Open "SELECT CustomerID, CompanyName, " & _
                    "ContactName, Address, City, Region, " & _
                    "PostalCode, Country FROM Customers"
        Set DataCombo1.RowSource = RSCustomers
        DataCombo1.ListField = "CompanyName"
        OrderControls
    End Sub
```

The OrderControls subroutine aligns the various controls on the Form. The user interface is not elaborate at all. You'd probably expect to be able to select the product by name in a list, but this isn't how invoices are issued. The product's code will most likely be scanned with a bar-code reader. At the very least, the user will have the product code at hand and will simply enter it. That's why the interface is so simple.

The user must select a customer name from the list at the top. The selected customer's address is displayed on a multiline TextBox control. This information should also be stored in the database (it's the order's shipping address and the user may actually change it), but it isn't.

To enter the details, the user must enter a product code in the ID box and move to the quantity box by pressing the Tab key. The program will display the product's description and price in the appropriate fields (which are locked) and will jump to the quantity box. After entering a quantity, the user can press Tab to move to the discount field. To add the line to the grid, the user must press Enter. Upon pressing Enter (equivalent to clicking the "Add this line" button on the Form), the program will add the new line to the grid and will move the focus to the ID field for the next line. You can actually enter details with a few keystrokes, and you never have to reach for the mouse. The interface is simple and functional, and it won't be difficult to adjust it to work with a bar-code reader.

When the user presses the Tab button in the ID box, the following code is executed. It retrieves the price and description of the product that corresponds to the specified ID and displays these two fields in the appropriate TextBox controls. Here's the code that accomplishes these tasks.

LISTING 17.13   Displaying a Product's Price and Name

```
Private Sub Text1_LostFocus()
    If Not IsNumeric(Text1.Text) Then Exit Sub
    RSProducts.MoveFirst
    RSProducts.Find "ProductID=" & CInt(Text1.Text)
    If RSProducts.EOF Then
        MsgBox "Invalid product ID!"
        Text1.Text = ""
    Else
        Text2.Text = RSProducts.Fields("ProductName")
        Text3.Text = RSProducts.Fields("UnitPrice")
    End If
    Text4.SetFocus
End Sub
```

The Find method is quite efficient with small Recordsets like the RSProducts Recordset. The Seek method would be a better choice, but this method doesn't work with client-side Recordsets. This project is based on the assumption that the product list is not too large. Unfortunately, even if your company sells a large number of different products, you must still download the entire table to the client.

To add a new detail line to the order, you can either click the "Add this line" button on the Form, or simply press Enter. This button is the default one on the Form; the next listing details its Click event handler, which adds the detail line to the grid at the bottom of the Form. The grid is an MSFlexGrid control.

LISTING 17.14   Adding a Detail Line

```
Private Sub bttnAddDetail_Click()
    If Not IsNumeric(Text1.Text) Then Exit Sub
    RSProducts.MoveFirst
    RSProducts.Find "ProductID=" & CInt(Text1.Text)
    If RSProducts.EOF Then
        MsgBox "Invalid product ID!"
        Text1.Text = ""
        Text1.SetFocus
        Exit Sub
    Else
        Text2.Text = RSProducts.Fields("ProductName")
    End If
    newRow = OrderGrid.Rows - 1
    OrderGrid.TextMatrix(newRow, 0) = Text1.Text
    OrderGrid.TextMatrix(newRow, 1) = Text2.Text
```

```
        OrderGrid.TextMatrix(newRow, 2) = Text3.Text
        OrderGrid.TextMatrix(newRow, 3) = Text4.Text
        OrderGrid.TextMatrix(newRow, 4) = Text5.Text
        OrderGrid.TextMatrix(newRow, 5) = _
                    Val(Text3.Text) * Val(Text4.Text) * _
                    (1 - Val(Text5.Text))
        Label6.Caption = Val(Label6.Caption) + _
                    OrderGrid.TextMatrix(newRow, 5)
        OrderGrid.Rows = OrderGrid.Rows + 1
        Text1.Text = ""
        Text2.Text = ""
        Text3.Text = ""
        Text4.Text = ""
        Text5.Text = ""
        Text1.SetFocus
    End Sub
```

The last operation is to add the order to the database. As mentioned already, the program must add a row to the Orders table and as many rows to the Order Details table as there are details. These actions must be performed as a transaction.

The program opens two Recordsets to access the Orders and Order Details tables in the database. These are server-side cursors, because you don't need to transfer information to the client. RSOrders is a keyset-type Recordset, because we want to be able to get back a single piece of information. When a new order is added to the Orders table, you need its number so you can insert it into the order's details in the Order Details table. RSDetails is a static cursor, because all it does is add a few lines to the Order Details table. Here's the code that adds the order to the database when the Save Order button is clicked.

LISTING 17.15   Adding an Invoice with VB Code

```
    Private Sub Command2_Click()
        Set RSOrders.ActiveConnection = NWConnection
        RSOrders.CursorLocation = adUseServer
        RSOrders.CursorType = adOpenKeyset
        RSOrders.LockType = adLockOptimistic
        RSOrders.Open "Orders"
        On Error GoTo TransactionFail
        NWConnection.BeginTrans
        RSOrders.AddNew
        RSOrders.Fields("CustomerID") = _
                    RSCustomers.Fields("CustomerID")
        RSOrders.Fields("OrderDate") = CDate(Now)
```

```
        RSOrders.Fields("EmployeeID") = 3
        RSOrders.Update
        OrderID = RSOrders.Fields("OrderID")
        Set RSDetails.ActiveConnection = NWConnection
        RSDetails.CursorLocation = adUseServer
        RSDetails.CursorType = adOpenStatic
        RSDetails.LockType = adLockOptimistic
        RSDetails.Open "[Order Details]"
        For i = 1 To OrderGrid.Rows - 2
            RSDetails.AddNew
            RSDetails.Fields("OrderID") = OrderID
            RSDetails.Fields("ProductID") = _
                    OrderGrid.TextMatrix(i, 0)
            RSDetails.Fields("UnitPrice") = _
                    OrderGrid.TextMatrix(i, 2)
            RSDetails.Fields("Quantity") = _
                    OrderGrid.TextMatrix(i, 3)
            RSDetails.Fields("Discount") = _
                    Val(OrderGrid.TextMatrix(i, 4))
            RSDetails.Update
        Next i
        NWConnection.CommitTrans
        MsgBox "The order was added successfully"
        Set RSOrders = Nothing
        Set RSDetails = Nothing
        Exit Sub

TransactionFail:
        NWConnection.RollbackTrans
        MsgBox "Could not add invoice. Transaction aborted with the error "
& Err.Number
        Set RSOrders = Nothing
        Set RSDetails = Nothing
End Sub
```

The code is straightforward and there's very little that could go wrong. The customer's ID and all product IDs are correct, because they are verified on the client. The only thing that could go wrong is to enter an invalid discount (a value less than zero or greater than one). This error can be easily caught on the client, but the program doesn't validate this value. Enter an invalid discount and see how the program will react. The transaction will fail because this value violates the constraint CK_Discount in the Order Details table, shown in Figure 17.6. Before you actually test the program's behavior, make sure you have added the constraint CK_Discount to the Order Details table.

FIGURE 17.6:

This constraint tells SQL Server that the discount must be a value between 0 and 1 and that it shouldn't accept any values outside this range.

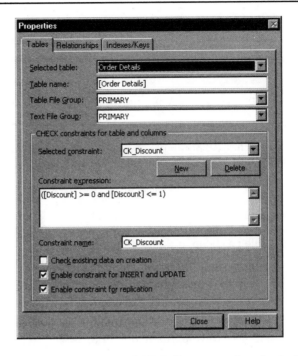

Let's test the transactional capabilities of ADO. Prepare an invoice in the Invoices project. Select a customer you don't mind removing from the database, because this is exactly what you'll do. Then switch to the Enterprise Manager (or Access, if you're using the Jet version of the database), open the Customers table, and delete the customer you've selected in the Invoices application. Return to the VB application and try to save the order. As expected, the transaction will fail with the error 3617. As you recall from Chapter 9, this error occurs when ADO attempts to read a row that has been deleted since it was read. The same will happen if you remove one of the products you've included in the details from the Products table.

OK, the code aborts the transaction and doesn't take any actions on its own. In situations where one user enters invoices and another removes rows from the Customers or Products table at the same time, then the problem is in the company's policies, not your code. The most common reasons for a transaction to fail are that a table has been locked, a network connection fails, and so on.

You can also modify the code so that it takes into consideration the current stock and doesn't process an invoice that would bring the stock of a product to a negative level. To handle this situation from within your VB code, you must read the current stock, compare it to the quantity, and add the detail line only if the stock exceeds the quantity ordered. This is not as simple as it sounds, though. You must lock the row of the Products table to make sure that other users will not be able to decrease the stock at the same time. Your VB application will become complicated and more difficult to test. You must use pessimistic locking to make sure that no other user gets a chance to modify the product's stock after you have read it and before you update it. At this point, you should consider a stored procedure that will perform all the necessary operations on the server. You will see how this is done in the section "Implementing Transactions with Stored Procedures," later in this chapter.

Insert the following line after the line that updates the RSOrders Recordset.

```
MsgBox "Orders table was updated, click OK to add the details."
```

This line is commented out in the project, and you should enable it for testing purposes only. *Never, never, interact with the user from within a transaction.* The transaction will lock several rows in the involved tables, and others will not even be able to read them.

The MsgBox line gives you a chance to look at the database after the Orders table has been updated and before the Order Details table is updated (in other words, before the transaction completes).

If you attempt to open the Orders table to see whether SQL Server has added the new row that corresponds to the order being processed, the Enterprise Manager will crash. The Enterprise Manager expects that all tables are available, because it's a tool for development, not for browsing or editing tables.

You can start the Query Analyzer and enter a query like the following to retrieve the last few orders:

```
USE Northwind
SELECT * FROM Orders WHERE orderdate >= GetDate() - 24
```

This statement will retrieve the orders placed in the last 24 hours.

While the message box is open, the query will not return! You may see the first few rows of the query, or you may see no rows in the Results pane. The reason is that the last few rows of the Orders table are locked and the Query Analyzer is waiting for the lock to be released. If you switch back to the Invoices application and close the dialog box, then the query will be able to complete.

The Jet Version of the Project

If you want to test the application with the Access version of the Northwind database, all you have to do is change the Connection object's ConnectionString property:

```
NWConnection.ConnectionString = _
        "Provider=Microsoft.Jet.OLEDB.4.0; " & _
        "Data Source=C:\Program Files\VB98\Nwind.mdb; " & _
        "Persist Security Info=False"
```

Other than that, the exact same code will work with the new provider (it's ADO that does all the work behind the scenes). Transactions are no different with the new provider. The row added to the Orders table is not visible until the entire transaction completes. However, unlike the Enterprise Manager, Access will not wait for the transaction to complete before displaying the entire table. You can open the Orders table from within Access and see all the rows, with the exception of the one being added as part of the transaction.

Access can place a lock on a single row, which is what happens during a transaction. Access only locks the rows involved in each step of the transaction and releases the locks when the transaction completes (successfully or otherwise).

Implementing Transactions with Stored Procedures

The most efficient method of updating tables, especially if the update involves a transaction, is to use stored procedures. Stored procedures are executed on the server and complete faster then the equivalent VB code. Let's say you have to make sure that the product IDs exist before you use them in updating tables. This step would require too many steps with Visual Basic. A stored procedure would verify the validity of the product IDs much faster. The major benefit of using stored procedures is that, once the stored procedure for adding an order and its details is in place, you don't have to worry about implementing transactions from within your VB code. In addition, you can incorporate business rules (such as aborting a transaction if it results in negative stocks) into the stored procedure.

Stored procedures do not interact with the user. When you write stored procedures, you must include all the necessary logic in the procedure and take any action without user involvement. You can do the same with Visual Basic, but you'll be tempted to display a message box or prompt the user for some action in the middle of a transaction. Besides, the longer your code gets, the more you increase the chance of errors. It's possible to have to roll back a perfectly valid transaction because of an error in the VB code!

Finally, stored procedures are transparent to VB programmers. All they have to do is set up a Command object and pass the appropriate parameter values, as if they were calling a built-in Visual Basic function. You can write and test your own stored procedures (or ask the DBA to write them for you) and pass them to the programming team to use. Doing so, you not only simplify programming tasks, you also make sure that the database is updated consistently, regardless of how well programmers have understood the structure of the database and the corporation's policies. If you decide later to keep track of who's entering each order, you can modify the appropriate stored procedure and the VB applications will not have to be touched.

The NewOrder Stored Procedure

Let's start with the stored procedure that adds an invoice to the Northwind database. This stored procedure must update two tables, the Order and Order Details tables, and it must do so in a transaction. If one operation fails, then the entire transaction must fail. You have seen this stored procedure in Chapter 7, "Transact-SQL," but here you'll see how it's used from within a VB application. For your convenience, the listing of the stored procedure is repeated here.

LISTING 17.16   The NewOrder Stored Procedure

```
CREATE PROCEDURE NewOrder
@custID nchar(5), @empID int, @orderDate datetime, @shipperID int,
@Details varchar(1000)
AS

DECLARE @ErrorCode int
DECLARE @OrderID int
- Add new row to the Orders table
DECLARE @shipcompany nvarchar(40), @shipAddress nvarchar(60),
        @shipCity nvarchar(15),
        @shipRegion nvarchar(15), @shipPCode nvarchar(10),
        @shipCountry nvarchar(15)
SELECT @shipCompany=CompanyName,
       @shipAddress=Address,
       @shipCity=City,
       @shipRegion=Region,
       @shipPCode=PostalCode,
       @shipCountry=Country
       FROM Customers
       WHERE CustomerID = @custID
IF @@ROWCOUNT = 0
   RETURN(-100)    - Invalid Customer!

SELECT * FROM Employees WHERE EmployeeID = @empID
IF @@ROWCOUNT = 0
   RETURN(-101)    - Invalid Employee!

SELECT * FROM Shippers
       WHERE ShipperID = @shipperID
IF @@ROWCOUNT = 0
   RETURN(-102)    - Invalid Shipper!

BEGIN TRANSACTION
INSERT Orders (CustomerID, EmployeeID, OrderDate, ShipVia,
               ShipName, ShipAddress, ShipCity, ShipRegion,
               ShipPostalCode, ShipCountry)
VALUES (@custID, @empID, @orderDate, @ShipperID,
        @shipCompany, @shipAddress, @ShipCity, @ShipRegion,
        @shipPCode, @shipCountry)
SET @ErrorCode=@@ERROR
IF (@ErrorCode <> 0)
   BEGIN
```

```
    ROLLBACK TRANSACTION
    RETURN (-@ErrorCode)
    END
SET @OrderID = @@IDENTITY

- Now add rows to the Order Details table
- All new rows will have the same OrderID
DECLARE @TotLines int
DECLARE @currLine int

SET @currLine = 0
SET @TotLines = Ceiling(Len(@Details)/18)

DECLARE @Qty smallint, @Dscnt real, @Price money
DECLARE @ProdID int

WHILE @currLine <= @TotLines
    BEGIN
        SET @ProdID = SUBSTRING(@Details, @currLine*18 + 1, 6)
        SET @Qty = SUBSTRING(@Details, @currLine*18 + 7, 6)
        SET @Dscnt = SUBSTRING(@Details, @currLine*18 + 13,6)
        SET @currLine = @currLine + 1
        IF @Qty > 0
        BEGIN
            SELECT @Price=UnitPrice FROM Products WHERE
                    ProductID=@ProdID
            INSERT [Order Details] (OrderID, ProductID, Quantity,
                    UnitPrice, Discount)
                    VALUES (@OrderID, @ProdID, @Qty, @Price, @Dscnt)
            SET @ErrorCode = @@ERROR
        END
        IF (@ErrorCode <> 0) GOTO DetailError
    END
    COMMIT TRANSACTION
    RETURN (0)
DetailError:
    ROLLBACK TRANSACTION
    RETURN(@ErrorCode)
```

The NewOrder stored procedure requires five parameter values:

- The ID of the customer that placed the order

- The ID of the employee that made the sale

- The order date

- The shipper ID

- The order's details

The date is not really needed—the stored procedure can insert the current date in the database—but I've included it to show you how to pass dates to stored procedures. The details of the order can't be passed as separate values, because each order can have any number of rows. Stored procedures, however, can't accept a varying number of parameters, so you must place all the information about the details into a single string and pass it to the stored procedure.

The stored procedure makes sure that the IDs of the customer, employee, and shipper are valid; if not, it returns the appropriate error code. Again, you don't have to perform these tests, as long as you're enforcing the appropriate relations in the database. If you enforce the relation between Orders and Customers tables (namely, that the two tables are linked with a common CustomerID field), then SQL Server will abort the insertion of a new row in the Order table if the specified customer ID does not exist. However, the error code you'll get back from SQL Server will not be nearly as descriptive as the one produced from within your stored procedure.

A transaction is initiated with the BEGIN TRANSACTION statement. First, it inserts a new row into the Order table. Then the code extracts each detail line's fields from the @Details parameter and appends a new line to the Order Details table. If any of these operations fails, the code aborts the transaction with the ROLLBACK TRANSACTION statement and returns the error code generated by the SQL Server.

Another shortcoming of the NewOrder stored procedure, shown in Figure 17.7, is that it uses the company's address as the shipping address. If you want to be able to specify different shipping addresses, you must create more input parameters for the stored procedure, one for each address field.

FIGURE 17.7:

Stored procedures are database objects that can be used by external applications.

Calling the NewOrder Stored Procedure

To insert a new order, you must set up a Command object to call the NewOrder stored procedure, prepare the parameters, and then execute the command. The code picks up the values of the various fields from the controls on the Form and stores them into separate Parameter objects. The information about the order's details is stored into a long string. Each detail line is made up of 18 characters and holds 3 fields of 6 characters each: the product ID, quantity, and discount. The program iterates through the rows of the grid at the bottom of the Form, extracts each value, and stores it into a string variable that was declared with a fixed length of 6 characters. The fields are concatenated to build a long string with the invoice's details. The NewOrder stored procedure uses the current product's price in the database, so you need not include this information in the *InvoiceStr* string.

To pass a parameter to a stored procedure through the Command object, you must first create a Parameter object; set its name, data type, value, size, and direction (whether it's a parameter to be passed to the procedure or a parameter returned by the procedure); and then append it to the Command object's Parameters collection. The same process must be repeated for each parameter. Finally, you call the Command object's Execute method to execute the stored procedure. Here's the code behind the Save Order button:

LISTING 17.17   **Adding an Invoice through the NewOrder Stored Procedure**

```
Private Sub bttnSaveOrder_Click()
Dim oParam As New ADODB.Parameter
Dim oCommand As ADODB.Command
Dim item As String * 6
Dim InvoiceStr As String

    Set oCommand = DataEnvironment1.Commands(1)
'   Output Parameter
    Set oParam = oCommand.CreateParameter
    oParam.Name = "RETURN_VALUE"
    oParam.Type = adInteger
    oParam.Direction = adParamReturnValue
    oCommand.Parameters.Append oParam

'   CustomerID
    Set oParam = oCommand.CreateParameter
    oParam.Name = "@CustID"
    oParam.Type = adChar
    oParam.Size = 5
    oParam.Direction = adParamInput
    oParam.Value = RSCustomers.Fields("CustomerID")
    oCommand.Parameters.Append oParam
```

```
'    EmployeeID
     Set oParam = oCommand.CreateParameter
     oParam.Name = "@EmpID"
     oParam.Type = adInteger
     oParam.Direction = adParamInput
     oParam.Value = 4
     oCommand.Parameters.Append oParam

'    Order Date
     Set oParam = oCommand.CreateParameter
     oParam.Name = "@OrderDate"
     oParam.Type = adDate
     oParam.Direction = adParamInput
     oParam.Value = "2/2/2002"
     oCommand.Parameters.Append oParam

'    Shipper ID
     Set oParam = oCommand.CreateParameter
     oParam.Name = "ShipperID"
     oParam.Type = adInteger
     oParam.Direction = adParamInput
     oParam.Value = 2
     oCommand.Parameters.Append oParam

'    Now build string with order details
     For i = 1 To OrderGrid.Rows - 2
         If Not (Val(OrderGrid.TextMatrix(i, 0)) = 0 Or _
                 Val(OrderGrid.TextMatrix(i, 3)) = 0) Then
             LSet item = Str(OrderGrid.TextMatrix(i, 0))
             InvoiceStr = InvoiceStr & item
             LSet item = Str(OrderGrid.TextMatrix(i, 3))
             InvoiceStr = InvoiceStr & item
             LSet item = Str(Val(OrderGrid.TextMatrix(i, 4)))
             InvoiceStr = InvoiceStr & item
         End If
     Next

     Set oParam = oCommand.CreateParameter
     oParam.Name = "Details"
     oParam.Type = adVarChar
     oParam.Size = Len(InvoiceStr)
     oParam.Direction = adParamInput
     oParam.Value = InvoiceStr
     oCommand.Parameters.Append oParam

     oCommand.CommandText = "NewOrder"
     oCommand.CommandType = adCmdStoredProc
```

```
On Error GoTo ExecError
    oCommand.Execute
    If oCommand.Parameters(0).Value <> 0 Then
        MsgBox "The stored procedure returned error # " & _
            oCommand.Parameters(0).Value
    Else
        MsgBox "Order added successfully!"
    End If
    For i = 0 To oCommand.Parameters.Count - 1
        oCommand.Parameters.Delete (0)
    Next
    Set oCommand = Nothing
    Exit Sub
ExecError:
    msg = "Could not add order." & vbCrLf & _
            "Error(s) returned by the provider:" & vbCrLf
    msg = msg & _
        DataEnvironment1.Connections(1).Errors(0). _
        Description & vbCrLf
    MsgBox msg
    Set oCommand = Nothing
End Sub
```

Some Housekeeping Chores

Notice the line that removes the parameters of the *oCommand* object. This object represents the first Command object in the DataEnvironment window. If you don't remove the parameters, the next time you add an order, the Parameter object will be added again and you'll end up calling the stored procedure with twice as many arguments. Alternatively, you could append the parameters in the Form's Load event and then set their properties (in other words, omit the lines that create a new Parameter object and then append it to the Parameters collection of the Command object).

The examples in this chapter were certainly not trivial, but they demonstrate two of the most common applications you'll be developing. Every database application requires several data-entry and browsing Forms. Transactions are essential to every application that must update multiple tables, and you should be able to implement transactions both in your VB code and with stored procedures in a SQL Server database.

CHAPTER

EIGHTEEN

Building an Online Store

This chapter describes a Web application, an online bookstore. It uses the titles stored in the Biblio database, so you have a wealth of data to test your site. The Biblio database doesn't contain any tables for storing customer and order information, so you must edit the database a little and add two tables for storing the orders.

The Online Bookstore sample application is stored in the ONLINE folder on the CD. You must copy the entire folder as is onto your computer's hard disk and clear the read-only attribute of all the files (so that you can edit the files later). Then, you must make the ONLINE folder the root folder of your Web site. This step is required, because the site uses a GLOBAL.ASA file, which is activated when the application starts. The GLOBAL.ASA file holds a "global" variable: the maximum number of rows that can be retrieved by any SQL statement in the application's scripts. In addition, when the application starts, two session variables are created. These variables hold the login information for a generic user. The first time a user logs in with a real user ID and password, these values replace the generic ones. Here's the application's GLOBAL.ASA file:

```
<SCRIPT LANGUAGE = VBScript RUNAT = Server>
Sub Application_OnStart
    Application("maxRecordsAllowed") = 500
End Sub

Sub Session_OnStart
    Session("UserID") = "GUEST"
    Session("Password") = "anonymous"
End Sub
</SCRIPT>
```

As you can understand, the application should not allow any user to register with the GUEST/anonymous combination. You must insert the corresponding validation code in the script that registers new users and records the information to the database.

Revising the Biblio Database

First, you must add two tables in the Biblio database, where customer and order information will be stored. They are the Customers and Orders tables:

Table Customers

Field Name	Field Type
EMail	Text (25)
Password	Text (15)

FirstName	Text (25)
LastName	Text (25)
Address1	Text (50)
Address2	Text (50)
City	Text (15)
Phone	Text (12)
FAX	Text (15)

Table Orders

Field Name	Field Type
UserID	Text (25)
OrderDate	Date/Time (short date format)
BookISBN	Text (12)
BookQTY	Integer

Customers are identified by their e-mail addresses so they won't have to memorize user IDs. You may apply some rules to the password, such as minimum length, one or more special characters required, and so on. There's no credit card information in the table, so all orders will ship COD. You can accept credit card information over the Web, as long as you use a secure Web server. You can use IIS as long as you specify the HTTPS protocol. The address prefix https:// tells the browser to encrypt the information before sending it to the server. The viewer will see the usual message box, informing them that they're about to switch to a secure connection. You can expect that they'll click the OK button and proceed.

I've modified the Titles table a little. I've changed the name of the Description column to Price, because if you look at the values stored in this column you'll realize that they're prices. I also added a new column, Discount, that stores discount information. The following query was used to populate this column with random discounts between 10 percent and 40 percent. The discount is stored as a real value between 0 and 1.

```
UPDATE Titles SET Discount = 0.1 + Int(Rnd(Price)*30)/100;
```

Make a copy of the Biblio database, implement the changes, and then create a DSN for the new database. I've named this DSN BIBLIO2000 on my system. That's because I've converted the database to Access 2000 format; the original database that comes with VB will work just as well. To set up a Data Source Name for the database, see the section "DSN-Based Connections" in Chapter 5.

The Web Application

The main page of the online bookstore is shown in Figure 18.1. The hyperlinks don't lead anywhere, except for the My Basket link. On this page, you can specify a part of the title and click the Now button to retrieve selected titles. The search capabilities of this page are limited; you can't specify isolated keywords to select titles. You can use the Titles component to perform more complicated searches—or build your own SQL statement that retrieves titles based on multiple keywords.

FIGURE 18.1:

The main page of the online bookstore

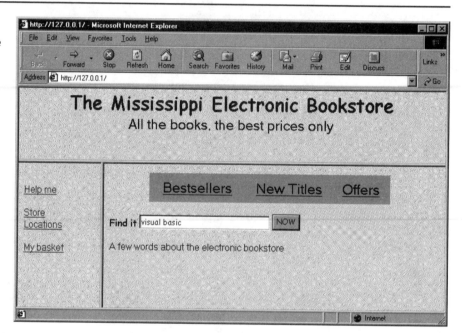

When the Now button is clicked, SRCHTITLES.ASP on the server is called, which processes the user-supplied string. Here's the FORM tag of the main page:

```
<FORM ACTION="SRCHTITLES.ASP" METHOD="POST" NAME="SRCHFORM">
```

This page is responsible for extracting displaying the titles that match the user-supplied criteria. It extracts the string entered by the user on the main page and builds a SELECT statement, which it executes against the database with the following statements:

```
ReqTitle = Request.QueryString("SRCHARG")
SQLArgument = "SELECT Titles.ISBN, Title, Price, Author "
SQLArgument = SQLArgument & "FROM Titles, Authors,
             [Title Author] "
SQLArgument = SQLArgument & "WHERE Titles.Title LIKE '%" &
             UCase(ReqTitle) & "%' AND "
```

```
    SQLArgument = SQLArgument & "Titles.ISBN=[Title Author].ISBN AND
[Title Author].Au_ID=Authors.Au_ID"
    connectString="DSN=BIBLIO2000"
    Set SelTitles=Server.CreateObject("adodb.Recordset")
```

The script retrieves the titles that contain the user-supplied string. You can modify the script so that it uses the TITLES component to retrieve titles by keywords and/or author names.

The selected titles are displayed (Figure 18.2) on a new page with 20 titles per page. The page allows the viewer to select any page with a group of 20 books. This arrangement is most useful when the titles are sorted. Titles can be sorted either by title or by selling order (start with the best-selling titles in the first page and proceed to the less-successful ones). This information does not exist in the Biblio database, but you can easily keep track of this information in a database with sales data.

FIGURE 18.2:

The titles on this page are hyperlinks to each individual title's page.

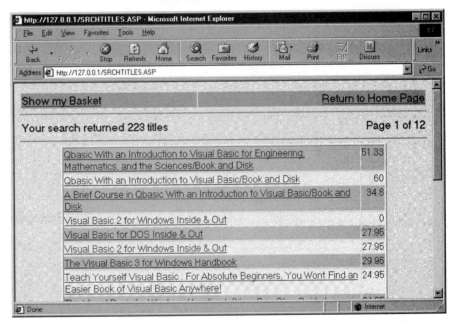

The trick to breaking a large page into smaller ones and create paged output is to manipulate the PageSize and AbsolutePage properties of a client-side Recordset. Here's the code of the SRCHTITLES.ASP script:

LISTING 18.1   The SRCHTITLES.ASP Server-Side Script

```
<HTML><FONT FACE='MS Sans Serif'>
<body BGCOLOR="#F0F0B0">
<%
    currentPage=Request.QueryString("whichpage")
```

```
If currentPage="" Then
   currentPage=1
End If
pageSize=Request.QueryString("pagesize")
If pageSize="" Then
   pageSize=20
End If

ReqTitle = Request.QueryString("SRCHARG")
SQLArgument = "SELECT Titles.ISBN, Title, Price, Author "
SQLArgument = SQLArgument &
              "FROM Titles, Authors, [Title Author] "
SQLArgument = SQLArgument &
              "WHERE Titles.Title LIKE '%" &
              UCase(ReqTitle) & "%' AND "
SQLArgument = SQLArgument &
              "Titles.ISBN=[Title Author].ISBN AND
              [Title Author].Au_ID=Authors.Au_ID"
connectString="DSN=BIBLIO2000"
adOpenStatic = 3
adUseClient = 3
Set SelTitles=Server.CreateObject("adodb.Recordset")
SelTitles.CacheSize=5
SelTitles.MaxRecords=Application("maxRecordsAllowed")

SelTitles.Open SQLArgument, connectString, adOpenStatic
If SelTitles.EOF Then
   Response.Write "Sorry, no title matches your search
                   criteria (" & ReqTitle & ")"
   Response.Write "<BR>"
   Response.Write "Please press Back to return to
                   the main page"
   Response.End
End If
SelTitles.MoveFirst
SelTitles.PageSize=pageSize
PageCount = CInt(SelTitles.PageCount)
If PageCount > CInt(Application("maxRecordsAllowed")) /
      PageSize) Then
   maxCount = CInt(Application("maxRecordsAllowed")) / PageSize)
Else
   maxCount = PageCount
End If
SelTitles.AbsolutePage=currentPage
totRecords=0
BooksTotal=SelTitles.RecordCount
```

```
'   BASKET ICONS HERE ................................................
    Response.Write "<TABLE WIDTH=100% BORDERCOLOR=cyan><TR>"
    Response.Write "<TD ALIGN=LEFT BGCOLOR=cyan><FONT SIZE=+1><A
HREF=BASKET.ASP" & ">Show my Basket</A></FONT>"
    Response.Write "<TD ALIGN=RIGHT BGCOLOR=cyan><FONT SIZE=+1><A
HREF=DEFAULT.HTM>Return to Home Page</A></FONT></TABLE>"
    Response.Write "<HR>"
'   ...................................................................
    Response.Write "<TABLE WIDTH=100% ><TR><TD ALIGN=LEFT>"
    Response.Write "<FONT SIZE=4>Your search returned " & booksTotal & "
titles</FONT>"
    Response.Write "<TD ALIGN=RIGHT>"
    Response.Write "<FONT SIZE=4> Page " & currentPage & " of " & max-
count & "<br>"
    Response.Write "</TABLE>"
    Response.Write "<HR>"
%>
<CENTER>
<TABLE RULES=none WIDTH=80%>
<%
    BooksFound = False
    bcolor = "lightyellow"
    Do While Not SelTitles.EOF And totRecords < SelTitles.PageSize
      If bcolor = "lightyellow" Then
          bcolor = "lightgrey"
        Else
          bcolor = "lightyellow"
        End If
%>
<TR BGCOLOR = <% =bcolor %>>
<TD> <A HREF="BookISBN.asp?ISBN=<% =SelTitles("ISBN") %>"> <%
          =SelTitles("Title") %></A>
<%
    currentISBN=SelTitles.Fields("ISBN")
    currentPrice=SelTitles.Fields("Price")
    BookISBN=SelTitles.Fields("ISBN")
    Authors=""
    Do
        If Not IsNull(SelTitles.Fields("Author")) Then
            Authors=Authors & SelTitles.Fields("Author") & ", "
        SelTitles.MoveNext
        If SelTitles.EOF Then
            currentISBN=""
        Else
            currentISBN = SelTitles.Fields("ISBN")
        End If
```

```
        Loop While currentISBN = BookISBN
        Authors = Left(Authors, Len(Authors)-2)
%>


<BR> <% =Authors %>
<TD ALIGN=RIGHT VALIGN=TOP> <% =currentPrice %>
<%
        BooksFound = True
        If Not SelTitles.EOF Then SelTitles.MoveNext
        totRecords = totRecords + 1
    Loop
%>
</TABLE>
<%
    If BooksFound=False Then
        Response.Write "No books were found"
    End If
    Set SelTitles = Nothing
%>
<P>
<%
    pad = "0"
    Scriptname = Request.ServerVariables("script_name")
    For pgCounter=1 to maxcount
        If pgCounter>=10 then pad=""
        ref="<a href='" & Scriptname & "?whichpage=" & pgCounter
        ref=ref & "&SRCHARG=" & ReqTitle & "&pagesize=" &
                pageSize & "'>" & pad & pgcounter &
                "</a>  "
        response.write ref & " "
    Next
    If PageCount > CInt(Application("maxRecordsAllowed") /
            PageSize) Then
        Response.Write "<HR>"
        Response.Write "<FONT SIZE=3>Your search for [" &
                ReqTitle & "] at the Mississippi bookstore returned "
                & booksTotal & " titles, "
        Response.Write "but you will see only the first " &
                Application("maxRecordsAllowed") & " of them. "
        Response.Write "Please specify better the titles you're
                interested in. </FONT>"
        Response.Write "<HR>"
    End If
%>
</HTML>
```

The script formats each title as a hyperlink. The destination of all hyperlinks is the BookISBN.asp script on the server. This script accepts the book's ISBN as a parameter, extract the book's complete information from the database, and displays it on a separate page. When a title is clicked, the book's details are displayed on a new page, which is shown in Figure 18.3. Here's the BookISBN.asp script:

LISTING 18.2   The BookISBN.asp Server-Side Script

```
<HTML><FONT FACE='MS Sans Serif'>
<%
   Set FSys=Server.CreateObject("Scripting.FileSystemObject")
   ReqISBN = Request.QueryString("ISBN")

'   BASKET ICON HERE
   Response.Write "<HTML>"
   Response.Write "<body BGCOLOR=#F0F0B0>"
   Response.Write "<TABLE WIDTH=100% BORDERCOLOR=cyan><TR>"
   Response.Write "<TD ALIGN=LEFT BGCOLOR=cyan><FONT SIZE=+0> _
                  <A HREF=BASKET.ASP" & "> _
                  Show my Basket</A></FONT>"
   Response.Write "<TD ALIGN=RIGHT BGCOLOR=cyan><FONT SIZE=+0> _
                  <A HREF=DEFAULT.HTM> _
                  Home Page</A></FONT></TABLE>"
   Response.Write "<HR>"
'''''''''''''''''''''''''''''''''''''''''''''''''''''''''''''''''''''''''''
   FName1="Images\" & ReqISBN & "S.GIF"
   FName2="Images\" & ReqISBN & "L.GIF"
   If Not FSys.FileExists(FName) Then
       FName1 = "Images\LOGOSMALL.JPG"
   End If
   Set DBConnection=Server.CreateObject("ADODB.Connection")
   DBConnection.Open "DSN=BIBLIO2000"
   SQLArgument = "SELECT Title, Notes, Price, Discount, _
                  [Company Name] FROM (Titles INNER JOIN _
                  Publishers ON Titles.PubID = Publishers.PubID) _
                  WHERE Titles.ISBN='" & ReqISBN & "'"
   Set SelTitle = DBConnection.Execute(SQLArgument)
   Response.write "<TABLE>"
   Response.Write "<TR ALIGN=center VALIGN=center><TD>"
   If FName1 = "Images\LOGOSMALL.JPG" Then
       Response.Write "<IMG SRC = " & chr(34) & _
               FName1 & chr(34) & " BORDER = 2 ALT = 'Book cover'>"
```

```
        Else
            Response.Write "<A HREF = " & chr(34) & FName2 &
                    chr(34) & "><IMG SRC = " & chr(34) & FName1 & _
                    " BORDER =2 ALT = 'Book cover'>"
        End If
        Response.Write "<TD ALIGN=left><H2>"
        Response.Write SelTitle.Fields("Title")
        ReqTitle = SelTitle.Fields("Title")
        Response.Write "</H2>"
        Response.Write "<TABLE><TR>"
        If Not IsNull(SelTitle.Fields("Company Name")) Then
                    Response.Write "<TD ALIGN=left> _
                    Published by <TD ALIGN=left>" & _
                    SelTitle.Fields("Company Name") & "<BR>"
        Response.write "<TR><TD ALIGN=left>Publisher's Price
                    <TD ALIGN=left>" & _
                    SelTitle.Fields("Price") & "<BR>"
        Response.write "<TR><TD ALIGN=left><FONT COLOR=red> _
                    Sale Price <TD ALIGN=left><FONT COLOR=red>" & _
                    FormatNumber((1 - _
                        CDbl(SelTitle.Fields("Discount"))) * _
                        SelTitle.Fields("Price"), 2) & _
                        "</FONT><BR>"
        Response.Write "</TABLE>"
        Response.Write "<TR><TD>"
        Response.Write "<FORM ACTION=ISBNOrder.ASP METHOD=POST>"
        Response.Write "<INPUT TYPE=HIDDEN NAME=ISBN VALUE='" & _
                    ReqISBN & "'>"
        Response.Write "<INPUT TYPE=HIDDEN NAME=TITLE VALUE='" & _
                    ReqTitle & "'>"
        Response.Write "<INPUT TYPE=Submit NAME=Order _
                    VALUE='Order this Title'>"
        Response.Write "</FORM>"
        Response.Write "<BR>"
        Response.Write "</TABLE>"
        Response.Write "<HR>"
        Response.Write SelTitle.Fields("Notes")
        Response.write "<HR>"
        Set DBConnection=Nothing
    %>
    </HTML>
```

The script assumes that the thumbnails of the book covers are stored in the folder IMAGES and their names are each book's ISBN with the character "S" (for small) or "L" (for large) appended. If the book's cover picture is missing, then the LOGOSMALL .JPG image is displayed.

FIGURE 18.3:

A book's page

The most interesting part of this script is the code that sets up the Order button. This is usual Submit button, but it passes the ISBN of the selected books to the ISBNOrder.ASP script through a hidden control. This trick allows you to pass information to a script with the POST method (so the values of the parameters won't appear along with the script's URL in the Address box). The POST method works with controls, but there are no controls on this Form. You can't just redesign the page so that it uses controls. The hidden box control solves the problem by allowing the script to retrieve the ISBN with the Request.Form collection. Notice that this page passes the selected book's title along with its ISBN (you'll see why shortly). The listing of the ISBNOrder.ASP script is shown next:

LISTING 18.3   **The ISBNOrder.ASP Server-Side Script**

```
<%
    OrderISBN=Request.Form("ISBN")
    OrderTitle=Request.Form("Title")
    CurQuantity = Request.Cookies("BasketItem")(OrderISBN)
    If CurQuantity = 0 Then
        Response.Cookies("BasketItem")(OrderISBN) = "1"
        BookFound = False
```

```
        Else
            BookFound = True
        End If
        Response.Cookies("BasketItem").Expires = Date + 365
        Response.Write "<HTML><FONT FACE='MS Sans Serif'>"
        Response.Write "<TABLE WIDTH=100% BORDERCOLOR=cyan><TR>"
        Response.Write "<TD ALIGN=LEFT BGCOLOR=cyan>
                        <FONT FACE='MS Sans Serif'>
                        <A HREF=BASKET.ASP" & ">
                        Show my Basket</A></FONT>"
        Response.Write "<TD ALIGN=RIGHT BGCOLOR=cyan>
                        <FONT FACE='MS Sans Serif'>
                        <A HREF=DEFAULT.HTM>
                        Home Page</A></FONT></TABLE>"
    %>
    <P>
    <CENTER><B>Title Order</B></CENTER>
    </FONT>
    <BR>
    <FONT SIZE=4>

    <% If BookFound = False Then %>
    The book <I> <% =OrderTitle %> </I> was added to your basket.<BR>
    Use the Back button to return to the book's page.
    You can always remove this title from your <A
    HREF=BASKET.ASP>basket</A>.
    <P>
    <% Else %>
    The title <I> <% =OrderTitle %> </I> has been selected already.<BR>
    View your <A HREF=BASKET.ASP>basket</A> and change the quantity, or
    the BACK button to return to this book's page.
    You can always cancel this title from your basket.
    <P>
    <% End If %>

    <H1>The titles you have chosen so far</H1>
    <%
    For Each cookie in Request.Cookies("BasketItem")
        Response.Write "ISBN=" & cookie &
                        "      "
        Response.Write "QUANTITY= " &
                        Request.Cookies("BasketItem")(cookie)
        Response.Write "<BR>"
    Next
    %>
```

This page retrieves the selected book's ISBN and title through the Request.Form collection. The script doesn't access the database, but it needs to display the book's title. To avoid an unnecessary trip to the server, the script passes the title along with its ISBN to the server.

The ISBNOrder script reads the values of the cookies sent by the client. The online bookstore stores the ordered items in the BasketItem array. This is an array of cookies that stores two pieces of information for each title ordered: its ISBN and its quantity. The script attempts to locate an existing cookie for the selected title. If one exists, the script doesn't change its quantity. It simply prompts the user (via the window shown in Figure 18.4) to visit the basket's page and change the quantity there.

FIGURE 18.4:

The order's confirmation page

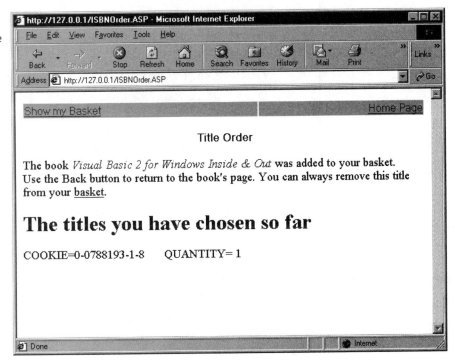

Finally, the script iterates through the site's cookies and displays them on the page. This segment of the script isn't required; it was inserted as a debugging aid, and you must redesign this page after testing your site. This script should update the cookies silently, as it does now, and then simply display a confirmation page.

This page contains two hyperlinks, which allow the viewer to jump to the site's main page or view the page with the basket's cookies—the page that displays all the titles ordered so far (Figure 18.5) and allows the viewer to change their quantities.

This page doesn't contain a client-side script to process the quantities. If the customer changes a quantity, they must click the Recalculate button at the bottom of the page to update the total.

FIGURE 18.5:

The viewer's basket page

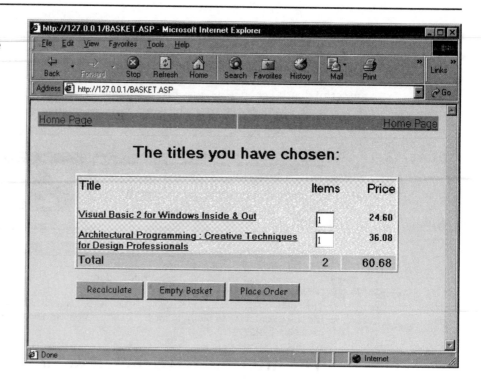

This is an interesting page. Each time the shopper clicks the Recalculate button, the same page must be displayed again, only this time with the new total. The statements that insert the buttons at the bottom of the Form are shown next:

```
<INPUT TYPE=SUBMIT NAME=RecalcBttn VALUE='Recalculate'>
<INPUT TYPE=SUBMIT NAME=RecalcBttn VALUE='Empty Basket'>
<INPUT TYPE=SUBMIT NAME=RecalcBttn VALUE='Place Order'>
```

All buttons call the same page, Recalc.asp, which examines the value of the button pressed to take the appropriate action. Here's the listing of the Recalc.asp page:

LISTING 18.4   **The Recalc.asp Server-Side Script**

```
<%
    HTMLText = "<HTML><FONT FACE='MS Sans Serif'>"
    HTMLText = HTMLText & "<HEAD>"
    HTMLText = HTMLText & "<META HTTP-EQUIV='Expires'
            CONTENT='0'>"
```

```
        HTMLText = HTMLText & "</HEAD>"
        HTMLText = HTMLText & "<BODY BGCOLOR=F0F0F0>"
        HTMLText = HTMLText & "<TABLE WIDTH=100%
                    BORDERCOLOR=cyan><TR>"
        HTMLText = HTMLText & "<TD ALIGN=LEFT BGCOLOR=cyan>
                    <FONT SIZE=+0><A HREF=DEFAULT.HTM>
                    Home Page</A></FONT>"
        HTMLText = HTMLText & "<TD ALIGN=RIGHT BGCOLOR=cyan>
                    <FONT SIZE=+0><A HREF=DEFAULT.HTM>
                    Home Page</A></FONT></TABLE>"
        HTMLText = HTMLText & "</TABLE>"
        HTMLText = HTMLText & "<CENTER>"
        HTMLText = HTMLText & "<FORM NAME=AllOrders
                    ACTION='ReCalc.asp' METHOD='POST'>"
        HTMLText = HTMLText & "<H2>The titles you have chosen:</H2>"
        HTMLText = HTMLText & "<TABLE BGCOLOR=lightyellow
                    WIDTH=80% RULES=none>"
        HTMLText = HTMLText & "<TR><TD VALIGN=top>
                    <FONT SIZE=+1>Title</FONT>"
        HTMLText = HTMLText & "<TD VALIGN=top ALIGN=center>
                    <FONT SIZE=+1>Items</FONT>"
        HTMLText = HTMLText & "<TD VALIGN=top ALIGN=right>
                    <FONT SIZE=+1>Price</FONT>"
    Set DBConnection=Server.CreateObject("ADODB.Connection")
    DBConnection.Open "DSN=Biblio2000"

'  DELETE ALL COOKIES, will be resent
    RequestedAction = Request.Form("RecalcBttn")
    If RequestedAction="Recalculate" Then
        Response.Cookies("BasketItem").Expires = Date-1
        For Each cookie in Request.Cookies("BasketItem")
            HTMLText = HTMLText & "<TR>"
            ISBN = cookie
            QTY=Request.Form("Q" & ISBN)
' RETRIEVE TITLE, PRICE AND PROCESS WITH NEW QUANTITY
            If QTY > 0 Then
                SQLArgument = "SELECT Title, Price,
                                Discount FROM Titles
                                WHERE Titles.ISBN='" & ISBN & "'"
                Set SelTitle = DBConnection.Execute(SQLArgument)
                BookTitle = SelTitle.Fields("Title")
                HTMLText = HTMLText & "<TD VALIGN=top>
                            <FONT SIZE=-1><B>" &
                            "<A HREF=BookISBN.asp?ISBN=" &
                             ISBN & ">" & BookTitle & "</A>"
                            & "    </B>"
```

```
                            HTMLText = HTMLText & "<TD VALIGN=top
                            ALIGN=center><FONT SIZE=-1>
                            <INPUT TYPE=TEXT SIZE=2 MAXSIZE=3
                            NAME='Q" & ISBN & "'"
                            HTMLText = HTMLText &
                            "VALUE = " & QTY & ">"
                            HTMLText = HTMLText &
                            "<TD ALIGN=right VALIGN=top>
                            <FONT SIZE=-1><B>" &
                            FormatNumber((1-SelTitle.Fields("Discount")) *
                            SelTitle.Fields("Price"), 2) & " </B>"
                            Cost = Cost + (1-SelTitle.Fields("Discount")) *
                                    SelTitle.Fields("Price") * QTY
                            Items = Items + CInt(QTY)
                            Response.Cookies("BasketItem")(ISBN) = CStr(QTY)
                            Response.Cookies("BasketItem").Expires =
                                    Date + 365
                    End If
                Next

    ' NOW PRINT BASKET'S CONTENTS
            HTMLText = HTMLText & "<TR><TD BGCOLOR=yellow>
                        <FONT COLOR=black><B>Total</B></FONT>
                        <TD BGCOLOR=yellow ALIGN=center>
                        <FONT COLOR=black><B>" & Items &
                        "</B></FONT>
                        <TD BGCOLOR = yellow ALIGN=right>
                        <FONT COLOR=black><B>    "
                        & FormatNumber(Cost, 2, , -1) &
                        " </B></FONT>"
            HTMLText = HTMLText &  "</TABLE>"
            Response.Write HTMLText
            DBConnection.Close
            Set DBConnection = Nothing
            Set SelTitle = Nothing
    %>
    <TABLE WIDTH=80%>
    <TR><TD>
    <FONT SIZE=+1>
    <INPUT TYPE=SUBMIT NAME=RecalcBttn VALUE='Recalculate'>
    <INPUT TYPE=SUBMIT NAME=RecalcBttn VALUE='Empty Basket'>
    <INPUT TYPE=SUBMIT NAME=RecalcBttn VALUE='Place Order'>
    </FONT>
    </TABLE>
    </FORM>
    </HTML>
    <%
```

```
            Else
                If RequestedAction="Empty Basket" Then
                    For Each ctrl in Request.Form
                        If ctrl <> "RecalcBttn" Then
                            ISBN = ctrl
                            Response.Cookies("BasketItem")(ISBN) = "0"
                            Response.Cookies("BasketItem").Expires =
                                            Date - 365
                        End If
                    Next
                    HTMLText = "<HTML>"
                    HTMLText = HTMLText & "<HEAD>"
                    HTMLText = HTMLText &
                            "<META HTTP-EQUIV='Expires' CONTENT='0'>"
                    HTMLText = HTMLText & "</HEAD>"
                    HTMLText = HTMLText & "<BODY BGCOLOR=F0F0F0 FONT=>"
                    HTMLText = HTMLText &
                            "<TABLE WIDTH=100% BORDERCOLOR=cyan><TR>"
                    HTMLText = HTMLText &
                            "<TD ALIGN=LEFT BGCOLOR=cyan>
                            <FONT SIZE=+1><A HREF=DEFAULT.HTM>
                             Home Page</A></FONT>"
                    HTMLText = HTMLText &
                            "<TD ALIGN=RIGHT BGCOLOR=cyan>
                            <FONT SIZE=+1><A HREF=DEFAULT.HTM>
                             Home Page</A></FONT></TABLE>"
                    HTMLText = HTMLText & "</TABLE>"
                    Response.Write HTMLText
                    Response.Write "<BR><BR><BR>"
                    Response.Write "<CENTER><H1>
                        Your basket has been emptied</H1></CENTER>"
                Else
                    ' The following statements
                    ' process the order. The matching End If statement
                    ' appears at the end of the script
%>
<HTML>
<HEAD>
<meta http-equiv="Content-Type"
content="text/html">
<TITLE>RegNew</TITLE>
</HEAD>

<BODY bgcolor="#FFFFFF">
<FONT SIZE=+1><H1>Place an order</H1>
<p>Please enter your ID and password in the boxes below. If this is the
```

```
first time you're ordering, write down your ID and password for future
use and make sure you don't share this information with anyone else.
<P>
Your ID must be your e-mail address and it will be used to confirm your
order.
<P>
<FORM NAME=GetCustomer ACTION="GetCustomer.ASP" METHOD="POST">
<HR>
<table border="0">
    <tr>
        <td>User ID (your e-mail address)
        <td><input type="text" size="20" maxsize=30 name="UserID">
        <td>Password
        <td><input type="password" size="15" maxsize=20
                name="Password">
</table>
<HR>
If you already have an ID and password, enter them and click here to
<INPUT TYPE=SUBMIT VALUE="Place Order">.
<BR>
If not, click here to see the <A HREF="RegNewCustomer.htm">New Cus-
tomer</A> page to request your personal ID and password.
</FORM>
</body>
</html>
<%
      End If
    End If
%>
```

When the customer decides to actually order the items in the basket, they must provide information that will enable us to charge them and deliver the items ordered. The application displays a login screen (Figure 18.6) where return customers must enter their e-mail address and password (the address is used as UserID to identify the customer). New customers must follow the link to the New Customer Registration page, where they can enter all the information needed to process and deliver the order. This information is entered once and stored in the Customers table. For the next order, the customer need enter only an e-mail address and password.

The page shown in Figure 18.7 is an HTML file. The New Customer Registration page displays a Form with the controls you see, and its Submit button calls the RegNewCustomer.htm (Listing 18.5), which stores the information entered by the viewer in the Customers table.

FIGURE 18.6:

The bookstore's login screen

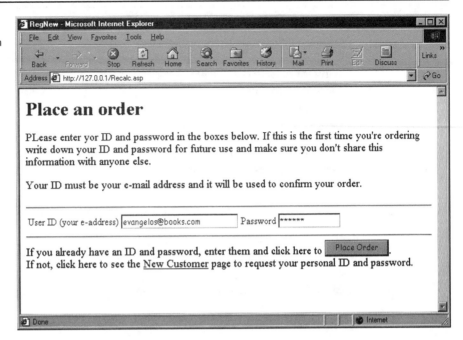

FIGURE 18.7:

The New Customer Registration page

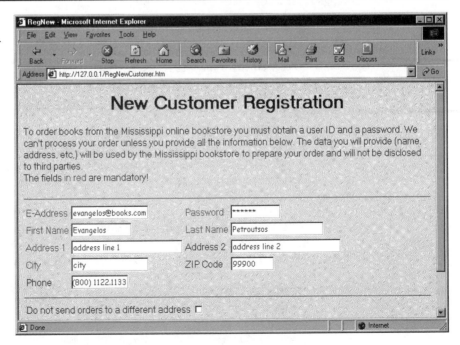

LISTING 18.5 The RegNewCustomer.htm Page

```html
<HTML><FONT FACE='MS Sans Serif'>
<HEAD>
<meta http-equiv="Content-Type"
content="text/html">
<TITLE>RegNew</TITLE>
</HEAD>
<body BGCOLOR=#F0F0B0>
<p align="center"><font size="6"><strong>New Customer
Registration</strong></font></p>

<p>To order books from the Mississippi online bookstore
you must obtain a user ID and a password.
We can't process your order unless you provide all the information
below.
The data you will provide (name, address, etc,) will be used by the
Mississippi bookstore
to prepare your order and will not be disclosed to third parties.
<BR>
The fields <FONT COLOR=red>in red</FONT> are mandatory!
<P>
<FORM NAME=RegNew ACTION=RegisterNew.ASP METHOD="POST">
<HR>
<table border="0">
    <tr>
        <td><FONT COLOR=red>E-Mail Address
        <td><input type="text" size="20" name="EAddress">
        <td><FONT COLOR=red>Password
        <td><input type="text" size="12" name="Password">
    <tr>
        <td><FONT COLOR=red>First Name
        <td><input type="text" size="15" name="FName">
        <td><FONT COLOR=red>Last Name
        <td><input type="text" size="25" name="LName">
    <tr>
        <td><FONT COLOR=red>Address 1
        <td><input type="text" size="30" name="Address1">
        <td>Address 2
        <td><input type="text" size="30" name="Address2">
    <tr>
        <td><FONT COLOR=red>City
        <td><input type="text" size="20" name="City">
        <td>ZIP Code
        <td><input type="text" size="10" name="ZIP">
```

```
        <tr>
            <td>Phone
            <td><input type="text" size="14" name="Tel">
        <tr>
    </table>
    <HR>
    <table border="0">
        <tr>
            <td>Do not send orders to a different address
            <td><input type="checkbox" VALUE=ON name="MyAddress">
        <tr>
            <td>Do not mail promotional material
            <td><input type="checkbox" VALUE=ON name="MailPromo">
    </table>
    <P>
    Fill out this form and click here to <INPUT TYPE=SUBMIT VALUE="Register">
    </FORM>
    </body>
    </html>
```

Once the customer logs in, a new page with the order is displayed (Figure 18.8). This is the customer's last chance to cancel the order. This is a plain HTML page and need not be listed here.

FIGURE 18.8:

The final order confirmation page

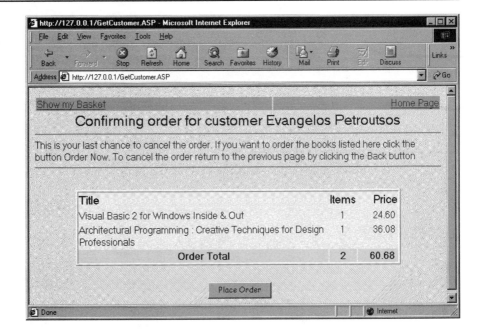

If the Place Order button is clicked, the application stores the order in the Orders table and displays the thank-you message seen in Figure 18.9. You can read the orders placed by a customer (they all have the same customer ID and date) and process the order. The database isn't nearly as complicated as the Northwind database, but you can add more features to the store. For example, you can create an Orders and an Order Details table and store the exact same information as we did with the Northwind database. You can also use similar Classes (or stored procedures, if you'd rather work with SQL Server) to enter new orders. By the way, if you port the Biblio database to SQL Server with the Data Transformation Wizard (discussed in Chapter 2) and then add the new tables as discussed in the first section of this tutorial, the same Web application will also work with the SQL Server database (that's because we use a DSN and the Active Data Objects to access the database).

FIGURE 18.9:

The order has been accepted.

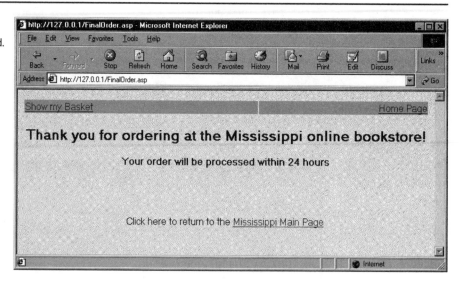

The last page of the application informs the user that the order has been accepted and the books are practically on their way.

Summary

This sample application concludes the book. While you work with ADO on your own, you may find an appendix with all ADO objects, their properties and methods useful. The appendix can be found on the companion CD. Just double-click its icon and it will open with Acrobat Reader. This is not a hyperlinked document. It's a PDF document with the same page layout as all the chapters in this book, and it's meant to be printed, rather than be read online.

INDEX

Note to the Reader: Throughout this index **boldfaced** page numbers indicate primary discussions of a topic. *Italicized* page numbers indicate illustrations.

(

E

G

M

N

Q

R

S

T

U

X

Y